MANPOWER PROFILE INDIA YEARBOOK 2009

MANPOWER PROFILE INDIA YEARBOOK 2009

Published by

INSTITUTE OF APPLIED MANPOWER RESEARCH

A-7, Narela Institutional Area, Delhi-110040 (India)

Manpower Profile India Yearbook, 2009
16th edition

IAMR Report No. 2/2009

Sixteenth Edition: 2009

Team for Manpower Profile India Yearbook:

Dr. M.R. Prasad, Chief
Boop Singh, Research Officer
Vijay K. Saxena, Research Associate
Dipika Sen, Sub-Editor

ISBN-978-812-906035-3-9

Published by
INSTITUTE OF APPLIED MANPOWER RESEARCH
A-7, Narela Institutional Area, Delhi-110040 (India)
Phone: 27787214-18, *Fax*: +91-11-27783467
Web site : http://iamrindia. gov. in
e-mail : iamrindia @ nic.in

Printed and Distributed by :
GYAN PUBLISHING HOUSE,
Gayn Kunj, 23 Main Ansari Road, Darya Ganj, New Delhi-110002
Phones : 23282060, 23261060 Fax No. : 23285914
e-mail : books@gyanbooks.com
website : gyanbooks. com

PREFACE

Manpower Profile – India Yearbook is being brought out annually since 1993, by the Institute of Applied Manpower Research to provide information on various dimensions of human resource development. The document provides a wide range of statistics and information on various characteristics of India's manpower on the basis of data available from different sources, namely, Office of the Census Commissioner and Registrar General of India; the National Sample Survey Organisation; the Central Statistical Organisation; the Ministry of Human Resource Development; the Directorate General of Employment and Training; the Labour Bureau; the Department of Science and Technology; the Directorate General of Health Services; the University Grants Commission; the National Technical Manpower Information System, funded by the All India Council for Technical Education and operated by this Institute; International Labour Office; United Nations Development Programmes Reports as well as the Institute's own research projects. As part of extending the scope and coverage of the data, information from other agencies such as Ministries of Agriculture, Rural Development, and Small & Medium Enterprises is also included in the present issue.

The Profile contains time-series data on crucial aspects such as human resource planning and development, and labour market features including utilisation, magnitude and nature of labour force. The data are presented, analysed and sequentially arranged in such a way that important interrelationships among relevant economic and manpower parameters become clearly visible.

The objective of the Manpower Profile is to present relevant data in tabular form from the national human resource point of view. It shows how the potential human resource—the outcome of prevailing demographic forces—is generated and transformed into manpower. Data on labour force and its participation in economic activities show the extent to which the available manpower is utilised. Educational and training statistics in terms of enrolment, outturn, teacher-pupil ratios, etc., and present manpower formation processes show how the quality and productivity of labour force is improved for performing various economic activities. The information on national accounts aggregates depicts how the optimum utilisation of manpower and other resources improves the growth performance of the national economy and its position globally.

The data presented in the Profile, which are drawn from various sources mentioned earlier, are not necessarily comparable among themselves because of variations in concept, coverage and methodology used. It is for this reason that a technical note has been provided preceding each statistical section. These brief technical notes bring out the main features of individual sections and attempt to show how the data contained in the section are related to the overall profile of India's manpower.

The figures presented in the publication are the latest available upto March, 2009. While updating the tables in certain cases, data pertaining to earlier periods could not be accommodated due to constraints of space. The interested users may refer to previous editions of the yearbook for the purpose. The footnotes in tables give source, scope, coverage and limitations of data.

Encouraged by the overwhelming response and support, the scope of the Manpower Profile is being enlarged every year. The current 16th edition of Profile is also enriched with more data pertaining to Population, Manpower formation and utilization characteristics.

It remains our constant endeavour to improve the coverage and depth of the information based on the feedback received from the users of the Profile as well as workshops organised periodically. Towards this end, we welcome further comments and suggestions from the users. It is hoped that the present edition will be found useful for planning, administration and research purposes in the area of human resources in the country, both at the national and state levels.

The Institute is grateful to all the concerned data producing agencies for their valuable cooperation and help in bringing out this publication. It is a great pleasure to put on record the contributions of faculty of IAMR by way of technical notes preceding the tables in each section: (alphabetically) Rashmi Agrawal, I.C. Awasthi, Shachi Joshi, Gayatri Pandey, M. R. Prasad, Vijay K Saxena, Mridula Sharma, and Anil K Yaadav.

July, 2009

R. SRIDHARAN
Director

CONTENTS

LIST OF TABLES AND CHARTS

SECTION 1: POPULATION CHARACTERISTICS

(i) Population Characteristics

SECTION III :
BASE FOR MANPOWER UTILISATION AND ITS CHARACTERISTICS

(i) Base for Manpower Utilisation

(ii) Employment Characteristics

SECTION IV : ECONOMIC RETURNS FROM MANPOWER UTILISATION

SECTION V : LABOUR MARKET FEATURES

(i) Wages, Salarics and Wage Differentials

SECTION VI: GENDER ISSUES

Table No.	Title	Page
	SECTION VII: INTERNATIONAL COMPARISONS	

SECTION 1

Population Characteristics

Dr. M. R. Prasad
Vijay K. Saxena

Section -I
Population Characteristics

At the end of six decades of independence and ten five-year plans, it is imperative to look at the development scenario of our country. As the eleventh five year plan (2007-2012) is in progress, it is interesting to review the progress of our country, discuss the challenges to be faced and the opportunities explored in the coming decades in the light of a growing population. There are different approaches to review the progress, and thereby draw inferences for the future, based on past trends and present status. One such approach is through the broad dimension of human resource development with particular emphasis on demography.

Human resource development as the ultimate goal of development was stressed by UNDP in 1990 and it received considerable attention across the globe thereafter. It was argued that the objective of development is not simply to produce goods and services but to increase the capabilities of people to lead full, productive and satisfying lives with enhanced quality of life. The concept of human development as put forward by the UNDP is highly significant for a country like India whose position is dismal among all the countries. However, some positive developments over the past decades in the demographic pattern has placed India comfortably among the Asian countries.

It is in this context that some important traits of population and demography are highlighted in the section on Population Characteristics through time-series data for the last ten decades and for each state/union territory presented individually. An important and notable addition in this section is the demographic data of disabled population. Through this new addition under the heading of 'Disabled Persons', an attempt is being made to capture the data on the type of disability, sex, literacy status, age group, level of education, type of activity etc. of the disabled persons for both rural and urban areas.

The section consists of 34 tables which are divided into two sections. The first section consists of 26 tables which broadly categorized into four types i.e., (i) Demographic trends (Tables 1.1.1 to 1.1.10), (ii) Literacy, health, and mortality trends (Tables 1.1.11 to 1.1.20), (iii) Migration trends of labor force (Tables 1.1.21 to 1.1.24), and (iv) Activity status of labor force etc. (Tables 1.1.25 to 1.1.26). The second section consists of 8 tables (Tables 1.2.1 to 1.2.8) which are exclusively devoted to capture important variables associated with the disabled persons. Observations on different sets of tables in terms of trends, inferences based on the time-series developments and future projections wherever possible are presented in the following paragraphs.

Tables 1.1.1 to 1.1.10 describe the demographic profile and characteristics over the period of a century and more in the intervals of decadal changes. Table 1.1.1 shows the increase of population by sex over a period of one century. From 972 in the year 1901, the sex ratio (number of females per 1000 males) has declined to 933 in 2001. During the last ten decades, the population has grown steadily except for the period 1911-21, as reported in the table. In case of sex ratio, it was alarmingly lowest at 927 during the decade 1981-91, but rose to 933 during 2001 thus arresting the trend of abnormal sex ratio.

Table 1.1.2 presents the important variables of population growth for India for the last ten decades. In all these decades, India has registered a declining birth and death rate which automatically reflects improvement in life expectancy at birth. As a result of these two factors, there has been a steep increase in the density of population for the past one century from 77 to 325. All these decades showed increase of population except the period 1911-1921 which saw a negative annual growth rate of 0.03 per cent. For the remaining period, the growth rate of population increased from 1.04 per cent to 2.22 per cent for the period from 1931 to 1981 and thereafter showed a decline in annual growth rate to 1.97 per cent during 2001.

Table 1.1.3 provides data on important attributes of population, viz. sex ratio, density, and share of urban population for each state and union territory of India during the year 2001. Among the states, Delhi and Kerala witnessed the lowest and highest sex ratio at 821 and 1058 respectively. In case of Union Territories, Daman and Diu and Pondicherry have witnessed minimum and maximum sex ratio at 710 and 1001 respectively. The population density, which is an important yardstick for each state, witnessed a minimum of 13 for Arunachal Pradesh and as high as 9340 for Delhi state. Again, in case of urban population, Delhi stood at the top with as high as 93 per cent of the population living in urban areas and Himachal Pradesh recorded the lowest urban population at 10 per cent.

Table 1.1.4 presents the population in absolute numbers by sex and by urban, rural divisions for all India and different states and union territories. It shows that states like Uttar Pradesh, Bihar, Andhra Pradesh, West Bengal, Maharashtra are major contributors of population whereas states like Tamil Nadu, Gujarat, Goa, Delhi, Mizoram and Maharashtra are contributing more in terms of urban population.

Table 1.1.5 presents the percentage distribution of population by sex and quinquennial age group which is an important factor that shows the labour force participation by different age groups. Over a period of three decades, there has been an increase of population in the age group of 15-59 years, from 52.9 per cent to 55.6 per cent for males and from 52.5 per cent to 56.5 per cent for females. There is a drastic change in the population pyramid especially in the age group of 0-4 and 20-24 during the past three decades.

Table 1.1.6 and 1.1.7 provides the percentage of population by size of the village and town respectively. In case of villages, it was observed that the smaller villages have witnessed sharp decline in terms of percentage of population in favour of a corresponding rise of population in bigger villages upto the year 1991. However, according to Table 1.1.6, the census 2001 data reveals that there is increase of population in rural areas in all categories of population.. The same trend is visible with towns as shown in Table 1.1.7 which shows an increasing concentration of population in bigger towns as compared to smaller towns when the urban population is considered over a period of three to four decades of time span.

Any data on demography for a multi-religious country like India are insufficient unless the data are captured religion-wise and analysed on regular basis. Table

1.1.8 gives the share of more than six religions and their progress in population for four decadal years starting from 1971. It is observed that population belonging to Hindu religion is dominant and steady at around 80 per cent, followed by Muslims at around 13 per cent. It is significant to note here that though the population figures have increased in absolute numbers, their percentages are almost stagnant.

Table 1.1.9 provides the percentage of population below poverty line (BPL) for more than two decades starting from 1983 in terms of urban and rural categorization. The data also include projections of BPL population for the year 2004-05. A noteworthy feature of the data is that there is a remarkable decline in the BPL population both in urban and rural areas by approximately 50 percent. The overall decline of BPL population, taking into consideration the projections for the year 2004-05, is from around 45 to 22 percent in a time span of two decades. The table shows the proof of economic sustenance of the population at the grass root level in both rural and urban areas.

Table 1.1.10 presents the estimated number of BPL population for all the states and union territories of India upto the period 2004-05 both for rural and urban areas of each state. According to the projections based on the reference year 1999-2000 and made by the Planning Commission, GOI with the assistance from different expert groups, states like Meghalaya, Karnataka, Tamil Nadu etc., will reduce the percentage of BPL population drastically to a single digit. States like Bihar, Madhya Pradesh, Nagaland, Orissa, Sikkim will however not have much impact in terms of reduction of BPL population, according to the estimated figures. There is a discerning note about states like Manipur and Mizoram which are apprehended to have an increased BPL population in the near future.

Table 1.1.11 elucidates the important indicators of literacy rate for overall population in each state and union territory for both male and female. It notes the attainment of literacy for three decadal periods starting from 1981. During this period, all India literacy rate has increased from 43 to 65 percent which is considered to be remarkable given the gigantic Indian population. There is also significant development towards enhancement of literacy among females from 29 to 54 percent over the same period. Every state and union territory has contributed towards the improvement in the literacy rate. States like Delhi, Goa, kerala, mizoram and all union territories except Dadra and Nagar Haveli recorded a literacy rate as high as 80 percent.

An important exercise is delineating population characteristics is the capturing of data concerning the under-privileged, and socially marginalized population of the country. In this direction, couple of tables have been presented concerning the literacy rate, and population of SC and ST compared to overall picture of the country. Table 1.1.12 again focuses on literacy rate for the SC and ST population in each state. The literacy rate in this case is much below the national average of overall population, with 54 percent and 47 percent for SC and ST population respectively according to the latest figures of 2001. States like Bihar, Jharkhand, and Uttar Pradesh have recorded dismal progress in literacy rates. It is again noticed that the gap in literacy rate between male and female is wider than that was observed for the all India average

Table 1.1.13 captures the percentage of SC and ST population vis-à-vis the overall population for all the states and union territories, according to the latest census report of 2001. There exists a wide variation in the percentage of SC and ST population in every state. Their overall percentage being 16 and 8 percent respectively, with almost all north eastern states dominating the list with their share of ST population.

Key indicators of demographic patterns like birth and death rate, infant mortality rate, age specific fertility rates are crucial in deciding the overall human development of any country. It is more significant to capture the above data for different states as the overall development of India is witnessed by uneven progress of different geographical regions. Tables 1.1.14 to 1.1.20 show the progress of different states in the above indicators.

Table 1.1.14 gives the three-year-moving average of birth and death rates across all the states of India. The latest figures of 2005-07 reveals that UP and Bihar are at the top of the birth rate with 29.5 and 29.4 percent respectively, where as Orissa and MP were recorded of having highest death rates among all the states. Significant reduction is observed for national average of birth and death rates with 23.1 7.4 percent respectively..

Age-specific fertility rates within the time gap of three decades is shown in Table 1.1.15. It is remarkable that the fertility rate of age groups of 40 - 44 and 45 – 49 were brought down by nearly one-fourth within a span of three decades. In the case of age group of 15 – 19, fertility rate was brought down by more than half from 100.8 to 46.1 for the same period.

Table 1.1.16 reveals the data of 2005 as per the Sample Registration System of Registrar General and Census Commissioner of India, pertaining to total fertility rate in major states by rural/urban classification. Uttar Pradesh is alarmingly much higher at 4.5 and 3.3 for both rural and urban respectively against the national average of 3.2 and 2.1. UP is followed by Bihar, Rajasthan, MP and Jharkhand with high fertility rate. Lowest fertility rates are observed in Kerala, Tamil Nadu and Andhra Pradesh.

Infant mortality rates which show a wide gap between rural and urban population has improved over a period of two-and-half decades both as average and rural-urban differences. Table 1.1.17 shows that the infant mortality rate which was as high as 119 and 62 for rural and urban areas, was brought down to 62 and 39 respectively. The data reassures that the human development has increased significantly in rural areas over the last two decades.

Table 1.1.18 captures the age-specific mortality rates in India for the last couple of decades. Noteworthy improvement did happen in the age group of 0-4 age group with drastic reduction upto 70 percent from 51.9 to 17.3. In the age group of 70-74, the mortality rate has fallen more than half from 109.4 to 52.8. For all the age groups, as an average also, the mortality rate was reduced to half of the prevailing rate during the past two-and-half decades.

Table 1.1.19 presents the age-specific mortality rates in rural India. For all the age groups ranging from 0-4 onwards, the improvement is significant as illustrated in the previous table. Indeed, the remarkable achievements shown in case of overall scenario for all India is a result of achievements in rural India which dominates the overall scenario.

Table 1.1.20 illustrates the age-specific mortality rates in urban India. In case of 0-4 age-group, the reduction is more than one-third during two decades. For all the age-groups upto 85+, there is a significant reduction in mortality rate. For the entire population as a whole, the mortality rate has come down by nearly 40 percent as was evident from the table.

The next segment of tables i.e., Tables 1.1.21 to 1.1.24 have captured the trends of migration by intra and inter-district and state, sex and rural-urban exodus. The data also highlight the types and reasons of migration from different parts of the country. Table 1.1.21 indicates that migration is predominant within the state and female migrants are out-numbering their male counterparts. Within the state, the intra-district migration is dominant accounting for two-thirds of the total migration. More than 11 percent of the migrants are going out of the state for livelihood. A noticeable feature of the migration trends is that the inter-state migration has reduced considerably, increasing in favour of intra-state migration. Another important feature is the drastic reduction of migrants to other countries by almost 70 percent during the past two decades from 1981 to 2001.

Table 1.1.22 captures the distribution of migrants by sex and type of migration for four decadal years from 1971. During the past three decades, there appears to be a continuous exodus of people from rural to urban, and from one urban region to another urban region with total migrants amounting to more than 241 millions according to the latest figures. The migration from urban to rural areas has remained at the same level over the same period. It is again noteworthy that female migrants are outnumbering their male counterparts in each category.

Table 1.1.23 captures the inter-state flow of migrants among all major states. Out-migration of labour force is maximum from Uttar Pradesh and Bihar. It is surprising to note that the migration from union territories is also significant which mainly a type of urban to urban migration. It is also observed that migration is widespread among the border states. Flow of migration into the states of Maharashtra, Gujarat, Punjab and West Bengal is predominant compared to other states.

Table 1.1.24 takes into account the reasons for migration, broadly categorizing them into economic and social factors. For people migrating from rural areas, social factors are predominant, whereas it is primarily economic factors like employment which determines migration from urban areas. Other causes like pursuing studies, health, etc. are also prime reasons for migrations.

Another important feature of the population characteristics is the actual trends of labour force in both rural and urban segments in comparison with the overall population trends. Table 1.1.25 captures the activity status of the population broadly in terms of labour force and out of the purview of labour force in percentage of population. Labour force participation has increased significantly during the five years both in rural and urban areas. This reflects a shift of different age groups and abnormality of the demographic pattern over the past few years considering the steady increase in the population.

Table 1.1.26 shows that female-headed families are maintaining small family norms both in rural and urban areas across all sections of society in India. The table presents the number of female-headed families per thousand families for each state and union territory.

India in its efforts to surge ahead in all walks of life, has been trying to provide equal opportunities to the disabled population, and bring them up to the mainstream by providing all amenities and incentives. The Indian polity as a whole has played a positive role in creating a conducive environment towards all the disabled persons and providing equal opportunities in addition to making positive discrimination by providing sizable quantity of jobs in all sectors of employment which are not a hindrance to physically challenged people. The sub-section on disabled population tries to capture the socio-economic trends among the disabled. Some of the typical features associated with the disabled like type of disability, prevalence rate, age-group wise prevalence, level of education, and activity status etc. provide useful information about the status of the disabled and demographic trends within the group.

Following tables, Table 1.2.1 to Table 1.2.8 elucidate the current status and statistics concerning the disabled. While arriving at accurate figures of the disabled from the main sources of data i.e., Census of India, and NSSO, it has to be noted that both the agencies are adopting effective and sound methodologies unique to each agency in collection, anticipation and estimation of the data. In the process, there is bound to be reasonable difference in the figures generated by the above agencies. Though, census data is exhaustive, several rounds of the NSSO have updated the data and captured the salient features of the population concerned like, their activity profile, rural–urban distribution, etc.

Table 1.2.1 gives the latest figures of different types of disability by sex, residence and literacy. Approximately two percent of the total population is disabled in our country according to the census report of 2001. Among them, nearly three-fourth are spread in rural areas and the prevalence is more among males as compared to females. More than half of the disabled are illiterates with 90 per cent illiteracy in rural areas. The table also gives another important feature, i.e., type of disability and their share of population. It is observed that more than half of the disabled are suffering from blindness. Among the disabled persons, 10 per cent are identified as mentally disabled. The trends are observed to be almost same with type of residential status, sex etc.

Capturing of data pertaining to different states and union territories by sex, by rural-urban distribution will help all government bodies in taking suitable remedial steps to mitigate the sufferings of disabled in different geographical areas of the country. Table 1.2.2 gives the distribution of disabled by state/union territory, by sex and by location. Uttar Pradesh is having maximum number of disabled persons followed by Bihar and West Bengal. Among union territories, Puducherry (formerly Pondicherry) is having maximum number of disabled.

Table 1.2.3 elucidates the prevalence rate and estimated number of disabled by type of disability, sex, and type of residence as recorded by the NSSO in various rounds of surveys. The December 2002 round indicates that there is a drastic reduction in the prevalence rate in case of visual, hearing and speech disability.

Again in case of rural population, women with visual impairment are 50 per cent more than their male counterparts.

Table 1.2.4 gives the distribution of the disabled according their age group. It is estimated according to the 58th round of NSSO, i.e. December 2002 that more than half of the disabled population are in the productive age group, i.e., 15 to 59 years and nearly one-fourth are in the age group of 60 and above. There is a re-adjustment of the disabled population resulting in increase in the age group of 15-34 over a period of two decades, which causes concern in terms of employment avenues to them.

Table 1.2.5 presents data on the disabled by level of general education, type of residence and sex. It is heartening to note that more than 50 per cent of the disabled are illiterates with high incidence of illiteracy among the rural women. Merely less than two percent are graduates and a sizable population among disabled is school pass-outs according to the available data.

Another important feature associated with the disabled is their activity status by type of sector and type of employment. The last two tables of this section deal with the status of the disabled, i.e. their distribution in different sectors of economy and the magnitude of unemployment prevalent among them.

Table 1.2.6 captures the type of employment e.g., regular or self-employment, casual employment, and employment in agricultural and non-agriculture based activities etc. It is observed that nearly three-fourths of the disabled population is out of the labour force. Among the employed, majority of them are earning their livelihood by some source of agricultural activity. The unemployed persons account for nearly 8 percent of the total labour force among the disabled.

Table 1.2.7 reveals that there is a remarkable shift in the activity status of the disabled with a reduction in their participation from around 65 to 56 percent in the primary sector which has resulted in increased participation of the disabled in other sectors mainly the tertiary sector over, a period of two decades.

Noteworthy among the data of disabled is the distribution of disabled workers by sex and broad industrial category. The last table, i.e., Table 1.2.8 gives the distribution of disabled workers in four broad types of activities i.e., cultivators, agricultural labour, household industry, and other workers. This data is available for all the 5 categories of disability and by sex, and location i.e., rural and urban division. Among them, visual impaired constitute around 50% of the disability in all gainful activities followed by locomotor disability. Among the disabled, most of them are settled as cultivators and agricultural labourers as per the census data - 2001.

(i) Population Characteristics

Table 1.1.1: Population by Sex

Year	*Population (Million)*			*Sex Ratio (Females per 1000 Males)*
	Person	*Male*	*Female*	
1901	238.4	120.8	117.4	972
1911	252.1	128.4	123.7	964
1921	251.3	128.5	122.8	955
1931	279.0	142.9	135.8	950
1941	318.7	163.7	154.7	945
1951	361.1	185.5	175.6	946
1961	439.2	226.3	212.9	941
1971	548.2	284.1	264.1	930
1981	683.3	353.3	330.0	934
1991	846.3	439.2	407.1	927
2001	1028.6	532.2	496.4	933

Note: Sex-wise breakup of population of Pondicherry is not available for the years 1901, 1931 and 1941. The figures (male and female) for these years are therefore exclusive of Pondicherry population.

Source: Registrar General and Census Commissioner of India, *Census of India*, for relevant years.

Table 1.1.2: Growth of Population and Changes in Population Characteristics

Year	*Total Population (Million)*	*Annual Growth Rate (Exponential)*	*Birth Rate (per 1000)*	*Death Rate (per 1000)*	*Life Expectancy at Birth (Years)*		*Density (Population per sq.km)*
					Male	*Female*	
1901	238.4	—	49.2	42.6	23.63	23.96	77
1911	252.1	0.56	48.1	47.2	22.59	23.31	82
1921	251.3	−0.03	46.4	36.3	19.42	20.91	81
1931	279.0	1.04	45.2	31.2	26.91	26.56	90
1941	318.7	1.33	39.9	27.4	32.09	31.37	103
1951	361.1	1.25	41.7	22.8	32.45	31.66	117
1961	439.2	1.96	41.2	19.0	41.89	40.55	142
1971	548.2	2.20	36.9	14.9	46.40	44.70	177
1981	683.3	2.22	33.9	12.5	54.10	54.70	216
1991	846.3	2.14	29.5	9.8	59.7(a)	60.9(a)	274
2001	1028.6	1.97	25.0*	8.1*	63.9(b)	66.9(b)	325

Notes: Birth rates and Death rates for the years 1901 to 1961 relate to census estimates and for 1971 onwards correspond to sample registration.
* Figures are provisional and related to the year 2002.
(a) Figures relate to the period 1991-95. (b) Projected values for the period 2001-06.

Source: Registrar General and Census Commissioner of India, *SRS Bulletin, Sample Registration System.*

Figure 1.1.A

MALE AND FEMALE POPULATION

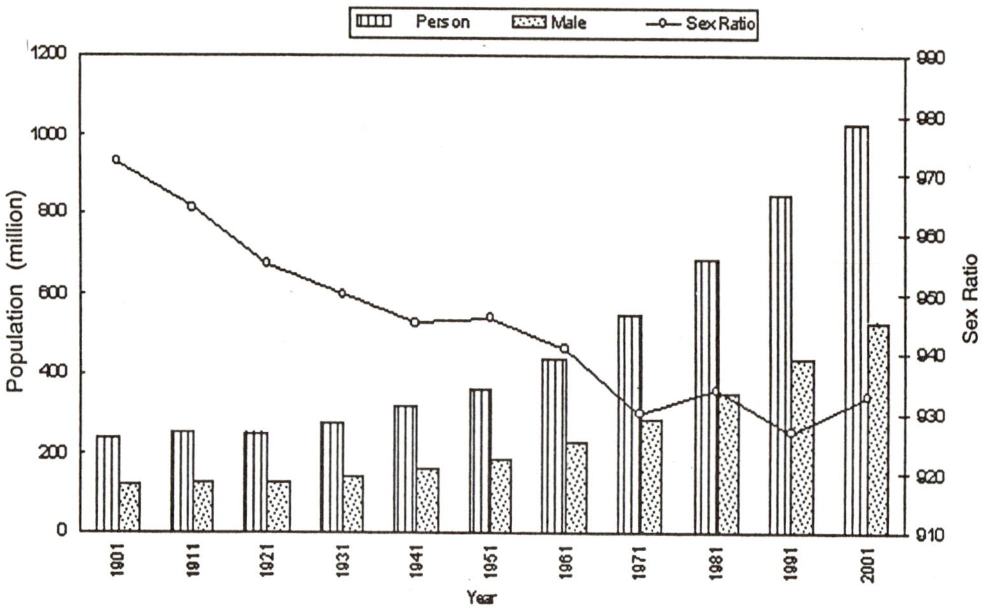

For details see Tables 1.1.1

Figure 1.1.B

BIRTH RATE AND DEATH RATE

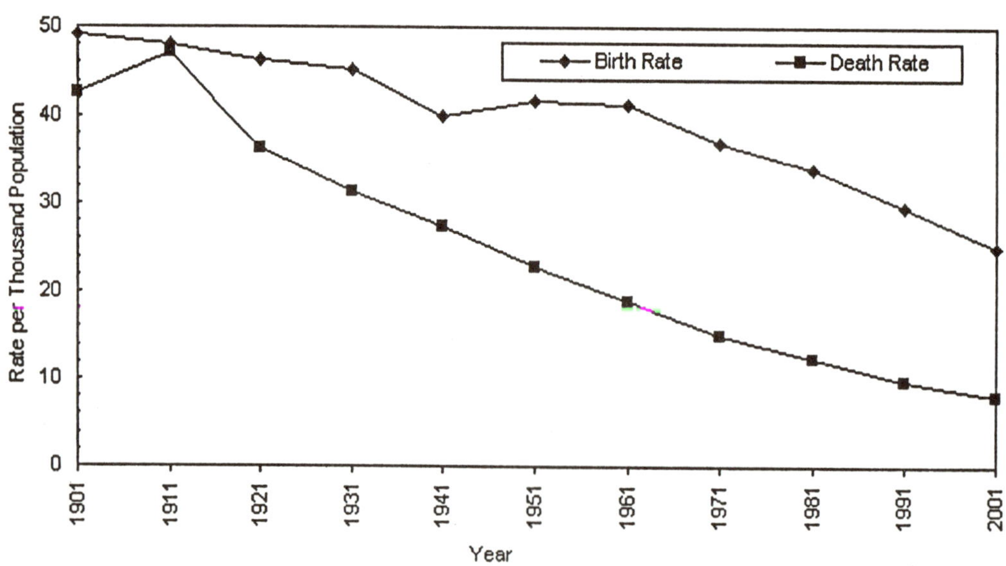

For details see Table 1.1.2

Table 1.1.3: Population Characteristics — State/Union Territory, 2001

State/Union Territory	Population(000)			Sex Ratio (Females per 1000 Males)	Density (Population per sq. km)	Percentage of Urban Population
	Person	Male	Female			
INDIA	1028,610	532,157	496,454	933	325	27.78
States						
1. Andhra Pradesh	76,210	38,527	37,683	978	277	27.08
2. Arunachal Pradesh	1,098	580	518	893	13	20.41
3. Assam	26,656	13,777	12,879	935	340	12.72
4. Bihar	82,999	43,244	39,755	919	881	10.47
5. Chhattisgarh	20,834	10,474	10,360	989	154	20.08
6. Delhi	13,851	7,607	6,243	821	9,340	93.01
7. Goa	1,348	687	660	961	364	49.77
8. Gujarat	50,671	26,386	24,285	920	258	37.35
9. Haryana	21,145	11,364	9,781	861	478	29.00
10. Himachal Pradesh	6,078	3,088	2,990	968	109	9.79
11. Jammu and Kashmir	10,144	5,361	4,783	892	100	24.88
12. Jharkhand	26,946	13,885	13,061	941	338	22.25
13. Karnataka	52,851	26,899	25,952	965	276	33.98
14. Kerala	31,841	15,469	16,372	1,058	819	25.97
15. Madhya Pradesh	60,348	31,444	28,904	919	196	26.67
16. Maharashtra	96,879	50,401	46,478	922	315	42.40
17. Manipur	2,167	1,096	1,071	978	103	23.88
18. Meghalaya	2,319	1,176	1,143	972	103	19.63
19. Mizoram	889	459	430	935	42	49.50
20. Nagaland	1,990	1,047	943	900	120	17.74
21. Orissa	36,805	18,661	18,144	972	236	14.97
22. Punjab	24,359	12,985	11,374	876	484	33.95
23. Rajasthan	56,507	29,420	27,087	921	165	23.38
24. Sikkim	541	289	252	875	76	11.10
25. Tamil Nadu	62,406	31,401	31,005	987	480	43.86
26. Tripura	3,199	1,642	1,557	948	305	17.02
27. Uttaranchal	8,489	4,326	4,163	962	159	25.59
28. Uttar Pradesh	166,198	87,565	78,633	898	690	20.78
29. West Bengal	80,176	41,466	38,710	934	903	28.03
Union Territories						
1. Andaman and Nicobar Islands	356	193	163	846	43	32.67
2. Chandigarh	901	507	394	777	7,900	89.78
3. Dadra and Nagar Haveli	221	122	99	812	449	22.89
4. Daman and Diu	158	92	66	710	1,413	36.26
5. Lakshadweep	61	31	30	948	1,895	44.47
6. Pondicherry	974	487	487	1,001	2,030	66.57

Note: Totals may not tally due to rounding off.

Source: Registrar General and Census Commissioner of India, *Census of India-2001, Primary Census Abstract, Total Population.*

Table 1.1.4: Rural and Urban Population by Sex and State/Union Territory, 2001

(Thousands)

State/Union Territory	Rural			Urban		
	Person	Male	Female	Person	Male	Female
INDIA	742,491	381,603	360,888	286,120	150,554	135,566
States						
1. Andhra Pradesh	55,401	27,937	27,464	20,809	10,590	10,219
2. Arunachal Pradesh	870	455	415	228	125	103
3. Assam	23,216	11,940	11,276	3,439	1,837	1,602
4. Bihar	74,317	38,595	35,721	8,681	4,649	4,033
5. Chhattisgarh	16,648	8,307	8,341	4,185	2,167	2,019
6. Delhi	945	522	423	12,906	7,085	5,821
7. Goa	677	341	337	671	347	324
8. Gujarat	31,741	16,318	15,423	18,930	10,068	8,862
9. Haryana	15,029	8,053	6,976	6,115	3,311	2,804
10. Himachal Pradesh	5,482	2,756	2,726	596	332	264
11. Jammu and Kashmir	7,627	3,978	3,649	2,517	1,383	1,132
12. Jharkhand	20,952	10,680	10,272	5,994	3,205	2,788
13. Karnataka	34,889	17,649	17,240	17,962	9,250	8,712
14. Kerala	23,574	11,451	12,123	8,267	4,017	4,250
15. Madhya Pradesh	44,381	23,031	21,350	15,967	8,413	7,555
16. Maharashtra	55,778	28,459	27,319	41,101	21,942	19,159
17. Manipur*	1,591	809	782	576	287	289
18. Meghalaya	1,865	947	918	454	229	225
19. Mizoram	448	233	215	441	226	215
20. Nagaland	1,647	860	788	343	187	155
21. Orissa	31,287	15,749	15,538	5,517	2,912	2,606
22. Punjab	16,096	8,517	7,580	8,263	4,468	3,794
23. Rajasthan	43,293	22,427	20,866	13,214	6,993	6,221
24. Sikkim	481	256	225	60	33	27
25. Tamil Nadu	34,922	17,532	17,390	27,484	13,869	13,615
26. Tripura	2,653	1,364	1,290	546	279	267
27. Uttaranchal	6,310	3,145	3,166	2,179	1,181	998
28. Uttar Pradesh	131,658	69,157	62,501	34,540	18,408	16,132
29. West Bengal	57,749	29,616	28,132	22,427	11,850	10,577
Union Territories						
1. Andaman and Nicobar Islands	240	129	111	116	64	52
2. Chandigarh	92	57	35	809	450	358
3. Dadra and Nagar Haveli	170	92	78	50	30	21
4. Daman and Diu	101	64	37	57	29	28
5. Lakshadweep	34	17	16	27	14	13
6. Pondicherry	326	164	162	648	323	325

Note: Totals may not tally due to rounding off.

Source: Registrar General and Census Commissioner of India, *Census of India-2001.*

Table 1.1.5: Percentage Distribution of Population by Sex and Quinquennial Age Group

Age Group	*1971*		*1981*		*1991*		*2001*	
	Male	*Female*	*Male*	*Female*	*Male*	*Female*	*Male*	*Female*
0-4	15.94	16.42	13.99	14.36	12.58	13.03	10.73	10.74
5-9	14.03	14.16	13.39	13.52	13.20	13.28	12.54	12.40
10-14	11.90	11.83	12.22	11.93	11.95	11.48	12.33	11.93
15-19	9.77	9.86	10.24	10.03	9.90	9.51	10.14	9.32
20-24	8.28	8.55	8.49	8.61	8.60	8.98	8.70	8.75
25-29	7.27	7.58	7.31	7.58	7.79	8.45	7.81	8.43
30-34	6.47	6.64	6.38	6.57	6.96	7.20	7.02	7.44
35-39	5.77	5.68	5.69	5.73	6.19	6.01	6.77	6.96
40-44	5.02	4.71	5.10	4.97	5.25	4.97	5.61	5.21
45-49	4.24	3.86	4.47	4.22	4.43	4.19	4.67	4.54
50-54	3.42	3.10	3.66	3.42	3.63	3.42	3.73	3.37
55-59	2.69	2.51	2.91	2.78	2.85	2.80	2.55	2.83
60-64	2.03	1.95	2.26	2.26	2.39	2.41	2.55	2.81
65-69	1.38	1.34	1.67	1.70	1.75	1.76	1.78	2.08
70+	1.79	1.81	2.22	2.32	2.53	2.49	3.06*	3.19*
All Ages	100.00	100.00	100.00	100.00	100.00	100.00	100.00	100.00

Note: * Includes 'Age not stated'.
Source: Registrar General and Census Commissioner of India, *Census of India*, for relevant years.

Table 1.1.6: Percentage of Total Population in Rural Areas by Size of Village

Size of Village in Terms of Populati..n	*1961*	*1971*	*1981**	*1991***	*2001****
Less than 200	3.83	2.68	1.78	1.18	-
200-499	12.55	9.91	7.49	5.48	-
500-999	18.33	16.45	14.21	11.78	-
1000-1999	19.80	19.90	19.25	18.13	-
2000-4999	17.22	18.68	20.09	21.34	-
5000-9999	5.05	5.94	6.90	8.17	-
10000 & above	2.80	4.07	4.56	5.16	-
Rural Population as per cent of total population	82.03	80.09	76.66	74.27	72.18
Total Population (Million)	439.24	548.16	683.33	846.30	1,028.61

Notes: Class-wise percentages do not add up to the percentage of total rural population:
- * Exclude figures for Assam in 1981 where census of 1981 was not held.
- ** Exclude figures for Jammu and Kashmir in 1991 where 1991 census was not conducted owning to distructure.
- *** Exclude figures of Mao Maram, Paomata and Pural sub-divisions of Sanapati Dist. of Manipur.

Source: Registrar General and Census Commissioner of India, *Census of India*, for relevant years.

Figure 1.1.C

EXPECTATION OF LIFE AT BIRTH

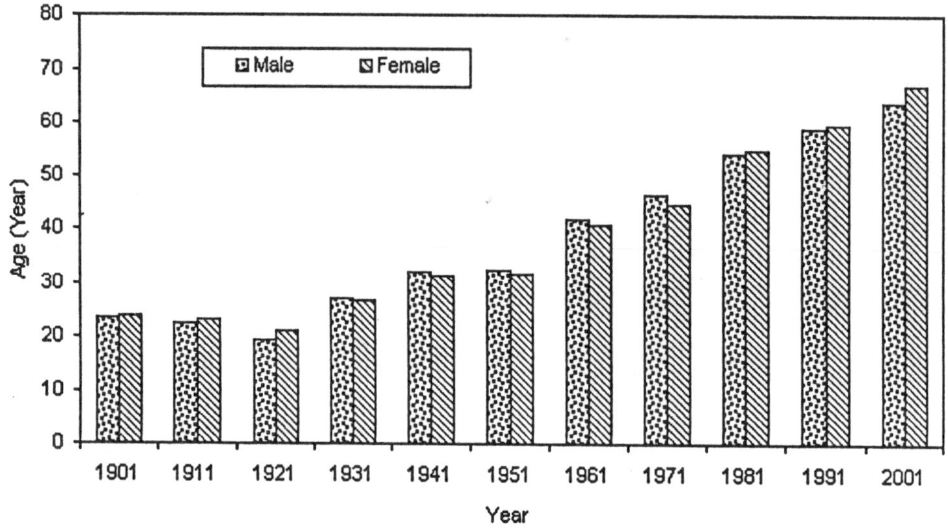

For details see Table 1.1.2

Figure 1.1.D

CHANGES IN POPULATION PYRAMID

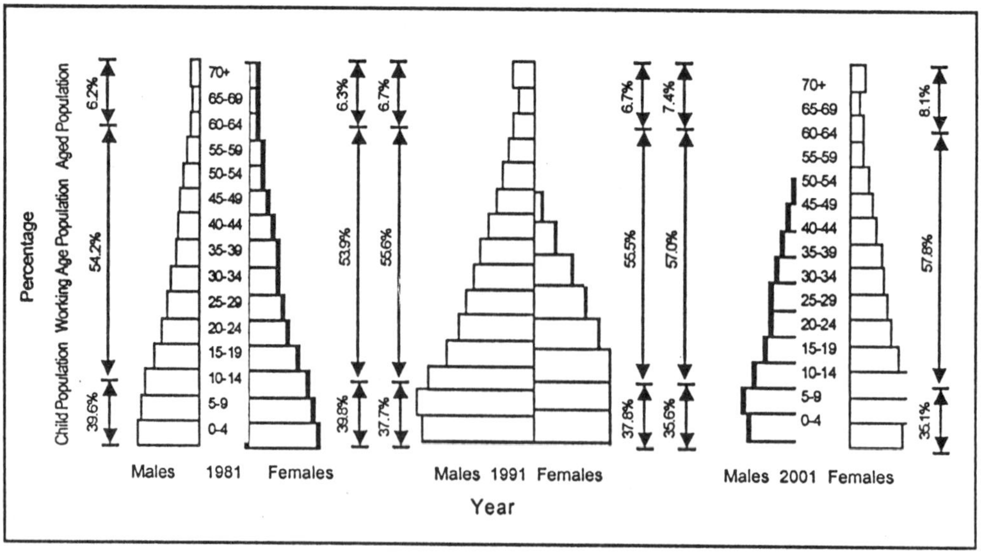

For details see Table 1.1.5

Table 1.1.7: Percentage of Total Population in Urban Areas by Size of Town

Class and Size of Town in Terms of Population	*1961*	*1971*	*1981**	*1991***	*2001****
Class I : 1,00,000 & above	9.08	11.17	13.83	16.55	17.33
Class II : 50,000 - 99,999	1.98	2.13	2.66	2.76	3.35
Class III : 20,000 - 49,999	2.99	3.12	3.28	3.31	4.09
Class IV : 10,000 - 19,999	2.25	2.14	2.18	1.96	2.20
Class V : 5,000 - 9,999	1.21	0.86	0.82	0.65	0.77
Class VI : Less than 5000	0.14	0.09	0.12	0.07	0.08
Urban Population as per cent of total Population	17.97	19.91	23.34	25.70	27.82
Total Population (Million)	439.24	548.16	683.33	846.30	1,028.61

Notes: Class-wise percentages do not add up to the percentage of total urban population :

* Exclude figures for Assam in 1981 where census of 1981 was not held.

** Exclude figures for Jammu & Kashmir in 1991 where 1991 census was not conducted owing to disturbance.

*** Exclude figures of Mao Maram, Paomata and Purul sub-divisions & Senapati Dist. of Manipur.

Source: Registrar General and Census Commissioner of India, *Census of India*, for relevant years.

Table 1.1.8: Distribution of Population by Religion, 1971 to 2001

Religion	*1971*		*1981*		*1991*		*2001*	
	Total (Million)	*Percentage*	*Total (Million)*	*Percentage*	*Total (Million)*	*Percentage*	*Total (Million)*	*Percentage*
Hindu	453.4	82.7	549.7	82.6	687.6	82.0	827.6	80.5
Muslim	61.4	11.2	75.6	11.4	101.6	12.1	138.2	13.4
Christian	14.3	2.6	16.2	2.4	19.6	2.3	24.1	2.3
Sikh	10.4	1.9	13.1	2.0	16.3	1.9	19.2	1.9
Buddhist	3.9	0.7	4.7	0.7	6.4	0.8	8.0	0.8
Jain	2.6	0.5	3.2	0.5	3.4	0.4	4.2	0.4
Others	2.2	0.4	2.8	0.4	3.7	0.5	7.3	0.7
Total	548.2	100.0	665.3**	100.0	838.6*	100.0	1028.6***	100.0

Notes:

* Exclude the figures of J & K.

** Exclude the figures of Assam.

*** Exclude the figures of Mao Maram, Paomata and Purul sub-divisions of Senapati Dist. of Manipur.

Sources: Registrar General and Census Commssioner of India :

(i) *Census of India, 1971,* Part II-C, Series I.

(ii) *Census of India, 1981,* Series I, 1984 (Religion) paper III.

(iii) *Census of India, 1991,* Series I, 1995 (Religion) paper I.

(iv) *Census of India, 2001,* (The First Report on Religion Data) Abstract.

Figure 1.1.E

POPULATION IN RURAL AREAS BY SIZE OF VILLAGE

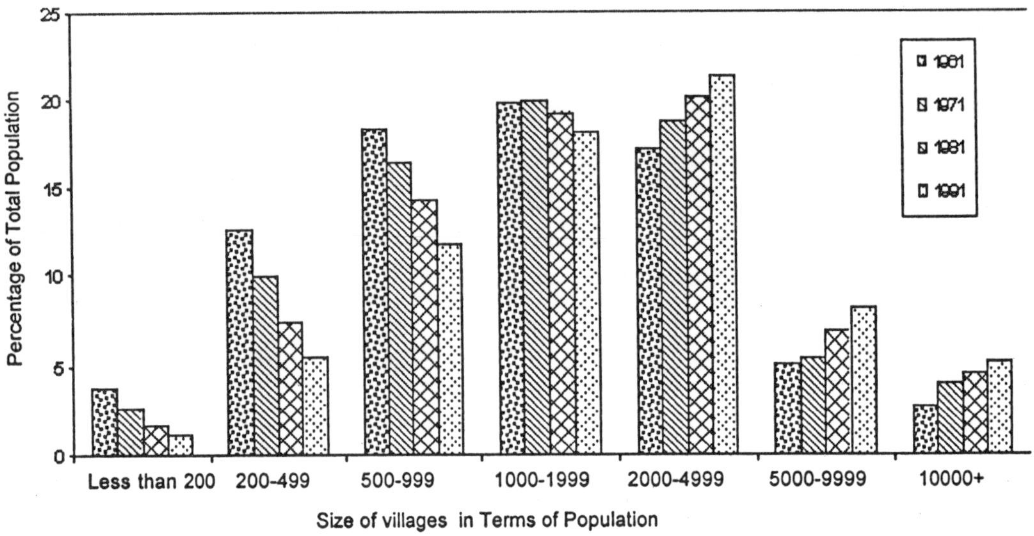

For details see Table 1.1.6

Figure 1.1.F

POPULATION IN URBAN AREAS BY SIZE OF TOWN

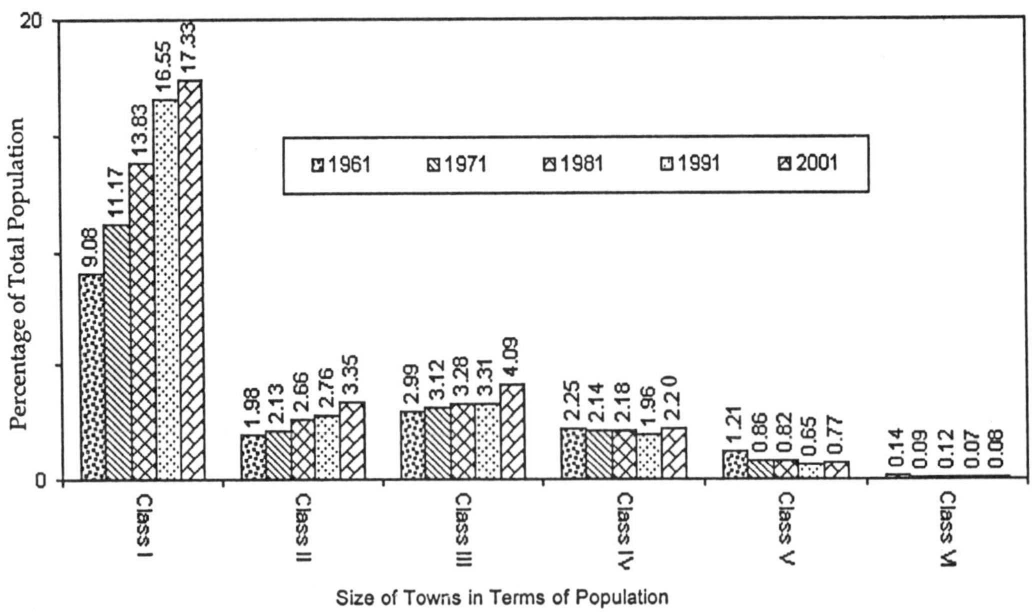

For details see Table 1.1.7

Table 1.1.9: Percentage of Population Below Poverty Line

Year	*Rural*	*Urban*	*Total*
1983 (38th Round)	45.65	40.79	44.48
1987-88 (43rd Round)	39.09	38.20	38.86
1989-90 (45th Round)	33.70	36.00	34.28
1990-91 (46th Round)	35.04	35.29	35.11
1992 (48th Round)	41.70	37.80	40.70
1993-94 (50th Round)	37.27	32.36	35.97
1994-95 (51st Round)	38.03	34.24	36.98
1995-96 (52nd Round)	38.29	30.05	36.08
1997 (53rd Round)	38.46	33.97	37.23
1999-00 (55th Round)			
30 day recall	27.10	23.60	26.10
7 day recall	24.00	21.60	23.30
2004-05 (61st Round)			
30 day recall	28.3	25.7	27.5
365 day recall	21.8	21.7	21.8

Note: Data related to 1989-90, 1990-91, 1992, 1994-95, 1995-96 and 1997 are based on thin samples.

Sources: (i) Central Statistical Organisation, *Statistical Pocket Book, 1999.*

(ii) Planning Commission, Government of India.

Table 1.1.10: Estimated Population Below Poverty Line by State/ Union Territory, 1999-2000* and 2004-05

State/ Union Territory	Rural				Urban				Combined			
	1999-2000		2004-05		1999-2000		2004-05		1999-2000		2004-05	
	No. of Persons (Lakh)	Percentage	No. of Persons (Lakh)	Percentage	No. of Persons (Lakh)	Percentage	No. of Persons (Lakh)	Percenstage	No. of Persons (Lakh)	Percentage	No. of Persons (Lakh)	Percentage
States												
1. Andhra Pradesh	58.13	11.05	43.21	7.5	60.88	26.63	44.50	20.7	119.01	15.77	88.71	11.1
2. Arunachal Pradesh	3.80	40.04	1.47	17.0	0.18	7.47	0.07	2.4	3.98	33.47	1.54	13.4
3. Assam	92.17	40.04	41.46	17.0	2.38	7.47	0.93	2.4	94.55	36.09	42.39	15.0
4. Bihar	376.51	44.30	262.92	32.9	49.13	32.91	27.09	28.9	425.64	42.60	290.01	32.5
5. Chhattisgarh	—	—	54.72	31.2	—	—	16.39	34.7	—	—	32.0	71.1
6. Delhi	0.07	0.40	0.01	0.1	11.42	9.42	15.83	10.0	11.49	8.23	15.83	10.2
7. Goa	0.11	1.35	0.13	1.9	0.59	7.52	1.62	20.9	0.70	4.40	1.74	12.0
8. Gujarat	39.80	13.17	46.25	13.9	28.04	15.59	21.18	10.1	67.89	14.07	67.43	12.5
9. Haryana	11.94	8.27	14.57	9.2	5.39	9.99	7.99	11.3	17.34	8.74	22.56	9.9
10. Himachal Pradesh	4.84	7.94	4.10	7.2	0.29	4.63	0.17	2.6	5.12	7.63	4.27	6.7
11. Jammu and Kashmir	2.97	3.97	2.20	2.7	0.49	1.98	2.34	8.5	3.46	3.48	4.54	4.2
12. Jharkhand	—	—	89.76	40.2	—	—	10.63	16.3	—	—	100.39	34.8
13. Karnataka	59.91	17.38	43.33	12.0	44.49	25.25	53.28	27.2	104.40	20.04	96.60	17.4
14. Kerala	20.97	9.38	23.59	9.6	20.07	20.27	13.92	16.4	41.04	12.72	37.51	11.4
15. Madhya Pradesh	217.32	37.06	141.99	29.8	81.22	38.44	68.97	39.3	298.54	37.43	210.97	32.4
16. Maharashtra	125.12	23.72	128.43	22.2	102.87	26.81	131.40	29.0	227.99	25.02	259.83	25.2
17. Manipur	6.53	40.04	2.86	17.0	0.66	7.47	0.14	2.4	7.19	28.54	3.00	13.2
18. Meghalaya	7.89	40.04	3.32	17.0	0.34	7.47	0.12	2.4	8.23	33.87	3.43	14.1
19. Mizoram	1.40	40.04	0.78	17.0	0.45	7.47	0.11	2.4	1.85	19.47	0.89	9.5
20. Nagaland	5.21	40.04	2.94	17.0	0.28	7.47	0.09	2.4	5.49	32.67	3.03	14.5
21. Orissa	143.69	48.01	129.29	39.8	25.40	42.83	24.30	40.3	169.09	47.15	153.59	39.9
22. Punjab	10.20	6.35	9.78	5.9	4.29	5.75	3.52	3.8	14.49	6.16	13.30	5.2
23. Rajasthan	55.06	13.74	66.69	14.3	26.78	19.85	40.50	28.1	81.83	15.28	107.18	17.5
24. Sikkim	2.00	40.4	0.85	17.0	0.04	7.47	0.02	2.4	2.05	36.55	0.87	15.2
25. Tamil Nadu	80.51	20.55	56.51	16.9	49.97	22.11	58.59	18.8	130.48	21.12	115.10	17.8
26. Tripura	12.53	40.04	4.70	17.0	0.49	7.47	0.14	2.4	13.02	34.44	4.85	14.4
27. Uttar Pradesh	412.01	31.22	357.68	25.3	117.88	30.89	100.47	26.3	529.89	31.15	485.15	25.5
28. Uttarakhand	—	—	21.11	31.7	—	—	7.75	32.0	—	—	28.86	31.8
29. West Bengal	180.11	31.85	146.59	24.2	33.38	14.86	26.64	11.2	213.49	27.02	173.23	20.6
Union Territories												
1. Andaman and Nicobar Islands	0.58	20.55	0.44	16.9	0.24	22.11	0.27	18.8	0.82	20.99	0.71	17.6
2. Chandigarh	0.06	5.75	0.04	3.8	0.45	5.75	0.36	3.8	0.51	5.75	0.40	3.8
3. Dadra and Nagar Haveli	0.30	17.57	0.62	36.0	0.03	13.52	0.16	19.2	0.33	17.14	0.77	30.6
4. Daman and Diu	0.01	1.35	0.03	1.9	0.05	7.52	0.14	20.8	0.06	4.44	0.16	8.0
5. Lakshadweep	0.03	9.38	0.04	9.6	0.08	20.27	0.05	16.4	0.11	15.60	0.09	12.3
6. Pondicherry	0.64	20.55	0.58	16.9	1.77	22.11	1.34	18.8	2.41	21.67	1.92	18.2
All India	1932.43	27.09	1702.99	21.08	670.07	23.62	682.0	21.7	2602.50	26.10	2384.99	21.8

Notes: * Estimates correspond to 30 day recall period.
(—) Not available.

Source: Planning Commission, Government of India.

Figure 1.1-G

NUMBER AND PERCENTAGE OF PERSONS BELOW POVERTY LINE

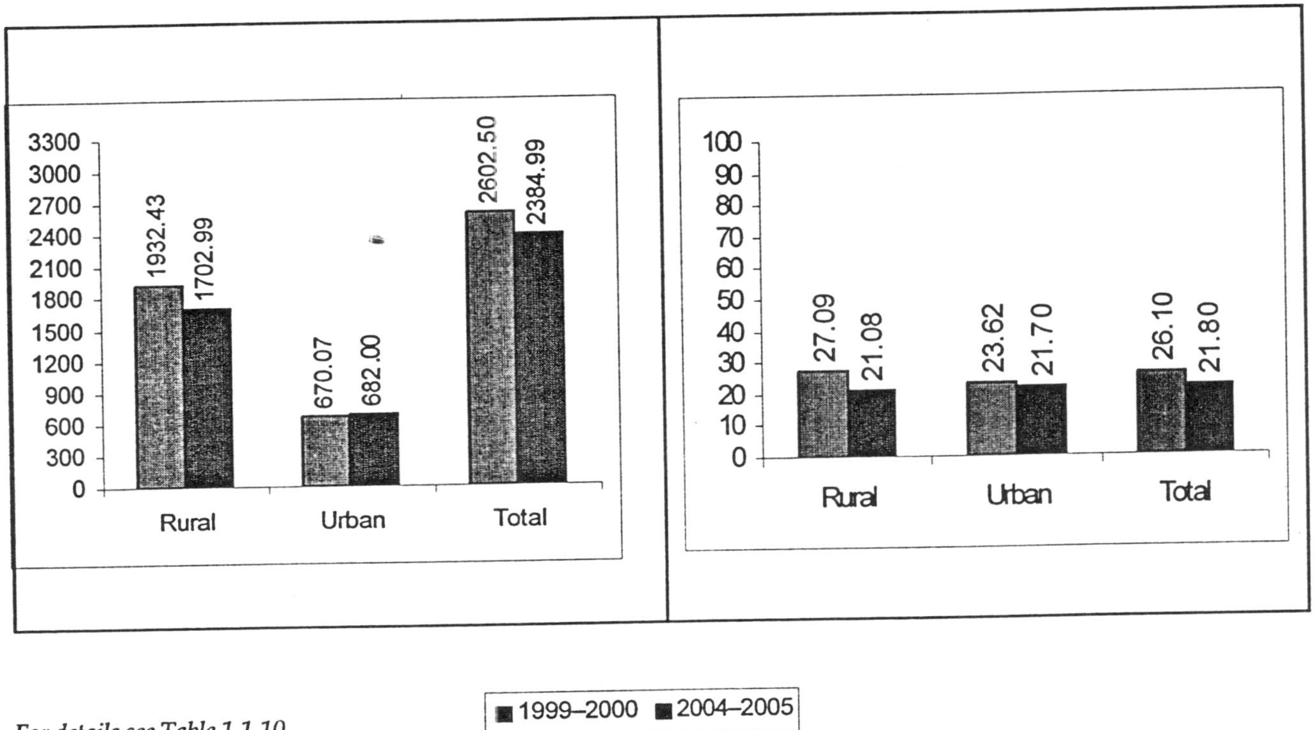

For details see Table 1.1.10

Table 1.1.11 : Literacy Rates by Sex and State/Union Territory, 1981-2001

State/Union Territory	1981			1991			2001		
	Person	Male	Female	Person	Male	Female	Person	Male	Female
INDIA*	43.56	56.37	29.75	52.20	64.13	39.29	65.38	75.85	54.16
States									
1. Andhra Pradesh	35.66	46.83	24.16	44.09	55.13	32.72	61.11	70.85	51.17
2. Arunachal Pradesh	25.54	35.11	14.01	41.59	51.45	29.69	54.74	64.07	44.24
3. Assam	NA	NA	NA	52.89	61.87	43.03	64.28	71.93	56.03
4. Bihar	32.03	46.58	16.51	38.48	52.49	22.89	47.53	60.32	33.57
5. Chhattisgarh	—	—	—	—	—		65.18	77.86	52.40
6. Delhi	71.93	79.28	62.57	75.29	82.01	66.99	81.82	87.37	75.00
7. Goa	65.71	76.01	55.17	75.51	83.64	67.09	82.32	88.88	75.51
8. Gujarat	52.21	65.14	38.46	61.29	73.13	48.64	69.97	80.50	58.60
9. Haryana	43.85	58.49	26.89	55.85	69.10	40.47	68.59	79.25	56.31
10. Himachal Pradesh	51.17	64.27	37.72	63.86	75.36	52.13	77.13	86.02	68.08
11. Jammu and Kashmir	32.68	44.18	19.55	NA	NA	NA	54.46	65.75	41.82
12. Jharkhand	—	—	—	—	—	—	54.13	67.94	39.38
13. Karnataka	46.20	58.72	33.16	56.04	67.26	44.34	67.04	76.29	57.45
14. Kerala	81.56	87.74	75.65	89.81	93.62	86.13	90.92	94.20	87.86
15. Madhya Pradesh	34.22	48.41	18.99	44.20	58.42	28.85	64.11	76.80	50.78
16. Maharashtra	55.83	69.66	41.01	64.87	76.56	52.32	77.27	86.27	67.51
17. Manipur	49.61	64.12	34.61	59.89	71.63	47.60	68.87	77.87	59.70
18. Meghalaya	42.02	46.62	37.15	49.10	53.12	44.85	63.31	66.14	60.41
19. Mizoram	74.26	79.37	68.60	82.27	85.61	78.60	88.49	90.69	86.13
20. Nagaland	50.20	58.52	40.28	61.65	67.62	54.75	67.11	71.77	61.92
21. Orissa	40.96	56.45	25.14	49.09	63.09	34.68	63.61	75.95	50.97
22. Punjab	48.12	55.52	39.64	58.51	65.66	50.41	69.95	75.63	63.55
23. Rajasthan	30.09	44.76	13.99	38.55	54.99	20.44	61.03	76.46	44.34
24. Sikkim	41.57	52.98	27.35	56.94	65.74	46.69	69.68	76.73	61.46
25. Tamil Nadu	54.38	68.05	40.43	62.66	73.75	51.33	73.47	82.33	64.55
26. Tripura	50.10	61.49	38.01	60.44	70.58	49.65	73.66	81.47	65.41
27. Uttaranchal	—	—	—	—	—	—	72.28	84.01	60.26
28. Uttar Pradesh	33.33	47.43	17.18	41.60	55.73	25.31	57.36	70.23	42.98
29. West Bengal	48.64	59.93	36.07	57.70	67.81	46.56	69.22	77.58	60.22
Union Territories									
1. Andaman and Nicobar Islands	63.16	70.28	53.15	73.02	78.99	65.46	81.18	86.07	75.29
2. Chandigarh	74.81	78.89	69.31	77.81	82.04	72.34	81.76	85.65	76.65
3. Dadra & Nagar Haveli	32.70	44.69	20.38	40.71	53.56	26.98	60.03	73.32	42.99
4. Daman and Diu	59.91	74.45	46.51	71.20	82.66	59.40	81.09	88.40	70.37
5. Lakshadweep	68.42	81.24	55.32	81.78	90.18	72.89	87.52	93.15	81.56
6. Pondicherry	65.14	77.09	53.03	74.74	83.68	65.63	81.49	88.89	74.13

Notes: Literacy rates are estimated on the basis of age 7 years and above population.
*Literacy rates for 1981 and 1991 exclude the states of Assam and Jammu and Kashmir respectively.

Source: Registrar General and Census Commssioner of India, *Census of India*, for relevant years.

Figure 1.1.H

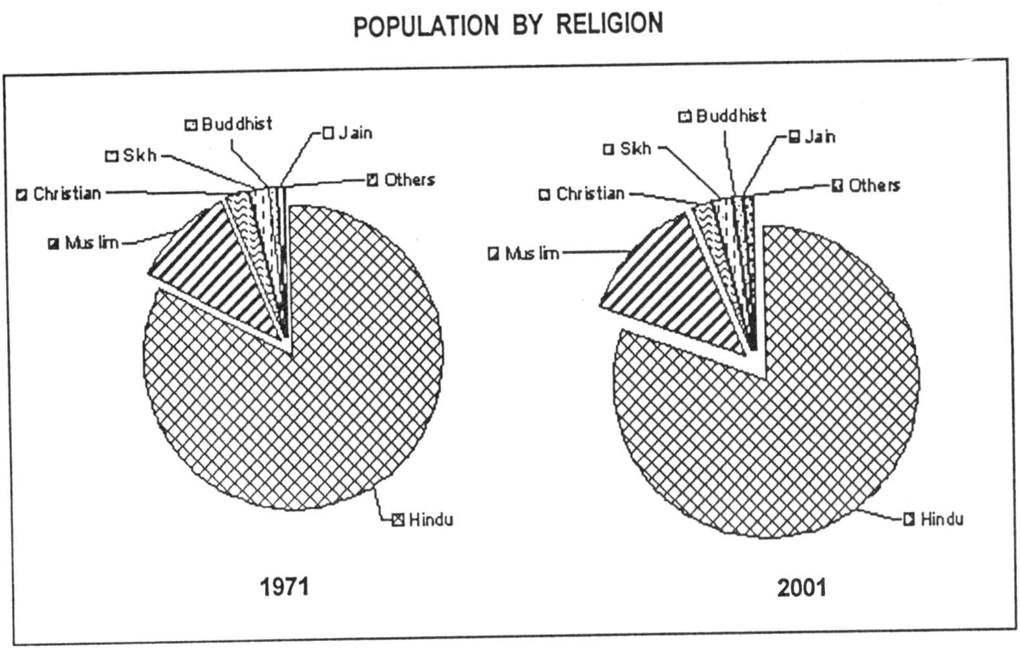

For details see Table 1.1.8

Figure 1.1.I

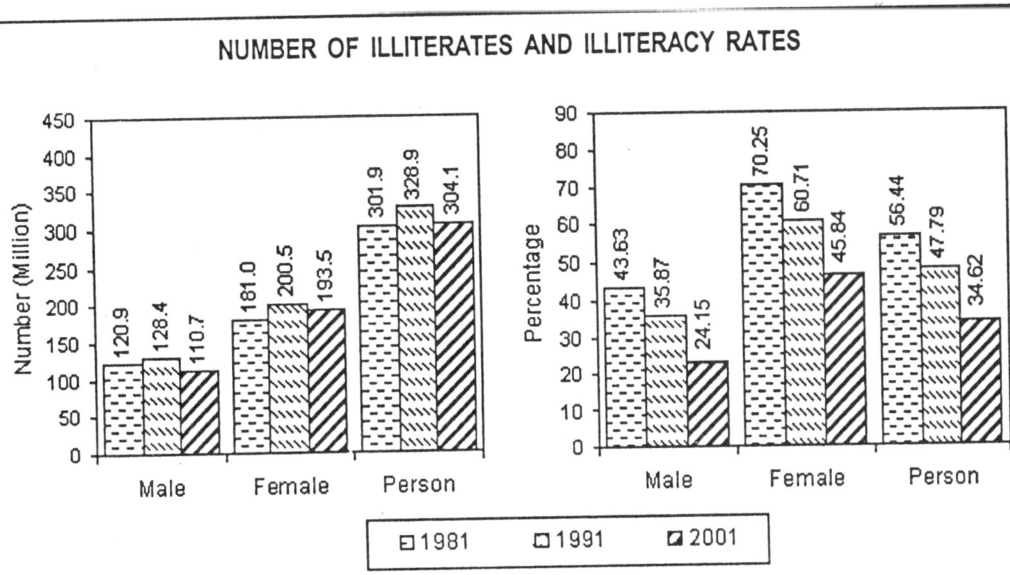

For details see Table 1.1.11, Census of India, 1981, 1991 and 2001.

Table 1.1.12 : Literacy Rates for Scheduled Caste/Scheduled Tribe Population by Sex, 2001

State/Union Territory	Scheduled Caste			Scheduled Tribe		
	Person	Male	Female	Person	Male	Female
INDIA	54.69	66.64	41.90	47.10	59.17	34.76
States						
1. Andhra Pradesh	53.52	63.51	43.35	37.04	47.66	26.11
2. Arunachal Pradesh	67.64	76.31	54.99	49.62	58.77	40.56
3. Assam	66.78	75.74	57.14	62.52	72.34	52.44
4. Bihar	28.47	40.23	15.58	28.17	39.76	15.54
5. Chhattisgarh	63.96	78.70	49.22	52.09	65.04	39.35
6. Delhi	70.85	80.77	59.07	—	—	—
7. Goa	71.92	81.56	62.05	55.88	63.49	47.32
8. Gujarat	70.50	82.56	57.58	47.74	59.18	36.02
9. Haryana	55.45	66.93	42.26	—	—	—
10. Himachal Pradesh	70.31	80.01	60.35	65.50	77.71	53.32
11. Jammu & Kashmir	59.03	69.57	46.46	37.46	48.16	25.51
12. Jharkhand	37.56	51.59	22.55	40.67	53.98	27.21
13. Karnataka	52.87	63.75	41.72	48.27	59.66	36.57
14. Kerala	82.66	88.07	77.56	64.35	70.78	58.11
15. Madhya Pradesh	58.57	72.33	43.28	41.16	53.55	28.44
16. Maharashtra	71.90	83.29	59.98	55.21	67.02	43.08
17. Manipur	72.32	81.78	62.97	65.85	73.16	58.42
18. Meghalaya	56.27	65.86	45.21	61.34	63.49	59.20
19. Mizoram	89.20	88.44	92.16	89.34	91.71	86.95
20. Nagaland	—	—	—	65.95	70.26	61.35
21. Orissa	55.53	70.47	40.33	37.37	51.48	23.37
22. Punjab	56.22	63.38	48.25	—	—	—
23. Rajasthan	52.24	68.99	33.87	44.66	62.10	26.16
24. Sikkim	63.04	70.15	55.71	67.14	73.81	60.16
25. Tamil Nadu	63.19	73.41	53.01	41.53	50.15	32.78
26. Tripura	74.68	81.85	67.24	56.48	67.97	44.60
27. Uttar Pradesh	46.27	60.34	30.50	35.13	48.45	20.70
28. Uttaranchal	63.40	77.26	48.74	63.23	76.39	49.37
29. West Bengal	59.04	70.54	46.90	43.40	57.38	29.15
Union Territories						
1. Andaman and Nicobar Islands	—	—	—	66.79	73.61	59.58
2. Chandigarh	67.66	76.20	57.22	—	—	—
3. Dadra & Nagar Haveli	78.25	88.37	67.05	41.24	55.97	26.99
4. Daman and Diu	85.13	94.03	75.82	63.42	74.23	51.93
5. Lakshadweep	—	—	—	86.14	92.16	80.18
6. Pondicherry	69.12	18.41	60.05	—	—	—

Source: Registrar General and Census Commssioner of India, *Census of India-2001.*

Table 1.1.13: Percentage of Scheduled Caste and Scheduled Tribe Population to Total Population, 2001

State/Union Territory	*Scheduled Caste Population (000)*	*Scheduled Tribe Population (000)*	*Percentage of Scheduled Caste Population to Total Population*	*Percentage of Scheduled Tribe Population to Total Population*
INDIA	166,636	84,326	16.23	8.21
States				
1. Andhra Pradesh	12,340	5,024	16.29	6.63
2. Arunachal Pradesh	6	705	0.55	64.62
3. Assam	1,826	3,309	6.85	12.42
4. Bihar	13,049	758	15.74	0.91
5. Chhattishgarh	2,419	6,617	11.63	31.82
6. Delhi	2,343	—	17.00	—
7. Goa	24	1	1.79	0.07
8. Gujarat	3,503	7,481	6.92	14.79
9. Haryana	4,091	—	19.40	—
10. Himachal Pradesh	1,502	245	24.72	4.03
11. Jammu & Kashmir	770	1,106	7.65	10.98
12. Jharkhand	3,189	7,087	11.85	26.34
13. Karnataka	8,564	3,464	16.24	6.57
14. Kerala	3,124	364	9.81	1.14
15. Madhya Pradesh	9,155	12,233	15.16	20.26
16. Maharashtra	9,882	8,577	10.21	8.86
17. Manipur	60	741	2.51	31.02
18. Meghalaya	111	1,993	4.81	86.43
19. Mizoram	N	839	0.03	94.16
20. Nagaland	—	1,774	—	89.19
21. Orissa	6,082	8,145	16.57	22.19
22. Punjab	7,029	—	28.94	—
23. Rajasthan	9,694	7,098	17.17	12.57
24. Sikkim	27	111	5.00	20.56
25. Tamil Nadu	11,858	651	19.09	1.05
26. Tripura	556	993	17.42	31.12
27. Uttaranchal	1,517	256	17.89	3.02
28. Uttar Pradesh	35,148	108	21.17	0.07
29. West Bengal	18,453	4,407	23.00	5.49
Union Territories				
1. Andaman and Nicobar Islands	—	29	—	8.15
2. Chandigarh	158	—	17.54	—
3. Dadra and Nagar Haveli	4	137	1.82	62.27
4. Daman and Diu	5	14	3.16	8.86
5. Lakshadweep	—	57	—	93.44
6. Pondicherry	158	—	16.22	—

Notes: '—'No Schedule Caste/Schedule Tribe notified.
N - Negligible.

Source: Registrar General & Census Commissioner of India, *Census of India-2001*.

Table 1.1.14: Three Year Moving Average of Birth and Death Rates — India and Major States, (2002-2004, 2004-2006 and 2005-07)

Major States	2002-2004[E]		2004-2006[E]		2005-2007[E]	
	Birth Rate	*Death Rate*	*Birth Rate*	*Death Rate*	*Birth Rate*	*Death Rate*
Andhra Pradesh	19.0	7.0	18.9	7.3	18.7	7.0
Assam	25.1	8.8	24.6	8.7	24.3	8.6
Bihar	30.2	8.1	29.9	7.7	29.4	7.5
Gujarat	24.3	6.9	23.5	7.3	23.0	7.2
Haryana	25.1	6.6	23.9	6.5	23.4	6.6
Karnataka	20.9	6.9	20.1	7.1	19.9	7.3
Kerala	15.2	6.1	14.9	6.7	14.7	6.8
Madhya Pradesh	29.8	9.2	29.1	8.9	28.5	8.7
Maharashtra	19.1	6.2	18.5	6.7	18.1	6.6
Orissa	22.7	9.6	21.9	9.3	21.5	9.2
Punjab	18.7	6.4	17.8	6.8	17.6	7.0
Rajasthan	29.0	7.0	28.3	6.9	27.9	6.8
Tamil Nadu	17.1	7.5	16.2	7.5	15.8	7.2
Uttar Pradesh	30.8	8.8	30.1	8.6	29.5	8.5
West Bengal	19.3	6.3	18.4	6.2	17.9	6.3
INDIA	24.1	7.5	23.5	7.5	23.1	7.4

Note: E Estimated.
Source: Registrar General and Census Commission of India, *Sample Registration System Bulletin*, for relavent years.

Table 1.1.15: Age-Specific Fertility Rates

Age-Group	*1971**	*1981*	*1986*	*1991***	*1997***	*1998***	*2000*	*2001*	*2003*
15-19	100.8	90.4	91.1	76.1	53.7	54.0	51.1	48.9	46.1
20-24	250.8	246.9	252.8	234.0	225.6	220.3	218.7	215.9	214.4
25-29	254.8	232.1	216.4	191.3	188.2	182.8	184.5	177.3	171.3
30-34	202.2	167.7	139.2	117.0	112.4	104.2	100.8	98.5	90.6
35-39	137.8	102.5	78.6	66.8	56.6	54.3	53.1	49.9	44.1
40-44	62.2	44.0	37.9	30.6	28.3	25.0	21.7	21.2	18.5
45-49	24.4	19.6	14.9	12.1	10.2	9.0	7.7	7.3	6.8
Total Fertility Rate	5.2	4.5	4.2	3.6	3.4	3.2	3.2	3.1	3.0

Notes: *Exclude Bihar and West Bengal.
**Excludes Jammu and Kashmir.
Source: Registrar General and Census Commissioner of India, *Sample Registration System, Statistical Report*, for relevant years.

Table 1.1.16: Total Fertility Rate in Major States by Residence in India, 2005

Major States	*Total Fertility Rate, 2005*		
	Rural	*Urban*	*Total*
Andhra Pradesh	2.2	1.7	2.0
Assam	3.1	1.6	2.9
Bihar	4.4	3.2	4.3
Chhattisgarh	3.7	2.2	3.4
Delhi	2.2	2.1	2.1
Gujarat	3.1	2.3	2.8
Haryana	3.0	2.3	2.8
Himachal Pradesh	2.2	1.5	2.2
Jammu & Kashmir	2.6	1.6	2.4
Jharkhand	3.9	2.3	3.5
Karnataka	2.5	1.8	2.2
Kerala	1.7	1.7	1.7
Madhya Pradesh	4.0	2.5	3.6
Maharashtra	2.4	1.9	2.2
Orissa	2.7	1.7	2.6
Punjab	2.2	1.9	2.1
Rajasthan	4.0	2.7	3.7
Tamil Nadu	1.8	1.6	1.7
Uttar Pradesh	4.5	3.3	4.2
West Bengal	2.4	1.4	2.1
All India	3.2	2.1	2.9

Source: Ragistrar General and Census Commissioner of India, sample Registration System, Statistical Report, 2005.

Table 1.1.17: Infant Mortality Rates in Rural and Urban Areas

Year	*Infant Mortality Rates (per thousand live births)*		
	Rural	*Urban*	*Total*
1981	119	62	110
1991*	87	53	80
1996*	77	46	72
1997*	77	45	71
1998[P]	77	45	72
2000*	74	43	68
2001[E]	72	42	66
2002**[E]	69	40	63
2003**[E]	66	38	60
2004**[E]	64	40	58
2006[E]	62	39	57
2007[E]	61	37	55

Notes: *Excludes Jammu and Kashmir and Nagaland (Rural).

**Excludes Nagaland (Rural).

P : Provisional.

E : Estimated.

Source: Registrar General and Census Commissioner of India, *Sample Registration System Bulletin*, for relevant years.

Table 1.1.18: Age-Specific Mortality Rates in India

Age-group	*1971**	*1981*	*1991***	*1996***	*2001*	*2002*	*2003*	*2004*	*2005*
0-4	51.9	41.2	26.5	23.9	19.3	17.8	17.3	17.0	17.3
5-9	4.7	4.0	2.7	2.3	1.9	1.5	1.4	1.5	1.6
10-14	2.0	1.7	1.5	1.3	1.3	1.0	1.0	0.9	1.1
15-19	2.4	2.4	2.1	1.6	1.7	1.5	1.6	1.6	1.7
20-24	3.6	3.1	2.8	2.3	2.3	2.3	1.9	2.0	2.0
25-29	3.7	3.2	3.1	2.5	2.7	2.6	2.3	2.3	2.2
30-34	4.6	4.0	3.1	2.9	2.9	2.8	2.6	2.8	2.5
35-39	5.7	4.4	3.9	3.9	3.6	4.1	3.3	3.1	3.2
40-44	6.7	5.8	4.8	4.9	4.4	4.4	4.4	4.2	4.0
45-49	9.5	8.5	7.4	6.7	6.2	6.7	5.9	5.9	6.0
50-54	16.8	13.2	13.3	10.9	9.9	9.5	9.8	7.6	8.4
55-59	21.2	20.6	17.6	15.7	15.9	15.3	15.0	12.4	13.3
60-64	34.9	3.3	28.5	26.7	22.3	22.0	23.8	20.9	22.2
65-69	48.4	46.4	41.6	38.9	38.6	38.3	36.7	30.1	32.6
70-74	109.4	97.4	91.4	61.5	51.3	51.5	54.1	50.0	52.8
75-79	NA	NA	NA	89.5	81.6	78.1	79.8	71.2	74.0
80-84	NA	NA	NA	120.4	99.5	98.6	109.0	108.3	106.7
85+	NA	NA	NA	182.2	171.5	165.5	175.1	184.0	169.3
All Ages	14.9	12.5	9.8	9.0	8.4	8.1	8.0	7.5	7.6

Notes: * Excludes Bihar and West Bengal.
** Excludes Jammu & Kashmir.
NA: Not available

Source: Registrar General and Census Commissioner of India, *Sample Registration System, Statistical Report*, for relevant years.

Table 1.1.19: Age-Specific Mortality Rates in Rural India

Age-group	*1971**	*1981*	*1991***	*1996***	*2001*	*2002*	*2003*	*2004*	*2005*
0-4	56.2	45.5	29.1	26.2	21.5	19.7	19.1	19.1	19.5
5-9	5.2	4.6	3.0	2.6	2.1	1.7	1.6	1.7	1.8
10-14	2.2	1.8	1.6	1.4	1.4	1.1	1.0	1.1	1.3
15-19	2.7	2.6	2.3	1.8	1.9	1.7	1.6	1.7	1.9
20-24	4.0	3.4	3.0	2.5	2.1	2.6	2.1	2.3	2.2
25-29	4.0	3.6	3.3	2.6	2.9	3.0	2.5	2.5	2.5
30-34	5.0	4.3	3.3	3.1	3.2	3.1	2.8	3.0	2.7
35-39	6.0	4.6	4.1	3.7	3.8	4.4	3.5	3.3	3.4
40-44	7.0	6.1	5.1	5.2	4.7	4.4	4.8	4.5	4.3
45-49	9.0	8.9	7.8	7.0	6.4	7.2	6.6	6.3	6.4
50-54	17.5	13.6	11.5	11.3	9.9	9.8	10.4	8.0	8.6
55.59	21.6	21.0	17.6	16.2	16.3	16.2	15.8	13.0	14.0
60-64	35.7	34.1	29.0	26.8	22.7	22.6	25.1	21.9	22.0
65-69	40.5	47.9	42.5	38.0	39.4	38.8	34.3	30.9	33.4
70-74	112.8	101.5	93.3	62.9	52.0	53.6	58.0	51.6	54.0
75-79	NA	NA	NA	88.6	83.2	79.7	84.7	73.0	72.8
80-84	NA	NA	NA	120.8	101.2	101.1	112.6	108.7	106.4
85+	NA	NA	NA	184.4	171.5	161.7	182.0	184.1	166.7
All Ages	16.4	13.7	10.6	9.7	9.1	8.7	8.7	8.2	8.1

Notes: * Excludes Bihar and West Bengal.
** Excludes Jammu & Kashmir.
NA : Not available

Source: Registrar General and Census Commissioner of India, *Sample Registration System, Statistical Report*, for relevant Years.

Table 1.1.20: Age-Specific Mortality Rates in Urban India

Age-group	*1971**	*1981*	*1991***	*1996***	*2001*	*2002*	*2003*	*2004*	*2005*
0-4	32.2	20.4	16.0	14.2	11.2	10.3	10.2	10.1	10.3
5-9	2.7	1.7	1.5	1.2	1.2	0.7	0.6	0.8	0.9
10-14	1.4	1.5	1.0	0.9	0.9	0.7	0.8	0.6	0.7
15-19	1.6	1.6	1.4	1.2	1.0	1.0	1.3	1.2	1.3
20-24	2.2	1.8	1.9	1.8	1.5	1.5	1.3	1.3	1.6
25-29	2.6	1.7	2.4	2.1	2.1	1.8	1.6	1.7	1.7
30-34	3.1	2.8	2.3	2.2	2.2	1.9	2.1	2.3	2.0
35-39	4.4	3.6	3.5	2.7	2.8	3.2	2.5	2.4	2.8
40-44	5.6	4.8	4.1	3.7	3.6	4.4	3.5	3.6	3.5
45-49	8.0	6.9	6.3	5.7	5.6	5.4	4.2	5.1	5.3
50-54	13.6	11.6	10.7	9.9	9.7	8.7	8.3	6.6	7.8
55-59	19.4	18.5	17.7	14.4	14.6	12.7	12.7	10.8	11.7
60-64	30.9	28.4	26.5	26.3	21.3	20.2	20.0	18.1	19.0
65-69	42.8	39.3	38.0	32.4	35.7	36.7	31.1	27.8	13.3
70-74	91.5	79.7	84.1	55.0	49.2	44.3	42.1	45.1	49.2
75-79	NA	NA	NA	83.2	75.6	72.3	63.7	66.0	77.2
80-84	NA	NA	NA	118.2	94.9	90.4	99.1	107.3	107.8
85+	NA	NA	NA	172.8	171.6	178.5	154.9	183.8	176.9
All Ages	9.7	7.8	7.1	6.5	6.3	6.1	6.0	5.8	6.0

Notes: * Excludes Bihar and West Bengal.
** Excludes Jammu & Kashmir.
NA: Not available

Source: Registrar General and Census Commissioner of India, *Sample Registration System, Statistical Report*, for relevant Years.

Table 1.1.21: Migrants by Place of Last Residence and Sex

(Proportion in per cent)

Place of last residence	1981			1991			2001		
	Person	Male	Female	Person	Male	Female	Person	Male	Female
A. Migrants within the state of enumeration to total migrants	85.7	76.8	89.5	85.8	76.6	89.4	85.3	76.7	88.9
(i) Migrants who have resided elsewhere in the district of enumeration to total migrants	61.3	48.5	66.7	60.5	47.9	60.3	61.5	50.7	66.1
(ii) Migrants who have resided in other districts of the state to total migrants	24.5	28.3	22.8	25.3	28.7	24.1	23.8	26.0	22.8
B. Migrants who have resided in other states to total migrants	11.3	18.0	8.5	11.5	18.5	8.8	13.6	21.3	10.4
C. Migrants who have resided in other countries to total migrants	2.9	5.2	2.0	2.7	4.9	1.8	1.1	2.0	0.7
Total	100.0	100.0	100.0	100.0	100.0	100.0	100.0	100.0	100.0
Number of Migrants (Million)	207.7	62.5	145.2	232.1	64.3	167.8	314.5	93.3	221.2

Notes: 1981 figures exclude Assam.
1991 figures exclude Jammu and Kashmir.

Source: Registrar General and Census Commissionerof India, *Census of India,* for relevant years.

Table 1.1.22: Percentage Distribution of Migrants by Sex and Type of Migration

Sex	Year	Rural to Rural	Rural to Urban	Urban to Urban	Urban to Rural	Total	Number of Migrants (Million)
Male	1971	51.4	24.2	16.8	7.6	100.0	49.1
	1981	46.0	27.6	18.9	7.5	100.0	59.7
	1991	43.5	30.0	19.0	7.5	100.0	60.8
	1999-2000	32.6	34.3	22.3	10.8	100.0	54.2[E]
Female	1971	77.0	10.3	7.5	5.2	100.0	109.6
	1981	73.5	12.0	9.0	5.5	100.0	141.4
	1991	72.3	13.2	9.1	5.4	100.0	164.1
	1999-2000	70.3	14.4	10.1	5.2	100.0	186.9[E]
Person	1971	69.1	14.6	10.4	5.9	100.0	158.7
	1981	65.3	16.7	11.9	6.1	100.0	201.1
	1991	64.5	17.7	11.8	6.0	100.0	224.9
	1999-2000	61.8	18.9	12.8	6.5	100.0	241.1[E]

Notes: Exclude the unclassifiable figures. E- Estimated.

Sources: (i) Registrar General and Census Commssioner of India, *Census of India,* for relevant years.
(ii) National Sample Survey Organisation: Report No. 470, *Migration in India - 1999-2000.*

Figure 1.1.J

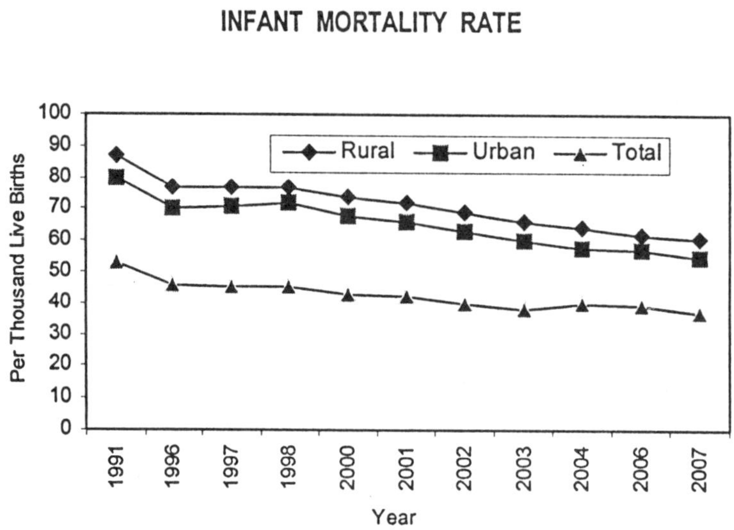

For details see Table 1.1.17

Figure 1.1.K

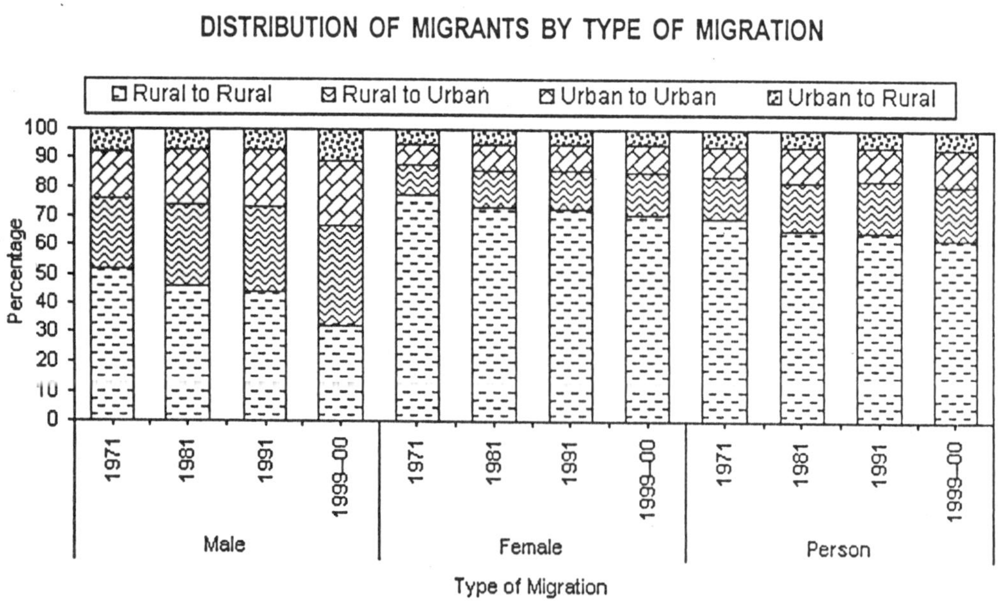

For details see Table 1.1.22

Table 1.1.23 : Inter-State Flow of Migrants (in'00) Among the Major States

To state / From State	Andhra Pradesh	Assam	Bihar	Gujarat	Haryana	Karnataka	Kerala	Madhya Pradesh	Mahara-shtra	Orissa	Punjab	Rajas-than	Tamil Nadu	Utter Pradesh	West Bengal	Others States/ Uts	All India
(1)	(2)	(3)	(4)	(5)	(6)	(7)	(8)	(9)	(10)	(11)	(12)	(13)	(14)	(15)	(16)	(17)	(18)
Andhra Pradesh	–	0	158	513	3	2944	241	530	3569	552	48	5	1521	278	308	389	11059
Assam	172	–	6	91	19	8	37	137	86	133	104	54	40	442	692	557	2578
Bihar	557	347	–	522	2608	51	50	1081	3389	2096	3389	548	66	9793	8313	1673	34483
Gujarat	127	12	154	–	47	108	252	545	6047	339	69	1608	0	311	57	319	9995
Haryana	0	0	58	0	–	5	1	154	399	45	3015	1769	14	1835	30	1342	8667
Karnataka	3364	0	22	46	16	–	1230	1044	8836	153	68	147	2117	177	135	1127	18482
Kerala	404	0	8	90	164	2119	–	203	1698	2	11	79	3118	114	181	307	8498
Madhya Pradesh	182	0	22	613	139	42	111	–	5364	590	199	2671	77	4656	131	452	15249
Maharashtra	1610	13	15	6746	205	2695	691	3722	–	476	174	850	900	2385	240	839	21561
Orissa	689	1	414	7	69	56	264	1131	1008	–	47	73	32	70	1420	137	5418
Punjab	78	1	129	19	3277	201	111	65	400	171	–	2553	227	2543	337	2736	12848
Rajasthan	614	82	106	2957	5043	261	174	1973	2965	49	907	–	408	2177	729	177	18622
Tamil Nadu	1732	165	60	68	26	3733	2903	180	3751	45	11	35	–	127	873	1836	15595
Uttar Pradesh	511	47	1294	3339	7612	157	154	9202	16174	68	4954	2796	270	–	1996	2746	51320
West Bengal	230	121	1130	122	19	132	20	785	1640	1563	238	366	258	2140	–	554	9 3 1 8
Other States/ UTs	1309	500	2035	2965	3946	1433	1596	1982	3839	794	3486	1341	2805	9885	3570	–	41536
All India	11579	1289	5611	18098	23193	14045	7835	22734	59165	7076	16720	14894	11853	36933	19012	15191	X

Note: For any state,'all-India' figure in cloumn 18 gives estimate for total out-migrants from that state to other States/UTs in India and row 'all-India' give of in-migrants in the state considering those from all states/Uts in India.

Source : National Sample Survey, Organisation : Report No. 470, *Migration in India*, 1999-2000.

Table 1.1.24: Percentage Distribution of Migrants by Reason for Migration & Location, 1999-2000

Reason for Migration		Rural			Urban			All India		
Code	Description	Male	Female	Person	Male	Female	Person	Male	Female	Person
A	**Economic Factors**	30.3	1.0	5.3	51.9	3.0	22.5	42.4	1.4	10.8
01	In Search of Employment	6.4	0.2	1.1	17.0	0.7	7.2	12.4	0.3	3.1
02	In Search of better Employment	10.4	0.4	1.8	15.6	0.8	6.7	13.3	0.5	3.4
03	To take up Employment/ better Employment	6.5	0.2	1.1	9.2	0.5	4.0	8.0	0.2	2.0
04	Transfer of Service/ Contract	6.0	0.2	1.1	9.1	0.9	4.2	7.7	0.4	2.0
05	Proximity to the place of Work	1.0	N	0.2	1.0	0.1	0.4	1.0	N	0.3
B	**Social Factors**	35.4	95.1	86.4	28.6	89.5	65.0	31.6	93.6	79.6
11	Marriage	9.4	88.8	77.3	1.6	58.5	35.6	5.0	81.3	64.1
12	Movement of Parents/ Earning Members	26.0	6.3	9.1	27.0	31.0	29.4	26.6	12.3	15.5
C	**Others**	34.1	3.9	8.3	19.5	7.5	12.5	25.9	5.0	9.6
06	Pursuing Studies	5.3	0.4	1.1	6.2	1.3	3.3	5.8	0.6	1.8
07	Acquision of house/Flat	3.9	0.3	0.9	4.1	1.4	2.5	4.0	0.6	1.4
08	Housing Problem	3.6	0.4	0.9	2.3	0.8	1.4	2.9	0.5	1.1
09	Social/Political Problem	3.9	0.5	1.0	1.4	0.7	1.0	2.5	0.6	1.0
10	Health	1.0	0.1	0.2	0.3	0.1	0.2	0.6	0.1	0.2
19	Other (including not else where classified)	16.4	2.2	4.2	5.2	3.2	4.1	10.1	2.6	4.1
	Total	100.0	100.0	100.0	100.0	100.0	100.0	100.0	100.0	100.0
	Estimated Migrants (Million)	24.0	142.6	166.6	31.2	46.4	77.6	55.2	189.0	244.2

Note: N — Nil.

Source: National Sample Survey Organisation : Report No. 470, *Migration in India, 1999-2000.*

Table 1.1.25: Population by Activity Status

Activity Status	1987-88 Rural	1987-88 Urban	1993-94 Rural	1993-94 Urban	1999-2000 Rural	1999-2000 Urban	2004-05 Rural	2004-05 Urban	2005-06 Rural	2005-06 Urban
Labour Force	44.3	35.6	44.9	36.3	42.3	35.4	44.6	38.2	44.1	36.8
Out of Labour Force	55.7	64.4	55.1	63.7	57.7	64.6	56.4	68.8	65.9	63.2
Total Population	100.0	100.0	100.0	100.0	100.0	100.0	100.0	100.0	100.0	100.0

Note: Figures relate to usual status of Individuals.

Sources: National Sample Survey Organisation:
Report No. 409, 458, 476, 515 & 522, *Employment and Unemployment situation in India.*

Table 1.1.26: Female Headed Households per 1000 Households and Average Household Size by Sex and State/Union Territory, 2004-05

State/Union Territory	Rural				Urban			
	Total No. of Households 2001(000's)	No. of Fh. Hhs. per 1000Hhs	Average Hh. Size		Total No. of Households 2001(000's)	No. of Fh. Hhs. per 1000Hhs	Average Hh.Size	
			Fh. Hhs.	all Hhs.			Fh. Hhs.	all Hhs.
INDIA	137,747	113	3.4	4.8	55,833	111	3.5	4.3
States								
1. Andhra Pradesh	12,607	136	2.6	3.3	4,397	132	3.0	3.9
2. Arunachal Pradesh	166	98	3.0	4.7	49	110	2.3	3.9
3. Assam	4,204	76	4.3	5.0	711	114	3.0	3.9
4. Bihar	12,407	111	3.8	5.1	1,337	74	4.1	4.7
5. Chhattisgarh	3,274	89	3.3	5.0	818	99	3.6	4.6
6. Delhi	180	4	3.6	4.7	2,554	79	3.7	4.0
7. Goa	145	264	3.6	4.1	150	158	3.6	4.5
8. Gujarat	5,942	104	3.0	4.8	3,750	95	2.8	4.4
9. Haryana	2,542	86	4.1	5.1	1,170	92	4.2	4.5
10. Himachal Pradesh	1,080	194	3.6	4.6	142	129	2.5	3.0
11. Jammu and Kashmir	1,167	56	4.3	5.6	401	67	3.5	5.0
12. Jharkhand	3,737	75	3.3	4.9	1,063	117	4.0	4.8
13. Karnataka	6,726	166	3.4	4.6	3,676	152	3.5	4.2
14. Kerala	5,010	233	3.9	4.2	1,716	251	3.9	4.1
15. Madhya Pradesh	7,996	62	3.3	5.2	2,916	71	3.3	5.0
16. Maharashtra	11,174	106	2.9	4.6	8,403	97	3.2	4.3
17. Manipur	273	115	4.6	5.0	102	163	4.2	4.8
18. Meghalaya	333	157	3.9	4.8	86	270	3.7	4.5
19. Mizoram	87	123	3.9	4.9	89	127	3.9	4.8
20. Nagaland	263	38	4.4	4.9	65	45	4.1	4.9
21. Orissa	6,619	96	3.2	4.7	1,120	100	3.4	4.3
22. Punjab	2,796	93	4.4	5.2	1,552	108	4.0	4.4
23. Rajasthan	7,054	105	3.8	5.4	2,263	79	3.9	5.1
24. Sikkim	101	89	3.3	4.2	13	114	2.3	3.4
25. Tamil Nadu	8284	163	2.5	3.7	6,382	146	2.8	3.6
26. Tripura	540	107	3.6	4.4	124	141	3.3	3.9
27. Uttaranchal	1,186	187	3.2	4.7	418	160	4.3	4.4
28. Uttar Pradesh	20,373	98	4.0	5.6	5,385	76	4.4	5.1
29. West Bengal	11,271	90	3.2	4.7	4,601	121	3.8	4.1
Union Territories								
1. Andaman and Nicobar Islands	52	92	3.8	4.2	26	111	3.4	3.8
2. Chandigarh	23	58	3.4	3.5	184	71	4.1	3.9
3. Dadra and Nagar Haveli	34	35	1.7	3.4	12	17	1.7	3.6
4. Daman and Diu	23	88	3.3	3.5	12	145	2.9	4.3
5. Lakshadweep	6	339	5.8	5.2	4	288	6.5	5.5
6. Pondicherry	73	243	3.0	3.7	143	188	3.2	3.7

Note: *Fh. Hhs*: Female Headed Households.

Sources: (i) National Sample Survey Orginsation : Report No. 515, *Employment and Unemployment Situation in India, 2004-2005.*

(ii) Registrar General and Census Commssioner of India, *Census of India-2001, Primacy Census Abstract* (for no. of household).

(ii) Disabled Persons

Table 1.2.1: Distribution of Disabled by Type of Disability, Sex, Literacy Status and Residence – 2001

(Thousands)

Type of disability	*Sex*	*Total Population*			*Literate*			*Illiterate*		
		Total	*Rural*	*Urban*	*Total*	*Rural*	*Urban*	*Total*	*Rural*	*Urban*
Total disabled population	Persons	21,907	16,388	5,518	10,801	7,277	3,524	11,106	9,112	1,994
	Males	12,606	9,410	3,196	7,330	5,092	2,238	5,276	4,319	957
	Females	9,301	6,978	2,323	3,471	2,185	1,286	5,830	4,793	1,037
In Seeing	Persons	10,635	7,873	2,762	5,301	3,430	1,872	5,334	4,444	890
	Males	5,732	4,223	1,510	3,414	2,288	1,126	2,318	1,935	383
	Females	4,903	3,651	1,252	1,887	1,142	745	3,015	2,509	507
In Speech	Persons	1,641	1,244	397	594	390	204	1,046	854	193
	Males	942	714	228	395	266	129	547	448	99
	Females	699	530	169	200	124	76	499	406	93
In Hearing	Persons	1,262	1,023	239	545	402	143	717	621	96
	Males	674	549	125	375	287	89	298	262	36
	Females	588	474	114	169	115	54	419	358	60
In Movement	Persons	6,105	4,655	1,451	3,503	2,501	1002	2,602	2,153	449
	Males	3,903	2,975	928	2,554	1,860	694	1,349	1,115	234
	Females	2,203	1,679	523	949	641	308	1,254	1,038	215
Mental	Persons	2,264	1,598	670	858	553	304	1,406	1,040	366
	Males	1,355	949	405	592	391	201	763	559	204
	Females	909	644	265	266	162	104	643	482	161

Source: Registrar General and Census Commission of India, *Census of India – 2001*

Table 1.2.2 : Rural and Urban Disabled Population by Sex and State/Union Territory, 2001

(Thousands)

State/Union Territory	Rural			Urban		
	Person	*Male*	*Female*	*Person*	*Male*	*Female*
INDIA	**16388**	**9410**	**6978**	**5518**	**3195**	2323
States						
1. Andhra Pradesh	1050	590	460	315	184	131
2. Arunachal Pradesh	27	18	9	6	4	2
3. Assam	468	261	207	62	36	26
4. Bihar	1692	1014	678	195	118	77
5. Chhattisgarh	345	189	156	75	43	32
6. Delhi	13	8	5	222	136	86
7. Goa	9	5	4	7	4	3
8. Gujarat	719	415	304	326	190	136
9. Haryana	340	205	135	115	69	46
10. Himachal Pradesh	145	84	61	11	7	4
11. Jammu & Kashmir	229	129	100	73	42	31
12. Jharkhand	349	203	146	99	61	38
13. Karnataka	661	376	285	279	162	117
14. Kerala	648	345	303	213	114	99
15. Madhya Pradesh	1060	618	442	348	206	142
16. Maharashtra	1020	600	420	549	333	216
17. Manipur*	21	11	10	7	4	3
18. Meghalaya	23	12	11	6	3	3
19. Mizoram	10	5	5	6	3	3
20. Nagaland	24	13	11	3	2	1
21. Orissa	878	486	392	144	84	60
22. Punjab	297	178	119	127	75	52
23. Rajasthan	1109	658	451	303	183	120
24. Sikkim	18	10	8	2	1	1
25. Tamil Nadu	945	447	498	698	345	353
26. Tripura	49	28	21	10	6	4
27. Uttaranchal	155	89	66	40	24	16
28. Uttar Pradesh	2706	1626	1080	748	451	297
29. West Bengal	1354	774	580	493	284	209
Union Territories						
1. Andaman and Nicobar Islands	5	3	2	2	1	1
2. Chandigarh	1.6	1.0	0.6	14	9	4
3. Dadra & Nagar Haveli	2	1	1	1.2	0.6	0.6
4. Daman and Diu	3	2	1	0.8	0.5	0.3
5. Lakshadweep	1	0.5	0.5	0.7	0.4	0.3
6. Pondicherry	9	5	4	16	9	7

Notes: * Excludes the figures of Mao Maram, Paomata and Purul sub-divisions of Senapati Dist.
Total may not tally due to rounding off.

Source: Registrar General and Census Commssioner of India, *Census of India-2001.*

Table 1.2.3: Prevalence Rate and Estimated Number (in 000's) of Disabled by Type of Disability, Sex and Residence

NSS Round and Level of Education	*Rural*			*Urban*			*Total*		
	Male	*Female*	*Persons*	*Male*	*Female*	*Persons*	*Male*	*Female*	*Persons*
1) Mental Disability									
36th Round July-December, 1981	Not Available								
47th Round July-December, 1991	Not Available								
58th Round July-December, 2002	241 (910)	160 (573)	202 (1483)	223 (302)	152 (188)	189 (490)	237 (1212)	158 (761)	199 (1973)
2) Visual Disability									
36th Round July-December, 1981	444 (1193)	670 (1715)	553 (2908)	294 (249)	425 (317)	356 (566)	409 (1442)	617 (2032)	509 (3474)
47th Round July-December, 1991	471 (1539)	584 (1796)	525 (3335)	263 (308)	346 (362)	302 (670)	416 (1847)	524 (2158)	467 (4005)
58th Round July-December, 2002	267 (1009)	325 (1162)	296 (2171)	162 (220)	228 (283)	194 (503)	239 (1230)	301 (1445)	269 (2674)
3) Hearing Disability (5 Yrs & above)									
36th Round July-December, 1981	595 (1366)	510 (1111)	553 (2477)	386 (288)	395 (254)	390 (542)	469 (1654)	414 (1365)	443 (3019)
47th Round July-December, 1991	498 (1409)	435 (1164)	467 (2573)	325 (339)	355 (330)	339 (669)	394 (1748)	362 (1494)	379 (3242)
58th Round July-December, 2002	319 (1203)	301 (1072)	310 (2275)	234 (317)	238 (295)	236 (612)	296 (1520)	285 (1367)	291 (2887)
4) Speech Disability									
36th Round July-December, 1981	379 (870)	228 (496)	304 (1366)	342 (255)	207 (133)	279 (388)	319 (1125)	191 (629)	257 (1754)
47th Round July-December, 1991	333 (942)	208 (557)	273 (1449)	285 (298)	182 (169)	237 (467)	279 (1240)	176 (726)	230 (1966)
58th Round July-December, 2002	242 (916)	176 (626)	210 (1542)	221 (298)	151 (187)	187 (485)	237 (1214)	169 (813)	204 (2027)
5) Locomotor Disability									
36th Round July-December, 1981	1047 (2814)	597 (1528)	828 (4342)	800 (679)	544 (406)	679 (1085)	990 (3493)	587 (1934)	796 (5427)
47th Round July-December, 1991	1345 (4396)	784 (2411)	1074 (6807)	1170 (1370)	728 (762)	962 (2132)	1299 (5766)	770 (3173)	1044 (8939)
58th Round July-December, 2002	1274 (4813)	804 (2863)	1046 (7676)	1058 (1430)	730 (905)	901 (2335)	121 (6243)	785 (3768)	1008 (10011)
6) Physical Disability									
36th Round July-December, 1981	2045 (5496)	1632 (4176)	1844 (9672)	1532 (1300)	1297 (967)	1420 (2267)	1928 (6796)	1557 (5143)	1750 (11939)
47th Round July-December, 1991	2277 (7442)	1694 (5210)	1995 (12652)	1774 (2078)	1361 (1424)	1579 (3502)	2144 (9520)	1610 (6634)	1887 (16154)
58th Round July-December, 2002	2118 (8001)	1556 (5544)	1846 (13545)	1670 (2259)	1311 (1624)	1499 (3883)	2000 (10260)	1493 (7168)	1755 (17428)

Note: Figures within the parenthesis are estimates of Disabled.

Sources: National Sample Survey Organisation :

(*i*) Report No. 305, *Report on Survey of Disabled Persons, 1981.*

(*ii*) Report No. 337, *Characteristics of Disabled Persons, 1981.*

(*iii*) Report No. 393, *A Report on Disabled Persons, 1991.*

(*iv*) Report No. 485, *Disabled Persons in India, 2002.*

Table 1.2.4: Distribution of Disabled (per thousand) by Broad Age-group

All-India

Age-group	*Rural*			*Urban*			*Total*		
	Male	*Female*	*Person*	*Male*	*Female*	*Person*	*Male*	*Female*	*Person*
36th Round									
July-December, 1981									
0-4	38	32	36	52	45	49	41	34	38
5-14	186	145	168	231	185	211	194	153	176
15-39	275	191	239	311	224	273	282	197	246
40-59	204	192	199	166	170	168	197	188	193
60+	297	440	358	240	376	299	286	428	347
All	1000	1000	1000	1000	1000	1000	1000	1000	1000
47th Round									
July-December, 1991									
0-4	36	35	35	41	37	39	37	35	36
5-14	204	173	191	218	196	209	207	178	195
15-34	240	171	212	281	195	247	249	176	219
35-44	97	70	86	96	79	89	97	72	87
45-59	151	156	153	130	141	134	146	153	149
60+	272	395	322	234	352	282	264	386	314
All	1000	1000	1000	1000	1000	1000	1000	1000	1000
58th Round									
July-December, 2002									
0-4	31	31	31	30	30	30	31	31	31
5-14	185	181	183	161	166	163	180	178	179
15-34	308	241	281	317	264	295	311	246	283
35-44	111	87	101	118	94	108	112	89	103
45-59	150	142	147	156	144	151	151	142	148
60+	216	317	257	218	302	253	216	314	256
All	1000	1000	1000	1000	1000	1000	1000	1000	1000

Sources: National Sample Survey Organisation :
(*i*) Report No. 305, *Report on Survey of Disabled Persons, 1981.*
(*ii*) Report No. 337, *Characteristics of Disabled Persons, 1981.*
(*iii*) Report No. 393, *A Report on Disabled Persons, 1991.*
(*iv*) Report No. 485, *Disabled Persons in India, 2002.*

Table 1.2.5: Distribution of Disabled (per thousand) by Level of General Education, Sex and Residence

All-India

NSS Round and Level of Education	Rural			Urban			Total		
	Male	Female	Person	Male	Female	Person	Male	Female	Person
36th Round July-December, 1981									
Illiterate	635	873	737	454	649	481	580	831	688
Literate but below Primary	183	71	135	235	156	201	193	87	147
Primary	90	26	62	151	87	123	102	37	74
Middle	53	12	35	131	56	98	68	20	47
Secondary/ Hr. Secondary	24	4	15	87	29	61	36	9	24
Graduate and above	4	–	3	36	9	24	10	2	7
Not Reported	11	14	13	11	14	12	11	14	13
Total	1000	1000	1000	1000	1000	1000	1000	1000	1000
47th Round July-December, 1991									
Illiterate	–	–	701	–	–	462	–	–	649
Literate but below Primary	–	–	117	–	–	163	–	–	127
Primary	–	–	86	–	–	135	–	–	97
Middle	–	–	53	–	–	110	–	–	65
Secondary/ Hr. Secondary	–	–	31	–	–	92	–	–	44
Graduate and above	–	–	4	–	–	31	–	–	10
Not Reported	–	–	8	–	–	8	–	–	8
Total	–	–	1000	–	–	1000	–	–	1000
58th Round July-December, 2002									
Illiterate	485	741	590	311	523	400	447	691	547
Primary*	293	174	244	309	258	288	297	193	254
Middle	128	52	97	160	104	137	135	64	106
Secondary/ Hr. Secondary	79	28	59	160	86	129	97	42	74
Graduate and above	13	4	10	59	27	46	23	9	18
Not Reported	1	1	1	1	2	1	1	1	1
Total	1000	1000	1000	1000	1000	1000	1000	1000	1000

Notes : Sex-wise data by level of education for 47th Round is not available.
* Includes the category 'Literate but below Primary' also.

Sources : National Sample Survey Organisation :
(*i*) Report No. 305, *Report on Survey of Disabled Persons, 1981.*
(*ii*) Report No. 337, *Characteristics of Disabled Persons, 1981.*
(*iii*) Report No. 393, *A Report on Disabled Persons, 1991.*
(*iv*) Report No. 485, *Disabled Persons in India, 2002.*

Table 1.2.6: Distribution of Disabled* (per thousand) by Broad Activity Status

All-India

Activity Status	*Rural*			*Urban*			*Total*		
	Male	*Female*	*Person*	*Male*	*Female*	*Person*	*Male*	*Female*	*Person*
36th Round									
July-December, 1981									
1. Employed	410	116	283	326	84	221	394	110	272
(a) Self-Employed	272	53	177	164	36	108	251	50	164
(b) Regular Employee	30	4	19	106	22	70	45	7	29
(c) Casual Employee	108	59	87	56	26	43	98	53	78
2. Unemployed	12	4	8	32	7	21	16	51	11
3. Not in Labour Force	578	880	709	642	909	758	590	885	717
Total	1000	1000	1000	1000	1000	1000	1000	1000	1000
47th Round									
July-December, 1991									
1. Employed	–	–	290	–	–	253	–	–	282
(a) Self-Emp. in Agriculture	–	–	133	–	–	19	–	–	108
(b) Self-Emp. in Non-Agriculture	–	–	42	–	–	102	–	–	55
(c) Regular Employee	–	–	20	–	–	77	–	–	32
(d) Casual Employee	–	–	95	–	–	55	–	–	86
2. Unemployed	–	–	7	–	–	17	–	–	9
3. Not in Labour Force	–	–	703	–	–	730	–	–	709
Total	–	–	1000	–	–	1000	–	–	1000
58th Round									
July-December, 2002									
1. Employed	369	109	263	347	88	238	364	104	257
(a) Self-Emp. in Agriculture	163	23	106	144	26	94	159	24	103
(b) Self-Emp. in Non-Agriculture	65	30	51	30	10	22	58	26	45
(c) Regular Employee	26	7	18	105	29	73	43	12	30
(d) Casual Employee	115	48	88	67	23	49	105	42	79
2. Unemployed	8	2	6	18	4	12	11	3	7
3. Not in Labour Force	623	889	731	635	908	750	625	893	736
Total	1000	1000	1000	1000	1000	1000	1000	1000	1000

Notes: Sex-wise data by activity status for 47th Round is not available.
* Data relate to 5 + age-group.

Sources: National Sample Survey Organisation :
(*i*) Report No. 305, *Report on Survey of Disabled Persons, 1981.*
(*ii*) Report No. 337, *Characteristics of Disabled Persons, 1981.*
(*iii*) Report No. 393, *A Report on Disabled Persons, 1991.*
(*iv*) Report No. 485, *Disabled Persons in India, 2002.*

Table 1.2.7: Distribution of Disabled Workers according to Usual Activity Status in Broad Industrial Sector

All-India

Industry Sector	*Rural*			*Urban*			*Total*		
	Male	*Female*	*Person*	*Male*	*Female*	*Person*	*Male*	*Female*	*Person*
36th Round July-December, 1981									
Primary Sector	770	770	770	147	182	152	651	660	655
Secondary Sector	77	70	75	247	280	253	109	109	109
Tertiary Sector	153	160	155	606	538	595	240	231	236
Total	1000	1000	1000	1000	1000	1000	1000	1000	1000
58th Round July-December, 2002									
Primary Sector	667	730	678	99	137	105	548	616	560
Secondary Sector	132	117	130	303	323	306	168	156	166
Tertiary Sector	193	146	185	587	531	578	276	220	266
Total*	1000	1000	1000	1000	1000	1000	1000	1000	1000

Notes: Industry-wise data in 47th Round of NSS July-December, 1991 is not available.
* Includes the Category 'not reported'.

Sources: National Sample Survey Organisation :
(*i*) Report No. 305, *Report on Survey of Disabled Persons, 1981.*
(*ii*) Report No. 337, *Characteristics of Disabled Persons, 1981.*
(*iii*) Report No. 393, *A Report on Disabled Persons, 1991.*
(*iv*) Report No. 485, *Disabled Persons in India, 2002.*

Table 1.2.8: Distribution of Disabled Workers by Sex & Broad Industrial Category, 2001

(Thousands)

S. No.	Typed of Disabled Workers	Cultivators			Agricultural Labour			Household Industry			Other Workers			Total Workers		
		Person	*Male*	*Female*	*Person*	*Male*	*Female*	*Person*	*Male*	*Female*	*Person*	*Male*	*Female*	*Person*	*Male*	*Female*
	ALL INDIA															
1.	Total Population	2432	1855	577	1966	1224	742	346	211	135	2811	2358	453	7556	5649	1907
2.	In Seeing	1382	1020	362	1099	643	456	185	106	79	1580	1313	267	4247	3083	1164
3.	In Speech	169	127	42	167	103	64	26	15	11	167	137	30	529	383	146
4.	In Hearing	191	144	47	142	85	57	24	14	10	134	106	28	491	349	142
5.	In Movement	530	438	92	414	296	118	90	63	27	767	664	103	1802	1461	341
6.	Mental	160	126	34	143	96	47	21	13	8	162	137	25	486	372	114
	RURAL															
1.	Total Population	2382	1816	566	1886	1173	713	252	151	101	1405	1141	264	5925	4281	1644
2.	In Seeing	1352	997	355	1050	614	436	130	73	57	743	593	150	3276	2278	998
3.	In Speech	165	124	41	161	99	62	19	11	8	86	68	18	432	302	130
4.	In Hearing	188	142	46	137	82	55	19	11	8	84	65	19	429	230	129
5.	In Movement	519	429	90	399	285	114	68	47	21	416	355	61	1403	1115	288
6.	Mental	156	123	33	138	93	45	15	9	6	76	61	15	386	286	100
	URBAN															
1.	Total Population	50	40	10	80	51	29	95	60	35	1406	1217	189	1631	1368	263
2.	In Seeing	30	23	7	49	29	20	54	33	21	837	720	117	971	805	166
3.	In Speech	3	2	1	6	4	2	7	4	3	81	70	11	98	81	17
4.	In Hearing	3	2	1	5	3	2	5	3	2	51	42	9	63	50	13
5.	In Movement	11	10	1	15	12	3	23	16	7	351	309	42	399	346	53
6.	Mental	3	2	1	5	4	1	6	4	2	86	76	10	100	86	14

Note: *Total may not tally due to rounding off.*

Source: Registrar General & Census Commissioner of India, *Census of India* 2001.

SECTION 2

Manpower Formation Process

Dr. Mridula Sharma
Vijay K. Saxena

Section-II
Manpower Formation Process

The Constitution of India provides directives regarding development of education in the country. Education being the concurrent subject, the constitution also identifies the domain of the central and state government with respect to sharing the responsibilities of development of education in the country. The central government establishes broad educational policies related to all important issues besides access, quality affordability and governance. The policies are evolved on the basis of (a) recommendations of various educational commissions and committees set up by the government from time to time and (b) extensive debates, seminar, findings of research and consultations organized at state, national and international levels on various educational issues. The policies serve as guidelines for educational development in the country.

The research in economics of educational in sixties (Shultz – Investment in Human Capital 1966) established by the positive contribution of education to the socio-economic development of a nation. Influenced by findings of the research, the countries in the world started giving importance to the development of education sector. India was no exception to this general phenomenon. The education Commission (1966) and the New Education Policy (1986) emphasized on increasing the allocations to education sector to the extent of 6% of the GDP. The idea was to develop the quality and stock of manpower which contributes positively to the growth and development of the country. As the development of quality and stock of manpower depends on the quantitative and qualitative achievements of education sector, it is essential from policy point of view to analyse the quantitative and qualitative achievements of education sector. The data in this section provide information on this aspect.

The quantitative achievements are seen in terms of expansion of the education sector and qualitative achievements are assessed through improvement in the system on the basis of certain qualitative indicators. Tables 2.1.1 to 2.1.20 provide information about quantitative achievements of education sector in terms of increase in the number of educational institutions, teachers, and enrolments by levels, types of education and gender, during 1980-81 to 2005-06. The information about qualitative development is available in the tables 2.1.19 to 2.1.27. These tables provide data on some of the qualitative indicators of the system, namely, gross enrolment ratio and net attendance ratio, dropouts and outturn of students with gender and regional focus. Tables 2.1.28 to 2.1.35 provide information related to apprentices training and vocational education. Tables 2.2.1 to 2.2.7 provide data on labour force participation rates and its educational composition which is the source of economically active stock in labour market during the last 30 years. Tables 2.3.1 to 2.3.4 provide data on investment in education during the same period. Some data about literacy rates, net enrolment rates, educational attainments as well as expenditure on education by households in the North-eastern part of India are available in the tables 2.4.1-2.4.15.

Data presented in the tables have been obtained mainly from the publications of various departments, ministries and other government organizations. Data on educational institutions, enrolment and teachers have been collected mainly from the reports titled, Education in India, and Selected Educational Statistics published annually by the Department of Education, Ministry of Human Resource Development. Data related to higher education was obtained from the annual reports of the University Grants Commission. The data on medical education was collected from the statistical reports of the Directorate General of Health Services and Medical Council of India. The published and unpublished documents of the National Technical Manpower Information System; IAMR, and the Department of Technical Education, Ministry of Human Resource Developent, Government of India were used for collecting information on engineering/technical education facilities and the outturn of technical institutions. The data in the tables 2.4.1-2.4.15 belong to IAMR project, Bench Marking Human Development in the North-eastern Region of India. The data in the report are collected from 46,220 households of the 72 districts in the seven states of North East. A broad analysis of the above set of tables is given under the following headings.

Quantitative Achievements

The indicators used for quantitative achievements of education sector are (a) increase in the number of educational institutions, (b) increase in enrolment, and (c) increase in teachers.

Institutions: Table 2.1.1 provides data related to educational institutions by level and type of education during 1981 to 2005. Analysis of the data reveals that there was a significant increase in the absolute number of all types of educational institutions at all levels during 1981-2005. However, the number of institutions declined as one moved from lower to higher levels of educational institutions, i.e. from schools to colleges and from colleges to universities. The rate of increase in the number of institutions also varied for different levels of education. The higher secondary schools increased by 2.13 per cent and the middle schools by 143 per cent. The increase in the primary schools was only 56 per cent. The highest increase 553 per cent was observed for pre-primary schools. It may however be mentioned that increase in the growth of pre-primary schools was not continuous during the period under consideration.

At the higher level, rate of growth of professional institutions was much higher than that of institutions providing general education during 1981-2005. The number of engineering, technology and architecture institutions increased by 813 per cent, while the number of institutions providing general education of the same level increased only by 242 per cent. The teachers training institutions increased by about 389 per cent and professional/vocational institutions at below degree level increased only by 56 per cent during the same period. Evidently, there is a growing demand for vocational/professional education.

Teachers: data regarding the number of teachers in different types of institutions over the period 1981 to 2005, indicate that although the number of teachers increased by 60 per cent at primary level, 96 per cent at middle and 136 per cent at secondary level, the student-teacher ratio did not improve, rather deteriorated at all the three levels of school education. Gender-wise data regarding the number of teachers indicate a higher increase in the number of female teachers 151 per cent at primary level, 166 per cent at middle level and 223 per cent at secondary level) as compared to the male teachers during 1981 to 2005.

Enrolment: Data in tables 2.1.4 to 2.1.19 related to enrolment in educational by type and level, during 1981 to 2005-06, the analyses of the data indicate a rapid increase in enrolment for all types of education and at all levels during the period under consideration. At the school level, highest increase in enrolment (336 per cent) was observed for the post-metric level, followed by the secondary education where percentage increase in enrolment was found to be 183. The increase in enrolment at middle and primary levels during 1981 to 2005 was observed as 152 and 79 per cent respectively.

The enrolment at degree and above level increase by 230 per cent during 1981 to 2005 (Table 2.1.4). The general courses had much higher enrolment at Undergraduate (UG), Postgraduate (PG) and Ph.D. levels as compared to the professional courses of same levels. In general education, arts and humanities accounted for more than half of the total enrolments (53 per cent) at Ph.D level and 63 per cent at PG level during 1981. Enrolment in sciences declined at the postgraduate level during 1981 to 1991 and increased during 1991 to 2001, but at the undergraduate level it has a continuously declining trend from 1981 to 1991 both in postgraduate and undergraduate levels, but declined trend from 1981 to 2001 at both levels.

The figures relating to enrolment by type of education at degree and above levels indicate that the highest increase in enrolment among the professional courses was for the engineering and technology courses followed by medicine. The enrolment in engineering/technology and architecture increased by 453 per cent during 1981 to 2004. Against this, the enrolment in medicine and veterinary courses varied between 158 to 103. The rate of increase in the enrolment in agriculture/forestry was even lower (42 percent) than the rate of increase in enrolment in agriculture/forestry was even lower (42 per cent) than the rate of increase in enrolment in medicine and veterinary science. The other courses in education showed an increase in enrolment by about 42 per cent during 20001 to 2004.

Gender specific data regarding enrolment indicate that enrolment of girls at the primary level increased by 116 per cent during 1981-2005. Against this, the enrolment of boys at this level increased by only 56 per cent. The increase in the enrolment of girls at middle and secondary levels was 243 per cent and 296 per cent, respectively which were much higher than the increase of enrolment of boys

107 per cent and 135 per cent during 1981 to 2005). Even at the higher level the rate of increase in enrolment of girls (548 per cent) was significantly higher than the increase in enrolment of boys (302 percent) (tables 2.1.5 to 2.1.6).

Putting all the three levels of higher education together (i.e. Ph.D, PG and UG), the enrolment of girls as a percentage of total enrolment increased in all the faculties during 1980-81 to 2000-01. Highest increase in the girls" enrolment (from 4.6 per cent to 22.2 per cent) as a percentage of total enrolment was observed in the faculty of engineering/technology. It was followed by commerce, where girls' enrolment as a percentage of total enrolment increased from 15.2 percent to 35.1 per cent during 1980-81 to 2003-06. Increase in the enrolments of girls in the faculty of arts was very insignificant as compared to commerce e and engineering. The faculties of science and medicine showed an increase of 12 to 21 percent in the girls' enrolments as a percentage of total enrolment during the period under consideration (Table 2.1.19).

Qualitative Achievements

Tables 2.1.20 to 2.1.35 and 2.3.1 to 2.3.8 provide data on the qualitative achievements of the system. A number of indicators, namely, gross enrolment ratios, gross and net attendance ratios, dropouts, intake capacity and outturn of institutions, labour force estimation and their participation rates and cost and expenditure on education have been analyzed to assess the qualitative a achievements of the sector.

Gross Enrolment Ratio: Table 2.1.20 provides gross enrolment ratios (GER) for primary, upper primary (middle) and secondary stages of education for different years, starting from 1980-81 to 2005-06. The gross enrolment ratios deteriorated, as we move from primary to secondary level of education. Gender wise data about gross enrolment ratios indicate that the gross enrolment ratios for boys were better at all levels of school education as compared to the gross enrolment ratios of girls. The gross enrolment ratio improved for girls significantly at primary and middle levels during 1980-81 to 2005-06. At higher secondary level the gross enrolment ratios improved for both girls and boys, but at a very slow pace.

Dropouts: 2.1.22 provide dropout rates by sex for primary, upper primary (Middle) and secondary levels for different years starting from 1980-81. The dropout rates at schools increased with an increase in the level of education throughout the period under considerations. About 60% of boys and 61% girls dropped out at secondary level of school education. The dropout rate was higher among girls as compared to boys at middle and secondary level. The situation was however reversing at primary levels.

Intake Capacity and Outturn: Tables 2.1.24 to 2.1.29 present data about intake capacity and outturn of the system during 1970-71 to 2001-02. It is seen from the tables that the number of admissions in engineering increased significantly at both degree and diploma levels, but the rate of increase in the number of admission in degree courses was much higher as compared to the rate of increase in number of admissions in the diploma both at degree and diploma levels during

1998-99. The outturn of engineering increased for both degree as well as diploma courses during 1970-71 to 2001-02, but the rate of increase of outturn was higher for diploma courses compared to the degree courses. As a result, the gap between admission and outturn became wider for degree level engineering courses in comparison to the gap at diploma level.

The increase in the number of admissions as well as outturn for medical (Allopathy) and dental degree courses was not very significant during the period under consideration. The admissions to medical (allopathy) courses increased from 12,029 to 18,168 during 1971 to 2001. The outturn of the medical courses (allopathy) also increased from 10,407 to 14,500 during the 1971-1992. The admissions to dental courses increased from 562 to 3301 and the outturn from 478 to 2548 during 1971 to 1998. The gap between the number of admissions and outturns of medical (allopathy) courses was less as compared to dental courses.

Details of the outturn of different types of engineering courses, indicate a decline in the number of outturns for civil/engineering at diploma level. The degree level engineering courses show an increasing trend in the number of outturns during 2002. The outturn of some of the diploma courses, namely, chemical, electrical, electronics, automobiles, leather technology, production and textile engineering, architecture, instrumentation and leather engineering was also more than double at the degree level. The outturn of nurses (diploma/certificate holders) doubled while the outturn of midwives, health workers and health visitors decline during 1970-1998.

The stagnation in the number of apprentices undergoing training in different industrial training centres during 1981-2002 led to an increase gap between the existing and utilized vacancies for apprentices in different trades.

Tables 2.1.31 to 2.1.35 provide data relating to industrial training and vocational education which develop the manpower. Table 2.1.34 to 2.1.35 present information regarding the number of persons trained by Khadi and Village Industry Commission by social groups.

Labour Force Estimation and their Participation Rates: The strength of the labour force as well as their participation rates for both males and females were found to be much higher in rural areas as compared to their urban counterparts during 1972-73 to 2005-06. Total labour force in rural areas increased from 199.6 million to 326.0 million and in urban areas from 40.6 million to 86.7 million during 1972-73 to 2005-06. The participation rate of labour force varied between 43.9 per cent to 44.1 per cent in rural areas and 34.5 per cent to 36.8 per cent in urban areas.

State-wise details of labour force participation rates in India indicate that very few states, namely Andhra Pradesh, Chhatisgarh, Dadra & Nagar Haveli, Gujarat, Himachal Pradesh, Meghalaya, Mizoram, Nagaland, Karnataka, Maharashtra and Tamil Nadu had labour force participation rates more than 40 per cent in rural areas and 37.7 per cent to 47.4 per cent for urban areas. The lowest rural female labour force participation rate (8.6 percent) is noted for Delhi followed by Goa (15.6 percent). The lowest urban female labour force participation rate (7.8 per cent) is recorded for Delhi, followed by Bihar (8.3 Percent). The highest urban female labour force participation rate (28.4 per cent) is seen for Goa and the highest rural female participation (50.5 per cent) for Himachal Pradesh. Against this, the lowest male labour force participation rates for rural and urban areas are noted to be (50.6 per cent) and (46.4 per cent) for Uttar Pradesh and Uttranchal respectively. The highest male labour force participation rate is observed as 69.7 per cent for urban areas and 65.5 per cent for rural areas.

Around six out of every 10 male labour forces were illiterate during 1977-78. The number declined to 3.3 during 2005-06. The percentage of male literate labour force decreased marginally. Illiteracy was more prevalent among the female labour force as compared to the male. Almost the entire female labour force (88.1 per cent in rural areas and 58.2 per cent in urban areas) was illiterate in 1977-78. Although, the percentage of illiterate female is still constituted about half the total female labour force even in the years 2005-06 only 4.5 per cent of the total female labour force had education up to secondary level and above till 2002-03. Only 7.6 per cent of the total rural female labour force and 14.6 per cent of the total urban female labour force had education above secondary level during 1999-2000.

Data regarding educated labour force participation indicate that through labour force participation rates for the male matriculates and graduates increased for rural areas and declined for urban areas during 1977-78 to 2005-06, the labour force participation rates for females' matriculates and graduates declined for both rural and urban areas during the same period.

Financing and Cost of Education: Tables 2.3.1 to 2.3.4 provide information about financing and cost of education in India during 1990-91 to 2004-05. It is important to note that the country is not able to reach its target of spending 6 percent of GDP on education even in the year 2005-06. The expenditure on education as a percentage of GDP decreased from 3.84 in 1990-91 to 3.49 during 2004-05.

Data about the allocation of budget to various stages of education indicate that elementary education received top priority throughout the 1990s. Almost half of the total budget allocation was for elementary education during 1993-94 to 2005-06. University and other higher education received nearly 11.02. The allocation for technical education remained in between 4.0 per cent and 4.8 percent during 1991-1992 to 2004-05.

Education in the North Eastern Region of India: The Table 2.4.1 to 2.4.15 provides data on literacy rates, net enrolment rates, educational attainments and private expenditure on education in the seven states of the North East. The analysis of these tables indicates that the states in the North East in general have done well in terms of achieving high literacy rates but their performances in terms of educational attainments are poor. A good point which emerges from the analysis of data related to private expenditure of education is that, poor spend relatively larger portion of their income on the education of their wards. This is a positive indication for development of education sector in the region.

The issues which emerge out of above analysis of the tables are:

- The expansion in education sector is still not able to bring all children to the schools at primary level. The schemes like Sarv Shiksha Abhiyan have not succeeded in achieving 100% literacy rate. The country still has 46% illiterate females and 204% illiterate males. There are a few states like Arunachal Pradesh, Bihar, Jammu and Kashmir, Jharkhand, Rajasthan, Uttar Pradesh, where more than half of the women are illiterates. The illiteracy among scheduled caste and scheduled tribes is still high as more than half of the scheduled tribe population is still illiterate. There is a need to evaluate the working of the schemes like SSA and give a fresh look so that the target set by SSA; namely (a) all children in the school by 2003, (b) all children completing five years primary education by 2007 (c) all children completing 8 years of schooling by 2010 (d) bridging of all gender and social category gap at primary stages of schooling by 2010 and (e) universal retention by 2010 may be achieved. The achievement of these targets require lots of challenges; particularly, improvement in infrastructure, as well quality and joyful learning.
- The enrolment at middle and secondary level has increased during 1981-2004 but high dropout rates (more than 50% at middle level and more than 60% at secondary level) keeps the gross enrolment ratio low at middle and secondary level. The gross enrolment ratio for the year 2004-05 were only 70% at middle level and 40% at secondary level. Further research is needed to find out the causes of high dropout rate and steps to reduce the dropout rate may be taken accordingly. A study by NUEPA – Elementary Education in India Progress: towards UEE, 2004-05 indicate that there exist wide variations in infrastructural facilities in most of the states. Rural-urban differences in terms of infrastructural facilities are also indicates. If lack of infrastructural facilities are the causes of high dropout rate, a careful structural programme with financial support for improvement of infrastructural facilities may help in reducing dropout rates. Some of the causes of dropouts in metropolitan slums rare also highlighted in study. (Why children drop out metro slums by Sunita Chugh-2004). The causes for dropouts may be taken care, while formulating the policy of development of education.
- Only 15% of the relevant age group population (18-23) is enrolled in the system of higher education in spite of an expansion of the system in terms of number of educational institutions as well as enrolment during 1981-82 – 2004-05. This percentage is extremely low as compared developed countries, mainly USA 76%, Finland 57%, New Zealand 50% and the France 46%. Even some of the developing countries like South Korea and Phillippines also have 46% and 28% of their population (in age 18-23) in the higher education. Higher Education provides R&D and technology base for the development of the country. Education and skill development contributes positively to the growth and development of the nation. Hence,

expansion in the system of higher education with quality is the need of the hour if the country has to achieve sustainable growth and development. The growth strategy of higher education can be based on the suggestions given by M. Ananda Krishan (in his paper – Revisiting Education Commission "Perspectives, Goals and Values", presented in Seminar, Education and National Development, Vigyan Bhawan, New Delhi, 17-19 December 2006) i.e. 15% of the eligible age group should get higher education by the year 2012, growing further to 25% in 2020 and 50% by 2030. The growth strategy must take into account the (a) growing demand for higher education (b) capacity for economy to absorb graduates and (c) cost implications.

- More students (54%) at higher level of education are enrolled in general education as compared to science and commerce education. Percentage of students opting for science and commerce education at undergraduation has declined during 1981-2001. There is a need to change these traditional pattern of course selection. However, redistribution of the present pattern of courses/programme will have to take an assessment of future manpower needs of the economy.
- The gender difference in terms of enrolment and courses opted for increases as one moves from undergraduate level of education to higher level of university education. Girls generally opt for Arts courses as 57% of the girls as against 51% of boys at undergraduate level have opted for general Arts courses. Enrolment of girls in engineering and technical education is extremely low (23% in 2003-04). Women candidates may be encouraged to opt for technical and professional courses, which may help them achieve empowerment through economic independence.
- An increase in the admissions of engineering education indicates an increasing demand for engineering and Technical education during 1991-2001. Highest demand is noticed for Electronics Telecommunications and electrical engineering. This could be due to boom in the IT industry. A proper planning based on the future demand for technical skill of technical and professional education, will help in reducing the mismatch of demand and supply of educated youth in the labour market.
- Existence of unutilized vacancies for apprentices in various trades is an indication of the obsolescence of thee trades in the present labour market. However, it has to be noticed that only 20% of the workforce in India have some skills. Remaining 80% of the workforce will have to be provided skill and education. The number and seating capacity of the ITI's is very limited in relation to the requirement of the skill development of the workforce. Further, the courses offered by these it is have not been revised and therefore have lost relevance to the demand of the labour market. As a result, these ITI's are neither able to meet the increasing demand nor trade requirement of the labour market. There is an urgent need to make and estimate of skill requirements at state and district levels and programmes of developing skills may be prepared accordingly.

- Khadi Village and Cottage industries play an important role in providing training to men and women in different industries. Though the number of beneficiaries under these industrial training programmes is less yet, a good percentage of women out of total beneficiaries have been taking training in industries like cotton, silk, woolen, cottage, match/agarbatti, food & vegetable processing, textile and processing of cereals and pulses etc. Highest percentage of women beneficiaries (77%) under these training is found in Assam followed by Orissa and Nagaland. More such training programmes may be introduced to generate income and employment in district and village levels. Such programmes will also help in empowerment of women.
- The higher labour force participation rates in rural areas as urban areas have to be taken with some caution because of the presence of disguised unemployment in rural areas. Lower labour force participation rates on younger age group may be due to shift in activity status i.e. this age group population is involved in the educational activities.
- Though the percentage of illiteracy among labour force has declined during 1983-2005, yet 66% of the females and 34% of males in rural labour force are still illiterate. The situation is not very good in urban areas where 34% of females and 13% of males in labour force are illiterate. The labour force participation rate is highest among the graduates. This may be due to higher rate of unemployment among graduates.
- The expenditure on education as a percentage of GDP though has increased from 2.80% in 1980-81 to 3.49% in 2004-05, it has not yet reached the target of 6% of GDP as suggested by Education Commission, 1966.
- Elementary Education has received highest priority in terms of receiving allocations during 1991-92 – 2005-06. The university and other higher education have not only received low priority but allocations to the higher education have declined from 13.2% of the total budget in 1991-92 to 11.11% in 2005-06 which is a matter of concern. Education at different level has complimentarily. The development of one level of education depends on the development of other level. Hence, equal importance has to be given to the development of all levels of education.

Health Status

The development of the social sector especially health and education is one of prime importance in the development strategy. This is so because the ultimate goal of development in any economy is the improving quality of life and best feasible satisfaction of human needs in terms of basic health care, pure drinking water and ensuring food security of the people. In order to achieve the above objective and the best possible planning for health sector huge data on several aspects of population regarding the currents status of health and need of manpower to ensure a healthy environment is required. The present section thoroughly highlights on some of the health aspects of population, and wherever possible depicts data by regions and by time series trends. Some of the major sources of data to obtain the above information include Central Bureau of health Intelligence, Directorate General of Health Service, Health Information of India, Department of Family Welfare, Ministry of Health and Family Welfare, Bulletin on Rural Health Statistics in India and Registrar General of India and Census Commissioner of India, Sample Registration System.

The initial section devotes basically on health infrastructure in the country and across regions. Tables 2.5.2 to 2.5.11 provide valuable information on several aspects of health infrastructure and development of primary health care services in rural India. Table 2.5.2 presents the number of doctors and population served per government doctor in various states and union territories during 2006-07. It reveals that in Assam, Haryana, Jharkhand and some of the highly populated states such as Andhra Pradesh, Maharashtra, Tamilnadu, Uttar Pradesh and West Bengal, the number of population served per doctor is highest. The average rural population covered by each sub-centre, primary health centre and community health centre also suggests that the poorer states such as Bihar, Jharkhand, Orissa, Uttar Pradesh lag behind the richer states. It may be recalled that the programme of establishing Primary Health Centres (PHCs) in the rural areas was launched as an integral part of Community Development Programme with the advent of planning era and priority was accorded to extension, expansion and consolidation of rural health infrastructure in view of rapidly changing socio-economic scenario. But little has been achieved in this respect since the growth of sub-centres, PHCs and CHCs have been stagnant. Even the doctors' population ratio has taken a declining trend over the years. Tables 2.5.7 to 2.5.10 depict the number of health manpower working in rural areas by states and union territories.

The population served per hospital and hospital beds is also taken as one of the important indicators of health infrastructure. Table 2.5.10 provides useful information in this regard. The states of Andhra Pradesh, Delhi, Gujarat, Kerala and J&K have made outstanding achievement in this aspect. On the other hand, the states like Bihar 28959,

Madhya Pradesh 3392, Orissa 2699, Uttar Pradesh 2593, Rajasthan 1977 lag far against the national average 2339 persons per bed. Subsequent Table 2.5.11 follows time series data on the number of hospitals, hospital beds and all types of beds from 1981 to 2002. It is clearly shown that no significant achievement has been made in this aspect over the years; in fact, the number of hospitals has taken a declining trend since 2000.

Table 2.5.12 presents data regarding distribution of live births by type of medical attention, received by the mother at the time of delivery for the period 1980 to 2000. It is evident from the table that the proportion of deliveries attended by trained hands is still low in the country. By the year 2000, about one half of total women in rural areas do not have access to trained personnel. Therefore, an urgent step in this direction is needed.

Morbidity by cause of sickness, the number of cases and deaths reported is depicted in Table 2.5.13. Most of the cases of sickness are reported from diarrhoeal diseases, malaria, acute respiratory infection and tuberculosis. The number of cases in malaria, however, declined significantly in 2004 even less than half of the total cases reported in 1998 indicating a step forward towards malaria eradication programme. It further reveals that Japanese Encephalitis, Meningitis, Tetanus emerge to be the most fatal diseases, where maximum deaths were reported. Morbidity rates by states and union territories suggest that Chandigarh (153), Kerala (118) and Tripura (117) have highest morbidity rate per thousand rural population. The data on morbidity rate and prevalence rate of ailment based on NSS 52nd round reveal no significant gap between rural and urban areas and that of male and female in the country. While in earlier rounds, especially in 42nd and 28th, there was a huge gap in morbidity rate being observed in rural and urban areas.

The percentage distribution of deaths by major cause (under medical certification) and by sex and age group is presented in Table 2.5.16. One can see that persons attaining the age above 70 are vulnerable to most of the diseases. On the other hand, the infants are most vulnerable in case of disease originating in the prenatal period and congenital anomalies. Tables 2.5.17 and 2.5.18 give an idea about the percentage distribution of deaths by type of medical attention received during 2000 by major states. It could be seen that maximum proportion of deaths were reported from non-institutional medical attention in most all states. It is also seen from Table 2.5.18 that maximum percentage of deaths reported if and when medical attention is received from non-institutional qualified professionals and untrained functionaries.

The 2.5.19 highlights one of the crucial issues on health aspects in the country. It reveals that total planned investment, though has been increasing over the years, and has not been enough to meet the growing needs of people. It might be seen from the table that the percentage allocations on health, family welfare and water supply have been stagnant over the years.

The percentage of couple protected by various family planning methods from 1991-92 to 2005-06 has been presented in Table 2.5.20. Taking all methods together, the percentage of couple protected remained static during 1990s but showed a decline in recent years. This indicates that the programme on health education and other awareness campaign have augmented declining birth rate in effective manner.

The per capita net availability of cereals and pulses per day in the country has also remained stagnant (Table 2.5.21). While the availability was 468.8 grams during 1971, it increased to 510.1 gram during 1991. The same however declined to 462.7 gram in 2004 and further to 444.4 gram according to the provisional estimates in 2006. This is a sorry state of affairs in Indian agricultural economy, which calls for raising agricultural productivity and ensuring food security to the people.

Table 2.5.22 presents social security schemes in important organized sectors. It contains information relating to medical facilities provided by the Central Government Health Schemes (CGHS), Employees State Insurance (ESI), Post and Telegraph (P&T), Mines and Railways to specific categories of their employees.

The on-going analysis reveals that the health status of people in general has not yet met adequate standard in the country. Therefore, there is an urgent need to push somewhat a higher proportion of expenditure on health and family welfare. Once the mission for health and food for all is achieved, we could get better place in the ranking of Human Development Index.

(i) Developmental Instruments

Table 2.1.1: Number of Educational Institutions

Type	*1981*	*1986*	*1991*	*1996**	*2001**	*2002**	*2003**	*2004**	*2005*	*2006*
Pre-Primary Schools	10,281	13,951	15,877	38,553	60,848	61,108	62,934	63,569	67,157	66,420#
Primary/Junior Basic schools	494,503	528,872	560,935	603,646	664,041	651,399	7,10,471	7,67,520	7,72,568	7,56,950
Middle/Senior Basic schools	118,555	134,846	151,456	180,293	219,626	245,710	2,62,649	2,74,731	2,88,493	3,00,008
High/Higher Secondary Schools/Pre-Degree	51,006	65,837	79,796	98,172	175,588	137,654	1,45,938	1,52,090	1,59,667	165,087
Universities/Deemed Universities/Institutions of National Importance	132	149	184	228	272	304	304	343	350	358
Research Institutions	—	47	49	65	79	81	85	136	140	140
Degree Standard and above General Educational Institutions	3,421	4,135	4,862	6,759	8,737	9166	9,427	10,377	11,698	12,754
Degree Standard and above Professional and Technical Institutions for										
(a) Agriculture and Forestry	61	70	80	90	102	NA	NA	NA	NA	NA
(b) Engineering, Technology and Architecture	171	248	282	418	838	978	1,068	1,302	1,562	1,627
(c) Medicine**	249	288	346@	655	725	759	783	817	2,053	2,082
(d) Veterinary Science	22	22	37	45	50	NA	NA	NA	NA	NA
(e) Teacher's Training	341	442	474	697	846	873	900	1,082	1,669	2,019
(f) Others***	—	—	673	1275	2004	1982	1.991	2,431	3,787	2,626
Below Degree Level Professional/ Vocational and Technical Institutional	4,808	5,381	5,739	6,542	6,637	7,022	7,285	7,750	7,486	7,686

Notes:

* As on September 30 of the relevant year.

** Medicine includes Allopathy, Homoeopathy, Ayurveda and Unani, Dental, Pharmacy, Nursing and Physiotherapy.

*** Includes law, Management, MCA/IT, Agriculture, etc.

@ Health Information of India, 1993, DGHS.

\# Many States have not shown Pre-Primary Schools reparately, they are attached with the Primary Schooles.

Sources:

1. Ministry of Human Resource Development: Department of Secondary and Higher Education, *Selected Educational Statistics.*
2. *Statistical Abstract*-2003 (for Agriculture and Veterinary Colleges).

Figure 2.1.A

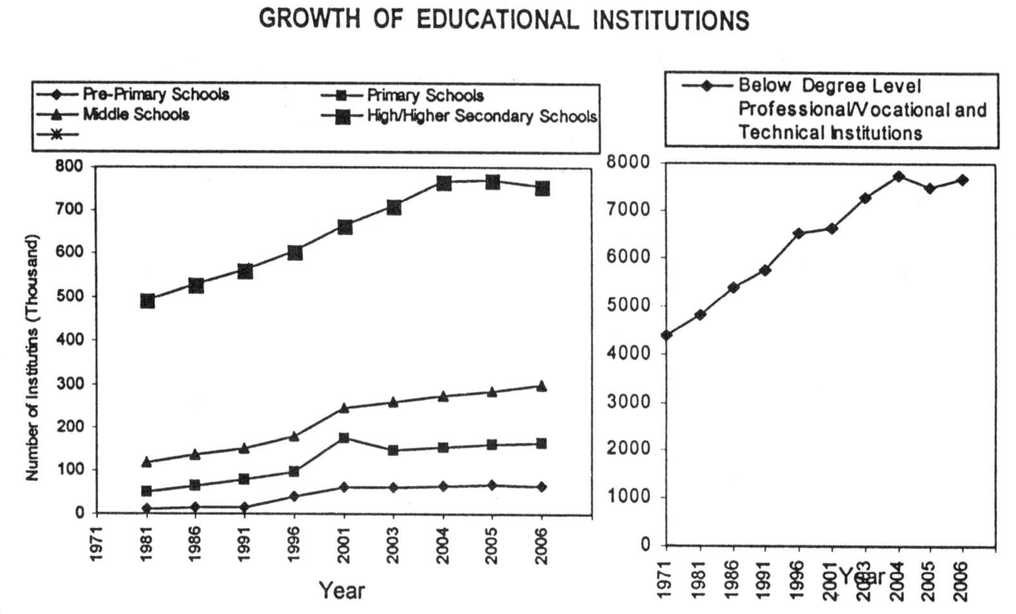

For details see Table 2.1.1

Figure 2.1.B

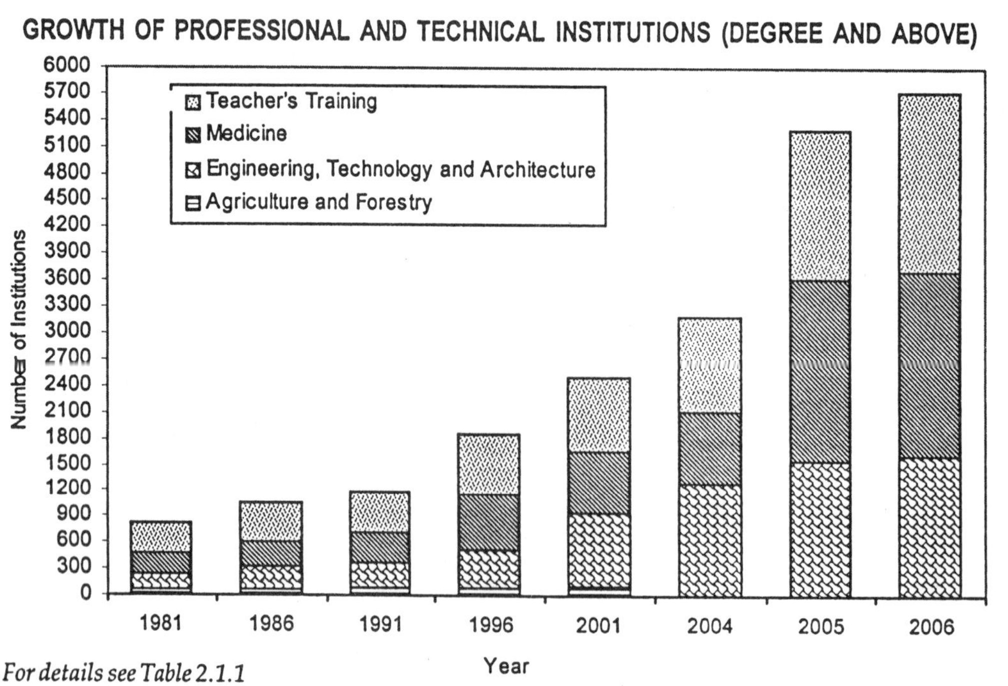

For details see Table 2.1.1

Table 2.1.2: Total Teachers by Type of Institution & Sex

Type	*Sex*	*1981*	*1986*	*1991*	*1996**	*2001**	*2002**	*2003**	*2004*	*2005*
Primary Schools	Total	1363,217	1495,812	1616,020	1789,733	1928,075	1912,934	2,160,666	2160,666	2183,479
	Male	1021,275	1094,168	1143,514	1204,780	1212,861	1164,575	1,308,660	1318,660	1325,640
	Female	341,942	401,644	472,506	584,953	715,214	743,799	842,006	842,006	857,839
Middle Schools	Total	851,527	968,348	1072,911	1195,845	1467,920	1579,774	1,589,280	1,589,280	1671,495
	Male	598,191	663,208	716,431	768,091	921,109	934,772	992,407	992,407	998,093
	Female	253,336	305,140	356,480	427,754	546,811	645,002	596,873	596,873	673,402
High/Higher Secondary Schools	Total	912,129	1131,505	1334,745	1542,360	1777,495	2039,753	2,082,990	2,082,990	2154,655
	Male	657,839	792,703	917,301	1003,371	1157,194	1227,388	1,281,816	1,281,816	1333,462
	Female	254,290	338,802	417,444	538,989	620,301	812,365	801,174	801,174	821,193
Graduate and above										
Total	Total	–	271,882	–	354,430	426,797	436,246	471,931	471,931	504,812
General Ecuation	Total	137,531	171,780	204,464	247,750	NA	NA	NA	NA	NA
Professional/Tech. Education/Special Education	Total	53,201	54,498	NA	NA	NA	NA	NA	NA	NA
University Teaching Deptt. & other National Important Research Institutions	Total	26,661	37,472	58,661	69,090	75,205[b]	72,543[b]	75,925[b]	78,819[b]	NA

Notes: Sex-wise data is available for school level only.
a As on September 30 of relevant year.
* Includes Intermediate and 10+2 stage Schools.
@ Included in High/Higher Secondary School Teachers.

Sources: 1.Ministry of Human Resource Development: *Selected Educational Statistics.*
2.[b]University Grants Commission : *Annual Report* for various years.

Figure 2.1.C

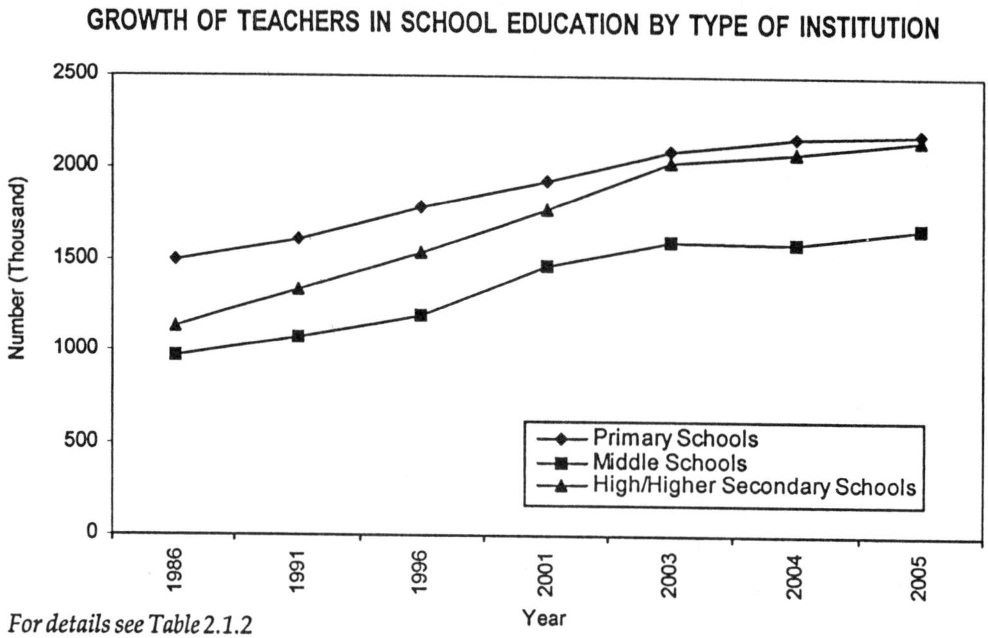

For details see Table 2.1.2

Figure 2.1.D

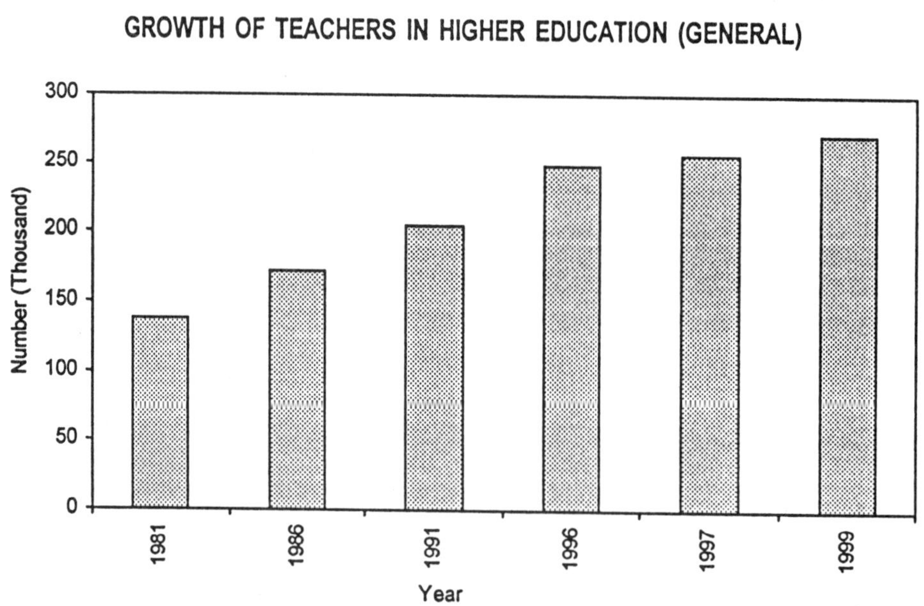

For details see Table 2.1.2

Table 2.1.3: Number of School Teachers by States/UTs, 2005-06

State/Union Territery	*Primary (I-V)*			*Middle/Upper Primary (VI-VIII)*			*High/Higher Secondary (IX-XII)*		
	Total	*Male*	*Female*	*Total*	*Male*	*Female*	*Total*	*Male*	*Female*
States									
1. Andhra Pradesh	1,66,790	91,079	75,711	1,06,215	62,034	44,181	1,86,867	1,17,596	69,271
	(100.0)	(54.6)	(45.4)	(100.0)	(58.4)	(41.6)	(100.0)	(62.4)	(37.1)
2. Arunachal Pradesh	3,790	2,511	1,279	3,494	2,359	1,135	3,823	2,923	900
	(100.0)	(66.2)	(33.8)	(100.0)	(67.5)	(32.5)	(100.0)	(76.5)	(23.5)
3. Assam	80,072	51,550	28,522	69,013	52,622	16,391	78,954	57,713	21,241
	(100.0)	(64.4)	(35.6)	(100.0)	(76.2)	(23.8)	(100.0)	(73.1)	(26.9)
4. Bihar	75,703	60,187	15,516	58,033	44,949	13,084	25,724	22,268	3,456
	((100.0)	(79.5)	(20.5)	(100.0)	(77.4)	(22.6)	(100.0)	(86.6)	(13.4)
5. Chhattisgarh	80,659	55,843	24,816	29,933	21,594	8,339	27,871	19,027	8,844
	(100.0)	(69.2)	(30.8)	(100.0)	(72.1)	(27.9)	(100.0)	(68.3)	(31.7)
6. Delhi	27,431	6,728	20,703	7,226	1,823	5,403	61,149	20,248	40,901
	(100.0)	(24.5)	(75.5)	(100.0)	(25.2)	(74.8)	(100.0)	(33.1)	(66.9)
7. Goa	3,232	433	2,799	2,148	635	1,513	5,069	2,294	2,775
	(100.0)	(13.4)	(86.6)	(100.0)	(29.6)	(70.4)	(100.0)	(45.3)	(54.7)
8. Gujarat	37,188	15,790	21,397	1,86,76	86,606	1,00,163	72,089	53,229	18,855
	(100.0)	(42.5)	(57.5)	(100.0)	(46.4)	(53.6)	(100.0)	(73.8)	(26.2)
9. Haryana	50,621	25,381	25,240	11,175	6,539	4,636	68,185	39,097	29,088
	(100.0)	(50.11)	(49.9)	(100.0)	(58.5)	(41.5)	(100.0)	(57.3)	(42.7)
10. Himachal Pradesh	30,948	15,266	15,682	13,417	8,572	4,845	31,905	18,926	12,979
	(100.0)	(49.3)	(50.7)	(100.0)	(63.9)	(36.1)	(100.0)	(59.3)	(40.7)
11. Jammu & Kashmir	38.686	2,288	15,805	32,773	18,773	14,000	29,519	17,898	11,621
	((100.0)	(59.1)	(40.9)	(100.0)	(57.3)	(42.7)	(100.0)	(60.6)	(39.4)
12. Jharkhand	32,764	25,144	7,620	31,619	22,077	9,542	14,478	9,170	5,308
	(100.0)	(76.7)	(23.3)	(100.0)	(69.8)	(30.2)	(100.0)	(63.3)	(36.7)
13. Karnataka	52,056	28,172	23,884	1,84,566	80,414	1,04,151	84,036	51,466	32,570
	(100.0)	(54.1)	(45.9)	(100.0)	(43.6)	(56.4)	(100.0)	(61.2)	(38.8)
14. Kerala	41,751	10,897	30,854	46,481	14,544	31,937	1,11,878	33,689	78,189
	(100.0)	(26.1)	(73.9)	(100.0)	(31.3)	(68.7)	(100.0)	(30.1)	(69.9)
15. Madhya Pradesh	23,0653	1,65,262	65,391	1,29,445	91,575	37,870	93,239	57,425	35,814
	(100.0)	(71.6)	(28.4)	(100.0)	(70.7)	(29.3)	(100.0)	(61.6)	(38.8)
16. Maharashtra	1,57,593	75,683	81,910	2,03,046	1,13,523	89,523	2,84,501	1,94,567	89,934
	(100.0)	(48.0)	(52.0)	(100.0)	(55.9)	(44.1)	(100.0)	(68.4)	(31.6)
17. Manipur	7,867	4,[illegible]33	3,034	8,673	5,113	3,560	11,966	7,039	4,927
	(100.0)	(61.4)	(38.6)	(100.0)	(59.0)	(41.0)	(100.0)	(58.8)	(41.2)
18. Meghalaya	1,37,45	7,300	6,445	7,407	3,994	3,413	6,204	3,512	2,692
	(100.0)	(53.1)	(46.9)	(100.0)	(53.9)	(46.1)	(100.0)	(56.6)	(43.4)
19. Mizoram	5,210	2,651	2,559	7,983	5,073	2,910	4,548	3,145	1,403
	(100.0)	(50.9)	(49.1)	(100.0)	(63.5)	(36.5)	(100.0)	(69.2)	(30.8)

State/Urban Territery	Primary (I-V)			Middle/Upper Primary (VI-VIII)			Higher/Higher Secondary (IX-XII)		
	Total	Male	Female	Total	Male	Female	Total	Male	Female
20. Nagaland	7,948	4,985	2,963	6,263	3,902	2,361	8,514	4,919	3,595
	(100.0)	(62.7)	(37.3)	(100.0)	(62.3)	(37.7)	(100.0)	(57.8)	(42.2)
21. Orissa	1,01,199	65,177	36,022	34,285	25,712	8,573	61,939	48,485	13,454
	(100.0)	(64.4)	(35.6)	(100.0)	(75.0)	(25.0)	(100.0)	(78.3)	(21.7)
22. Punjab	37,028	13,856	23,172	12,910	6,175	6,735	66,511	28,800	37,711
	(100.0)	(37.4)	(62.6)	(100.0)	(47.8)	(52.2)	(100.0)	(43.3)	(56.9)
23. Rajasthan	1,21,737	86,697	35,040	1,91,208	1,34,354	56,854	1,26,741	92,244	34,497
	(100.0)	(71.2)	(28.8)	(100.0)	(70.3)	(29.7)	(100.0)	(72.8)	(27.2)
24. Sikkim	5,388	2,663	2,725	1,177	766	411	1,477	967	510
	(100.0)	(49.4)	(50.6)	(100.0)	(65.1)	(34.9)	(100.0)	(65.5)	(34.5)
25. Tamil Nadu	1,15,568	53,190	62,378	92,156	19,371	72,785	2,26,742	89,754	1,36,988
	(100.0)	(46.0)	(54.0)	(100.0)	(21.1)	(79.0)	(100.0)	(39.6)	(60.4)
26. Tripura	12,207	6,027	6,180	8,439	6,701	1,738	17,313	11,804	5,509
	(100.0)	(49.4)	(50.6)	(100.0)	(79.4)	(20.6)	(100.0)	(68.2)	(31.2)
27. Uttranchal	46,415	21,682	24,733	18,715	11,880	6,835	34,436	24,473	9,963
	(100.0)	(46.7)	(53.3)	(100.0)	(63.5)	(36.5)	(100.0)	(71.1)	(28.9)
28. Utter Pradesh	4,12,080	2,94,956	1,17,124	1,66,344	1,30,778	35,566	1,92,053	1,61,100	30,953
	(100.0)	(71.6)	(28.4)	(100.0)	(78.6)	(21.4)	(100.0)	(83.9)	(16.1)
29. West Bengal	1,49,764	1,09,243	40,521	10,895	8,137	2,758	1,30,418	92,522	37,896
	(100.0)	(72.9)	(27.1)	(100.0)	(74.7)	(25.3)	(100.0)	(70.9)	(29.1)
Union Territories									
1. Andaman &	891	383	508	726	337	389	2,692	1,326	1,366
Nicobar Islands	(100.0)	(43.0)	(57.0)	(100.0)	(46.4)	(53.6)	(100.0)	(49.3)	(50.7)
2. Chandigarh	231	46	125	36	11	25	3,029	655	2,374
	(100.0)	(19.9)	(80.1)	(100.0)	(30.6)	(69.4)	(100.0)	(21.6)	(78.4)
3. Dadra and	553	268	285	288	174	114	316	169	147
Nagar Haveli	(100.0)	(17.1)	(82.9)	(100.0)	(47.1)	(52.9)	(100.0)	(58.4)	(41.6)
4. Daman and Diu	467	80	387	259	122	137	298	174	124
	(100.0)	(17.1)	(82.9)	(100.0)	(47.1)	(52.9)	(100.0)	(58.4)	(41.6)
5. Lakshadweep	283	182	101	113	76	37	419	281	138
	(100.0)	(64.3)	(35.7)	(100.0)	(67.3)	(32.7)	(100.0)	(67.1)	(32.9)
6. Pondicherry	2,853	707	2,146	1,534	624	910	6,045	2,629	3,416
	(100.0)	(24.8)	(75.2)	(100.0)	(40.7)	(59.3)	(100.0)	(43.5)	(56.5)
All India	21,141,183	13,11,943	8,02,244	14,97,995	9,05,334	5,92,661	20,80,943	12,91,534	7,89,409
	(100.0)	(62.1)	(37.9)	(100.0)	(60.4)	(39.6)	(100.0)	(62.1)	(37.9)

Note : Figures are Provisional as on 30.9.2005.
Figures within the Parenthesis indicates the percentage.
Source : Ministry of Human Resource Development : Annual Report, 2007-08

Table 2.1.4: Enrolment by Level of Education

(Thousands)

Stage	1981	1986	1991	1996[a]	2001[a]	2002[a]	2003[a]	2004[a]	2005[a]	2006[a]
Pre-Primary	*1,158*	*1,426*	*1,635*	*2,382*	*4,623*	*5,484*	*5,059*	*4,761*	*5,264*	*5,358*
Primary	73,774	87,441	97,375	110,394	113,883	122,136	128,407	130,763	1,32,049	1,33,526
Middle	20,724	27,310	34,026	41,065	44,828	46,947	48,821	51,245	52,195	54,359
High/Higher Secondary (Class IX-X)	8,807	12,18,73	14,365	17,862	20,054	21,906	23,292	24,330	24,971	25,859
Post-Matric but below Degree level*	3,079	4,336	3,658	9,175	10,453	11,397	11,715	12,745	13,414	13,583
Degree and above	2,320	3,159	3,672	5,373	7,143[N]	7,652[b]	8,316[b]	9,220[b]	7,667[n]	9,483
B. Professional/ Tech./ Vocational Education										
Post-Matric but below Degree level**	519	540	666	NA	1,105	1,200	1,191	1.255	690[e]	940
Degree and above	623	743	901	1,184	1,421	1,575	1,637	1,808	5,193	6,069
(a) Engineering/ Technology/ Architecture	130	197	241	328	606	692[b]	717[b]	795[b]	1,668	2,504
(b) Medicine***	121	138	179[b]	230[b]	276	301[b]	313[b]	348[b]	306	319
(c) Agriculture/ Forestry	40	43	55[b]	74[b]	53	55[b]	59[b]	64[b]	NA	NA
(d) Education	75	88	92	116	115	133[b]	146[b]	161[b]	245	272
(e) Veterinary Science	7	9	13[b]	20[b]	14[b]	15[b]	15[b]	16[b]	NA	NA
(f) Others	250	268	321[b]	412[b]	358[b]	379[b]	387[b]	424[b]	2,974	2,974

Notes:
- a As on September 30 of relevant year.
- N Includes enrolment of Ph.D/DSc/M.Phil cources for which bifercation on General and Professional is not available.
- * Pre-Degree/Junior Colleges and Class XI-XII.
- ** Includes Teacher Training Schools, Polytechnic and Art & Craft Schools.
- *** Medicine includes Allopathy, Homoeopathy, Ayurveda and Unani.
- @ Polytechnic, estimated on the basis of intake Capacity communicated by AICTE.

Sources:
1. Ministry of Human Resource Development :
   - *(i) Education in India.*
   - *(ii) Selected Educational Statistics.*
2. [b]University Grant Commission : *Annual Report* for various years.

Figure 2.1.E

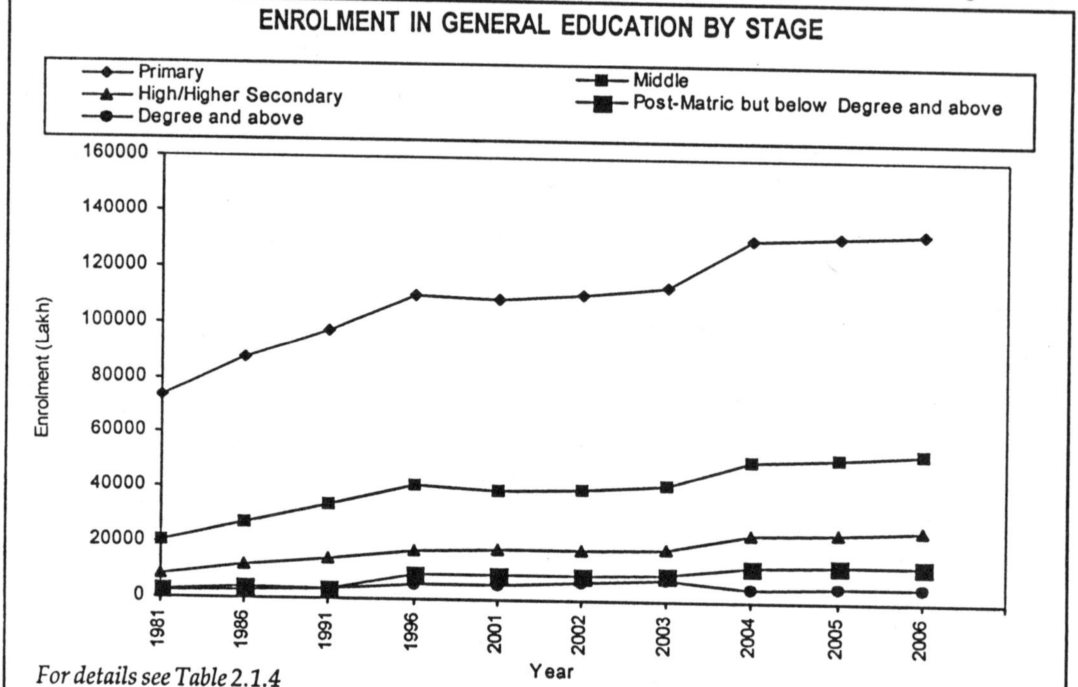

For details see Table 2.1.4

Figure 2.1.F

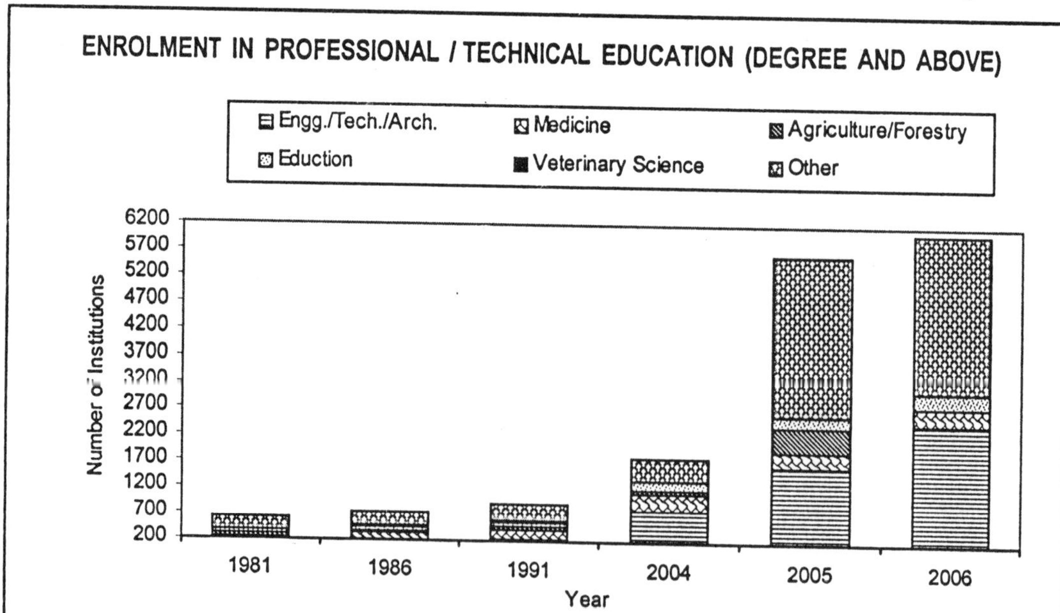

For details see Table 2.1.4

Table 2.1.5: Enrolment of Boys by Level of Education

(*Thousands*)

Stage	*1981*	*1986*	*1991*	*1996*[a]	*2001*[a]	*2002*[a]	*2003*[a]	*2004*[a]	*2005*[a]	*2006*[a]
A. General Education										
Pre-Primary	635	776	890	1,267	2,480	2865	2,654	2,494	2,756	2,860
Primary	45,286	52,247	56,955	62,502	63,619	64,946	68,442	69,675	70,496	70,986
Middle	13,934	17,736	21,487	24,706	26,089	26,336	27,333	28,504	28,865	29,783
High/Higher Secondary	6,157	8,437	9,571	11,234	12,148	12,846	13,699	14,222	14,474	14,905
Post-Matric but below Degre level*	2,245	3,027	4,326	6,011	6,296	6,727	6,914	7,465	7,817	7,772
Degree and above	1,631	2,099	2,408	3,376	4,178[N]	4,416	4,807	6,562	4,422	9,594
B. Professional/Tech./ Vocational Education										
Post-Matric but below Degree level	408	418	513	NA	879	976	1,006	NA	539	654
Degree and above	513	606	728	937	1,008	1,115	1,143	NA	3,368	1,876

Notes:
a As on September 30.
N Includes Ph.D/D.Sc./M.Phill of General & Professional.
* Includes 10+2 / Intermediate / Junior Colleges / Pre-university.

Sources:
1. Ministry of Human Resource Development: *(i) Education in India (ii) Selected Educational Statistics.*
2. University Grants Commission : *Annual Report* for various years.

Table 2.1.6: Enrolment of Girls by Level of Education

(*Thousands*)

Stage	*1981*	*1986*	*1991*	*1996*[a]	*2001*[a]	*2002*[a]	*2003*[a]	*2004*[a]	*2005*[a]	*2006*[a]
A. General Education										
Pre-Primary	523	650	745	1,115	2,143	2,619	2,405	2,267	2,509	2,498
Primary	28,488	35,194	40,420	47,892	50,264	57,190	59,965	61,089	61,552	62,540
Middle	6,790	9,574	12,439	16,359	18,739	20,610	21,488	22,742	23,330	24,576
High/Higher Secondary	2,650	3,735	4,794	6,628	7,906	9,059	9,593	10,108	10,498	10,954
Post-Matric but below Degre level*	834	1,308	2,032	3,164	4,157	4,669	4,801	5,280	5,598	5,811
Degree and above	689	1,060	1,264	1,997	2,965[N]	3,236	3,509	4,466	3,245	5,959
B. Professional/Tech./ Vocational Education										
Post-Matric but below Degree level	111	122	153	NA	226	224	185	NA	151	285
Degree and above	110	137	173	243	413	460	494	NA	1,824	630

Notes:
a As on September 30.
N Includes Ph.D/D.Sc./M.Phil of General and Professional.
* Includes 10+2 / Intermediate / Junior Colleges / Pre-university.

Sources:
1. Ministry of Human Resource Development: *(i) Education in India (ii) Selected Educational Statistics.*
2. University Grants Commission : *Annual Report* for various years.

Table 2.1.7: Total Enrolment by Educational Level and State/Union Territory, 2005-2006*

(Thousands)

State/Union Territory	*School Level*					*Graduate & above****
	Pre-Primary	*Primary*	*Middle*	*Sec./Sr. Secondary*** General*	*Sec./Sr. Secondary*** Vocational*	
States						
1. Andhra Pradesh	478	7,392	3,731	3,288	49	1,411
2. Arunachal Pradesh	32	196	64	43	0.7	9
3. Assam	785	3,551	1,463	816	3	218
4. Bihar	0.2	10,525	2,384	1,332	7	525
5. Chhattisgarh	51	3,168	1,055	607	5	196
6. Delhi	66	1,787	866	691	9	867
7. Goa	0	105	72	60	3	24
8. Gujarat	105	6,557	2,492	1,760	40	664
9. Haryana	122	1,997	1,160	873	19	298
10. Himachal Pradesh	49	661	411	691	2	109
11. Jammu and Kashmir	106	1,135	479	363	7	159
12. Jharkhand	0.9	3,828	986	414	5	261
13. Karnataka	0	5,758	2,886	2,098	97	952
14. Kerala	0	2,545	1,601	1,467	27	451
15. Madhya Pradesh	0	11,274	4,253	2,194	24	969
16. Maharashtra	2,524	11,558	6,311	4,831	101	1,682
17. Manipur	116	360	142	100	0.8	38
18. Meghalaya	181	508	154	81	0.6	39
19. Mizoram	0	162	74	36	0.8	15
20. Nagaland	104	225	92	55	0.3	29
21. Orissa	0	4,701	1,602	1,386	17	413
22. Punjab	37	1,872	1,064	862	29	348
23. Rajasthan	132	9,412	3,361	1,924	8	488
24. Sikkim	29	91	32	18	0.8	9
25. Tamil Nadu	0	6,378	3,634	3,008	174	1,324
26. Tripura	236	500	197	123	0.7	25
27. Uttaranchal	0	1,197	561	511	7	164
28. Uttar Pradesh	48	25,187	7,272	6,071	26	1,761
29. West Bengal	0	9,150	3,624	2,535	19	787
Union Territories						
1. Andaman and Nicobar Islands	6	38	23	19	0.5	3
2. Chandigarh	14	67	37	45	1	55
3. Dadra and Nagar Haveli	0	36	12	7	0	0
4. Daman and Diu	2	16	9	6	0.6	1
5. Lakshadweep	0.8	7	4	5	0	0
6. Pondicherry	36	106	66	62	3	31
ALL INDIA	5,264	1,32,049	55,195	38,386	690	14,324

Notes: Totals may not tally due to rounding off.
* As on September 30, 2005.
** Covers Intermediate/Junior Colleges/Pre-Degree/Pre- niversity and classes IX-X, XI-XII under + 2 stage/Vocational/Technical Education. (As on Sept. 2003)
*** Includes Ph.D./D.Sc./M.Phill level.

Source: Ministry of Human Resource Development : *Selected Educational Statistics*—2005-06.

Table 2.1.8: Enrolment of Boys by Educational Level and State/Union Territory 2005-2006*

(*Thousands*)

State/Union Territory	*School Level*					*Graduate & above****
	Pre-Primary	*Primary*	*Middle*	*Sec./Sr. Secondary***		
				General	*Vocational*	
States						
1. Andhra Pradesh	267	3,743	1,948	1,823	27	885
2. Arunachal Pradesh	18	106	35	24	0.5	5
3. Assam	386	1,805	775	469	3	145
4. Bihar	0.1	6,186	1,512	906	6	431
5. Chhattisgarh	27	1,801	572	362	4	112
6. Delhi	33	938	467	354	7	477
7. Goa	0	55	38	30	2	11
8. Gujarat	63	3,704	1,446	1,056	33	374
9. Haryana	66	1,067	633	496	16	168
10. Himachal Pradesh	26	346	216	368	1	59
11. Jammu and Kashmir	58	602	270	204	5	91
12. Jharkhand	0.5	2,089	579	256	5	159
13. Karnataka	0	2,967	1,503	1,110	69	565
14. Kerala	0	1,300	834	732	19	207
15. Madhya Pradesh	0	5,942	2,365	1,393	19	658
16. Maharashtra	1,313	6,052	3,281	2,654	81	1,039
17. Manipur	60	187	75	52	0.6	21
18. Meghalaya	88	259	75	40	0.5	20
19. Mizoram	0	84	38	17	0.4	9
20. Nagaland	55	117	47	29	0.3	19
21. Orissa	0	2,442	886	839	14	337
22. Punjab	22	999	571	468	21	186
23. Rajasthan	77	5,019	2,087	1,319	6	327
24. Sikkim	16	46	15	10	0.6	5
25. Tamil Nadu	0	3,295	1,893	1,524	155	770
26. Tripura	118	261	101	67	0.5	14
27. Uttaranchal	0	617	291	281	4	86
28. Uttar Pradesh	30	13,567	4,271	3,851	20	1,095
29. West Bengal	0	4,728	1,978	1,477	15	506
Union Territories						
1. Andaman and Nicobar Islands	3	19	12	10	0.4	2
2. Chandigarh	8	37	20	24	0	28
3. Dadra and Nagar Haveli	0	19	7	4	0	0
4. Daman and Diu	1	9	4	3	0.6	0.8
5. Lakshadweep	0.4	4	2	2	0	
6. Pondicherry	19	54	35	31	2	17
INDIA	2,756	70,496	28,865	22,290	539	8,832

Notes: Totals may not tally due to rounding off.
* As on September 30, 2005.
** Covers Intermediate/Junior Colleges/Pre-Degree/Pre-University and classes IX-X, XI-XII under + 2 stage./Vocational/Technical Education (As on Sept. 2003)
*** Includes Ph.D./D.Sc./M.Phill level.

Source: Ministry of Human Resource Development : *Selected Educational Statistics*—2004-2005.

Table 2.1.9: Enrolment of Girls by Educational Level and State/Union Territory 2005-2006*

(*Thousands*)

State/Union Territory	*School Level*			*Sec./Sr. Secondary***		*Graduate & above****
	Pre-Primary	*Primary*	*Middle*	*General*	*Vocational*	
States						
1. Andhra Pradesh	211	3,649	1,783	1,465	22	526
2. Arunachal Pradesh	14	90	29	17	0.2	3
3. Assam	399	1,746	688	387	0.7	73
4. Bihar	0.1	4,339	872	426	0.9	94
5. Chhattisgarh	24	1,366	483	245	1	84
6. Delhi	33	849	419	338	1.8	391
7. Goa	0	50	33	30	0.3	13
8. Gujarat	42	2,853	1,045	704	7	290
9. Haryana	56	931	527	376	3	130
10. Himachal Pradesh	24	315	195	323	0.8	50
11. Jammu and Kashmir	48	532	209	159	2	67
12. Jharkhand	0.3	1,739	407	158	0.4	101
13. Karnataka	0	2,791	1,383	987	28	386
14. Kerala	0	1,246	767	735	8	244
15. Madhya Pradesh	0	5,332	1,889	802	5	311
16. Maharashtra	1,212	5,505	3,030	2,177	21	642
17. Manipur	56	173	67	47	0.2	17
18. Meghalaya	94	250	78	40	0.1	19
19. Mizoram	0	79	36	17	0.4	6
20. Nagaland	49	107	45	27	0.1	10
21. Orissa	0	2,259	735	546	3	76
22. Punjab	15	873	493	393	8	161
23. Rajasthan	55	4,363	1,274	605	2	161
24. Sikkim	13	45	17	10	02	4
25. Tamil Nadu	0	3,084	1,740	1,484	19	555
26. Tripura	118	238	96	56	0.3	11
27. Uttaranchal	0	580	270	231	3	77
28. Uttar Pradesh	18	11,620	3,001	2,220	6	666
29. West Bengal	0	4,422	1,646	1,058	4	281
Union Territories						
1. Andaman and Nicobar	3	18	11	9	0.2	2
2. Chandigarh	6	30	17	21	1	27
3. Dadra and Nagar Haveli	0	17	5	3	0	0
4. Daman and Diu	1	8	4	3	0.1	0.1
5. Lakshadweep	0.4	3	2	2	0	0
6. Pondicherry	18	52	32	32	0.8	14
INDIA	2,508	61,552	23,330	16,096	151	5,492

Notes: Totals may not tally due to rounding off.
* As on September 30, 2005
** Covers Intermediate/Junior Colleges/Pre-Degree/Pre-University classes IX-X, XI-XII under + 2 stage./Vocational/Teachnical Education (As on Sept. 2003)
*** Includes Ph.D/D.Sc./M.Phill level.

Source: Ministry of Human Resource Development : *Selected Educational Statistics*—2005-2006.

Table 2.1.10: Enrolment in Engineering/Technology/ Architecture by Level

Level	*1981*		*1986*		*2001*		*2006*	
	Boys	*Girls*	*Boys*	*Girls*	*Boys*	*Girls*	*Boys*	*Girls*
Doctorate	1,995	169	2,207	405	10,625*	2,215*	NA	NA
Postgraduate	10,792	567	11,229	1,271	18,885	3,543	NA	NA
Graduate	1,11,064	4,942	1,69,388	13,061	4,23,147	1,18,234	NA	NA
Total	1,23,851	5,678	1,82,824	14,737[b]	4,52,657	1,23,992[b]	6,51,461[b]	1,85,800[b]

Notes: NA : Not Availabe..

* Includes M.Phil, Ph.D. and D.Sc.

Sources: 1. Ministry of Human Resource Development:
(*i*) *Selected Educational Statistics.*
2. [b]University Grants Commission :
(*i*) *Annual Report*, relevent years.

Table 2.1.11: Enrolment in Medicine by Level

Level	*1981*		*1986*		*2001*		*2006*	
	Boys	*Girls*	*Boys*	*Girls*	*Boys*	*Girls*	*Boys*	*Girls*
Doctorate	338	118	488	234	9,019*	4,751*	NA	NA
Postgraduate	11,930	3,129	14,844	4,344	14,956	7,846	NA	NA
Graduate	81,192	24,712	82,259	37,805	1,23,221	1,02,960	NA	NA
Total	93,460	27,959	97,591	42,383	14,7,196[b]	1,15,557[b]	2,04,379[b]	1,62,575[b]

Notes: NA : Not Availabe..

* Includes M.Phil, Ph.D. and D.Sc.

Sources: 1. Ministry of Human Resource Development:
(*i*) *Selected Educational Statistics.*
2. [b]University Grants Commission :
(*i*) *Annual Report*, relevent years.

Table 2.1.12: Enrolment in Agriculture and Forestry by Level

Level	*1981*		*1986*		*2001*		*2006*	
	Boys	*Girls*	*Boys*	*Girls*	*Boys*	*Girls*	*Boys*	*Girls*
Doctorate	2,030	119	1,991	232	3,127*	616*	NA	NA
Postgraduate	6,773	432	6,997	887	7,543	1,749	NA	NA
Graduate	30,140	1,085	32,750	2,243	30,865	6,408	NA	NA
Total	38,943	1,636	41,738	3,362	41,535[b]	8,773[b]	56,633[b]	10,719[b]

Notes: NA : Not Availabe..

* Includes M.Phil, Ph.D. and D.Sc.

Sources:
1. Ministry of Human Resource Development :
   (*i*) Selected Educational Statistics.
2. [b]University Grants Commission :
   (*i*) *Basic facts and Figures, 1995-96 to 2000-01.*
   (*ii*) *Annual Report,* relevent years.

Table 2.1.13: Enrolment in Education (Teacher's Training) by Level

Level	*1981*		*1986*		*2001**		*2006*	
	Boys	*Girls*	*Boys*	*Girls*	*Boys*	*Girls*	*Boys*	*Girls*
Doctorate	404	194	NA	NA	1025*	1050*	NA	NA
Postgraduate	3185	3465	NA	NA	2348	2110	NA	NA
Graduate	36340	31509	51453	40764	49900	52763	NA	NA
Total	36952	22345	39,929	35,168	NA	NA	86915[b]	82627[b]

Notes: NA : Not Availabe.

* Includes M.Phil, Ph.D. and D.Sc.

Sources:
1. Ministry of Human Resource Development:
   (*i*) *Selected Educational Statistics.*
2. [b]University Grants Commission :
   (*i*) *Annual Report,* relevent years.

Table 2.1.14: Enrolment in Veterinary Science by Level

Level	*1981*		*1986*		*2001*		*2006*	
	Boys	*Girls*	*Boys*	*Girls*	*Boys*	*Girls*	*Boys*	*Girls*
Doctorate	334	6	333	11	636*	133*	NA	NA
Postgraduate	1091	22	1228	84	1836	419	NA	NA
Graduate	5650	224	5650	224	7071	632	NA	NA
Total	7075	252	8632	727	10,750[b]	2,838[b]	13,845[b]	3,573[b]

Notes: NA : Not Availabe..

* Includes M.Phil, Ph.D. and DSc.

Sources:

1. Ministry of Human Resource Development :
   (*i*) Selected Educational Statistics.
2. [b]University Grants Commission :
   (*i*) *Basic facts and Figures, 1995-96 to 2000-01,*
   (*ii*) *Annual Report,* relevent years.

Table 2.1.15: Enrolment in Other* by Level

Level	*1986*		*2001*		*2002*		*2006*	
	Boys	*Girls*	*Boys*	*Girls*	*Boys*	*Girls*	*Boys*	*Girls*
Doctorate	621	169	1062	420	8,661**	6,992**	NA	NA
Postgraduate	18,173	4,147	18,612	4,987	14,284	8,297	NA	NA
Graduate	1,90,515	35,513	2,12,047	35,872	2,36,824	65,917	NA	NA
Total	2,09,309	39,829	2,31,721	41,279	2,59,769[b]	81,206[b]	3,40,783[b]	1,06,299[b]

NA: Not Available.

Notes:

* Others include Business Management, Journalism, Law, Library Science, Music and Dance, Physical Education, Oriental Studies, Social Work and Others.

** Includes M.Phil, Ph.D. and D.Sc.

Sources:

1. Ministry of Human Resource Development :
   (*i*) Selected Educational Statistics.
2. [b]University Grants Commission :
   (*i*) *Basic facts and Figures, 1995-96 to 2000-01.*
   (*ii*) *Annual Report,* relevent years.

Table 2.1.16: Total Enrolment in Higher Education (General) by Faculty and Level

Faculty	*Doctorate/Research*			*Postgraduate*			*Graduate*		
	1981	*1991⁺*	*2001*[N]	*1981*	*1991*	*2001*[N]	*1981*	*1991*	*2001*[N]
Arts	13003 (53.34)	@	@	160673 (63.17)	202831 (57.26)	410730 (63.48)	1016036 (49.76)	1534348 (46.70)	3447745 (53.51)
Science	10403 (42.68)	@	@	52809 (20.76)	71891 (20.30)	148393 (22.94)	489415 (23.97)	756896 (23.03)	1449244 (22.50)
Commerce	971 (3.98)	@	@	40879 (16.07)	79494 (22.44)	87893 (13.58)	536217 (26.27)	994532 (30.27)	1545800 (23.99)
Total	24377 (100.00)	27815 (100.00)	53119 (100.00)	254361 (100.00)	354216 (100.00)	647016 (100.00)	447359 (100.00)	328577 (100.00)	6442789 (100.00)

Notes : Figures in brackets are percentages in relation to total.
[N] As on September 30.
@ Break-up of Arts, Science and Commerce is not available.

Sources : Ministry of Human Resource Development:
(i) *Education in India* (ii) *Selected Educational Statistics.*

Table 2.1.17: Enrolment of Boys in Higher Education (General) by Faculty and Level

Faculty	*Doctorate/Research*			*Postgraduate*			*Graduate*		
	1981	*1991⁺*	*2001*[N]	*1981*	*1991*	*2001*[N]	*1981*	*1991*	*2001*[N]
Arts	8194 (48.76)	@	@	101910 (57.64)	125935 (52.93)	246978 (63.87)	633745 (44.07)	918955 (42.81)	1922917 (51.17)
Science	7790 (46.35)	@	@	37255 (21.07)	47542 (19.98)	81240 (21.01)	353052 (24.55)	475861 (22.17)	891715 (23.73)
Commerce	821 (4.89)	@	@	37638 (21.29)	64451 (27.09)	58449 (15.12)	451223 (31.38)	751596 (35.02)	943074 (25.10)
Total	16805 (100.00)	18696 (100.00)	33820 (100.00)	176803 (100.00)	237928 (100.00)	386667 (100.00)	1438020 (100.00)	2146412 (100.00)	3757706 (100.00)

Notes: Figures in brackets are percentages in relation to total.
[N] As on September 30.
@ Break-up of Arts, Science and Commerce is not available.

Sources: Ministry of Human Resource Development :
(*i*) *Education in India.*
(*ii*) *Selected Educational Statistics.*

Table 2.1.18: Enrolment of Girls in Higher Education (General) by Faculty and Level

Faculty	Doctorate/Research			Postgraduate			Graduate		
	1981	1991+	2001N	1981	1991	2001N	1981	1991	2001N
Arts	4809 (63.51)	@	@	58763 (75.77)	76896 (66.12)	163752 (62.90)	382291 (63.33)	615393 (54.01)	1524828 (56.79)
Science	2613 (34.51)	@	@	15554 (20.05)	24349 (20.94)	67153 (25.79)	136363 (22.59)	281035 (24.67)	557529 (20.76)
Commerce	150 (1.98)	@	@	3241 (4.18)	15043 (12.94)	29444 (11.31)	84994 (14.08)	242936 (21.32)	602726 (22.45)
Total	7572 (100.00)	9129 (100.00)	19,299 (100.00)	77558 (100.00)	116288 (100.00)	260349 (100.00)	603648 (100.00)	1139364 (100.00)	2685083 (100.00)

Notes: NAs on September 30.
+ Figures relate to 1989-90.
@ Break-up of Arts, Science and Commerce is not available.
Figures in brackets are percentages in relation to total.

Sources: Ministry of Human Resource Development:
(i) *Education in India.*
(ii) *Selected Educational Statistics.*

Table 2.1.19: Enrolment of Girls as percent of Total Enrolment in University Education by Faculty

Year	Arts	Science	Commerce	Education*	Engg./Tech.*	Medicine @*
1980-81	37.5	27.9	15.2	46.7	4.6	23.8
1985-86	37.9	29.8	20.9	43.9	5.9	29.5
1990-91	39.8	36.8	24.0	44.2	10.9	34.3
1993-94	39.4	32.9	26.7	44.6	11.1	36.5
1994-95	39.8	33.3	28.0	43.2	13.1	33.9
1995-96	41.5	35.5	29.0	41.2	14.2	34.5
1996-97	41.9	34.6	29.7	43.1	14.8	35.4
1997-98	41.5	35.6	30.6	43.1	16.9	36.1
1998-99	44.7	35.6	31.6	42.5	14.9	33.7
1999-00	44.9	37.4	34.0	42.6	22.1	37.8
2000-01	38.0	38.0	35.6	42.8	22.3	40.6
2001-02	43.8	39.1	38.7	43.5	24.9	40.6
2002-03*	45.4	40.2	36.7	50.6	22.2	44.7
2003-04**	45.5	39.8	36.7	52.1	23.1	46.3
2006-2007***	45.8	38.0	35.1	48.7	22.2	44.3

Notes: @ Excludes dentistry, public health, nursing, midwifery and pharmacy.
* Only for degree level, not postgraduate. ** Estimated. ***Provisional.

Source: University Grant Commission : *Annual Report,* relevent years.

Figure 2.1.G

ENROLMENT IN HIGHER EDUCATION BY FACULTY AND LEVEL

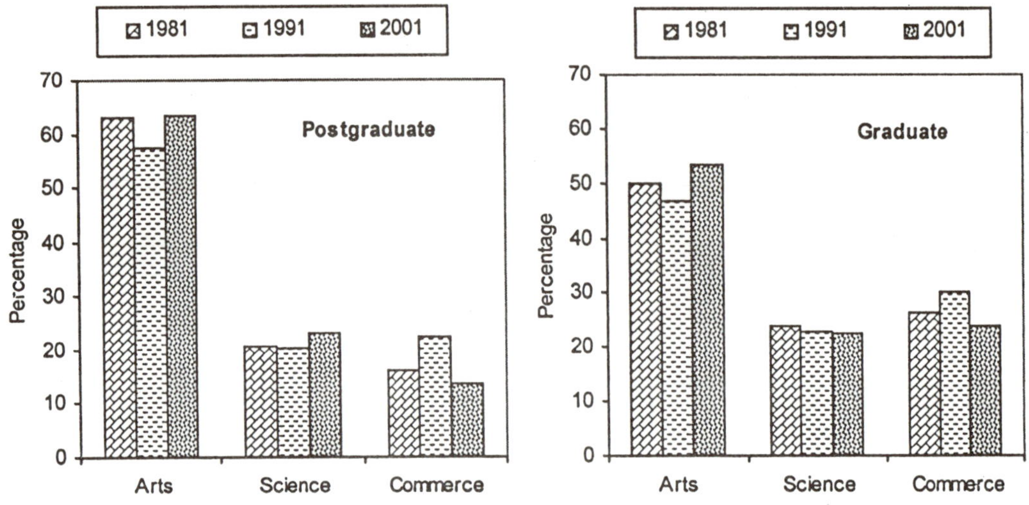

For details see Table 2.1.16

Figure 2.1.H

PERCENTAGE OF GIRLS' ENROLMENT TO TOTAL ENROLMENT IN UNIVERSITY EDUCATION BY FACULTY

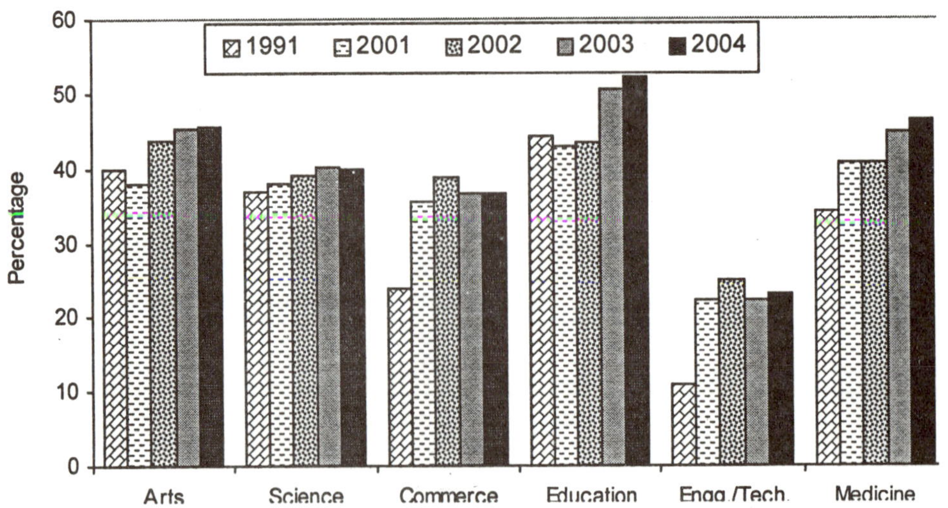

For details see Table 2.1.19

Table 2.1.20: Gross Enrolment Ratio in Different Stage of School Education

Year	*Primary Classes I-V (6-11 Years)*			*Middle Classes VI-VIII (11-14 Years)*			*High/Higher Secondary Classes IX-XI/XII (14-18 Years)*		
	Boys	*Girls*	*Total*	*Boys*	*Girls*	*Total*	*Boys*	*Girls*	*Total*
1981-82	98.9	66.2	83.0	56.0	29.7	43.3	24.1	11.3	18.0
1982-83	103.0	69.6	86.8	58.3	31.7	45.5	25.1	11.6	18.6
1983-84	106.9	72.6	90.2	60.6	33.2	47.3	25.4	12.1	19.0
1984-85	110.3	75.9	93.6	61.3	34.0	48.1	31.7	14.7	23.5
1985-86	111.1	79.2	95.6	61.8	35.3	49.0	32.7	15.5	24.4
1986-87	110.0	79.8	95.3	61.0	34.7	48.2	30.8	15.6	24.0
1987-88	114.0	83.2	99.0	63.1	36.6	50.2	29.5	14.5	22.2
1988-89	109.2	86.3	95.1	61.4	35.8	48.9	28.4	15.3	22.1
1989-90	109.7	81.3	95.9	72.0	42.2	57.4	31.2	16.3	24.0
1990-91	115.3	86.0	101.0	73.4	46.1	60.1	NA	NA	NA
1991-92	116.6	88.1	102.7	74.2	47.4	61.2	NA	NA	NA
1992-93	118.1	92.7	105.7	80.5	53.8	67.5	NA	NA	NA
1993-94P	115.3	92.9	104.5	79.3	55.2	67.7	NA	NA	NA
1994-95P	114.8	92.5	104.0	78.9	54.5	67.2	NA	NA	NA
1995-96P	114.5	93.3	104.3	79.5	54.9	67.6	NA	NA	NA
1996-97P	98.7	81.9	90.6	70.9	52.8	62.4	NA	NA	NA
1997-98P	97.7	81.2	89.7	66.4	49.5	58.4	NA	NA	NA
1998-99P	100.9	82.9	92.1	65.3	49.1	57.6	NA	NA	NA
1999-00P	104.1	85.2	94.9	67.2	49.7	58.8	NA	NA	NA
2000-01P	104.9	85.9	95.7	66.7	49.9	58.6	NA	NA	NA
2001-02P	105.3	86.9	96.3	67.8	52.1	60.2	38.2	27.7	33.3
2002-03P	97.3	92.9	95.2	65.5	56.3	61.1	41.5	33.2	37.6
2003-04P	100.7	95.7	98.3	66.9	57.7	62.5	42.9	34.3	38.9
2004-05P	110.7	104.7	107.8	74.3	65.1	69.9	44.3	35.1	39.9
2005-06P	112.8	105.7	109.4	75.1	66.4	70.9	44.5	35.8	40.4
2006-07P	114.4	107.8	111.2	77.4	69.5	73.6	44.4	36.4	40.6

Notes: P — Provisional.
As on September 30.
NA: Not available.

Sources: Ministry of Human Resource Development :
(i) *Selected Educational Statistics*, relevent years.
(ii) *Annual Report, 2007-08.*

Table 2.1.21: Educational Composition of Population by Number of Years of Schooling in India

Year	No education or less than three years		3-6 years		7-11 years		12-14 years		15+ years		Total	
	Female	Person	Female	Person	Female	Person	Female	Person	Female	Person	Female	Person
Number (million)												
1971	214.7	386.8	36.9	110.5	9	33	2.8	14.6	0.7	3.3	264.1	548.2
1981	247.9	435	55.4	154.5	17.6	56.7	7.1	29.1	2	8	330	683.3
1991[R]	278.1	489.6	75.4	189.8	41.3	123.7	5.9	20.3	6.3	23	407.1	846.3
2001[E]	273.1	469.5	123.3	284.7	72.3	198.3	13	40.5	11.4	34.1	495.7	1027
Percentage distribution												
1971	81.2	70.5	14	20.2	3.4	6	1.1	2.7	0.3	0.6	100	100
1981	75.1	63.6	16.8	22.6	5.3	8.3	2.2	4.3	0.6	1.2	100	100
1991[R]	68.3	57.8	18.5	22.4	10.1	14.6	4.2	6.8	1.6	2.7	100	100
2001[E]	55.1	45.7	24.9	27.7	14.6	19.3	2.6	3.9	2.3	3.3	100	100

Notes: The revised figures for the year 1991 were prepared by taking the actual figure of total population (excluding Jammu & Kashmir where census could not be held) by level of education available from "Social and Cultural Tables, Census of India, 1991". Then the estimated population of Jammu & Kashmir was added to the total population and distributed by level of education in the same proportion.

The estimated figures for 2001 were prepared by taking the total (provisional) population figures by broad level of education (Illiterate and literate) available from "Provisional Population Totals, Census of India, 2001". Then the literate population of 2001 was distributed in different level of education by applying the NSSO's proportions of 2000-01. For the number of years of schooling, the appropriate grouping of levels of education was done.

R—Revised. E—Estimated.

Sources: (*i*) Registrar General and Census commissioner of India.
(*ii*) National Sample Survey Organisation.

Table 2.1.22: Drop-out Rate by Sex and Stages of School Education

Year	Boys			Girls		
	Primary (I-V Classes)	*Middle (I-VIII Classes)*	*Secondary (I-X Classes)*	*Primary (I-V Classes)*	*Middle (I-VIII Classes)*	*Secondary (I-X Classes)*
1980-81	56.20	68.00	79.80	62.50	79.40	86.60
1981-82	51.10	68.50	79.44	57.30	77.70	86.81
1990-91	40.10	59.12	67.50	45.97	65.13	76.96
1991-92	40.30	56.10	69.60	44.30	62.40	76.30
1992-93	43.80	58.20	70.00	46.70	65.20	77.30
1994-95P	35.18	50.02	67.15	37.79	56.53	73.78
1995-96P	37.92	54.99	66.36	41.31	61.70	74.07
1996-97P	39.37	51.89	66.82	38.35	52.77	73.64
1998-99P	38.62	54.40	65.44	41.22	60.09	70.22
1999-00P	38.67	51.96	66.58	42.28	58.00	68.28
2000-01	39.71	50.33	66.41	41.90	57.95	71.51
2001-02P	38.36	52.91	64.16	39.88	56.92	68.59
2002-03P	35.85	52.28	60.72	33.72	53.45	64.97
2003-04P	33.66	51.74	60.97	28.44	52.84	64.92
2004-05P	31.81	50.49	60.41	25.42	51.28	63.88
2005-06	29.52	49.64	60.41	22.50	50.36	63.44
2006-07	24.41	45.58	58.62	26.56	45.33	61.47

Notes: Total drop-out during a course (stage) has been taken as percent of intake in the first year of the course (stage).
P – Provisional.

Sources: Ministry of Human Resource Development:
(i) Selected Educational Statistics.
(ii) Annual Report, 2007-08.

Table 2.1.23: Progress of Educational Institutions in Select Professional Courses

Year	Engineering		Medical (Allopathy)	Dental
	Degree	*Diploma*		
1971	134	301	95	15
1981	171	363	109	16
1986	248	680	122	29
1991	351	910	128	54
1992	354	911	146	57
1993	370	988	146	63
1994	422	1029	146	67
1997	607	1135	165	100
1999	776	1215	147*	110
2000	880	1225	147*	121
2001	880	1225	189	135
2002	1347	1228	NA	149
2003	NA	NA	NA	164
2004	NA	NA	NA	185
2005	NA	NA	229	189
2006	NA	NA	242	205
2007	NA	NA	262	240
2008	NA	NA	266	268

Note: * Only the numbers of recognised medical Colleges.

Sources: (i) Ministry of Human Resource Development: *Technical Education in India-Survey of Facilities;* (ii) Medical Council of India; (iii) Dental Council of India; (iv) All India Council for Technical Education; (v) University Grants Commission; (vi) Ministry of Health & Family Welfare: (a) Directorate General of Health Services, Central Bureau of Health Intelligence, (b) Health Information of India, 2006.

Figure 2.1.I

DROP OUT RATE IN DIFFERENT STAGES OF SCHOOL EDUCATION

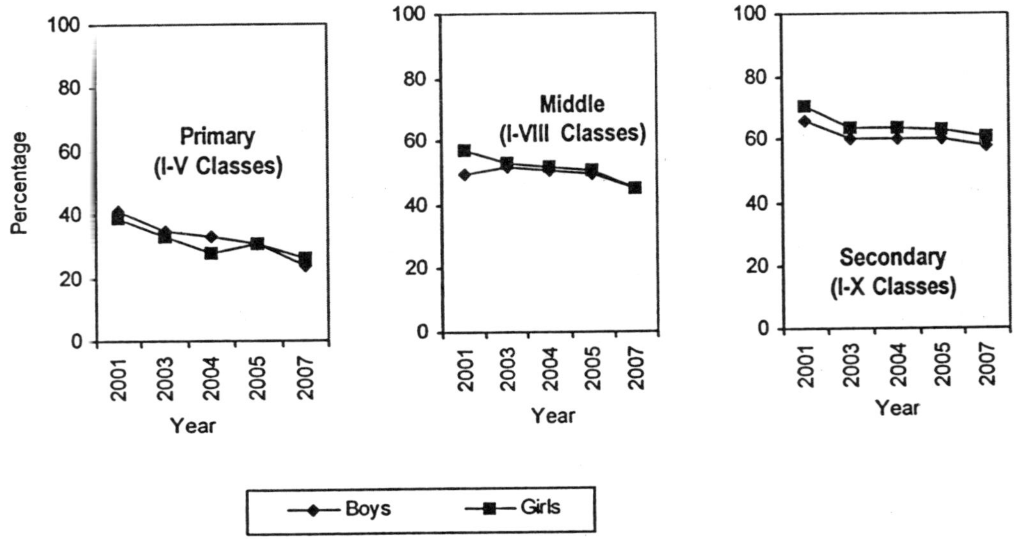

For details see Table 2.1.22

Table 2.1.24: Admission and Outturn in Select Professional Courses

Year	Engineering				Medical (Allopathy)		Dental	
	Degree		Diploma					
	Admission	Outturn	Admission	Outturn	Admission	Outturn	Admission	Outturn
1971	18,207	18,223	33,154	17,699	12,029	10,407	562	478
1981	34,835	19,012	61,114	35,487	11,431	12,170	705	501
1986	36,328	29,291	94,728	50,390	12,860*	12,490*	1,059	567
1991	70,481	44,724	117,835	65,325	14,700*	14,300*	2,160*	1,500*
1996	103,933	75,450**	161,125	94,554**	NA	NA	2,562	2,065
1999	185,360	72,247	100,893	82,338	NA	NA	6,100	NA
2000	197,081	74,323	159,555	92,323	NA	NA	7,100	NA
2001*	262,882*	94,639*	201,093*	102,549*	18,168	NA	8,340	NA
2002*	305,370	101,914	184,989	1,03,563*	NA	NA	9,550	NA
2003	NA	NA	NA	NA	NA	NA	10,970	NA
2004	NA	NA	NA	NA	NA	NA	12,960	NA
2005	NA	NA	NA	NA	24,690	NA	13,300	NA
2006	NA	NA	NA	NA	26,449	NA	14,700	NA
2007	NA	NA	NA	NA	28,928	NA	18,180	NA
2008	NA	NA	NA	NA	30,290	NA	20,080	NA

Notes: * Provisional. ** Estimated.

Sources: (i) Ministry of Human Resource Development: *Technical Education in India-Survey of Facilities.*; (ii) Medical Council of India; (iii) Dental Council of India; and (iv) NTMIS, AICTE, Government of India.

Table 2.1.25: Outturn at Diploma Level in Engineering and Technology

Discipline	1991	1992	1996	1997	1998	1999	2000	2001*	2002*
Civil	15,337	14,413	11,599	12,155	12,672	12,213	14,211	11,379	13,389
Mechanical	14,592	14,264	18,337	18,604	19,201	17,944	21,090	20,982	21,244
Electrical	10,362	7,545	11,427	11,869	12,997	11,333	12,701	9,823	13,938
Chemical	727	561	1,483	1,662	1,647	1,979	1,996	1,974	1,856
Electronics and Telecommunication	7,357	6,903	24,360	24,707	25,625	15,693	16,495	13,485	15,152
Metallurgy	213	208	361	300	376	427	385	501	421
Mining	420	471	681	498	520	563	558	453	268
Automobile	1,741	1,764	1,951	1,828	1,847	1,915	2,171	2,458	2,270
Agriculture	116	124	108	136	145	145	145	150	81
Hotel Management	321	393	518	523	543	534	534	477	35
Leather Tech.	98	72	174	212	225	327	327	242	216
Production	428	435	629	617	647	655	655	458	730
Textile Tech.	836	833	1,453	1,472	1,472	1,981	1,990	1,118	1,476
Printing Tech.	526	366	536	418	425	445	449	579	625
Others	12,251	15,536	20,937	18,123	18,299	16,184	18,616	38,470	31,862
Total	65,325	63,888	94,554	93,121	96,641	82,338	92,323	102,549	103,563

Note: * Provisional.

Sources: (*i*) Ministry of Human Resource Development : *Facilities for Technical Education.* (*ii*) NTMIS, AICTE, Govt. of India.

Figure 2.1.J

GROWTH OF ENGINEERING, MEDICAL AND DENTAL EDUCATIONAL INSTITUTIONS

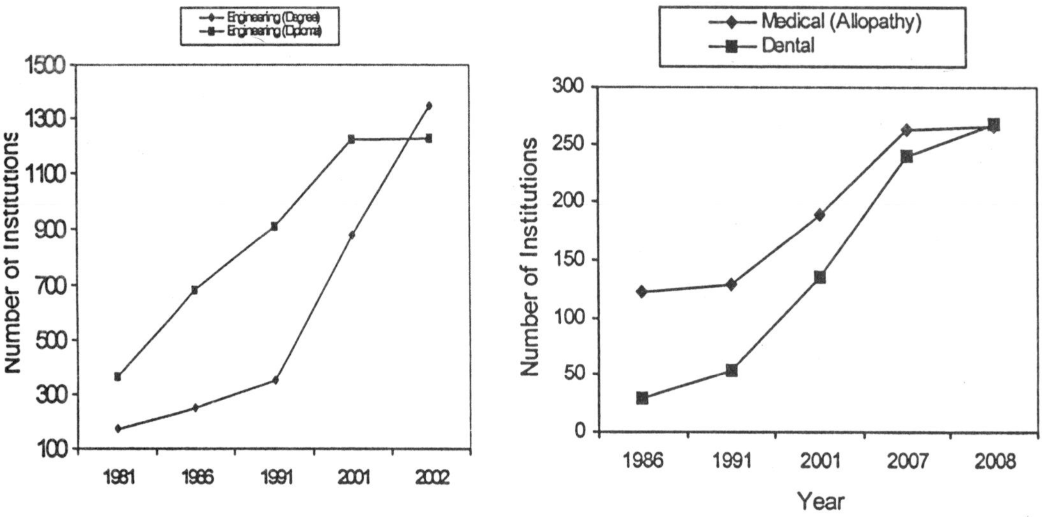

For details see Table 2.1.23

Figure 2.1.K

ADMISSION AND OUTTURN IN SELECT PROFESSIONAL COURSES

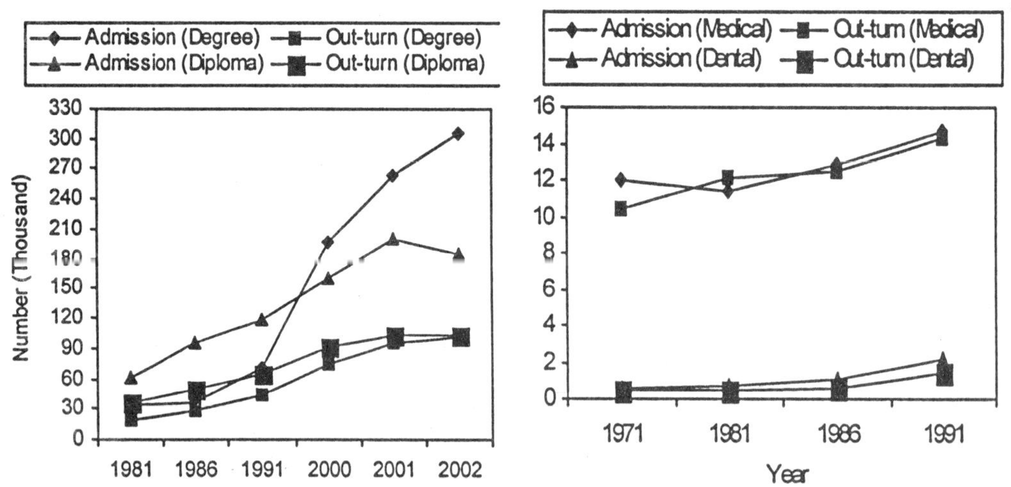

For details see Table 2.1.24

Table 2.1.26: Outturn at Degree Level in Engineering and Technology

Discipline	*1991*	*1992*	*1996*	*1997*	*1998*	*1999*	*2000*	*2001**	*2002**
Civil	8,514	8,147	8,875	8,998	8,787	9,119	9,336	7,422	7,471
Mechanical	9,257	9,538	13,582	12757	12,877	13,800	14,191	17,674	18,132
Electrical	5,399	3,716	8,160	7,787	7,982	8,309	8,309	8,198	12,199
Chemical	1,734	1,587	2,411	2,563	2,622	2,856	2,901	3,982	3,886
Electronics and Telecommunication	6,746	7,322	18,543	18,758	18,942	13,500	13,610	13,485	18,639
Metallurgy	497	469	788	965	987	927	928	849	759
Mining	348	536	508	522	537	542	552	509	419
Automobile	154	207	336	265	281	286	304	286	314
Aeronautical	58	75	102	113	117	90	90	132	127
Agriculture	202	164	359	295	306	265	265	426	337
Production	1,112	1,030	2,132	2,086	2,092	2,173	2,173	2,414	2,706
Sugar	15	15	128	52	56	56	56	24	97
Oil Tech.	45	46	57	38	39	39	39	54	31
Textile	459	414	581	657	745	804	826	822	921
Architecture	815	743	1,391	1,379	1,373	1,597	1,650	1,672	1,788
Food Tech.	29	43	85	94	97	111	111	146	600
Instrumentation	863	845	1,924	1,987	2,080	2,040	2,142	2,004	1,727
Ceramics	62	60	89	74	68	73	78	315	44
Leather	43	45	61	49	49	69	69	121	124
Others	8,372	9,139	15,538	14,497	15,173	15,591	16,693	34,104	31,593
Total	44,724	44,141	75,450	73,936	75,210	72,247	74,323	94,639	101,914

Note: * Provisional.

Source: NTMIS; AICTE, Govt. of India.

Figure 2.1.L

OUTTURN AT DIPLOMA LEVEL IN ENGINEERING AND TECHNOLOGY

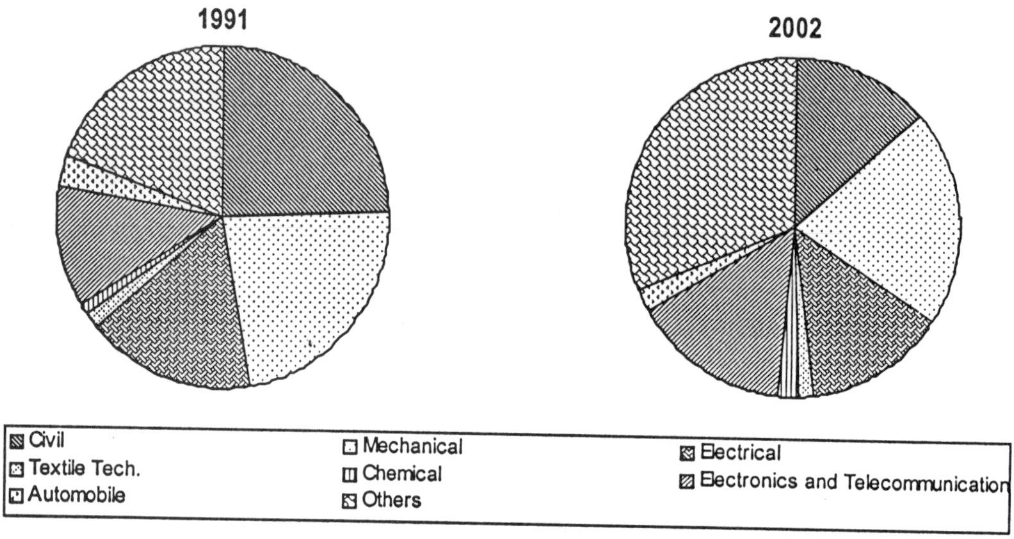

For details see Table 2.1.25

Figure 2.1.M

OUTTURN AT DEGREE LEVEL IN ENGINEERING AND TECHNOLOGY

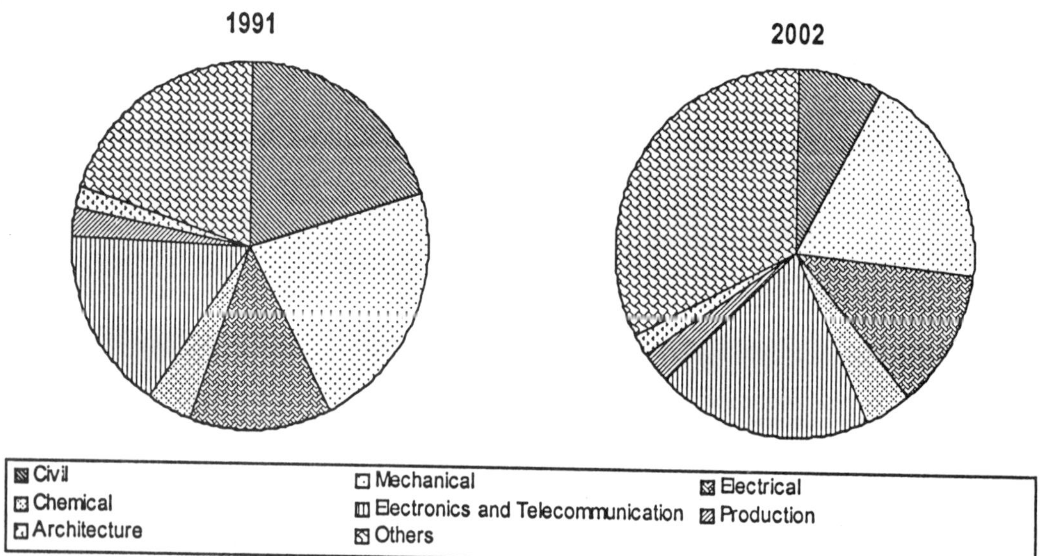

For details see Table 2.1.26

Table 2.1.27: Outturn in Select Paramedical Courses

Year	Nurses (Diploma Certificate Holders)	Midwives	Auxiliary Nurse-midwives (Health workers Female)	Health Visitors
1970	6,257	5,416	5,104	479
1980	7,256	6,541	4,264	483
1985	8,956	7,364	9,694	1,435
1990	11,032	9,366	12,377	1,185
1991	10,753	7,852	10,890	754
1992	11,686	7,893	9,390	508
1993	10,908	6,402	8,401	470
1994	11,938	6,933	6,258	511
1995	11,601	5,859	6,262	463
1996	11,431	6,256	6,541	475
1997	13,109	4,011	5,686	489
1998	13,331	3,725	4,988	412

Source : Indian Nursing Council.

Table 2.1.28: Number of Apprentices in Trades

(Thousand)

Year	Number of Establishment having Training Facilities	Number of Apprentices Under-going training	Number of Apprentices Appeared in Trade Tests	Number of Apprentices passed
1981	–	118.95	45.90	34.32
1986	–	132.30	52.10	37.20
1991	–	129.28	42.54	27.76
1992	–	133.32	36.70	26.11
1993	–	134.37	45.44	27.14
1994*	26	136.11	50.90	34.00
1995*	26	148.82	47.71	32.50
1997*	27	156.31	44.21	29.77
1998*	27	161.14	49.67	34.31
1999*	28	168.65	53.19	33.78
2000*	29	162.85	104.69	65.52
2001*	28	157.65	103.91	64.62
2002*	29	152.88	103.72	62.73
2003*	29	154.03	NA	NA
2004*	32	168.82	85.79	50.93

Notes: Data relate to 30th September. * As on March 31.
The Apprentices appear and pass out in various trade tests held twice a year in April/May and November-December.

Source: Ministry of Labour and Employment : D.G.E. & T. (Survey and Study Division), *Trade Apprenticeship Training in India under Apprenticeship Training Scheme.*

Table 2.1.29: Number of Vacancies Available and Utilised for Apprentices in Various Trades

Year	Vacancy		Vacancy Utilised by Weaker Section				Physically Handicapped
	Available	Utilised	SC	ST	Minorities	Women	
1985	189,013	134,074	13,101	3,781	15,296	3,457	–
1991	186,219	135,860	16,090	3,343	14,032	2,285	–
1996*	225,254	149,181	16,740	4,688	10,572	3,621	–
1997**	235,797	157,361	19,908	6,467	12,430	4,005	–
1998**	232,572	160,757	20,687	6,785	10,914	4,107	–
1999*	233,056	169,733	20,889	7,569	9,295	4,623	–
2000**	227,501	165,474	21,910	7,024	10,964	4,997	–
2002**	216,564	153,503	19,388	7,562	8,914	5,576	–
2003**	232,745	162,221	20,196	7,713	11,383	4,138	–
2004*	253,541	170,848	19,638	7,753	12,322	5,225	–
2006**	2,40,256	172,747	21,812	7,349	13,246	6,394	
2007**	2,58,163	185,224	22,274	7,821	12,895	6,695	1,067

Notes: Data relate to September 30.
SC – Scheduled Caste.
ST – Scheduled Tribe.
* As on 30th March ** As on 30th June.

Source: Ministry of Labour and Employment : *Annual Reports* relevent years.

Table 2.1.30: Teacher-Pupil Ratio

Year	Primary	Upper Primary	High/Hr. Secondary
1950-51	1:24	1:20	1:21
1960-61	1:36	1:31	1:25
1970-71	1:39	1:31	1:25
1980-81	1:38	1:33	1:27
1990-91	1:43	1:37	1:31
1995-96	1:43	1:37	1:32
2000-01*	1:43	1:38	1:32
2001-02*	1:43	1:34	1:34
2002-03*	1:42	1:34	1:30
2003-04*	1:45	1:35	1:35
2004-05*	1:46	1:35	1:33
2005-06	1:46	1:34	1:33
2006-07	1:45	1:35	1:33

Note: * Provisional.

Sources: Ministry of Human Resource Development :
(i) Education in India, (ii) Selected Educational Statistics relevent years.

Figure 2.1.N

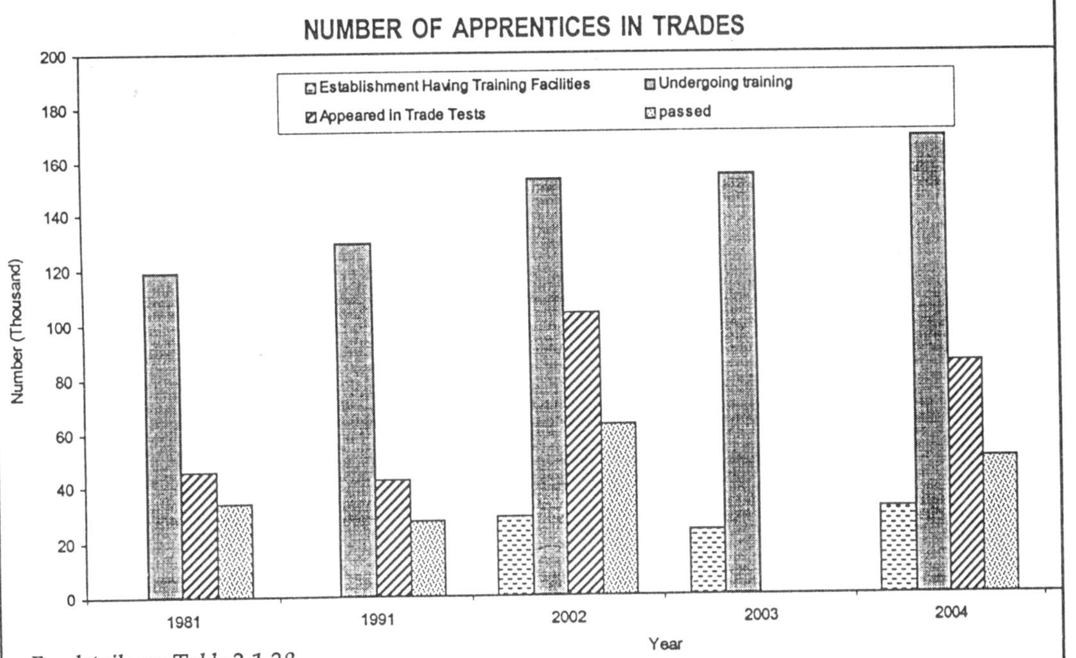

For details see Table 2.1.28

Figure 2.1.O

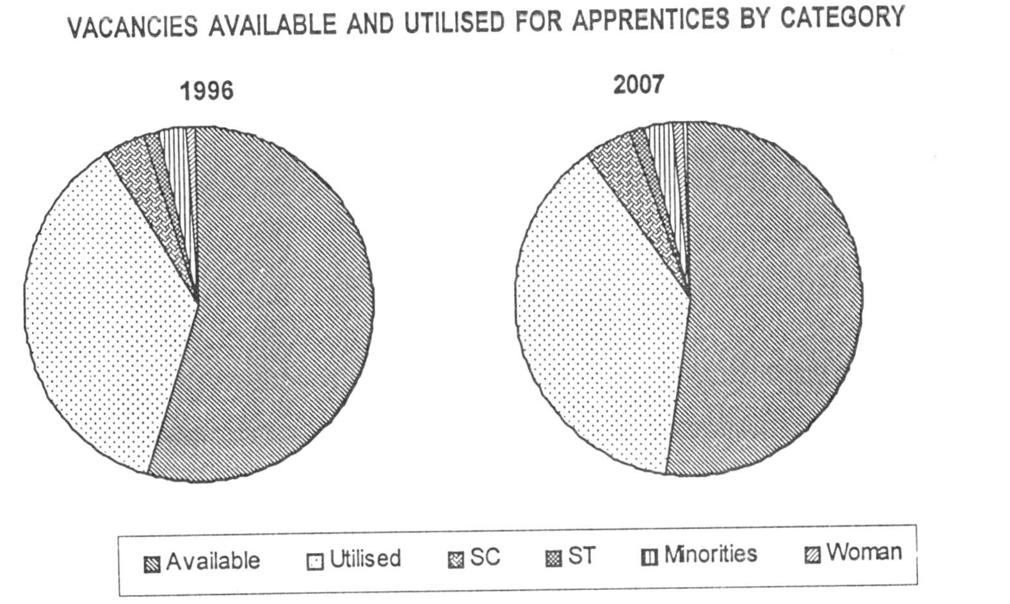

For details see Table 2.1.29

Table 2.1.31: Number of ITIs and their Seating Capacity by State/ Union Territory, 2008

State/Union Territory	*Total Number of ITIs*				*Seating Capacity*			
	Govt.	*Private*	*Total*	*WITIS/* Wings*	*Govt.*	*Private*	*Total*	*WITIS/* Wings*
States								
Andhra Pradesh	87	448	535	54	21780	83528	105308	3980
	(92)	(476)	(568)	(54)	(24.239)	(87346)	(111585)	(3980)
Arunachal Pradesh	5	0	5	1	512	0	512	80
	(2)	(0)	(2)	(1)	(368)	(0)	(368)	(112)
Assam	28	3	31	11	5696	80	5776	864
	(24)	(3)	(27)	(27)	(4536)	(84)	(4620)	(1104)
Bihar	34	59	93	7	11154	8070	19224	432
	(29)	(29)	(58)	(7)	(10496)	(4472)	(14968)	(432)
Chhattisgarh	68	23	91	13	8896	2184	11080	488
	(80)	(57)	(137)	(8)	(8984)	(5880)	(14864)	(406)
Delhi	16	55	71	41	9516	3516	13032	2760
	(14)	(48)	(62)	(41)	(9364)	(2548)	(11912)	(2760)
Goa	10	4	14	0	3056	265	3321	0
	(11)	(4)	(15)	(0)	(2652)	(420)	(3072)	(0)
Gujarat	136	202	338	33	56020	16784	72804	2160
	(135)	(129)	(264)	(33)	(70500)	(16626)	(87126)	(2144)
Haryana	79	43	122	39	15684	3252	18936	2460
	(81)	(25)	(106)	(39)	(13477)	(1428)	(14905)	(2556)
Himachal Pradesh	50	28	78	16	5186	1786	6927	1140
	(55)	(8)	(63)	(16)	(5649)	(980)	(6629)	(1102)
Jammu & Kashmir	37	1	38	54	4332	48	4380	1246
	(38)	(0)	(38)	(54)	(4332)	(0)	(4332)	(1245)
Jharkhnd	14	37	51	6	4512	5088	9600	544
	(14)	(22)	(36)	(9)	(2564)	(3124)	(5688)	(537)
Karnataka	115	738	853	28	20568	48848	69416	2260
	(131)	(610)	(741)	(29)	(21340)	(38576)	(59916)	(2224)
Kerala	34	376	410	9	14217	46314	60531	1334
	(82)	(467)	(549)	(9)	(16176)	(43946)	(60121)	(1524)
Madhya Pradesh	149	34	183	14	18680	2716	21396	846
	(136)	(33)	(169)	(13)	(19538)	(2860)	(22398)	(1044)
Maharashtra	369	207	576	588	67240	25328	92568	13702
	(347)	(267)	(614)	(311)	(67390)	(29794)	(97184)	(11704)
Manipur	7	0	7	8	540	0	540	192
	(7)	(0)	(7)	(8)	(540)	(0)	(540)	(192)
Meghalya	5	2	7	1	622	320	942	52
	(5)	(2)	(7)	(1)	(622)	(320)	(942)	(52)
Mizoram	1	0	1	0	294	0	294	0
	(1)	(0)	(1)	(–)	(294)	(0)	(294)	(0)
Nagaland	7	0	7	1	928	0	928	112
	(3)	(0)	(3)	(6)	(404)	(0)	(404)	(240)
Orissa	25	208	233	15	6776	31534	38310	928
	(27)	(147)	(174)	(15)	(7328)	(16660)	(23988)	(912)

(Contd...

State/Union Territory	Total Number of ITIs				Seating Capacity			
	Govt.	Private	Total	WITIS/* Wings	Govt.	Private	Total	WITIS/* Wings
Punjab	93	104	197	70	21635	8288	29923	4564
	(110)	(71)	(181)	(70)	(14351)	(4716)	(19067)	(4564)
Rajasthan	99	134	233	17	8588	9965	18553	928
	(91)	(45)	(236)	(16)	(9472)	(3868)	(13340)	(816)
Sikkim	1	0	1	0	212	0	212	0
	(1)	(0)	(1)	(—)	(140)	(0)	(140)	(0)
Tamil Nadu	50	608	664	27	19064	56684	75748	2568
	(71)	(605)	(676)	(24)	(24812)	(62191)	(87003)	(2716)
Tripura	8	0	8	1	816	0	816	116
	(4)	(0)	(4)	(1)	(416)	(0)	(416)	(116)
Uttaranchal	58	19	77	9	6251	2036	8287	560
	(57)	(16)	(73)	(6)	(6088)	(1592)	(7680)	(480)
Uttar Pradesh	258	191	449	67	23736	20520	44256	3852
	(185)	(128)	(313)	(67)	(38644)	(13284)	(51928)	(3852)
West Bengal	51	20	71	17	11388	984	12372	640
	(49)	(18)	(67)	(12)	(11956)	(964)	(12920)	(596)
Union Territories								
Andaman and Nicobar	1	0	1	0	241	0	241	0
Islands	(1)	(0)	(1)	(0)	(220)	(0)	(220)	(0)
Chandigarh	2	0	2	1	804	0	804	280
	(2)	(0)	(2)	(1)	(1048)	(0)	(1048)	(280)
Dadra & Nagar Haveli	1	0	1	1	228	0	228	16
	(1)	(0)	(1)	(1)	(228)	(0)	(228)	(16)
Daman and Diu	2	0	2	0	388	0	388	(0)
	(2)	(0)	(2)	(0)	(388)	(0)	(388)	(0)
Lakshadweep	1	0	1	0	96	0	96	0
	(1)	(0)	(1)	(1)	(96)	(0)	(96)	(16)
Pondicherry	6	8	14	3	1224	492	1716	232
	(7)	(8)	(15)	(3)	(1336)	(664)	(2000)	(292)
TOTAL	1913	3552	5465	1152	370880	378630	749510	49336
	(1896)	(3218)	(5114)	(883)	(399988)	(342342)	(742330)	(48014)

Notes: As on 31st January, 2007. (–) Nil. *As on October, 2007
WITIs/Women Wings—Woman Industrial Training Institutes/Women Wings.
Figure in parenthesis indicates for the year 2007.

Source: Ministry of Labour and Employment : *Annual Report*—2007-2008.

Table 2.1.32 : Trade-wise Seating Capacity in Various Vocational Institutes

Trade Courses for Women	*Seating Capacity* NVTI	RVTI	Total
Basic Cources			
Sec. Practice	32 (32)	176 (192)	208 (224)
Hair & Skin Care	32 (32)	208 (240)	240 (272)
Dress Making	—	256 (272)	256 (272)
Fruit & Veg. Prac.	—	16 (16)	16 (16)
Electronics	32 (32)	288 (256)	320 (288)
C.O.P.A.	80 (80)	340 (320)	420 (400)
Instrument Mech.	—	32 (32)	32 (32)
Arch. D'Man	48 (48)	288 (272)	336 (320)
D.T.P.	16 (16)	128 (112)	144 (112)
Steno (Hindi)	—	80 (64)	80 (64)
Fashion Technology	16 (16)	64 (98)	80 (64)
Total	256 (256)	1808 (1916)	2132 (2064)
Advance Skills			
Sec. Practice	20 (20)	120 (100)	160 (140)
Hair & Skin Care	40 (20)	100 (40)	160 (120)
Dress Making	120 (120)	320 (200)	420 (440)
Embroidery	40 (40)	— (—)	40 (40)
Electronics	20 (20)	120 (120)	140 (140)
Arch. Assist	20 (20)	140 (120)	180 (160)
Sec. Practice (Hindi)	—	40 (60)	40 (60)
Total	260 (240)	860 (580)	1140 (1100)
Post Advanaced			
P.O.T.	40 (40)	120 (120)	180 (160)
Business Services	20 (20)	—	20 (20)
Total	60 (60)	120 (120)	200 (180)
Grand Total	576 (556)	2788 (2,616)	3472 (3344)
Number of NVTI & RVTI Institutions	1	10	11

Trade Courses for Craft Instructors	*Seating Capacity* ATI	CTI	Total
Carpenter*	10	—	10
Cutting & Tailoring*	20	—	20
Draugftman(Civil)@	10	10	20
Draugftman(Mech.)@	40	—	40
Electrician@	90	10	100
Mechanic Electronics@	16	—	16
Engineering Tech.***	30	30	60
Fitter@	116	10	126
Forger and Heat Theater	—	—	—
Grinder@	8	—	8
Machinist@	86	10	96
Mech.(Radio & T.V.)@	20	—	20
Mech. Agri. Machinery@	20	—	20
Mechanic (Diesel)*	—	10	10
Mechanic Insturment@	20	—	20
Mechanic Ref. & Air.@ Cond.	20	—	20
Mechanic M.V.@	68	10	78
Moulder*	10	—	10
Reading of Drawing*	20	—	20
Sheet Metal Worker*	10	—	10
Tool & Die Maker @@	16	—	16
Training Methodology**	30	30	60
Turner@	80	8	88
Welder*	48	—	48
Wireman@	40	—	40
Foundaryman*	—	10	10
Welder-G/E*	—	8	8
Grand Total	828	146	974£
Number of ATI & CTI Institutions	5	1	6

Notes: £: Present Seating Capacity–1050 in 27 trades.
* The duration of course is one year.
** The duration of course is three month.
*** The duration of course is six months
@ The duration of course is 2 years
@ The duration course is 3 years.
— One year courses to provide comprehensive training both in skill development and principles of teaching.
— Refresher courses.
NVTI - National Vocational Training Institute
RVTI - Regional Vocational Training Institute
ATI - Advance Training Institute
CTI - Central Training Institute

Source: Ministry of Labour and Employment : *Annual Report 2007-08.*

Table 2.1.33 : Number of Schools Imparting Voational Education by Section and Enrolment Capacity, State/Union Territory

Sl. No.	State/ Union Territory	Number of Schools	Number of Sections	Enrolment Capacity
	States			
1.	Andhra Pradesh	668	1,880	94,000
2.	Arunachal Pradesh	4	4	200
3.	Assam	225	510	25,500
4.	Bihar	251	752	37,600
5.	Chhattisgarh	—	—	—
6.	Delhi	38	93	4,650
7.	Goa	43	106	5,300
8.	Gujarat	364	1,023	51,600
9.	Haryana	170	876	43,350
10.	Himachal Pradesh	40	82	4,100
11.	Jammu & Kashmir	38	38	1,900
12.	Jharkhand	—	—	—
13.	Karnataka	564	1,427	71,350
14.	Kerala	363	1,008	50,400
15.	Madhya Pradesh	465	1,307	65,350
16.	Maharashtra	1,141	3,480	174,000
17.	Manipur	19	57	2,850
18.	Meghalya	10	20	1,000
19.	Mizoram	17	51	2,550
20.	Nagaland	8	16	800
21.	Orissa	231	924	46,200
22.	Punjab	282	846	42,300
23.	Rajasthan	155	465	23,250
24.	Sikkim	7	9	450
25.	Tamil Nadu	700	2,140	107,000
26.	Tripura	12	12	600
27.	Uttaranchal	910	2,350	117,500
28.	Uttar Pradesh	—	—	—
29.	West Bengal	39	39	1,950
	Union Territories			
1.	Andaman & Nicobar Islands	3	3	150
2.	Chandigarh	17	58	2,900
3.	Dadra and Nagar Haveli	2	2	100
4.	Daman and Diu	2	5	250
5.	Lakshadweep	—	—	—
6.	Pondicherry	12	16	800
	Total	6,800	19,599	979,950

Source: Ministry of Human Resource Development: *Annual Report*, 2002-03.

Table 2.1.34: Industry-wise Number of Persons Trained by KVIC by Social Group

Sl. No.	Name of Programme/ Industry	Social Group											
		2004-05						2006-07					
		SC	ST	OBC	Gen	Total	Women	SC	ST	OBC	Gen	Total	Women
	KHADI												
1.	Cotton	75	63	236	124	498	405 (71.6)	62	192	115	107	476	370 (70.2)
2.	Silk	3	24	19	1	47	45 (8.0)	14	10	15	12	51	51 (9.7)
3.	Woolen	5	1	11	3	20	14 (2.5)	—	—	—	—	—	— (0.0)
	Total Khadi	83 (14.7)	88 (15.7)	266 (47.1)	128 (22.7)	565 (100.0)	464 (82.1)	76 (14.4)	202 (38.3)	130 (24.7)	119 (22.6)	527 (100.0)	421 (79.9)
	VILLAGE INDUSTRIES												
1.	Bee-Keeping	94	104	207	542	947	253 (1.0)	897	460	760	727	2844	632 (2.9)
2.	Cottage Match/Agarbatti	302	147	616	688	1753	1127 (4.6)	524	203	647	532	1906	1325 (6.1)
3.	Electronics	3	6	18	12	39	0 (0.0)	128	1	28	10	167	12 (0.0)
4.	Forest Based	36	52	47	72	207	95 (0.4)	24	79	16	4	123	72 (0.3)
5.	Fibre	82	26	36	141	285	172 (0.7)	49	87	28	50	214	102 (0.5)
6.	Food & Veg. Proc.	45	33	91	168	337	221 (0.9)	310	97	206	219	832	566 (2.6)
7.	Hand-made-paper	120	56	204	238	618	266 (1.1)	144	96	259	277	776	332 (1.5)
8.	Marketing	3	1	13	48	65	11 (0.0)	1	0	25	34	60	6 (0.0)
9.	Mineral Based Industry-Lime	6	0	57	58	121	66 (0.3)	—	—	—	—	—	— (0.0)

Contd.

Sl. No.	Name of Programme/ Industry	Social Group											
		2004-05						2006-07					
		SC	ST	OBC	Gen	Total	Women	SC	ST	OBC	Gen	Total	Women
10.	Mineral Based Industry-Pottery	23	17	127	89	256	62 (0.2)	27	15	133	58	233	101 (0.5)
11.	Non Conventional Energy	53	284	91	9640	10070	415 (1.7)	233	190	721	267	1411	245 (1.1)
12.	Non Edible Oil & Soap	247	123	469	846	1685	980 (4.0)	433	341	432	573	1779	953 (4.4)
13.	Processing of Cereals & Pulses	278	79	439	390	1186	780 (3.2)	365	138	513	415	1431	910 (4.2)
14.	Palm Gur Industry	104	7	348	600	1059	502 (2.1)	22	51	70	29	172	11 (0.0)
15.	Plastic	4	0	15	19	38	0 (0.0)	14	10	17	29	70	11 (0.0)
16.	Polymer	147	168	503	611	1429	643 (2.6)	269	97	222	494	1082	598 (2.7)
17.	Rural Engineering	57	53	109	166	385	5 (0.0)	134	181	206	50	571	22 (0.0)
18.	Service	170	49	490	353	1062	366 (1.5)	858	76	694	469	2097	646 (3.0)
19.	Textile	122	87	475	364	1048	1000 (4.1)	881	245	685	399	2210	1904 (8.8)
20.	Village Leather	64	19	36	43	162	92 (0.4)	148	42	31	38	259	79 (0.4)
21.	Village Oil	13	0	11	7	31	0 (0.0)	19	80	18	13	130	0 (0.0)
22.	Information Tech.	52	13	238	173	476	178 (0.7)	194	79	65	228	566	226 (1.0)
23.	Peripatetic	—	—	—	—	—	—	117	30	69	2376	2592	374 (1.7)
24.	Other Village Industry	122	300	232	431	1085	284 (1.2)	34	17	54	98	203	110 (0.5)
	Total Village Industry	2147 (8.8)	1624 (6.7)	4872 (20.0)	15701 (64.5)	24344 (100.0)	7518 (30.9)	5825 (26.8)	2615 (12.0)	5899 (27.2)	7389 (34.0)	21728 (100.0)	9237 (42.5)

Sl. No.	Name of Programme/ Industry	Social Group											
		2004-05						2006-07					
		SC	*ST*	*OBC*	*Gen*	*Total*	*Women*	*SC*	*ST*	*OBC*	*Gen*	*Total*	*Women*
	OTHER												
1.	EAP/EDP	949	427	1,821	14,722	17,969	3,981 (19.8)	3,966	6,015	7,135	12,618	29,734	11,336 (33.7)
2.	In-service	7	6	26	1461	1500	81 (0.4)	20	8	34	548	610	52 (0.1)
3.	Sponsored Programme	0	0	0	658	658	0 (0.0)	1,946	18	1,062	353	3,379	1,632 (4.8)
	Total Others	956 (4.7)	433 (2.2)	1,847 (9.2)	16,891 (83.9)	20,127 (100.0)	4,062 (20.2)	5,932 (17.6)	6,041 (17.9)	8,231 (24.4)	13,519 (40.1)	33,723 (100.0)	13,020 (38.6)
	Grand Total	3,186 (7.1)	2,145 (4.8)	6,985 (15.5)	32,720 (72.6)	45,036 (100.0)	12044 (26.7)	11,833 (21.1)	8,858 (15.8)	14,260 (25.5)	21,038 (37.6)	55,989 (100.0)	22,769 (40.7)

Contd.

Notes: SC: Scheduled Caste.
ST: Scheduled Tribes.
OBC: Other Backward Class.
Gen.: General.
EAP: Entrepreneures Awareness Programme.
EDP: Entrepreneures Development Programme.
Figures with in the parenthesis represent percentage of total.

Source: Khadi and Village Industry Commission : *Annual Reports* for the years 2004-05 & 2006-07.

Table 2.1.35 : State-wise Number of Persons Trained by KVIC by Social Group–2006-07

S.No.	Name of States	*Social Group*					
		SC	*ST*	*OBC*	*Gen.*	*Total*	*Women*
1.	Andhra Pradesh	609	67	1142	719	2537	1818
		(138)	(38)	(306)	(566)	(1048)	(466)
							71.7 [44.5]
2.	Arunachal Pradesh	1	676	18	26	721	415
		(0)	(100)	(9)	(2080)	(2189)	(108)
							57.6 [4.9]
3.	Assam	139	174	243	2288	2844	519
		(22)	(96)	(44)	(25)	(187)	(145)
							18.2 [77.5]
4.	Bihar	711	2	759	605	2077	373
		(67)	(2)	(235)	(344)	(648)	(106)
							18.0 [16.4]
5.	Chhattisgarh	—	—	—	—	—	—
		(7)	(63)	(39)	(16)	(125)	(73)
							0.0 [58.4]
6.	Delhi	80	0	622	716	1418	424
		(31)	(1)	(56)	(583)	(671)	(210)
							29.9 [31.3]
7.	Jharkhand	122	510	101	22	755	321
		(13)	(286)	(67)	(177)	(543)	(186)
							42.5 [34.3]
8.	Karnataka	814	311	751	1920	3796	1965
		(468)	(155)	(493)	(1616)	(2732)	(1344)
							51.8 [49.2]
9.	Kerala	671	185	2431	1549	4836	2511
		(390)	(53)	(979)	(1834)	(3256)	(1821)
							51.9 [55.9]
10.	Madhya Pradesh	567	526	727	499	2319	1091
		(273)	(135)	(249)	(199)	(856)	(391)
							47.0 [45.7]
11.	Maharashtra	3105	668	1294	5730	10797	4628
		(479)	(512)	(1042)	(15259)	(17292)	(1974)
							42.9 [11.4]
12.	Manipur	0	472	0	0	472	0
		(0)	(0)	(0)	(0)	(0)	(0)
13.	Meghalaya	0	718	0	0	718	0.0 [0.0]
		(0)	(0)	(0)	(0)	(0)	(0)
							0.0 [0.0]
14.	Mizoram	0	2846	0	0	2846	784
		(0)	(200)	(0)	(0)	(200)	(0)
							27.5 [0.0]
15.	Nagaland	0	385	0	0	385	190
		(0)	(0)	(0)	(200)	(200)	(141)
							49.4 [70.5]
16.	Orissa	363	311	743	1042	2459	963
		(261)	(162)	(551)	(839)	(1813)	(1316)
							39.2 [72.6]

S.No.	Name of States	Social Group					
		SC	ST	OBC	Gen.	Total	Women
17.	Rajasthan	72	99	132	202	505	254
		(31)	(17)	(73)	(96)	(217)	(22)
							50.3 [10.1]
18.	Tamil Nadu	1048	563	3341	956	5908	2945
		(204)	(44)	(873)	(3344)	(4465)	(863)
							48.2 [19.3]
19.	Tripura	0	0	0	0	0	0
		(0)	(0)	(0)	(640)	(640)	(0)
							0.0 [0.0]
20.	Uttaranchal	90	0	748	1559	2397	298
		(181)	(258)	(1513)	(2165)	(4117)	[1986]
							12.4 [48.2]
21.	Uttar Pradesh	2885	277	1048	1384	5594	2909
		(179)	(0)	(340)	(586)	(1105)	(223)
							52.0 [20.2]
22.	West Bengal	556	68	160	1821	2605	663
		(442)	(23)	(116)	(2151)	(2732)	(669)
							24.3 [24.5]
	Total All States	11833(3186)	8858(2145)	14260(6985)	21038(32720)	55989(45036)	22769(12044)
	Percentage	21.1[7.1]	15.8[4.8]	25.5[15.5]	37.6[72.6]	100.0[100.00]	40.7[26.8]

Notes: SC: Scheduled Castes, ST: Scheduled Tribes, OBC: Other Backward Class
Gen.: General.
Figures within parenthesis ( ) represent for the year 2004-05.
Figures within [ ] Bracket represent percentage for the year 2004-05 and before this [ ] Bracket for the year 2006-07

Source: Khadi and Village Industry Commission : *Annual Reports*, 2006-07.

(ii) Participation in Labour Force

Table 2.2.1: Labour Force Participation Rates (LFPR) and Estimates of Labour Force

Year	*Rural*			*Urban*			*Total*		
	Male	*Female*	*Total*	*Male*	*Female*	*Total*	*Male*	*Female*	*Total*
1972-73									
LFPR	55.1	32.1	43.9	52.1	14.2	34.5	54.5	28.6	42.0
Labour Force (Million)	128.7	70.9	199.6	32.9	7.7	40.6	161.6	78.6	240.2
1977-78									
LFPR	56.5	34.5	45.8	54.3	18.3	37.5	56.0	31.0	44.0
Labour Force (Million)	144.5	83.6	228.1	41.4	12.1	53.5	185.9	95.7	281.6
1983									
LFPR	55.5	34.2	45.2	54.0	15.9	36.2	55.1	29.9	43.0
Labour Force (Million)	155.9	91.3	247.2	50.2	13.0	63.2	206.1	104.3	310.4
1987-88									
LFPR	54.9	33.1	44.3	53.4	16.2	35.6	54.5	28.8	42.1
Labour Force (Million)	165.0	95.1	260.1	58.5	15.8	74.3	223.5	110.9	334.4
1993-94									
LFPR	56.1	33.0	44.9	54.3	16.5	36.3	55.6	28.7	42.7
Labour Force (Million)	189.3	104.7	294.0	67.3	18.4	85.7	256.6	123.1	379.7
1999-00									
LFPR	54.0	30.2	42.3	54.2	14.7	35.4	54.1	25.8	40.4
Labour Force (Million)	200.2	105.0	305.2	80.7	20.0	100.7	280.8	125.1	405.9
2000-01									
LFPR	55.2	28.8	42.3	55.3	14.4	35.8	55.1	25.2	40.7
Labour Force (Million)	211.2	104.2	315.4	83.7	19.6	103.3	294.9	123.8	418.7
2004-05									
LFPR	55.5	33.3	44.6	57.0	17.8	38.2	55.9	29.4	43.0
Labour Force (Million)	204.9	118.8	323.2	73.5	21.1	94.7	278.5	139.4	417.9
2005-06									
LFPR	56.0	31.4	44.1	56.5	15.3	36.8	56.2	27.5	42.3
Labour Force (Million)	212.6	113.3	326.0	69.6	17.1	86.7	282.3	130.4	412.7

Notes: @ The results of 2000-01, and 2005-06 (46th, and 62nd rounds respectively) are based on thin samples. Figures relate to usual status of individuals. Labour force covers those involved in gainful activity regularly + those involved in gainful activity occasionally + those unemployed.
The LFPR represent the size of labour force as per cent of population.

Sources: National Sample Survey Organisation :
Sarvekshana, Vol. V, July 77-June 78.
Vol. XI, Jan-Dec. 1983.
Special Issue, July 87-June., 88.
Vol. XX, 1993-94.
Report No. 458, *Employment and Unemployment Situation in India-1999-2000.*
Report No. 476, *Household Consumer Expenditure and Employment-Unemployment Situation in India-2000-01.*
Report Nos. 515 & 522 *Employment and Unemployment Situation in India, 2004-05 & 2005-06.*

Figure 2.2.P

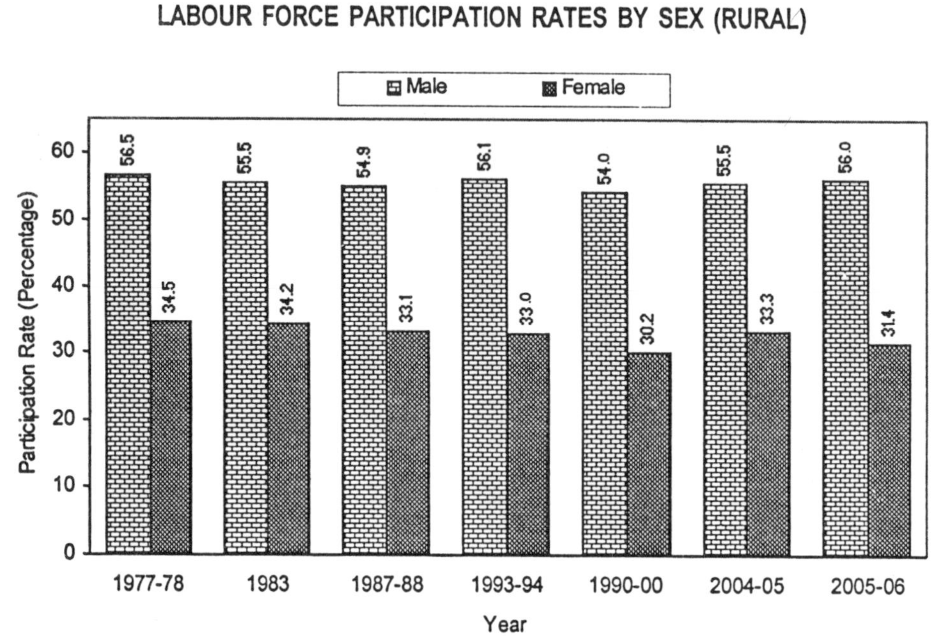

For details see Table 2.2.1

Figure 2.2.Q

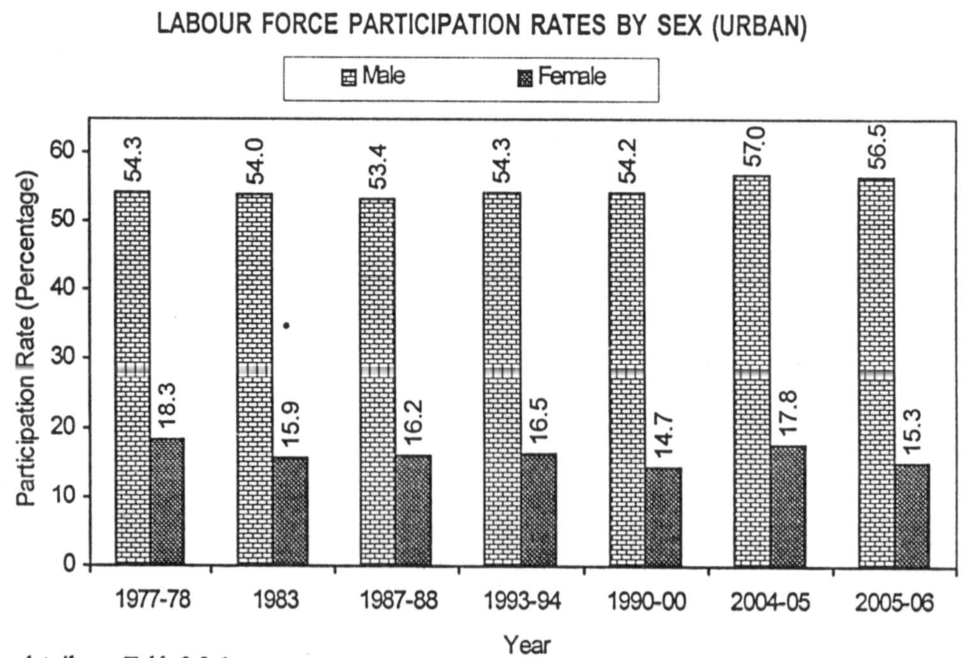

For details see Table 2.2.1

Table 2.2.2: Labour Force Participation Rates by State/Union Territory, 1999-2000, 2004-05 and 2005-06

States/ Union Territory	Rural									Urban								
	Male			Female			Total			Male			Female			Total		
	July 1999 June, 2000	July 2004 June 2005	July 2005 June 2006	July 1999 June, 2000	July 2004 June 2005	July 2005 June 2006	July 1999 June, 2000	July 2004 June 2005	July 2005 June 2006	July 1999 June, 2000	July 2004 June 2005	July 2005 June 2006	July 1999 June, 2000	July 2004 June 2005	Julu 2005 June 2006	July 1999 June, 2000	July 2004 June 2005	July 2005 June 2006
States																		
Andhra Pradesh	61.1	61.2	61.9	48.0	48.5	45.7	54.6	54.8	53.5	53.2	58.1	59.1	18.4	23.2	19.9	36.2	40.6	39.7
Arunachal Pradesh	42.5	50.5	NE	31.0	41.3	NE	37.1	46.2	NE	40.6	46.6	NE	11.0	15.1	NE	27.5	32.3	NE
Assam	54.6	56.4	55.6	16.1	21.6	21.4	36.4	40.1	39.1	56.5	59.1	60.3	13.8	12.0	12.0	36.8	36.2	38.3
Bihar	50.3	48.6	49.5	17.4	13.8	10.7	34.4	32.0	30.8	46.6	48.5	47.5	8.2	6.8	8.3	28.7	29.0	29.4
Chhattisgarh	NA	56.9	61.2	NA	45.5	47.6	NA	51.2	54.3	NA	55.0	56.9	NA	18.5	18.7	NA	37.7	38.5
Delhi	54.1	52.6	50.0	3.6	4.7	•8.6	32.4	31.7	33.1	54.6	56.1	50.6	10.9	9.4	7.8	34.3	35.1	32.3
Goa	57.8	57.6	53.9	21.5	22.2	15.6	39.5	38.5	33.5	58.5	57.8	59.0	15.9	21.4	28.4	37.9	39.8	44.1
Gujarat	58.7	59.8	58.7	41.3	42.8	37.9	50.1	51.6	48.7	54.7	59.2	59.7	13.8	15.5	12.5	35.2	38.7	37.9
Haryana	48.1	53.7	51.0	20.2	32.1	31.7	34.9	43.4	42.0	52.0	52.8	55.2	10.1	14.3	16.9	32.2	35.3	37.7
Himachal Pradesh	54.6	56.5	56.0	47.4	51.6	50.5	50.9	54.0	53.2	53.3	63.0	59.7	14.2	26.8	23.1	34.4	47.4	42.5
Jammu & Kashmir	55.4	56.1	54.0	33.0	27.1	23.3	44.7	42.2	39.2	50.0	54.6	55.9	6.8	12.6	11.2	29.6	34.8	35.0
Jharkhand	NA	54.6	53.9	NA	31.3	32.6	NA	43.3	42.5	NA	51.0	52.1	NA	13.7	11.0	NA	33.3	32.5
Karnataka	60.1	62.8	60.8	38.1	46.2	41.6	49.1	54.6	51.3	56.2	58.7	59.0	18.6	19.2	18.8	37.8	39.7	39.4
Kerala	58.7	58.9	59.5	27.3	32.1	30.1	42.2	44.8	44.2	59.1	58.3	59.3	25.4	30.1	26.1	41.5	44.0	42.4
Madhya Pradesh	54.0	54.8	55.6	38.3	36.6	34.7	46.4	46.1	45.6	50.9	54.2	52.4	13.6	15.6	13.1	33.1	35.7	33.8
Maharashtra	54.2	57.5	59.5	43.7	47.5	42.5	49.0	52.7	51.3	56.3	58.0	57.4	14.6	19.8	15.7	36.7	39.9	37.5
Manipur	50.6	53.1	NE	25.7	35.4	NE	38.7	44.5	NE	47.8	48.2	NE	22.5	23.6	NE	35.3	35.8	NE
Meghalaya	55.9	57.2	NE	41.9	48.0	NE	48.8	52.7	NE	40.7	47.0	NE	21.1	31.4	NE	31.0	38.7	NE
Mizoram	56.3	59.7	NE	44.1	44.1	NE	50.3	52.3	NE	48.7	49.1	NE	26.5	28.8	NE	37.4	39.0	NE
Nagaland	53.2	56.1	NE	45.1	51.1	NE	49.4	53.7	NE	43.3	47.9	NE	21.7	27.7	NE	33.5	38.5	NE
Orisqa	56.4	60.4	62.7	30.2	35.1	35.4	43.2	47.6	48.8	51.1	55.3	58.2	15.3	20.2	13.8	33.9	38.6	37.4
Punjab	54.3	56.7	55.0	28.2	33.8	29.6	41.7	45.8	43.1	56.5	58.9	56.8	12.8	15.5	13.2	36.3	38.5	36.9
Rajasthan	50.3	51.6	53.0	38.9	40.7	40.3	44.8	46.3	46.8	49.9	52.3	52.1	14.1	18.8	11.8	33.2	35.9	32.9
Sikkim	51.9	57.0	NE	24.5	32.3	NE	39.1	45.3	NE	55.7	56.4	NE	22.5	17.7	NE	40.7	38.3	NE
Tamil Nadu	61.0	60.4	61.8	43.4	46.7	45.1	52.3	53.4	53.3	58.5	61.1	61.4	22.7	25.3	23.1	41.0	43.4	42.3
Tripura	50.7	60.7	NE	7.6	NE	12.5	30.7	37.3	NE	52.2	60.5	NE	8.1	23.0	NE	31.3	41.4	NE
Uttranchal	NA	53.3	51.1	NA	42.9	40.6	NA	48.0	45.9	NA	54.2	46.4	NA	14.2	8.9	NA	35.1	27.8

	Male			Female			Total			Male			Female			Total		
	July 1999 June, 2000	*July 2004 June 2005*	*July 2005 June 2006*	*July 1999 June, 2000*	*July 2004 June 2005*	*July 2005 June 2006*	*July 1999 June, 2000*	*July 2004 June 2005*	*July 2005 June 2006*	*July 1999 June, 2000*	*July 2004 June 2005*	*July 2005 June 2006*	*July 1999 June, 2000*	*July 2004 June 2005*	*June 2005 July 2006*	*July 1999 June, 2000*	*July 2004 June 2005*	*July 2005 June 2006*
Uttar Pradesh	48.6	49.9	50.6	20.1	24.1	22.4	34.8	37.3	37.3	51.2	54.2	52.7	9.7	12.0	8.3	31.7	34.2	31.5
West Bengal	54.9	58.7	60.5	16.5	18.4	20.0	35.9	38.9	40.9	61.2	63.0	62.2	12.9	16.9	15.5	37.8	41.0	40.2
North-Eastern States	NA	NA	57.3	NA	NA	27.2	NA	NA	42.6	NA	NA	52.2	NA	NA	23.3	NA	NA	38.0
Union Territories																		
Group of UTs	NA	NA	61.2	NA	NA	26.0	45.6	NA	NA	NA	NA	52.1	NA	NA	17.6	NA	35.7	NA
Andaman & Nicobar Islands	56.0	65.5	@	19.3	27.7	@	38.4	47.1	@	65.3	61.7	@	24.9	18.8	@	45.4	41.6	@
Chandigarh	79.0	61.8	@	12.8	5.6	@	63.9	39.9	@	56.6	52.8	@	15.3	15.4	@	36.9	35.8	@
Dadra & Nagar Haveli	59.2	56.4	@	35.4	49.5	@	47.5	53.3	@	66.4	69.7	@	11.2	21.4	@	40.9	46.6	@
Daman & Diu	66.5	59.2	@	30.0	16.8	@	50.9	40.3	@	55.7	67.1	@	20.3	23.3	@	38.7	42.8	@
Lakshadweep	55.1	61.6	@	19.9	11.4	@	35.6	40.8	@	46.0	49.5	@	22.1	23.0	@	34.3	36.3	@
Pondicherry	58.7	62.7	@	29.4	37.4	@	44.3	49.5	@	57.4	55.9	@	18.1	19.1	@	36.8	37.3	@
All India	54.0	55.5	56.0	30.2	33.3	31.4	44.1	44.6	44.1	54.2	57.0	56.5	14.7	17.8	15.3	35.4	38.2	36.8

Notes: Figures relate to usual status of individuals.
@ included in Group of UTs.
NE: included in North Eastern States.
NA: Not Available.

Sources: National Sample Survey Organization: (*i*) Report No. 458, *Employment and Unemployment Situation in India*, 1999-2000.
(*ii*) Report Nos. 515 & 522 *Employment and Unemployment Situation in India*, 2004-05 and 2005-06.

Table 2.2.3: Labour Force Participation Rates in Broad Age-Group

Age-Group	*Year*	*Male*			*Female*			*Total*		
		Rural	*Urban*	*Total*	*Rural*	*Urban*	*Total*	*Rural*	*Urban*	*Total*
15-29	1987-88	82.4	71.0	79.5	47.8	21.1	41.4	65.1	47.2	60.7
	1993-94	80.3	68.4	77.0	45.5	20.4	39.0	63.2	45.6	58.4
	1999-00	77.4	66.3	74.2	41.1	17.3	34.7	59.3	43.2	54.8
	2004-05	78.0	68.3	74.6	43.0	21.7	37.1	60.1	46.6	56.4
	2005-06	75.7	66.9	73.3	38.5	19.1	33.3	57.9	44.1	54.2
30-44	1987-88	98.8	98.7	98.8	60.3	30.1	53.3	79.7	66.5	76.5
	1993-94	98.9	98.6	98.8	60.0	30.0	52.1	79.7	66.1	76.0
	1999-00	98.6	98.2	98.5	57.2	27.1	49.1	77.9	64.0	74.0
	2004-05	98.8	98.5	99.1	61.9	32.2	54.0	80.0	66.1	76.2
	2005-06	98.8	98.5	98.8	58.5	25.9	50.2	78.2	63.0	74.2
45-59	1987-88	96.4	93.3	95.5	53.8	27.5	48.1	75.2	62.4	72.4
	1993-94	96.8	93.7	96.0	54.3	28.3	48.3	75.7	63.4	72.8
	1999-00	95.8	92.5	94.9	51.8	25.2	45.2	74.3	61.3	70.9
	2004-05	96.3	93.0	95.4	57.0	25.3	48.6	77.3	60.9	72.9
	2005-06	97.1	92.2	95.8	54.7	22.3	46.8	76.3	59.6	72.1
60 and above	1987-88	67.0	48.2	63.3	22.0	12.3	20.0	55.1	30.0	50.0
	1993-94	70.0	44.3	64.4	24.1	11.3	21.1	47.4	27.3	42.9
	1999-00	64.0	40.2	58.7	21.8	9.4	18.8	43.0	24.1	38.6
	2004-05	64.5	36.6	57.8	25.4	10.0	21.5	44.8	22.8	39.4
	2005-06	65.0	37.3	58.8	24.6	7.7	20.7	44.5	21.9	39.4
All (15 Years +)	1987-88	87.9	81.0	86.2	49.6	23.9	43.7	68.9	53.8	65.0
	1993-94	87.6	80.1	85.6	49.0	23.8	42.7	68.6	53.3	64.6
	1999-00	85.5	78.7	83.6	45.7	20.9	39.1	65.7	51.0	61.7
	2004-05	85.9	79.2	84.0	49.4	24.4	42.7	67.7	53.0	63.7
	2005-06	45.3	78.7	83.6	46.1	20.6	39.6	65.9	50.7	62.0

Notes: Figures relate to usual status of individuals. Labour force covers those involved in gainful activity regularly + those involved in gainful activity occasionally + those unemployed. The figures represent size of labour force of a given age-group as percent of population of that age-group.

Sources: National Sample Survey Organisation :
Sarvekshana, Special Number, 1987-88.
Report No. 409, *Employment and Unemployment Situation in India-1993-94.*
Report No. 455, *Employment and Unemployment Situation in India-1999-2000,* Key Results.
Report No. 515, *Employment and Unemployment Situation in India, 2004-05.*
Report No. 522, *Employment and Unemployment Situation in India, 2005-06.*

Table 2.2.4: Age-specific Labour Force Participation Rates, 2005-06

Age-Group	*Male*			*Female*			*Persons*		
	Rural	*Urban*	*Total*	*Rural*	*Urban*	*Total*	*Rural*	*Urban*	*Total*
15-19	59.9	36.7	47.3	28.2	12.0	24.0	40.7	25.5	36.8
20-24	87.2	76.5	84.3	39.3	21.3	34.5	63.8	50.2	60.1
25-29	97.8	95.0	97.0	49.2	24.4	42.6	73.2	59.7	69.6
30-34	99.1	98.3	98.8	56.0	24.4	47.9	76.2	61.9	72.3
35-39	99.0	99.1	99.1	60.7	27.1	52.2	79.7	64.1	75.6
40-44	98.3	98.2	98.3	59.2	26.5	50.7	79.0	63.0	74.8
45-49	98.4	97.0	98.0	58.3	24.6	50.0	78.7	63.0	74.7
50-54	97.8	93.3	96.7	53.0	21.4	44.8	77.3	59.7	72.8
55-59	93.8	82.7	90.7	50.8	19.6	43.8	71.1	53.5	66.7
60 and above	65.0	37.3	58.8	24.6	7.7	20.7	44.5	21.9	39.4
All (15 years+)	85.3	78.7	83.6	46.1	20.6	39.6	65.9	50.7	62.0.

Notes: Figures relate to usual status of individuals. Labour force covers those involved in gainful activity regularly + those involved in gainful activity occasionally + those unemployed. The figures represent size of labour force of a given age group as percent of population of that age group.

Sources: National Sample Survey Organisation :
Report No. 522, *Employment-Unemployment Situation in India, 2005-06.*

Table 2.2.5: Educational Composition of Rural Labour Force

Educational Level	*1977-78*		*1987-88*		*1993-94*		*1999-2000*		*2004-05*		*2005-06*	
	Male	*Female*	*Male*	*Female*	*Male*	*Female*	*Male*	*Female*	*Male*	*Female*	*Male*	*Female*
Illiterate	55.0	88.1	48.3	82.3	43.7	79.0	39.7	73.9	33.6	66.2	31.6	64.0
Literate but up to Primary	30.8	9.1	29.6	12.0	29.0	13.7	27.4	15.7	29.4	18.0	29.6	19.4
Middle	8.5	1.6	11.6	3.2	13.6	3.9	16.0	5.8	18.0	8.2	19.2	9.9
Secondary	4.7	1.0	8.4	2.0	10.9	2.7	13.5	3.6	9.2	3.7	9.5	3.7
Graduate and above	1.0	0.2	2.1	0.4	2.8	0.7	3.4	1.0	9.8	3.9	10.1	3.0
Total	100.0	100.0	100.0	100.0	100.0	100.0	100.0	100.0	100.0	100.0	100.0	100.0

Notes: Figures relate to usual status of individuals. Figures for the year 1977-78 and 1999-2000 relate to the population age 5 year and above while figures for the years 1983, 1987-88, 1993-94, 2004-05 and 2005-06 relate to the population age 15 years and above.

Sources: National Sample Survey Organisation :
Sarvekshana, Vol. V, July 77-June 78.
Sarvekshana, Vol. XI, Jan-Dec. 1983
Sarvekshana, Special Issue, July 87-June 88.
Sarvekshana, Vol. XX, 1993-94.
Report No. 458, *Employment and Unemployment in India, 1999-2000.*
Report No. 515, *Employment and Unemployment Situation in India, 2004-05.*
Report No. 522, *Employment and Unemployment Situation in India, 2005-06.*

Figure 2.2.R

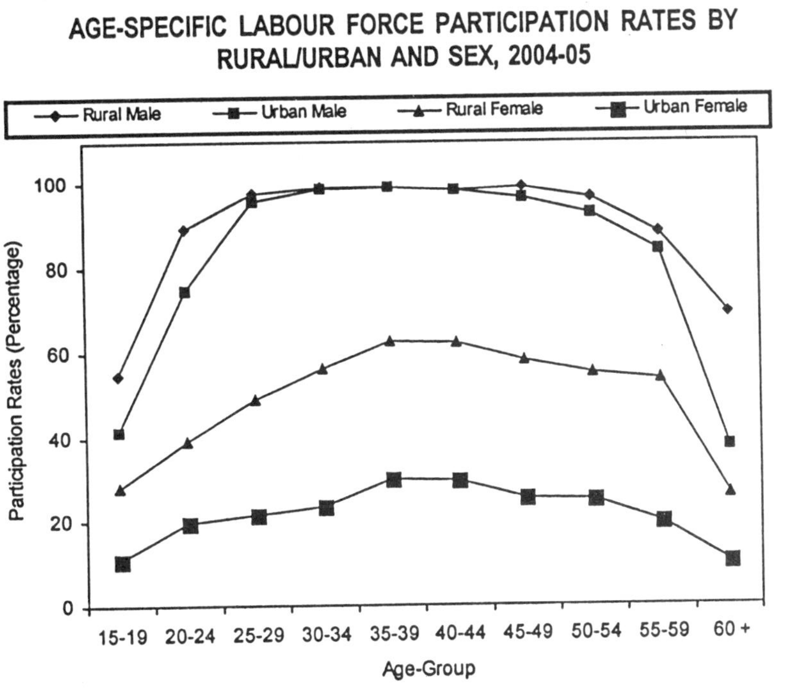

For details see Table 2.2.4

Figure 2.2.S

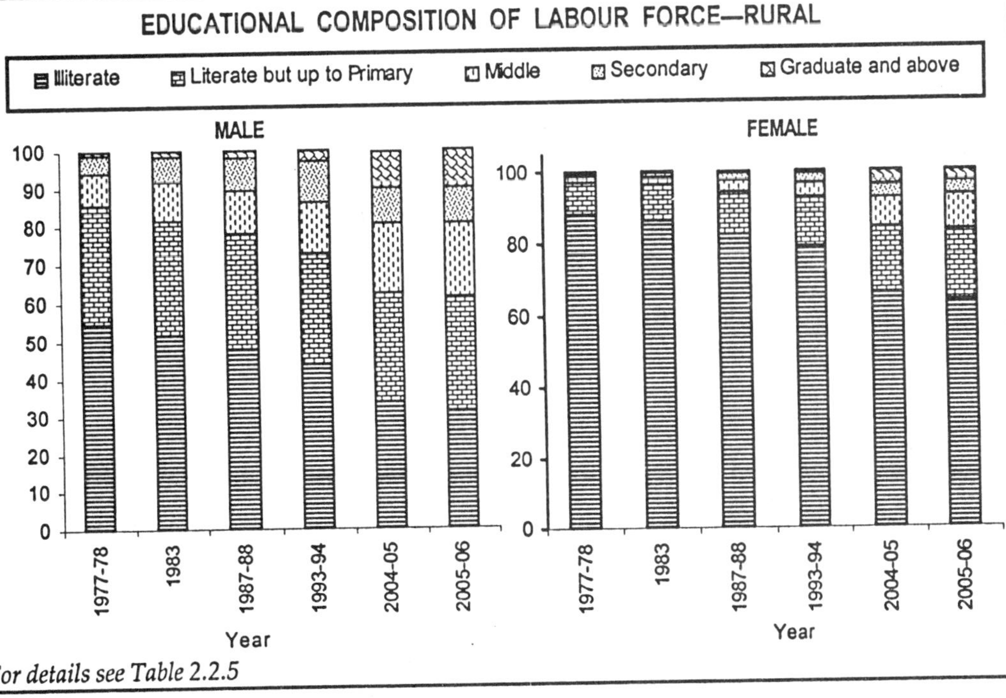

For details see Table 2.2.5

Table 2.2.6: Educational Composition of Urban Labour Force

Educational Level	1977-78		1987-88		1993-94		1999-2000		2004-05		2005-06	
	Male	Female	Male	Female	Male	Female	Male	Female	Male	Female	Male	Female
Illiterate	22.1	58.2	19.6	51.8	17.9	44.5	16.0	41.2	12.8	34.4	11.9	32.2
Literate upto Primary	33.6	17.9	30.5	19.0	25.4	17.7	21.9	17.0	22.4	18.8	21.1	19.4
Middle	17.2	6.7	16.4	7.3	17.5	8.1	18.8	9.7	19.5	10.9	21.7	12.6
Secondary	18.4	10.8	21.8	12.3	24.6	15.1	26.4	15.7	15.0	7.7	14.6	8.1
Graduate & above	8.7	6.4	11.7	9.6	14.6	14.6	16.9	16.4	30.3	28.2	30.7	27.7
Total	100.0	100.0	100.0	100.0	100.0	100.0	100.0	100.0	100.0	100.0	100.0	100.0

Notes: Figures relate to usual status of individuals. Figures for the year 1977-78 and 1999-2000 relate to the population age 5 years and above while figures for the years 1983, 1987-88 and 1993-94 relate to the population age 15 years and above.

Sources: National Sample Survey Organisation:
(i) *Sarvekshana* Vol. V, July 77-June 78. 32nd Round, *Sarvekshana* special Number 1987-88. (ii) Report No. 409, *Employment and Unemployment in India-1993-94*. (iii) Report No. 515, *Employment and Unemployment Situation in India*, 2004-05, (iv) Report No. 522, Employment and Unemployment in India, 2005-06.

Table 2.2.7: Labour Force Participation Rates for Educated Persons

Year	Educational Level	Male Rural	Male Urban	Female Rural	Female Urban
1977-78	Below Matric	N.A	N.A	N.A	N.A
	Matric*	75.27	72.32	33.66	22.26
	Graduate	89.05	87.97	55.55	43.65
1987-88	Below Matric	87.56	82.90	39.05	18.47
	Matric*	74.20	70.70	26.30	16.20
	Graduate	90.10	86.40	39.90	37.70
1993-94	Below Matric	88.35	83.38	35.82	18.60
	Matric*	72.08	68.33	20.01	14.48
	Graduate	91.30	86.20	44.80	35.50
1999-2000	Below Matric	57.91	51.90	26.99	12.59
	Matric*	74.38	67.83	19.39	12.58
	Graduate & above	89.97	85.21	40.28	30.24
2004-05	Below Matric	87.79	83.68	50.88	25.13
	Matric*	75.13	67.44	32.70	14.67
	Graduate & above	90.64	84.38	46.81	35.02
	Diploma/Certificate Course	91.71	85.94	63.83	57.55
2005-06	Below Matric	90.85	87.88	51.41	22.85
	Matric*	73.59	68.94	27.79	12.94
	Graduate & above	93.11	91.10	41.97	34.42
	Diploma Certificate Course	90.20	84.10	55.80	43.00

Notes: The Figures represent the size of labour force of given educational level as percent of population of that educational level.

* Matric includes Higher Secondary.

Sources: National Sample Survey Organisation:
(*i*) *Sarvekshana*, Vol. V, July 77-June 78. 32nd Round.
(*ii*) *Sarvekshana*, Special Number 1987-88. (*iii*) Report No. 409, *Employment and Unemployment in India-1993-94*. (*iv*) Report No. 455, *Employment and Unemployment in India-1999-2000*, Key Results. (*v*) Report No. 515 and 552, *Employment and Unemployment in India-2004-05, and 2005-06*.

Figure 2.2.T

EDUCATIONAL COMPOSITION OF LABOUR FORCE—URBAN

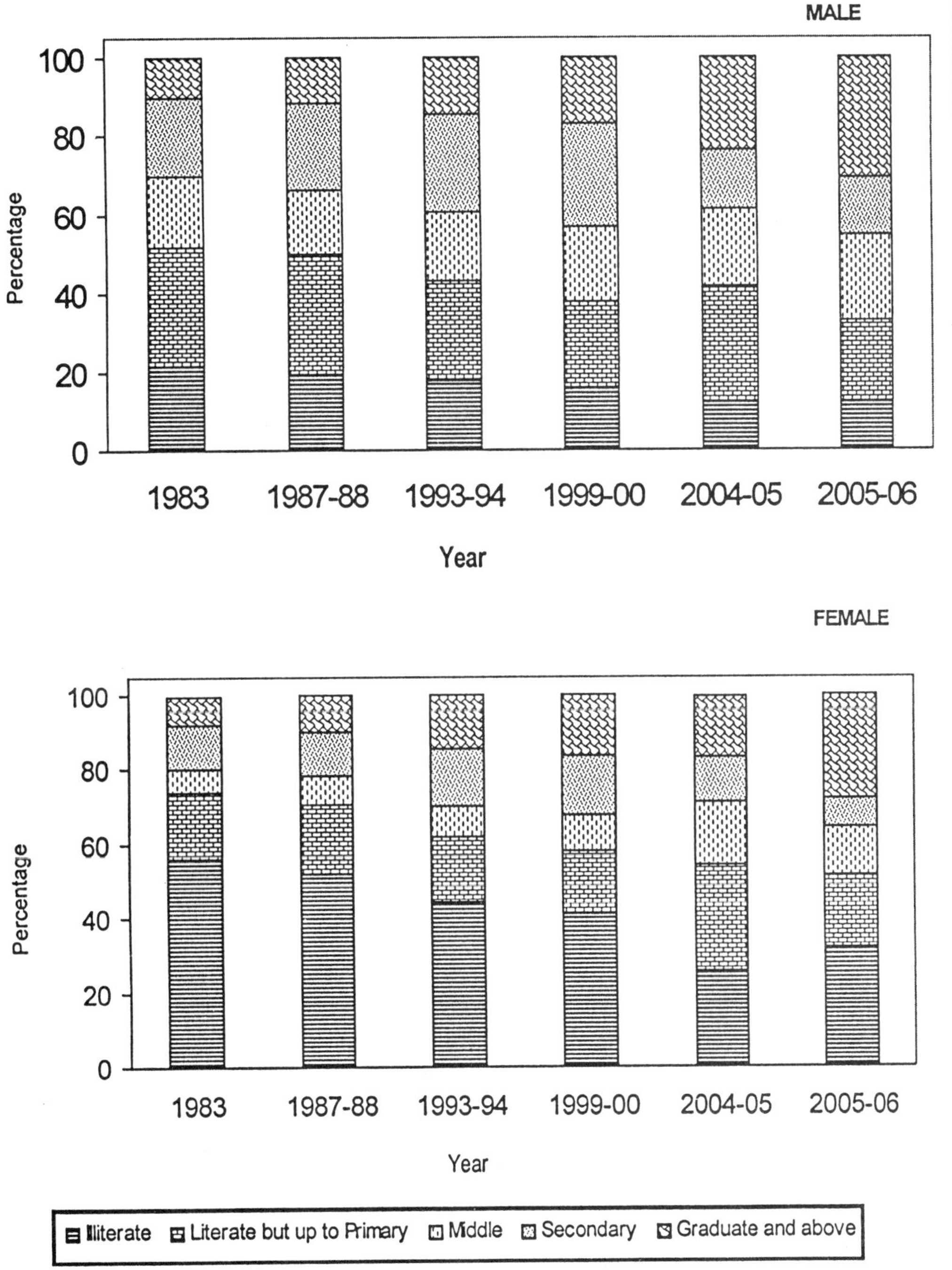

For details see Table 2.2.6

Figure 2.2.U

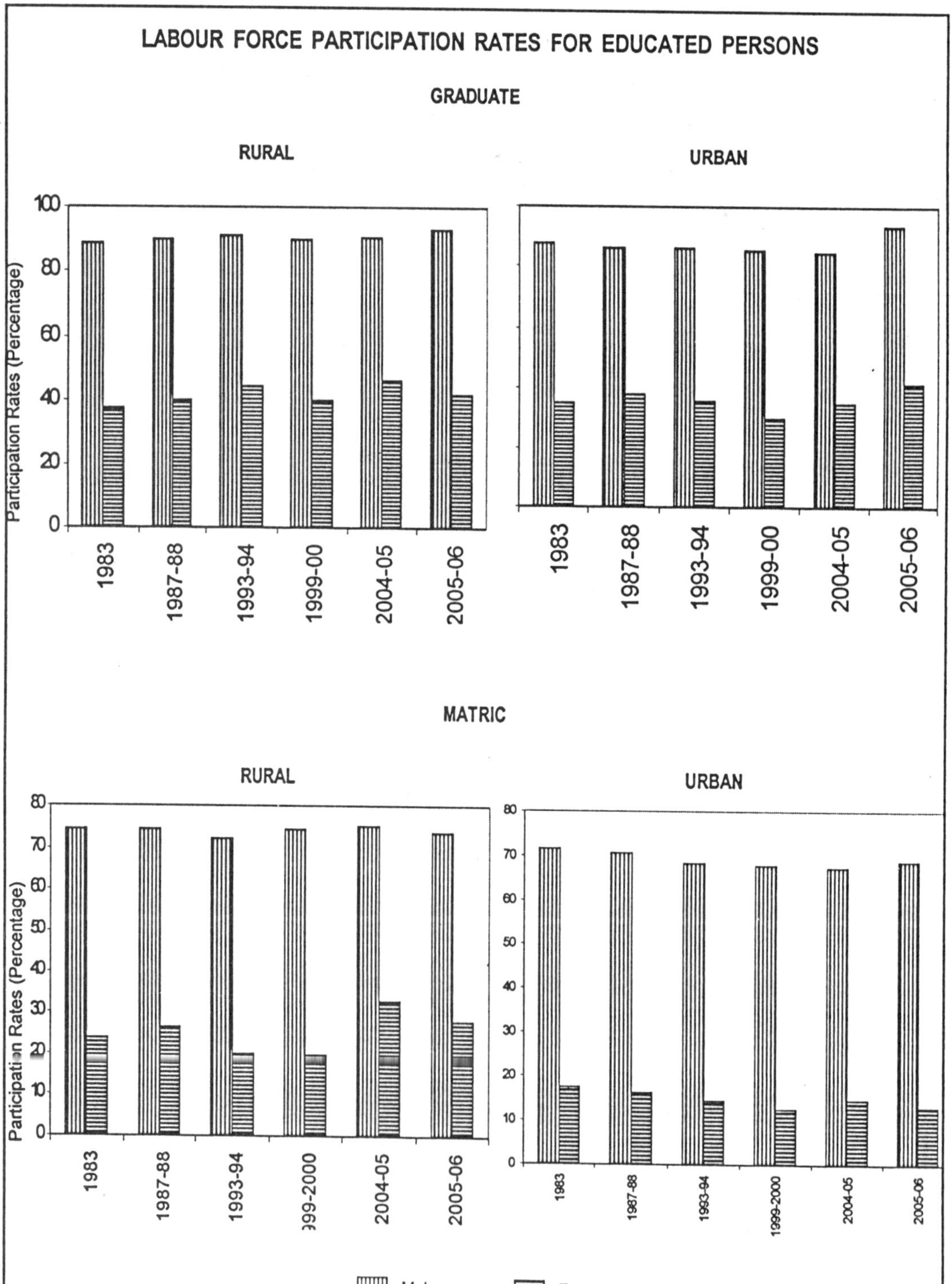

For details see Table 2.2.7

(iii) Educational Expenditure

Table 2.3.1: Total Budgeted Educational Expenditure* (Revenue Account) as percentage of GDP

Year	*GDP at Current Prices (Rs. Crore)*	*Total Educational Expenditure (Rs. Crore)*	*Expenditure as Percentage of GDP*
1980-81	130,176	3645	2.80
1985-86	249,547	7457	2.99
1990-91	510,954	19615.85	3.84
1993-94	781,345	28279.69	3.62
1995-96	1073,271	38178.09	3.56
1997-98	1390,148	48552.14	3.49
1998-99	1598,127	61578.91	3.85
1999-00	1761,838	74816.09	4.25
2000-01	1902,999	82486.48	4.33
2001-02	2081,474	84179.46	4.04
2002-03	2254,888	85507.34	3.79
2003-04	2519,785 (Q)	94652.50 (RE)	3.76
2004-05	2838,123 (A)	99054.65 (BE)	3.49

Notes: Q : Quick Estimate. (*)- Indues expenditure on education by education and other Departments.
A : Advance. RE : Revised Estimate. BE : Budget Estimate. GDP : Gross Domestic Product.

Sources: (*i*) Central Statistical Organisation : *National Accounts Statistics—2005.*
(*ii*) Ministry of Human Resource Development, (Dept. of Secondary and Higher Education) : *Analysis of Budgeted Expenditure on Education.*

Table 2.3.2: Expenditure on Education by Education Department to Total Expenditure on all Sectors (Revenue Account)

(Percentage)

Year	*State/Union Territory*	*Centre*	*Total*
1980-81	20.6	1.6	11.6
1990-91	21.2	2.2	11.7
1995-96	19.3	2.4	11.0
1996-97	19.2	2.3	11.0
1997-98	19.0	2.6	11.1
1998-99	20.2	2.9	11.7
1999-00	20.5	2.9	12.0
2000-01	18.5	2.9	10.9
2001-02	18.5	2.7	11.0
2002-03	17.6	2.7	10.1
2003-04	18.9	4.7	12.0
2004-05	19.1	4.7	12.1
2005-06 (RE)	19.3	5.5	12.7
2006-07	19.2	6.4	13.0

Notes: RE : Revised Estimate; BE : Budget Estimate

Source: Ministry of Human Resource Development; (Dept. of Secondary and Higher Education) : *Analysis of Budgeted Expenditure on Education.*

Figure 2.3.V

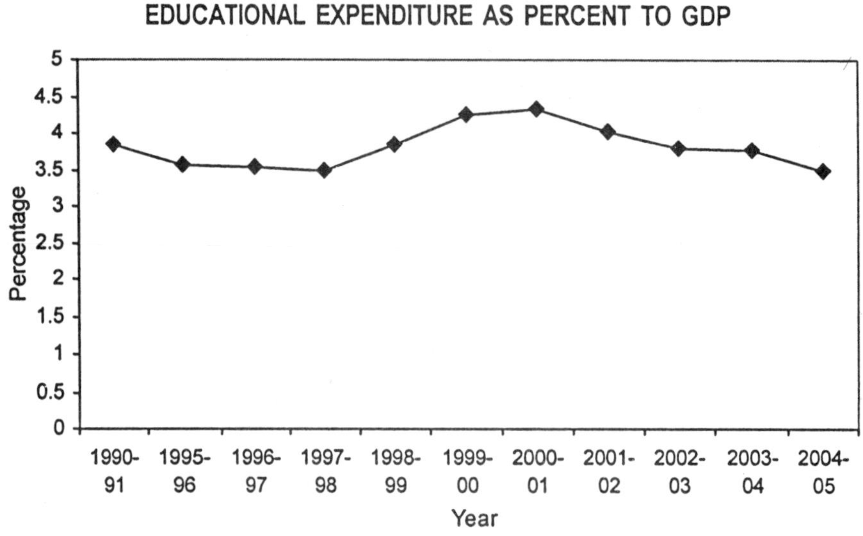

For details see Table 2.3.1

Figure 2.3.W

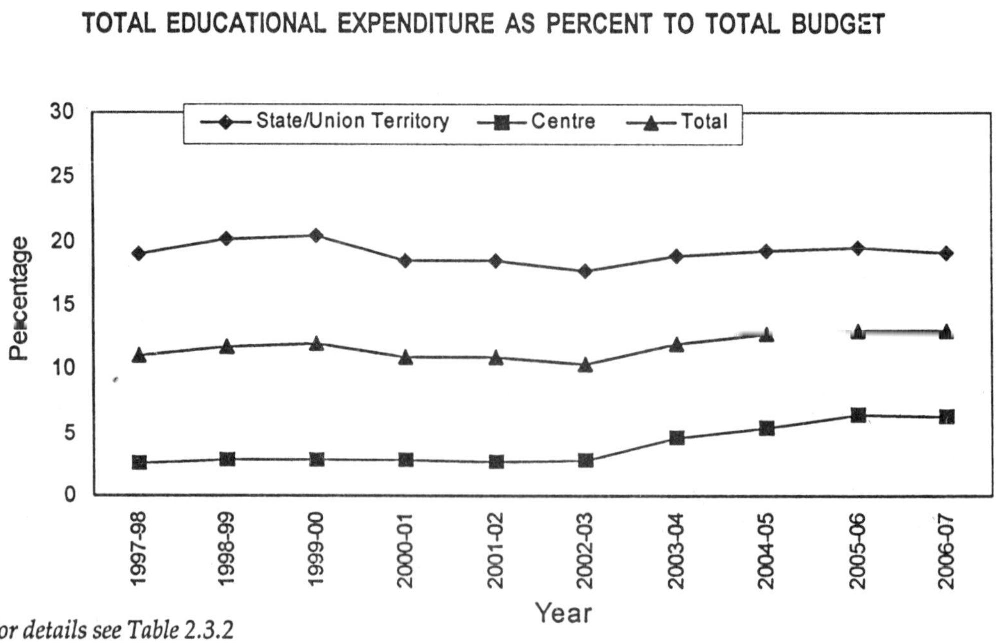

For details see Table 2.3.2

Table 2.3.3: Expenditure on Education to Total (Revenue Account) State Budget, 2006-07 (B.E.)

State/Union Territory	Total State Budget (Rs.Million)	Expenditure on Education & Training by Education & other Department (Rs. Million)	% Expenditure on Education to the total Budget	Percentage of Total Budgeted Educational Expenditure of Education Department on					
				Elementary Education	Secondary Education	University & Higher Education	Technical Education	Other *	Total
States									
Andhra Pradesh	453270.10	57298.44	12.64	49.24	31.00	14.63	3.58	1.56	100.00
	(373886.70)	(52353.81)	(14.00)	(48.22)	(31.92)	(14.82)	(3.41)	(1.63)	(100.00)
Arunachal Pradesh	18095.10	2110.36	11.66	59.27	25.70	11.71	—	3.30	100.00
	(17024.20)	(2344.77)	(13.77)	(63.46)	(23.00)	(10.51)	(—)	(3.03)	(100.00)
Assam	160962.40	41281.32	25.65	61.38	25.46	10.17	0.91	2.08	100.00
	(146165.20)	(37220.01)	(25.41)	(63.38)	(24.10)	(9.59)	(0.88)	(2.10)	(100.00)
Bihar	217795.60	52585.46	24.14	64.69	17.04	15.78	0.84	1.65	100.00
	(192685.30)	(47762.39)	(24.79)	(63.65)	(16.86)	(17.15)	(0.52)	(1.82)	(100.00)
Chattisgarh	95972.80	27730.34	28.89	64.31	19.91	10.57	2.24	2.97	100.00
	(86026.70)	(26209.13)	(30.47)	(64.81)	(19.68)	(12.45)	(2.23)	(0.83)	(100.00)
Delhi	75356.60	18976.42	25.18	25.76	62.74	2.45	4.01	5.03	100.00
	(71901.70)	(17399.07)	(24.20)	(26.53)	(61.99)	(2.43)	(4.09)	(5.26)	(100.00)
Goa	31762.70	3832.65	12.07	21.42	55.00	12.86	7.18	3.53	(100.00
	(22585.40)	(3724.88)	(16.49)	(21.59)	(54.10)	(14.44)	(7.06)	(2.81)	(100.00)
Gujarat	262755.40	48817.38	18.58	56.71	28.47	8.95	3.69	2.18	100.00
	(254631.30)	(45990.49)	(18.06)	(55.14)	(29.97)	(9.08)	(3.22)	(2.59)	(100.00)
Haryana	140666.50	25666.30	18.25	49.22	34.84	11.53	3.56	0.84	100.00
	(132491.30)	(23751.56)	(17.93)	(50.31)	(34.32)	(10.97)	(3.56)	(0.84)	(100.00)
Himachal Pradesh	67753.20	13515.27	19.95	57.91	35.47	4.97	0.91	0.73	100.00
	(64267.50)	(12588.32)	(19.59)	(53.68)	(38.29)	(6.27)	(0.96)	(0.80)	(100.00)
Jammu & Kashmir	96300.00	13120.42	13.62	49.60	37.51	10.03	1.99	0.87	100.00
	(97240.10)	(12184.20)	(12.53)	(46.36)	(39.34)	(11.23)	(2.17)	(0.90)	(100.00)
Jharkhand	108571.90	23938.28	22.05	68.45	16.07	9.89	5.36	0.23	100.00
	(97559.40)	(21786.20)	(22.33)	(64.77)	(14.27)	(14.86)	(5.75)	(0.35)	(100.00)
Karnataka	343405.50	60613.85	17.65	55.44	29.21	9.70	3.48	2.17	100.00
	(284980.40)	(53500.46)	(18.77)	(56.33)	(27.41)	(10.62)	(3.57)	(2.07)	(100.00)
Kerala	245548.30	55374.04	22.55	40.32	39.78	13.96	4.70	1.24	100.00
	(210902.10)	(39107.47)	(18.54)	(41.19)	(36.75)	(15.41)	(5.07)	(1.58)	(100.00)

(Contd.)

Contd.

Table 2.3.3: Expenditure on Education to Total (Revenue Account) State Budget, 2006-07 (B.E.)

State/Union Territory	*Total State Budget (Rs.Million)*	*Expenditure on Education & Training by Education & other Department (Rs. Million)*	*% Expenditure on Education to the total Budget*	*Percentage of Total Budgeted Educational Expenditure of Education Department on*					
				Elementary Education	*Secondary Education*	*University & Higher Education*	*Technical Education*	*Other **	*Total*
Madhya Pradesh	225099.70	41366.05	18.38	72.33	14.24	10.16	2.63	0.65	100.00
	(213699.10)	(39936.22)	(18.69)	(68.96)	(15.25)	(11.75)	(3.21)	(0.83)	(100.00)
Maharashtra	588400.40	128811.51	21.89	42.06	43.36	10.14	3.59	0.85	100.00
	(536175.00)	(126436.95)	(23.58)	(42.20)	(42.42)	(10.29)	(4.20)	(0.89)	(100.00)
Manipur	19947.20	3667.89	18.39	52.26	23.57	20.50	0.81	2.87	100.00
	(13511.00)	(4307.39)	(31.88)	(45.50)	(21.04)	(29.46)	(0.88)	(3.12)	(100.00)
Meghalaya	21177.60	3467.87	16.38	51.13	28.73	14.65	1.46	4.03	100.00
	(18757.10)	(3586.61)	(19.12)	(54.06)	(24.22)	(10.36)	(7.47)	(3.89)	(100.00)
Mizoram	15581.90	2478.36	15.91	54.76	23.26	10.78	3.38	7.83	100.00
	(17048.30)	(2373.26)	(13.92)	(55.49)	(22.72)	(10.28)	(3.95)	(7.56)	(100.00)
Nagaland	21895.90	3092.48	14.12	64.70	22.14	6.96	2.54	3.65	100.00
	(21181.10)	(2940.94)	(13.88)	(61.41)	(20.93)	(7.81)	(6.49)	(3.36)	(100.00)
Orissa	159398.80	26276.14	16.48	56.40	26.37	15.46	1.13	0.64	100.00
	(146384.40)	(25583.22)	(17.48)	(55.12)	(28.38)	(14.69)	(1.12)	(0.69)	(100.00)
Punjab	214462.50	28205.98	13.15	28.23	60.47	9.08	1.44	0.77	100.00
	(196037.60)	(27174.48)	(13.86)	(25.17)	(61.46)	(10.88)	(1.52)	(0.97)	(100.00)
Rajasthan	240343.40	51639.40	21.49	59.71	31.81	6.04	0.90	1.55	100.00
	(216112.00)	(48963.95)	(22.66)	(60.34)	(30.79)	(6.29)	(0.97)	(1.61)	(100.00)
Sikkim	19226.60	2011.56	10.46	47.57	45.44	2.76	1.23	3.00	100.00
	(18133.80)	(1967.61)	(10.85)	(47.32)	(44.85)	(2.96)	(1.80)	(3.07)	(100.00)
Tamil Nadu	398608.10	74071.00	18.58	43.69	38.52	10.48	3.01	4.30	100.00
	(332641.30)	(58268.00)	(17.52)	(40.86)	(36.96)	(11.26)	(3.42)	(7.50)	(100.00)
Tripura	27629.90	5780.08	20.92	52.72	36.25	5.27	0.80	4.95	100.00
	(25614.60)	(5350.81)	(20.89)	(52.86)	(36.05)	(5.35)	(0.80)	(4.94)	(100.00)
Uttaranchal	75962.40	15770.36	20.76	40.63	43.19	10.46	4.98	0.74	100.00
	(68204.50)	(13782.85)	(20.21)	(43.39)	(43.89)	(8.01)	(4.00)	(0.71)	(100.00)

Contd.

Contd.

Table 2.3.3: Expenditure on Education to Total (Revenue Account) State Budget, 2006-07 (B.E.)

State/Union Territory	*Total State Budget (Rs.Million)*	*Expenditure on Education & Training by Education & other Department (Rs. Million)*	*% Expenditure on Education to the total Budget*	*Percentage of Total Budgeted Educational Expenditure of Education Department on*					
				Elementary Education	*Secondary Education*	*University & Higher Education*	*Technical Education*	*Other **	*Total*
Uttar Pradesh	550212.20	109930.31	19.98	55.49	33.65	7.88	1.67	1.31	100.00
	(498723.50)	(97434.12)	(19.54)	(58.12)	(31.40)	(7.91)	(0.99)	(1.58)	(100.00)
West Bengal	350420.40	67127.32	19.16	37.97	46.82	11.64	1.73	1.84	100.00
	(332519.70)	(58632.95)	(17.63)	(38.13)	(45.83)	(11.77)	(1.77)	(2.50)	(100.00)
Union Territories									
Andaman & Nicobar Islands	13010.20	1288.80	9.91	48.55	34.92	6.76	5.41	4.36	100.00
	(14820.70)	(1229.83)	(8.30)	(48.34)	(34.45)	(6.93)	(5.80)	(4.48)	(100.00)
Chhandigarh	11477.80	2501.73	21.80	29.42	19.90	37.19	12.02	1.47	100.00
	(10927.90)	(2351.68)	(21.52)	(29.43)	(19.74)	(37.64)	(11.67)	(1.52)	(100.00)
Dadra & Nagar Haveli	8012.00	2370.05	2.96	65.55	23.38	0.04	5.51	5.51	100.00
	(5794.00)	(239.30)	(4.13)	(69.63)	(20.80)	(0.04)	(4.53)	(5.00)	(100.00)
Daman & Diu	2734.60	229.30	8.39	40.13	36.24	7.45	11.06	5.12	100.00
	(2583.90)	(219.97)	(8.51)	(41.01)	(36.57)	(6.46)	(10.51)	(5.45)	(100.00)
Lakshadweep	2494.70	285.56	11.45	2.98	89.34	4.34	—	3.34	100.00
	(2340.90)	(260.39)	(11.12)	(3.10)	(93.56)	(0.16)	(—)	(3.18)	(100.00)
Pondicherry	19594.85	2659.99	13.58	37.47	34.58	16.63	8.56	2.78	100.00
	(28144.94)	(2380.82)	(13.12)	(39.04)	(33.73)	(15.88)	(8.74)	(2.61)	(100.00)
Total (States & UTs)	5303906.78	1015759.31	19.15	50.57	34.44	10.55	2.69	1.75	100.00
	(4761702.64)	(91934.09)	(19.31)	(50.46)	(33.76)	(11.05)	(2.74)	(1.99)	(100.00)

Notes: BE- Budget Estimate. RE : Revised Estimate.
* Includes Adult Education, Physical Education, Language Development and other general Educational Programmes.
Figures in the parenthesis indicates for the year 2005-06 (RE).

Source: Ministry of Human Resource Development (Dept. of Secondary & Higher Education) : *Analysis of Budgeted Expenditure on Education 2004-05 to 2006-07.*

Table 2.3.4: Stage-wise Percentage Distribution of Budgeted Expenditure on Education by Education Department (Revenue Account)

Stage	*1991-92*	*1995-96*	*1998-99*	*2000-01*	*2001-02*	*2002-03*	*2004-05*	*2005-06*
Elementary Education	43.8	48.3	49.0	48.6	49.9	49.3	50.6	53.0
Secondary Education	30.5	32.8	32.6	30.1	31.0	31.3	31.1	28.8
University and Other Higher Education	13.2	12.3	11.9	14.6	12.4	12.6	11.9	11.1
Technical Education	4.8	4.1	4.1	3.9	4.1	4.0	4.2	3.9
Others*	7.7	2.5	2.4	2.9	2.6	2.8	1.8	3.3
Total	100.0	100.0	100.0	100.0	100.0	100.0	100.0	100.0

Notes: * Includes Adult Education, Language Development, Physical Education and Other General Educational Programmes.

Source: Ministry of Human Resource Development : *Analysis of Budgeted Expenditure on Education.*

Figure 2.3.X

DISTRIBUTION OF BUDGETED EXPENDITURE BY STAGE

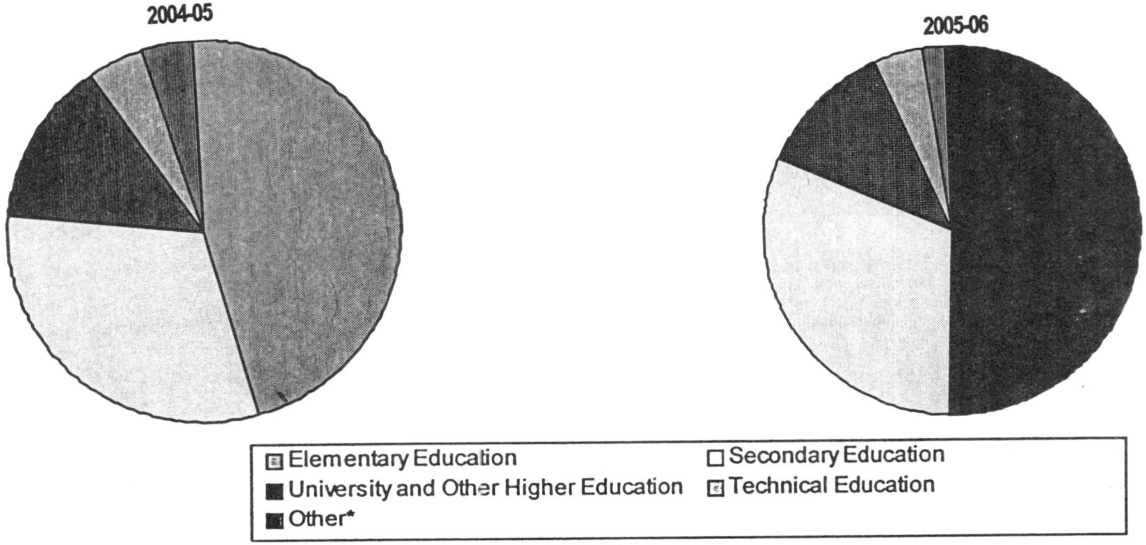

For details see Table 2.3.4

(IV) Education in the North Eastern Region of India

Table 2.4.1: Literacy Rate and Net Enrolment Rate Combined in Arunachal Pradesh (2003-2004)

District	*Literacy Rate*			*Net Enrolment*
	Male	*Female*	*Total*	*Rate Combined*
Changlang	74.8	52.9	64.4	84.8
Dibang Valley	66.0	60.7	63.2	76.9
East Kameng	51.9	40.8	46.5	78.6
East Siang	74.6	65.7	70.5	76.8
Kurung Kumey	31.7	19.9	26.1	56.0
Lohit	68.3	58.3	63.5	83.9
Lower Dibang Valley	72.9	61.8	67.9	71.9
Lower Subansiri	82.0	72.0	77.2	87.5
Papum Pare	76.4	67.7	71.9	86.5
Tawang	62.5	43.3	52.2	76.2
Tirap	43.4	27.9	36.3	69.6
Upper Siang	52.1	39.1	45.7	72.0
Upper Subansiri	67.7	54.1	61.3	78.0
West Kameng	86.4	78.5	82.9	96.9
West Siang	66.4	58.1	62.4	90.8
Total Rural	66.9	54.1	60.8	81.7
Urban	89.9	84.9	87.4	86.7

Source: IAMR Report No.: 12/2006.

Table 2.4.2: Literacy Rate and Net Enrolment Rate Combined in Assam (2003-2004)

District	*Literacy Rate*			*Net Enrolment*
	Male	*Female*	*Total*	*Rate Combined*
Bongaigaon	73.0	62.9	68.2	87.1
Barpeta	54.8	46.0	50.7	81.3
Cachar	76.9	67.0	72.1	91.5
Darrang	61.1	53.2	57.4	73.13
Dhemaji	68.6	60.1	64.6	86.7
Dhubri	50.2	43.5	47.1	69.9
Dibrugarh	68.7	66.3	67.5	78.8
Goalpara	63.5	59.3	61.6	88.8
Golaghat	71.3	61.1	66.3	80.10
Hailakandi	60.8	56.1	58.7	86.9
Jorhat	80.3	82.9	81.6	99.0
Kamrup	81.9	70.5	76.5	93.2
Karimganj	68.9	65.7	67.4	74.3
Kokrajhar	62.1	49.4	55.9	80.8
Lakhimpur	63.4	55.5	59.8	71.7
Marigaon	55.2	51.8	53.6	77.3
Nagaon	75.8	69.2	72.7	90.4
Nalbari	76.9	68.1	72.7	92.5
North Cachar Hills	56.1	51.2	53.7	92.8
Sibsagar	83.0	78.9	81.1	92.7
Sonitpur	69.3	61.9	65.8	87.6
Tinsukia	67.9	55.1	61.7	85.2
Total Rural	68.0	60.3	64.3	84.4
Urban	91.7	89.3	90.6	96.3

Source: IAMR Report No. : 13/2006.

Table 2.4.3: Literacy Rate and Net Enrolment Rate Combined in Manipur (2003-2004)

District	*Literacy Rate*			*Net Enrolment*
	Male	*Female*	*Total*	*Rate Combined*
Bishnupur	76.8	66.9	71.8	92.2
Chandel	60.9	54.9	57.8	86.8
Churachandpur	75.4	70.6	73.0	86.8
Imphal East	80.4	69.6	75.1	87.6
Imphal West	88.9	80.3	84.7	96.7
Senapati	75.3	66.4	71.0	89.9
Tamenglong	81.6	75.3	78.4	95.5
Thoubal	72.0	55.8	63.9	89.4
Ukhrul	70.6	65.6	68.1	94.9
Total Rural	76.8	67.3	72.1	90.0
Urban	84.7	76.5	80.5	90.3

Source: IAMR Report No. : 14/2006.

Table 2.4.4: Literacy Rate and Net Enrolment Rate Combined in Meghalaya (2003-2004)

District	*Literacy Rate*			*Net Enrolment Rate Combined*
	Male	*Female*	*Total*	
East Garo Hills	79.9	75.0	77.5	94.1
East Khasi Hills	70.8	73.4	72.1	91.8
Jaintia Hills	38.2	45.2	41.7	72.3
Ri Bhoi	60.1	59.8	59.9	80.9
South Garo Hills	77.6	71.9	75.0	96.6
West Garo Hills	61.6	55.1	58.4	79.9
West Khasi Hills	56.6	55.3	56.0	66.4
Total Rural	62.5	61.8	62.2	82.9
Total Urban	88.6	85.3	86.9	96.1

Source: IAMR Report No. : 15/2006.

Table 2.4.5: Literacy Rate and Net Enrolment Rate Combined in Mizorm (2003-2004)

District	*Literacy Rate*			*Net Enrolment Rate Combined*
	Male	*Female*	*Total*	
Aizawl	95.5	93.6	94.7	90.0
Lunglei	68.9	59.3	64.0	74.0
Chhimtuipui	79.5	70.4	75.2	79.3
Total rural	86.9	82.4	84.7	81.0
Urban	99.4	99.2	99.3	88.3

Source: IAMR Report No. : 16/2006.

Table 2.4.6: Literacy Rate and Net Enrolment Rate Combined in Nagaland (2003-2004)

District	*Literacy Rate*			*Net Enrolment Rate Combined*
	Male	*Female*	*Total*	
Dimapur	84.6	85.5	85.1	97.6
Kohima	61.5	48.0	55.1	91.5
Mokokchung	85.1	85.3	85.2	94.7
Mon	69.1	66.3	67.8	78.2
Peren	80.8	78.2	79.4	89.3
Phek	73.8	65.4	69.9	86.3
Tuensang	71.2	66.1	68.9	94.0
Wokha	83.0	78.6	80.8	97.5
Zunheboto	73.9	70.7	72.4	93.3
Total Rural	76.4	73.3	74.9	91.9
Urban	86.2	84.4	85.3	98.9

Source: IAMR Report No. : 17/2006.

Table 2.4.7: Literacy Rate and Net Enrolment Rate Combined in Tripura (2003-2004)

District	*Literacy Rate*			*Net Enrolment Rate Combined*
	Male	*Female*	*Total*	
Dhalai	65.7	50.5	58.2	80.8
North Tripura	77.4	65.8	71.7	81.2
South Tripura	75.2	64.6	70.1	90.0
West Tripura	76.7	68.7	72.9	91.9
Total Rural	75.1	65.3	70.4	89.2
Urban	86.6	84.8	85.7	94.7

Source: IAMR Report No. : 18/2006.

Table 2.4.8: Percentage Distribution of Literate Population According to Education Standard, Arunachal Pradesh

Standard of education attained (in percent)	Gender	District															Total	
		Chang-lang	Dibang Valley	East Kameng	East Siang	Kurung Kumey	Lohit	Lower Dibang Valley	Lower Subansiri	Papum Pare	Tawang	Tirap	Upper Siang	Upper Subansiri	West Kameng	West Siang	Rural	Urban
Below Primary	Male	4.7	Neg.	1.1	6.6	4.5	4.2	8.5	3.8	1.5	8.8	8.1	5.8	8.4	5.0	3.4	4.8	5.4
	Female	7.2	Neg.	1.4	6.2	4.7	5.0	9.2	4.9	1.2	34.8	4.5	4.1	13.8	7.9	1.7	6.7	7.0
	Total	5.7	Neg.	1.2	6.4	4.6	4.5	8.8	4.3	1.3	22.6	6.9	5.1	10.7	6.2	2.6	5.7	6.2
Primary School	Male	44.7	41.9	65.3	34.5	49.5	47.8	36.9	37.2	46.1	39.6	55.5	39.5	42.6	40.0	37.4	43.3	25.0
	Female	46.9	47.7	77.1	41.2	70.3	53.3	39.8	38.9	52.8	33.1	66.4	59.0	46.9	44.2	42.9	48.2	29.2
	Total	45.6	44.9	70.4	37.4	57.1	50.2	38.1	37.9	49.3	36.2	59.2	47.6	44.5	41.8	39.8	45.5	27.0
Middle School	Male	29.1	27.4	23.7	33.3	32.4	23.8	15.6	23.9	21.9	19.5	21.3	31.4	23.2	26.7	28.3	26.2	20.3
	Female	25.8	29.2	17.4	35.3	21.9	23.4	18.4	30.6	26.0	16.9	25.5	27.0	24.1	24.2	31.8	26.2	21.8
	Total	27.8	28.3	21.0	34.2	28.6	23.6	16.7	26.9	23.9	18.1	22.7	29.6	23.6	25.6	29.9	26.2	21.0
High School	Male	10.9	8.1	3.2	11.1	5.4	13.8	14.9	14.8	13.8	14.5	9.5	10.5	10.0	12.2	15.2	12.0	16.3
	Female	12.3	10.8	1.4	9.2	3.1	13.1	10.2	14.5	12.0	7.9	Neg.	9.0	9.7	14.7	13.9	11.2	16.9
	Total	11.5	9.4	2.4	10.3	4.6	13.5	13.0	14.6	12.9	11.0	6.2	9.9	9.9	13.3	14.6	11.6	16.6
Higher Second-ary	Male	6.9	14.5	4.2	8.2	5.4	6.0	8.5	12.5	9.7	6.9	3.8	7.0	10.5	11.1	10.2	8.1	14.6
	Female	6.0	10.8	1.4	5.3	Neg.	2.8	12.2	8.3	4.4	4.5	3.6	0.8	2.1	4.2	6.5	4.9	13.9
	Total	6.5	12.6	3.0	6.9	3.4	4.6	10.0	10.6	7.1	5.6	3.7	4.4	6.9	8.2	8.6	6.8	14.3
Degree/ Diploma & above	Male	3.7	8.1	2.6	6.3	2.7	4.5	15.6	7.9	7.1	10.7	1.9	5.8	5.3	5.0	5.4	5.5	18.4
	Female	1.9	1.5	1.4	2.7	0.0	2.5	10.2	2.8	3.6	2.8	0.0	0.0	3.4	4.9	3.1	2.7	11.2
	Total	3.0	4.7	2.1	4.8	1.7	3.6	13.4	5.6	5.4	6.5	1.2	3.4	4.5	5.0	4.4	4.3	14.9

Source: IAMR Report No. : 12/2006.

Table 2.4.9: Percentage Distribution of Literate Population According to Education Standard, Assam

Standard of education attained (in percent)	Gender	District																							Total	
		Bongai-gaon	Bar-peta	Cac-har	Dar-rang	Dhe-maji	Dhubri	Dibru-garh	Gol-para	Gola ghat	Haila Kandi	Jorhat	Kam-rup	Karim ganj	Kokr-ajhar	Lakhim pur	Mari-gaon	Nagaon	Nal bari	North Chchar	Sib-sagar Hills	Sonit-pur	Tin-sukia	Rural	Urban
Below Primary	Male	5.4	6.0	1.8	5.7	9.1	9.6	1.4	2.9	5.5	8.8	2.4	1.9	8.0	6.1	4.9	2.9	5.1	2.4	12.7	1.5	4.8	4.1	4.6	0.8
	Female	5.3	5.6	2.9	5.4	10.7	9.1	1.5	3.4	4.1	8.9	1.2	1.8	5.5	7.0	5.1	1.5	5.8	2.6	10.6	1.2	5.3	3.8	4.5	0.9
	Total	5.4	5.9	2.3	5.6	9.8	9.4	1.4	3.1	4.9	8.9	1.8	1.9	6.9	6.5	5.0	2.2	5.4	2.5	11.8	1.4	5.0	4.0	4.6	0.8
Primary School	Male	38.0	42.2	42.9	28.5	30.8	48.6	32.4	43.6	33.3	45.0	26.8	29.5	35.3	42.5	29.1	41.6	39.0	29.2	34.5	21.6	35.2	36.4	35.9	13.6
	Female	42.7	50.1	44.1	39.1	37.5	56.0	37.6	47.4	42.8	47.0	30.8	35.6	41.3	48.1	32.9	49.7	45.2	35.8	48.9	21.2	36.8	44.6	41.4	17.0
	Total	40.1	45.5	43.4	33.1	33.8	51.8	34.9	45.3	37.6	45.9	28.8	32.2	38.0	44.9	30.7	45.3	41.8	32.2	41.2	21.4	35.9	39.9	38.4	15.1
Middle School	Male	35.7	28.5	38.8	32.8	28.9	25.9	41.7	35.7	41.5	29.4	42.8	34.7	30.9	29.6	30.9	37.1	34.4	36.2	38.2	33.6	31.3	41.6	34.4	25.0
	Female	38.2	31.5	40.9	38.4	30.7	22.8	42.6	39.1	35.9	32.0	42.4	40.5	34.9	28.5	30.6	35.8	32.5	41.8	31.9	42.6	36.5	38.3	36.2	31.3
	Total	36.8	29.8	39.8	35.2	29.7	24.5	42.1	37.2	39.0	30.6	42.6	37.3	32.7	29.2	30.7	36.5	33.6	38.7	35.3	37.7	33.6	40.2	35.2	27.8
High School	Male	12.0	12.7	11.0	16.2	15.5	8.8	13.5	8.3	12.4	10.8	13.6	15.7	18.2	12.9	17.7	7.9	11.1	15.0	8.2	24.6	16.2	10.5	13.4	18.9
	Female	10.8	8.1	8.5	12.2	12.6	6.7	10.8	5.3	11.4	10.1	13.6	12.2	12.3	12.0	17.0	6.3	10.1	12.8	7.4	19.5	12.0	8.7	11.0	21.0
	Total	11.5	10.8	9.9	14.5	14.2	7.9	12.2	7.0	11.9	10.5	13.6	14.2	15.5	12.5	17.4	7.2	10.7	14.0	7.8	22.2	14.3	9.7	12.3	19.8
Higher Secondary	Male	6.1	6.7	4.5	10.5	10.1	4.5	6.9	7.5	5.5	4.6	7.2	11.7	3.6	5.4	12.2	6.2	7.4	10.6	5.5	11.9	8.1	5.6	7.7	17.8
	Female	2.2	2.7	2.7	2.8	6.3	4.4	4.6	3.6	4.6	1.7	7.2	6.8	3.8	3.3	12.1	4.8	5.4	4.7	1.1	10.9	6.7	3.9	5.1	14.9
	Total	4.4	5.0	3.7	7.2	8.4	4.4	5.8	5.7	5.1	3.3	7.2	9.6	3.7	4.5	12.1	5.6	6.5	7.9	3.4	11.4	7.5	4.9	6.5	16.5
Degree/ Diploma & above	Male	2.7	3.9	1.0	6.2	5.6	2.7	4.2	2.1	1.9	1.3	7.2	6.4	4.0	3.5	5.4	4.3	2.9	6.7	0.9	6.8	4.4	1.7	3.9	23.9
	Female	0.8	2.0	0.9	2.1	2.2	0.9	2.9	1.2	1.1	0.2	4.8	3.1	2.1	1.1	2.4	1.9	1.0	2.4	0.0	4.7	2.7	0.7	1.9	15.0
	Total	1.8	3.1	1.0	4.5	4.1	1.9	3.6	1.7	1.6	0.9	6.0	4.9	3.1	2.4	4.1	3.2	2.0	4.7	0.5	5.8	3.6	1.3	3.0	19.9

Source: IAMR Report No. :13/2006.

Table 2.4.10: Percentage Distribution of Literate Population According to Education Standard, Manipur

Standard of education attained (in percent)	Gender	District									Total	
		Bishnupur	Chandel	Churachandeur	Imphal East	Imphal West	Senapati	Tamenglong	Thoubal	Ukhrul	Rural	Urban
Below Primary	Male	23.2	39.1	24.6	19.6	11.1	24.7	18.4	28.0	29.4	23.2	2.7
	Female	33.1	45.1	29.4	30.4	19.7	33.6	24.7	44.2	34.4	32.7	4.5
	Total	28.2	42.2	27.0	24.9	15.3	29.0	21.6	36.1	31.9	27.9	3.6
Primary School	Male	16.3	16.2	37.8	18.9	20.4	25.7	25.3	24.8	15.5	22.4	14.2
	Female	15.2	18.3	36.7	17.6	19.0	25.5	26.8	21.4	19.4	21.7	15.3
	Total	15.7	17.3	37.3	18.2	19.7	25.6	26.1	23.1	17.5	22.0	14.7
Middle School	Male	17.2	19.8	20.9	27.0	27.0	27.9	25.2	23.7	25.8	24.4	19.8
	Female	17.3	18.8	18.5	24.4	25.8	22.6	24.7	18.6	23.8	21.9	19.2
	Total	17.2	19.3	19.7	25.7	26.4	25.3	24.9	21.1	24.8	23.1	19.5
High School	Male	12.3	12.2	9.8	15.7	11.6	10.4	14.3	10.1	12.7	12.4	15.1
	Female	13.5	7.5	9.3	12.8	12.2	8.9	11.5	9.9	10.7	11.0	13.2
	Total	12.9	9.8	9.5	14.3	11.9	9.7	12.9	10.0	11.7	11.7	14.1
Higher Secondary	Male	14.1	6.3	5.3	9.6	13.1	5.9	5.9	7.9	8.0	8.6	13.3
	Female	13.4	5.1	4.6	8.5	12.1	5.8	7.6	3.8	7.9	7.6	12.7
	Total	13.8	5.7	5.0	9.0	12.6	5.9	6.7	5.9	8.0	8.1	13.0
Degree/ Diploma & above	Male	16.9	6.4	1.7	9.2	16.7	5.4	10.9	5.6	8.6	9.0	22.3
	Female	7.6	5.1	1.4	6.3	11.2	3.6	4.8	2.0	3.8	5.2	16.1
	Total	12.2	5.8	1.6	7.8	14.0	4.5	7.8	3.8	6.2	7.1	19.2

Source: IAMR Report No.: 14/2006.

Table 2.4.11: Percentage Distribution of Literate Population According to Education Standard, Meghalaya

Standard of education attained (in per cent)		*District*							*Total*	
	Gender	*East Garo Hills*	*East Khasi Hills*	*Jaintia Hills*	*Ri Bhoi*	*South Garo Hills*	*West Garo Hills*	*West Khasi Hills*	*Rural*	*Urban*
Below Primary	Male	2.8	6.8	10.0	9.0	5.4	4.0	5.5	6.0	2.4
	Female	3.7	4.7	6.3	11.6	5.0a	3.5	6.2	5.4	3.1
	Total	3.2	5.7	8.1	10.3	5.2	3.8	5.8	5.7	2.8
Primary School	Male	48.8	47.2	56.4	51.4	53.5	43.8	41.1	47.4	17.0
	Female	54.1	42.2	54.5	50.7	50.5	51.8	40.0	47.8	17.7
	Total	51.4	44.6	55.4	51.1	52.2	47.4	40.6	47.6	17.4
Middle School	Male	34.9	23.3	17.0	27.1	28.8	26.7	32.0	26.1	28.0
	Female	29.7	25.2	21.2	27.9	28.7	28.8	36.9	27.4	28.0
	Total	32.4	24.3	19.3	27.5	28.8	27.6	34.4	26.7	28.0
High School	Male	9.6	10.3	9.8	5.3	9.2	19.0	11.5	12.2	15.0
	Female	9.0	15.2	10.8	4.3	12.9	13.0	8.2	11.9	13.0
	Total	9.3	12.8	10.3	4.8	10.8	16.3	9.9	12.0	14.0
Higher Secondary	Male	2.8	7.6	4.7	5.1	2.7	4.1	4.1	5.2	14.3
	Female	3.0	8.0	6.1	3.5	3.0	2.2	5.1	5.1	11.5
	Total	2.9	7.8	5.4	4.3	2.8	3.3	4.6	5.1	12.8
Degree/ Diploma & above	Male	1.1	4.8	2.1	2.0	0.4	2.3	5.8	3.1	14.3
	Female	0.5	4.8	1.0	2.1	0.0	0.8	2.5	2.5	15.1
	Total	0.8	4.8	1.5	2.0	0.2	1.6	2.8	2.8	14.8

Source: IAMR Report No.: 15/2006.

Table 2.4.12: Percentage Distribution of Literate Population According to Education Standard, Mizoram

Standard of education attained		*District*			*Total*	
		Aizawl	*Lunglei*	*Chhim tuipui*	*Rural*	*Urban*
Below primary	Male	3.9	1.5	12.9	5.7	1.9
	Female	3.7	3.1	14.5	6.1	3.3
	Total	3.8	2.3	13.7	5.8	2.6
Primary school	Male	3.6	32.9	29.0	33.6	20.8
	Female	36.6	29.3	26.4	33.0	23.5
	Total	36.3	31.1	27.8	33.3	22.3
Middle school	Male	36.7	25.4	21.2	30.8	33.9
	Female	36.7	24.1	19.3	30.5	32.7
	Total	36.7	24.7	20.3	30.6	33.4
High school	Male	10.1	6.1	11.7	9.9	19.3
	Female	11.4	2.4	9.0	9.3	20.8
	Total	10.7	4.2	10.4	9.6	20.1
Higher secondary	Male	3.7	3.1	2.8	3.4	10.4
	Female	3.5	0.8	1.6	2.6	10.2
	Total	3.6	2.0	2.2	3.0	10.4
Degree/ diploma & above	Male	5.2	1.4	1.7	3.5	13.1
	Female	1.8	Neg.	Neg.	1.0	8.8
	Total	3.6	0.7	0.9	2.4	10.5

Source: IAMR Report No.:16/2006.

Table 2.4.13: Percentage Distribution of Literate Population According to Education Standard, Nagaland

Standard of education attained (in percent)	*Gender*	*District*									*Total*	
		Dimapur	*Kohima*	*Mokokchung*	*Mon*	*Peren*	*Phek*	*Tuensang*	*Wokha*	*Zunheboto*	*Rural*	*Urban*
Below Primary	Male	3.1	13.2	4.2	5.3	3.2	3.5	5.4	5.2	2.5	4.6	1.6
	Female	2.2	17.2	2.5	4.6	3.0	7.6	7.5	6.4	5.9	5.2	2.0
	Total	2.6	14.9	3.4	5.0	3.1	5.3	6.4	5.8	4.2	4.9	1.8
Primary School	Male	29.2	36.8	25.1	33.5	27.0	37.5	33.5	30.5	43.4	32.0	15.3
	Female	31.0	46.5	24.7	44.8	36.1	37.2	32.9	35.5	41.2	34.0	13.5
	Total	30.1	40.9	24.9	38.7	31.7	37.4	33.3	32.9	42.3	32.9	14.4
Middle School	Male	36.3	37.5	35.3	47.0	46.0	32.7	35.0	33.1	37.4	36.8	31.6
	Female	39.0	33.3	41.4	40.2	39.1	35.2	39.3	41.1	40.6	39.2	34.3
	Total	37.7	35.7	38.1	43.8	42.5	33.8	37.0	36.9	39.0	38.0	32.9
High School	Male	11.6	6.6	16.0	7.5	13.5	9.9	16.6	16.2	6.6	12.8	19.8
	Female	12.0	2.0	15.8	5.9	9.8	6.0	12.5	9.2	3.7	10.4	22.0
	Total	11.8	4.7	15.9	6.7	11.6	8.2	14.8	12.9	5.2	11.7	20.9
Higher Secondary	Male	8.8	3.7	9.1	3.9	1.6	5.8	6.5	6.5	5.6	6.7	14.4
	Female	9.1	1.0	7.0	2.9	9.8	9.2	5.2	3.5	4.3	6.5	12.6
	Total	9.0	2.6	8.1	3.5	5.8	7.3	5.9	5.1	4.9	6.6	13.5
Degree/ Diploma & above	Male	10.9	2.2	10.2	2.8	8.7	10.6	2.9	8.4	4.5	7.1	17.3
	Female	6.7	Neg.	8.6	1.7	2.3	4.8	2.5	4.3	4.3	4.7	15.5
	Total	8.8	1.3	9.5	2.3	5.4	8.0	2.7	6.4	4.4	6.0	16.4

Source: IAMR Report No. : 17/2006.

Table 2.4.14: Percentage Distribution of Literate Population According to Education Standard, Tripura

Standard of education attained	*Gender*	*District*				*Total*	
		Dhalai	*North Tripura*	*South Tripura*	*West Tripura*	*Rural*	*Urban*
Below Primary	Male	7.7	5.9	5.7	7.8	7.3	1.8
	Female	9.5	8.0	8.1	8.9	8.8	3.1
	Total	8.5	6.9	6.8	8.3	7.9	2.4
Primary School	Male	44.4	41.9	40.4	35.5	37.9	15.3
	Female	41.1	44.6	45.7	40.9	42.1	20.9
	Total	43.0	43.1	42.8	38.0	39.8	18.1
Middle School	Male	28.5	32.5	32.5	31.7	31.5	27.9
	Female	32.1	32.0	29.1	32.2	31.6	28.3
	Total	30.0	32.3	31.0	31.9	31.6	28.1
High School	Male	11.3	10.7	11.2	15.2	13.7	16.9
	Female	10.7	9.5	9.0	12.1	11.2	18.8
	Total	11.0	10.2	10.2	13.8	12.5	17.9
Higher Secondary	Male	3.1	3.0	5.0	5.5	4.9	14.2
	Female	3.7	1.8	4.2	3.5	3.5	11.9
	Total	3.4	2.5	4.6	4.6	4.3	13.0
Degree/ Diploma & above	Male	5.0	5.9	5.2	4.3	4.7	23.9
	Female	3.0	4.0	3.9	2.3	2.8	17.1
	Total	4.2	5.0	4.6	3.4	3.8	20.4

Source: IAMR Report No. : 18/2006.

Table 2.4.15: Percentage Distribution Group of Income on Education with Respect to Total Income by States and Rural/Urban in North Eastern Region

Income Group	*Arunachal Pradesh*		*Assam*		*Manipur*		*Meghalaya*		*Mizoram*		*Nagaland*		*Tripura*	
	Rural	*Urban*	*Rural*	*Urban*	*Rural*	*Urban*	*Rural*	*Urban*	*Rural*	*Urban*	*Rural*	*Urban*	*Rural*	*Urban*
< 30,000	10.6	3.8	28.0	12.2	24.4	22.6	51.4	55.0	6.7	31.4	50.1	40.2	39.6	53.9
30,000 – 60,000	8.3	2.7	5.8	5.1	13.3	9.7	13.2	12.3	6.0	7.8	28.2	19.2	8.3	5.5
60,000 – 90,000	9.7	3.2	8.5	5.7	10.7	8.8	9.2	12.5	5.9	6.8	16.9	13.6	3.5	6.3
> 90,000	6.9	2.1	5.1	3.5	15.6	8.3	6.2	8.9	5.1	7.7	13.9	10.2	6.3	6.4
Total	8.6	2.3	12.8	4.5	16.1	9.1	17.7	11.3	5.4	7.8	24.1	12.9	21.8	7.6

Sources: IAMR Report Nos. : 12, 13, 14, 15, 16, 17 and 18/2006.

(v) Health Status

Table 2.5.1: Doctor-Population Ratio by Category

Year	*Allopathy**	*Ayurveda***	*Unani***	*Siddha***	*Homeopathy*	*All*
1981	2,543	2,942	24,404	NA	6,241	1,041
1986	2,374	2,872	26,484	65,668	5,801	1,005
1987	2,342	2,859	26,700	66,790	5,650	994
1988	2,232	2,588	26,723	68,164	5,536	937
1989	2,200	2,568	23,244	69,207	5,447	922
1990	2,169	2,451	23,434	70,197	5,571	905
1991	2,148	2,495	23,750	72,863	5,549	907
1992	2,101	2,436	21,870	71,993	5,529	887
1993	2,064	2,488	22,119	73,403	5,409	885
1994	2,015	2,532	22,705	75,494	5,374	887
1995	1,993	2,639	22,658	73,640	5,444	894
1996	1,964	2,666	22,461	74,570	5,454	888
1997	1,928	2,710	22,959	75,822	5,494	888
1998	1,916	2,740	23,195	77,075	5,343	885
2001	NA	2,383	23,824	60,070	5,207	NA
2002	NA	2,387	23,702	59,051	5,134	NA
2005	1,658	NA	NA	NA	NA	NA
2006	1,629	2,452	23,888	1,74,296	5,105	NA
2007	1,620	NA	NA	NA	NA	NA

Notes: Figures are provisional.

* Institutionally qualified (MBBS) only.

** Institutionally as well as Non Institutionally qualified registered practitioners.

NA Not Available.

Sources : (i) Medical Council of India.

(ii) Ministry of Health and Family Welfare:

(a) Rural Health Division.

(b) Directorate General of Health Services : *Health Information of India.*

Table 2.5.2: Government Allopathic, Doctors Dentists and Doctor-Population Ratio by State/Union Territory*

State/Union Territory	*Population served per Dental Surgeon*	*Doctors Engaged*	*Dental Surgeons Engaged*	*Population served per Govt. Doctor*	*Reference Period*
States					
Andhra Pradesh	6,16,122	4,487	131	17,988	1.1.2007
Arunachal Pradesh	29,600	405	40	2,923	1.1.2008
Assam	13,73,900	2,103	20	13,066	1.1.2004
Bihar	NA	NA	NA	NA	NA
Chattisgarh	NA	NA	NA	NA	NA
Delhi	2,01,028	3,629	71	3,933	1.1.2003
Goa	33,909	562	44	2,655	1.1.2007
Gujarat	12,19,279	2,712	43	19,332	1.1.2004
Haryana	78,360	1,802	303	13,176	1.1.2008
Himachal Pradesh	22,015	NA	272	NA	1.1.2000
Jammu and Kashmir	NA	2,869	NA	NA	1.1.2007
Jharkhand	23,65,667	1,234	12	23,005	1.1.2005
Karnataka	2,45,668	4,175	229	13,475	1.1.2007
Kerala (a)	4,41,250	3,315	76	10,116	1.1.2008
Madhya Pradesh	NA	3,662	NA	18,451	1.1.2008
Maharashtra	23,26,279	5,061	43	19,765	1.1.2004
Manipur	66,743	653	35	3,577	1.1.2008
Meghalaya	1,31,579	580	19	4,310	1.1.2008
Mizoram	36,846	247	26	3,879	1.1.2008
Nagaland	1,37,867	293	15	7,058	1.1.2005
Orissa	24,54,750	5,079	16	7,733	1.1.2008
Punjab	1,11,843	3,545	230	7,256	1.4.2005
Rajasthan	5,98,189	5,979	106	10,605	1.1.2008
Sikkim	22,423	220	26	2,650	1.1.2008
Tamil Nadu (a)	3,95,355	7,107	166	9,234	1.1.2008
Tripura	95,806	719	36	4,797	1.1.2008
Uttar Pradesh	NA	6,766	NA	23,986	1.1.2000
Uttaranchal	1,70,722	1,051	54	8,772	1.1.2007
West Bengal	1,93,975	6,113	444	14,089	1.1.2008
Union Territories					
Andaman and Nicobar Islands	72,733	113	6	3,841	1.1.2008
Chandigarh	16,382	1,414	55	637	1.1.2002
Dadra and Nagar Haveli	2,81,000	16	1	17,562	1.1.2008
Daman and Diu	1,08,000	27	2	8,000	1.1.2007
Lakshadweep	69,000	22	1	3,136	1.1.2005
Pondicherry	NA	582	65	1969	1.1.2008
All India Total		76,542	2,993		

Notes: Provisional.

Govt. Agency includes Central/State Govt. Hospitals, Public Sector undertaking Hospitals etc. but generally the figures from states include only state agencies and figures fromUnion Territories cover only central agencies excepting Delhi, Pondichery and Manipur where both state and central agencies are included.

(*a*) Tamil Nadu information relates to only the allopathic doctors in PHCs-sanctioned strength.

(*b*) Uttar Pradesh figure for 1.1.2000 includes Uttaranchal.

NA – Not available.

Source: Central Bureau of Health Intelligence, Directorate General of Health Services : National Health Profile, 2007.

Table 2.5.3: State-wise Number of Allopathic Doctors with Recognised Medical Qualifications (Under IMC Act)

State Medical Councils	Years							
	2000	2001	2002	2003	2004	2005	2006	2007
1. Andhra Pradesh	43102	44575	46398	48035	48676	48649	@	@
2. Assam	14253	14586	15060	15526	15849	16401	16800	17121*
3. Bhopal	18181	19021	27440	28247	29003	29649	30430	31234*
4. Bihar	32226	33070	33720	34583	35111	35510	35979	36630*
5. Chattisgarh#	–	–	1	101	285	470	654	899*
6. Goa	1916	2030	2128	2236	2360	2469	2550*	@
7. Gujarat	32177	33653	35174	36012	37194	38642	40230	41458*
8. Haryana	1065	1146	1234	1285	1332	1380	1406*	@
9. Himachal Pradesh	—	—	—	—	—	123	256	283*
10. Jammu and Kashmir	6344	6875	7317	7900	8284	8557	9222	9669*
11. Jharkhand#	—	—	—	91	183	553	756	851*
12. Karnataka	57464	61163	64012	65789	67864	68987	71909	74525*
13. Traveen Core-Cochin	29087	30173	31353	@	33418	34561	35477	@
14. Maharashtra	77278	80764	84536	88378	92327	96560	100428	@
15. Orissa	14009	14315	14640	14707	14973	15219	15573	15728*
16. Punjab	31859	32558	33206	33417	34104	34967	36100	@
17. Rajasthan	19744	20438	21198	21885	22567	23459	24777	24955*
18. Tamil Nadu	63434	65771	68209	70357	72077	73211	75415	77780*
19. Uttar Pradesh	42452	43492	45295	46309	46604	47871	49527	50808*
20. West Bengal	49261	49941	50794	51961	53068	53521	54513	55200*
21. MCI Delhi	21694	23055	24435	25737	26468	27347	28525	30954
22. Delhi##	4	468	925	1514	2197	2750	3470	4042*
Total	555550	577094	607075	625423	643964	660856	682646	696747

Notes : Data as on 31st December of the concerned year.

\# Chhattisgarh Medical Council started Registration work in year 2002.

\# Jharkhand Medical Council started Registration work in year 2003.

\## Delhi Medical Council established in year 2000.

@ Information not received for the concerned year.

* Incomplet Information received.

— Information not received.

Source : Medical Council of India.

Table 2.5.4: State-wise Number of Registered Dental Surgeons*

State	Dental Surgeons
1. Andhra Pradesh	3726
2. Assam	843
3. Bihar	2396
4. Chattisgarh	85
5. Delhi	3848
6. Goa	580
7. Gujarat	2558
8. Haryana	1723
9. Himachal Pradesh	406
10. Jammu and Kashmir	1090
11. Karnataka	19757
12. Kerala	5735
13. Madhya Pradesh	1643
14. Maharashtra	6857
15. Orissa	463
16. Punjab	3953
17. Rajasthan	364
18. Tamil Nadu	9876
19. Uttar Pradesh	4637
20. West Bengal	1957
Total	72497

Notes : * Data as on 31st Decembar, 2006.

Dentists Registration Tribunals/State Dental Council are yet to be formed in the following States/UTs: 1.Andaman & Nicobar, 2. Manipur, 3. Nagaland, 4. Dadra and Nagar Haveli, 5. Mizoram, 6. Arunachal Pradesh, 7. Lakshadweep, 8. Tripura, 9. Meghalaya, 10. Jharkhand.

Source : Dental council of India

Table 2.5.5: State–wise Number & Registered AYUSH Doctors

State	*Ayurveda*	*Unani*	*Siddha*	*Naturapathy*	*Homoeopathy*	*Total*
1. Andhra Pradesh*	15231	5022	0	374	9422	30049
2. Arunachal Pradesh	0	0	0	0	94	94
3. Assam	442	0	0	0	669	1111
4. Bihar	132981	4202	0	0	27864	165047
5. Chattisgarh	794	9	0	0	221	1024
6. Delhi	3088	1625	0	0	3149	7862
7. Goa	290	0	0	0	274	564
8. Gujarat	20985	256	0	0	8503	29744
9. Haryana	18726	2212	0	0	5570	26508
10. Himachal Pradesh	7236	456	0	0	1111	8803
11. Jammu & Kashmir	1952	1956	0	0	0	3908
12. Karnataka	20352	1121	4	234	5003	26714
13. Kerala	15068	64	1326	0	9273	25731
14. Madhya Pradesh*	47602	609	0	2	9380	57593
15. Maharashtra	63030	4079	0	0	38407	105516
16. Meghalaya	0	0	0	0	240	240
17. Nagaland*	0	0	0	0	1997	1997
18. Orissa*	4448	17	0	0	3106	7571
19. Punjab	18424	4033	0	0	3742	26199
20. Rajsthan*	23861	1619	0	0	4778	30258
21. Tripura	0	0	0	0	145	145
22. Tamil Nadu	3612	1014	5051	278	17268	27223
23. Uttar Pradesh	51240	13289	0	0	27790	92319
24. Uttarachal	1065	41	0	0	0	1106
25. West Bengal	3234	4934	0	0	39547	47715
26. Chandigarh*	0	0	0	0	297	297
Total	453661	46558	6381	888	217850	725338

Note : *Data as on 1.1.2007 (Provisional).

Source : Department of AYUSH, National Health Profile, 2007.

Table 2.5.6: Government Health Facility for Rural Population

State/Union Territory	*Health Facility (No.)*			*Average Rural Population (2001) covered by one*		
	Sub Centre	*PHC*	*CHC*	*Sub Centre*	*PHC*	*CHC (In Lakh)*
States						
Andhra Pradesh	12,522	1,570	167	4,424	35,287	3.32
Arunachal Pradesh	379	85	31	2,296	10,236	0.28
Assam	5,109	610	100	4,544	38,059	2.32
Bihar	8,909	1,648	70	8,342	45,287	10.62
Chhatisgarh	4,692	518	118	3,548	32,139	1.41
Delhi	41	8	0	23,042	118,091	–
Goa	172	19	5	3,937	35,636	1.35
Gujarat	7,274	1,073	273	4,364	29,609	1.16
Haryana	2,433	411	86	6,177	36,836	1.83
Himachal Pradesh	2,071	443	71	2,647	12,488	0.83
Jammu and Kashmir	1,888	374	80	4,040	20,393	0.95
Jharkhand	3,958	330	194	5,294	63,491	10.80
Karnataka	8,143	1,679	254	4,285	20,780	1.37
Kerala	5,094	909	107	4,628	25,934	2.20
Madhya Pradesh	8,834	1,149	270	5024	37,232	1.94
Maharashtra	10,453	1,800	407	5,336	30,988	1.37
Manipur	420	72	16	3,788	22,095	0.99
Meghalaya	398	103	26	4,685	18,462	0.75
Mizoram	366	57	9	1,223	7,852	0.50
Nagaland	397	84	21	4,149	19,610	0.78
Orissa	5,927	1,279	231	5,279	24,462	1.35
Punjab	2,858	484	126	5,632	33,257	1.28
Rajasthan	10,612	1,499	337	4080	25,273	1.33
Sikkim	147	24	4	3,272	20,041	1.20
Tamil Nadu	8,683	1,181	236	4,022	27,893	2.11
Tripura	579	75	10	4,583	36,349	2.65
Uttaranchal	1765	232	49	3,575	28,425	1.29
Uttar Pradesh	20,521	3,660	386	6,416	35,972	3.41
West Bengal	10,356	922	346	5,576	62,634	1.67
Union Territories						
Andaman and Nicobar Islands	108	20	4	2,222	11,998	0.60
Chandigarh	13	0	2	7,086	–	0.92
Dadra and Nagar Haveli	38	6	1	4,474	28,338	1.70
Daman and Diu	21	3	1	4,803	33,619	1.01
Lakshadweep	14	4	3	2,406	8,421	0.11
Pondicherry	77	39	4	4,230	8,352	0.81
All India	1,45,272	22,370	4,045	5,111	32,754	1.90

Notes: As on March 2007 (Figures are provisional).
One Sub-centre : For every 5000 population in plain areas and 3000 population in tribal and hilly areas. One Primary Health Centre (PHC) : For every 30,000 population in plain areas and 20,000 population in hilly and tribal areas.
One Community Health Centre (CHC) : For every 120,000 population in plain areas, and 20,000 population in hilly and tribal areas, serving as a referral institution for four Primary Health Centres.

Source: Ministry of Health and Family Welfafe: Department of Family Welfare, *Bulletin on Rural Health Statistics in India,2007 (Special Revised Edition).*

Figure 2.5.Y

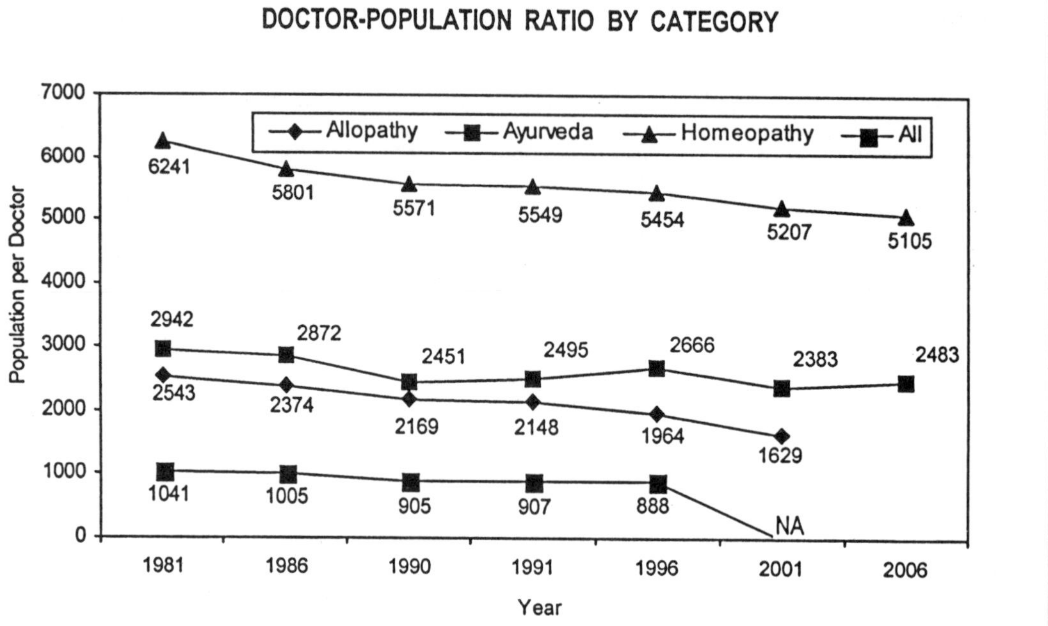

For details see Table 2.5.1

* All includes Unani and Siddha.

Figure 2.5.Z

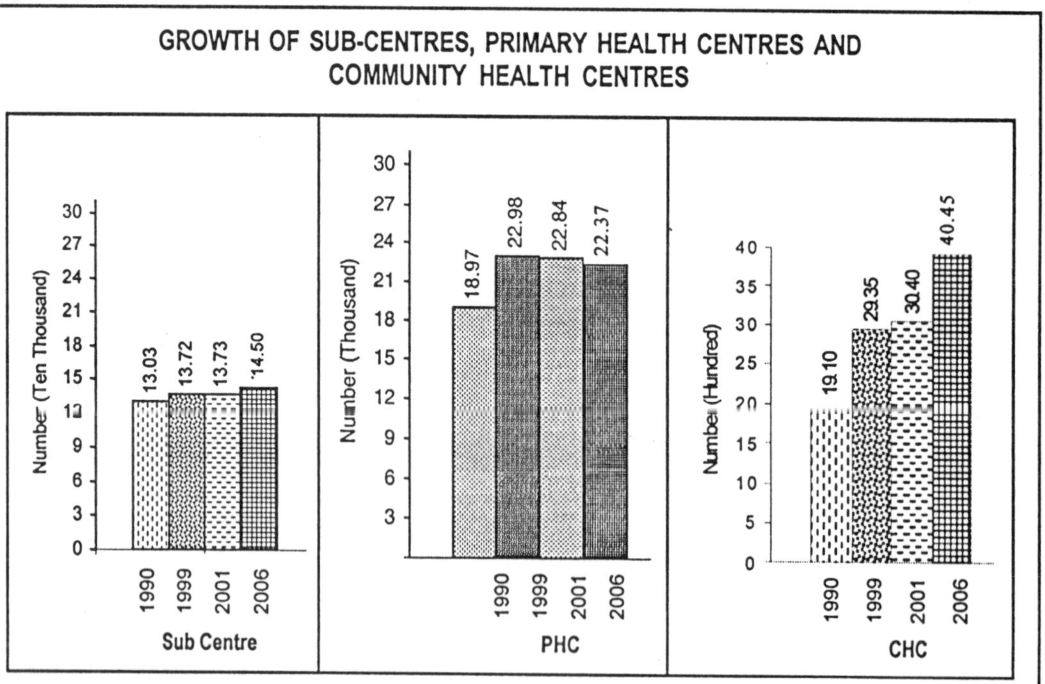

For details see Table 2.5.4

Table 2.5.7: Specialists and Doctors Working in CHC and PHC in Rural Areas

State/Union Territory	*Specialists@ at CHCs*						
	Surgeons	*Obst. & Gynaes*	*Physi-cians*	*Peadia-trician*	*Total*	*Doctors at PHCs*	*Total*
States							
Andhra Pradesh	22(89)	62(49)	5(106)	77(34)	166(278)	2214(283)	2380(561)
Arunachal Pradesh	0 (0)	0 (2)	0 (0)	0 (2)	0 (4)	78 (0)	78 (4)
Assam	NA (NA)	NA (NA)	NA (NA)	NA (NA)	NA (NA)	NA (NA)	NA (NA)
Bihar	28 (42)	21 (49)	38 (32)	17 (53)	104 (176)	1,850 (228)	1954 (404)
Chattisgarh	6 (169)	26 (149)	10 (165)	7 (168)	49 (651)	1,154 (388)	1203 (1039)
Delhi	0 (0)	0 (0)	0 (0)	0 (0)	0 (0)	23 (8)	23 (8)
Goa	1 (4)	2 (3)	0 (3)	0 (1)	3 (1)	46 (0)	49 (1)
Gujarat	70 (184)	6 (28)	0 (0)	6 (28)	82 (240)	1,034 (39)	1,116 (279)
Haryana	13 (10)	7 (19)	12 (13)	7 (14)	39 (56)	350 (230)	389 (286)
Himachal Pradesh	NA (NA)	NA (NA)	NA (NA)	NA (NA)	NA (NA)	628 (0)	628 (0)
Jammu & Kashmir	37 (32)	26 (43)	46 (23)	33 (36)	142 (134)	643 (25)	785 (159)
Jharkhand	37 (*)	61 (*)	22 (*)	19 (*)	139 (*)	2,323 (1,604)	2,462 (1604)
Karnataka	168 (22)	215 (39)	192 (62)	116 (29)	691 (152)	2,041 (196)	2,732(348)
Kerala	18 (88)	28 (78)	31 (75)	38 (68)	115 (309)	1558 (*)	1,673 (309)
Madhya Pradesh	126 (141)	41 (115)	287 (122)	49 (66)	503 (444)	869 (280)	1,372 (724)
Maharashtra	88 (319)	202 (205)	52 (355)	106 (301)	448 (1180)	1,191 (609)	1,639 (1789)
Manipur	1 (9)	0 (10)	0 (10)	0 (0)	1 (29)	103 (*)	104 (29)
Meghalaya	0 (0)	0 (1)	1 (0)	0 (0)	1 (2)	106 (21)	107 (23)
Mizoram	0 (0)	0 (0)	0 (0)	0 (0)	0 (0)	39 (18)	39 (18)
Nagaland	0 (0)	0 (0)	0 (0)	0 (0)	0 (0)	53 (0)	53 (0)
Orissa	NA (NA)	NA (NA)	NA (NA)	NA (NA)	NA (NA)	1,353 (0)	1,353 (0)
Punjab	62 (22)	41 (48)	44 (51)	30 (45)	177 (166)	350 (284)	527 (450)
Rajasthan	203 (115)	111 (44)	208 (100)	78 (19)	600 (278)	1,318 (209)	1,908 (487)
Sikkim	1 (3)	1 (3)	1 (3)	1 (3)	5 (11)	38 (10)	43 (21)
Tamil Nadu	NA (NA)	NA (NA)	NA (NA)	NA (NA)	725 (96)	1,984 (276)	2709(372)
Tripura	0 (0)	0 (0)	2 (0)	0 (0)	2 (0)	150 (11)	152(11)
Uttaranchal	17 (27)	37 (7)	4 (30)	21 (20)	79 (84)	182 (90)	261(174)
Uttar Pradesh	154 (216)	123 (247)	123 (247)	13 (NA)	413 (697)	NA (NA)	413 (697)
West Bengal	0 (0)	346 (0)	0 (0)	278 (68)	624 (68)	811 (111)	1,435 (179)
Union Territories							
Andaman and Nicobar Islands	0 (4)	0 (4)	0 (4)	0 (0)	0 (12)	36 (0)	36 (12)
Chandigarh	1 (0)	1 (0)	1 (0)	1 (0)	4 (0)	0 (0)	4 (0)
Dadra and Nagar Haveli	1 (0)	0 (0)	0 (0)	0 (0)	1 (0)	6 (0)	7 (0)
Daman and Diu	0 (0)	0 (0)	0 (0)	0 (0)	0 (0)	5 (0)	5 (0)
Lakshadweep	0 (0)	0 (0)	0 (0)	0 (0)	0 (0)	4 (0)	4 (0)
Pondicherry	0 (0)	0 (0)	4 (0)	0 (0)	4 (0)	63 (0)	67 (0)
All India	1054 (1497)	1,357 (1143)	1083 (1401)	898 (954)	5117 (5078)	22608 (4920)	26,252 (10482)

Notes: @ As on March, 2007.

NA : Not available. * Surplus.

The figures in parenthesis indicate vacant position.

Source: Ministry of Health and Family Welfare : Department of Family Welfare, *Bulletin on Rural Health Statistics in India,2007.*

Table 2.5.8: Select Paramedical Health Manpower Working in Rural Areas

State/Union Territory	*Health Assistant (Male)*	*Health Assistant (Female)/ LHVs*	*Health Workers (Male)/ MPW*	*Health Workers (Female)/ ANM*
States				
Andhra Pradesh	1,920 (242)	1,564 (50)	6,127 (1213)	12000 (623)
Arunachal Pradesh	26 (0)	16 (0)	23 (0)	454 (0)
Assam	NA (NA)	NA (NA)	NA (NA)	5,719 (0)
Bihar	634 (15)	491 (359)	1,240 (895)	8,904 (1653)
Chattisgarh	2,940 (611)	709 (70)	2852 (966)	3,667 (668)
Delhi	NA (NA)	19 (7)	0 (0)	51 (9)
Goa	15 (7)	12 (8)	134 (16)	196 (0)
Gujarat	2421 (797)	267 (214)	3347 (1959)	7,071 (203)
Haryana	106 (131)	73 (134)	425 (384)	1,909 (*)
Himachal Pradesh	361 (52)	283 (68)	1270 (738)	1,836 (372)
Jammu & Kashmir	334 (0)	62 (58)	377 (4)	1,588 (376)
Jharkhand	118 (154)	278 (183)	4291 (1153)	4372 (1177)
Karnataka	837 (465)	1,170 (39)	3762 (1247)	7244 (1512)
Kerala	794 (8)	740 (90)	4266 (80)	5634 (36)
Madhya Pradesh	1168 (24)	350 (116)	6560 (610)	8590 (1393)
Maharashtra	1,800 (0)	1718 (82)	6097 (4356)	9598 (2655)
Manipur	52 (10)	55 (*)	420 (0)	487 (5)
Meghalaya	87 (15)	75 (10)	273 (0)	608 (59)
Mizoram	57 (0)	57 (0)	303 (63)	421 (21)
Nagaland	15 (0)	15 (0)	300 (*)	342 (0)
Orissa	168 (8)	726 (0)	3,392 (1519)	6,768 (353)
Punjab	208 (81)	264 (27)	1375 (1483)	2515 (667)
Rajasthan	714 (224)	1358 (0)	2,528 (1440)	12271 (0)
Sikkim	8 (22)	18 (6)	147 (0)	267 (0)
Tamil Nadu	303 (81)	1612 (56)	1503 (3287)	10351 (16)
Tripura	93 (60)	62 (7)	268 (181)	642 (0)
Uttaranchal	417 (135)	159 (1)	656 (199)	1785 (165)
Uttar Pradesh	4,061 (1651)	2128 (407)	5,732 (3348)	21900 (1756)
West Bengal	550 (946)	1,227 (499)	5178 (4482)	9900 (456)
Union Territories				
Andaman and Nicobar Islands	0 (0)	20 (0)	0 (26)	127 (0)
Chandigarh	0 (0)	0 (0)	8 (0)	22 (0)
Dadra and Nagar Haveli	3 (3)	3 (4)	9 (0)	38 (0)
Daman and Diu	3 (0)	3 (0)	17 (0)	24 (0)
Lakshadweep	4 (0)	0 (0)	1 (13)	22 (0)
Pondicherry	17 (5)	12 (2)	0 (0)	116 (0)
All India	20,234 (5,747)	15,546 (2,497)	62,881 (29,653)	147,439 (14,180)

Notes: Data As on March, 2007.
NA: Not Available.
* Surplus.
The figures in parenthesis indicate vacant position.
LHVs — Lady Health Visitors.
ANM — Auxiliary Nurse-midwives. MPW- Multipurpose Worker.

Source: Ministry of Health and Family Welfare : Department of Family Welfare, *Bulletin on Rural Health Statistics in India, 2007*

Table 2.5.9: Select Paramedical Manpower Working in Rural Areas

State/Union Territory	*Radio-grapher*	*Phar-macists*	*Laboratory Tech-nicians*	*Nurse Midwife*	*Block Extension Educator*
States					
Andhra Pradesh	59 (44)	1614 (72)	1363 (228)	2373 (369)	1397 (110)
Arunachal Pradesh	22 (0)	31 (0)	18 (0)	105 (0)	0 (2)
Assam	NA (NA)	NA (NA)	NA (NA)	NA (NA)	NA (NA)
Bihar	15 (74)	439 (550)	135 (548)	1425 (237)	80 (314)
Chattisgarh	95 (21)	467 (282)	348 (285)	540 (136)	183 (27)
Delhi	0 (0)	11 (2)	5 (3)	4 (6)	6 (3)
Goa	6 (1)	26 (1)	27 (0)	141 (0)	8 (0)
Gujarat	124 (131)	814 (550)	899 (429)	1585 (1184)	0 (0)
Haryana	63 (38)	372 (91)	216 (202)	411 (278)	29 (9)
Himachal Pradesh	54 (12)	303 (140)	318 (125)	484 (715)	60 (24)
Jammu & Kashmir	61 (0)	456 (0)	395 (0)	68 (176)	67 (56)
Jharkhand	24 (*)	310 (379)	239 (308)	451 (23)	NA (NA)
Karnataka	30 (21)	1472 (463)	1242 (408)	3,100 (129)	428 (103)
Kerala	15 (2)	995 (43)	336 (32)	3064 (*)	145 (16)
Madhya Pradesh	NA (NA)	215 (1204)	489 (87)	901 (40)	21 (19)
Maharashtra	294 (113)	1976 (391)	769 (34)	2774 (1355)	286 (53)
Manipur	7 (3)	26 (53)	41 (47)	169 (*)	11 (*)
Meghalaya	25 (3)	113 (32)	130 (7)	174 (49)	23 (0)
Mizoram	9 (0)	35 (34)	31 (38)	243 (148)	12 (8)
Nagaland	11 (0)	85 (0)	45 (0)	520 (0)	14 (1)
Orissa	8 (18)	1,984 (56)	311 (33)	637 (20)	284 (36)
Punjab	67 (50)	680 (56)	523 (159)	448 (292)	39 (103)
Rajasthan	269 (0)	2,355 (20)	2065 (88)	8425 (1466)	15 (217)
Sikkim	9 (3)	0 (28)	32 (4)	90 (*)	3 (6)
Tamil Nadu	NA (NA)	1349 (93)	955 (93)	NA (NA)	213 (169)
Tripura	4 (0)	56 (*)	42 (13)	268 (*)	14 (4)
Uttaranchal	30 (10)	281 (0)	32 (58)	129 (16)	13 (71)
Uttar Pradesh	NA (NA)	NA (NA)	NA (NA)	NA (NA)	110 (898)
West Bengal	425 (65)	1341 (273)	1031 (382)	858 (86)	600 (300)
Union Territories					
Andaman and Nicobar Islands	4 (0)	28 (0)	24 (0)	108 (0)	0 (0)
Chandigarh	1 (0)	2 (0)	2 (0)	13 (0)	1 (0)
Dadra and Nagar Haveli	1 (0)	6 (0)	6 (0)	20 (*)	4 (0)
Daman and Diu	1 (0)	4 (0)	4 (0)	12 (0)	2 (0)
Lakshadweep	3 (0)	11 (0)	7 (1)	13 (0)	0 (0)
Pondicherry	4 (0)	62 (1)	21 (0)	223 (2)	0 (0)
All India	1740 (609)	17919 (4814)	12101 (3672)	29776 (6727)	4068 (2549)

Notes: * Data as on March, 2007.
NA : Not Available. * Surplus.
The figures in parenthesis indicate vacant position.

Source: Ministry of Health & Family Welfare : Department of Family Welfare, *Bulletin on Rural Health Statistics in India, 2007*

Table 2.5.10: Hospitals and Beds by Organisation

State/Union Territory	Government (Including Local Bodies)*		Private and Voluntary Organisation@		Total		Population Served per	
	Hospital	Bed	Hospital	Bed	Hospital	Bed	Hospital	Bed
States								
Andhra Pradesh	359	34333	2802	42192	3161	76525	224825	2351
Arunachal Pradesh	66	2053	0	0	66	2053	17288	556
Assam	100	3,000	80	1992	180	4992	278780	9293
Bihar	101	3030	90	8519	191	11549	868712	28959
Chhitsgarh	138	5566	—	—	138	5566	156181	3873
Delhi	123	21192	23	3414	146	24607	134016	778
Goa	20	2579	91	1781	111	4360	74600	579
Gujarat	1712	41032	2152	36867	3864	77899	32598	1360
Haryana	149	7662	20	2232	169	9894	159349	3099
Himachal Pradesh	149	8109	9	345	158	8454	43799	805
Jammu & Kashmir	92	2245	2	140	94	2385	NA	NA
Jharkhand	47	1410	—	—	47	1410	604000	20133
Karnataka	868	42591	56	9999	924	52590	64815	1321
Kerala	250	28395	1958	67517	2208	95912	134140	1217
Madhya Pradesh	377	19918	0	0	377	19918	179228	3392
Maharashtra	666	45973	2583	37758	3249	83731	157363	2280
Manipur	28	1920	5	100	33	2020	83429	1067
Meghalaya	34	2619	4	720	38	3339	72647	943
Mizoram	20	1224	5	350	25	1574	47900	783
Nagaland	135	2752	0	0	135	2752	15511	761
Orissa	1707	14550	14	201	1921	14751	23009	2699
Punjab	249	11027	39	3782	288	14809	104655	2363
Rajasthan	475	32067	0	0	475	32067	133491	1977
Sikkim	32	1520	0	0	32	1520	18219	384
Tamil Nadu	581	47198	119	10366	700	57564	112959	1391
Tripura	31	2262	0	0	31	2262	111258	1525
Uttar Pradesh	925	32460	159	12026	1084	44486	198143	5646
Uttranchal	118	5513	—	—	118	5513	78127	1672
West Bengal	383	49681	133	6729	516	56410	224869	1734
Union Territories								
Andaman and Nicobar Islands	7	805	2	37	9	842	59857	520
Chandigarh	7	2200	0	0	7	2200	136714	435
Dadra and Nagar Haveli	2	160	2	40	4	200	140500	1756
Daman and Diu	4	192	2	50	6	242	45500	948
Lakshadweep	5	160	0	0	5	160	13800	431
Pondicherry	16	3425	21	674	37	4099	71625	335
Total	9976	482522	10371	247631	20347	730153	113124	2339

Note: * As on 01-03-2007. @ Figures for the year 1998 is available.

Source: Directorate General of Health Services : National Health Profile, 2007

Table 2.5.11: Number of Hospitals, Hospital Beds and All Types of Beds Alongwith Ratios

Year	*Number of Hospitals*	*No. of Hospital Per Million Population*	*No. of Hospital beds*		*No. of Beds (All Types)*	
			Actual	*Ratio per Lakh Population*	*Actual*	*Ratio per Lakh Population*
1986	8,067	10	555,264	72	694,121	91
1991	11,571	13	629,453	75	806,409	97
1996	15,097	16	623,819	67	849,431	91
1997	15,170	16	662,372	70	892,738	94
1999	15,501	16	NA	NA	908,000	92
2000	18,218	13	598,059	74	909,000	95
2001	17,952	13	602,490	74	904,000	97
2002	15,393[a]	NA	NA	NA	914,543	89
2003	5479[b]	NA	NA	NA	381,000[c]	NA
2004	7029[b]	NA	NA	NA	470,000	NA
2005	7008[b]	NA	NA	NA	470,000	NA
2006	7663	NA	NA	NA	493,000	NA

Notes: As on December 31.
P — Provisional. NA — Not Available.
(*a*) Total Hospitals reduced from 2001 due to exclusion on CHCs and non reporting.
(*b*) Related to Government Allopathic Hospitals only.
(*c*) Estimated at 30 beds per one CHC.

Sources: (*i*) Directorate General of Health Services : *Health Information of India —1997 and 1998.*
(*ii*) Central Statistical Organisation : *Statistical Abstract-2007.*

Table 2.5.12: Percentage Distribution of Live Births by Type of Medical Attention

Type of Medical Attention at the time of Delivery	*Location*	*1980*	*1986*	*1990*	*1993*	*1995*	*1996*	*1998*	*1999*	*2000*
Institution like Hospitals, Maternity/Nursing Homes, Health Centres, etc.	Rural	11.0	14.3	16.2	20.2	17.4	17.7	18.0	18.2	17.5
	Urban	37.7	47.8	52.8	56.5	59.6	59.5	59.6	59.7	55.0
	Total	17.4	20.7	22.9	24.5	25.2	25.2	25.4	26.6	25.1
Delivery conducted in the Home by Doctor, Trained Dai, Midwife, Nurse etc.	Rural	13.2	17.7	20.2	23.3	27.6	27.9	28.2	28.3	27.1
	Urban	27.3	25.0	26.1	31.6	30.9	31.1	31.4	31.5	34.0
	Total	16.7	19.1	21.3	24.3	28.2	28.5	28.8	28.9	29.0
Delivery conducted in the Home by untrained Dai or other traditional attendents	Rural	55.4	48.3	62.0	56.5	49.8	49.5	49.2	49.3	50.9
	Urban	26.5	18.6	20.6	11.8	7.8	7.8	7.6	7.7	10.0
	Total	48.4	42.6	54.4	51.3	42.1	41.9	41.8	40.9	42.0
Delivery conducted in the Home by Relatives or others excluding the above	Rural	20.4	19.7	1.5	*	5.2	5.0	4.6	4.5	4.5
	Urban	8.5	8.6	0.6	*	1.7	1.6	1.4	1.4	1.0
	Total	17.5	17.6	1.4	*	4.6	4.4	4.1	39	3.9

Note: * Included in category 3.

Source: Registrar General and Census Commissioner of India, *Sample Registration System : Statistical Reports.*

Figure 2.5.ZA

NUMBER OF HOSPITALS AND BEDS

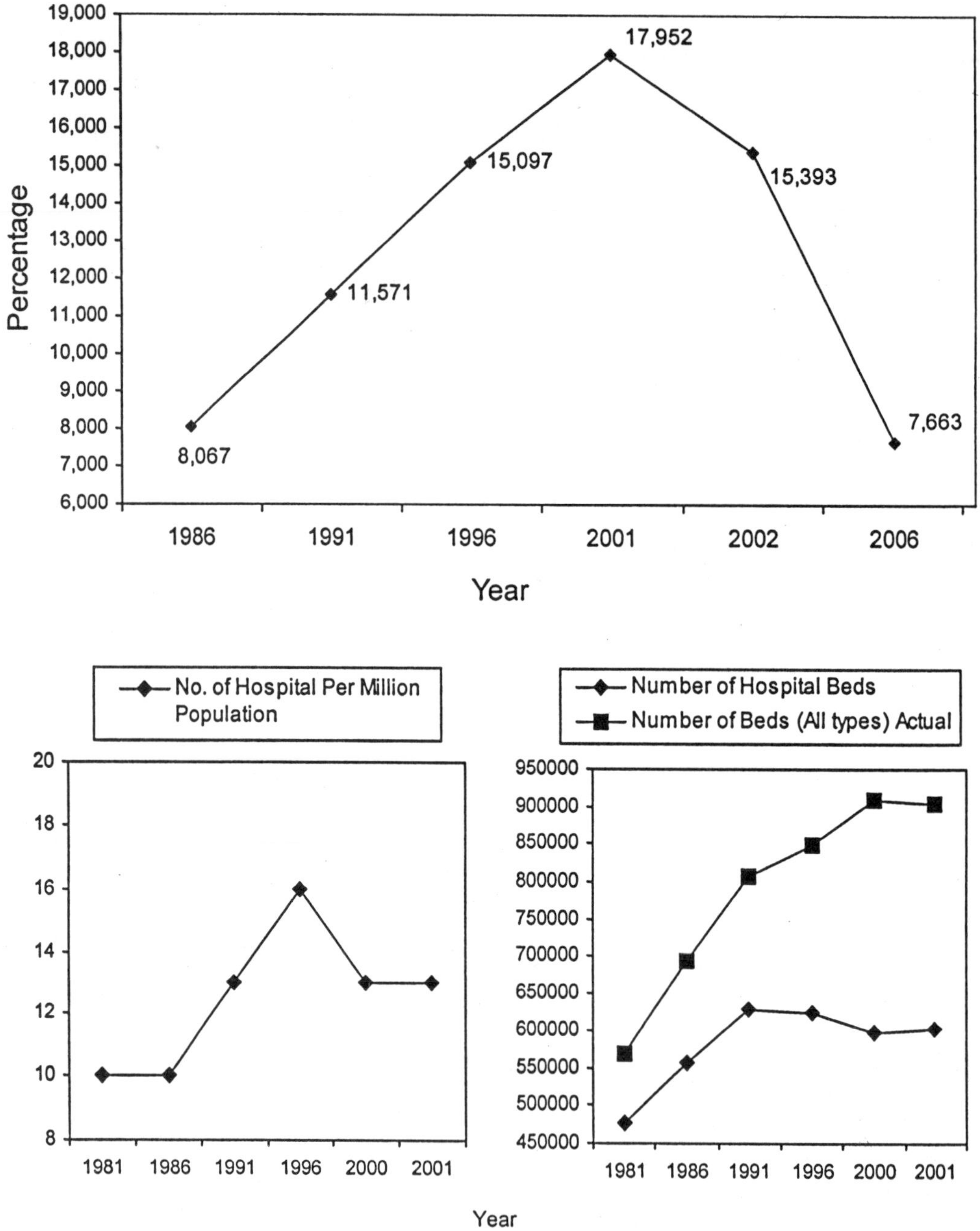

For details see Table 2.5.11

Figure 2.5.ZB

PERCENTAGE DISTRIBUTION OF LIVE BIRTHS BY TYPE OF MEDICAL ATTENTION

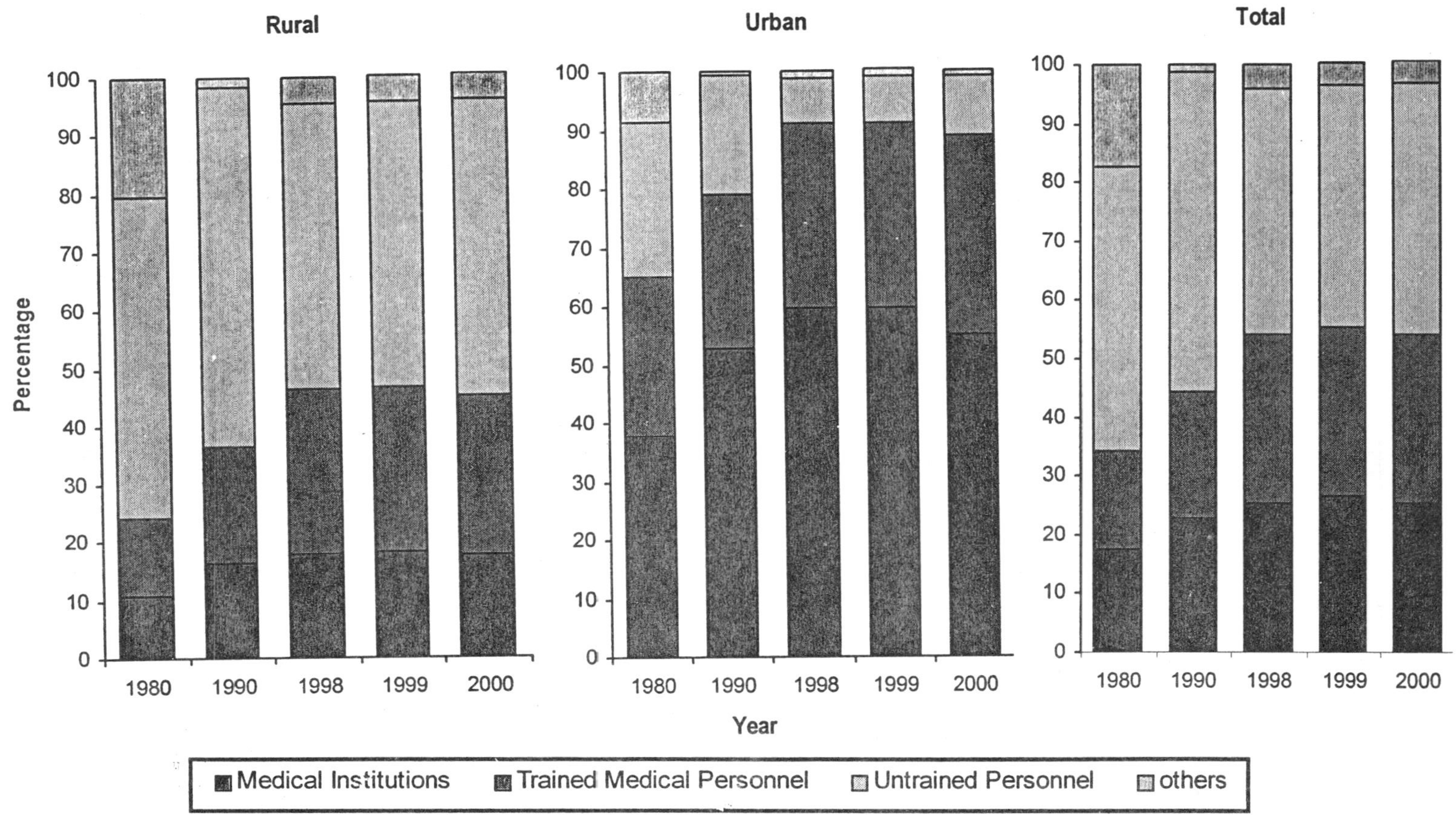

For details see Table 2.5.12

Table 2.5.13: Morbidity by Cause of Sickness, Number of Sick and Deaths

Cause of Sickness	*Cases*			*Deaths*		
	2004P	*2006*	*2007P*	*2004P*	*2006*	*2007P*
Diarrhoeal diseases	9575112	10213917	9478813	2855	3176	2328
Malaria	1915363	1780777	1363279	949	1704	1066
Cholera	4728	NA	2635	9	NA	3
Kala-azar	24479	39178	44001	155	187	189
Japanese Encephalitis	1714	2842	4017	367	658	989
Meningitis	8999	3438	4472	541	312	252
Kayasanur Forest diseases	112	NA	NA	2	NA	NA
Diphtheria	8465	2834	3354	126	66	37
Poliomyelitis	218	116	238	4	1	4
Tetanus-Neonatal	1087	625	937	141	80	93
Tetanus Others	3743	2815	7005	474	365	272
Whooping Cough	32786	30088	40729	19	17	15
Measles	51546	64185	36900	140	96	50
Dengue	4153	12317	5395	45	184	69
Plague	8	NA	NA	3	NA	NA
Acute Respiratory Infection	25571757	26152957	23379578	5223	3736	4019
Pneumonia	675888	681560	660390	3463	3342	2865
Enteric Fever (Typhoid)	65830	789004	694862	805	658	393
Viral Hepatitis	203939	152623	97827	1122	694	480
Dog Bites/Rabies	536	361	221	536	361	221
Syphilis	56473	60122	47718	26	6	8
Gonococcal Infection	162946	128373	153050	2310	15	11
Tuberculosis	731952	834037	720395	7800	7244	6037
Other Diseases	NA	NA	NA	NA	NA	NA

Notes: P : Provisional (Reference Period Dec., 2006/2007)
NA : Not Available

Source: Ministry of Health and Family Welfare, Directorate General of Health Services, Central Bureau of Health Intelligence : National Health People, 2007

Table 2.5.14: Morbidity Rates* for **Each Type of Ailment by State/Union Territory, 1995-96

States/UT	*Rural*			*Urban*		
	Male	*Female*	*Person*	*Male*	*Female*	*Person*
States						
Andhra Pradesh	66	63	64	58	63	61
Arunachal Pradesh	24	24	24	45	39	42
Assam	68	95	80	71	104	86
Bihar	33	39	36	40	42	41
Delhi	23	22	23	45	40	43
Goa	30	58	44	36	31	34
Gujarat	46	45	46	34	37	36
Haryana	57	65	61	47	80	63
Himachal Pradesh	84	96	90	71	59	66
Jammu & Kashmir	52	53	52	51	57	54
Karnataka	41	48	44	39	42	40
Kerala	116	119	118	88	88	88
Madhya Pradesh	40	43	41	38	37	38
Maharashtra	51	52	52	45	51	48
Manipur	10	6	8	3	2	2
Meghalaya	35	34	35	29	40	34
Mizoram	12	25	18	10	13	12
Nagaland	30	33	31	47	44	46
Orissa	64	61	62	56	69	62
Punjab	71	81	76	84	86	85
Rajasthan	31	24	28	34	33	33
Sikkim	37	39	38	14	30	22
Tamil Nadu	52	53	52	50	66	58
Tripura	112	123	117	90	103	96
Uttar Pradesh	60	63	61	63	82	72
West Bengal	61	70	65	61	68	65
Union Territories						
Andaman and Nicobar Islands	30	24	27	18	11	15
Chandigarh	140	173	153	127	141	133
Dadra and Nagar Haveli	47	69	57	59	54	57
Daman and Diu	35	51	43	41	44	43
Lakshadweep	63	51	57	50	47	48
Pondicherry	78	103	91	62	72	67
All India	54	57	55	51	58	54

Notes: * Number (per 1000) of persons reporting ailment (PAP) during 15 days perceeding the date of Survey is known as Morbidity Rate.

** Each type of ailment means Acute + Chronic ailment.

Source : National Sample Survey Organisation : *Sarvekshana*, Vol. 23, No. 3, 82nd Issue, January-March 2000.

Table 2.5.15: Morbidity Rate and Prevalence Rate of Ailment

Sex	*1995-96 (52nd round)*			*1986-87 (42nd round)*	*1973-74 (28th round)*	*1961-61 (17th round)*
	PAP (15 days recall)	*PR (derived) (30 days)*	*PAP (derived (15 days)*	*PR (30 days)*	*PAP (15 days)*	
			Rural			
Male	54	84	54	64	47	139
Female	57	89	58	63	40	123
Person	55	86	56	64	43	132
			Urban			
Male	51	81	52	30	43	133
Female	58	89	58	33	41	128
Person	54	84	55	31	42	131

Notes: Recall periods used in different rounds are shown in column headings in parenthesis.
PAP-Proportion of Ailing Person per 1000 persons (Morbidity Rate).
PR- Prevalance Rate.

Source: National Sample Survey Organisation : *Sarvekshana,* Vol. 23, No. 3, 82nd Issue, 52nd Round.

Table 2.5.16: Percentage Distribution of Medically Certified Deaths over Various Age-Groups by Major Causes and Sex During 1998

Major Causes	Sex	Age Groups											
		<1	1to4	5 to 14	15 to 24	25 to 34	35 to 44	45 to 54	55 to 64	65 to 69	70+	NS	Total
1. Infectious and parasitic diseases	M	6.4	5.7	5.3	6.9	13.2	16.2	14.0	12.3	5.2	9.5	5.1	100.0
	F	8.0	8.6	7.7	12.4	15.0	11.4	9.2	9.3	4.9	10.0	3.5	100.0
2. Neoplasm	M	0.5	1.0	3.1	4.2	6.1	11.2	19.0	23.8	11.0	18.4	1.7	100.0
	F	0.4	1.0	2.2	3.9	6.9	14.4	21.1	21.5	10.0	17.4	1.1	100.0
3. Endocrine, nutritional, metabolic and immunity disorder diseases	M	4.6	3.3	1.8	2.0	4.3	8.3	15.1	23.7	11.9	22.9	2.2	100.0
	F	4.8	4.8	2.3	2.8	4.0	6.0	13.2	22.0	13.2	25.4	1.3	100.0
4. Diseases of blood and blood forming organs	M	4.2	7.2	7.0	8.8	10.1	11.4	11.8	12.3	6.2	15.9	5.1	100.0
	F	2.9	6.4	7.1	14.4	16.9	10.0	8.6	9.2	4.1	17.7	2.7	100.0
5. Mental disorders	M	1.5	0.6	0.6	3.4	11.7	23.9	22.9	18.0	7.5	9.0	0.8	100.0
	F	2.0	2.0	3.1	11.2	11.2	13.3	12.2	11.2	10.2	20.4	3.1	100.0
6. Diseases of the nervous system and sense organs	M	12.4	12.8	12.5	8.0	9.7	10.0	8.8	9.3	4.2	9.2	3.2	100.0
	F	10.4	15.6	15.4	10.3	10.1	7.9	6.9	7.1	4.0	9.9	2.4	100.0
7. Diseases of the circulatory system	M	1.1	0.8	1.4	3.1	6.0	10.8	16.5	21.3	11.2	25.8	2.0	100.0
	F	1.1	1.1	1.9	4.4	6.3	8.2	11.9	18.1	11.4	34.3	1.2	100.0
8. Diseases of respiratory system	M	9.5	7.4	4.6	4.2	5.9	8.1	10.7	15.1	7.9	22.4	4.0	100.0
	F	11.3	9.6	5.8	5.0	6.1	6.4	7.8	11.4	7.4	26.1	3.1	100.0
9. Disease of digestive system	M	1.4	2.0	2.9	4.3	10.6	20.9	21.6	16.7	6.5	10.3	2.7	100.0
	F	2.2	4.5	5.2	9.3	12.9	12.7	14.1	14.0	7.8	14.5	2.8	100.0
10. Diseases of the Genitourinary system	M	2.0	2.1	3.1	6.2	9.4	12.2	15.0	17.5	8.7	20.8	2.9	100.0
	F	1.5	2.7	3.8	8.3	12.1	12.6	13.4	15.5	7.4	19.4	3.1	100.0
11. Complications of pregnancy and child birth	F	0.0	0.0	0.2	38.9	44.3	12.2	1.0	0.4	0.0	0.1	2.9	100.0

Cotd.

Major Causes	Sex	Age Groups											
		<1	1to4	5 to 14	15 to 24	25 to 34	35 to 44	45 to 54	55 to 64	65 to 69	70+	NS	Total
12. Diseases of skin and subcutaneous tissue	M	2.2	2.9	2.9	5.7	7.9	17.4	13.0	17.4	6.2	21.3	3.3	100.0
	F	3.0	3.0	6.5	5.2	13.0	13.0	10.8	20.8	4.3	20.3	0.0	100.0
13. Diseases of the musculoske etal system and connective tissue	M	5.6	1.9	4.3	4.3	8.1	17.4	19.9	13.0	11.8	11.2	2.5	100.0
	F	3.7	2.2	6.7	8.9	14.1	8.9	11.1	18.5	9.6	14.1	2.2	100.0
14. Congenital anomalies	M	72.3	8.9	5.7	4.2	1.0	1.6	1.0	0.5	0.3	1.0	3.6	100.0
	F	69.4	11.5	7.7	4.4	2.2	0.7	1.1	0.5	0.4	0.5	1.8	100.0
15. Disease originating in the perinatal period	M	98.5	0.8	0.0	0.0	0.0	0.0	0.0	0.0	0.0	0.0	0.7	100.0
	F	98.2	1.1	0.2	0.0	0.0	0.0	0.0	0.0	0.0	0.0	0.5	100.0
16. Symptoms signs and ill defined conditions	M	6.5	3.9	3.0	6.5	9.5	11.4	12.9	14.4	8.1	21.9	1.8	100.0
	F	7.7	4.4	3.6	8.1	9.6	7.5	8.5	10.5	7.8	30.7	1.6	100.0
17. Injury and poisoning (External cause/injury)	M	1.0	2.3	4.6	17.3	23.8	19.2	12.6	8.2	2.7	4.5	3.9	100.0
	F	0.9	2.6	5.5	29.2	27.6	13.8	6.8	4.9	2.0	3.8	2.8	100.0
All Causes	M	11.6	3.3	3.4	6.1	9.7	12.3	13.4	14.5	7.1	15.8	2.9	100.0
	F	12.4	4.3	4.3	10.2	11.6	9.0	9.1	11.2	6.7	19.1	2.1	100.0
	T	11.9	3.7	3.7	7.6	10.4	11.0	11.8	13.3	6.9	17.0	2.6	100.0

Notes: M - Male, F - Female, T - Total.

Source : Central Bureau of Health Intelligence, Directorate General of Health and Services : *Health Information India-2004.*

Table 2.5.17 : Percentage Distribution of Death in Major States by Type of Medical Attention Received, 2000

States	Institutional			Medical Attention Other than Institution			No Medical Attention		
	Total	Rural	Urban	Total	Rural	Urban	Total	Rural	Urban
All India	20.9	17.4	35.9	65.9	67.5	58.9	12.7	14.6	4.6
Andhra Pradesh	23.7	20.4	39.4	59.5	60.4	55.1	16.6	19.0	5.4
Assam	9.8	8.7	26.2	78.1	78.4	73.2	11.8	12.6	0.5
Bihar	16.8	14.9	34.9	78.7	80.6	60.5	4.4	4.4	4.2
Gujarat	26.0	21.9	38.6	60.9	62.9	57.1	12.8	15.6	4.2
Haryana	20.5	19.9	23.5	68.2	67.4	71.8	11.0	12.4	4.6
Himachal Pradesh	43.7	43.6	45.3	44.7	44.2	52.2	11.6	12.2	2.2
Karnataka	32.8	28.9	46.2	35.9	33.8	43.1	31.2	37.3	10.5
Kerala	80.4	88.5	54.5	15.3	6.5	43.6	4.0	4.8	1.6
Madhya Pradesh	14.3	11.6	30.0	73.2	74.5	65.4	12.3	13.6	5.1
Maharashtra	35.6	29.9	49.1	56.4	58.9	50.5	7.9	11.1	0.4
Orissa	12.2	11.1	25.2	43.2	42.6	50.3	44.3	46.0	24.3
Punjab	23.4	24.5	19.3	75.2	74.6	77.6	1.5	1.1	3.0
Rajasthan	10.8	8.4	26.3	81.2	83.2	68.6	7.9	8.4	5.0
Tamil Nadu	27.4	21.3	44.3	36.3	32.6	46.5	36.1	45.9	8.9
Utter Pradesh	10.6	9.8	15.7	85.1	85.9	80.2	4.1	4.1	3.9
West Bengal	22.4	14.6	46.3	68.9	74.1	52.9	8.6	11.1	0.7

Source: Registrar General and Census Commissioner of India : Sample Registration System, *Statistical Report 2000*.

Table 2.5.18 : Percentage Distribution of Death in Major States by Type of Medical Attention Received, 2005

States	Government Hospital			Private Hospital			Qualified Professional			Untrained Functionary & others		
	Total	Rural	Urban	Total	Rural	Urban	Total	Rural	Urban	Total	Rural	Urban
All India	15.9	12.8	27.1	12.0	10.0	19.1	38.6	39.4	35.9	33.5	37.9	18.0
Andhra Pradesh	12.0	9.2	21.1	16.1	15.2	19.0	33.2	32.7	34.7	38.7	42.9	25.2
Assam	11.0	10.0	20.4	10.1	9.9	11.5	55.8	56.1	53.3	23.1	23.9	14.8
Bihar	10.6	9.9	18.1	7.2	6.3	17.3	44.2	44.0	46.8	37.9	39.8	17.8
Chhattisgarh	16.4	12.7	34.7	8.8	7.7	14.4	25.5	23.2	37.0	49.3	56.4	13.9
Delhi	38.9	16.6	43.6	10.7	6.0	11.7	29.0	49.5	24.7	21.4	27.9	20.0
Gujarat	18.6	14.7	27.1	14.2	12.1	18.6	49.7	52.9	42.7	17.5	20.3	11.6
Haryana	13.6	12.9	15.6	11.1	10.7	12.2	56.2	57.3	53.1	19.1	19.1	19.1
Himachal Pradesh	42.2	43.1	28.6	10.2	9.3	23.0	27.3	27.9	18.5	20.4	19.7	29.9
Jammu & Kashmir	35.4	30.0	57.0	8.1	7.6	10.0	33.5	34.6	28.8	23.0	27.8	4.2
Jharkhand	9.7	6.5	28.9	9.6	7.7	20.6	36.1	35.7	38.7	44.6	50.1	11.8
Karnataka	23.0	19.2	32.8	14.5	11.5	22.9	18.8	21.5	12.0	43.7	47.9	32.8
Kerala	36.0	37.6	31.3	33.2	35.4	26.7	12.7	7.6	28.0	18.1	19.4	14.0
Madhya Pradesh	13.9	11.0	29.2	13.7	12.5	20.1	34.1	34.4	32.7	38.3	42.1	18.0
Maharashtra	22.5	18.4	29.6	15.2	12.1	20.6	42.1	45.0	36.9	20.3	24.5	12.9
Orissa	16.0	14.8	26.7	2.9	2.5	6.0	22.7	22.4	25.2	58.4	60.3	42.1
Punjab	11.6	10.8	13.2	30.7	25.6	41.1	48.5	52.7	39.9	9.2	10.9	5.8
Rajasthan	15.3	11.7	27.8	8.1	6.9	12.3	45.8	45.4	47.4	30.7	35.9	12.5
Tamil Nadu	15.8	11.8	22.8	14.6	10.3	22.3	22.3	20.3	25.9	47.3	57.6	29.0
Utter Pradesh	9.8	7.9	20.6	11.1	9.1	22.3	46.2	47.2	40.4	32.9	35.8	16.7
West Bengal	22.3	17.3	35.0	6.1	3.5	12.6	46.4	47.4	44.0	25.1	31.8	8.4

Source : Ministry of Health & Family Welfare, Directorate General of Health Services, Central Bureau of Health Intelligence : *Mortality Statistics in India* 2006

Table 2.5.19: Percentage Expenditure on Health, Family Welfare and Water Supply to Total Investment/Outlay

Year	*Total Plan Investment/ outlay (Rs. Crore)*	*Health*	*Family Welfare*	*Sub-total*	*Water Supply*
1991-92	65855.8	1.6	1.3	2.9	3.4
1994-95	98167.3	1.7	1.7	3.4	3.1
1995-96	107380.4	1.8	1.6	3.4	3.5
1996-97	118976.4	2.0	1.7	1.9	3.5
1997-98	129757.3	2.0	1.4	3.4	3.3
1998-99	151580.4	3.6	1.5	5.1	3.4
1999-2000	160,608.2	2.2	1.8	4.0	3.2
2000-2001	185736.8	2.2	1.7	3.9	2.9
2001-2002	186315.2	2.4	1.9	4.3	NA
2002-2003	210202.9	2.1	1.8	3.9	NA
2003-2004	224827.0	2.1	1.9	4.0	NA
2004-2005	263665.2	2.3	1.8	4.1	NA
2005-2006	351629.5	2.4	1.5	3.9	NA
2006-2007 (RE)	441285.2	2.6	1.7	4.3	NA
2007-2008 (BE)	559314.0	NA	NA	NA	NA

Notes: RE : Revised Estimates. BE : Budget Estimates. NA : Not Available

Source: Economic Survey, 2007-08.

Table 2.5.20: Couples Effectively Protected by Family Planning Methods (Percent)

Year	*Eligible Couples ('000's)*	*Percentage of Couples Protected by*				
		Sterilisation	*IUD*	*Oral Pill*	*CC*	*All Methods*
1991-92	148,430	30.3	6.3	2.2	4.7	43.6
1992-93	151,720	30.3	6.3	2.0	4.9	43.5
1993-94	155,020	30.3	6.8	2.7	5.6	45.4
1994-95	158,310	30.2	7.2	–	8.4	45.8
1995-96	161,593	30.2	7.8	3.2	5.3	46.5
1996-97	164,749	29.6	7.4	3.1	5.2	45.4
1997-98	165,868	29.3	7.3	3.8	5.0	45.4
1999-00	172,700	29.0	7.3	3.9	4.5	46.2
2000-03*	NA	4.7	6.1	8.2	22.0	41.7
2003-04*	NA	4.9	6.1	8.7	18.7	38.3
2004-05*	NA	4.9	6.2	7.6	18.3	37.1
2005-06*	NA	4.7	6.2	9.2	26.0	46.1

Notes: IUD : Intra Uterine Devices * Provisional
CC : Conventional contraceptives.

Source: Ministry of Health and Family Welfare : Department of Family Welfare, *Annual Report* relevent years.

Figure 2.5.ZC

EXPENDITURE ON HEALTH, FAMILY WELFARE AND WATER SUPPLY TO TOTAL INVESTMENT/OUTLAY

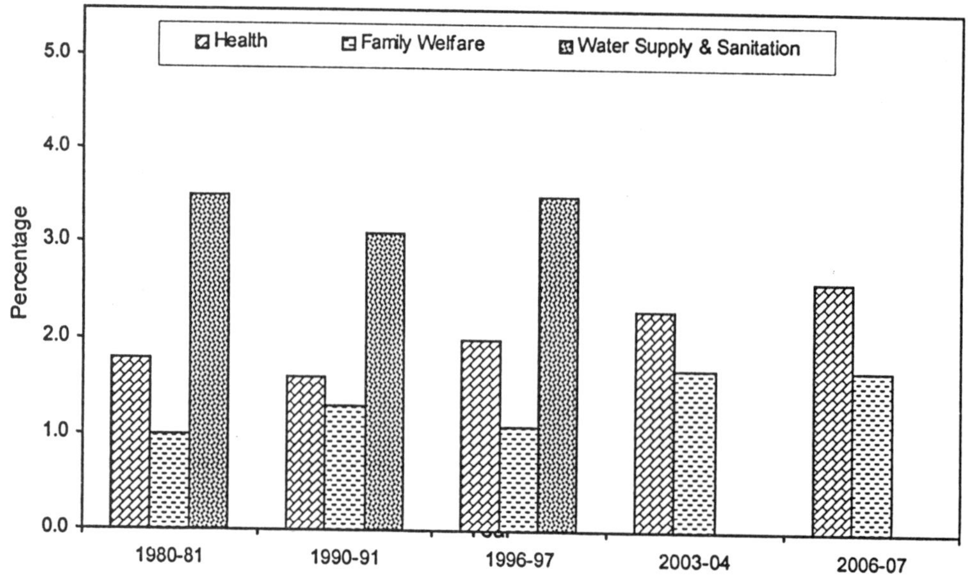

For details see Table 2.5.19

Table 2.5.21: Percapita Net Availability per Day of Cereals and Pulses in India

(in Grams)

Year	*Cereals*	*Pulses*	*Total*
1971	417.6	51.2	468.8
1981	417.3	37.5	454.8
1991	468.5	41.6	510.1
1996	442.5	32.7	475.2
1997	466.0	37.1	503.1
1998	414.2	32.8	447.0
1999	429.2	36.5	465.7
2000	422.7	31.8	454.4
2001	386.2	30.0	416.2
2002	458.1	35.4	494.1
2003	408.5	29.1	437.6
2004	426.9	35.8	462.7
2005	390.9	31.5	422.4
2006*	412.1	32.5	444.5

Note : * Provisional.
Source : *Economic Survey—2006-2007.*

Table 2.5.22: Social Security Schemes in Important Organised Sectors

Description	*Year*	*Number*
1. Central Government Health Scheme (CGHS)	31st March, 2005	
(i) Number of Dispensaries		311 (333)
(a) Allopathy		246 (247)
(b) Ayurveda		32 (33)
(c) Homeopathy		36(36)
(d) Unani		10 (10)
(e) Sidha		3 (3)
(f) Yoga		4 (4)
(ii) No. of Families covered (Lakhs)		10.32 (10.66)
(iii) No. of beneficiaries (Lakhs)		42.86 (45.59)
2. Employees State Insurance Scheme (ESIS)	31st March, 2005	
(i) No. of Hospitals/Annexes		186 (185)
(ii) No. of Dispensaries		1427 (1452)
(iii) No. of Insured Persons/Family Units (Lakhs)		84.98 (79.13)
(iv) No. of beneficiaries (including insured person for medical benefits) (Lakhs)		329.73 (307.01)
3. Post and Telecommunications	November, 2003	
(i) No. of Dispensaries (Including First Aid Centres)		62 (62)
4. Mines and Beedi Workers	2005	
I Mines		
(i) No. of Central/Regional Hospitals and PHCs		7 (14)
(ii) No. of Dispensaries		62 (60)
(iii) No. of Beds		365(375)
II. Beedi Workers		
(i) No. of Hospitals/T.B. Hospital/Chest Clinic		4 (4)
(ii) No. of Dispensaries (including of Ayurvedic)		210 (206)
(iii) No. of Beds		160 (160)
5. Railways	December, 2004	
(i) No. of Hospitals		120
(ii) No. of Health units (including lockup dispensaries)		661
(iii) No. of Beds		13,504
(iv) No. of Medical Beneficiaries (Lakhs)		55.89
(v) No. of Medical Staff Employed		47050

Note : Figures in the parenthesis indicate for the previous year.

Source : Central Bureau of Health Intelligence, Directorate General of Health Service : *Health Information of India, 2005.*

SECTION 3

Base for Manpower Utilisation and Its Characteristics

Dr. I. C. Awasthi
Vijay K. Saxena

Section-III
Base for Manpower Utilisation and Its Characteristics

The global meltdown has significant adverse impact across all sectors of economy barring mining & quarrying and community, social and personal services. The overall growth plummeted to 6.7 per cent in 2008-09 registering a substantive decline from 9.7 per cent achieved during 2006-07. Despite economic recession, Indian economy has posted a reasonable growth rate in 2008-09. Yet, the economic scenario continues to be grim because of wide-ranging challenges in terms of social and economic infrastructure and also because of the pressing needs felt for increasing the productivity in agriculture and industry. One of the direct manifestations of slowdown of the economy has been huge job losses across industries that have profound implication in the labour market.

The other important associated problem is a growing number of educated unemployed on the one hand and an acute shortage of skilled manpower on the other. It is, therefore of paramount importance to look into the whole process of formation, maintenance and utilisation of manpower resources in order to sustain the process of economic reforms and taking the economy into a higher trajectory of growth. This process necessarily calls for the maintenance of manpower that includes preservation and renewal of capabilities and skills through appropriate educational, training and retraining interventions on a continuous basis. It is important from the policy point of view to respond to this challenge in order to sustain India's growing economy.

This section provides some basic information on various aspects of the utilisation pattern of manpower that has been organised in the following sub-sections:

(i) Base for Manpower Utilisation

(ii) Employment Characteristics

(iii) Manpower Utilisation in Scientific and Technical Fields

(iv) Child Labour (5-14 years)

(v) Activities of Population Aged 60+

(vi) Activities of Youth (15-34 years)

Major sources of data used here are the Census, National Sample Survey (NSS) and Economic Census, and the departmental statistics. Currently available information from these sources has been presented in the section. The information provided in this section would enable researchers and policy makers to draw inferences and make generalisation regarding the structure and trends in manpower utilisation. In this section, some of the main inferences and issues brought out by the data are highlighted in the following discussion.

The data organised in the sub-section (i) (tables 3.1.1 to 3.1.11) provide some indicators for assessing the utilisation potential in the economy. The data on land utilisation show that there has been a significant increase in the gross irrigated area (about 66%), and also the area sown more than once (56%) during 1980-81 to 2005-06. Yet, the gross cropped area increased only by about 11.5 per cent and the net sown area increased marginally by 1.3 per cent. It may be noted that the population increased by about 50 per cent during 1981-2001. The number of operational holdings in general increased by 70 per cent, whereas the number of operational holdings below 1 hectare increased by about 111 per cent during 1970-71 to 2000-01, indicating an increasing pressure on land.

The proportion of the workforce dependent on agriculture has declined from about 74 per cent in 1972-73 to about 58.5 per cent in 2004-05, while the share of national income originating from agriculture has declined from about 45 per cent to 18 per cent during the same period. This kind of structural change has resulted in low productivity in agriculture. Therefore, from the long-term perspective, land-based activities seem to have limited employment potential for the growing population and labour force.

There has been a continuous increase in the number of enterprises between 1980 and 2005, as reported by the Economic Census. Of the total number of enterprises, rural areas accounted for about 61 per cent and urban areas about 39 per cent in 2005. The share of own account enterprises was significantly higher than that of non-directory and directory establishments, indicating low employment generating capacity for hired workers. Own account enterprises constituted about 71 per cent in the rural areas and 54 per cent in the urban areas. The directory establishments constituted only a small proportion of the total enterprises (about 3.2 % in rural areas and 4.6 per cent in urban areas). Among the non-agricultural enterprises, maximum number of enterprises has been recorded in retail trade, followed by manufacturing and community, social & personnel services in both rural and urban areas. The lowest number of enterprises has been recorded in electricity, gas and water both in rural and urban areas. An overwhelmingly large number of non-agricultural enterprises (97 %) have employment size of 1-5, and a very small proportion of enterprises (1%) have employment size of 10 and above. During the period 1980-90, the number of units had increased by 36 per cent and between 1998 and 2005 the increase had been by 38 per cent. Correspondingly, employment per enterprise had declined from 2.9 to 2.4 between 1980 and 2005. Employment declined relatively faster during 1998-2005 as compared to that of 1980-90. By and large, a similar declining trend in employment has also been observed at the state level for the period 1998-2005. There has been thus a relatively faster decline of employment per enterprise during 1998-2005 than it was during 1980 and 1990. The increase in the number of units associated with declining employment per enterprise amply indicates that the enterprises are operating at a low productivity level.

Small-scale industries (SSI) have been playing an important role in the economy in terms of output growth, employment generation and export performance. The larger significance of this sector lies in its employment generating potential in the face of overall deceleration in employment growth. The annual compound growth of SSI (registered) has been 3.8 per cent during 1987-88 and 2001-02, while the overall employment in the economy had been about 1.7 per cent during 1987-88 and

1999-00. The growth of working units has shown a significant progress over time. It had recorded about 8.2 per cent growth per annum during 1972-73 to 2001-02. This growth was about 10 per cent during 1972-73 to 1987-88. However, the growth has decelerated to about 6.3 per cent during 1987-88 to 2001-02.

The significant changes noticed in the growth of SSI units are the increasing intensity of closed units and substantial decline in the employment per unit. Per unit employment declined from 11.8 in 1972-73 to 6.3 in 1987-88 and 4.5 in 2001-02. Across states, majority of states have experienced a fall in the share of working units and a consequent rise in the share of closed units during last three census periods. Employment per unit has declined in almost all the states. In recent years the performance of SSI units has declined, which is believed to be a result of opening up of the economy. This raises the central concern for creating an environment conducive to business and removing of policy constraints.

Sub-section (ii) (tables 3.2.1 to 3.2.38) presents information on employment characteristics by sector, location, sex, and age group and by level of education. In certain cases information is also provided across states. A striking feature observed is the significant decline in workforce participation rate (WPR) between 1993-94 and 1999-2000, particularly in rural areas. Female participation rate has declined relatively faster than their male counterparts both in rural and urban areas. But in rural areas, there has been a sharper fall in female WPR, with near stagnation in absolute numbers. Not only this, the decline is observed in all the age groups both in rural and urban areas. To some extent it may be attributed to higher attendance of children in educational institutions, and also to withdrawal of elderly persons from the labour force. Decline in WPR at younger age groups and withdrawal of elderly persons from the labour force has been generally regarded beneficial in the development process.

Recent NSS data, however, show (2004-05) a significant up-trend in the WPRs compared to 1999-00 levels. Annual growth of employment (UPSS) has shown perceptible increase from about 0.98 per cent in 1994-2000 to 2.89 per cent in 2000-05, more particularly in female employment. Female employment increased from 0.3 to 4.0 per cent while male employment rose from 1.4 to 2.6 per cent during 1994-2000 to 2000-05.

Explanation for such increase is worth examining. A cursory look into the age-specific WPRs for the year 2004-05 shows an increase in participation of rural female population and urban population (both males and females) in the age-group of 15-19. This is a major trend reversal, as a growing number of youth are not being retained in educational institutions. The decline in the WPR in the younger age-groups has been generally regarded beneficial in the process of development as it indicates higher attendance in middle, secondary education or even higher level of education. There has been also a fall in WPR in the age-group 59 and above during 1993-94 to 1999-00, which might be attributed to some extent due to retirement and voluntary withdrawal from the labour market as a result of enhanced earnings of younger population. However, this trend seems to have reversed in 2004-05 – in rural areas both male and female WPR increased and in urban area male WPR declined, but female WPR increased. This trend shows an increasing pressure in the labour market and whether school/college going and older-age (59+) population has actually reverted back into the labour market under duress conditions seem to be the most worrisome concern.

Unemployment by current daily status (CDS) which captures underemployment intensity more precisely shows a consistently higher rate of unemployment both for males and females indicating a huge unutilised labour time. Results of NSS (61st round) provide evidence of increasing unemployment rates (CDS) compared to 1999-00 levels, both for males and females in rural and urban areas. Female unemployment increased from 7 to 8.7 per cent and male unemployment rose by 7.2 to 8 per cent in rural areas, while in urban areas corresponding male unemployment and female unemployment increased from 7.3 to 7.5 and 9.4 to 11.6 respectively during 1999-00 to 2004-05.

The long-term shift in the structure of employment in rural areas shows that self-employment base has eroded systematically both for males and females. A distinct sign of increasing casualisation has also been noticed, and it is more conspicuous among females than for males. The share of regular employment has declined for males and has stagnated for females. In urban areas, however, a somewhat different trend has been noticed for both males and females. The share of self-employment has remained more or less constant for males but declined for females. The share of regular employment has declined and that of casual employment increased for males; whereas, for females the share of regular employment has increased and that of casual employment declined over the period.

Recent quinquennial survey results (61st round 2004-05), however, show distinct changes in the earlier pattern observed in 55th round (1999-00). The self-employment base in rural area is showing improvement and the share of casual employment is declining, which is more visible among females than males. Regular employment share however did not witness any significant change, it remained almost constant. In the urban area too the share of self-employment increased and that of casual employment declined both for males and females. Regular employment share increased for females but declined for males. The share of casual employment declined relatively faster for females compared to that of males.

The rise in self-employment, by and large, is indicative of low quality of employment with low wages. It is important from the policy point of view to make the employment productive and efficient through specific interventions that could help develop more dynamic and better-protected unorganised/informal sector for its progressive integration into the society.

The indicators of judging quality of employment are income levels, labour productivity, status of employment and wage rate. Some broad indication from recent NSS data reveals that wages (constant prices) declined in regular/ salaried employment in rural area (marginal increase in male wages and sharp decline in female wages) and marginal increase in casual employment in other than public works. While in the urban areas wages of both regular and casual workers declined for males and females during 1999-00 to 2004-05.

The available evidence indicates that about 34 per cent male and 68 per cent female in the rural area and 13 per cent male and 38 per cent female workforce in the urban area are illiterate. Marketable skills are dismally low among the workforce. When a substantively large proportion of workforce is illiterate with low skills, the group of persons depending on irregular or casual form of employment would have no opportunities for acquiring skills for further development. At the policy plane such situation raises issues of concern.

The sectoral distribution of workforce shows a decline from 72.5 per cent to 58.5 per cent (14 percentage points) in the share of primary sector during 1977-78 to 2004-05 – a consequent gain of 6.0 percentage points by the secondary sector and about 8.0 percentage points by the tertiary sector.

The occupational distribution of the workforce shows that there has been a continuous decline in the number of farmers, fishermen and related workers and an increase in that of administrative, executive and managerial workers; sales workers and production and related workers in rural areas. While in the urban areas professional, technical and related workers; administrative, executive and managerial workers; sales workers; service workers etc. continue to show an increasing trend in the proportion of clerical and related workers; farmers and fishermen and production workers etc. showing declining trend. The employment data show a predominance of the unorganised sector as it accounts for about 92 per cent of total employment. In any case, public sector employment is not likely to increase in the foreseeing future and one can, therefore, visualize that the major part of employment is likely to be generated in the unorganised sector. The unorganised sector is unprotected with insecure employment, absence of social security and deterioration of labour standards. There is, therefore, need to make this sector productive in the face of competitive environment and generate employment on sustainable basis through comprehensive social security system. In this connection, National Commission for Enterprises in the Unorganised Sector (NCEUS) has submitted two draft bills – one on social security and other on conditions of work and livelihood promotion for unorganised sector workers.

The Parliament has passed the Unorganised Workers' Social Security Bill 2008 which is expected to provide social security to 92 per cent unorganised workers across the country.

It is widely believed that the NSS captures the workers in a much better way than the census survey does and, therefore, the WPR reported by the NSS is higher than that of the census. In spite of this, it is often argued that the NSS -provided workforce statistics are not able to capture the work pattern and workers adequately, particularly in the invisible and informal sector activities. The significant fall in WPR as per the NSS during the 1990s, for example, does not fully explain the reasons for such a sizeable decline. It is well known that the conventional economic surveys do not capture non-market or unremunerated economic activities, hence the underestimation of workforce and income statistics; though they contribute substantially to human welfare. The Time Use Survey (TUS) has been considered comprehensive and a better measure for netting entire spectrum of work activities and work pattern of the labour force at disaggregated levels. For the first time, the Central Statistical Organisation (CSO) conducted TUS in 1998-99 and it provided estimates on WPR in six states (Haryana, Madhya Pradesh, Gujarat, Orissa, Tamil Nadu and Meghalaya) and for combined states. The WPRs observed by TUS are higher than that of conventional surveys. Female WPR, in particular, is much higher as per TUS than that the corresponding NSS rate. The time disposition by System of National Accounts (SNA), extended SNA and non-SNA brings out some interesting results. For example, females spend about ten times more time in extended SNA activities than their male counterparts, while in SNA activities females spend less than males by a little over two times. State-wise time use pattern also brings out perceptible variation in the time spent, particularly in SNA and non-SNA activities among rural and urban females.

Utilisation of manpower in research and development (R&D) establishments and expenditure is presented in sub-section (iii) (tables 3.3.1 to 3.3.14). The R&D establishments including administration and auxiliary employed 2.96 lakh persons in 2000. The employment share of R&D is about 32 per cent and the remaining pertains to other activities. The share of female employment is 11 per cent and it shows a continuous increase over time. The institutional sector employs a relatively higher proportion of R&D personnel than the industrial sector. However, there has been a significant fall in the absorption capacity of both the sectors during 1992-2005. Female R&D personnel are still mostly employed in the institutional sector. Investment in R&D is minuscule as the government spent 0.59 per cent of gross domestic product (GDP) during 2005-06. In order to withstand global competition, the government has taken various initiatives to encourage investment on R&D, both in public institutions and industry through several measures. The S&T Plan outlay of scientific departments/agencies has been increased almost three times higher in the Eleventh Five Year Plan as compared to that of Tenth Five Year Plan (Rs.25, 243 crore).

Information about working children by sex, location, activity, educational level and state is given in sub-sections (iv) (tables 3.4.1 to 3.4.6). An overall decline in the number of working children has been noted during 1981-2001. This is primarily due to improvements in the access to schooling and other complementary measures undertaken. The share of child labour in agricultural activities has declined, though in non-agricultural activities it has increased. Also, there has been a distinct shift away of working children from casual employment to self-employment pursuits while regular employment remains almost constant during 1999-00 to 2004-05.

Census 2001 figure, however, shows an increase in the number of working children over 1991 Census if marginal workers are included (12.26 million working children in the age group of 5-14 years in 2001 as compared to 11.3 million in 1991). The NSS estimates for 2004-05 (61st round) suggests that child labour in the country is around 8.9 million with a WPR of 3.4 per cent.

This is a cause of serious concern from the policy plane and requires concerted efforts to tackle the problem through three components of policy objectives enunciated in the National Policy on Child Labour (1987). First, legislative action plan emphasizing strict and effective enforcement of legal provisions relating to child labour second, focus on general development programmes for benefiting children and their families and third, project-based plan of action focusing on area with high concentration of child labour through implementation of national child labour project.

Information about population aged 60 years and above (by sex, location, workforce participation rate, industrial category, and educational level) has been provided in sub-section (v) (tables 3.5.1 to 3.5.8). Population aged 60+ accounted for about 7.4 per cent of the total population as per 2001 Census. About 35 per cent of rural and 23 per cent of urban population constituted the workforce aged 60+. Majority of these workers (80%) at the aggregate level was employed in agriculture and related activities. About 75 per cent of urban non-agricultural workers were employed in activities such as trade and commerce (28%), manufacturing (20%), services (18%), etc. About 5 per cent of workers aged 60+ has educational qualification at the level of matriculates and above. The dependency ratio in this age group has been observed to be increasing over time both in rural and in urban areas.

The last sub-section (vi) (tables 3.6.1 to 3.6.6) presents information about youth (15-34 years). The youth population constituted 33.8 per cent as per the total population in 2001 Census. The proportion of youth population has shown an overall increase and it is relatively higher among females than males. Overall youth participation rate has declined during 1991-2001. The male and female youth WPR in the rural area has declined but male WPR has declined more sharply than female WPR. Whereas, in the urban area, male WPR declined but female WPR increased marginally during the period. The proportion of female youth employed in rural areas is almost three times higher than their urban counterparts. Unemployment rate in the urban areas is higher than that of rural areas, and in particular among females. Illiteracy among women is still a problem of large magnitude in this age-group.

(i) Base for Manpower Utilisation

Table 3.1.1: Land Utilisation Pattern

(in Million Hectare)

	Item	*1970-71*	*1980-81*	*1990-91*	*2000-01P*	*2003-04P*	*2004-05P*	*2005-06P*
	Total Reported Area (I)-(IX)	**303.76**	**304.16**	**304.86**	**305.17**	**305.40**	**305.31**	**305.27**
(i)	Forests	63.92 (21.0)	67.47 (22.2)	67.80 (22.2)	69.53 (22.8)	69.73 (22.8)	69.72 (22.8)	69.79 (22.9)
(ii)	Area put to Non-Agricultural Uses	16.48 (5.4)	19.66 (6.4)	21.09 (6.9)	23.86 (7.8)	24.66 (8.1)	24.76 (8.1)	25.03 (8.2)
(iii)	Barren and Unculturable Land	28.16 (9.3)	19.96 (6.6)	19.39 (6.4)	17.60 (5.8)	17.58 (5.8)	17.58 (5.8)	17.48 (5.7)
(iv)	Permanent Pastures and Other Grazing Lands	13.26 (4.4)	11.97 (3.9)	11.40 (3.7)	10.66 (3.5)	10.44 (3.4)	10.42 (3.4)	10.42 (3.4)
(v)	Land Under-Misc. Tree Crops and Groves	4.30 (1.4)	3.61 (1.2)	3.82 (1.3)	3.43 (1.1)	3.40 (1.1)	3.38 (1.1)	3.38 (1.1)
(vi)	Culturable Waste	17.50 (5.8)	16.74 (5.5)	15.00 (4.9)	13.61 (4.5)	13.13 (4.3)	13.16 (4.3)	13.12 (4.3)
(vii)	Old Fallows	8.76 (2.9)	9.92 (3.3)	9.66 (3.2)	10.31 (3.4)	11.21 (3.7)	10.71 (3.5)	10.50 (3.4)
(viii)	Current Fallows	11.12 (3.7)	14.83 (4.9)	13.70 (4.5)	14.77 (4.8)	14.48 (4.7)	14.43 (4.7)	13.67 (4.5)
(ix)	Net Sown Area	140.27 (46.2)	140.08 (46.0)	143.00 (46.9)	141.40 (46.3)	140.97 (46.2)	141.14 (46.2)	141.89 (46.5)
(x)	Gross Cropped Area	165.79	172.63	185.74	187.37	190.20	190.42	192.80
(xi)	Area Sown More than Once	25.52	32.63	42.74	43.97	49.23	49.26	50.90
(xii)	Gross Irrigated Area	38.19	49.78	63.20	76.57	78.00	80.00	82.63

Notes: P — Provisional,
Figure within the Parentheses indicated percentage of Reported Area.

Source: Ministry of Agriculture, (Directorate of Economics and Statistics) : *Agriculture Statistics at a Glance.*

Table 3.1.2: Operational Holdings and Area Operated by Size of Holding

Size Class (Hectares)	*Number (Lakh)*					*Area Operated (Lakh Hectare)*				
	1970-71	*1980-81*	*1990-91*	*1995-96*	*2000-01**	*1970-71*	*1980-81*	*1990-91*	*1995-96*	*2000-01**
Marginal (Below 1.0)	357	501	634	712	754	146	197	249	281	298
Small (1.0-2.0)	134	161	201	216	227	193	232	288	307	321
Semi-Medium (2.0-4.0)	107	124	139	143	140	300	347	384	390	382
Medium (4.0-10.0)	79	81	76	71	66	482	485	447	414	382
Large (10.0 and above)	28	22	16	14	12	501	377	287	242	211
All Holdings	705	889	1066	1156	1199	1621	1638	1655	1634	1594

Note : * Excluding Jharkhand

Source: Ministry of Agriculture, (Directorate of Economics & Statistics) : *Agriculture Statistics at a Glance.*

Figure 3.1.A

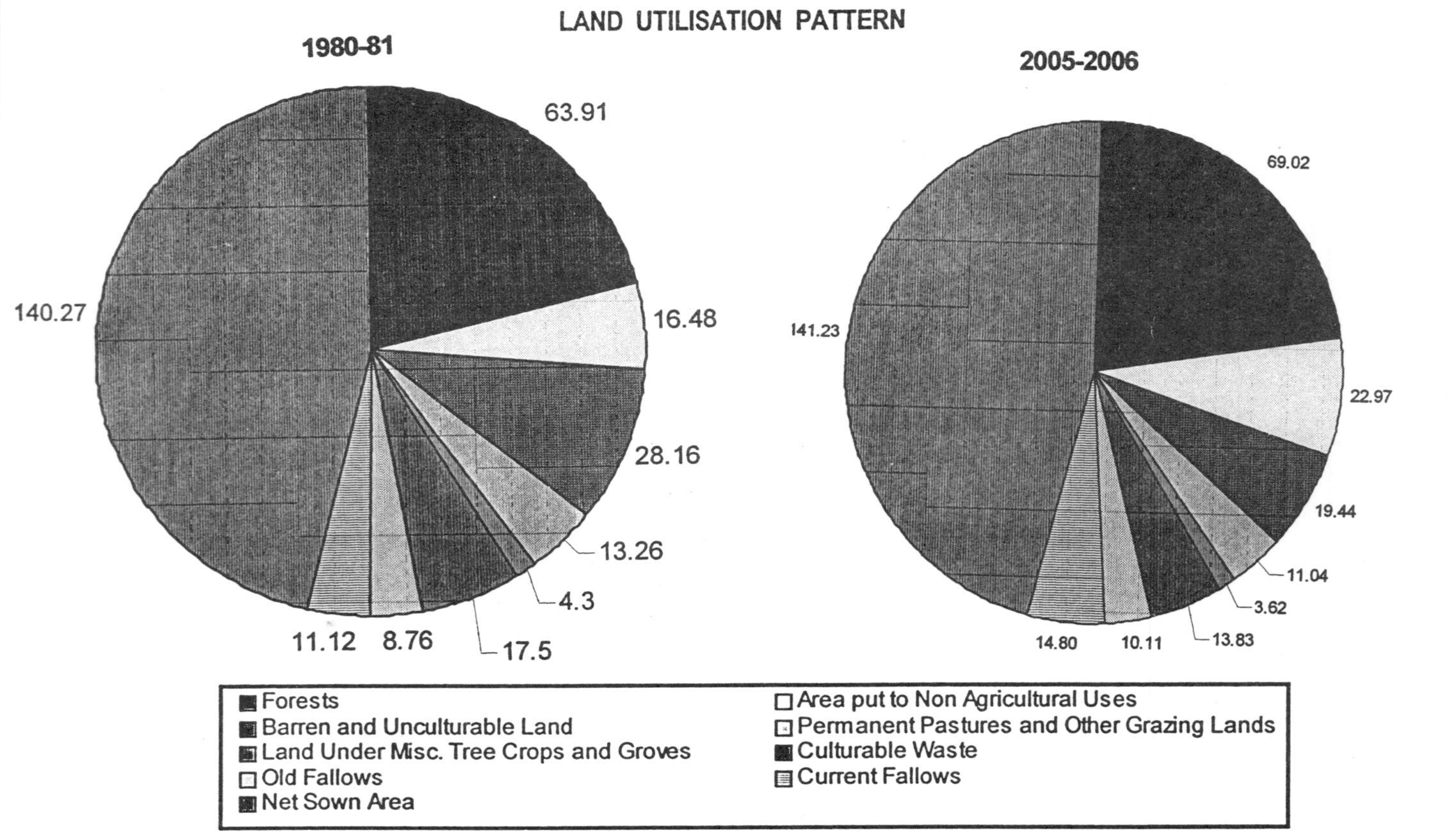

For details see Table 3.1.1

Table 3.1.3: Number of Enterprises and Employment per Enterprise, 2005

Industry	*Number of Enterprises (00)*			*Employment per Enterprise*		
	Own Account Enterprise	*Establish-ment*	*Total*	*Own Account Enterprise*	*Establishment*	
					All	*Hired*
Agriculture	51,322	9,478	60,800	1.5	1.8	3.2
Mining and Quarrying	423	425	848	1.6	6.9	12.1
Manufacturing	50,930	32,292	83,222	1.5	3.1	5.6
Electricity, Gas and Water Supply	140	512	652	1.2	6.7	8.2
Construction	2,049	1,154	3,203	1.1	2.3	4.5
Sale, Maint. & Repair of Motor Vehicles, Motor Cycles	3,203	3,964	7,167	1.2	2.6	3.8
Wholesale Trade	4,701	3,823	8,524	1.2	2.5	4.0
Retail Trade	1,05,658	43,872	1,49,530	1.2	1.7	2.8
Hotel & Restaurants	8,321	6,598	149,18	1.3	2.5	3.8
Transport & Storage	10,875	4,250	15,125	1.1	1.9	4.1
Post & Telecommunications	4,289	2,685	6,974	1.1	2.1	3.8
Financial Intermediation	995	1,926	2,921	1.5	5.6	7.8
Real Estate, Renting & Business Services	5,390	4,760	10,150	1.2	2.7	4.5
Public Administration and Defence, Compulsory Social Security	450	5,283	5,734	1.6	10.2	10.9
Education	1,991	12,423	14,414	1.4	5.2	5.8
Health and Social Work	3,113	4,694	7,807	1.2	3.4	4.8
Other Communicty, Social and Personal Service Activities	15,541	10,721	26,262	2.1	1.9	1.8
Other Sectors (Unspecified)	9	9	18	2.0	3.1	3.9
Non-Agriculture Activities	**2,18,078**	**1,39,392**	**3,57,470**	**1.3**	**2.5**	**4.5**
All Agricultural & Non Agricultural Activities	**2,69,400**	**1,48,870**	**4,18,270**	**1.3**	**2.4**	**4.3**

Notes: Total may not tally with all due rounding off.

(i) Agricultural enterprise has been defined as one engaged forming of animals, agricultural services, hunding trapping and game propagation, forestry and logging and fishing.

Source: Ministry of Statistics and Programme Implementation, Central Statistical Organisation: *Economic Census–2005.*

Table 3.1.4: Growth of Enterprises* and Employment per Enterprise

State/Union Territory	*Number of Enterprises (Lakh)*				*Employment per Enterprise*			
	1980	*1990*	*1998*	*2005*	*1980*	*1990*	*1998*	*2005*
States								
Andhra Prdesh	16.14	24.87	29.02	39.97	2.92	2.71	2.59	2.80
Arunachal Pradesh	0.11	0.21	0.21	0.28	4.01	4.48	3.89	3.93
Assam	@	4.95	5.93	9.84	@	3.41	3.70	2.24
Bihar	10.45	12.28	14.43	12.25	2.66	2.81	2.38	1.85
Chattisgarh	—	—	—	6.37	—	—	—	2.38
Delhi	2.88	4.55	6.86	7.58	5.08	4.58	5.10	4.69
Goa	0.48	0.61	0.72	0.73	3.54	3.60	3.01	3.12
Gujarat	11.88	14.98	19.15	24.26	3.07	3.16	2.75	2.76
Haryana	3.20	4.57	5.33	8.33	3.05	2.96	2.93	2.69
Himachal Pradesh	1.39	1.83	2.25	2.68	2.47	2.56	2.56	2.46
Jammu & Kashmir	2.00	@	2.16	3.25	2.49	@	2.20	2.31
Jharkhand	—	—	—	4.91	—	—	—	2.35
Karnataka	13.75	16.94	19.12	25.39	2.81	3.00	2.75	2.50
Kerala	8.72	12.29	15.65	28.04	2.81	2.68	2.46	2.05
Madhya Pradesh	13.41	18.73	21.24	17.35	2.45	2.61	2.47	2.29
Maharashtra	18.39	26.24	32.34	42.25	3.67	3.42	3.23	2.68
Manipur	0.33	0.61	0.80	1.05	2.92	2.57	2.49	2.25
Meghalaya	0.32	0.50	0.56	0.83	3.35	3.40	3.26	2.92
Mizoram	0.13	0.23	0.25	0.48	3.40	3.13	3.11	2.23
Nagaland	0.16	0.24	0.30	0.35	4.76	5.46	5.91	5.00
Orissa	8.04	10.94	14.50	18.30	2.43	2.39	2.13	2.02
Punjab	4.63	5.99	7.17	10.72	2.88	2.95	2.93	2.52
Rajasthan	9.64	11.69	15.31	19.61	2.41	2.43	2.31	2.19
Sikkim	0.08	0.11	0.13	0.19	3.70	4.43	3.64	3.58
Tamil Nadu	17.68	21.11	25.14	44.33	2.91	2.95	2.86	2.27
Tripura	0.54	0.85	1.04	1.89	2.51	2.58	2.57	2.04
Uttarakhand	—	—	—	3.25	—	—	—	2.27
Uttar Pradesh	21.66	26.33	30.43	40.21	2.65	2.62	2.46	2.03
West Bengal	17.04	27.50	32.34	42.05	3.14	2.71	2.71	2.39
Union Territories								
Andaman and Nicobar Islands	0.07	0.12	0.14	0.13	5.25	4.56	4.56	4.08
Chandigarh	0.16	0.33	0.40	0.64	7.64	6.09	5.47	3.92
Dadra and Nagar Haveli	0.02	0.03	0.01	0.08	3.04	5.36	8.27	8.38
Daman and Diu	0.04	0.05	0.06	0.10	3.00	3.81	5.07	6.20
Lakshadweep	0.05	0.05	0.05	0.03	3.01	3.54	3.48	4.00
Pondicherry	0.23	0.31	0.43	0.50	3.56	3.94	4.25	3.90
All India	183.62	250.02	303.49	418.27	2.92	2.88	2.74	2.41

Notes: * Include own-account enterprises.
@ Census could not be conducted.

Source: Ministry of Statistics and Programme Implementation, Central Statistical Organisation : *Economic Census–1980, 1990, 1998 and 2005.*

Table 3.1.5: Number of Enterprises by Type of Enterprise and Major Industry Division, 2005

(Thousands)

Activity Group	*Rural*				*Urban*				*Combined*			
	OAE	*NDE*	*DE*	*ALL*	*OAE*	*NDE*	*DE*	*ALL*	*OAE*	*NDE*	*DE*	*ALL*
Agricultural Activities	4,848	802	59	5,709	284	77	10	371	5132	880	68	6,080
Mining & Quarrying	31	16	14	61	11	10	3	24	42	25	17	85
Manufacturing	3,578	1,334	247	5,159	1,515	1,328	320	3,163	5,093	2,661	568	8,322
Electricity, Gas and Water	9	29	5	43	5	11	6	23	14	39	12	65
Construction	116	45	9	171	88	49	12	149	205	94	21	320
Sale, Maint & Repair of Moter Vehicies, Moterecycles	135	93	9	238	185	259	35	479	320	352	44	717
Wholesale Trade	261	97	11	368	209	240	35	484	470	336	46	852
Retail Trade	6,170	1,562	57	7,789	4,396	2,595	174	7,164	10,566	4,156	231	14,953
Hotels & Restaurants	526	248	22	796	306	320	70	696	832	567	93	1,492
Transport & Storage	640	197	16	853	448	183	28	659	1087	380	45	1513
Post & Telecommunication	186	115	5	307	243	132	16	391	429	247	21	697
Financial Intermediation	45	62	22	129	55	61	48	164	99	123	70	292
Real Estate, Renting and Business Services	263	130	12	405	275	286	49	610	539	416	60	1,015
Public Administration and Defence, Compulsory Social Security	31	299	60	390	14	73	96	183	45	372	156	573
Education	94	764	218	1,076	106	134	126	365	199	898	344	1,441
Health and Social Work	181	223	24	428	130	177	46	353	311	400	70	781
Other Community, Social & Personal Service Activities	997	586	32	1,615	557	411	43	1,011	1,554	997	75	2,626
Others (Unspecified)	1	N	N	1	N	N	N	1	1	1	N	2
All Non-agricultural	13,262	5,800	765	19,827	8,546	6,265	1,109	15,920	21,808	12,066	1,874	35,747
All Agricultural and Non Agricultural Activities	18,110	6,603	823	25,536	8,830	6,343	1,118	16,291	26,940	12,945	1,942	41,827

Notes: N : Negligible.
OAE : Own-Account Enterprises.
DE : Directory Establishment.
NDE : Non Directory Establishment.

Source: Ministry of Statistics and Programme Implementation, Central Statistical Organisation : *Economic Census–2005,* All India Report.

Table 3.1.6: Number of Enterprises by Size of Employment and State/Union Territory, 2005

(in Hundred)

State/Union Territory	*Size class of Employment*			
	1-5	*6-9*	*10 and above*	*All Classes*
States				
Andhra Pradesh	37,764	1,319	887	39,970
Arunachal Pradesh	257	14	16	287
Assam	9,353	374	110	9,837
Bihar	11,947	244	55	12,246
Chhattisgarh	6,082	192	99	6,373
Delhi	6,496	892	189	7,577
Goa	681	35	19	735
Gujarat	23,037	885	339	24,260
Haryana	7,914	251	174	8,339
Himachal Pradesh	2,526	85	67	2,678
Jammu & Kashmir	3,085	104	60	3,249
Jharkhand	4,721	141	52	4914
Karnataka	23,751	1258	380	25,389
Kerala	26,975	625	438	28,038
Madhya Pradesh	16,570	599	184	17,353
Maharashtra	39,693	1,730	830	42,253
Manipur	1,002	33	12	1,047
Meghalaya	770	41	21	832
Mizoram	451	16	10	477
Nagaland	295	44	17	356
Orissa	17,643	467	193	18,303
Punjab	10,174	367	176	10,717
Rajasthan	18,749	631	235	19,615
Sikkim	176	10	8	194
Tamil Nadu	42,372	1,281	31	44,334
Tripura	1,830	33	31	1,894
Uttarakhand	3,120	84	48	3,252
Uttar Pradesh	38,992	954	260	40,206
West Bengal	39,879	1,521	647	42,047
Union Territories				
Andaman and Nicobar Islands	120	8	6	135
Chandigarh	597	31	20	648
Dadra and Nagar Haveli	69	6	10	85
Daman and Diu	81	9	11	102
Lakshadweep	27	3	2	32
Pondicherry	450	23	22	496
Total Enterprises	397,649	14,311	6,310	418,270

Note: Totals may not tally due to rounding off.

Source: Ministry of Statistics and Programme Implementation. Central Stastical Organisation, *Economic Census–2005,* All India Report.

Table 3.1.7: Number of Own-Account Enterprises by Size of Employment, 2005

Location	*Item*	*Size of Employment*			
		1-5	*6-9*	*10 and above*	*All*
		Agriculture			
Rural	Enterprises(000)	4,824.3 (99.5)	21.3 (0.4)	2.4 (0.1)	4,848.0 (100.0)
	Employment (Lakh)	72.4 (97.5)	1.4(1.9)	0.4 (0.6)	74.2 (100.0)
Urban	Enterprises(000)	282.6 (99.4)	1.5 (0.5)	0.0 (0.1)	284.2 (100.0)
	Employment (Lakh)	4.0 (97.1)	0.1 (2.4)	0.0 (0.5)	4.1 (100.0)
Total	Enterprises(000)	5,106.9 (99.5)	22.8 (0.4)	2.5 (0.5)	5,132.2 (100.0)
	Employment (Lakh)	76.5 (97.5)	1.5 (1.9)	0.4 (0.6)	78.4 (100.0)
		Non-Agriculture			
Rural	Enterprises(000)	13,198.2 (99.5)	50.3 (0.4)	13.7 (0.1)	13,262.2 (100.0)
	Employment (Lakh)	167.1 (96.6)	3.6 (2.0)	2.3 (1.4)	173.0 (100.0)
Urban	Enterprises(000)	8,514.5 (99.6)	27.1 (0.3)	4.0 (0.1)	8,545.7 (100.0)
	Employment (Lakh)	103.1 (97.4)	1.9 (1.8)	0.9 (0.8)	105.9 (100.0)
Total	Enterprises(000)	21,712.7 (99.5)	77.4 (0.4)	17.7 (0.1)	21,807.8 (100.0)
	Employment (Lakh)	270.2 (96.9)	5.5 (2.0)	3.2 (1.1)	278.9 (100.0)

Notes: (*i*) Agricultural enterprise has been defined as one engaged livestock production, agricultural services, hunting, trapping and game propagation, forestry and logging and fishing. Establishment engaged in activities pertaining to crop production and plantation are excluded from the coverage.

(*ii*) Figures within Parantheses are percentage to are classes respectively.

(*iii*) Figures mey not tally with all due to rounding off.

Source: Ministry of Statistics and Programme Implemention, Central Statistical Organisation : *Economic Census–2005.*

Table 3.1.8: Number of Establishments by Size of Employment, 2005

Location	*Item*	*Size of Employment*			
		1-5	*6-9*	*10 and above*	*All*
		Agriculture			
Rural	Establishments (000)	802.3 (93.2)	42.9 (5.1)	15.8 (1.7)	861.0 (100.0)
	Employment (Lakh)	17.9 (65.3)	3.0 (10.9)	6.6 (23.8)	27.5 (100.0)
Urban	Establishments (000)	77.3 (89.0)	7.3 (8.4)	2.2 (2.6)	86.8 (100.0)
	Employment (Lakh)	1.9 (59.5)	0.5 (15.8)	0.8 (24.7)	3.2 (100.0)
Total	Establishments (000)	879.5 (92.8)	50.1 (5.3)	18.2 (1.9)	947.8 (100.0)
	Employment (Lakh)	19.9 (64.7)	3.5 (11.4)	7.3 (23.9)	30.7 (100.0)
		Non-Agriculture			
Rural	Establishments (000)	5800.3 (88.3)	520.9 (7.9)	243.7 (3.8)	6,564.9 (100.0)
	Employment (Lakh)	122.5 (49.8)	37.9 (15.4)	85.5 (34.8)	245.9 (100.0)
Urban	Establishments (000)	6265.4 (85.0)	759.9 (10.0)	349.0 (5.0)	7,374.3 (100.0)
	Employment (Lakh)	159.7 (42.4)	54.9 (14.6)	161.0 (43.0)	375.0 (100.0)
Total	Establishments (000)	12,065.7 (86.6)	1280.8 (9.2)	592.7 (4.2)	13,939.2 (100.0)
	Employment (Lakh)	281.6 (45.4)	92.8 (14.9)	246.6 (39.7)	621.0 (100.0)

Notes: (*i*) Agricultural enterprise has been defined as one engaged livestock production, agricultural services, hunting, trapping and game propagation, forestry and logging and fishing. Establishment engaged in activities pertaining to crop production and plantation are excelueded from the coverage.

(*ii*) Figures within Parantheses are percentage to all clesses respectively.

(*iii*) Figures may not tally with all due to rounding off.

Source: Ministry of Statistics and Programme Implementation, Central Statistical Organisation : *Economic Census*–2005.

Figure 3.1.B

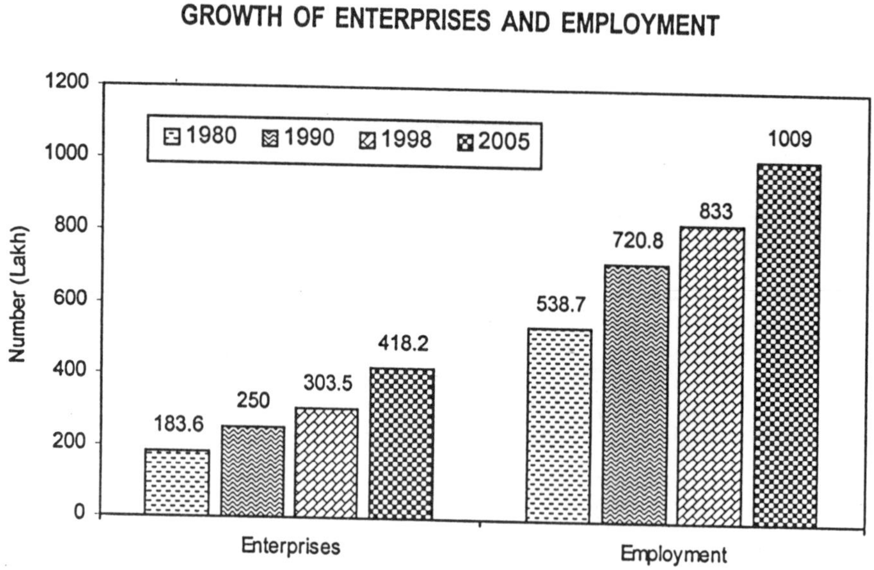

For details see Table 3.1.4

Figure 3.1.C

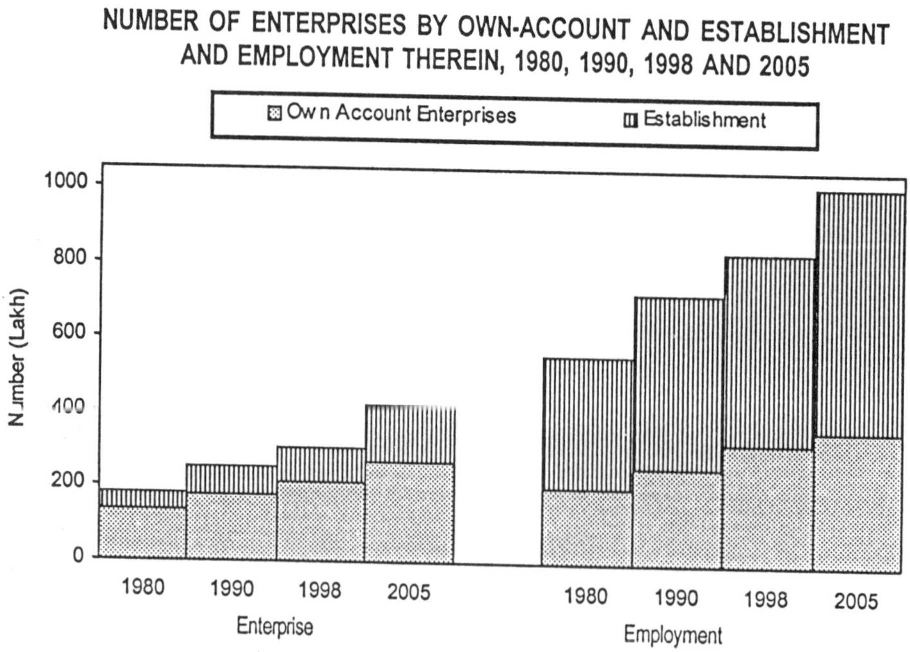

For details see Table 3.1.7 and 3.1.8

Table 3.1.9 : State-wise Performance of Small Scale Industries(Registered)

State/Union Territory	1st Census (1972-73)			2nd Census(1987-88)			3rd Census(2001-02)		
	Working* Units	Closed Units	Employment (00)	Working* Units	Closed Units	Employment (00)	Working Units	Closed Units	Employment (00)
States									
Andhra Pradesh	8091	2917	787	39210	14813	2761	62917	38582	3834
Arunachal Pradesh	11	11	2	326	36	28	255	248	12
Assam	1648	402	197	4430	1732	345	14453	10338	647
Bihar	5260	1975	615	34822	14812	1818	52170	20525	1368
Chhattishgarh	-	-	-	-	-	-	33909	27830	912
Delhi	5102	1828	649	10038	5020	1220	7360	8357	863
Goa	637	172	73	2772	957	199	2139	2327	166
Gujarat	9904	4107	1145	34453	18977	2770	138537	39159	5788
Haryana	4591	2876	485	23356	20981	1057	39584	27546	2410
Himachal Pradesh	1495	634	59	6983	2856	255	10891	6509	376
Jammu & Kashmir	1039	706	96	9080	4031	407	14625	22709	505
Jharkhand	-	-	-	-	-	-	18322	13822	709
Karnataka	5618	2645	644	40525	14629	2440	110487	46611	4771
Kerala	6205	3885	1265	25717	11763	1693	146988	74832	5405
Madhya Pradesh	7701	5585	596	73892	35479	1588	101939	65649	2496
Maharashtra	15358	5019	2398	29856	10925	3559	83098	54243	6311
Manipur	485	130	34	2078	169	102	4599	1226	197
Meghalaya	164	68	12	587	136	38	1939	1908	105
Mizoram	61	-	3	917	306	42	2733	1313	92
Nagaland	38	7	4	183	83	31	568	129	49
Orissa	1799	412	186	8287	3607	693	12366	9708	807
Punjab	13675	7466	1235	45339	21701	2062	65015	82731	3371
Rajasthan	7062	4916	457	29043	17528	1226	43145	36847	1997
Sikkim	NA	-	NA	66	36	10	174	155	12
Tamil Nadu	16002	6071	2152	57213	24825	5364	180032	127185	8826
Tripura	246	82	17	809	603	101	959	1077	117
Uttaranchal	-	-	-	-	-	-	15285	12100	407
Uttar Pradesh	12851	8471	1600	53282	37249	3489	162938	122282	5824
West Bengal	13931	5835	1762	45954	36607	3118	42148	26080	2546
Union Territories									
Andaman and Nicobar Islands	NA	-	NA	323	88	17	673	515	25
Chandigarh	284	160	29	1310	640	106	1281	1405	105
Dadra and Nagar Haveli	25	9	4	149	33	21	693	423	129
Damanand Diu	-	-	-	147	46	12	1026	454	253
Lakshadweep	-	-	-	-	-	-	68	16	-
Pondicherry	294	171	26	1221	722	87	1721	2586	197
All India* Total	139577	66560	16532	582368	301390	36658	1374174	887427	61635

Notes: Total registered SSI units cover all small scale sector units registered with Directorters of Industries and falling within the purview of Small Industries Development Organisation.

* SSI units for which data were tabulated.

Sources: Development Commissioner, Small Scale Industries, Ministry of Industry:

(i) *Report on Census of Small Scale Industrial Units, 1972-73, Vol. I & II.*

(ii) *Report on the Second All India Census of Small Scale Industrial Units, 1987-88.*

(iii) *Final Results, Third All India Census of Small Scale Industries, 2001-02.*

Table 3.1.10: Number of Mines				
Year	*Fuel*	*Metallic Minerals*	*Non-Metallic Minerals*	*All Minerals*
1986	501	776	3,148	4,425
1991	525	758	3,017	4,300
1996	565	696	2,374	3,635
1997	578	683	2,280	3,541
1998	575	612	2,166	3,352
1999	567	622	2,095	3,283
2000	611	572	2,027	3,210
2001	596	565	2,030	3,191
2002	570	574	2,049	3,193
2003	562	591	1,992	3,145
2004	562	612	1,958	3,132
2005(P)	562	615	1,991	3,168
2006 (P)	572	589	1,801	2,970

Note: @ Following nationalisation and amalgamation in 1974, the number of coal mines dropped to 394 in 1976.

Source: Central Statistical Organisation : *Statistical Abstract, 2007.*

Table 3.1.11: Monthly Average of Electricity Generated (Crore KWH)				
Year	*Thermal Plants*	*Hydel Plants*	*Nuclear Plants*	*Total*
1985-86	951.0	424.5	41.5	1,417.0
1990-91	1,553.8	596.1	52.0	2,201.9
1995-96	2,496.9	604.3	66.3	3,167.5
1996-97	2,635.8	574.0	74.7	3,284.5
1997-98	2,805.5	621.4	84.1	3,511.5
1998-99	2,945.1	694.9	98.9	3,738.9
1999-00	3,189.6	678.0	109.0	3,976.6
2000-01	3,396.5	619.6	139.9	4,156.0
2001-02	3,508.9	614.0	160.4	4,283.3
2002-03	3,738.0	531.9	160.4	4,430.3
2003-04	3,889.1	615.0	147.7	4,651.8
2004-05	4,466.8	661.0	164.5	5,292.3
2005-06	4,648.7	675.9	144.9	5,469.5
2006-07	4,911.8	803.1	169.6	5,884.5
2007-08	5,212.0	763.6	133.9	6,109.5

Note: Data relates to public utilities.
* Includes data for gas, diesel plants also.

Source: Central Statistical Organisation : *Monthly Abstract of Statistics.*

(ii) Employment Characteristics

Table 3.2.1: Educational Composition of Rural Workforce

Educational Level	*1987-88*		*1993-94*		*1999-2000*		*2004-05*		*2005-06*	
	Male	*Female*	*Male*	*Female*	*Male*	*Female*	*Male*	*Female*	*Male*	*Female*
Illiterate	48.9	82.9	43.7	78.5	39.6	73.9	34.2	67.8	32.4	64.9
Literate but up to Primary	29.8	12.1	29.1	14.2	27.3	15.5	29.6	18.1	30.1	19.5
Middle	11.4	3.1	13.7	4.3	16.3	6.2	18.0	8.0	19.2	9.7
Secondary/ Higher Secondary	8.0	1.6	10.8	2.5	13.5	3.7	13.4	4.5	14.1	4.8
Graduate and above	1.9	0.3	2.6	0.4	3.3	0.6	4.8	1.6	4.2	1.1
Total	100.0	100.0	100.0	100.0	100.0	100.0	100.0	100.0	100.0	100.0

Note: Figures relate to usual status of individuals. Figures for the years 1987-88, 1993-94 and 1999-2000 relate to population age 15 years and above.

Sources: National Sample Survey Organisation :
Sarvekshana, Special No., July 87-June 88, (43rd Round).
Vol. XX, July 93-June 94, (50th Round).
Report No. 458, 515 & 522 *Employment and Unemployment in India,* 1999-2000, (55th Round.) 2004-05, (61st Round) and 2005-06 (62nd Round).

Table 3.2.2: Educational Composition of Urban Workforce

Educational Level	*1987-88*		*1993-94*		*1999-2000*		*2004-05*		*2005-06*	
	Male	*Female*	*Male*	*Female*	*Male*	*Female*	*Male*	*Female*	*Male*	*Female*
Illiterate	20.3	55.1	18.4	48.9	16.0	44.0	13.2	37.7	12.6	34.9
Literate but up to Primary	30.9	19.4	25.8	19.7	21.9	17.8	22.9	19.8	22.1	20.7
Middle	16.0	6.4	17.3	8.4	18.9	9.3	19.4	10.6	22.1	12.8
Secondary/Hr. Sec.	21.3	10.7	24.2	12.3	26.4	14.2	24.0	10.9	24.5	13.3
Graduate and above	11.5	8.5	14.3	10.6	16.8	14.7	20.5	21.0	18.7	18.3
Total	100.0	100.0	100.0	100.0	100.0	100.0	100.0	100.00	100.0	100.0

Sources: National Sample Survey Organisation :
Sarvekshana, Special No., July 87-June 88, (43rd Round).
Vol. XX, July 93-June 94, (50th Round).
Report No. 458, 515 and 522 *Employment and Unemployment in India,* 1999-2000, (55th Round.) 2004-05, (61st Round) and 2005-06 (62nd Round).

Figure 3.2.D

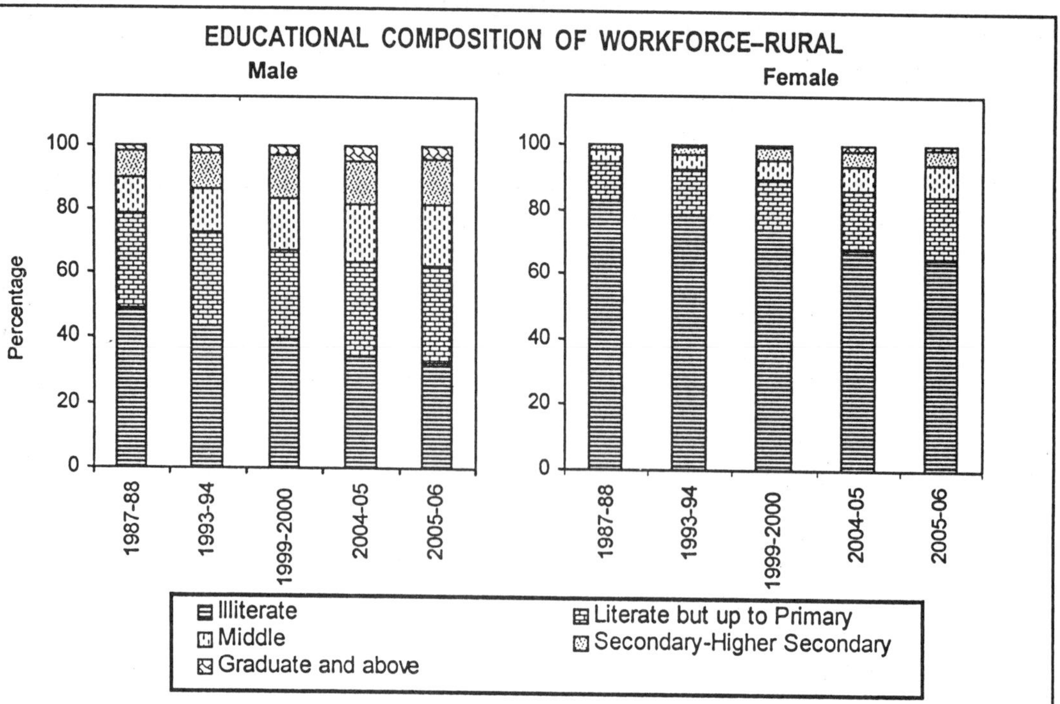

For details see Table 3.2.1

Figure 3.2.E

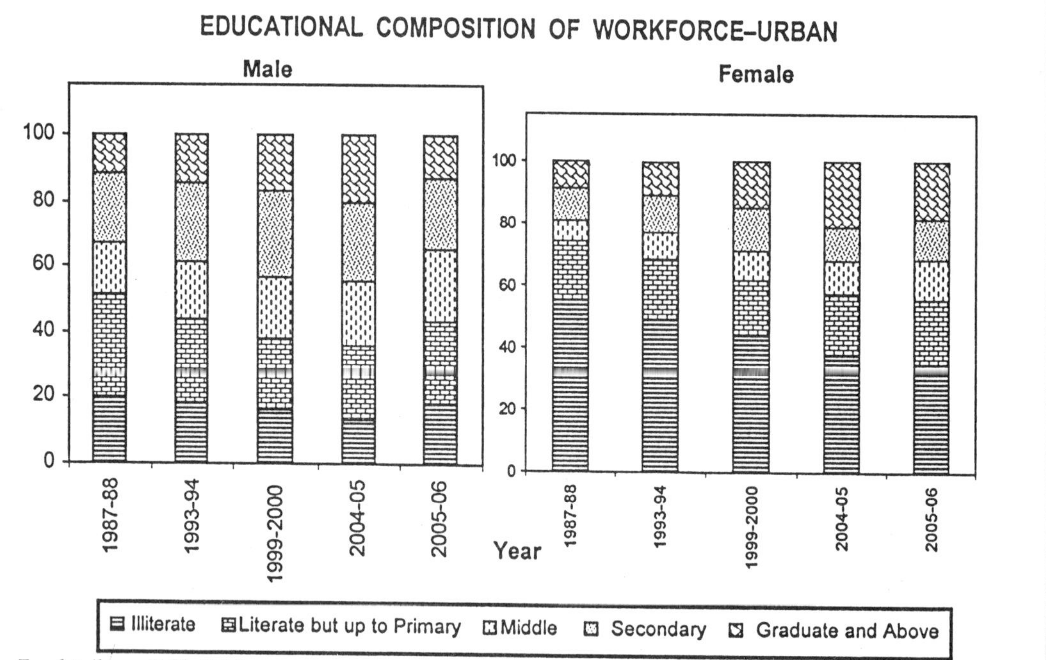

For details see Table 3.2.2

Table 3.2.3 : Workforce Participation Rates (WFPR) and Estimates (Million) of Employment

Year	Rural			Urban			Total		
	Male	*Female*	*Person*	*Male*	*Female*	*Person*	*Male*	*Female*	*Person*
1977-78									
WFPR	55.2	33.1	44.4	50.8	15.6	34.1	54.3	29.7	42.3
Employment	141.4	80.1	221.5	38.8	10.4	49.2	180.2	90.5	270.7
1987-88									
WFPR	53.9	32.3	43.4	50.6	15.2	33.7	53.1	28.5	41.2
Employment	160.5	92.0	252.5	55.0	14.5	69.5	215.5	106.5	332.0
1993-94									
WFPR	55.3	32.8	44.4	52.1	15.5	34.7	54.5	28.6	42.0
Employment	186.6	103.7	290.3	64.5	17.3	81.8	251.1	121.0	372.1
1999-2000									
WFPR	53.1	29.9	41.7	51.8	13.9	33.7	52.7	25.9	39.7
Employment	196.8	104.0	300.8	77.1	18.9	96.0	273.9	122.9	396.8
2001-02									
WFPR	54.6	31.4	43.3	55.3	13.9	35.5	54.8	27.4	41.5
Employment	210.0	114.3	324.3	84.7	19.2	103.9	294.7	133.5	428.2
2004-05									
WFPR	54.6	32.7	43.9	54.9	16.6	36.5	54.7	28.7	42.0
Employment	201.7	116.1	317.8	70.7	19.7	90.4	272.4	135.8	408.2
2005-06									
WFPR	54.9	31.0	43.3	54.0	14.3	35.0	54.7	27.0	41.3
Employment	208.5	111.9	320.4	66.4	16.1	82.5	274.9	128.0	402.9

Notes: Figures relate to usual status of individuals. The WFPR represent size of workforce as percent of population.
These rates were applied to the Estimated Population of the relavant Year based on Census.

Sources: National Sample Survey Organisation :
(*i*) *Sarvekshana*, Vol. V, July 77-June 78, 32nd Round. (*ii*) Report No. 481, *Household Consumer Expenditure and Employment-Unemployment Situation in India*, 2001-2002. (*iii*) Report No. 458, 515 and 522, *Employment and unemployment Situation in India*, 1999-2000, 2004-05 and 2005-06.

Table 3.2.4: Workforce Participaton Rates according to Current Weekly Status and Current Daily Status

Year	Current Weekly Status				Current Daily Status			
	Rural		Urban		Rural		Urban	
	Male	*Female*	*Male*	*Female*	*Male*	*Female*	*Male*	*Female*
1977-78	51.9	23.2	49.0	12.5	48.8	19.4	47.2	10.9
1983	51.1	22.7	49.2	11.8	48.2	19.8	47.3	10.6
1987-88	50.4	22.0	49.2	11.9	50.1	20.7	47.7	11.0
1993-94	53.0	26.7	51.1	13.9	50.4	22.0	49.8	12.0
1999-00	51.0	25.3	50.9	12.8	47.8	20.4	49.0	11.1
2004-05	52.4	27.5	53.7	15.2	48.8	21.6	51.9	13.3
2005-06	52.4	25.7	52.9	13.2	49.1	20.3	51.3	11.8

Note: NA — Not Available

Sources: National Sample Survey Organisation :
(*i*) Sarvekshana, Vol, V, July 77-June 78, 32nd Round.
(*i*) Report No. 455, 515 and 522 *Employment and Unemployment in India*, 1999-2000, 2004-05 and 2005-065.

Figure 3.2. F

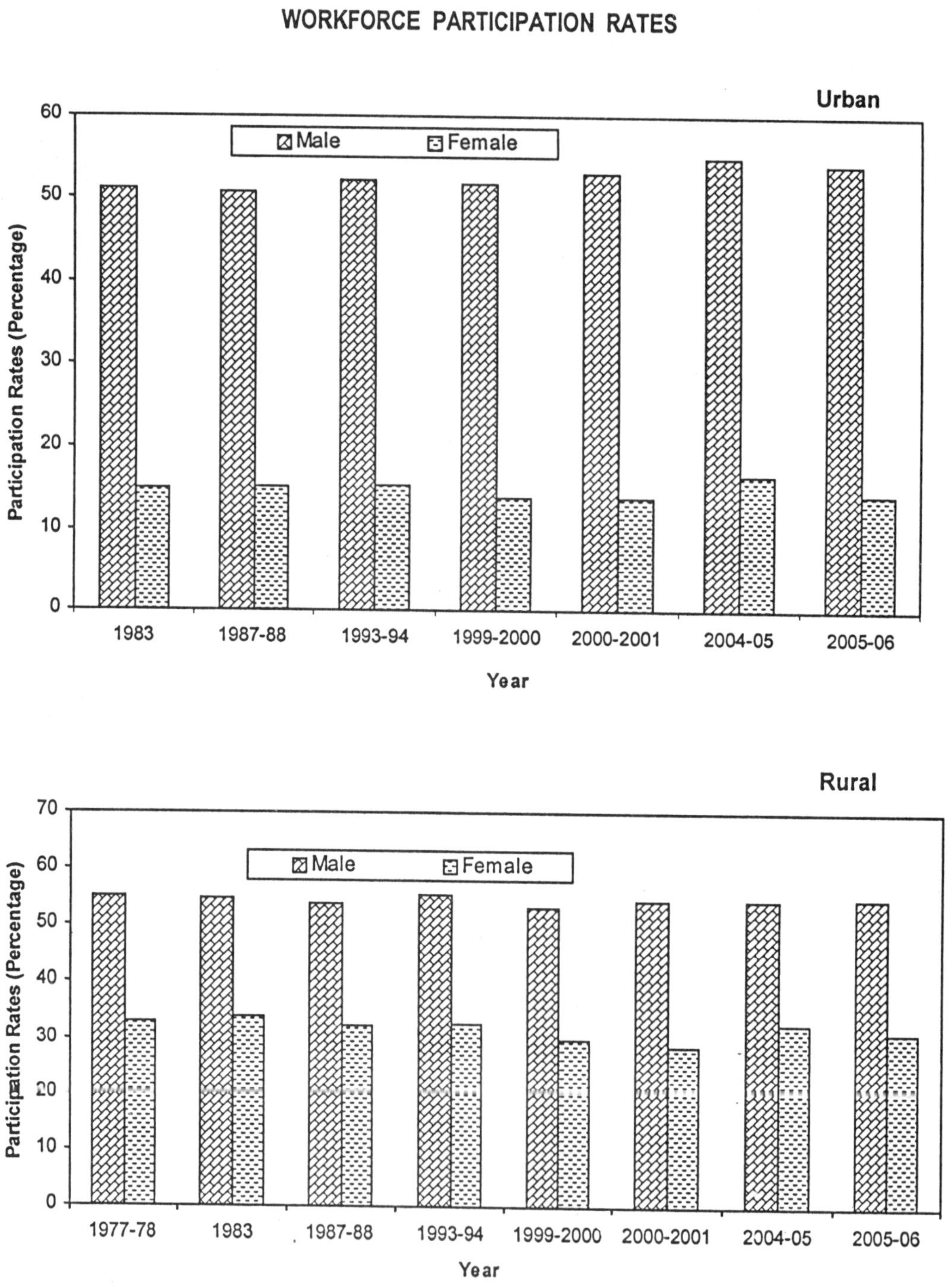

For details see Table 3.2.3

Table 3.2.5: Workforce Participation Rates by State/Union Territory, 2005-06

State/Union Territory	*Rural*			*Urban*		
	Male	*Female*	*Person*	*Male*	*Female*	*Person*
States						
1. Andhra Pradesh	61.3 (60.5)	45.4 (48.3)	53.1 (54.4)	56.4 (56.0)	19.3 (22.7)	38.0 (39.2)
2. Arunachal Pradesh	NE (50.0)	NE (41.0)	NE (45.8)	NE (46.1)	NE (14.8)	NE (31.9)
3. Assam	54.2 (55.1)	20.7 (20.9)	38.1 (39.1)	56.3 (55.1)	10.1 (10.9)	38.2 (33.6)
4. Bihar	48.8 (47.7)	10.6 (13.8)	30.4 (31.6)	43.4 (55.2)	7.8 (6.5)	27.0 (27.2)
5. Chattisgarh	61.1 (56.5)	47.5 (45.4)	54.2 (50.9)	54.0 (52.9)	17.7 (18.1)	36.5 (36.4)
6. Delhi	49.2 (51.6)	8.6 (4.7)	32.6 (31.1)	49.4 (53.5)	7.5 (8.8)	31.5 (33.4)
7. Goa	50.2 (52.4)	10.8 (18.8)	29.2 (34.2)	53.3 (53.4)	24.7 (18.8)	39.4 (36.3)
8. Gujarat	57.9 (59.3)	37.8 (42.7)	48.2 (51.3)	57.7 (57.8)	12.5 (15.1)	36.5 (37.7)
9. Haryana	48.8 (52.2)	31.7 (31.7)	40.8 (42.4)	53.1 (51.1)	16.3 (13.2)	36.3 (35.9)
10. Himachal Pradesh	55.2 (55.5)	50.0 (50.6)	52.6 (53.0)	58.2 (61.9)	21.5 (24.1)	41.0 (45.6)
11. Jammu and Kashmir	52.3 (55.2)	23.3 (26.7)	38.3 (41.6)	52.2 (52.6)	10.2 (11.2)	32.6 (33.1)
12. Jharkhand	52.6 (53.5)	32.5 (31.3)	42.8 (42.2)	47.2 (47.2)	8.1 (13.4)	23.0 (31.1)
13. Karnataka	59.6 (62.3)	41.4 (45.9)	50.6 (54.2)	56.2 (57.6)	17.9 (18.1)	37.5 (38.6)
14. Kerala	56.5 (55.9)	25.4 (25.6)	40.3 (40.0)	57.3 (54.7)	19.4 (20.0)	35.2 (37.1)
15. Madhya Pradesh	55.0 (54.4)	34.7 (36.6)	45.3 (45.9)	50.3 (52.5)	12.9 (15.4)	32.5 (34.7)
16. Maharashtra	58.5 (56.6)	42.3 (47.4)	50.7 (52.1)	54.5 (56.0)	14.5 (19.0)	35.4 (38.4)
17. Manipur	NE (52.4)	NE (35.1)	NE (44.0)	NE (45.6)	NE (22.1)	NE (33.8)
18. Meghalaya	NE (57.2)	NE (47.8)	NE (52.5)	NE (45.4)	NE (30.3)	NE (37.3)
19. Mizoram	NE (59.4)	NE (44.1)	NE (52.1)	NE (48.4)	NE (28.1)	NE (38.3)
20. Nagaland	NE (54.9)	NE (50.4)	NE (52.7)	NE (45.7)	NE (25.7)	NE (36.4)
21. Orissa	59.9 (58.6)	34.2 (32.2)	46.8 (45.2)	54.4 (50.4)	12.1 (14.8)	34.6 (33.4)
22. Punjab	52.7 (54.9)	28.8 (32.2)	41.5 (44.0)	54.5 (57.2)	11.9 (13.3)	35.0 (36.5)
23. Rajasthan	52.4 (51.0)	40.3 (40.7)	46.5 (45.9)	50.2 (50.8)	11.6 (18.2)	31.8 (34.9)
24. Sikkim	NE (55.4)	NE (31.8)	NE (44.3)	NE (54.5)	NE (16.8)	NE (36.9)
25. Tamil Nadu	60.7 (59.4)	44.6 (46.1)	52.5 (52.8)	59.1 (59.3)	22.1 (24.1)	40.6 (41.8)
26. Tripura	NE (54.9)	NE (8.5)	NE (32.3)	NE (50.4)	NE (10.0)	NE (29.8)
27. Uttaranchal	51.0 (52.3)	40.6 (42.7)	45.9 (47.4)	45.5 (51.9)	8.4 (12.7)	21.1 (33.2)
28. Uttar Pradesh	50.0 (49.6)	22.4 (24.0)	37.0 (37.1)	50.9 (52.4)	8.1 (11.7)	30.4 (33.1)
29. West Bengal	58.3 (57.4)	19.0 (17.8)	39.7 (37.9)	58.6 (59.5)	14.9 (15.5)	38.0 (38.4)
30. North-Eastern States	55.2 (NA)	26.3 (NA)	41.1 (NA)	49.2 (NA)	19.7 (NA)	34.8 (NA)
Union Territores	58.7 (NA)	25.5 (NA)	44.3 (NA)	50.4 (NA)	15.6 (NA)	33.7 (NA)
Group of UTs						
31. Andaman and Nicobar Islands	@ (63.2)	@ (24.3)	@ (44.2)	@ (57.8)	@ (15.5)	@ (37.9)
32. Chandigarh	@ (60.2)	@ (5.4)	@ (38.8)	@ (51.2)	@ (14.2)	@ (34.3)
33. Dadra and Nagar Haveli	@ (54.7)	@ (47.8)	@ (51.6)	@ (68.9)	@ (19.4)	@ (45.2)
34. Daman and Diu	@ (59.1)	@ (16.8)	@ (40.2)	@ (65.2)	@ (22.5)	@ (41.5)
35. Lakshadweep	@ (61.1)	@ (5.0)	@ (37.9)	@ (43.6)	@ (10.8)	@ (27.4)
36. Pondicherry	@ (56.9)	@ (36.1)	@ (46.1)	@ (53.6)	@ (15.4)	@ (34.3)
All India	54.9 (54.6)	31.0 (32.7)	43.3 (43.9)	54.0 (54.6)	14.3 (16.6)	35.0 (36.5)

Notes: Figures relate to usual status of individuals.
The figures represent size of workforce as percent of population.
Figures with in the parenthesis represent the figures for 2004-2005.
@ – Included in group of UTs.
NE – Included in North-Eastern Estates.
NA – Data Not Available.

Sources: National Sample Survey Organisation :
Report Nos. 515 and 522 *Employment and Unemployment in India*, 2004-05 and 2005-06.

Table 3.2.6: Age-specific Workforce Participation Rates, 1999-2000, 2004-05 and 2005-06

Age-Group	*Rural*						*Urban*					
	Male			*Female*			*Male*			*Female*		
	1999-2000	*2004-05*	*2005-06*	*1999-2000*	*2004-05*	*2005-06*	*1999-2000*	*2004-05*	*2005-06*	*1999-2000*	*2004-05*	*2005-06*
5—9	0.6	0.3	0.4	0.7	0.3	0.5	0.3	0.2	0.2	0.2	0.3	0.1
10—14	9.1	6.8	6.5	9.6	7.4	6.6	4.9	4.8	4.0	3.6	3.3	2.4
15—19	50.3	49.7	47.5	30.4	31.9	27.1	31.4	33.5	30.4	10.5	12.8	10.5
20—24	84.4	84.9	82.5	40.9	41.0	37.7	65.8	68.4	67.1	15.5	20.1	17.2
25—29	95.0	96.6	95.4	49.1	51.3	48.2	88.3	90.9	89.6	19.4	22.9	21.9
15—29	74.1	74.2	72.6	40.0	41.0	37.7	59.3	62.3	59.8	14.9	18.4	16.5
30—34	97.9	98.1	98.2	55.5	58.4	55.6	96.0	96.9	96.2	23.5	29.0	23.1
35—39	98.4	98.9	99.0	57.9	63.9	60.5	97.5	97.7	98.3	28.5	32.8	26.5
40—44	98.3	98.3	98.2	58.6	62.5	59.2	97.4	98.0	97.5	28.3	31.2	26.5
30—44	98.2	98.4	98.4	57.2	61.4	58.4	96.9	97.5	97.3	26.6	31.0	25.4
45—49	98.0	98.1	98.3	56.6	61.5	58.2	96.9	96.8	96.4	26.7	26.7	24.6
50—54	95.3	96.3	97.7	51.5	56.1	53.0	93.5	93.1	92.5	26.2	25.8	21.3
55—59	92.9	93.0	93.5	45.0	50.9	50.8	80.9	83.0	82.4	20.7	21.8	19.6
45—59	95.8	96.2	96.5	51.8	56.9	54.0	92.1	92.3	90.4	25.0	25.2	21.8
60 and above	63.9	64.4	64.9	21.8	25.3	24.5	40.2	36.6	37.2	9.4	10.0	7.7
All(0+)	53.1	54.6	54.9	29.9	32.7	31.0	51.8	54.9	54.0	13.9	16.6	14.3

Notes: Figures relate to usual status of individuals.
Workforce covers those involved in gainful activity regularly + those involved in gainful activity occasionally. The figures represent the size of workforce of a given age-group as per cent of population of the age-group.

Sources: National Sample Survey Organisation :
Report No. 458 *Employment and Unemployment Situation in India,* 1999-2000.
Report No. 515, *Employment and Unemployment Situation in India,* 2004-2005.
Report No. 522, *Employment and Unemployment Situation in India,* 2005-06

Table 3.2.7: Workforce Participation Rates for Educated Persons

Year		*Male*		*Female*	
		Rural	*Urban*	*Rural*	*Urban*
1977-78	Below Matric	N.A.	N.A.	N.A.	N.A.
	Matric *	65.48	64.99	18.23	12.83
	Graduate & above	71.45	79.83	30.65	27.96
1983	Below Matric	87.31	80.32	37.81	18.22
	Matric *	66.50	65.20	15.80	13.40
	Graduate & above	77.40	81.00	22.00	27.90
1987-88	Below Matric	85.94	78.87	37.95	17.58
	Matric *	66.40	64.50	17.50	12.50
	Graduate & above	76.60	79.90	25.00	29.70
1993-94	Below Matric	87.55	80.85	35.62	18.00
	Matric *	66.57	63.44	15.50	11.45
	Graduate & above	79.20	80.70	29.30	28.20
1999-2000	Below Matric	57.3	50.0	26.8	12.2
	Matric *	70.1	63.3	15.9	10.6
	Graduate & above	80.3	79.7	27.8	25.2
2004-2005	Below Matric	87.2	81.4	50.5	24.5
	Matric	72.4	64.6	28.7	12.5
	Graduate & above	84.8	79.5	34.5	29.0
	Diploma/Certificate course	82.1	80.5	52.2	49.2
2005-06	Below Matric	51.99	45.74	31.41	13.03
	Matric*	69.48	62.75	24.80	11.04
	Graduate and above	84.50	81.03	34.63	29.00
	Diploma Certificate Course	83.10	74.50	43.10	34.90

Notes: Figures relate to usual status of individuals. The figures represent size of workforce of a given educational level as percent of population of that educational level.

* Includes Higher Secondary.

Sources: National Sample Survey Organisation :

Sarvekshana, Vol. V, July 77-June 78, 32nd Round.

Vol. XI, Jan-Dec. 1983, 38th Round.

Special No., July 87-June, 88, 43rd Round.

Vol. XX, July 93-June 94, 50th Round.

Report No. 458, *515 and 522 Employment and Unemployment in India,* 1999-2000, 2004-05 and 2005-06.

Figure 3.2.G

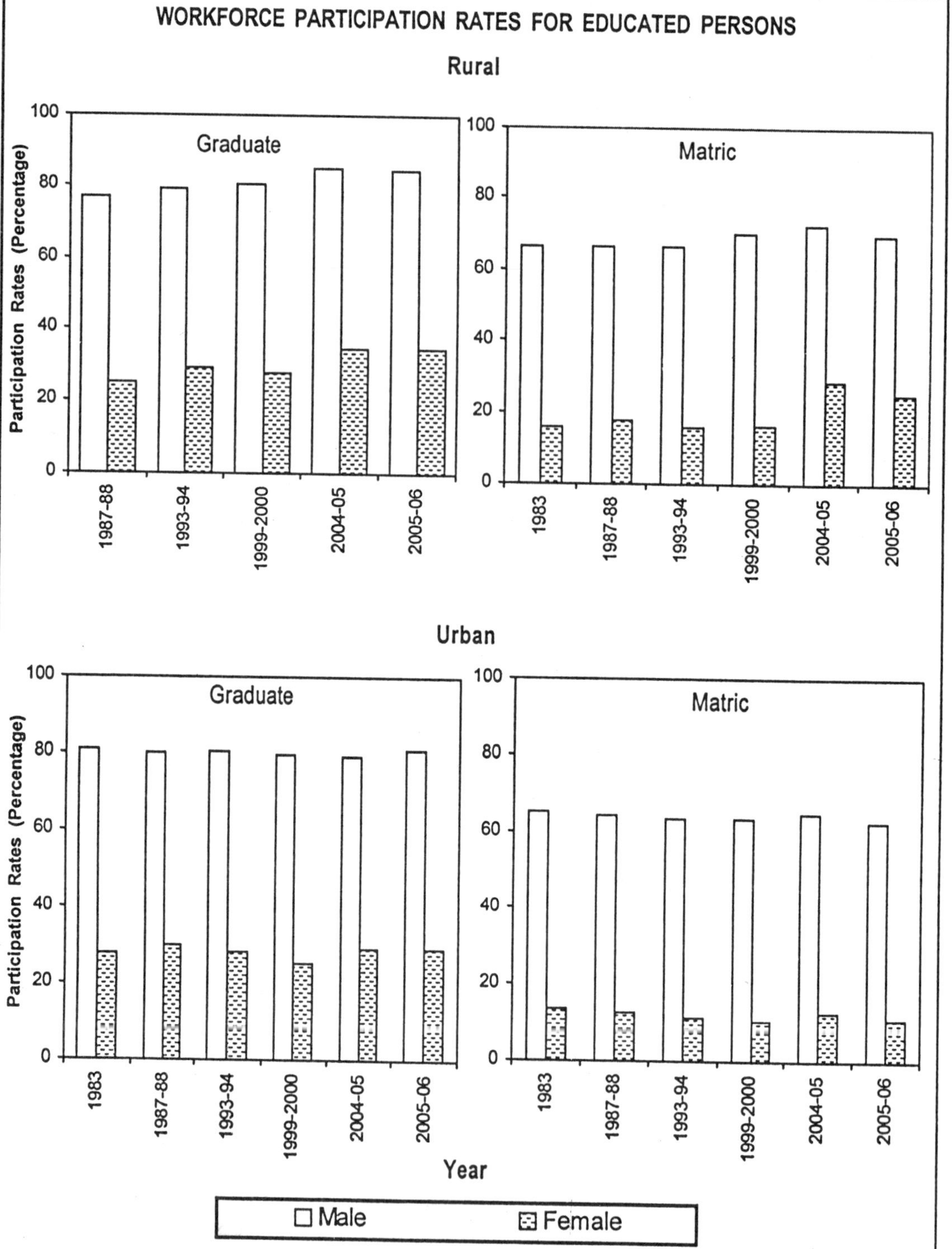

For details see Table 3.2.7

Table 3.2.8: Percentage Distribution of Employment by Status

Employment Status and year	*Rural*		*Urban*		*Total*	
	Male	*Female*	*Male*	*Female*	*Male*	*Female*
(*i*) Self-Employed						
1972-73	65.9	64.5	39.2	48.4	60.6	63.0
1977-78	62.8	62.1	40.4	49.5	58.0	60.7
1983	60.5	61.9	40.9	45.8	55.9	60.0
1987-88	58.6	60.8	41.7	47.1	54.3	58.9
1993-94	57.9	58.5	41.7	45.4	52.9	56.7
2000-01	58.9	59.3	41.4	44.4	54.5	57.2
2001-02	58.0	58.9	43.0	44.1	54.4	57.2
2004-05	58.1	63.7	44.8	47.7	NA	NA
2005-06	56.7	62.2	42.4	43.8	NA	NA
(*ii*) Regular Employees						
1972-73	12.1	4.1	50.7	27.9	19.7	6.3
1977-78	10.6	2.8	46.4	24.9	18.3	5.3
1983	10.3	2.8	43.7	25.8	18.2	5.6
1987-88	10.0	3.7	43.7	27.5	18.6	6.9
1993-94	8.3	2.8	42.1	28.6	17.0	6.3
1999-2000	8.8	3.1	41.7	33.3	14.0	7.3
2000-01	9.5	3.2	41.1	31.5	17.5	7.1
2001-02	8.1	2.9	41.5	29.8	16.2	8.0
2004-05	9.0	3.7	40.6	35.6	NA	NA
2005-06	10.0	3.9	42.0	39.7	NA	NA
(*iii*) Casual Labour						
1972-73	22.0	31.4	10.1	23.7	19.7	30.7
1977-78	26.6	35.1	13.2	25.6	23.7	34.0
1983	29.2	35.3	15.4	28.4	25.9	34.4
1987-88	31.4	35.5	14.6	25.4	27.1	34.2
1993-94	33.8	38.7	16.2	26.2	30.1	37.0
2000-01	31.6	37.5	17.5	24.1	28.0	35.7
2001-02	33.9	38.2	15.4	26.1	29.4	36.8
2004-05	32.9	32.6	14.6	16.7	NA	NA
2005-06	33.3	33.9	15.7	16.5	NA	NA
Total	*100.0*	*100.0*	*100.0*	*100.0*	*100.0*	*100.0*

Notes: Figures relate to usual status of individuals.

Workforce covers those involved in gainful activity regularly + those involved in gainful activity occasionally.

The results of 2000-2001, 2001-2002 and 2005-06 are based on thin samples.

Sources: National Sample Survey Organisation :

(i) *Sarvekshana*, Vol. V, July 77-June 78, 32nd Round.

(ii) Report No. 481, *Household Consumer Expenditures and Employment-Unemployment Situation in India–2001-2002.*

(iii) Report Nos. 515 and 522 *Employment and Unemployment Situation in India*, 2004-05 and 2005-06.

Figure 3.2.H

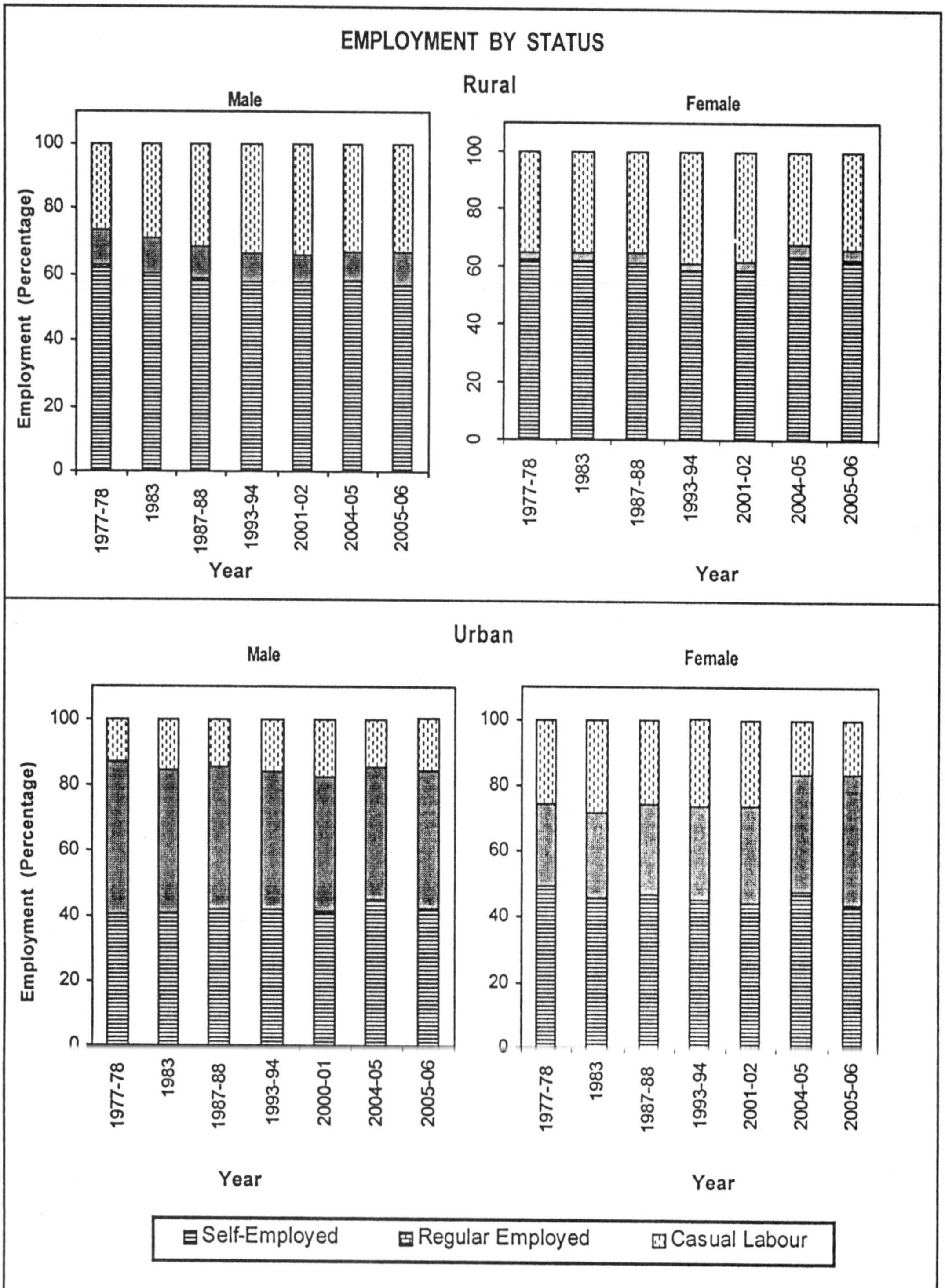

For details see Tables 3.2.8

Table 3.2.9: Percentage Distribution of Total Employment by Broad Economic Sector

Sectors	Person							Male							Female						
	1977-78	*1983*	*1987-88*	*1993-94*	*1999-2000*	*2004-05*	*2005-06*	*1977-78*	*1983*	*1987-88*	*1993-94*	*1999-2000*	*2004-05*	*2005-06*	*1977-78*	*1983*	*1987-88*	*1993-94*	*1999-2000*	*2004-05*	*2005-06*
Primary	72.5	68.7	64.8	64.6	61.7	58.5	58.0	67.8	62.3	58.6	58.3	54.9	50.8	51.0	82.6	81.1	77.6	77.8	76.2	73.9	72.9
Secondary	12.0	13.3	15.5	14.2	15.8	18.1	18.8	13.1	15.0	16.8	15.9	17.8	20.5	20.8	9.2	9.8	12.5	10.8	11.8	13.9	14.6
Tertiary	15.5	18.0	19.7	21.2	22.5	23.4	23.2	19.1	22.7	24.6	25.8	27.3	28.6	28.2	8.2	9.1	9.9	11.4	12.0	12.8	12.5
Total	100.0	100.0	100.0	100.0	100.0	100.0	100.0	100.0	100.0	100.0	100.0	100.0	100.0	100.0	100.0	100.0	100.0	100.0	100.0	100.0	100.0

Notes: Figures relate to usual status of individuals.

Workforce covers those involved in gainful activity regularly + those involved in gainful activity occasionally.

Sources: National Sample Survey Organisation :

(i) *Sarvekshana*, Vol. V, July 77-June 78, 32nd Round.

Vol. XI, Jan-Dec. 1983, 38th Round.

Special No., July 87-June 88, 43rd Round.

Vol. XX, July 93-June 94, 50th Round.

(ii) Report No. 458, *Employment and Unemployment in India*, 1999-2000.

(iii) Report No. 515, *Employment and Unemployment in India*, 2004-05.

(iv) Report No. 522, *Employment and Unemployment in India*, 2005-06.

Table 3.2.10: Percentage Distribution of Rural Employment by Broad Economic Sector

Sectors	Person							Male							Female						
	1977-78	1983	1987-88	1993-94	1999-2000	2004-05	2005-06	1977-78	1983	1987-88	1993-94	1999-2000	2004-05	2005-06	1977-78	1983	1987-88	1993-94	1999-2000	2004-05	2005-06
Primary	83.8	81.7	78.9	79.0	76.2	72.7	70.8	81.1	78.1	75.2	74.8	71.4	66.5	65.2	88.3	87.8	85.1	86.6	85.3	83.3	81.3
Secondary	7.6	8.5	10.7	9.6	11.3	13.6	14.9	.3	9.4	11.4	10.5	12.6	15.6	16.5	6.6	7.1	9.6	7.9	9.0	10.1	12.0
Tertiary	8.6	9.8	10.4	11.4	12.5	3.7	14.3	10.6	12.5	13.4	14.7	16.0	17.9	18.3	5.1	5.1	5.3	5.5	5.7	6.5	6.8
Total	100.0	100.0	100.0	100.0	100.0	100.0	100.0	100.0	100.0	100.0	100.0	100.0	100.0	100.0	100.0	100.0	100.0	100.0	100.0	100.0	100.0

Notes: Figures relate to usual status of individuals.
Workforce covers those involved in gainful activity regularly + those involved in gainful activity occasionally.

Sources: National Sample Survey Organisation :

(i) *Sarvekshana*, Vol. V, July 77-June 78, 32nd Round.
Vol. XI, Jan-Dec. 1983, 38th Round.
Special No., July 87-June 88, 43rd Round.
Vol. XX, July 93-June 94, 50th Round.

(ii) Report No. 458, *Employment and Unemployment in India*, 1999-2000.

(iii) Report No. 515, *Employment and Unemployment in India*, 2004-05.

(iv) Report No. 522, *Employment and Unemployment in India*, 2005-06.

Table 3.2.11 Percentage Distribution of Urban Employment by Broad Economic Sector

Sectors	*Person*							*Male*							*Female*						
	1977-78	*1983*	*1987-88*	*1993-94*	*1999-2000*	*2004-05*	*2005-06*	*1377-78*	*1983*	*1987-88*	*1993-94*	*1999-2000*	*2004-05*	*2005-06*	*1977-78*	*1983*	*1987-88*	*1993-94*	*1999-2000*	*2004-05*	*2005-06*
Primary	16.1	15.6	14.6	13.5	8.6	8.8	8.0	11.5	11.4	10.4	10.3	6.6	6.1	6.3	32.4	31.7	30.2	25.2	17.7	18.1	14.8
Secondary	32.6	32.3	32.4	30.9	32.2	34.0	34.1	32.8	32.9	32.7	31.7	32.8	34.5	34.3	32.1	30.1	30.9	28.5	29.3	32.4	33.0
Tertiary	51.3	52.1	53.0	55.6	59.2	57.2	58.0	55.7	55.7	56.9	58.0	60.6	59.4	59.4	35.5	38.2	38.9	46.3	52.9	49.5	52.2
Total	100.0	100.0	100.0	100.0	100.0	100.0	100.0	100.0	100.0	100.0	100.0	100.0	100.0	100.0	100.0	100.0	100.0	100.0	100.0	100.0	100.0

Notes: Figures relate to usual status of individuals.
Workforce covers those involved in gainful activity regularly + those involved in gainful activity occasionally.

Sources: National Sample Survey Organisation :
(i) *Sarvekshana*, Vol. V, July 77-June 78, 32nd Round.
Vol. XI, Jan-Dec. 1983, 38th Round.
Special No., July 87-June 88, 43rd Round.
Vol. XX, July 93-June 94, 50th Round.
(ii) Report No. 458, *Employment and Unemployment in India*, 1999-2000.
(iii) Report No. 515, *Employment and Unemployment in India*, 2004-05.
(iv) Report No. 522, *Employment and Unemployment in India*, 2005-06.

Table 3.2.12: Percentage Distribution of Total Employment by Industry Division

Industry Division	*Total*									
	1972-73	*1977-78*	*1983*	*1987-88*	*1990-91*	*1993-94*	*1999-2000*	*2001-02*	*2004-05*	*2005-06*
Agriculture Forestry, Fishing and Hunting	74.0	72.0	68.1	64.1	62.0	63.9	61.7	60.8	58.5	58.0
Mining and Quarrying	0.4	0.5	0.6	0.7	0.7	0.7	0.6	0.5	0.6	0.6
Manufacturing	8.8	10.2	10.7	11.3	11.5	10.6	10.6	11.9	11.7	12.1
Electricity, Gas and Water	0.2	0.2	0.3	0.4	0.6	0.4	0.3	0.2	0.3	0.3
Construction	1.8	1.7	2.3	3.8	2.8	3.2	4.3	4.5	5.6	5.8
Wholesale and Retail Trade and Restaurants and Hotels	5.0	5.8	6.9	7.3	6.8	7.6	9.8	10.5	10.3	10.0
Transport, Storage and Communication	1.8	1.9	2.5	2.7	2.8	2.9	3.5	3.5	3.8	4.1
Services	7.8	7.7	8.8	9.5	12.8	10.7	9.2	8.1	9.3	9.0
Activities not classified	0.2	–	0.4	0.2	–	–	–	–	–	–
Total	100.0	100.0	100.0	100.0	100.0	100.0	100.0	100.0	100.0	100.0
Total Employment (Million)	236.3	270.7	302.8	322.0	341.9	355.8	372.1	411.5	428.2	402.9

Notes: Figures relate to usual status of individuals.

Workforce covers those involved in gainful activity regularly + those involved in gainful activity occasionally.

Sources: National Sample Survey Organisation :

(i) *Sarvekshana*, Vol. V, July 77-June 78, 32nd Round.

Vol. XI, Jan-Dec. 1983, 38th Round.

Special No., July 87-June 88, 43rd Round.

Vol. XX, July 93-June 94, 50th Round.

(ii) Report No. 453, *Employment and Unemployment in India*, 1999-2000.

(iii) Report No. 481, *Employment and Unemployment in India*, 2001-02.

(iv) Report No. 515, *Employment and Unemployment in India*, 2004-05.

(iv) Report No. 522, *Employment and Unemployment in India*, 2005-06.

Figure 3.2.I

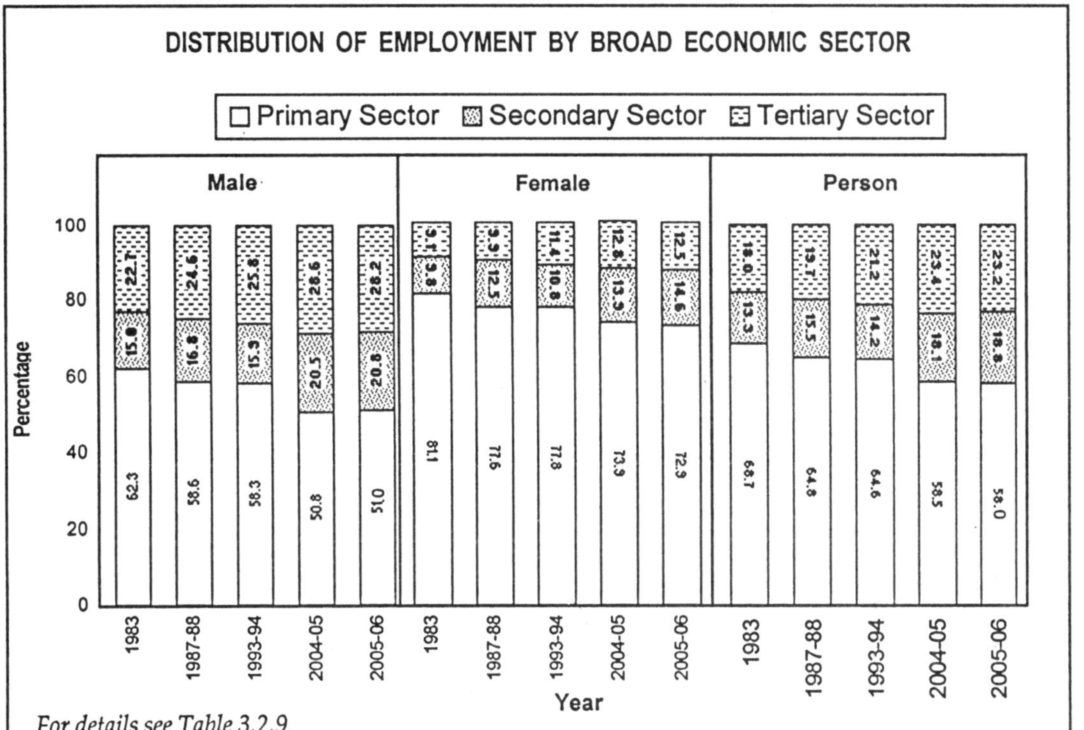

For details see Table 3.2.9

Figure 3.2.J

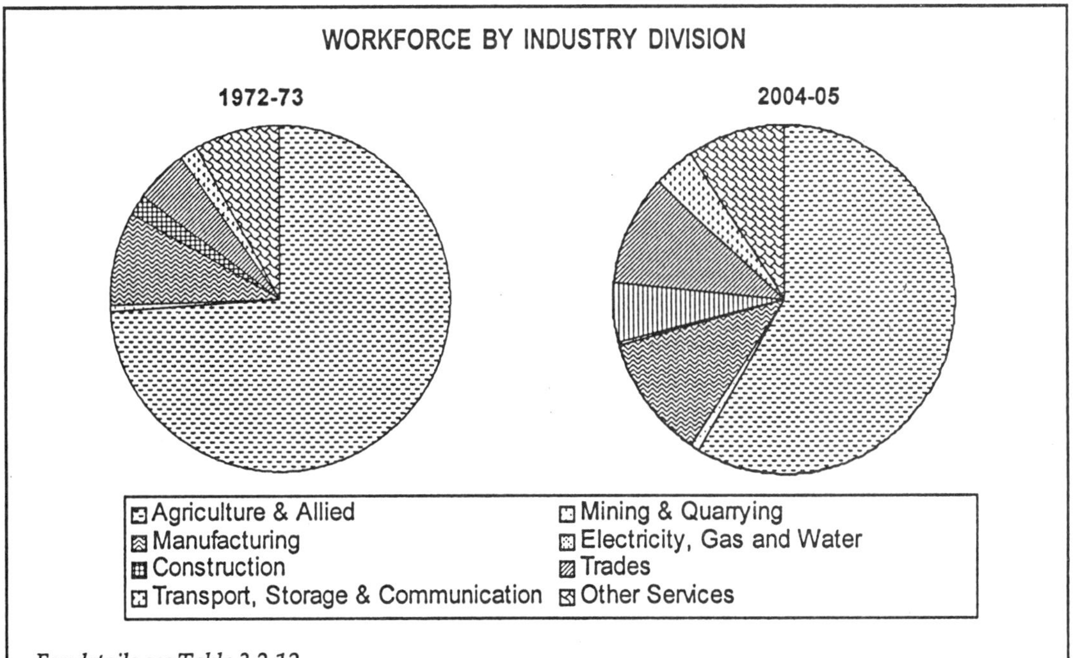

For details see Table 3.2.12

Table 3.2.13: Percentage Distribution of Total Employment by Rural/Urban and Industry Division

Industry Division	*Rural*						*Urban*					
	1983	*1987-88*	*1993-94*	*1999-2000*	*2004-05*	*2005-06*	*1983*	*1987-88*	*1993-94*	*1999-2000*	*2004-05*	*2005-06*
Agriculture, Forestry Fishing and Hunting	81.2	78.3	78.4	76.3	72.7	70.8	14.6	13.4	12.3	8.6	8.8	8.0
Mining and Quarrying	0.5	0.6	0.6	0.5	0.5	0.6	1.0	1.2	1.2	0.8	0.8	0.7
Manufacturing	6.7	7.2	7.0	7.3	8.1	9.0	26.7	26.0	23.6	22.7	24.6	24.0
Electricity, Gas and Water	0.1	0.2	0.2	0.2	0.2	0.2	0.9	1.0	1.0	0.7	0.7	0.7
Construction	1.7	3.3	2.4	3.3	4.9	5.0	4.7	5.4	6.3	8.0	8.0	8.7
Wholesale & Retail Trade & Restaurants & Hotels	3.5	4.0	4.3	5.1	6.1	6.1	18.4	19.0	19.4	26.9	24.6	25.0
Transport, Storage and Communication	1.1	1.3	1.4	2.1	2.5	2.9	8.1	7.8	8.0	8.7	8.6	9.0
Services	4.9	5.0	5.7	5.2	5.0	5.1	25.0	25.7	28.2	23.6	24.0	26.4
Activities not classified	0.3	0.1	–	–	–	0.4	–	0.6	0.5	–	–	–
Total	100.0	100.0	100.0	100.0	100.0	100.0	100.0	100.0	100.0	100.0	100.0	100.0
Total Estimated Employment (Million)	243.1	252.5	290.3	300.8	317.8	320.4	59.6	69.5	81.8	96.0	90.4	82.5

Notes: Figures relate to usual status of individuals.
Workforce covers those involved in gainful activity regularly + those involved in gainful activity occasionally.

Sources: National Sample Survey Organisation :
(i) *Sarvekshana*, Vol. XI, Jan Dec. 1983, 38th Round.
Special No., July 87-June 88, 43rd Round.
Vol. XX, July 93-June 94, 50th Round.
(ii) Report No. 458, *Employment and Unemployment in India*, 1999-2000.
(iii) Report No. 515, *Employment and Unemployment in India*, 2004-05.
(iv) Report No. 522, *Employment and Unemployment in India*, 2005-06.

Table 3.2.14: Percentage Distribution of Total Employment by Occupational Division

Occupational Division	*Rural*					*Urban*				
	1987-88	*1993-94*	*1999-2000*	*2004-05*	*2005-06*	*1987-88*	*1993-94*	*1999 2000*	*2004-05*	*2005-06*
0-1. Professional, Technical and Related Workers	1.7	2.3	2.1	2.2	2.2	8.0	9.0	8.9	9.2	9.7
2. Administrative, Executive and Managerial Workers	0.7	0.9	1.4	1.6	2.0	5.0	5.9	8.4	9.1	9.2
3. Clerical and Related Workers	1.3	1.4	1.5	1.2	1.2	10.2	9.7	9.2	7.6	7.9
4. Sales Workers	3.9	4.2	4.1	4.7	4.6	16.8	17.0	16.7	17.6	17.4
5. Service Workers	2.3	2.0	2.5	2.3	2.4	9.9	9.2	9.7	10.0	10.1
6. Farmers, Fishermen and Related Workers	75.1	76.7	74.2	72.3	70.6	10.7	10.7	8.3	8.8	7.9
7-8-9. Production and Related Workers, Transport Equipment Operators and Labourers	12.7	12.4	14.2	15.7	16.8	38.5	38.7	38.9	37.7	37.6
10. Workers not classified by Occupation	2.4	–	–	–	0.2	–	–	–	–	0.2
Total	100.0	100.0	100.0	100.0	100.0	100.0	100.0	100.0	100.0	100.0
Total Estimated Employment (Million)	224.0	255.0	273.8	317.8	320.4	56.0	65.1	76.9	90.4	82.5

Notes : Figures relate to usual status of individuals.
Workforce covers those involved in gainful activity regularly + those involved in gainful activity occasionally.

Sources : National Sample Survey Organisation :

(i) *Sarvekshana,* Special No., July 87-June 88, 43rd Round.
Vol. XX, July 93-June 94, 50th Round.

(ii) Report No. 458, *Employment and Unemployment in India,* 1999-2000.

(iii) Report No. 515, *Employment and Unemployment in India,* 2004-05.

(iv) Report No. 522, *Employment and Unemployment in India,* 2005-06.

Table 3.2.15: Percentage Distribution of Total Employment by Occupational Division and Sex, 2005-06

Occupational Division	Rural			Urban			Total		
	Male	Female	Person	Male	Female	Person	Male	Female	Person
0-1. Professional, Technical and Related Workers	2.6 (2.5)	1.4 (1.8)	2.2 (2.2)	8.2 (7.8)	15.7 (14.3)	9.7 (9.2)	4.0 (3.9)	3.2 (3.6)	3.7 (3.8)
2. Administrative, Executive and Managerial Workers	2.2 (1.9)	1.7 (1.0)	2.0 (1.6)	10.0 (10.2)	5.8 (5.2)	9.2 (9.1)	4.1 (4.1)	2.2 (1.6)	3.5 (3.3)
3. Clerical and Related Workers	1.6 (1.6)	0.5 (0.3)	1.2 (1.2)	8.2 (8.1)	6.7 (5.7)	7.9 (7.6)	3.2 (3.3)	1.2 (1.1)	2.5 (2.6)
4. Sales Workers	5.9 (6.2)	2.0 (2.1)	4.6 (4.7)	19.6 (19.9)	8.5 (9.2)	17.4 (17.6)	9.2 (9.8)	2.9 (3.1)	7.2 (7.6)
5. Service Workers	2.4 (2.4)	2.4 (2.2)	2.4 (2.3)	8.0 (7.8)	18.8 (18.1)	10.1 (10.0)	3.8 (3.8)	4.5 (4.5)	4.0 (4.0)
6. Farmers, Fishermen and Related Workers	65.0 (66.1)	80.9 (83.0)	70.6 (72.3)	6.3 (6.2)	14.7 (18.1)	7.9 (8.8)	50.8 (50.1)	72.6 (73.6)	57.7 (58.2)
7-8-9. Production and Related Workers, Transport Equipment Operators and Labourers	20.0 (19.3)	10.9 (9.6)	16.8 (15.7)	39.5 (40.0)	29.8 (29.4)	37.6 (37.7)	24.7 (25.0)	13.2 (12.5)	21.1 (20.5)
Total	100.0 (100.0)	100.0 (100.0)	100.0 (100.0)	100.0 (100.0)	100.0 (100.0)	100.0 (100.0)	100.0 (100.0)	100.0 (100.0)	100.0 (100.0)
Total Employment (Million)	208.5 (201.7)	111.9 (116.1)	320.4 (317.8)	66.4 (70.7)	16.1 (19.7)	82.5 (90.4)	274.9 (272.4)	128.0 (135.8)	402.9 (408.2)

Notes: Figures relate to usual status of individuals.
Figures in paranthesis indicase for the year 2004-05.
Workforce covers those involved in gainful activity regularly.

Sources: National Sample Survey Organisation :
(i) Report No. 515, *Employment and Unemployment in India, 2004-05.*
(ii) Report No. 522, *Employment and Unemployment in India, 2005-06.*

Table 3.2.16: Percentage Distribution of Main Workers by Census Industrial Category, 2001

Industrial Division	Rural			Urban			Total		
	Male	*Female*	*Person*	*Male*	*Female*	*Person*	*Male*	*Female*	*Person*
I. Cultivators	45.23	41.53	44.26	2.57	3.59	2.73	32.62	34.89	33.15
II. Agricultural Labourers	23.15	35.66	26.43	2.80	7.78	3.56	17.14	30.78	20.31
III. Livestock Forestry Fishing, Hunting and Plantations, Orchards and Allied Activities	3.20	5.51	3.80	1.77	2.49	1.88	2.78	4.98	3.29
IV. Mining and Quarrying	0.67	0.40	0.60	1.10	0.54	1.02	0.80	0.43	0.71
V. Manufacturing, Processing, Servicing and Repairs									
(a) Household Industry	2.98	5.45	3.63	3.46	10.97	4.60	3.12	6.42	3.89
(b) Other than Household Industry	5.21	2.95	4.62	20.06	13.15	19.01	9.06	4.74	8.47
VI Electricity, Gas and water Supply	0.36	0.04	0.28	1.13	0.43	1.02	0.59	0.11	0.48
VI. Construction	3.07	0.77	2.47	8.00	4.83	7.52	4.53	1.48	3.82
VII. Trade and Commerce	5.83	1.71	4.75	24.06	9.13	21.79	11.22	3.00	9.30
VIII. Transport, Storage and Communication	2.83	0.17	2.13	9.93	2.14	8.75	4.93	0.52	3.90
IX. Other Services	7.47	5.87	7.03	25.10	44.95	28.12	12.68	12.66	12.68
Total	100.00	100.00	100.00	100.00	100.00	100.00	100.00	100.00	100.00
Total Employment (Million)	169.01	59.97	228.98	70.91	12.74	83.65	239.92	72.71	312.63

Notes: The data excludes Jammu & Kashmir.
Main workers are those who work for 183 days or more in a year.

Source: Registrar General and Census Commission of India : *Census of India, 2001.*

Table 3.2.17: Classification of Workers by Broad Industrial Category, 1981, 1991 & 2001

(Thousand)

Year	Type of worker	Cultivators		Agricultural Labourers		Household Industry		Other Workers		Total	
		Male	Female	Male	Female	Male	Female	Male	Female	Male	Female
						ALL INDIA					
1981	Main	77591	14932	34732	20768	5647	2064	59573	7209	177543	44973
	Marginal	1468	8848	1187	7722	102	756	780	1226	3537	18552
	Total	79,059	23,780	35919	28490	5749	2820	60353	8435	181,080	63525
		(43.66)	(37.43)	(19.84)	(44.85)	(3.17)	(4.44)	(33.33)	(13.28)	(100.00)	(100.00)
										[52.65]	[19.77]
1991	Main	88481	22221	46165	28433	4555	2249	82458	11371	221659	64274
	Marginal	1154	12828	864	10531	76	674	611	1461	2705	25494
	Total	89635	35049	47029	38964	4631	2923	83069	12832	224364	89768
		(39.95)	(39.04)	(20.96)	(43.41)	(2.06)	(3.26)	(37.03)	(14.29)	(100.00)	(100.00)
										[51.55]	[22.26]
2001	Main	78259	25367	41119	22378	7509	4697	113261	20415	240148	72857
	Marginal	7158	16529	16210	27068	1235	3516	10264	7250	34867	54363
	Total	85417	41896	57329	49446	8744	8213	123525	27665	275015	127220
		(31.06)	(32.93)	(20.85)	(38.87)	(3.18)	(6.46)	(44.91)	(21.74)	(100.00)	(100.00)
										[51.68]	[25.63]
						RURAL					
1981	Main	75,476	14,682	32,835	19,878	3932	1501	24,588	3,542	136,831	39,603
	Marginal	1427	8,722	1,126	7,523	77	594	460	946	3,090	17,785
	Total	76,903	23,404	33,961	27,401	4009	2095	25048	4,488	139,921	57,388
		(55.0)	(40.8)	(24.3)	(47.7)	(2.9)	(3.7)	(17.9)	(7.8)	(100.00)	(100.00)
										[53.8]	[23.2]
1991	Main	85,771	21,797	43,187	27,151	3183	1627	34,152	5,421	166,294	55,996
	Marginal	1098	12,561	793	10,200	56	536	358	1,137	2,305	24,434
	Total	86,869	34,358	43,980	37,351	3,239	2,163	34,510	6,558	168,599	80,430
		(51.5)	(42.7)	(26.1)	(46.4)	(1.9)	(2.7)	(20.5)	(8.2)	(100.0)	(100.0)
										[52.5]	[26.7]
2001	Main	76436	24909	39130	21387	5036	3294	48499	10494	169101	60085
	Marginal	7040	16334	15576	26338	955	2857	6167	5503	29738	51032
	Total	83476	41243	54706	47725	5991	6151	54666	15997	198839	111117
		(41.98)	(37.12)	(27.51)	(42.95)	(3.01)	(5.53)	(27.49)	(14.40)	(100.00)	(100.00)
										[52.10]	[30.79]
						URBAN					
1981	Main	2115	250	1897	890	1716	563	34984	3667	40712	5370
	Marginal	41	127	61	199	25	162	320	279	447	767
	Total	2,156	377	1958	1089	1741	725	35304	3946	41,159	6137
		(5.2)	(6.1)	(4.8)	(17.8)	(4.2)	(11.8)	(85.8)	(64.3)	(100.0)	(100.0)
										[49.2]	[8.3]
1991	Main	2710	424	2977	1282	1372	623	48306	5950	55365	8278
	Marginal	56	267	72	330	20	138	252	324	400	1059
	Total	2766	691	3049	1612	1392	761	48558	6274	55765	9337
		(5.0)	(7.4)	(5.5)	(17.3)	(2.5)	(8.1)	(87.1)	(67.2)	(100.0)	(100.0)
										[48.9]	[9.2]
2001	Main	1823	458	1989	991	2473	1403	64762	9921	71047	12772
	Marginal	117	195	634	731	280	659	4097	1747	5129	3331
	Total	1940	653	2623	1722	2753	2062	68859	11668	76176	16103
		(2.55)	(4.05)	(3.44)	(10.69)	(3.61)	(12.81)	(90.39)	(72.46)	(100.00)	(100.00)
										[50.60]	[11.88]

Note: Figures within the brackets ( ) show the industrial distribution (per cent) of workers where as figures within [ ] bractet show workforce participation rate.

Sources: Registrar General and Census Commissioner of India :
Census of India, 1981, Series I India: Part III-A(i) General Economic Tables B-1 to B-5.
Census of India, 1981, Series I India: Part III-A(ii), General Economic Tables B-6 to B-10.
Census of India, 1991, Series I India: Part III-B, Series Economic Tables, Vol. I.
Census of India, 1991, Series I India: Part III-B Series, Economic Tables, Vol. 3 (Part 2).
Census of India, 2001, Series I India: Primary Census Abstract.

Table 3.2.18: Distribution of Main Workers by Industry/ Occupation, 1991

(Thousand)

Occupation/ Industry	*Sex*	*0-1 Profes-sional, Technical and Related Workers*	*2 Adminis-trative Executive & Mana-gerial Workers*	*3 Clerical & Rela-ted Workers*	*4 Sales Workers*	*5 Service Workers*	*6 Farmers, Fishermen & Related Workers*	*7-8-9 Production & Related Workers, Transport Equipment Operators & Labourers*	*X Workers not Classi-fied by Occupation Industry*	*Total*
Agriculture, Forestry, Fishing and Hunting	Person	122	1.6	231	187	118	190324	241	116	191341
	Male	113	1.5	217	158	112	138445	224	90	139361
Mining and Quarrying	Person	54	29	85	10	39	1.1	1509	24	1751
	Male	50	28	81	9	36	1.0	1312	20	1537
Manufacturing Household Industry	Person	13	26	13	72	86	—	6481	113	6804
	Male	11	23	12	53	54	—	4323	79	4555
Manufacturing Other than Household Industry	Person	475	590	1002	422	337	18	18836	187	21867
	Male	449	571	918	395	318	16	16581	167	19415
Construction	Person	166	298	238	25	90	5	4677	44	5543
	Male	159	294	220	23	84	4	4298	40	5122
Trade and Commerce	Person	533	1018	1715	15591	1681	12	578	168	21296
	Male	503	974	1528	14592	1557	11	544	154	19863
Transport, Storage and Communication	Person	119	171	1685	32	163	3	5755	90	8018
	Male	110	167	1580	30	147	2.8	5688	84	7810
Other Services	Person	8676	787	4797	212	5809	79	6318	2634	29312
	Male	6231	738	4295	198	4393	73	5627	2440	23995
Total	Person	10157	2923	9767	16550	8322	190442	44396	3375	285932
	Male	7627	2795	8852	15459	6701	138553	38597	3074	221658

Notes: Excludes Jammu & Kashmir.
Totals may not tally due to rounding off.
Main workers are those who work for 183 days or more in a year.

Source: Registrar General and Census Commissioner of India : *Census of India, 1991.*

Table 3.2.19: Share of Female Main Workers by Occupation and Education, 1981 and 1991

(Thousand)

Education / *Occupation*	*Year*	*Educational Level*											
		Illiterate		*Literate up to Primary*		*Middle*		*Secondary*		*Graduate and above*		*Total Main Workers*	
		Person	*Female*	*Person*	*Female*	*Person*	*Female*	*Person*	*Female*	*Person*	*Female*	*Person*	*Female*
0-1. Professional, Technical and Related Workers	1981	173	44	523	63	585	133	3212	753	2551	452	7044	1445
	1991	181	41	769	117	674	172	4076	1172	4457	1027	10157	2530
2. Administrative, Executive and Managerial Workers	1981	131	12	452	7	345	4	859	13	578	18	2365	54
	1991	155	23	354	14	335	10	952	27	1127	54	2923	128
3. Clerical and Related Workers	1981	11	-	1007	30	1034	21	3719	245	1559	176	7330	472
	1991	19	1	982	69	1356	64	4405	367	3005	414	9767	915
4. Sales Workers	1981	2516	530	3374	97	1759	22	2145	23	400	7	10194	679
	1991	3576	704	4247	204	3241	77	4187	76	1299	31	16550	109
5. Service Workers	1981	2967	959	2052	190	866	39	778	18	86	3	6749	1209
	1991	2940	1086	2193	311	1374	110	1533	94	282	20	8322	1621
6. Farmers, Fishermen and Related Workers	1981	106749	33036	32336	2932	8415	437	4934	107	383	3	152817	36515
	1991	122375	44169	39961	5681	16169	1492	10633	509	1304	39	190442	51889
7-8-9. Production and Related Workers, Transport Equipment Operators and Labourers	1981	14115	3212	10958	795	4381	187	3932	106	312	8	33698	4308
	1991	15339	3663	12902	1306	7732	491	7344	293	1079	46	44396	5799
10. Workers not Classified by occupation	1981	1257	234	427	27	203	9	327	14	106	7	2320	291
	1991	1083	228	433	25	562	13	1053	20	244	14	3375	301
Total	1981	127919	38027	51129	4141	17588	852	19906	1279	5975	674	222517	44973
	1991	145668	49915	61841	7727	31443	2429	34183	2558	12797	1645	285932	64274

Notes: Excludes Assam in 1981 and Jammu & Kashmir in 1991. Totals may not tally due to rounding off.

Main workers are those who work for 183 days or more in a year.

Source: Registrar General and Census Commissioner of India : *Census of India, 1981* and 1991.

Table 3.2.20: Employment* in Organised and Unorganised Sector

Year	*Employment (Million)*			*Organised as percent of Total*
	Organised	*Unorganised*	*Total*[E]	
1973	18.82	217.48	236.30	7.96
1978	21.24	249.46	270.70	7.85
1983	24.01	278.69	302.70	7.93
1988	25.71	296.29	322.00	7.99
1991	26.73	315.17	341.90	7.82
1994	27.38	344.72	372.10	7.36
2000	27.96	368.84	396.80	7.05
2001	27.79	383.71	411.50	6.75
2002	27.21	NA	NA	NA
2003	27.00	NA	NA	NA
2004	26.44	NA	NA	NA
2005	26.45	NA	NA	NA
2006	26.99	NA	NA	NA

Notes: Organised Sector includes all the establishments in the public sector and non-agricultural establishments employing 10 or more persons in the private sector. While data on employment in the public sector and the non-agricultural establishments in the private sector employing 25 or more persons are collected under the provisions of Employment Exchanges (Compulsory Notification of Vacancies) Act, 1959, the same from the non-agricultural establishments in the private sector employing 10-24 persons are being collected on voluntary basis.

*As on March 31. E – Estimated. NA – Not available.

Sources: (*i*) National Sample Survey Organisation.

(*ii*) Directorate General of Employment and Training.

Table 3.2.21: Employment* in Organised Sector

Year	Employment **(Lakh)			Percentage of Women Employment to total
	Public	Private	Total	
1971	107.31	67.42	174.73	11.00
1981	154.84	73.95	228.79	12.20
1986	176.84	73.74	250.58	13.00
1988	183.20	73.92	257.12	13.40
1989	185.09	74.53	259.62	13.60
1990	187.72	75.82	263.54	14.10
1991	190.57	76.76	267.33	14.10
1992	192.10	78.46	270.56	14.40
1993	193.26	78.51	271.77	14.80
1994	194.45	79.30	273.75	15.20
1995	194.66	80.59	275.25	15.40
1996	194.29	85.12	279.41	15.80
1997	195.59	86.86	282.45	16.40
1998	194.18	87.48	281.66	16.90
1999	194.15	86.98	281.13	17.20
2000	193.14	86.46	279.60	17.60
2001	191.38	86.52	277.89	17.81
2002	187.73	84.32	272.06	18.43
2003	185.80	84.21	270.00	18.40
2004	181.97	82.46	264.43	18.66
2005	180.06	84.52	264.58	18.96
2006	181.88	88.05	269.93	18.97

Notes: * As on March 31.

** Sikkim, Arunachal Pradesh, Dadar & Nagar Haveli and Lakshdweep are not covered under the Employment Market Information (EMI) Programme.

Source: Directorate General of Employment and Training : *Employment Review* for various years.

Figure 3.2.K

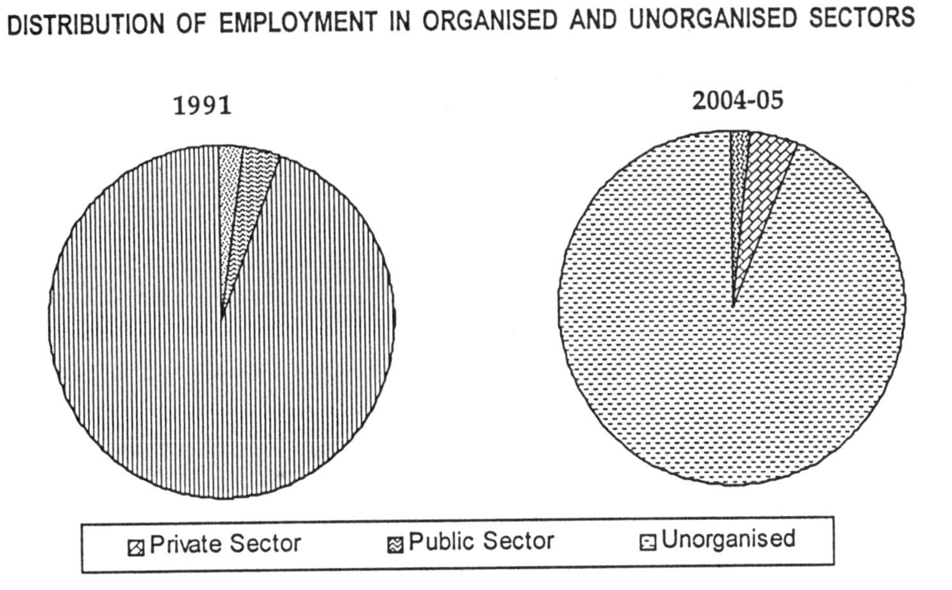

For details see Tables 3.2.20 and 3.2.21

Figure 3.2.L

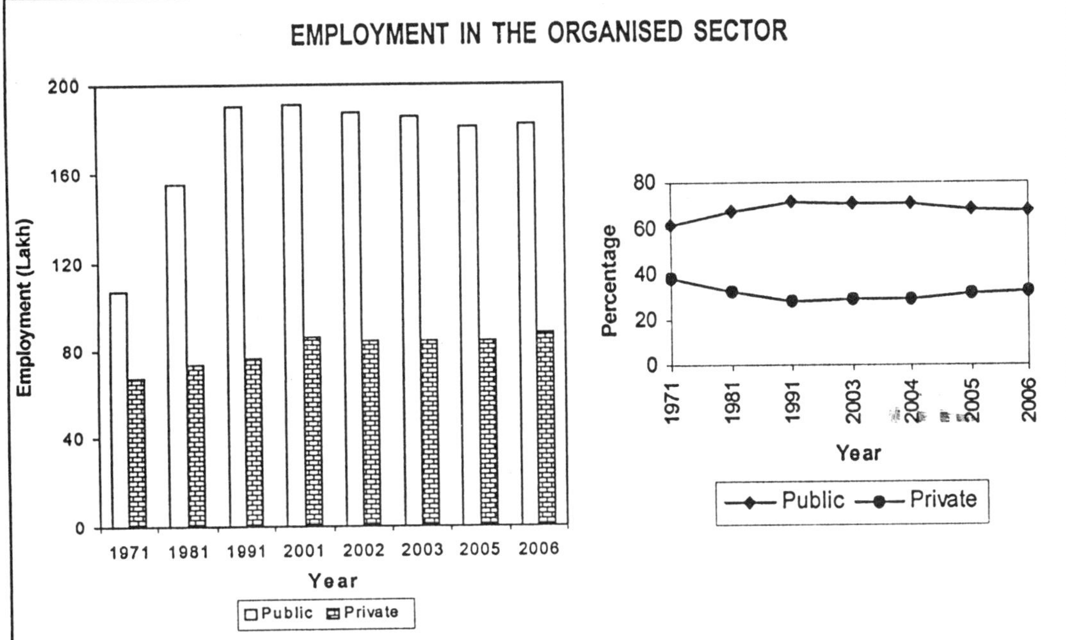

For details see Table 3.2.21

Table 3.2.22: Employment* in Organised Sector by Industry Division

Industry Division	*Employment (Lakh)*															
	Public Sector								*Private Sector*							
	1998	*2000*	*2001*	*2002*	*2003*	*2004*	*2005*	*2006*	1998	2000	2001	2002	2003	2004	2005	2006
0. Agriculture, Forestry, Fishing and Hunting	5.30	5.14	5.02	4.83	5.06	4.93	4.96	4.69	9.04	9.04	9.33	8.55	8.95	9.17	9.83	10.28
1. Mining and Quarrying	9.37	9.24	8.75	8.61	8..47	11.30	10.14	11.46	0.91	0.81	0.79	0.68	0.66	0.65	0.79	0.94
2&3. Manufacturing	16.16	15.31	14.30	13.50	12.60	11.89	11.30	10.92	52.33	50.85	50.13	48.67	47.44	44.89	44.89	45.49
4. Electricity, Gas and Water	9.54	9.46	9.35	9.23	9.13	8.74	8.60	8.50	0.42	0.41	0.52	0.42	0.51	0.47	0.49	0.40
5. Construction	11.08	10.92	10.8	10.26	9.48	9.32	9.11	8.94	0.74	0.57	0.57	0.56	0.44	0.45	0.49	0.55
6. Wholesale and Retail Trade and Restaurants and Hotels	1.64	1.63	1.63	1.57	1.82	1.81	1.84	1.82	3.21	3.30	3.39	3.35	3.60	3.51	3.75	3.87
7. Transport, Storage and Communications	30.84	30.77	30.42	30.09	29.39	28.15	27.51	26.75	0.65	0.70	0.76	0.76	0.79	0.81	0.85	0.87
8. Financing, Insurance, Real Estate and Business Services	12.88	12.96	12.81	12.30	13.77	14.08	14.08	13.90	3.41	3.58	3.70	3.91	4.26	4.58	5.23	6.52
9. Community, Social and Personal Services	97.37	97.71	98.30	97.34	96.09	92.78	92.52	91.76	16.77	17.23	17.37	17.42	17.56	17.92	18.20	18.79
Total	194.18	193.14	191.38	187.73	185.80	181.97	180.07	178.73@	87.48	86.46	86.52	84.32	84.21	82.46	84.52	87.71@

Notes : * As on March 31.

@ Due to non availability of data as per NIC 1998, information in respect of J & K, Meghalaya, Mizoram, Daman & Diu not included in totals.

Source: Directorate General of Employment and Training : *Employment Review* of the relevant various years.

Table 3.2.23: Employment in Organised Sector by State/ Union Territory

State/Union Territory	Employment (Lakh)													
	Public Sector							Private Sector						
	1998	2000	2001	2002	2003	2005	2006	1998	2000	2001	2002	2003	2005	2006
States														
1. Andhra Pradesh	15.09	15.03	14.89	14.62	14.75	13.96	13.88	5.42	5.69	5.86	5.89	6.25	5.47	5.96
2. Assam	5.35	5.36	5.37	5.25	5.28	5.31	5.24	5.57	5.49	5.79	5.38	5.51	5.81	6.27
3. Bihar	13.79	13.61	13.60	13.60	13.60	4.95	4.06	2.55	2.53	2.53	2.53	2.53	0.32	0.25
4. Chhathisgarh	@	@	3.17	3.24	3.24	3.07	3.09	@	@	0.31	0.30	0.30	0.32	0.32
5. Delhi	6.25	6.26	6.24	6.21	6.24	6.15	6.05	2.21	2.21	2.18	2.15	2.12	2.16	2.21
6. Goa	0.69	0.70	0.70	0.36	0.36	0.70	0.81	0.39	0.41	0.41	0.25	0.25	0.41	0.46
7. Gujarat	9.55	9.20	9.34	8.49	8.51	8.32	8.25	8.34	7.70	7.62	7.35	7.80	8.61	9.35
8. Haryana	4.24	4.21	4.16	4.10	4.00	3.90	3.88	2.33	2.31	2.36	2.56	2.55	2.58	2.61
9. Himachal Pradesh	2.50	2. 63	2.57	2.48	2.48	3.58	2.50	0.43	0.48	0.48	0.50	0.50	0.59	0.65
10. Jammu & Kashmir	2.00	2.00	2.00	2.00	2.00	1.99	2.00	0.11	0.11	0.11	0.11	0.11	0.10	0.11
11. Jharkhand	@	@	@	@	@	8.92	12.01	@	@	@	@	@	1.50	2.76
12. Karnataka	10.86	11.13	11.13	10.90	10.75	10.59	10.52	7.57	7.51	7.67	7.66	7.75	8.03	8.64
13. Kerala	6.30	6.45	6.45	6.45	6.34	6.14	6.15	5.60	5.65	5.97	5.76	5.77	5.25	4.96
14. Madhya Pradesh	14.05	13.67	9.93	9.68	9.48	9.15	9.06	2.48	2.27	1.86	1.74	1.62	1.56	1.51
15. Maharashtra	23.32	22.90	22.61	22.32	22.05	21.38	21.39	15.17	14.70	14.33	14.02	13.88	14.03	14.68
16. Manipur	0.78	0.79	0.80	0.80	0.81	0.78	0.76	0.02	0.03	0.03	0.03	0.03	0.03	0.03
17. Meghalaya	0.70	0.73	0.73	0.73	0.73	0.73	0.73	0.08	0.09	0.09	0.09	0.09	0.09	0.09
18. Mizoram	0.40	0.40	0.40	0.40	0.40	0.40	0.40	0.01	0.01	0.01	0.01	0.01	0.01	0.01
19. Nagaland	0.73	0.74	0.74	0.74	0.68	0.68	0.72	0.03	0.03	0.03	0.03	0.03	0.04	0.04
20. Orissa	7.07	7.12	7.44	6.93	6.68	6.60	6.48	0.94	0.86	0.85	0.84	0.83	0.90	0.90
21. Punjab	5.99	5.90	5.86	5.81	5.56	5.20	5.54	2.48	2.56	2.61	2.55	2.44	2.53	2.83
22. Rajasthan	10.09	10.17	9.92	9.60	9.35	9.33	9.47	2.64	2.59	2.56	2.50	2.45	2.48	2.58
23. Tamil Nadu	16.29	15.97	15.86	16.12	15.70	15.13	15.04	9.32	9.27	9.20	9.04	8.32	7.66	7.34
24. Tripura	1.00	1.10	1.10	1.10	1.10	1.10	1.34	0.11	0.13	0.13	0.13	0.13	0.13	0.12

Table 3.2.23: *(Contd.)*

State/Union Territory	*Employment (Lakh)*													
	Public Sector							*Private Sector*						
	1998	*2000*	*2001*	*2002*	*2003*	*2005*	*2006*	*1998*	*2000*	*2001*	*2002*	*2003*	*2005*	*2006*
25. Uttaranchal	@	@	2.35	2.28	2.27	2.24	2.26	@	@	0.35	0.37	0.35	0.37	0.37
26. Uttar Pradesh	20.88	20.29	17.58	17.18	16.92	16.50	16.36	5.36	5.10	4.66	4.56	4.52	4.37	4.55
27. West Bengal	14.87	15.42	15.25	15.17	15.16	12.86	12.51	7.98	8.11	8.00	7.47	7.47	7.52	7.79
Union Territories														
28. Andaman and Nicobar Islands	0.32	0.33	0.33	0.35	0.35	0.35	0.36	0.04	0.05	0.05	0.05	0.05	0.03	0.03
29. Chandigarh	0.64	0.64	0.64	0.63	0.62	0.60	0.60	0.19	0.25	0.27	0.28	0.28	0.28	0.28
30. Pondicherry	0.42	0.38	0.20	0.20	0.37	0.40	0.41	0.09	0.08	0.05	0.05	0.14	0.18	0.22
31. Daman and Diu	0.02	0.02	0.02	0.02	0.02	0.02	0.02	0.09	0.12	0.13	0.13	0.13	0.12	0.13
All India	194.18	193.14	191.38	187.73	185.80	180.61	181.88	87.48	86.46	86.52	84.32	84.21	84.52	88.05

Notes: As on March 31.
Totals may not tally due to rounding off.
Sikkim, Arunachal Pradesh, Dadra and Nagar Haveli and Lakshadweep are not covered under the EMI Programme.
@ Figures are incuded in their parent state.

Source: Directorate General of Employment and Training : *Employment Review* for the relevant years.

Table 3.2.24: Women Employment in Organised Sector by Industry Division

(*Thousand*)

Industry Division	*Public Sector*								*Private Sector*							
	1998	*2000*	*2001*	*2002*	*2003*	*2004*	*2005*	*2006*	*1998*	*2000*	*2001*	*2002*	*2003*	*2004*	*2005*	*2006*
Agriculture, Forestry, Fishing and Hunting	47.5	48.1	48.3	43.6	47.8	47.7	53.7	58.2	442.5	461.9	464.4	419.8	418.7	411.0	430.5	438.5
Mining and Quarrying	58.3	57.6	55.6	55.3	54.3	66.0	65.0	77.0	12.7	8.9	8.4	6.9	6.6	7.3	12.4	8.5
Manufacturing	105.5	99.1	93.0	88.1	86.6	81.5	80.0	77.7	930.6	933.9	937.0	928.0	923.2	867.9	859.3	812.7
Electricity, Gas and Water	41.7	43.6	44.7	45.4	46.3	49.7	50.5	50.4	1.4	0.9	1.3	1.2	1.4	2.4	2.5	2.2
Construction	60.7	64.1	63.2	63.7	60.5	62.6	63.6	61.4	6.3	4.0	4.0	3.8	3.7	3.4	3.4	4.2
Wholesale and Retail Trade and Restaurants and Hotels	16.3	16.6	17.4	17.3	14.0	14.0	14.3	13.9	27.4	29.4	29.4	30.3	30.5	32.0	35.3	34.6
Transport, Storage and Communications	168.4	170.2	174.9	178.1	180.3	179.0	181.1	180.4	6.1	6.8	8.1	8.3	8.7	10.4	10.5	10.2
Financing, Insurance, Real Estate and Business Services	177.9	181.1	184.8	191.1	202.0	206.0	207.9	205.7	48.8	53.9	60.2	65.1	72.3	81.2	94.3	124.0
Community, Social and Personal Services	2,086.4	2,176.1	2,177.2	2,204.1	2,212.9	2,183.6	2,205.0	2,231.8	535.1	566.1	537.3	585.4	598.7	628.8	647.1	675.0
Total	2,762.7	2,857.0	2,090.1	2,886.7	2,904.7	2,890.0	2,921.0	2,956.46	2,010.9	2,065.8	2,839.2	2,048.7	2,063.7	2,044.4	2,095.21	2,109.8

Source: Directorate General of Employment and Training : *Employment Review* for relevant years.

Figure 3.2.M

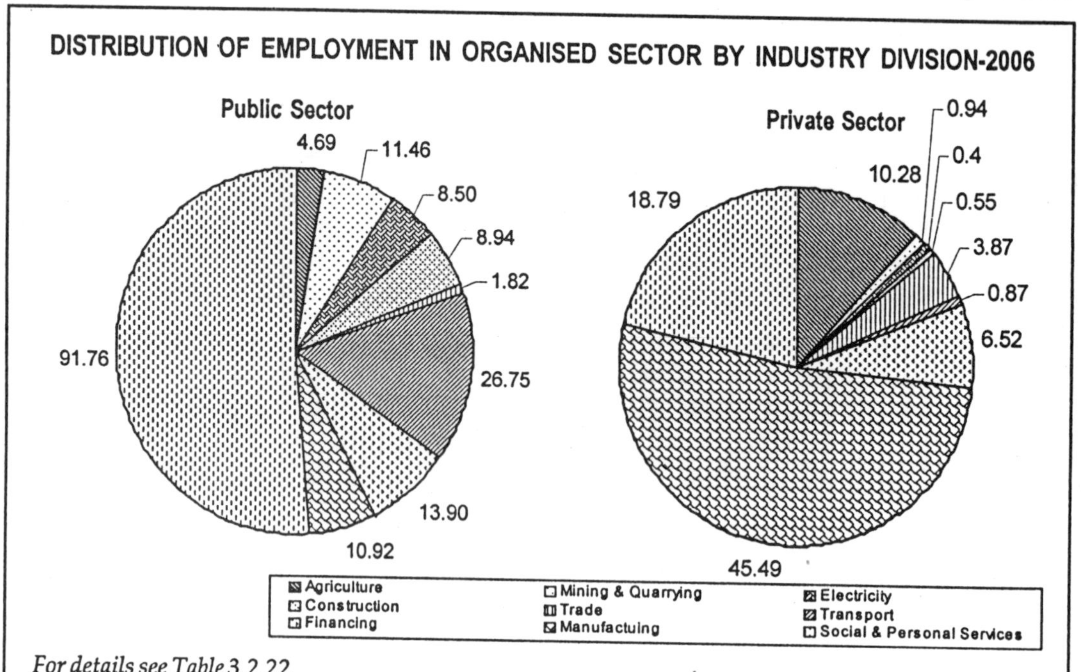

For details see Table 3.2.22

Figure 3.2.N

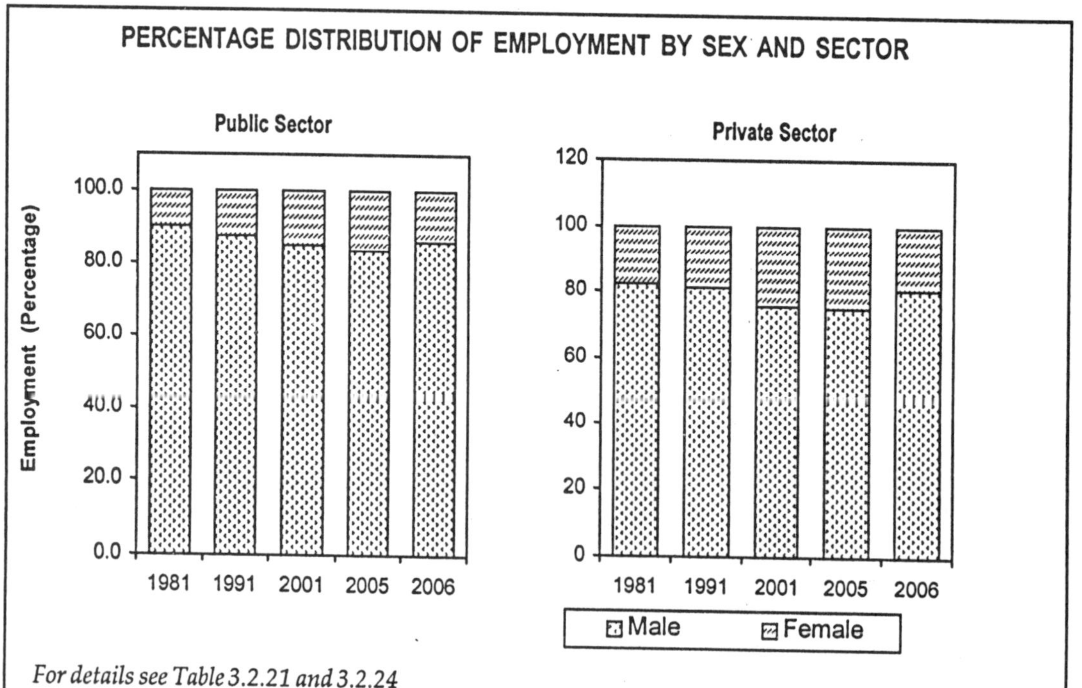

For details see Table 3.2.21 and 3.2.24

Table 3.2.25: Women Employment in Organised Sector by State/Union Territory

(Thousand)

State/Union Territory	Public Sector							Private Sector						
	1998	2000	2001	2002	2003	2005	2006	1998	2000	2001	2002	2003	2005	2006
States														
1. Andhra Pradesh	205.2	220.0	223.7	226.0	248.3	241.8	241.5	181.1	198.6	195.4	198.2	225.7	231.8	194.2
2. Assam	71.4	77.2	79.1	75.8	77.4	81.7	83.6	253.1	271.6	288.7	250.8	241.2	284.9	295.6
3. Bihar	91.7	90.0	89.9	89.9	89.9	29.5	20.5	17.5	17.3	17.2	17.2	17.2	2.0	1.9
4. Chhattisgarh	@	@	36.8	37.8	37.8	36.9	38.0	@	@	4.7	4.6	4.6	5.0	4.9
5. Delhi	91.1	91.4	91.5	91.9	92.9	92.6	93.0	29.6	30.3	30.1	30.4	30.2	32.9	33.8
6. Goa	14.8	14.9	14.9	10.3	10.3	13.3	10.2	7.2	7.4	7.4	4.6	4.6	9.0	6.9
7. Gujarat	148.2	138.1	136.4	128.6	133.7	144.7	147.5	76.8	70.7	69.3	70.5	80.3	90.2	94.2
8. Haryana	62.3	63.3	62.7	62.4	61.1	60.7	60.5	23.5	25.9	27.5	34.3	37.0	38.2	38.7
9. Himachal Pradesh	37.0	41.0	42.2	40.6	40.6	44.7	44.2	5.7	5.5	4.9	6.3	6.3	7.5	9.2
10. Jammu and Kashmir	20.7	20.7	20.7	20.7	20.7	20.7	20.7	1.9	1.9	1.9	1.9	1.9	1.9	1.9
11. Jharkhand	@	@	@	@	@	61.8	85.8	@	@	@	@	@	13.7	24.6
12. Karnataka	223.0	246.3	254.5	255.5	259.6	268.4	267.7	308.6	306.0	314.2	320.6	321.4	309.9	323.6
13. Kerala	190.5	191.5	193.5	193.5	191.6	187.6	187.3	262.3	275.2	292.4	282.3	283.5	262.0	240.5
14. Madhya Pradesh	157.5	165.2	129.2	127.8	121.3	124.0	123.7	27.8	27.4	21.3	20.6	19.7	19.2	18.8
15. Maharashtra	348.7	353.0	357.7	353.8	355.6	357.7	373.8	206.8	205.1	207.0	205.6	206.3	215.4	233.4
16. Manipur	16.7	17.7	18.0	18.2	18.2	18.0	18.4	0.8	1.0	1.0	1.0	1.0	1.0	0.6
17. Meghalaya	13.9	15.0	15.0	15.0	15.0	15.0	15.0	3.3	4.4	4.4	4.4	4.4	4.4	4.4
18. Mizoram	10.0	10.4	10.4	10.4	10.4	10.4	10.4	0.6	0.6	0.6	0.6	0.6	0.6	0.6
19. Nagaland	11.1	11.4	11.2	12.0	11.5	12.4	14.3	1.0	1.2	1.4	1.3	1.2	1.4	1.7
20. Orissa	79.3	84.3	88.3	91.8	92.1	98.1	104.4	10.7	10.2	10.4	9.7	10.1	10.5	10.6
21. Punjab	97.4	97.9	99.5	101.6	107.6	89.8	101.8	29.6	33.1	34.4	34.8	32.9	39.1	44.8
22. Rajasthan	129.0	133.1	131.7	127.6	125.8	138.1	150.9	41.9	40.9	40.9	40.8	38.9	40.8	42.4
23. Tamil Nadu	407.9	425.9	402.0	440.3	420.3	419.3	423.1	324.5	328.1	327.5	322.1	305.7	288.3	293.3

Table 3.2.25 *(Contd.)*

(Thousand)

State/Union Territory	*Public Sector*							*Private Sector*						
	1998	*2000*	*2001*	*2002*	*2003*	*2005*	*2006*	*1998*	*2000*	*2001*	*2002*	*2003*	*2005*	*2006*
24. Tripura	17.5	21.0	21.0	21.0	21.0	21.0	27.7	4.7	5.8	5.8	5.8	5.8	5.8	6.0
25. Uttaranchal	@	@	28.8	28.8	28.8	29.1	32.2	@	@	4.3	4.6	4.6	4.9	6.3
26. Uttar Pradesh	184.9	188.3	159.8	162.2	166.5	171.1	173.0	53.6	53.2	48.5	48.5	49.7	50.1	53.0
27. West Bengal	112.0	115.5	119.8	122.2	122.2	106.4	107.2	131.5	135.6	133.7	119.4	119.4	113.6	120.1
Union Territories1														
1. Andaman and Nicobar Islands	3.1	5.0	5.3	5.5	5.6	7.4	6.4	0.1	0.2	0.2	0.2	0.2	6.8	0.2
2. Chandigarh	11.1	12.5	12.7	12.8	12.9	13.4	13.4	3.8	6.2	6.3	5.9	5.9	6.5	6.2
3. Pondicherry	6.6	6.1	2.3	2.3	5.6	6.5	6.5	1.5	1.4	0.6	0.6	2.4	3.3	4.3
4. Daman and Diu	0.2	0.5	0.4	0.3	0.3	0,3	0.3	1.3	1.2	1.5	1.0	1.0	1.0	1.0
All India	2,762.7	2,857.0	2,859.2	2,886.7	2,904.7	2,921.0	3,002.8	2,010.9	2,065.8	2,090.1	2,048.7	2,063.7	2,095.2	2,117.7

Notes: Sikkim, Arunachal Pradesh, Dadra & Nagar Haveli and Lakshadweep are not covered under the EMI Programme.

@ The figures for these states were included in their parent states.

Source: Directorate General of Employment and Training : *Employment Review,* of the relevant Year.

Table 3.2.26: Number of Registered Working Factories and Estimated Average Daily Employment

State/Union Territory	*Total Number of Registered Working Factories*					*Total Estimated Average Daily Employment (in Thousand)*				
	1999	*2000*	*2002*	*2003*	*2004*	*1999*	*2000*	*2002*	*2003*	*2004*
States										
1. Andhra Pradesh	33,066	28,924	30,762	27,427	28,016	833	715	731	717	764
2. Assam	1,528	1,574	1,554	1,526	1,671	98	98	96	94	99
3. Bihar	46,424	46,424(R)	–	–	–	519	519 (R)	–	–	–
4. Delhi	6,612	6,641	–	–	–	228	228 (R)	–	–	–
5. Goa	543	591	695	696	661	33	36	42	45	43
6. Gujarat	19,879	19,879(R)	–	–	–	864	864 (R)	–	–	–
7. Haryana	7469	7,469(R)	8,794	6,303	9,170	419	419 (R)	448	361	558
8. Himachal Pradesh	1,825	1,825(R)	–	–	–	87	87 (R)	–	–	–
9. Jammu & Kashmir	651(R)	651(R)	–	–	–	27 (R)	27 (R)	–	–	–
10. Karnataka	9,647	9,647(R)	9,542	9,750	10,063	970	970 (R)	1,048	1,004	890
11. Kerala	18,511	18,554	–	–	18,221	437	441	–	–	408
12. Madhya Pradesh	10,961	7,869	7,806	7,893	7,586	611	403	392	417	473
13. Maharashtra	28,753	29,637	28,783	28,892	29,332	1,281	1,279	1,227	1,216	1,235
14. Manipur	1,177(R)	1,177(R)	–	–	–	9 (R)	9(R)	–	–	–
15. Meghalaya	53(R)	71	–	–	74	2 (R)	3	–	–	4
16. Orissa	1,909	1900	1,899	1,933	1,994	143	139	133	131	130
17. Punjab	13,389	13,596	13,791	14,109	14,670	448	451	451	462	480
18. Rajasthan	8,853	9,186	9,347	9,406	9,711	361	317	363	373	386
19. Tamil Nadu	21,875(R)	21,875(R)	24,811	–	25,843	1,153 (R)	1,153 (R)	1,252	–	1,283
20. Tripura	1,331	1,349	1,481	1,522	1,542	29	31	32	32	33
21. Uttar Pradesh	15,300(R)	15,300(R)	–	–	–	1,025 (R)	1,025	–	–	–
22. West Bengal	8,981(R)	8,981(R)	–	–	–	905 (R)	905	–	–	–
Union Territories										
1. Andaman and Nicobar Islands	48(R)	48(R)	48	33	–	6(R)	6 (R)	8	5	–
2. Chandigarh	534	529	494	484	437	16	17	15	15	14
3. Dadra and Nagar Haveli	50(R)	50(R)	–	–	–	2(R)	2 (R)	–	–	–
4. Pondicherry	1,627	1,774	1284	1,421	–	49	40	55	55	–
Total (Estimated)	260,248	255,521	141085	1,11,895	1,58,991	10,548	10,195	6,330	4,927	6,802

Notes: Factories registered under Indian Factories Act.
Figures are provisional.
R — Due to non receipt of returns the previous year's figures have been repeated.
P — Provisional.

Sources: Labour Bureau : (*i*) *Indian Labour Year Book—2004.*
(*ii*) Pocket Book of Labour Statitics, 2007.

Table 3.2.27: Employment in Select Organisations/Departments

(Thousand)

Year	*Banking**	*Insurance*	*Railways*	*Mines*	*Plantations***	*Shops and Commercial Establishment*
1993	1,039	202	1,649	779	1,680	4,123
1994	1,059	210	1,628	750	1,800	5,032
1995	1,063	206	1,605	736	1,809	5,197
1996	1,069	210	1,590	716	1,846	5,816
1997	1,066	212	1,587	705	1,854	6,118
1998	1,068	211	1,582	686	1,878	5,934
1999	1,066	209	1,582	659	2,060	6,503
2000	1,056	207	1,581	639	2,093	6,878
2001	958	203	1,549	599	2,133	6,928
2002	NA	201	1,515	582	2106	7364
2003	NA	198	1,476	572	2156	6995
2004	907	189	1,446	568	2163	NA
2005	923	187	1,425	554	2187	NA
2006	922	185	1,412	NA	NA	NA

Notes: * After 1991 it does not include the employees of non-scheduled banks.
** In terms of average daily employment. NA- Data not available

Source: Central Statistical Organisation : *Statistical Abstract, 2005 & 2006*

Table 3.2.28: Number* of Central Government Employees by Sex

Year	*Total Employment (in lakhs)*	*Index of Employment (witn 1971 as base)*	*No. of Women Employees (lakhs)*	*Percentage of Women Employees Total*
1971	26.99	100.00	0.67	2.51
1976	30.45	112.80	0.99	3.26
1981	34.07	126.20	1.24	3.64
1984	36.14	133.90	1.42	3.93
1988	36.99	137.10	2.39	6.46
1989	37.48	138.90	2.47	6.60
1990	37.74	139.80	2.83	7.52
1991	38.13	141.30	2.89	7.58
1995	39.82	147.50	2.96	7.43
2001	38.76	143.61	2.92	7.53
2004	31.64	117.23	3.06	9.68

Note: *31st March of the reference year.

Source: Directorate General of Employment and Training : *Census of Central Government Employees, 2004.*

Table 3.2.29. Distribution of SSI Units* by Industiral Categeory & Employment

NIC	Description of Industry Emp./Unit	Working Units			Employment			Employment/Unit		
		1st Census 1972-73	2nd Census 1987-88	3rd Census 2001-02	1st Census 1972-73	2nd Census 1987-88	3rd Census 2001-02	1st Census 1972-73	2nd Census 1987-88	3rd Census 2001-02
20/21.	Food & Food Products	6,577	96,123	1,04,489	1,31,220	4,81,682	4,03,113	20	5	4
22.	Beverages,Tobacco & Tobacco Products	469	3,669	5,851	4,577	73,375	35,863	10	20	6
23.	Cotton Textiles	–	1,451	10,876**	–	24,725	79,312**	–	–	7**
24.	Wool Silk & Synth. Fibre Textiles	–	1,158	–	12,314	–				
25.	Jute, Hemp & Mesta Textiles	–	219	–	2,599	–				
26.	Hosiery & Garments	6,178	39,778	1,07,565	75,346	1,98,387	3,74,836	11	5	3
27.	Wood Products	12,188	54,975	77,110	94,703	2,29,061	2,90,696	8	4	4
28.	Paper Products & Printing	8,332	33,320	26,104	89,146	1,99,389	1,19,658	11	6	5
29.	Leather & Leather Products	5,040	24,028	17,027	31,775	81,667	65,174	6	3	4
30.	Rubber & Plastic Products	7,688	25,819	18,228	81,690	1,88,784	1,17,934	11	7	6
31.	Chemical & Chemical Products	11,837	25,941	11,177	1,59,013	3,13,986	96,209	13	12	9
32.	Non-Mettalic Mineral Products (Glass & Ceramic)	7,794	3,15,891	25,128	2,02,269	4,46,218	2,58,627	26	14	10
33.	Basic Metal Products	5,073	14,937	7,876	1,09,626	2,02,463	84,830	22	14	11
34.	Metal Products	34,011	65,868	80,636	3,00,060	3,72,711	3,58,629	9	6	4
35.	Machinery & Parts Except Electrical	12,701	40,802	8,776	1,45,333	2,79,292	37,242	11	7	4
36.	Electrical Machinery/Apparatus	4,409	12,283	5,626	65,908	1,37,260	33,104	15	11	6
37.	Transport Equipment & Parts	6,049	11,325	2,100	83,492	1,00,360	36,208	14	9	17
38.	Misc Manufacturing Industries	3,489	8,852	4,726	40,025	65,322	–	5	7	–
97.	Repair Services	7,197	80,412	75,385	38,995	1,92,267	1,61,728	11	2	2
99.	Services not e.c.	–	613	1,200	–	2,720	–	–	4	–
OT	Other Service & Products	–	9,206	1,60,222	–	61,228	8,95,193	–	7	6
	Total	1,39,577	5,82,368	7,50,102	16,53,178	36,65,810	34,48,356	12	6	4.6

Notes: Concordance Table was applied for converting NIC-98 based data of IIIrd Census in terms of NIC-87, at two digit level of Ist & IInd Small Scale Induatrial Census data.

* All registered SSI Working Units for which data has been tabulated.

** Includes data related to code no. 24 and 25 also.

Sources: Development Commissioner, Small Scale Industries, Ministry of Industry:

(*i*) Report on Census of Small Scale Industrial Units, 1972-73, Vol. I & II.

(*ii*) Report on the Second All India Census of Small Scale Industrial Units.

(*iii*) Quick Results, Third All India Census of Small Scale Industries, 2001-02.

Table 3.2.30: Percentage of Employed Persons* with Changed Employment Status by Educational Level and Sex, 2004-2005

Usual Status	Male										Female									
	Not Literate		Literate and Below Primary		Primary, Middle & Secondary		Higher Secondary & Above		All		Not Literate		Literate and below Primary		Primary, Middle & secondary		Higher Secondary & Above		All	
	Esta-blish-ment	Work Status	Esta-blish-ment	Work Status	Esta-blish-ment	Work Status	Esta-blish-ment	Work Status	Esta-blish-ment	Work Status	Esta-blish-ment	Work Status	Esta-blish-ment	Work Status	Esta-blish-ment	Work Status	Esta-blish-ment	Work Status	Esta-blish-ment	Work Status
Rural																				
Self Employed	1.6	0.3	2.0	0.4	1.8	0.6	2.0	1.0	1.8	0.5	1.5	0.2	1.6	0.2	1.8	0.2	1.5	0.4	1.6	0.2
Regular Wage/ Salaried	8.4	2.6	3.5	0.8	6.3	2.1	4.5	1.5	5.8	1.9	6.1	0.5	4.5	0.3	3.1	2.0	3.2	0.9	4.1	1.1
Casual Labour	15.4	0.5	18.0	1.0	20.2	0.8	23.3	2.2	17.7	0.7	18.1	0.3	22.5	0.6	25.1	0.5	47.6	0.0	19.6	0.4
All	8.0	0.4	8.3	0.6	7.4	0.8	4.3	1.3	7.4	0.7	8.8	0.3	10.1	0.4	8.3	0.4	4.9	0.7	8.7	0.3
Urban																				
Self Employed	2.6	0.6	2.2	0.8	2.9	1.1	2.2	1.3	2.6	1.1	1.7	0.2	3.1	0.4	1.3	0.6	2.1	1.5	1.7	0.6
Regular Wage/ Salaried	9.3	1.2	6.9	0.6	6.1	1.3	4.0	0.8	5.5	1.0	8.2	0.5	5.3	0.0	6.9	0.8	3.5	0.3	5.5	0.5
Casual Labour	20.2	0.4	20.4	1.2	21.7	2.2	23.1	3.0	21.1	1.6	19.4	0.3	30.6	1.2	19.6	0.5	29.1	0.0	20.6	0.4
All	9.6	0.7	8.2	0.8	7.0	1.4	3.7	1.0	6.5	1.1	8.7	0.3	9.3	0.4	6.0	0.7	3.4	0.6	6.6	0.5

Notes: The change has been observed for the two years preceeding the survey.

* Figures relate to principal usual status of individuals of age 15 years and above.

Source: National Sample Survey Organisation : Report No. 515, *Employment and Unemployment Situation in India, 2004-05.*

Table 3.2.31: Percentage of Employed Persons* with Changed Occupation by Location and Sex, 2004-05

Occupation	Rural		Urban	
	Male	Female	Male	Female
0-1. Professional, Technical and Related Workers	1.0 (0.5)	0.7 (1.2)	1.0 (0.8)	0.4 (0.4)
2. Administrative, Executive and Managerial Workers	1.4 (2.8)	1.2 (0.1)	1.4 (1.5)	0.5 (1.1)
3. Clerical and Related Workers	1.5 (1.9)	2.3 (1.5)	1.7 (1.3)	0.8 (0.5)
4. Sales Workers	2.0 (1.7)	1.4 (1.1)	1.6 (1.3)	0.8 (0.6)
5. Service Workers	2.0 (1.6)	1.2 (1.3)	1.6 (1.4)	0.8 (0.8)
6. Farmers, Fisherman, Hunters, Loggers and Related Workers	0.6 (0.6)	0.3 (0.4)	0.9 (1.0)	0.4 (0.2)
7-8-9. Production and Related Workers, Transport Equipment Operators and Labourers	1.7 (1.7)	1.0 (1.6)	1.5 (1.5)	0.8 (0.7)
10. Workers not Classified by Occupation**	– (0.5)	– (0.0)	– (0.0)	– (0.0)
All	1.0 (0.9)	0.4 (0.6)	1.5 (1.3)	0.7 (0.6)

Notes: The change has been observed for the two years preceding the survey.
* Figures relate to Principle usual status of individuals of age 15 years and above.
** Includes 'not recorded' cases also.
Figures in Parenthetis indidicate for year 1999-2000.

Source: National Sample Survey Organisation : Report No. 515, *Employment and Unemployment Situation in India, 2004-05.*

Table 3.2.32: Percentage of Employed Persons* with Changed Industry Division by Location and Sex 2004-05

Broad Industry	Rural		Urban	
	Male	Female	Male	Female
Primary Sector	0.4 (0.5)	0.1 (0.3)	0.7 (0.8)	1.3 (0.1)
Secondary Sector	1.9 (2.1)	1.0 (1.5)	1.6 (1.8)	1.5 (0.8)
Tertiary Sector	1.7 (1.6)	1.2 (0.9)	1.6 (1.2)	0.7 (0.8)
All	0.9 (0.9)	0.3 (1.3)	1.6 (1.4)	0.9 (0.7)

Notes: The change has been observed for the two years preceding the survey.
* Includes 'not recorded' cases also. Figures relate to Principle usual status of individuals of age 15 years and above.
Figures in Parenthetis indidicate for year 1999-2000.

Source: National Sample Survey Organisation : Report No. 515, *Employment and Unemployment Situation in India, 2004-05.*

Table 3.2.33: Percentage of Employed Persons* with Changed Nature of Work by State/Union Territory, 2004-05 (Rural)

State/Union Territory	Male				Female			
	Establish-ment	Status	Industry	Occu-pation	Establish-ment	Status	Industry	Occu-pation
States								
Andhra Pradesh	3.0	0.7	1.0	1.1	2.2	0.2	0.3	0.4
Arunachal Pradesh	1.4	0.0	0.2	0.5	1.4	0.0	0.0	0.5
Assam	1.8	0.5	0.7	0.9	0.4	0.1	0.3	0.3
Bihar	2.8	0.3	0.2	0.3	3.7	0.3	0.2	0.1
Chhattisgarh	14.9	0.8	0.8	1.1	16.1	0.1	0.3	0.3
Delhi	1.7	0.0	0.0	0.0	0.0	0.0	0.0	0.0
Goa	12.9	2.8	3.9	2.0	11.6	0.0	0.0	0.0
Gujarat	9.9	0.8	1.2	1.2	13.0	0.0	0.1	0.1
Haryana	11.8	1.1	1.8	2.0	4.3	0.3	1.5	1.5
Himachal Pradesh	3.9	0.8	1.3	1.0	0.6	0.2	0.2	0.2
Jammu and Kashmir	1.0	0.7	0.6	0.6	0.3	0.0	0.0	0.0
Jharkhand	1.7	0.4	0. 6	0.6	1.6	0.2	0.3	0.4
Karnataka	4.4	0.9	0.7	0.9	5.2	0.6	0.3	0.4
Kerala	13.0	1.9	2.9	2.5	8.7	1.4	0.4	0.5
Madhya Pradesh	11.5	0.2	0.6	0.4	12.9	0.1	0.1	0.1
Maharashtra	17.2	1.1	1.1	1.2	19.1	0.4	0.2	0.6
Manipur	0.9	0.7	0.9	0.8	0.9	0.6	0.8	0.9
Meghalaya	0.8	0.7	0.8	0.7	0.0	0.3	0.2	0.0
Mizoram	3.0	0.3	0.1	0.1	3.7	0.0	0.0	0.0
Nagaland	0.7	0.2	0.4	0.2	0.2	0.7	0.3	0.3
Orissa	3.1	0.4	0.4	0.4	5.2	0.0	0.0	0.0
Punjab	5.9	0.4	1.2	1.0	8.7	0.1	1.2	1.2
Rajasthan	8.4	0.8	0.8	1.0	4.1	0.4	0.1	0.4
Sikkim	0.6	0.2	0.4	0.4	0.2	0.7	0.1	0.1
Tamil Nadu	19.0	1.1	1.4	1.7	18.4	0.4	0.4	0.6
Tripura	1.1	0.3	0.4	0.4	0.5	0.5	0.4	0.5
Uttar Pradesh	3.2	0.6	0.7	0.8	1.2	0.1	0.1	0.2
Uttaranchal	2.6	0.3	0.2	0.3	0.1	0.0	0.0	0.0
West Bengal	8.4	0.8	1.2	1.2	7.8	1.1	0.8	0.9
Union Territories								
Andman and Nicobar Islands	3.1	0.8	2.7	2.3	0.8	0.9	0.0	0.0
Chandigarh	13.1	0.0	0.3	0.0	0.0	0.0	0.0	0.0
Dadra & Nagar Haveli	3.6	3.6	3.6	3.6	0.0	0.0	0.0	0.0
Daman and Diu	1.1	0.2	0.6	0.2	0.0	0.0	0.0	0.0
Lakshadweep	0.4	0.0	0.0	0.0	0.0	0.0	0.0	0.0
Pondicherry	12.8	1.3	3.0	3.0	10.7	0.0	0.0	0.0
All India	7.4	0.7	0.9	1.0	8.7	0.3	0.3	0.4

Notes: The Change has been observed for the two years preceding the survey.

* Figures relate to principal usual status of individuals of age 15 years and above.

Sources: National and Sample Survey Organisation :

Report Nos. 458 & 515, *Employment and Unemployment Situation in India, 1999-2000 and 2004-05.*

Table 3.2.34: Percentage of Employed Persons* with Changed Nature of work by State/Union Territory, 2004-2005 (Urban)

State/Union Territory	*Male*				*Female*			
	Establishment	*Status*	*Industry*	*Occupation*	*Establishment*	*Status*	*Industry*	*Occupation*
States								
Andhra Pradesh	3.6	1.2	2.1	2.4	2.1	0.3	0.5	0.5
Arunachal Pradesh	7.4	2.9	3.1	6.4	0.4	0.0	0.0	0.3
Assam	1.1	0.9	0.6	0.4	0.1	0.0	0.0	0.1
Bihar	2.2	0.3	1.8	1.6	0.3	0.0	0.0	0.0
Chhattisgarh	9.0	1.2	2.6	2.2	16.1	1.1	1.3	0.4
Delhi	2.2	0.1	0.4	0.2	1.9	0.0	0.0	0.0
Goa	10.8	1.1	1.6	1.6	1.1	0.7	0.8	0.8
Gujarat	7.9	1.7	2.5	2.2	13.4	1.8	1.5	1.5
Haryana	4.3	0.8	1.6	1.0	5.2	0.0	1.0	0.0
Himachal Pradesh	1.8	0.4	0.7	0.7	0.1	0.0	0.0	0.0
Jammu & Kashmir	1.2	0.3	0.5	0.3	1.4	0.2	0.2	0.2
Jharkhand	1.3	1.3	0.7	0.8	2.0	0.5	0.2	0.0
Karnataka	2.3	0.2	0.7	0.5	2.4	0.4	0.4	0.4
Kerala	10.0	2.4	3.1	3.7	5.8	2.6	2.6	2.1
Madhya Pradesh	8.5	2.1	2.0	2.2	7.2	1.0	0.4	0.5
Maharashtra	12.2	1.9	2.5	1.9	9.8	0.2	1.6	1.0
Manipur	0.8	0.6	0.6	0.8	0.4	0.4	0.4	0.4
Meghalaya	0.1	2.2	0.1	0.1	0.8	0.4	0.1	0.2
Mizoram	1.5	0.4	0.3	0.1	0.3	0.0	0.0	0.0
Nagaland	1.5	0.3	0.7	0.9	1.0	0.0	1.0	1.0
Orissa	2.9	0.8	1.1	0.9	2.4	0.1	0.0	0.0
Punjab	3.6	0.3	0.5	0.5	1.4	0.0	0.0	0.0
Rajasthan	7.8	1.5	1.7	1.7	4.0	0.3	0.8	0.8
Sikkim	1.2	0.5	0.3	0.3	0.0	0.0	0.0	0.0
Tamil Nadu	11.5	1.0	1.9	1.9	11.8	0.4	0.9	0.9
Tripura	0.7	0.2	0.1	0.1	1.1	0.6	1.1	1.7
Uttar Pradesh	3.0	0.8	0.7	0.8	0.3	0.0	0.0	0.0
Uttaranchal	3.7	0.2	0.3	0.4	5.5	0.0	0.0	0.0
West Bengal	5.2	0.6	0.9	0.9	9.3	0.3	1.2	0.5
Union Territories								
Andman and Nicobar Islands	6.1	1.1	1.9	3.4	2.8	0.1	0.1	0.1
Chandigarh	3.0	0.1	0.3	0.1	8.6	0.0	0.0	0.0
Dadra & Nagar Haveli	0.3	0.0	0.3	0.0	0.0	0.0	0.0	0.0
Daman and Diu	0.0	0.4	0.0	0.0	0.0	0.0	0.0	0.0
Lakshadweep	1.7	0.0	0.0	0.0	0.0	0.0	0.0	0.0
Pondicherry	8.0	1.9	2.7	1.7	5.2	0.0	3.1	3.1
All India	6.5	1.1	1.6	1.5	6.6	0.5	0.9	0.7

Notes: The Change has been observed during the two years preceding the survey.

* Figures relate to principal usual status of individuals of age 15 years and above.

Sources: National Sample Survey Organisation : Report Nos. 458 & 515, *Employment and Unemployment Situation in India, 1999-2000 & 2004-05.*

Table 3.2.35: Percentage of Weekly Average Time Spent on Various Activities by Sex and Place of Residence (All) – 1998-99

States	*Activities*	*Rural*			*Urban*			*Total*		
		Male	*Female*	*Total*	*Male*	*Female*	*Total*	*Male*	*Female*	*Total*
Haryana	SNA	22.61	13.98	18.67	21.75	6.67	14.86	22.45	12.65	17.97
	Extended SNA	1.04	18.26	8.88	1.85	19.49	9.93	1.18	18.49	9.07
	Non-SNA	76.32	67.74	72.43	76.38	73.86	75.21	76.33	68.85	72.93
	Total	100.00	100.00	100.00	100.00	100.00	100.00	100.00	100.00	100.00
	Total hours	(168)	(168)	(168)	(168)	(168)	(168)	(168)	(168)	(168)
	Total persons	1919	1603	3522	687	588	1275	2606	2191	4797
Madhya Pradesh	SNA	25.92	13.46	20.02	21.64	5.06	13.91	25.04	11.82	18.77
	Extended SNA	2.63	21.11	11.38	2.64	22.02	11.67	2.64	21.30	11.44
	Non-SNA	71.42	65.39	68.57	75.71	72.93	74.42	72.30	66.89	69.76
	Total	100.00	100.00	100.00	100.00	100.00	100.00	100.00	100.00	100.00
	Total hours	(168)	(168)	(168)	(168)	(168)	(168)	(168)	(168)	(168)
	Total persons	6832	6186	13018	2275	1963	4238	9107	8149	17256
Gujarat	SNA	26.68	14.23	20.68	24.89	4.18	15.15	25.97	10.48	18.60
	Extended SNA	1.93	22.35	11.74	1.84	24.74	12.61	1.90	23.26	12.07
	Non-SNA	71.39	63.40	67.55	73.27	71.11	72.61	72.10	66.29	69.31
	Total	100.00	100.00	100.00	100.00	100.00	100.00	100.00	100.00	100.00
	Total hours	(168)	(168)	(168)	(168)	(168)	(168)	(168)	(168)	(168)
	Total persons	3244	2988	6232	2913	2652	5565	6157	5640	11797
Orissa	SNA	23.54	11.33	17.42	25.11	4.98	15.75	23.88	10.16	17.08
	Extended SNA	2.58	21.00	11.80	2.98	22.39	12.01	2.66	21.25	11.85
	Non-SNA	73.87	67.66	70.79	71.91	72.65	72.27	73.48	68.57	71.05
	Total	100.00	100.00	100.00	100.00	100.00	100.00	100.00	100.00	100.00
	Total hours	(168)	(168)	(168)	(168)	(168)	(168)	(168)	(168)	(168)
	Total persons	4131	4157	8288	957	877	1834	5088	5034	10122
Tamil Nadu	SNA	25.01	13.96	19.51	25.76	6.56	16.13	25.32	11.29	18.26
	Extended SNA	2.09	17.57	9.84	1.61	19.10	10.38	1.90	18.13	10.04
	Non-SNA	72.88	68.45	70.66	72.58	74.34	73.49	72.78	70.60	71.70
	Total	100.00	100.00	100.00	100.00	100.00	100.00	100.00	100.00	100.00
	Total hours	(168)	(168)	(168)	(168)	(168)	(168)	(168)	(168)	(168)
	Total persons	5507	5541	11048	3204	3186	6390	8711	8727	17438
Meghalaya	SNA	28.74	17.33	22.89	21.08	8.58	14.42	27.35	15.68	21.36
	Extended SNA	4.18	20.57	12.58	4.74	20.47	13.09	4.26	20.55	12.67
	Non-SNA	67.08	62.09	64.51	74.17	70.98	72.48	68.32	63.78	65.98
	Total	100.00	100.00	100.00	100.00	100.00	100.00	100.00	100.00	100.00
	Total hours	(168)	(168)	(168)	(168)	(168)	(168)	(168)	(168)	(168)
	Total persons	652	655	1307	269	283	552	921	938	1859
Combined States	SNA	25.18	13.41	19.48	24.44	5.45	15.34	24.98	11.14	18.30
	Extended SNA	2.23	20.21	10.95	2.05	21.69	11.46	2.17	20.61	11.13
	Non-SNA	72.61	66.37	69.58	73.49	72.88	73.23	72.87	68.20	70.61
	Total	100.00	100.00	100.00	100.00	100.00	100.00	100.00	100.00	100.00
	Total hours	(168)	(168)	(168)	(168)	(168)	(168)	(168)	(168)	(168)
	Total persons	22285	21130	43415	10305	9549	19854	32590	30679	63269

Notes: Totals may not tally due to rounding error.
'Total persons' gives sample number of persons participating.
Source: Central Statistical Organisation : *Time Use Survey Report, April 2000.*

Table 3.2.36: Statewise Distribution of Time Spent (in hour) in SNA Activities by Mode of Payment and Sex, 1998-99

States	*Male*			*Female*			*Total*		
	Paid	*Unpaid*	*% time on Unpaid Activities*	*Paid*	*Unpaid*	*% time on Unpaid Activities*	*Paid*	*Unpaid*	*% time on Unpaid Activities*
Haryana	33.09	18.12	35.38	4.13	25.34	85.99	20.06	21.37	51.58
	(1152)	(1347)	(53.90)	(215)	(1494)	(87.42)	(1367)	(2841)	(67.51)
Madhya Pradesh	29.41	23.34	44.25	14.31	15.75	52.40	22.99	20.12	46.67
	(5247)	(6311)	(54.60)	(3072)	(4391)	(58.84)	(8319)	(10702)	(56.26)
Gujarat	44.37	14.17	24.21	17.18	13.87	44.67	33.26	14.05	29.70
	(3959)	(3897)	(49.61)	(1747)	(2541)	(59.26)	(5706)	(6438)	(53.01)
Orissa	31.25	22.42	41.77	8.00	18.18	69.44	20.55	20.47	49.90
	(2103)	(2589)	(55.18)	(583)	(3235)	(84.73)	(2686)	(5824)	(68.44)
Tamil Nadu	41.42	13.36	24.39	21.48	10.32	32.45	32.74	12.04	26.89
	(5633)	(4863)	(46.33)	(3034)	(4280)	(58.52)	(8667)	(9143)	(51.34)
Meghalaya	17.34	35.39	67.12	7.83	25.34	76.39	12.65	30.44	70.64
	(374)	(740)	(66.43)	(196)	(692)	(77.93)	(570)	(1432)	(71.53)
Combined States	36.54	18.12	33.15	14.87	15.18	50.52	27.16	16.85	38.29
	(18468)	(19747)	(51.67)	(8847)	(16633)	(65.28)	(27315)	(36380)	(57.12)

Note: Figures in paranthesis in the second line give sample number of persons participating in the activity.

Source: Central Statistical Organisation : *Time Use Survey Report, April 2000.*

Table 3.2.37: Number of Casualties in Select Industries

Year	*Factories*			*Mines*			*Railways*		
	Fatal Injuries	*Non-Fatal Injuries*	*Total Injuries*	*Fatal Injuries*	*Non-Fatal Injuries*	*Total Injuries*	*Fatal Injuries*	*Non-Fatal Injuries*	*Total Injuries*
1987	487	1,51,321	1,51,808	250	1,356	1,606	232	21,875	22,107
1988	694	1,99,564	2,00,256	250	1,120	1,370	237	17,633	17,870
1989	706	1,61,331	1,62,037	232	1,201	1,433	245	17,262	17,507
1990	665	1,29,068	1,29,733	242	1,316	1,558	249	15,225	15,474
1991	690	76,262	76,952	245	1,176	1,421	234	13,609	13,843
1996P	907	60,328	61,935	229	1,006	1,244	172	2,139	2,311
1997	901	53,260	54,161	242	1,011	1,253	155	2,096	2,251
1998	862	57,789	58,651	211	833	1,044	111	1,491	2,602
1999	NA	NA	NA	210	901	1,111	117	1,775	1,892
2000	486	23,490	23,976	199	901	1,100	145	1,674	1,819
2001	NA	NA	NA	222	928	1,150	123	1,570	1,693
2002	540	19,913	NA	161	874	1,035	114	1,421	1,535
2003	525	15,907	NA	NA	NA	NA	152	4,528	1,324
2004	562	14,458	15,020	NA	NA	NA	83	4,257	4,340
2005	NA	NA	NA	169	1,251	1,420	91	3,927	4,018
2006	NA	NA	NA	NA	NA	NA	121	2,817	2,938

Note: P — Provisional.

Sources: (i) Labour Bureau : *Indian Labour Pocket Year Book, 2007.*

(ii) *Central Statistical Organisation : Statistical Abstract, 2003.*

Table 3.2.38: Compensated Accidents and the Amount Paid

Year	*Average daily No.of workers employed in establish-ments submitting returns*	*Number of compensated Accidents resulting in*				*Amount of Compensation Paid (Rs. Thousand)*			
		Death	*Perma-nent Disabl-ement*	*Temporary Dis-ablement*	*Total*	*Death*	*Perma-nent Disable-ment*	*Temporary Dis-ablement*	*Total*
1971	4,130,359	1,101	3,046	53,199	57,346	7,506	3,711	4,698	15,915
1981	4,222,968	1,493	2,632	30,321	34,446	20,874	7,000	13,562	41,436
1986	3,691,589	536	2,111	22,572	25,219	24,712	9,709	5,882	40,303
1987	1,948,619	480	1,109	14,035	15,624	20,847	10,129	12,353	43,329
1988	967,870	354	1,675	93,008	95,037	15,563	6,438	5,183	27,184
1989	4,545,648	1,151	2,393	1,67,631	1,71,175	61,238	21,984	17,455	1,00,677
1990	3,805,754	1,200	1,269	12,825	15,294	56,618	15,344	11,672	83,634
1991	3,669,567	1,409	1,538	10,597	13,544	72,086	24,639	10,369	1,07,094
1992	3,041,244	1,503	1,365	7,377	10,245	80,743	23,336	11,355	1,15,434
1993	1,255,895	474	237	3,027	3,738	17,283	6,407	7,142	30,831
1994	728,381	545	418	3,373	4,336	28,104	10,003	3,692	41,799
1995	157,922	231	151	892	1,274	15,782	4855	901	21,537
1996	1,153,149	1,050	748	2,048	3,846	79,057	36,395	19,148	1,34,601
1997	1,930,441	947	1,391	2,117	4,455	1,21,299	38,626	26,398	1,86,323
1998	2,375,654	896	1,231	42,598	44,725	1,98,053	1,23,727	2,49,452	5,71,232
1999	2,645,387	1,023	1,557	8,747	11,327	1,46,698	81,789	1,09,526	2,27,963
2000	2,697,581	1,377	1,587	4,765	7,649	1,93,004	1,04,783	32,016	3,29,802
2001	1,726,834	1,346	1,520	4,381	7,247	2,21,595	1,26,183	32,923	3,80,701
2002	3,330,367	1,501	1,592	3,649	6,742	2,89,912	1,50,619	28,297	4,68,828
2003	2,139,535	1,663	1,912	4,136	7,706	3,71,091	2,22,800	45,075	6,44,964
2004	3,275,362	1,581	1,662	3,507	6,750	3,28,612	1,27,335	23,599	4,79,546
2005	NA	1,780	1,522	2,814	6,116	3,80,510	1,87,074	49,922	6,17,506

Note: Figures relate to only those States/Union Territories which have submitted the returns.

Sources: Labour Bureau : (i) *Indian Labour Year Book, 2004.*
(*ii*) Pocket Book of Labour Statistics, 2007.

(iii) Manpower Utilisation in Scientific and Technical Field

Table 3.3.1: Personnel in Research and Development Establishments by Activity

Activity	*1984*	*1986*	*1988*	*1990*	*1992*	1994	1996	1998	2000
Research & Development	78,036	85,309	96,927	105,936	95,486	114,403	127,226	95,428	93,836
Auxiliary	72,233	70,233	80,956	96,737	98,202	98,769	108,817	100,656	90,045
Administration	71,680	79,093	86,398	98,204	99,660	101,317	99,029	112,308	112,462
Break-up Not Available	–	6,062	3,335	–	–	–	–	–	–
Total	221,949	240,697	267,616	300,877	293,348	314,489	335,072	308,392	296,343

Notes: As on Ist April.
Data Exclude Higher Education Sector.

Sources: Department of Science and Technology:
(*i*) *Pocket Data Book—1995.*
(*ii*) *Research and Development Statistics.*

Table 3.3.2: Level of Qualification of Personnel in Research and Development by Sex

Qualification	*1980*		*1986*		*1988*		*1992*		*1996*	
	Total	*Women*	*Total*	*Women*	*Total*	*Women*	*Total*	*Women*	*Total*	*Women*
Ph. D.	6,653	378	9,361	858	10,337	664	15,243	1,260	16,839	2,406
Post-Graduate	19,165	1,246	17,549	1,502	20,400	1,727	26,004	3,111	21,129	2,761
Graduate	18,866	846	17,696	1,070	19,046	1,227	25,469	2,205	18,625	1,628
Diploma Holder	7,899	186	5,944	408	6,561	385	8,497	731	11,467*	756*
Others	8,713	240	9,449	537	15,335	890	8,679	430	–	–
Total	61,296	2,896	59,999	4,375	71,679	4,893	83,892	7,737	68,060	7,551

Notes: As on Ist April.
Data Exclude Higher Education Sector.
* Include others also.

Sources: Department of Science and Technology:
(*i*) *Pocket Data Book—1995*
(*ii*) *Research and Development Statistics.*

Figure 3.3.O

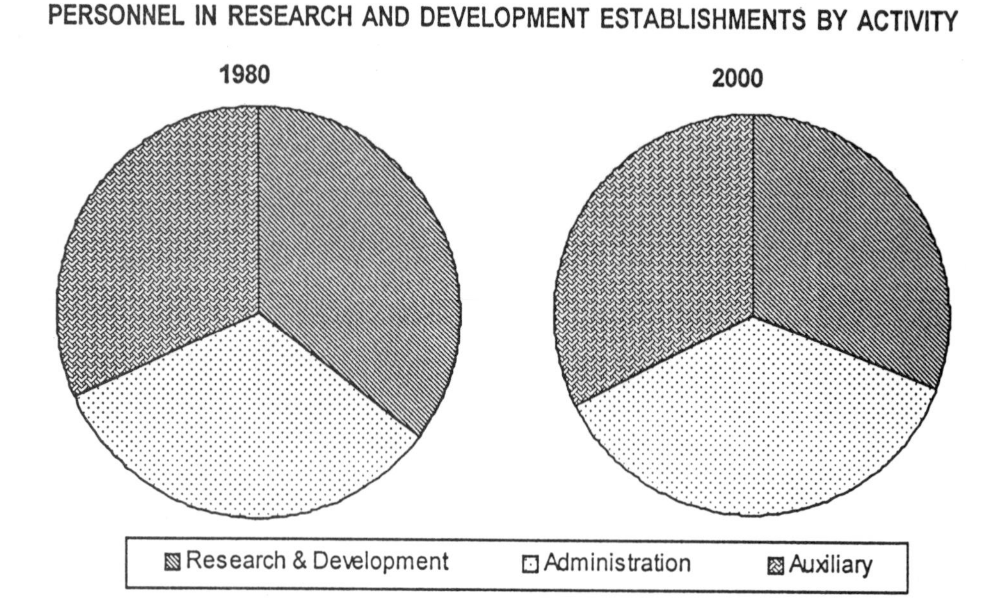

For details see Table 3.3.1

Figure 3.3.P

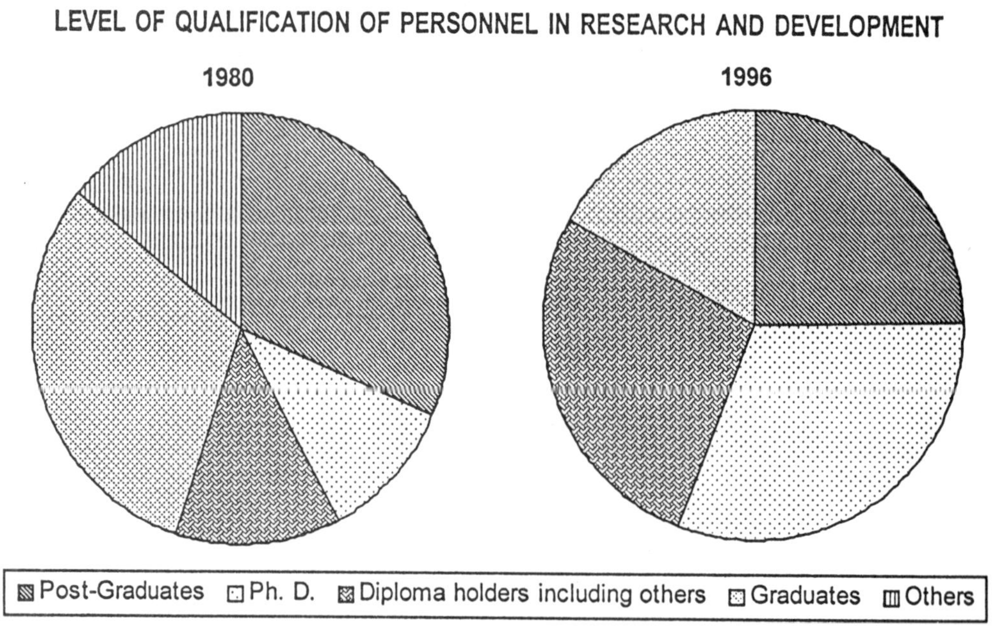

For details see Table 3.3.2

Table 3.3.3 : Level of Qualification of Personnel in Research and Development by Sector

Qualification	*Institutional Sector*			*Industrial Sector*			*Total*		
	1992	*1996*	*2005*	*1992*	*1996*	*2005*	*1992*	*1996*	*2005*
Ph. D.	12,521	14,350	15,627	2,722	2,489	4,772	15,243	16,839	20,399
Postgraduate	17,993	14,333	24,392	8,011	6,796	19,975	26,004	21,129	44,367
Graduate	11,533	8,879	13,330	13,936	9,746	21,840	25,469	18,625	35,170
Diploma Holder	4,004	5,010*	3,264	4,493	6,457*	6,503	8,497	11,467*	9,767
Others	2,842	–	2,202	5,837	–	4,270	8,679	–	6,472
Total	48,893	42,572	58,815	34,999	25,488	57,360	83,892	68,060	1,16,175

Notes: As on Ist April.
* Include 'others' also.

Sources: Department of Science and Technology:
(*i*) *Pocket Data Book—1995.*
(*ii*) *Research and Development Statistics—1996-97.*

Table 3.3.4: Level of Qualification of Women Research and Development Personnel by Sector

Qualification	*Institutional Sector*			*Industrial Sector*			*Total*		
	1988	*1992*	*1996*	*1988*	*1992*	*1996*	*1988*	*1992*	*1996*
Ph.D.	586	1,042	2,165	78	218	241	664	1,260	2,406
Post-Graduate	1,335	2,293	2,044	392	818	7,171	1,727	3,111	2,761
Graduate	544	1,104	807	683	1101	821	1,227	2,205	1,628
Diploma Holder	243	445	453*	142	286	303*	385	731	756*
Others	645	179	–	245	251	–	890	430	–
Total	3,353	5,063	5,469	1,540	2,674	2,082	4,893	7,737	7,551

Notes: As on Ist April.
Excluding Higher Education Sector.
* Include 'others' also.

Sources: Department of Science and Technology:
(i) *Pocket Data Book—1995.*
(ii) *Research and Development Statistics—1996-97.*

Table 3.3.5: Educational Qualification of Personnel in R & D by Sex, Sector, Discipline and Level

Discipline	Institutional Sector		Industrial Sector		Total	
	Total	*Women*	*Total*	*Women*	*Total*	*Women*
Natural Sciences	10522	1582	7488	642	18010	2224
Ph.D.	4006	618	1341	118	5347	736
Postgraduate	4286	712	2707	315	6993	1027
Graduate	1593	220	2687	201	4280	421
Diploma Holder and Others	637	32	753	8	1390	40
Agricultural Sciences	13185	1993	761	30	13946	2023
Ph.D.	8721	1392	106	6	8827	1398
Postgraduate	3552	562	246	13	3798	575
Graduate	554	25	209	9	763	34
Diploma Holder and Others	358	14	200	2	558	16
Engineering and Technology	16066	1225	14830	973	30896	2198
Ph.D.	1109	58	685	58	1794	116
Postgraduate	5318	409	3004	193	8322	602
Graduate	6295	453	6180	4080	12475	933
Diploma Holder and Others	3344	305	4961	242	8305	547
Medical Sciences	1367	471	1195	328	2562	799
Ph.D.	358	77	236	51	594	128
Postgraduate	737	275	615	177	1352	452
Graduate	172	58	249	85	421	143
Diploma Holder and Others	100	61	95	15	195	76
Social Sciences	1432	198	1214	109	2646	307
Ph.D.	156	20	121	8	277	28
Postgraduate	440	86	224	19	664	105
Graduate	265	51	421	46	686	97
Others	571	41	448	36	1019	77

Note: As on 1st April, 1996.

Source: Department of Science and Technology : *Research and Development Statistics—1996-97.*

Table 3.3.6: Full Time Equivalent of Manpower Employed in Research & Development Establishment, 2000

Name of Establishment	*Personnel engaged Primaricy in R & D Activities*		*Personnel engaged in Auxilitary Activities*		*Personnel engaged in Administrative Activities*		*Total*	
	Total	*Women*	*Total*	*Women*	*Total*	*Women*	*Total*	*Women*
Institutional Sector	56112 (19.95)	7675 (2.59)	80162 (27.05)	8855 (2.99)	103661 (34.98)	18073 (6.10)	242935 (81.98)	34603 (11.68)
Major Scientisfic Agencies	33165 (11.19)	4381 (1.48)	45718 (15.43)	4511 (1.52)	41495 (14.00)	8006 (2.70)	120378 (40.62)	16898 (5.70)
Central Government Ministries/ Department	7954 (2.67)	1032 (0.35)	16288 (5.50)	2676 (0.90)	19217 (6.48)	2355 (0.79)	43459 (14.66)	6063 (2.04)
State Government	17993 (6.07)	2262 (0.76)	18156 (6.13)	1668 (0.56)	42949 (14.49)	7712 (2.60)	79098 (26.69)	11642 (3.93)
Industrial Sector	34724 (11.72)	3629 (1.22)	9883 (3.33)	1508 (0.51)	8801 (2.97)	1458 (0.49)	53408 (18.02)	6595 (2.22)
Public Sector Including Joint Sector	8767 (2.96)	757 (0.25)	2580 (0.87)	188 (0.06)	2327 (0.78)	261 (0.09)	13674 (4.61)	1206 (0.41)
Private Sector	25957 (8.76)	2872 (0.97)	7303 (2.46)	13.20 (0.44)	6474 (2.18)	1197 (0.40)	39734 (13.41)	5389 (1.82)
Total	94836 (31.66)	11304 (3.81)	90045 (30.38)	10363 (3.50)	112462 (37.95)	19531 (6.59)	296343 (100.00)	41198 (13.90)

Notes: *As on 1st April, 2000.*

1. Data for private sector refers to 1174 in house R & D.
   Units including 212 Indian Space Research Organisation.
2. Data does not include Small Scale Industries, Higher Education and Private Research and Development (R & D) firms covered in Central Monitoring of Indian Economy (MIE) database.
3. Figures with in Perenthesis represent Percentage of total.

Source: Department of Science and Technology : Research and Development Statistics, 2006

Table 3.3.7: Application filed by Indian Manpower in Scientific and Technical field for Patents (1980-81 to 2006-07)

Selected States	*1980-81*	*1985-86*	*1990-91*	*1995-96*	2000-2001	2005-06	2006-07
Andhra Pradesh	34	14	35	53	100	408	385
Assam	NA	NA	NA	NA	NA	15	14
Bihar	36	29	26	21	31	29	14
Chandigarh	NA	NA	NA	NA	NA	15	23
Chhattisgarh	NA	NA	NA	NA	NA	3	17
Dadara & Nagar Haveli	NA	NA	NA	NA	NA	NA	1
Daman & Diu	NA	NA	NA	NA	NA	Na	01
Delhi	333	230	364	499	663	1018	1310
Gujarat	72	53	44	75	147	203	337
Haryana	15	3	9	7	20	93	93
Himachal Pradesh	NA	NA	NA	NA	NA	10	10
Jammu & Kashmir	NA	NA	NA	NA	NA	4	3
Jharkhand	NA	NA	NA	NA	NA	15	131
Karnataka	38	53	69	57	112	428	596
Kerala	35	35	60	72	77	96	128
Madhya Pradesh	13	18	18	29	30	55	33
Maharashtra	296	291	283	381	545	1233	1607
Meghalaya	NA	NA	NA	NA	NA	NA	3
Mizoram	NA	NA	NA	NA	NA	NA	1
Pondicherry	NA	NA	NA	NA	NA	5	2
Orissa	NA	NA	NA	NA	NA	NA	19
Punjab	17	9	9	16	15	29	74
Rajasthan	10	15	3	17	7	17	44
Tamil Nadu	112	81	109	125	174	433	2
Uttar Pradesh	37	38	39	35	90	193	205
Uttarakhand	NA	Na	NA	NA	NA	3	17
West Bengal	110	110	96	192	143	214	244
Total	1178	999	1180	1606	2179	4512	5314

Note : NA- Data Not Available

Source: Controller General of Patents, Designs and Trade Marks : *Annual Reports* of the relevent years.

Table 3.3.8: Number of Indian Students Going Abroad by Field of Study and Sex

Field of Study	*Sex*	*1991-92*	*1992-93*	*1993-94*	*1994-95*	*1995-96*	*1996-97*	*1997-98*	*1998-99*
Engineering and Architect	Person	2390	2460	709	792	703	1473	1014	1156
	Female	158	217	68	68	42	103	96	113
Science	Person	1384	1447	575	340	387	631	789	921
	Female	231	238	104	63	62	109	128	158
Technology and Industry	Person	121	115	43	141	98	381	325	540
	Female	17	17	3	43	13	36	35	86
Commerce, Business Administration, Business Management	Person	946	795	341	646	957	1777	2592	2342
	Female	122	107	45	55	102	179	292	293
Arts	Person	204	191	130	111	177	235	302	351
	Female	94	91	79	33	48	89	127	158
Agriculture and Forestry	Person	94	66	12	16	15	80	11	6
	Female	17	9	1	3	3	12	6	2
Medicine, Pharmacy & Veterinary Science	Person	350	449	85	327	370	907	607	645
	Female	94	106	30	50	37	116	102	87
Law	Person	26	21	9	18	23	43	55	66
	Female	5	5	2	6	8	3	16	20
Bank/Banking Institutions	Person	14	6	9	2	25	38	15	35
	Female	3	—	4	—	3	3	1	7
Fine Arts	Person	30	69	—	42	39	69	62	46
	Female	14	33	—	24	15	34	29	18
Others	Person	905	880	371	548	684	792	962	810
	Female	130	130	61	133	144	119	229	170
Total	Person	6466	6499	2284	2983	3478	6426	6734	6918
	Female	887	953	397	478	477	803	1061	1112

Source: Ministry of Human Resource Development, *Indian Student'/ Trainees Going Abroad, 1998-99.*

Table 3.3.9: Number of Indian Students Going Abroad by Field of Study and Continent, 1998-99

Field of Study	*America*	*Europe*	*Asia*	*Oceania*	*Others*	*Total*
Engineering and Architect	707	160	94	189	6	1156
Science	552	147	22	184	16	921
Technology and Industry	118	73	14	332	3	540
Commerce, Business Administration, Management	577	467	64	1208	26	2342
Arts	193	98	5	49	6	351
Agriculture and Forestry	3	1	—	2	—	6
Medicine, Pharmacy, Dentistry and Veterinary Sciences	73	37	481	42	12	645
Law	17	43	—	5	1	66
Banking Services	9	10	1	14	1	35
Fine Arts	33	2	—	10	1	46
Others	298	121	23	319	49	810
Total	2580	1159	704	2354	121	6918

Source: Ministry of Human Resource Development, *Indian Students and Trainess Going Abroad, 1998-99.*

Table 3.3.10: Scientific Manpower

Year	*Scientists, Engineers and Technicians per thousand Population*	*Scientists, Engineers and Technicians engaged in research and development as per thousand Population*	*Scientists, Engineers and Technicians engaged in research and development as percentage of total number of scientists, engineers and technicians*
1978	2.97	0.10	3.37
1980	2.63	0.10	3.80
1985	3.43	0.13	5.83
1990	3.76	0.15	5.85
1996	6.91	0.16	2.32
1999	7.27	0.10*	1.38

Note: *Data relate to 1998.

Sources: Department of Science and Technology:

(*i*) *Research and Development Statistics.*

(*ii*) *S & T Data Book.*

Table 3.3.11: GNP and National Expenditure on Research and Development

(Rs. in Crore)

Year	*GNP at factor cost*	*Expenditure on Research and Development*	*Expenditure on Research and Development as percent of GNP*
		Old Series (At 1993-94 Prices)	
1994-95	824,816	6,042.53	0.73
1995-96	886,961	6,263.44	0.71
1996-97	959,359	6,949.70	0.72
1997-98	1,005,946	7,750.76	0.77
1998-99	1,070,773	8,724.01	0.81
		New Series (At 1999-2000 Prices)	
1999-00	1,771,094	14,397.62*	0.82
2000-01	1,841,755	16,198.78*	0.86
2001-02	1,951,935	17,038.15*	0.82
2002-03	2,029,482	18,000.16*	0.80
2003-04	2,204,913	19,726.99*	0.79
2004-05(P)	2,366,886	21,639.58*	–
2005-06(P)	2,593,160	–	–
2006-07 (Q)	2,845,155	–	–

Notes: GNP—Gross National Product. – Data not available. * at current Prices.
P – Provisional estimates. Q – Quick estimates.

Sources: (i) Department of Science and Technology : *Research and Development Statistics, 2000-01*
(ii) *Economic Survey, 2007-08.*

Table 3.3.12: National Expenditure on Research and Development by Sector

(Rs. in Crore)

Year	*Central Government*	*State Government*	*Public Sector Industry*	*Private Sector Industry*	*Higher Educatonion*	*Total*
			Constant Price (Base 1993-94)			
1980-81	1521.73	182.75	265.99	371.69	–	2342.16
1985-86	2997.81	335.29	409.11	518.93	–	4261.14
1990-91	3590.41	496.92	562.96	746.95	–	5397.24
1992-93	3459.50	552.82	564.30	918.16	–	5494.78
1993-94	3986.17	561.50	542.81	982.54	–	6073.02
1994-95	3919.72	541.13	378.30	1203.38	–	6042.53
1995-96	3993.98	549.88	357.85	1361.73	–	6263.44
1996-97	4066.04	666.67	399.76	1817.22	–	6949.70
1997-98	4899.01	676.93	393.87	1780.95	264.07	7750.76
1998-99	5702.78	694.15	440.21	1886.87	255.98	8724.01
2002-03	11,268.10	1530.10	810.01	3654.03	738.01	18000.16

Note: The total expenditure at constant prices is available from R & D Statistics 2004-05, whereas distribution among the sectors is estimated by applying the same deflator of current price to constant price as that of total.

Source: Department of Science and Technology : Research and Development Statistics.

Figure 3.3.Q

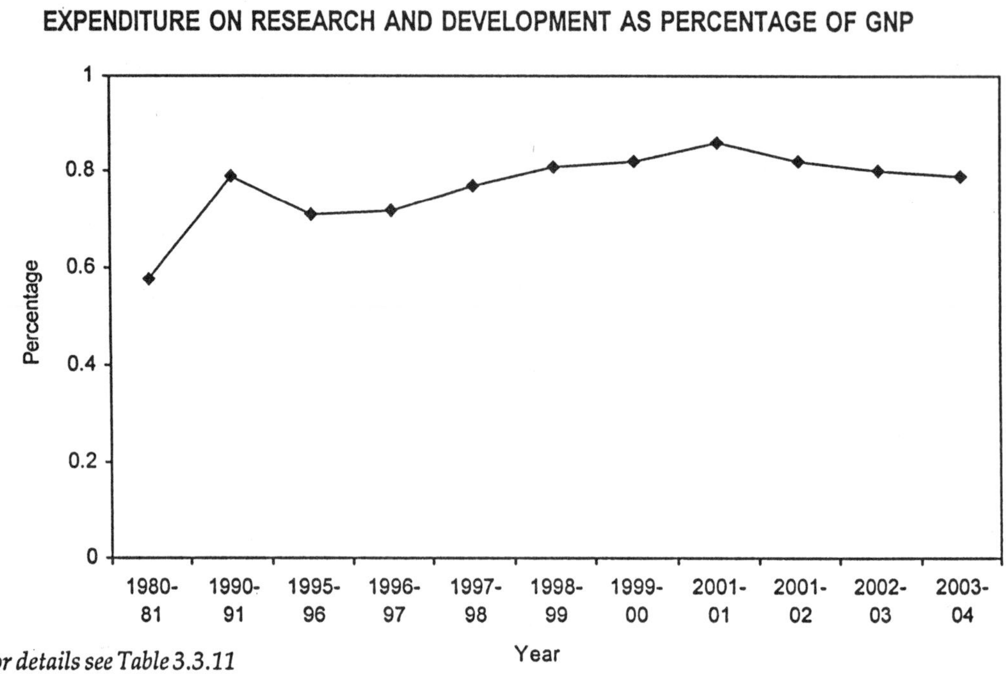

For details see Table 3.3.11

Figure 3.3.R

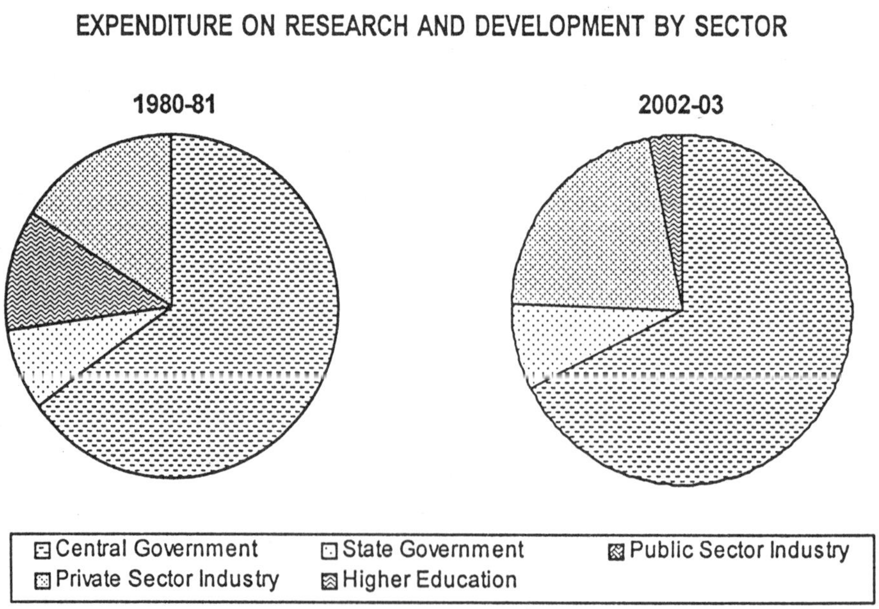

For details see Table 3.3.12

(iv) Child Labour

Table 3.4.1: Working Children by State and Union Territory, 1981, 1991 and 2001

(Thousand)

State/Union Territorary	1971	1981	1991	2001**
States				
1. Andhra Pradesh	1627	1,951	1,662	1,363
2. Arunachal Pradesh	18	18	12	18
3. Assam	239*	@	328	351
4. Bihar	1059	1,102	942	1,118
5. Chhattisgarh	—	—	—	365
6. Delhi	17	26	27	42
7. Goa	—	—	5	4
8. Gujarat	518	617	524	485
9. Haryana	138	194	110	253
10. Himachal Pradesh	71	100	56	108
11. Jammu & Kashmir	70	258	@@	176
12. Jharkhand	—	—	—	407
13. Karnataka	809	1,132	976	823
14. Kerala	112	93	35	26
15. Madhya Pradesh	1112	1,699	1,353	1,065
16. Maharashtra	988	1,558	1,068	764
17. Manipur	16	20	16	29
18. Meghalaya	30	45	35	54
19. Mizoram	*	6	16	26
20. Nagaland	14	16	16	46
21. Orissa	492	702	452	378
22. Punjab	233	217	143	177
23. Rajasthan	587	820	774	1,263
24. Sikkim	16	9	6	16
25. Tamil Nadu	713	975	579	419
26. Tripura	17	24	16	22
27. Uttaranchal	—	—	—	70
28. Uttar Pradesh	1327	1,435	1,410	1,928
29. West Bengal	511	6051	712	857
Union Territories				
1. Andaman and Nicobar Island	1	1	1	2
2. Chandigarh	1	2	2	4
3. Dadra and Nagar Haveli	3	4	4	4
4. Daman and Diu	7	9	1	1
5. Lakshadweep	—	—	—	—
6. Pondicherry	4	4	3	2
Total	10754	13,641	11,285	12,666

Notes: Data relate to age group 5-14 years.
*Includes figures of Mizoram. ** Includes marginal workers also.
@1981 Census could not be conducted in Assam.
@@1991 Census could not be conducted in Jammu and Kashmir.

Source: Registrar General and Census Commissioner of India : *Census of India, 1971, 1981, 1991 and 2001.*

Table 3.4.2: Working Children by Rural/Urban and Sex, 2001

(Million)

Location	Main Workers Male	Main Workers Female	Main Workers Person	Marginal Workers Male	Marginal Workers Female	Marginal Workers Person	Total Workers Male	Total Workers Female	Total Workers Person
Rural	2.93	1.89	4.82	3.00	3.52	6.52	5.93	5.41	11.34
	(4.96)	(3.17)	(8.13)	(0.50)	(1.63)	(2.13)	(5.46)	(4.80)	(10.24)
Urban	0.67	0.29	0.96	0.21	0.15	0.36	0.88	0.44	1.32
	(0.70)	(0.25)	(0.95)	(0.03)	(0.05)	(0.08)	(0.73)	(0.30)	(1.03)
Total	3.60	2.18	5.78	3.21	3.67	6.88	6.81	5.85	12.66
	(5.66)	(3.42)	(9.08)	(0.53)	(1.68)	(2.21)	(6.19)	(5.10)	(11.29)

Notes: Data relate to age group 5-14 years.
Main workers are those who work for 183 days or more in a year.
Figures in the Parenthesis relate to the year 1991.

Source: Registrar General and Census Commissioner of India : *Census of India, 1991 & 2001.*

Table 3.4.3: Percentage Distribution of Working Children (Main Workers) by Educational Level, 2001

Educational Level	Rural Male	Rural Female	Rural Person	Urban Male	Urban Female	Urban Person	Total Male	Total Female	Total Person
1. Illiterate	49.57	61.97	54.45	39.02	48.69	41.91	47.61	60.23	52.37
	(72.38)	(82.63)	(76.38)	(56.10)	(68.38)	(59.34)	(70.37)	(81.59)	(74.59)
2. Literate (without Educational level)	2.86	2.78	2.83	2.82	3.11	2.91	2.86	2.82	2.84
	(11.39)	(7.90)	(10.03)	(15.21)	(13.26)	(14.69)	(11.86)	(8.30)	(10.52)
3. Primary	–	–	–	–	–	–	–	–	–
	(12.60)	(7.74)	(10.70)	(20.68)	(13.94)	(18.90)	(13.61)	(8.19)	(11.57)
4. Middle	–	–	–	–	–	–	–	–	–
	(3.32)	(1.63)	(2.66)	(7.14)	(4.01)	(6.32)	(3.79)	(1.80)	(3.04)
5. Literate but Below Matric/Secondary	47.57	35.25	42.72	58.16	48.20	55.18	43.53	36.95	44.99
	(–)	(–)	(–)	(–)	(–)	(–)	(–)	(–)	(–)
6. Matriculation/ Secondary	–	–	–	–	–	–	–	–	–
	(0.26)	(0.08)	(0.19)	(0.71)	(0.33)	(0.61)	(0.31)	(0.10)	(0.23)
7. Higher Sec./ Inter./Pre-University/ Non Technical/ Technical Certificate/ Diploma	–	–	–	–	–	–	–	–	–
	(0.05)	(0.02)	(0.04)	(0.16)	(0.08)	(0.14)	(0.06)	(0.02)	(0.05)
Total	100.00	100.00	100.00	100.00)	100.00	100.00)	100.00	100.00)	100.00
Number* (Million)	2.93	1.89	4.82	0.67	0.28	0.95	3.60	2.18	5.78
	(4.96)	(3.17)	(8.13)	(0.70)	(0.25)	(0.95)	(5.66)	(3.42)	(9.08)

Notes: Data relate to age group 5-14 years.
Main workers are those who work for 183 days or more in a year.
* Includes main workers only. Figures within the Parenthesis relate to the year 1991.

Source: Registrar General and Census Commissioner of India : *Census of India, 1991 and 2001.*

Figure 3.4.S

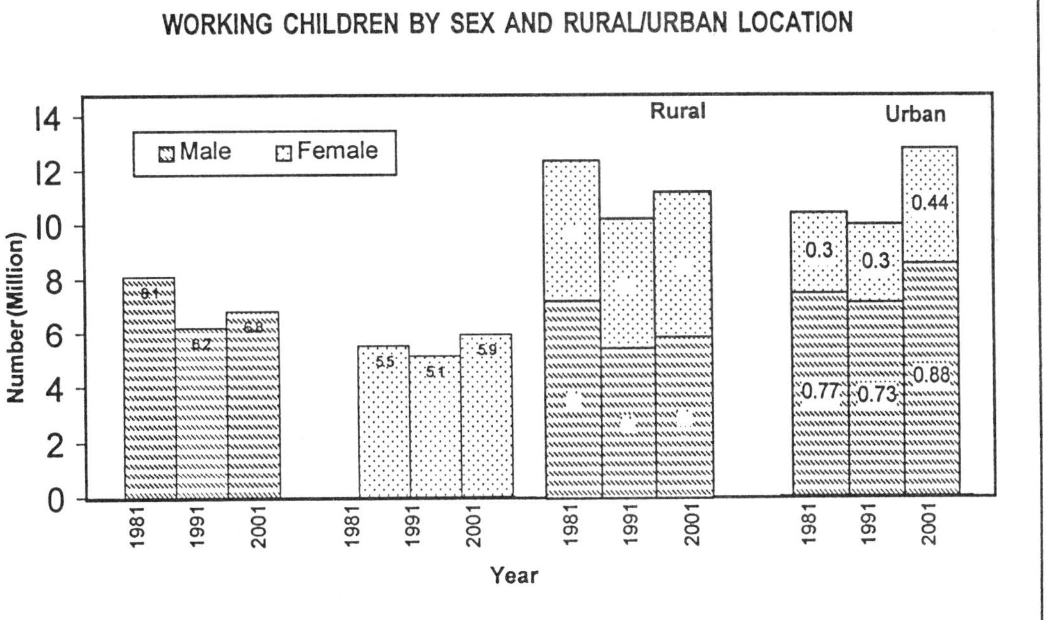

For details see Table 3.4.1 and Census Reports

Figure 3.4.T

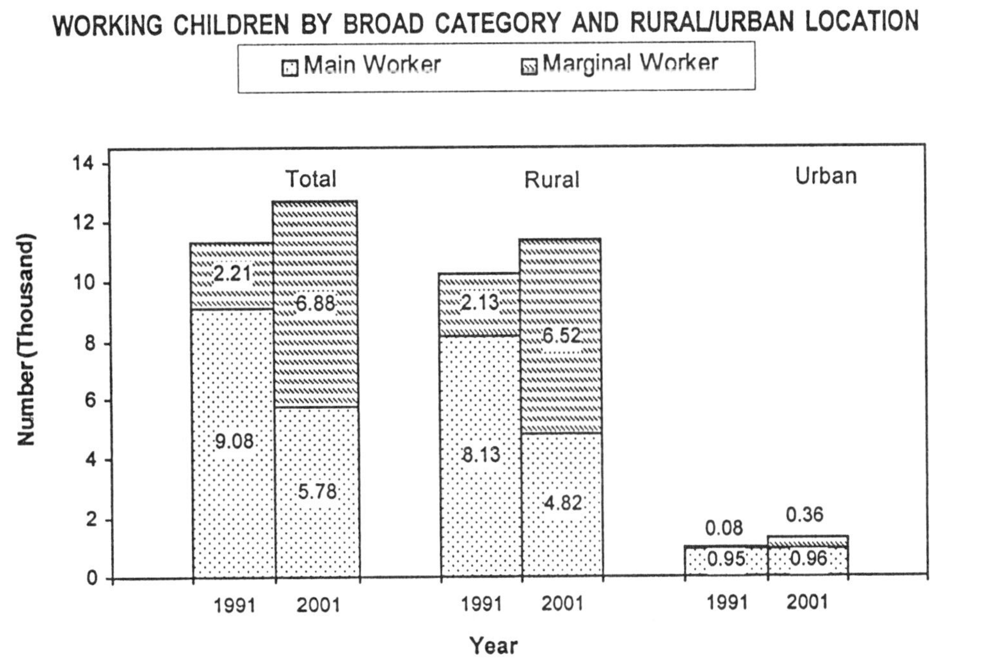

For details see Table 3.4.2 (Based of 1991 and 2000 Census)

Table 3.4.4: Percentage Distribution of Working Children*, by Industrial Category and Sex 1991

	Industrial Category	*Rural*			*Urban*			*Total*		
		Male	*Female*	*Person*	*Male*	*Female*	*Person*	*Male*	*Female*	*Person*
I.	Cultivators	42.57	33.06	38.86	6.18	5.58	6.02	38.14	31.10	35.49
II.	Agricultural Labourers	43.37	54.54	47.72	13.43	22.68	15.84	39.73	52.27	44.45
III.	Livestock, Forestry, Fishing, Hunting and Plantation, Orchard and Allied Activities	4.85	2.83	4.07	2.34	1.18	2.04	4.55	2.72	3.86
IV.	Mining and Quarrying	0.27	0.30	0.28	0.34	0.47	0.37	0.28	0.31	0.29
V.	Manufacturing, Processing, Servicing and Repairs	4.73	7.26	5.71	34.68	36.26	35.09	8.37	9.33	8.73
	(a) Household Industry	1.73	3.93	2.58	5.42	14.47	7.78	2.18	4.68	3.12
	(b) Other than Household Industry	3.00	3.33	3.13	29.26	21.79	27.31	6.19	4.65	5.61
VI.	Construction	0.49	0.24	0.39	4.53	3.14	4.17	0.98	0.44	0.78
VII.	Trade & Commerce	1.62	0.34	1.13	20.40	3.83	16.08	3.91	0.59	2.66
VIII.	Transport, Storage and Communication	0.21	0.02	0.14	2.75	0.44	2.15	0.52	0.05	0.34
IX.	Other Services	1.89	1.41	1.70	15.35	26.42	18.24	3.52	3.19	3.40
	Total	100.00	100.00	100.00	100.00	100.00	100.00	100.00	100.00	100.00
	Number**(Million)	4.96	3.17	8.13	0.70	0.25	0.95	5.66	3.42	9.08

Notes: Totals may not tally due to rounding off.
Main workers are those who work for 183 days or more in a year.
* Data relate to age group 5-14 years.
** Includes main workers only.

Source: Registrar General and Census Commissioner of India : *Census of India, 1991.*

Table 3.4.5: Percentage Distribution of Working Children*, by Industrial Category and Sex, 2001

Industrial Category	*Rural*			*Urban*			*Total*		
	Male	*Female*	*Total*	*Male*	*Female*	*Total*	*Male*	*Female*	*Total*
I. Cultivators	36.63	33.42	35.37	3.64	5.09	4.08	30.47	29.68	30.17
II. Agricultural Labourers	35.55	41.16	37.75	5.28	8.06	6.11	29.90	36.80	32.50
III. Plantation, Livestock, Forestry, Fishing, Hunting and Allied Activities	7.99	6.05	7.23	2.25	1.80	2.12	6.92	5.49	6.38
IV. Mining and Quarrying	0.62	0.60	0.61	0.50	0.53	0.51	0.60	0.59	0.59
V. Manufacturing, Processing, Servicing and Repairs :	8.90	12.78	10.42	29.09	33.27	30.34	12.67	17.48	13.74
(a) Household Industry	4.56	8.72	6.19	9.05	19.30	12.12	5.40	10.12	7.18
(b) Other than Household Industry	4.34	4.06	4.23	20.04	13.97	18.22	7.27	5.36	6.56
VI. Electricity, Gas and Water supply	0.03	0.01	0.02	0.17	0.06	0.14	0.05	0.01	0.04
VII. Construction	1.94	0.85	1.51	7.87	4.44	6.84	3.05	1.32	2.40
VIII. Wholesale and Retail Trade	3.27	0.96	2.37	24.04	8.70	19.44	7.15	1.98	5.20
IX. Hotels and Restourants	0.72	0.07	0.47	4.03	0.39	2.94	1.34	0.11	0.88
X. Transport, Storage and Communication	0.67	0.09	0.44	3.44	0.63	2.60	1.19	0.16	0.80
XI. Financial Intermediation, Real Estate, Renting and Business Activities	1.64	1.64	1.64	11.09	13.86	11.92	3.40	3.26	3.34
XII. Other Services***	2.03	2.37	2.17	8.60	23.17	12.96	3.26	5.12	3.96
Total	100.00	100.00	100.00	100.00	100.00	100.00	100.00	100.00	100.00
Number**(Million)	2.92	1.88	4.80	0.67	0.28	0.95	3.58	2.17	5.75

Notes: Totals may not tally due to rounding off.
Main workers are those who work for 183 days or more in a year.
* Data relates to age group 5-14 years.
** Includes Main Workers only.
*** Public Administration, Defence, Compulsory Social Security, Education, Health and Social, Work, Other Community, Social and Personel Service, Activities, Private Households with Employed Persons, Extra-Terriitoriol Organisations and Bodies

Source: Registrar General and Census Commissioner of India : *Census of India, 2001.*

Table 3.4.6: Percentage Distribution of Working Children* by Occupational Division, 1991

	Occupational Division	*Rural*			*Urban*			*Total*		
		Male	*Female*	*Person*	*Male*	*Female*	*Person*	*Male*	*Female*	*Person*
0-1.	Professional Technical and Related Workers'	0.11	0.04	0.08	0.51	0.57	0.53	0.16	0.07	0.12
2.	Administrative Executive and Managerial Workers'	0.03	0.01	0.02	0.38	0.13	0.30	0.07	0.02	0.05
3.	Clerical and Related Works	0.05	0.01	0.03	0.65	0.22	0.52	0.12	0.02	0.07
4.	Sales Workers	1.22	0.29	0.79	14.49	3.08	11.18	2.76	0.45	1.72
5.	Service Workers	1.07	0.71	0.90	10.79	18.01	12.88	2.20	1.70	1.97
6.	Farmers, Fishermen, Hunters, Loggers & Related Workers	91.07	92.38	91.68	23.19	36.11	26.94	83.19	89.14	85.88
7-8-9	Production and Related Workers, Transport Equipment Operators and Labourers	5.98	6.24	6.10	47.27	39.76	45.10	10.77	8.17	9.59
10.	Workers not Classified by Occupation	0.47	0.32	0.40	2.72	2.12	2.55	0.73	0.43	0.60
	Total	100.00	100.00	100.00	100.00	100.00	100.00	100.00	100.00	100.00
	Number**(Million)	5.46	4.80	10.26	0.73	0.30	1.03	6.19	5.10	11.29

Notes: Main workers are those who work for 183 days or more in a year.

* Data relate to age group 5-14 years.

** Includes main and marginal workers only.

Source: Registrar General and Census Commissioner of India : *Census of India 1991.*

Table 3.4.7: Employment Status of Working Children by Industry, 1999-00 and 2004-05

Status	*Industry*	*Year*	*Rural*			*Urban*			*Total*		
			Male	*Female*	*Person*	*Male*	*Female*	*Person*	*Male*	*Female*	*Person*
Self-Employed	0	1999-00	47.51	49.67	48.55	5.79	8.12	6.70	41.50	45.38	43.32
		2004-05	53.52	53.28	53.40	6.02	8.42	6.99	45.56	47.53	40.49
	1-9	1999-00	9.24	13.49	11.29	30.76	43.23	35.61	12.34	16.57	14.33
		2004-05	12.68	14.25	13.43	35.81	60.70	45.87	16.55	20.20	18.27
	0-9	1999-00	56.75	63.16	59.48	36.55	51.35	42.31	53.84	61.95	57.65
		2004-05	66.19	67.53	66.84	41.82	69.12	52.86	62.11	67.73	64.76
Regular Salaried/Wage Employee	0	1999-00	3.08	–	1.60	–	–	–	2.63	–	1.40
		2004-05	1.40	–	0.73	–	–	–	1.17	–	0.62
	1-9	1999-00	3.08	0.96	2.06	30.76	21.67	27.22	7.07	3.10	5.21
		2004-05	2.82	1.30	2.08	34.10	16.82	27.12	8.05	3.29	5.81
	0-9	1999-00	6.61	0.96	3.66	30.76	21.67	27.22	9.70	3.10	6.60
		2004-05	4.22	1.30	2.81	34.10	16.82	27.12	9.23	3.29	6.43
Casual Labour	0	1999-00	28.81	31.19	30.30	1.93	5.42	3.28	24.94	29.17	26.93
		2004-05	21.13	28.58	24.72	2.00	8.42	4.60	17.93	26.00	21.72
	1-9	1999-00	8.29	3.96	6.20	30.76	21.56	27.18	11.52	5.78	8.82
		2004-05	8.45	2.59	5.63	22.07	5.63	15.42	10.73	2.98	7.09
	0-9	1999-00	37.10	35.87	36.50	32.69	26.98	30.47	36.46	34.95	35.75
		2004-05	29.58	31.18	30.35	24.07	14.03	20.01	28.66	28.98	28.81
Total	0	1999-00	79.40	81.58	80.45	7.72	13.54	9.98	69.07	74.55	71.65
		2004-05	76.05	81.86	78.85	8.02	16.85	11.59	64.66	73.53	68.83
	1-9	1999-00	20.60	18.42	19.55	92.28	86.46	90.02	30.93	25.45	28.35
		2004-05	23.95	18.14	21.15	91.98	83.41	88.41	35.34	26.47	31.17
	0-9	1999-00	100.00	100.00	100.00	100.00	100.00	100.00	100.00	100.00	100.00
		2004-05	100.00	100.00	100.00	100.00	100.00	100.00	100.00	100.00	100.00

Notes: Data relate to age group 5-14 years. Figures include Principal as well as Subsidiary usual status workers.
0-Agriculture, 1-9—Non-Agriculture.

Sources: National Sample Survey Organiation :
(i) Report No. 408, *Employment and Unemployment in India, 1999-2000.*
(ii) Report No. 515, *Empolyment and Unemployment in India, 2004-2005.*

Figure 3.4.U

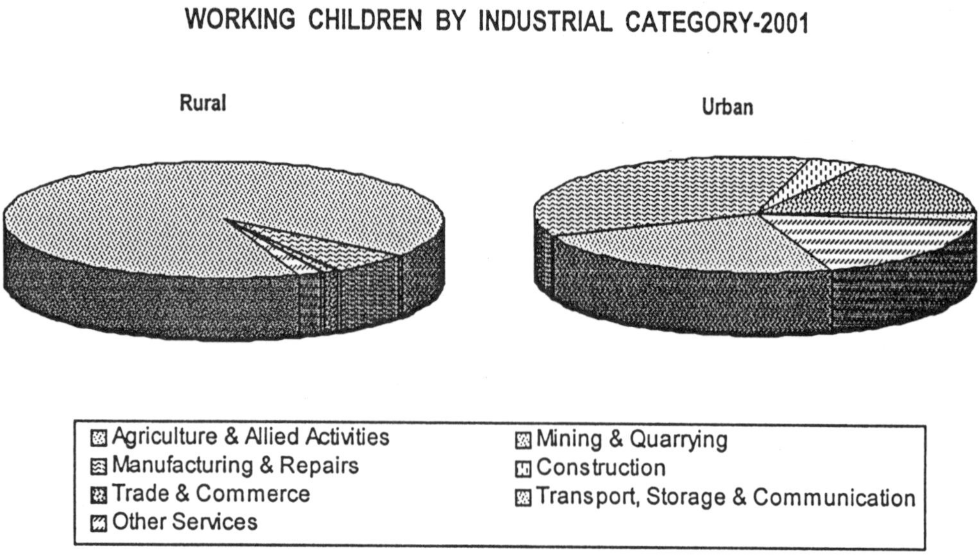

For details see Table 3.4.5

Figure 3.4.V

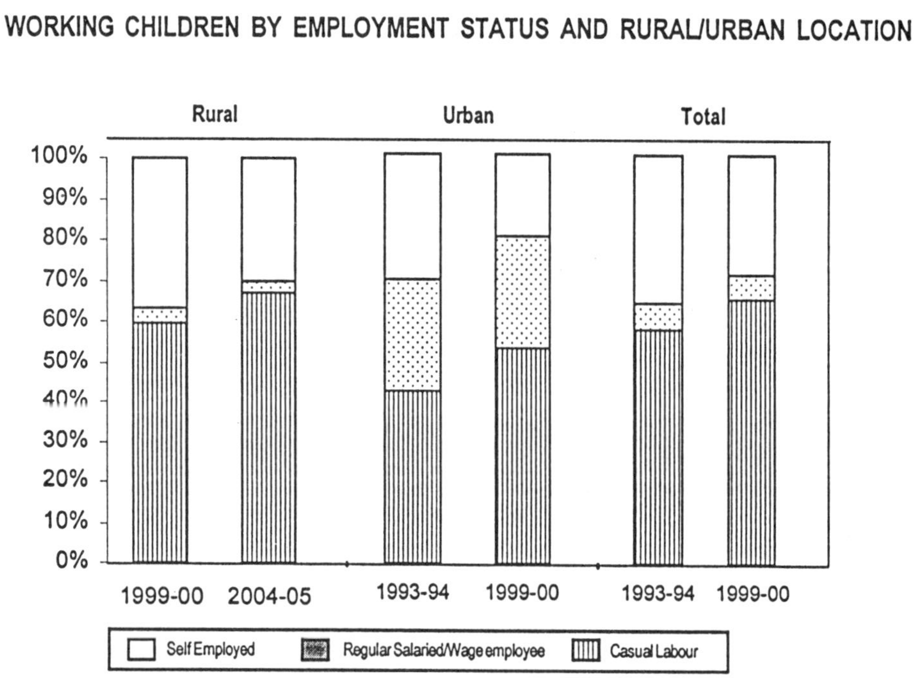

For details see Table 3.4.7

(v) Activities of Population Aged 60+

Table 3.5.1: Workforce Participation Rates of 60+ Population by Age Group, 2001

Age group	Population (Million)			Workers (Million)			Workforce Participation Rates		
	Male	Female	Person	Male	Female	Person	Male	Female	Person
				TOTAL					
60-69	23.06	24.26	47.32	14.19	3.66	17.85	61.53	15.09	37.72
70-79	10.79	10.47	21.26	4.59	0.78	5.37	42.54	7.45	25.20
80+	3.92	4.12	8.04	1.17	0.21	1.38	29.85	5.10	17.16
60+	37.77	38.83	76.62	19.95	4.66	24.61	52.82	1.99	32.12
				RURAL					
60-69	17.22	18.25	35.47	11.42	3.16	14.58	66.32	17..31	41.10
70-79	8.16	7.80	15.96	3.76	0.66	4.42	46.08	8.46	27.69
80+	2.98	3.03	6.01	0.93	0.17	1.10	31.21	5.61	18.30
60+	28.36	29.08	57.44	16.12	3.99	20.11	56.34	13.72	35.01
				URBAN					
60-69	5.84	6.01	11.85	2.76	0.50	3.26	47.26	8.32	27.51
70-79	2.63	2.67	5.30	.083	0.12	0.95	31.56	4.49	17.92
80+	0,93	1.09	2.02	0.24	0.04	0.28	25.81	3.67	13.86
60+	9.41	9.77	19.18	3.83	0.66	4.49	40.70	6.75	23.41

Note: Main Workers are those who work for 183 days or more in a year.
Source: Registrar General and Census Commissioner of India : *Census of India, 2001*

Table 3.5.2: Percentage Distribution of 60+ Population by Broad Activity Status in Agriculture & Non-agriculture Sector

Rural India

Activity Status	1999-2000			2004-05		
	Male	Female	Person	Male	Female	Person
A. Employed	63.90	21.80	43.00	64.5	25.3	44.8
i) Self employed						
- Agriculture	41.00	12.30	26.70	43.8	16.1	29.8
- Non Agriculture	8.20	2.00	5.20	8.3	2.4	5.4
Total	49.20	14.30	31.90	52.1	18.5	35.2
ii) Regular Employees						
- Agriculture	0.30	0.10	0.20	0.3	0.0	0.2
- Non Agriculture	0.70	0.20	0.40	0.9	0.4	0.6
Total	1.00	0.30	0.60	1.3	0.4	0.8
iii) Casual Wage Labou						
- Agriculture	12.20	6.80	9.50	9.5	5.8	7.6
- Non Agriculture	1.50	0.40	1.00	1.6	0.6	1.1
Total*	13.70	7.20	10.50	11.1	6.4	8.7
B. Unemployed	0.10	—	—	0.1	0.1	0.1
C. Out of Labour Force	36.00	78.20	57.00	35.5	74.7	55.7
Total	100.00	100.00	100.00	100.00	100.00	100.00

Note: * Include casual wage labour in public works.
Sources: National Sample Survey Organisation:
Report No. 458 and 515, *Employmaent and Unemployment Situation in India, 1999-2000 & 2004-05*

Table 3.5.3: Percentage Distribution of 60+ Population by Broad Activity Status in Agriculture and Non-Agriculture Sector

Urban India

Activity Status	1999-2000			2004-05		
	Male	Female	Person	Male	Female	Person
A. Employed	40.20	9.40	24.10	36.60	10.00	22.80
i) Self employed						
– Agriculture	5.50	1.10	3.20	6.40	1.90	4.10
– Non Agriculture	23.70	5.00	13.90	21.30	4.30	1240
Total	29.20	6.10	17.10	27.70	6.20	16.50
ii) Regular Employees						
– Agriculture	0.20	–	0.10	0.10	-	0.10
– Non Agriculture	5.60	1.40	3.40	5.50	1.90	3.60
Total	5.80	1.40	3.50	5.60	1.90	3.70
iii) Casual Wage Labour						
– Agriculture	1.50	1.00	1.20	0.80	0.90	0.90
– Non Agriculture	3.70	0.90	2.30	2.50	0.90	1.70
Total*	5.20	1.90	3.50	3.30	1.80	2.60
B. Unemployed	–	–	–	–	–	–
C. Out of Labour Force	59.80	90.60	75.90	63.40	90.00	77.20
Total	100.00	100.00	100.00	100.00	100.00	100.00

Note: * Include casual wage labour in public works.
Source: National Sample Survey Organisation :
Report No. 458and 515, *Employmaent and Unemployment Situation in India, 1999-2000 & 2004-05*

Table 3.5.4: Percentage Distribution of 60+ Main Workers by Industrial Category, 1981

Industrial Category	Rural			Urban			Total		
	Male	Female	Person	Male	Female	Person	Male	Female	Person
Cultivators	70.21	42.99	66.48	14.41	9.70	13.91	62.17	39.31	59.15
Agricultural Labourers	17.21	46.49	21.22	7.00	20.68	8.44	15.74	43.64	19.43
Livestock, Forestry, Fishing, Hunting and Plantations orchards and Allied Activities	1.55	1.05	1.48	1.97	1.27	1.90	1.62	1.07	1.54
Mininig and Quarrying	0.12	0.05	0.11	0.35	0.42	0.35	0.15	0.09	0.14
Manufacturing Processing, Servicing and Repairs									
(a) Household Industry	2.97	3.30	3.01	6.76	10.97	7.20	3.51	4.15	3.60
(b) Other than Household Inductry	1.90	1.20	1.81	17.86	9.70	17.01	4.20	2.14	3.93
Construction	0.50	0.21	0.47	3.75	1.69	3.53	0.97	0.37	0.89
Trade and Commerce	2.58	2.36	2.55	27.43	17.30	26.37	6.16	4.01	5.88
Transport Storage and Communication	0.37	0.05	0.32	4.93	1.27	4.55	1.02	0.19	0.91
Other Services	2.59	2.30	2.55	15.54	27.00	16.74	4.46	5.03	4.53
	100.00	100.00	100.00	100.00	100.00	100.00	100.00	100.00	100.00
Total Main Workers (Million)	12.04	1.91	13.95	2.03	0.23	2.26	14.07	2.147	16.21

Note: Main Workers are those who work for 183 days or more in a year.
Source: Registrar General and Census Commissioner of India : *Census of India, 1981.*

Table 3.5.5: Percentage Distribution of 60+ Main Workers by Industrial Category, and Sex 1991

Industrial Category	*Rural*			*Urban*			*Total*		
	Male	*Female*	*Person*	*Male*	*Female*	*Person*	*Male*	*Female*	*Person*
Cultivators	66.95	44.02	63.36	13.34	9.73	12.95	58.64	40.35	55.91
Agricultural Labourers	20.53	46.68	24.62	8.27	22.49	9.80	18.63	44.09	22.42
Livestock, Forestry, Fishing, Hunting and Plantations, orchards and Allied Activities	1.58	1.31	1.54	2.02	1.52	1.97	1.65	1.34	1.61
Mining and Quarrying	0.18	0.11	0.17	0.51	0.30	0.49	0.23	0.13	0.22
Manufacturing Processing Servicing and Repairs									
(a) Household Industry	1.99	2.48	2.07	3.97	8.81	4.49	2.30	3.16	2.42
(b) Other than Household Industry	1.96	1.24	1.84	16.43	10.33	15.77	4.20	2.20	3.90
Construction	0.56	0.11	0.50	4.23	2.13	4.00	1.13	0.33	1.01
Trade and Commerce	2.98	1.93	2.81	29.58	16.72	28.20	7.09	3.52	6.56
Transport Storage and Communication	0.38	0.04	0.33	4.70	0.61	4.26	1.06	0.10	0.92
Other Services	2.89	2.08	2.76	16.95	27.36	18.07	5.07	4.78	5.03
	100.00	100.00	100.00	100.00	100.00	100.00	100.00	100.00	100.00
Total Main Workers (Million)	14.83	2.74	17.57	2.72	0.33	3.05	17.55	3.07	20.62

Note: Main workers are those who work for 183 days or more in a year.
Source: Registrar General and Census Commissioner of India : *Census of India, 1991*.

Table 3.5.6: Percentage Distribution of 60+ Main Workers by Industrial Category & Sex, 2001

Industrial Category	*Rural*			*Urban*			*Total*		
	Male	*Female*	*Total*	*Male*	*Female*	*Total*	*Male*	*Female*	*Total*
I. Cultivators	63.22	48.67	60.34	7.62	6.80	7.50	52.56	42.69	50.69
II. Agricultural Labourers	18.55	33.80	21.57	4.79	11.70	5.81	15.91	30.65	18.70
III. Plantation, Livestock, Forestry, Fishing, Hunting and Allied Activities	2.60	4.64	3.01	2.46	3.30	2.58	2.57	4.45	2.93
IV. Mining and Quarrying	0.23	0.18	0.22	0.57	0.36	0.54	0.30	0.20	0.28
V. Manufacturing, Processing, Servicing and Repairs :	5.20	5.68	5.30	19.83	21.38	20.06	8.01	7.91	7.99
(a) Household Industry	2.92	4.18	3.17	5.18	11.75	6.15	3.35	5.25	3.71
(b) Other than Household Industry	2.28	1.50	2.13	14.65	9.63	13.91	4.66	2.66	4.28
VI. Electricity, Gas and Water supply	0.09	0.01	0.07	0.45	0.13	0.40	0.16	0.03	0.13
VII. Construction	1.25	0.40	1.08	6.32	4.04	5.98	2.22	0.92	1.98
VIII. Wholesale and Retail Trade	3.55	2.12	3.27	26.71	14.90	24.96	7.99	3.95	7.23
IX. Hotels and Restourants	0.36	0.21	0.33	2.08	1.42	1.98	0.69	0.38	0.63
X. Transport, Storage and Communication	0.73	0.09	0.60	5.85	1.28	5.18	1.71	0.26	1.44
XI. Financial Intermediation, Real Estate, Renting and Business Activities	1.16	1.11	1.15	9.74	7.85	9.48	2.81	2.08	2.67
XII. Other Services**	3.06	3.09	3.06	13.58	26.84	15.53	5.07	6.48	5.33
Total	100.00	100.00	100.00	100.00	100.00	100.00	100.00	100.00	100.00
Number*(Million)	16.12	3.98	20.10	3.83	0.66	4.49	19.94	4.65	24.59

Notes: Totals may not tally with all due to rounding off.
Main Workers are those who work for 183 days or more in a year.
* Includes Main Workers only.
** Public Administration, Defence, Compulsory Social Security, Education, Health and Social Work, Other Community, Social and Personel Service Activities, Private Households with Employed Persons, Extra-Territorial Organisations and Bodies

Source: Registrar General and Census Commissioner of India : *Census of India, 2001.*

Table 3.5.7: Old Age Dependency Rates* by Sex

Sex	1971			1981[1]			1991[2]			2001[3]		
	Rural	Urban	Total	Rural	Urban	Total	Rural	Urban	Total	Rural	Urban	Total
Male	12.33	8.20	11.39	13.06	8.53	11.84	13.34	9.21	12.16	13.59	9.93	12.45
Female	12.02	9.74	11.57	12.93	10.08	12.24	12.97	10.19	12.23	14.65	11.67	13.77
Person	12.18	8.89	11.47	12.99	9.24	12.04	13.16	9.66	12.19	14.11	10.75	13.08

Notes: * The dependency rates for the elderly is the percentage of populations of aged 60 years and above to the population in the age group 15-59 years.

1. Excludes figures for Assam
2. Excludes figures for Jammu & kashmir.
3. Excludes three sub-divisions of Senapati district of Manipur.

Source: Registrar General and Census Commissioner of India, *Census of India, Ageing Poprlation of India, An Analysis of the Census data.*

Table 3.5.8: Percentage Distribution of 60+ Main Workers by Educational Level and Sex, 1981

Industrial Category	Rural			Urban			Total		
	Male	Female	Person	Male	Female	Person	Male	Female	Person
Illiterate	71.22	96.96	74.75	43.32	87.76	47.97	67.20	95.99	71.01
Literate without educational level	13.01	1.73	11.46	14.11	4.22	13.07	13.17	2.00	11.69
Primary	10.66	1.05	9.35	18.55	3.37	16.96	11.80	1.30	10.41
Middle	3.55	0.21	3.10	10.06	1.27	9.14	4.49	0.32	3.94
Matriculation/Secondary	1.13	0.05	0.98	8.78	1.27	8.0	2.23	0.18	1.96
Higher Secondary	0.18	—	0.16	1.53	0.42	1.41	0.38	0.04	0.33
Non Technical Diploma or certificate not equal to degree	0.03	—	0.02	0.05	—	0.04	0.03	0.01	0.02
Technical Diploma or certificate not equal to Degree	0.05	—	0.04	0.35	0.42	0.35	0.09	0.03	0.09
Graduate and above	0.17	—	0.14	3.25	1.27	3.06	0.61	0.13	0.55
	100.00	100.00	100.00	100.00	100.00	100.00	100.00	100.00	100.00
Total Main Workers (Million)	12.04	1.91	13.95	2.03	0.24	2.26	14.07	2.15	16.21

Note: Main Workers are those who work for 183 days or more in a year.

Source: Registrar General and Census Commssioner of India : *Census of India, 1981.*

Figure 3.5 W

For details see Table 3.5.2 and 3.5.3

Figure 3.5 X

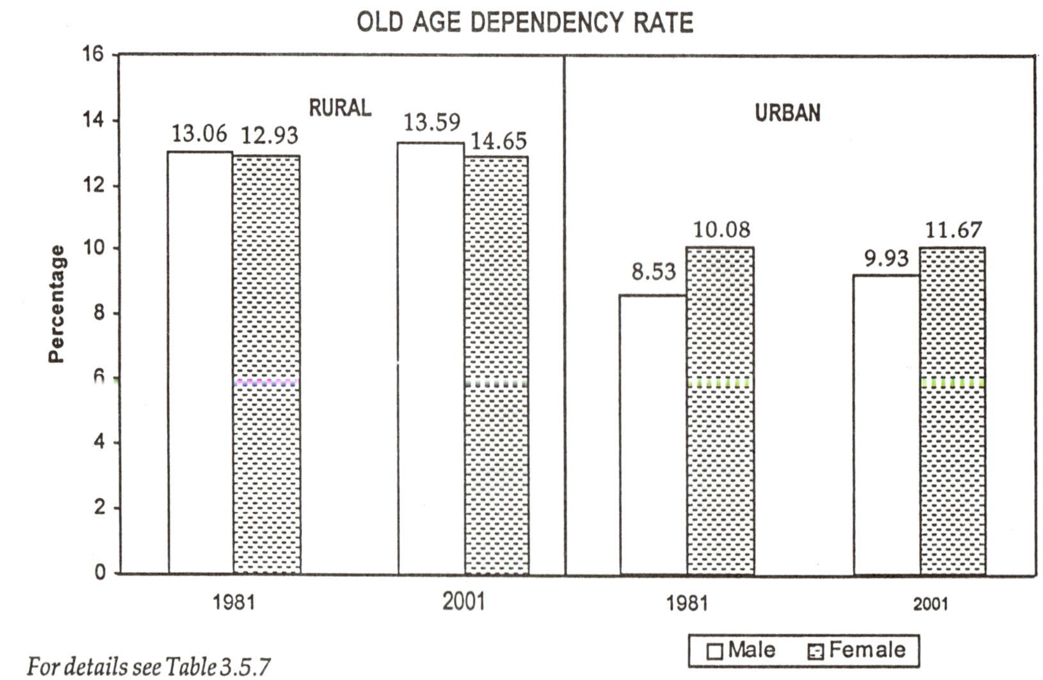

For details see Table 3.5.7

Table 3.5.9: Percentage Distribution of 60+ Main Workers by Educational Level and Sex, 1991

Educational Level	Rural			Urban			Total		
	Male	Female	Person	Male	Female	Person	Male	Female	Person
Illiterate	66.75	94.74	71.13	38.51	79.70	43.02	62.41	93.13	67.00
Literate without educational level	11.66	2.37	10.21	10.99	5.45	10.38	11.56	2.70	10.24
Primary	13.22	2.12	11.48	19.74	6.36	18.28	14.22	2.57	12.47
Middle	0.51	4.63	12.14	2.42	11.08	6.43	0.72	5.58	5.40
Matriculation/ Secondary	2.09	0.15	1.78	10.50	2.42	9.62	3.38	0.39	2.93
Higher Secondary	0.39	0.04	0.33	2.20	0.61	2.02	0.67	0.10	0.58
Non-Technical Diploma or Certificate not equal to Degree	0.05	—	0.05	0.11	—	0.10	0.06	—	0.06
Technical Diploma or Certificate not equal to Degree	0.05	—	0.05	0.34	0.30	0.33	0.10	0.03	0.09
Graduate and above	0.39	0.07	0.34	5.47	2.74	5.17	1.17	0.36	1.05
	100.00	100.00	100.00	100.00	100.00	100.00	100.00	100.00	100.00
Total Main Workers (Million)	14.83	2.74	17.57	2.72	0.33	3.05	17.55	3.07	20.62

Note: Main workers are those who work for 183 days or more in a year

Source: Registrar General and Census Commissioner of India : *Census of India, 1991.*

Table 3.5.10: Percentage Distribution of 60+ Main Workers by Educational Level & Sex, 2001

Industrial Category	Rural			Urban			Total		
	Male	Female	Person	Male	Female	Person	Male	Female	Person
Illiterate	53.21	88.16	60.15	27.22	67.76	33.22	48.22	85.25	55.23
Literate (without Educational Level)	3.63	2.32	3.36	3.59	3.47	3.56	3.62	2.46	3.40
Literate but below Matric/Secondary	36.34	8.80	30.88	39.86	18.64	36.72	37.02	10.21	31.94
Matriculation/Secondary below Graduate	5.62	0.55	4.61	18.72	5.04	16.70	8.13	1.20	6.82
Technical Diploma or Certificate not equal to Degree or Graduate and above	0.14	0.05	0.12	0.66	0.44	0.63	0.24	0.11	0.22
Other than Technical Degree	0.90	0.09	0.74	8.15	3.43	7.45	2.29	0.57	1.97
Technical Degree or Diploma equal to Degree or Post Graduate Degree	0.16	0.03	0.14	1.80	1.22	1.72	0.48	0.20	0.42
	100.00	100.00	100.00	100.00	100.00	100.00	100.00	100.00	100.00
Total Main Workers (Million)	16.12	3.99	20.11	3.83	0.66	4.99	19.95	4.65	24.60

Notes: Total may not tally due to rounding off.

Main Workers are those who work for 183 days or more in a year.

Source: Registrar General and Census Commssioner of India : *Census of India, 2001.*

(vi) Youth

Table 3.6.1: Youth* Population by Sex

Year	*Population* (Million)			*Youth Population* (Million)			*Proportion of Youth Population to Total Population*		
	Male	Female	Person	Male	Female	Person	Male	Female	Person
1971	284.05	264.11	548.16	85.50	82.14	167.67	30.1	31.1	30.6
1981	353.37	329.95	683.32	113.43	107.24	220.67	32.1	32.5	32.2
1991	439.23	407.07	846.30	146.04	138.97	285.00	33.1	34.0	33.6
2001	532.16	496.45	1028.61	179.18	168.50	347.68	33.7	33.9	33.8

Note: * Relates to the Population of Age-group15-34.

Source: Registrar General and Census Commissioner of India : *Census of India, 1971, 1981, 1991* and *2001* .

Table 3.6.2: Workforce Participation Rates of Youth*

Year	*Population (Million)*			*Workers (Million)*			*Work force Participation Rates*		
	Male	*Female*	*Person*	*Male*	*Female*	*Person*	*Male*	*Female*	*Person*
				Rural					
1981	97.30	77.52	156.82	63.37	19.40	82.77	79.91	25.03	52.78
1991	102.51	99.10	201.61	78.75	28.55	107.30	76.82	28.81	53.22
2001	122.94	118.08	240.97	74.86	28.15	103.01	60.89	23.85	42.75
				Urban					
1981	31.06	26.70	57.76	20.35	2.69	23.04	65.52	10.07	39.89
1991	41.70	37.84	79.54	26.69	4.09	30.78	64.00	10.81	38.70
2001	56.24	50.46	106.70	31.82	5.58	37.40	56.58	11.06	35.05
				Total					
1981	110.36	104.22	214.58	83.72	22.09	105.81	75.86	21.20	49.31
1991	144.21	136.94	281.15	105.44	32.64	138.08	73.12	28.84	49.11
2001	179.18	168.50	347.68	106.67	33.73	140.40	59.53	20.02	40.38

Notes: 1981 Census figures exclude Assam.
1991 Census figures exclude Jammu and Kashmir.
2001 Census figures exclude 3 Sub- division of Senapati District of Manipur.
* Relates to the Population of Age-group15-34.

Source: Registrar General and Census Commissioner of India : *Census of India,* 1981, 1991 and 2001.

Table 3.6.3: Percentage Distribution of Youth* Population by Broad Activity Status, 1999-2000, 2004-05

Activity Status	*Year*	*Rural* Male	*Rural* Female	*Rural* Person	*Urban* Male	*Urban* Female	*Urban* Person	*All India* Male	*All India* Female	*All India* Person
Employed	1999-2000	79.07	43.43	61.17	66.83	16.83	42.38	75.55	36.28	56.08
	2004-05	79.14	40.96	59.64	69.50	18.86	45.11	76.32	35.01	55.56
Unemployed	1999-2000	2.76	0.93	1.84	6.09	2.08	4.17	3.72	1.23	2.49
		(3.37)	(2.09)	(2.92)	(8.36)	(10.98)	(8.86)	(4.67)	(3.29)	(4.25)
	2004-5	2.55	1.96	2.25	5.11	3.66	4.41	3.30	2.42	2.85
		(3.12)	(4.56)	(3.62)	(6.85)	(76.26)	(8.91)	(4.14)	(6.45)	(4.89)
Student	1999-2000	15.22	7.66	11.42	24.09	18.73	21.52	17.77	10.64	14.23
	2004-05	16.29	10.32	13.24	23.54	22.49	23.03	18.41	13.60	15.99
Others	1999-2000	2.95	47.98	25.57	2.99	62.36	31.43	2.96	51.85	27.20
	2004-05	2.02	46.67	24.83	1.85	54.99	27.44	1.97	48.91	25.56
Total		100.00	100.00	100.00	100.00	100.00	100.00	100.00	100.00	100.00

Notes: Figures within parantheses are the unemployment rates with respect to Labour Force.
'Others' include domestic duties, rentiers, disabled, beggars, etc.
*Relates to the Population of Age-group 15-34.

Sources: National Sample Survey Organisation :
Report No. 458 and 515 *Employment and Unemployment Situatio in India, 1999-00 and 2004-05.*

Table 3.6.4: Percentage Distribution of Youth* Population by Sex and Education Level and Sex, 1981 and 1991

Education Level	*1981* Male	*1981* Female	*1981* Person	*1991* Male	*1991* Female	*1991* Person
Illiterate	36.11	64.70	50.00	30.44	56.52	43.15
Literate (without educational Level)	8.51	5.43	7.01	6.71	4.84	5.80
Primary	16.78	11.54	14.24	15.15	15.86	13.55
Middle	16.16	8.36	12.36	19.49	11.84	15.76
Matriculation/Secondary	12.57	5.88	9.33	14.56	8.04	11.38
Higher Secondary/ Intermediate/Pre-university	5.21	2.06	3.69	7.10	3.50	5.35
Non-Technical Diploma/Certificate not equal to Degree	0.05	0.04	0.04	0.15	0.11	0.13
Technical Diploma/Certificatenot equal to Degree	0.55	0.16	0.36	0.73	0.19	0.46
Graduate and above	4.06	1.83	2.97	5.67	3.10	4.42
Total	100.00	100.00	100.00	100.00	100.00	100.00

Note: *Relates to the Population of Age-group 15-34.

Source: Registrar General and Census Commissioner of India : *Census of India , 1981* and *1991.*

Table 3.6.5: Percentage Distribution of Youth* Population by Educational Level and Sex, 2001

Industrial Category	*2001*		
	Male	*Female*	*Total*
Illiterate	18.95	39.63	28.97
Literate (without Educational Level)	2.56	2.47	2.52
Literate	8.105	60.37	71.03
Below Primary	7.67	7.05	7.37
Primary	16.55	14.68	15.64
Middle	18.26	12.40	15.43
Matriculation/Secondary	18.05	12.42	15.31
High Secondar/ Intermediate/Pre-University/Senior Secondary	9.69	6.37	8.08
Non-Technical Diploma or Certificate not Equal to Degree or	0.08	0.04	0.06
Graduate and above Other than Technical Dgree	7.21	4.68	5.98
Technical Diploma or Certificate equal to Degree	0.97	0.26	0.63
Unclassified	0.01	0.01	0.01
Total	100.00	100.00	100.00
Total Main Workers (Million)	179.18	168.50	347.68

Notes: Total may not tally due to rounding off.

* Date relates to the Population of Age-group 15–34.

Source: Registrar General and Census Commssioner of India : *Census of India, 2001.*

Table 3.6.6: Percentage Distribution of Youth Workers by Level of Education, 1981, 1991 and 2001

Education Level	*1981*			*1991*			*2001*		
	Male	*Female*	*Person*	*Male*	*Female*	*Person*	*Male*	*Female*	*Person*
Illiterate	43.81	79.38	51.23	38.25	72.64	49.39	23.04	52.93	30.22
Literate but below Matric/Secondary	39.30	14.69	34.17	40.50	19.61	35.56	46.11	32.96	42.95
Matric/Secondary/ Higher Secondary/ Intermediate/Pre-University	12.84	3.40	10.86	15.80	4.47	13.12	22.73	8.78	19.38
Technical Deploma or certificate not equal to Degree	0.50	0.43	0.49	0.58	0.37	0.53	0.86	0.48	0.77
Graduate and above othter than technical Degree	3.55	0.10	3.25	4.87	2.91	4.40	6.26	3.84	5.68
Technical Degree or Deploma equal to Degree or Post-graduate Degree	—	—	—	—	—	—	1.00	1.01	1.00
Total	100.00	100.00	100.00	100.00	100.00	100.00	100.00	100.00	100.00
Workers (Million)	83.72	22.09	105.81	105.44	32.64	138.08	106.67	33.73	140.40

Note: — *Data Not Available.*

Source: Registrar General and Census Commissioner of India : *Census of India, 1981, 1991 and 2001.*

Table 3.6.7: Percentage Distribution of Youth Workers by Status of Employment and Broad Industry, 1999-2000

Status of Employment	*Industry Code*	*Rural*			*Urban*			*Total*		
		Male	*Female*	*Person*	*Male*	*Female*	*Person*	*Male*	*Female*	*Person*
Self-Employed	(0)	38.28	45.78	40.94	3.05	8.09	4.00	29.32	41.05	33.08
	(1-9)	12.92	9.39	11.69	37.25	35.98	37.02	19.11	12.76	17.00
	(0-9)	51.20	55.17	52.63	40.30	44.07	41.01	48.43	53.82	50.16
Regular Salaried/ Wage Employee	(0)	1.23	0.56	0.99	0.31	0.43	0.33	1.00	0.54	0.85
	(1-9)	7.04	2.67	5.48	38.24	34.06	37.45	14.97	6.59	12.28
	(0-9)	8.27	3.23	6.47	38.55	34.49	37.79	15.97	7.13	13.13
Casual Labour	(0)	29.94	38.30	32.90	2.18	7.82	3.24	22.88	34.46	26.59
	(1-9)	10.59	3.30	8.00	18.97	13.62	17.96	12.72	4.59	10.12
	(0-9)	40.53	41.60	40.90	21.15	21.44	21.20	35.60	39.05	36.71
Total Workers	(0)	69.45	84.64	74.84	5.54	16.34	7.57	53.19	76.06	60.53
	(1-9)	30.55	15.36	25.16	94.46	83.66	92.43	46.81	23.94	39.47
	(0-9)	100.00	100.00	100.00	100.00	100.00	100.00	100.00	100.00	100.00

Notes: 0 Agriculture; 1-9 — Non-agriculture.

Source: National Sample Survey Organisation :
Report No. 458, *Employment and Unemployment Situation in India—1999-2000.*

SECTION 4

Economic Returns from Manpower Utilisation

Gayatri Pandey
Vijay K. Saxena

Section IV
Economic Returns From Manpower Utilisation

For several decades the Indian economy remained almost stagnant. But with the implementation of planning, the economy that was stagnant started growing. Till 1990-91, the rate of growth of GDP hovered around 4 per cent. The economic reforms, which began in early 90's, consisted of policies for attaining macro-economic stabilisation and structural reforms to put the economy on the higher growth path. The economy has now started reaping the fruits of these economic reforms with attaining the higher growth rate (approximately 8 per cent GDP growth during Tenth Five Year Plan and 8.7 percent in the first year of Eleventh Plan). The optimum use of national manpower along with other national resources helps in accelerating the economic development of a country. The working population of the country is engaged in production of goods and services with the use of available limited national resources. The economic returns from these activities is measured (in value terms) in the form of gross domestic product (GDP), gross national product (GNP), net domestic product (NDP), net national product (NNP) (national income), per capita income, capital formation and labour productivity, etc.

The national output depends upon various factors such as demographic conditions of people, their knowledge, quality and working environment in general, and the quality of life, which the people are leading in particular. In the previous sections of the document it has been described how the human resources are generated through prevailing demographic conditions (Section-I) and transformed into manpower through development process of education and training (Section-II), and then utilised in economic activities with the available resource base (Section-III). Section-IV presents the macro information regarding the economic contribution arising out of manpower utilisation in the national economy. The data have been drawn from the M/O Finance, Central Statistical Organisation (CSO), National Sample Survey Organisation (NSSO), State Directorate of Economics & Statistics (SDES) and the National Productivity Council (NPC).

The total output of all economic activities (avoiding duplicate counting) which are performed by the manpower of the country, measured in terms of value gives the national output, defined as gross domestic product, which is a crude indicator of the economic position of a country in a particular time period. Table 4.1 presents growth performance of Indian economy since the inception of planning. Data reveals that India's GDP grew at an annual average rate of around 4 per cent during 1950-51 to 1990-91 and about 6.0 per cent per annum during 1990-91 to 2001 which further raised to about 7.6 per cent per annum during 2002-07 (Tenth Plan Period). The growth of GDP during 2002-07 remained slightly below the targeted growth of 8.0 per cent. Again in the first year of Eleventh Plan 2007-08 the growth of GDP raised to 8.7 per cent even after global slow down. The gradual increase in the rate of investment over the period of more than five decades (10.6 per cent during 1951-56 to 24.2 per cent during 1997-2002 at 1993-94 prices and 30.1 per cent during 2002-07 at 1999-2000 prices) indicates that proportionately a greater share of the increase in GDP goes towards capital formation. This is one of the important indicators of an economy's ability to produce more income. It is also assumed that higher the rate of capital formation, the more rapid is the growth of economy. But it is also evident from the data that higher growth rate is no longer solely due to higher investment. During the Ninth Plan (1997-2002), the growth rate of 5.35 per cent with an investment rate of the order of 24.2 per cent is much lower as compared to the Eighth Plan growth rate of 6.7 per cent with investment rate of 24.0 per cent. Hence, there are other macro-economic parameters such as estimated savings rate, investment rate, growth rate of total consumption, per capita private consumption and capital output ratio which influence the growth of economy. These factors are presented in Table 4.2 for the period 1992-93 to 2007-12.

If one has to restrict to one single figure as measure of economic returns from the economic activities in the country, the most comprehensive figure would be that of the national income, i.e. gross domestic product adjusted for transaction with the rest of the world. Table 4.3 presents the information about national income, per capita income, private consumption and net capital formation from 1981-82 to 1998-99 on the basis of old series at 1993-94 prices and 1999-000 to 2007-08 on the basis of new series at 1999-00 prices. Growing national income (at factor cost) over the period indicates that there is net increase in the total production of the country, and growing per capita income at factor cost indicates that the economic welfare of the people has also increased. It is just the one side of economic welfare of the society. The consumption pattern and its level determine the overall economic welfare of the society. As the private consumption level is also increasing over the period along with national income, it shows that the country is achieving greater economic welfare of the community. This fact is further substantiated through the consumption pattern data from NSSO presented in Table 4.8 that depicts that per capita expenditure on education, health, fuel&light, and goods& services has raised steadily over the time both in rural and urban areas.

The macro level economic development of a country is reflected in the development of its states and people. Tables 4.4 and 4.5 present the net state domestic product (NSDP) and per capita net state domestic product (PCNSDP) at constant price respectively which are growing over the period 1999-00 to 2007-08, although it is not uniform in all the states. It is observed that Maharashtra has been able to maintain highest NSDP during 1999-00 to 2006-07. But it is Arunachal Pradesh which performed better over the previous year followed by Chhatishgarh State with more than 11.0 percent growth rate. Only Bihar State did not perform well during 2007-08. In terms of PCNSDP , it is Chandigarh which is able to maintain the highest followed by Goa and Delhi during the period under consideration and Bihar is the laggard state.

Table 4.6 presents data about net domestic product (NDP) by industry at current prices. It shows that the contribution of rural areas in net domestic product has continuously declined from 58.91 per cent in 1980-81 to 54.27 per cent in 1993-94 and to 48.09 per cent during 1999-2000 which is mainly due to the declining contribution of most of the industries in NDP. The potential sectors in rural areas whose contribution in the NDP during 1999-2000 have grown are: manufacturing, electricity, gas & water supply. Due to structural changes in the economy there is a shift in the pattern of production also. The contribution of agriculture to NDP has continuously declined from 26.5 per cent in 1999-00 to 19.5 per cent in 2006-07 and this shrinkage has been shared by a marginal growth in secondary sector and higher growth in the tertiary sector especially in Financing, Insurance, Real Estate and Business Services and transport, storage and communication industries (Table 4.7).

Table 4.8 presents the trends in monthly per capita consumer expenditure pattern in rural and urban areas. There is a declining trend in the share of expenditure on food items, from 72.9 per cent in 1972-73 to 55.1 percent in 2004-05 in rural areas and from 64.5 per cent to 42.5 per cent in urban areas. There is a corresponding increasing trend in the expenditure of non-food items. Among the non-food items the major share is spent on goods and services followed by expenditure on fuel and light, health and education both in rural and urban areas of the country. Hence, increasing per capita income and expenditure with changing consumer expenditure pattern indicate the economic and social development of the society.

Increasing investment rate in the country has led to growth in the gross value of output in potential sectors such as agriculture and allied activities, mining and quarrying, manufacturing (registered) and construction. The value of output in mining and quarrying, manufacturing (registered) and construction has increased steadily (Table 4.9). During the period 2002-07 the construction sector registered the highest growth in value of output (79.9 percent) followed by manufacturing (registered)(43.1 percent). The gross value of output in registered manufacturing is highest among the select sectors. Its share in NDP has gone up from 62.5 per cent in 1999-00 to 65.8 per cent in 2006-07 at 1999-2000 prices (Table 4.10). It is observed in Section III that in the total employment the proportion of organised sector employment is continuously declining. But the share of the organised sector in NDP has increased from 35.1 per cent in 1985-86 to 42.6 percent in 2005-06 (Table 4.11). Hence, the corresponding decline in the share of unorganised sector. This indicates an increasing capital investment and technical progress and hence higher productivity in the organised sector.

Labour Productivity, which is a measurement of direct contribution of labour in economic development has been presented from 1987-88 to 1993-94 for manufacturing industries and from 1985 to 1994 for various economic sectors in Table 4.12 and 4.13 respectively. It is observed that barring in 1991-92, labour productivity has consistently increased in Indian manufacturing. Growth of labour productivity is not uniform among all the economic sectors. It is highest in electricity, gas and water followed by transport, storage and communication, manufacturing, mining & quarrying, and trade, hotels & restaurants indicating the employment generation potential in these sectors. Agriculture and allied activities as well as the construction sector have recorded a marginal increase in labour productivity, which indicates that increasing labour force in these sectors will result in little or no increase in the output.

The true meaning of economic development lies in the economic welfare of the community. This depends on the distribution of national income in favour of poor to reduce inequalities and provide them a better quality of life. From the facts presented in the present as well previous sections, it is evident that there has been a steady improvement in the socio-economic conditions of human resources. Still Indian economy has to fight with chronic problems of illiteracy, poverty and unemployment. The economy has targeted growth rate of 9.0 per cent during Eleventh Five Year Plan period (2007-2012). Unless these basic problems are addressed, specifically, the growth rate of 9.0 per cent has little significance. Hence, to maximise the economic returns from manpower it is desirable that investment in human capital formation and in agriculture sector be increased simultaneously with the investment in physical capital and infrastructure. The macro-economic stability observed in the recent years needs to be sustained. It is a well-known fact that stability brings progress and prosperity.

Table 4.1: Change in GDP, GNP and Rate of Investment in Indian Economy (1951-2008)

S.No.	Period	Growth in GDP at Factor Cost	Growth in GNP at Factor Cost	Investment Rate (At current prices)
		Old Series (At 1993-94 Prices)		
1.	1951-56	3.6	3.7	10.6
2.	1961-66	2.8	2.8	15.5
3.	1969-74	3.3	3.4	16.0
4.	1974-79	4.8	5.0	17.9
5.	1980-85	5.6	5.5	20.8
6.	1985-90	5.9	5.8	24.2
7.	1990-91	5.6	5.5	23.2
8.	1992-97	6.7	6.8	24.0
9.	1997-02	5.4	5.5	24.2
		New Series (At 1999-2000 Prices)		
1.	2000-01	4.4	4.0	NA
2.	2001-02	5.8	6.0	22.2
3.	2002-03	3.8	3.9	25.0
4.	2003-04	8.5	8.7	27.7
5.	2004-05	7.5	7.3	30.6
6.	2005-06	9.4	9.6	33.4
7.	2006-07	9.6(Q)	9.7(Q)	33.8
8.	2007-08	8.7(A)	9.0 (A)	NA

Notes: Q : Quick Estimates.
A : Advance Estimates. NA : Not Available

Source: Economic Survey, 2007-08.

Table 4.2: Select Macro-Parameters of Growth (1992-93 to 2007-12)

Period	GDP Growth rate		Savings rate	Investment rate (% of GDP at Market Price)	Growth rate of total Consumption	Growth rate of per Capita Pvt. Consumption	Incremental Capital Output Ratio
	Target	Actual					
1992-93 to 1996-97	5.6	6.7	23.8	24.9	5.6	3.5	3.4
1997-98 to 2001-02	6.5	5.4	23.3	24.2	5.6	4.3	4.5
2002-03 to 2006-07	7.9	7.6	30.9	32.4	6.2	5.3	3.6
2007-12	9.0	34.8	NA	NA	NA	NA	4.1

Note: At 2006–07 Prices

Sources: (*i*) Planning Commission, *Tenth Five Year* Plan, 2002-2007.

(*ii*) Planning Commission, Eleventh Five Year Plan, 2007-12 (Vol. I.)

Table 4.3: National Product, Consumption and Capital Formation

Years	*Net National Product**		*Private Final Consumption in Domestic Market*	*Net Domestic Capital Formation*
	Total (Rs. Crore)	*Per capita (Rs.)*	*(Rs. Crore)*	*(Rs. Crore)*
	Old Series (At 1993-94 Prices)			
1981-82	384,392	5,555	362,552	59,649
1985-86	459,187	6,082	422,916	71,240
1986-87	477,158	6,189	436,262	68,689
1987-88	493,312	6,260	451,215	84,055
1988-89	545,572	6,777	479,378	99,127
1989-90	582,518	7,087	503,167	106,456
1990-91	614,206	7,321	525,641	126,185
1991-92	617,372	7,212	536,980	97,782
1992-93	648,182	7,433	550,828	109,285
1993-94	685,912	7,690	574,772	115,059
1994-95	734,358	8,070	601,481	153,424
1995-96	787,809	8,489	638,938	171,863
1996-97	852,085	9,007	689,566	161,160
1997-98	891,086	9,244	707,285	174,198
1998-99	948,581	9,650	752,440	168,778
	New Series (At 1999-2000 Prices)			
1999-00	1,589,672	15,881	1,257,541	324,823
2001-02	1,647,903	16,172	1,300,494	294,803
2002-03	1,743,466	16,764	1,377,316	265,979
2003-04	1,905,830	17,101	1,413,594	331,632
2004-05	1,963,544	18,317	1,496,866	424,254
2005-06	2,104,520	19,325	1,579,747	533,276
2006-07	2,306,894	20,858	1,710,739	663,836
2007-08	2,530,494	22,553	1,833,673	738,664

Note : * At Factor Cost.

Source: Central Statistical Organisation : *National Accounts Statistics, 2008.*

Figure 4.A

ANNUAL GROWTH RATE OF GROSS DOMESTIC PRODUCT AT FACTOR COST

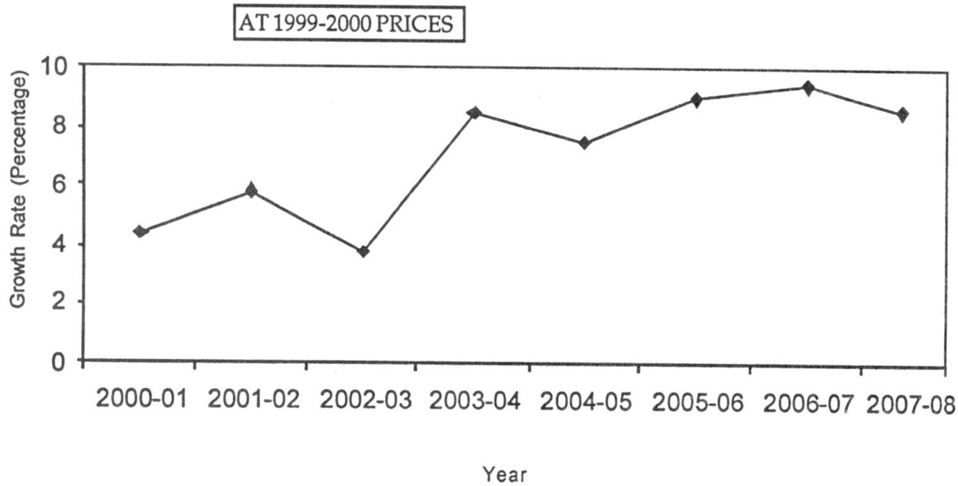

For details see Economic Survey, 2006-07

Figure 4.B

GROWTH IN PER CAPITA INCOME

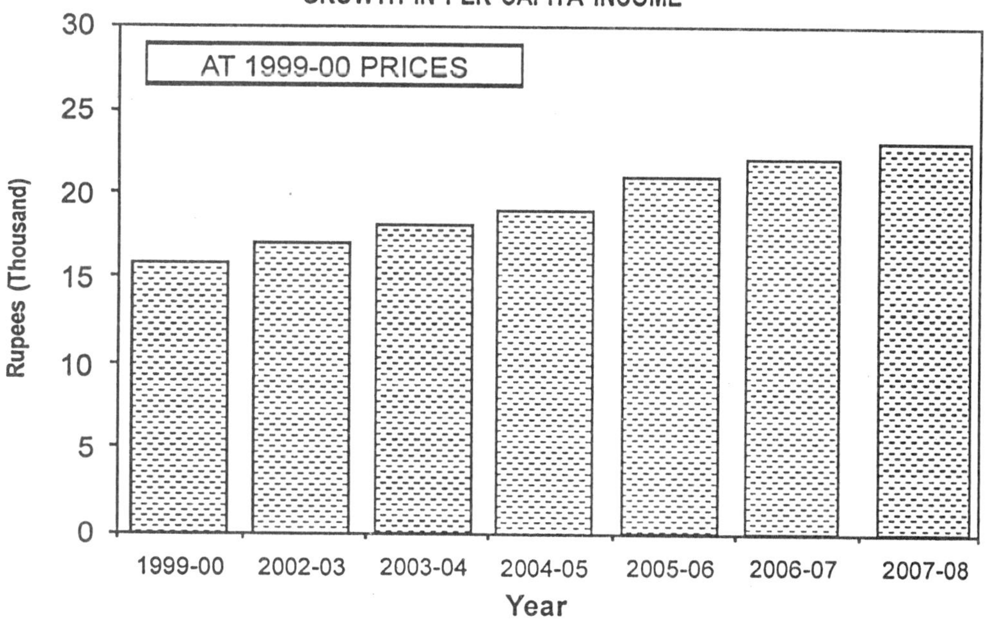

For details see Table 4.3

Table 4.4: Net State Domestic Product
(At 1999-00 Prices)

(Rs. Crores)

State/Union Territory	*1999-00*	*2000-01*	*2001-02*	*2002-03*	*2003-04*	*2004-05*	*2005-06*	*2006-07*	*2007-08**
States									
1. Andhra Pradesh	116966	126402	132108	135881	149067	157975	171462	185462	205486
2. Arunachal Pradesh	1497	1607	1864	1775	1968	2222	2139	2401	2684
3. Assam	32011	32821	33668	35708	37950	39207	41103	43782	46433
4. Bihar	46097	53684	50607	57009	53367	59613	60994	73818	73781
5. Chhattisgarh	23840	22372	25503	25072	29781	31739	34997	39653	44216
6. Delhi	50859	52697	54657	58818	61151	67306	73200	82375	NA
7. Goa	5570	5287	5492	5826	6225	6891	7563	8447	NA
8. Gujarat	92541	86431	93455	101603	118525	125599	139265	149933	NA
9. Haryana	47123	50891	54863	58135	63441	69260	75722	84327	92916
10. Himachal Pradesh	12467	13262	13938	14617	15596	17099	18037	19036	20654
11. Jammu and Kashmir	13533	13917	14185	14907	15673	16519	17497	18557	19687
12. Jharkhand	30229	26663	28500	29298	31515	36886	37631	41348	44752
13. Karnataka	86396	91413	93340	97389	100563	108948	116834	124233	132801
14. Kerala	61359	63052	66123	70879	75467	82575	90244	100427	111059
15. Madhya Pradesh	72655	66750	71525	67795	75400	78101	81006	84380	NA
16. Maharashtra	217198	210526	217807	232745	249458	270350	296155	325148	NA
17. Manipur	2954	2765	2937	2921	3240	3540	3668	3866	4000
18. Meghalaya	3211	3422	3651	3759	3993	4270	4548	4800	5060
19. Mizoram	1410	1463	1555	1705	1760	1839	1965	2110	2247
20. Nagaland	2556	3061	3380	3677	4053	4304	4566	NA	NA
21. Orissa	38200	37395	39678	39658	45319	51086	54167	59241	64310
22. Punjab	61094	63182	64000	65360	68842	72446	76491	81376	86888
23. Rajasthan	74174	71764	79936	70333	92712	90445	96082	103249	110918
24. Sikkim	765	814	881	947	1022	1102	1201	1299	1409
25. Tamil Nadu	119704	126346	123895	124512	132268	147976	161720	177335	188038
26. Tripura	4496	4778	5433	5796	6136	6639	7297	7889	NA
27. Uttaranchal	11187	12582	13179	14413	15553	17599	18645	20636	NA
28. Uttar Pradesh	156331	159668	162577	167761	176348	182870	192867	207345	NA
29. West Bengal	124808	12922	138639	143496	151204	161015	173047	188287	NA
Union Territory									
30. A & N Islands	838	838	857	948	1048	1088	1183	NA	NA
31. Chandigarh	3792	4274	4649	5235	5804	6397	7142	7986	9035
32. Pondicherry	2929	3326	3569	3930	4125	3633	3864	4164	4512
All-India GDP	1605104	1670448	1764137	1824635	1981317	2126269	2328675	2554712	2779648

Notes: * : Position as 09-02.2009
NA — Not Available.

Source: Directorate of Economics & Statistics of respective State Governments, and for All India — Central Statistical Organisation.

Table 4.5: Per Cepita Net State Domestic Product (At 1999-00 Prices)

(Rupees)

State/Union Territory	*1999-00*	*2000-01*	*2001-02*	*2002-03*	*2003-04*	*2004-05*	*2005-06*	*2006-07*	*2007-08**
States									
1. Andhra Pradesh	15507	16622	17260	17486	18961	19871	21334	22835	25044
2. Arunachal Pradesh	13990	14726	16793	15832	17340	19339	18390	20380	22518
3. Assam	12282	12447	12529	13072	13675	13946	14419	15152	15857
4. Bihar	5789	6557	5997	6662	6125	6724	6765	8056	7928
5. Chhattisgarh	11629	10808	12202	11716	13661	14233	15417	17166	18815
6. Delhi	38673	38623	38627	40492	40898	43745	46239	50565	NA
7. Goa	42296	38989	39339	40602	42206	45394	48419	52530	NA
8. Gujarat	18864	17227	18200	19509	22387	23346	25487	27027	NA
9. Haryana	23121	24328	25557	26622	28484	30502	32724	35779	38720
10. Himachal Pradesh	20806	21824	22543	23234	24377	26278	27232	28236	30097
11. Jammu and Kaskmir	13816	13859	13784	14341	14848	15414	16086	16817	17590
12. Jharkhand	11549	9980	10451	10563	11173	12869	12925	13984	14913
13. Karnataka	16703	17405	17505	18045	18400	19692	20866	21931	23180
14. Kerala	19461	19854	20681	21942	23156	25118	27220	30044	32961
15. Madhya Pradesh	12384	11150	11715	10880	11870	12068	12290	12577	NA
16. Maharashtra	23011	21892	22242	23422	24707	26359	28433	30750	NA
17. Manipur	13260	12157	12641	12319	13389	14334	14559	15047	15270
18. Meghalaya	14355	14910	15518	15882	16658	17595	18501	19292	20094
19. Mizoram	16443	16635	17245	18429	18555	18904	19691	20618	21400
20. Nagaland	13819	15746	16540	17122	17958	18147	18318	NA	NA
21. Orissa	10567	10211	10701	10575	11951	13329	13967	15096	16195
22. Punjab	25611	25990	25994	26065	26955	27851	28872	30158	31616
23. Rajasthan	13619	12840	13933	12054	15579	14908	15543	16401	17310
24. Sikkim	14890	15305	15953	17065	18159	19332	20777	22167	23761
25. Tamil Nadu	19432	20318	19747	19660	20705	22972	24906	27101	28526
26. Tripura	14119	14933	16947	17752	18554	19825	21524	22987	NA
27. Uttaranchal	13516	14932	15364	16530	17542	19524	20355	22178	NA
28. Uttar Pradesh	9719	9700	9651	9780	10080	10250	10605	11188	NA
29. West Bengal	15826	16185	17173	17515	18232	19191	20396	21953	NA
Union Territory									
30. A & N Islands	24005	23658	23869	25487	27229	27267	28637	NA	NA
31. Chandigarh	44502	48292	50476	55991	59406	62352	66134	70361	75480
32. Pondicherry	30865	34408	36230	39159	40338	34863	36397	38488	40931
All-India NDP(99-00 base)	15881	16172	16764	17101	18301	19331	20868	22580	24295

Notes: * : Position as 09.02.2009
NA — Not Available.

Source: Directorate of Economics & Statistics of respective State Governments, and for All India — Central Statistical Organisation.

Table 4.6: Net Domestic Product by Industry in Rural and Urban Areas (At Current Prices)

(*Rs. Crores*)

Industry	*1980-81*				*1993-94*				*1999-2000*			
	Rural	*Urban*	*Total*	*Rural as Percent to Total*	*Rural*	*Urban*	*Total*	*Rural as Percent to Total*	*Rural*	*Urban*	*Total*	*Rural as Per cent to Total*
1. Agriculture, Forestry & Fishing	41837	2254	44091	94.89	215890	13939	229829	93.94	395888	28670	424558	93.25
2. Minning and Quarrying	807	667	1474	54.75	9849	5105	14959	65.88	13978	18997	22975	42.39
3. Manu-facturing	5954	12744	18698	31.84	30885	72854	103739	29.77	85665	120461	206126	41.56
4. Electricity, Gas & Water Supply	365	547	912	40.02	3334	5467	8801	37.88	10998	13206	24204	45.44
5. Construction	2633	3138	5771	45.62	17480	21269	38749	45.11	43019	56293	99312	43.32
6. Wholesale Trade, Hotel & Restaurant	4645	9977	14322	30.34	29424	67203	96627	30.45	67152	181045	248197	27.06
7. Transport, Storage and Communi-cation	856	2868	3724	22.91	12933	24788	37721	34.29	30997	74796	105793	29.30
8. Banking & Insurance	525	2819	3344	15.70	6565	33545	40110	16.37	14895	87716	102611	14.52
9. Real Estate, Ownership of dwelling & Business Services	2959	2961	5920	49.98	16130	24301	40431	39.90	35415	75004	110419	32.07
10. Community, Social and Personal Services	4723	7361	12084	39.08	36301	50734	87035	41.71	71959	174779	246738	29.16
Total	64004	45336	110340	58.91	378791	319201	697992	54.27	769967	830966	1600933	48.09

Source: Central Statistical Organisation : *National Accounts Statistics-2007.*

Table 4.7: Net Domestic Product by Economic Activity (At 1999-2000 Prices)

(Rs.Crores)

Industry	*1999-00*	*2000-01*	*2001-02*	*2002-03*	*2003-04*	*2004-05*	*2005-06*	*2006-07*
Agriculture, Forestry, Fishing	424952 (26.5)	422756 (25.3)	448904 (25.5)	413072 (22.6)	455329 (23.0)	453582 (21.3)	480469 (20.7)	497759 (19.5)
Mining and Quarrying	33001 (2.1)	33819 (2.0)	34349 (1.9)	38036 (2.1)	39114 (2.0)	42385 (2.0)	44122 (1.9)	46463 (1.8)
Manufacturing	207186 (12.9)	223086 (13.4)	226460 (12.8)	242017 (13.3)	257105 (13.0)	278099 (13.1)	300438 (12.9)	335189 (13.2)
Electricity, Gas and Water Supply	24217 (1.5)	24076 (1.4)	23736 (1.4)	24952 (1.4)	25899 (1.3)	28708 (1.4)	29805 (1.3)	31619 (1.3)
Construction	99367 (6.2)	105463 (6.3)	109370 (6.2)	117828 (6.5)	131824 (6.7)	153197 (7.2)	178505 (7.7)	199792 (7.8)
Trade, Hotels and Restaurants	248337 (15.4)	261158 (15.6)	286360 (16.2)	306139 (16.8)	336883 (17.0)	362411 (17.1)	396623 (17.0)	430112 (16.9)
Transport, Storage and Communication	107913 (6.6)	121298 (7.3)	131733 (7.5)	151662 (8.3)	177063 (8.9)	206875 (9.7)	240044 (10.3)	283735 (11.1)
Financing, Insurance, Real Estate and Business Services	213443 (13.2)	220523 (13.2)	234756 (13.3)	252490 (13.8)	264902 (13.4)	287576 (13.5)	321109 (13.8)	367436 (14.4)
Community, Social and Personal Services	246688 (15.4)	258270 (15.5)	268469 (15.2)	278439 (15.2)	293270 (14.7)	313185 (14.7)	335466 (14.4)	357543 (14.0)
Total NDP (at Factor Cost)	1605103 (100.0)	1670448 (100.0)	1764137 (100.0)	1824635 (100.0)	1981389 (100.0)	2126018 (100.0)	2326581 (100.0)	2549648 (100.0)

Note: Figures in brackets are percentage to total.
Source: Central Statistical Organisation : *National Accounts Statistics*—2008.

Figure 4.C

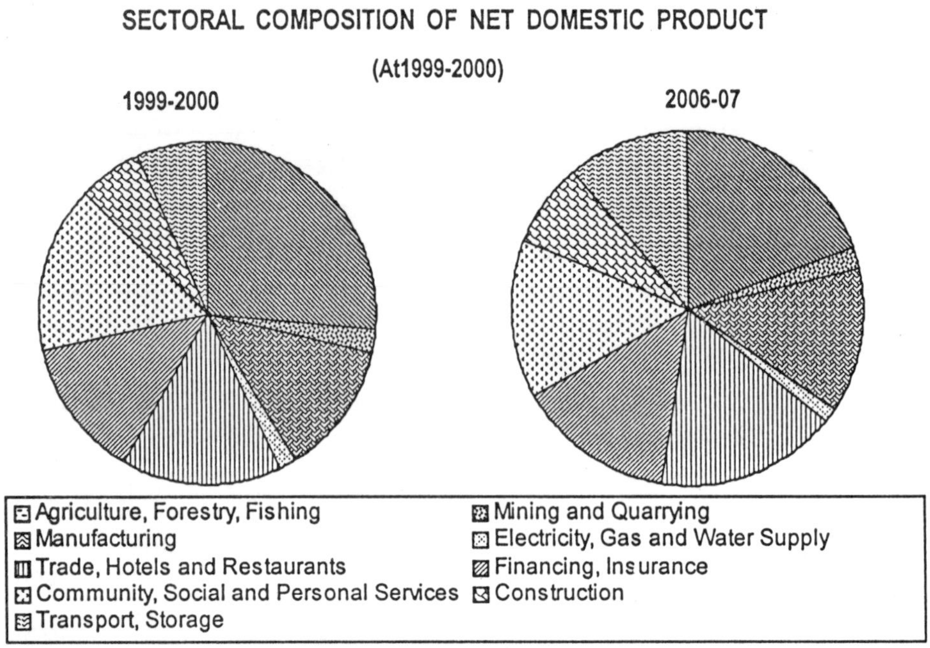

For details see Table 4.7

Figure 4.D

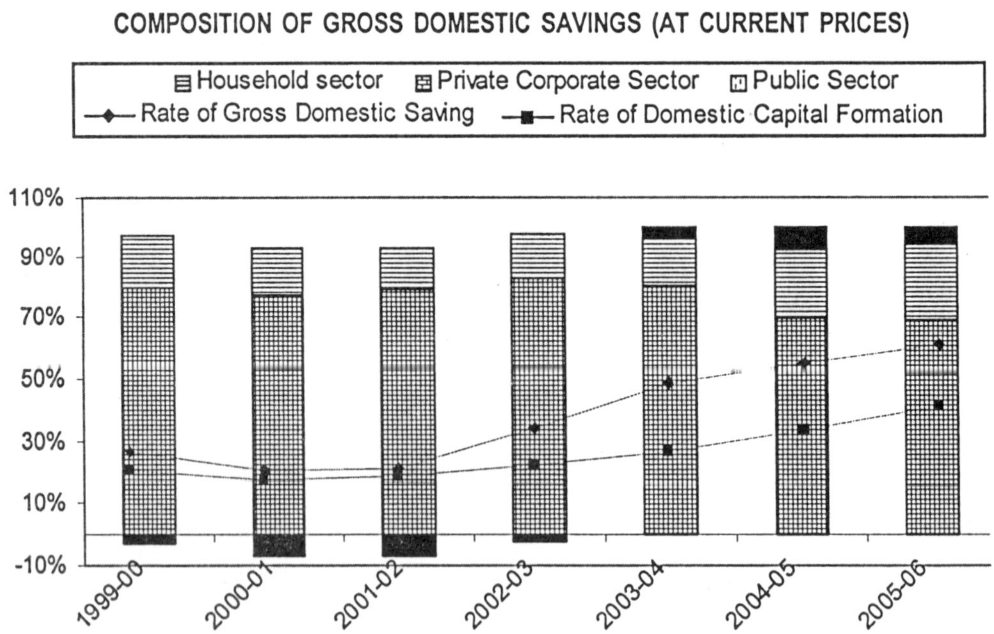

For details see Economic Survey 2006-2007

Table 4.8 : Distribution of Monthly per Capita Consumer Expenditure

(*Percent*)

Item	*Rural*								*Urban*							
	1972-73	*1977-78*	*1983*	*1987-88*	*1993-94*	*1999-2000*	*2003*	*2004-05*	*1972-73*	*1977-78*	*1983*	*1987-88*	*1993-94*	*1999-2000*	*2003*	*2004-05*
Food Total	72.9	64.3	65.6	64.0	63.2	59.4	54.0	55.1	64.5	60.0	59.1	56.4	54.7	48.1	42.0	42.5
Pan, Tobacco & Intoxicants	3.1	2.9	3.0	3.2	3.2	2.9	2.6	2.7	2.8	2.4	2.4	2.6	2.3	1.9	1.6	1.6
Fuel and Light	5.6	6.0	7.0	7.5	7.4	7.5	9.2	10.2	5.6	6.4	6.9	6.8	6.6	7.8	9.2	10.0
Clothing	7.0	8.7	8.6	6.7	5.4	6.8	6.9	5.4@	5.3	7.1	7.6	5.9	4.7	6.1	5.9	4,7@
Footwear	0.5	0.7	1.0	1.0	0.9	1.1	1.0	–	0.4	0.6	1.1	1.1	0.9	1.2	1.1	–
Education	–	–	–	1.5	1.4	1.9	–	2.7	–	–	–	3.5	4.2	4.3	–	5.0
Health	–	–	–	4.2	5.3	6.1	–	6.6	–	–	–	3.3	4.6	5.1	–	5.2
Misc. Consumer Goods & Services*	8.7	10.3	12.5	14.5	17.3	19.6	13.0	14.0	19.2	14.6	20.5	23.2	27.5	31.5	24.1	26.9
Durable Goods	2.2	7.0	2.3	3.1	2.7	2.6	3.3	3.4	2.2	8.9	2.3	4.1	3.3	3.6	4.1	4.1
Non-Food Total	27.1	35.7	34.4	36.0	36.8	40.6	46.0	44.9	35.5	40.0	40.9	43.6	45.3	51.9	58.0	57.5
Total	100.0	100.0	100.0	100.0	100.0	100.0	100.0	100.00	100.0	100.0	100.0	100.0	100.0	100.0	100.0	100.0
Total (Rs.)	44.2	68.9	112.5	158.1	281.4	486.1	556.0	55.9	63.3	96.2	164.0	249.9	458.0	855.0	1023.0	1052.0

Notes: * Also includes rents, taxes. @ Includes MPCE on Footwear.

Sources: National Sample Survey Organisation :

(*i*) Report No. 458, *Household Consumer Expenditure and Employment-Unemployment Situation in India—1999-2000*

(*ii*) Report No. 490, *Household Consumer Expenditure and Employment-Unemployment Situation in India—2003.*

(*iii*) Report No. 515, *Employment and Unemployment Situation in India, 2004-05.*

Table 4.9: Gross Value of Output in Select Sectors

(Rs. Crores)

Year	*Agriculture and Allied Activities*	*Mining and Quarrying*	*Manufacturing (Registered)*	*Construction*
		Old Series (At 1980-81 Prices)		
1980-81	56,875	2,482	58,787	16,038
1985-86	66,428	3,996	87,948	17,444
1990-91	80,565	5,732	139,780	23,354
1991-92	79,524	6,098	139,083	23,751
1992-93	83,626	6,262	142,288	24,362
		Old Series (At 1993-94 Prices)		
1993-94	271,839	27,796	395,434	106,458
1995-96	284,273	32,257	504,231	118,518
1997-98	302,399	33,982	586,428	136,118
1998-99	323,017	33,819	590,710	144,144
		New Series (At 1999-2000 Prices)		
1999-00	512,363	53,016	894,459	279,464
2000-01	506,870	54,862	952,831	295,589
2001-02	538,548	56,308	984,746	304,704
2002-03	500,644	59,941	1,057,997	336,345
2003-04	549,531	62,953	1,137,883	376,189
2004-05	552,608	66,717	1,239,900	452,791
2005-06	586,595	71,428	1,347,818	532,623
2006-07	611,120	76,269	1,514,439	605,163

Source: Central Statistical Organisation : *National Accounts Statistics—2008.*

Figure 4.E

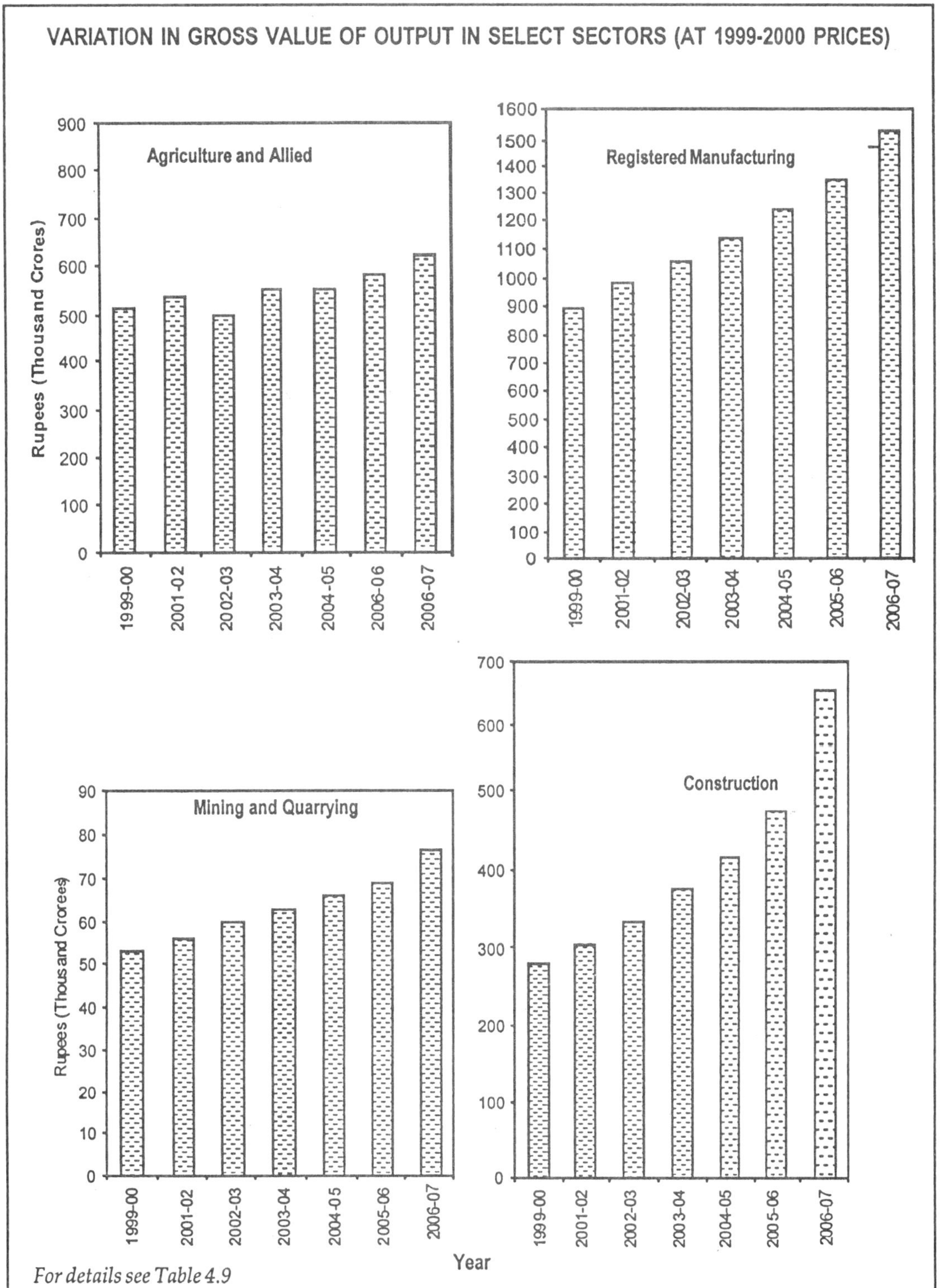

For details see Table 4.9

Table 4.10: Share of Registered and Unregistered Manufacturing in the Net Domestic Product

Year	Percent share of	
	Registered	Unregistered
	Old Series (At 1980-81 Prices)	
1980-81	53.7	46.3
1985-86	58.9	41.1
1990-91	60.0	40.0
1995-96	62.1	37.9
	Old Series (At 1993-94 Prices)	
1993-94	63.4	36.6
1996-97	65.5	34.5
1997-98	62.8	37.2
1998-99	61.7	38.3
	New Series (At 1999-2000 Prices)	
1999-00	62.5	37.5
2000-01	62.6	37.4
2001-02	64.0	36.0
2002-03	64.7	35.3
2003-04	65.2	34.8
2004-05	65.7	34.3
2005-06	65.8	34.2
2006-07	65.8	34.2

Source: Central Statistical Organisation : *National Accounts Statistics — 2008.*

Table 4.11: Net Domestic Product from Organised and Unorganised Sector (At Current Prices)

Year	Percent share of	
	Organised	Unorganised
1985-86	35.1	64.9
1986-87	36.8	63.2
1987-88	37.0	63.0
1988-89	35.8	64.2
1989-90	36.3	63.7
1990-91	36.2	63.8
1992-93	36.5	63.5
1993-94	36.9	63.1
1994-95	37.5	62.5
1995-96	39.6	60.4
1996-97	38.7	61.3
1997-98	39.2	60.8
1998-99	39.7	60.3
1999-00	38.8	61.2
2000-01	39.5	60.5
2001-02	40.1	59.9
2002-03	41.4	58.6
2003-04	40.6	59.4
2004-05	42.0	58.0
2005-06	42.6	57.4

Source: Central Statistical Organisation : *National Accounts Statistics — 2008.*

Table 4.12: Labour Productivity in Indian Manufacturing Industries (Base 1986-87 = 100)

Industry	*Labour Productivity*						
	1987-88	*1988-89*	*1989-90*	*1990-91*	*1991-92*	*1992-93*	*1993-94*
Food Products (20-21)	99	121	136	122	123	114	143
Beverages, Tobacco Products (22)	90	103	84	95	101	97	116
Cotton Textiles (23)	96	101	119	130	113	112	121
Wool, Silk, Synthetic Fibre Textiles (24)	90	103	139	165	148	160	198
Jute, Hemp and Mesta Textiles (25)	88	88	76	78	86	89	96
Textile Products (26)	100	118	126	138	163	162	195
Wood and Wood Products, Furniture and Fixtures (27)	112	131	124	185	185	96	108
Paper, Paper Products and Printing (28)	98	108	125	136	126	115	140
Leather and Fur Products (29)	125	102	113	135	152	169	241
Rubber and Plastics (30)	103	106	108	121	106	139	158
Chemicals and Chemical Products (31)	111	120	144	163	157	186	201
Non-Metallic Mineral Products (32)	112	123	140	166	190	153	60
Basic Metal and Alloy Industry (33)	116	157	154	185	148	182	381
Metal Products and Parts (34)	117	123	99	97	108	102	128
Machine Tools and Parts (35)	102	100	117	122	145	150	152
Electrical Machinery (36)	115	122	139	143	*	*	*
Transport Equipment (37)	99	105	120	140	128	134	145
Other Manufacturing Industry (38)	104	94	120	112	144	154	242
All Industries	102	114	121	132	129	142	161

Notes : Two-digit National Industrial Codes are given in brackets.
* Included in Machine Tools and Parts.

Source : National Productivity Council : *Productivity*, Vol. 38, No. 1, April-June, 1997.

Table 4.13: Labour Productivity in Economic Sectors (Base 1984 = 100)

Economic Sector	*1985*	*1986*	*1987*	*1988*	*1989*	*1990*	*1991*	*1992*	*1993*	*1994*
Agriculture, Forestry and Fishing	98.31	96.98	93.72	92.52	105.35	105.87	108.06	103.25	106.05	06.72
Mining and Quarrying	98.65	101.31	112.03	112.94	126.68	132.66	142.54	145.54	143.68	146.47
Manufacturing	105.70	109.14	115.90	123.48	133.28	149.06	155.63	155.63	151.08	154.27
Electricity,Gas and Water	107.69	112.55	121.21	127.59	137.63	147.3	152.16	152.16	169.03	174.14
Construction	100.50	101.98	103.57	103.32	107.54	109.3	117.95	117.95	111.46	107.99
Trade, Hotels and Restaurants	100.70	105.07	107.56	108.56	112.37	116.97	118.90	118.90	117.64	118.06
Transport Storage and Communication	106.75	113.93	119.02	126.66	131.72	140.28	143.87	143.87	151.59	156.39
Total*	102.76	105.53	108.31	110.88	120.02	125.01	127.81	127.81	126.01	128.37

Note : * Includes the 'Other Services' and 'Finance' Sectors.
Source : National Productivity Council : *Productivity*, Vol. 37, No.1, April-June, 1996.

SECTION 5

Labour Market Features

Dr. Anil K. Yadav
Vijay K. Saxena

Section V
Labour Market Features

In the aftermath of Economic reforms, India provides an insight into the macro and micro shifts in the labour market trends as a result of rapid changes taking place in the process of labour formation and its dynamics. There are several features of formation and development of labour force, e.g., demographic transition from traditional sector to modern ones, migration from village to the city, less literate to more literate, less skilled to more skilled and from field to factory etc.

Due to the ongoing of technological transformation and its significant contribution to the economy of any nation, especially the Indian economy, there has been a profound effect on the skills of labour force, which in turn has led to increased per capita productivity and sustained economic growth.

The labour and employment sector addresses the conditions under which the economically active population i.e., the labour force, exchanges its services with the economic population system, which in turn triggers off demand for more and more labour force at different skill levels. These type of conditions vary across different segments of labour force, i.e. rural-urban; organized and unorganized; informal and formal, small, medium, and large industrial sectors. The wage pattern and developments in the labour market get further influenced due to internal structural changes which are forced by global compulsions.

The present section consists of tables relating to the operation of labour market forces in India. The sections placed before this present data showing the manpower formation process and the manner in which the manpower get absorbed in various economic spheres. The manpower formation process is dependent on demographic forces which determine the aggregate size of labour force and distribution by age and sex. Further distribution of labour force does depend upon, and/or is determined by, the availability of facilities for education and training in the country. The absorption of various components of labour force in various economic activities therefore depends on the forces operating in the economy.

However, the transition of manpower supply to manpower utilisation is effected through the labour market. The forces of demand and supply interact in the market, and through this process the wage rates and the wage differentials get determined. It is indeed this process through which the entire supply of labour could be absorbed gainfully. In a perfect labour market with full flexibilities in all regards, the market is expected to establish appropriate wages and wage ratios. It is in fact, the only basis on which the full level of employment could be attained. The existence of unemployment therefore signifies possible rigidities in the system. Hence, in the market-based economies a great deal of interest is taken on labour market information systems (LMIS), which monitor changes in the labour market and also the status of parameters like wages and wage ratios. The LMIS also monitors the cost of living indices and the structural characteristics like the trade union, industrial relations and various similar features which may affect the degree of competition in the market.

Till 1991 India had not been following the market friendly system, and hence the sizes of employment and unemployment were largely dependent on the planning process. Although India has been following the mixed economy system where forces of socialism and capitalism operate together, most of the important decisions were taken by way of planning process, leaving little scope for the market. Hence, only a limited segments of the economy, market process operated, and a proper labour market information system could not develop in the country. The Indian economy has been restructured since 1991 and a market friendly environment established. This generates a need for development of a proper labour market information system in the economy.

The data presented in this section, therefore, are very limited. Most information has been taken from an engineering labour market information system generated under an ongoing programme of the National Technical Manpower Information System (NTMIS). The NTMIS covers only the degree and diploma holding engineers and collects data on their enrolment, outturn and utilisation. Information on engineering labour market is generated out of the data bank under NTMIS.

The data available with respect to other manpower categories are not comprehensive. However, the National Sample Survey Organisation (NSSO) collects data on employment and unemployment and information on average earning in different industries are compiled from the data collected by the Central Statistical Organisation (CSO). under its survey programme Annual Survey of Industries. Some estimates are also prepared at the Institute of Applied Manpower Research (IAMR) on stocks of manpower categories. The Labour Bureau and the Directorate General of Employment and Training also generate some data relating to the labour market information. These are however produced for supporting regulatory activities primarily, and thus do not form a comprehensive labour market information system. The Profile has brought together all relevant information available on the subject, but due to the above features of the data system, the overall structure of the data in the publication has been disproportionate and not sufficient.

The available data series on labour market features are presented under four sub- head:

- 5.1 Wages, salaries and wage differentials (13 tables)
- 5.2 Unemployment (31 tables)
- 5.3 Supply (7 tables)
- 5.4 Industrial relations (3 tables)
- 5.5 Tables together provide very valuable data on labour market features. Data on earnings and earning differentials and consumer price indices have been presented in 13 tables.

Table 5.1.1 presents average annual earnings of employees from 1980-81 to 2000-2001 in manufacturing industries at all India level. Despite it also shows that cotton, textile and transport sector has the highest and lowest annual earning respectively.

Table 5.1.2 gives the industry-wise and education wise average wage/salary of regular employees in rural India for the years 2004-2005 and table 5.1.3 presents the same relative earnings in urban India as in table 5.1.2, by industry, for the same year.

Table 5.1.4 contains data on average wages for casual labourer in public and other workers by type of occupation in rural India for the years 1999-2000 and 2004-05.

Table 5.1.5 presents average wages received by casual labourers by industry in urban India for the years 1999-2000 and 2004-05.

Table 5.1.6 presents the emoluments of engineers with degree, relative to the emoluments of those with a diploma for the year 1997. The emolument relatives are given for five branches of engineering in nineteen states.

Table 5.1.7 presents average labourer cost per manday for the census and sample sector for selected (31) states/union territories for the years, 1999-2000 and 2000-01.

Tables 5.1.8 to 5.1.12 provide data on average monthly emoluments of newly employed degree holding and diploma holding engineers in five branches of engineering. The data are given for 18 states at five different periods; 1988-90, 1998-2000, 2001-03 and 2002-04. However, the information is not available for several states.

Table 5.1.13 gives data on consumer price indices for (i) agricultural labourers, (ii) industrial workers and (iii) urban non-manual employees, for the years 1980-81 to 1992-93 with 1980-81 = 100; 1993-94, to 1998-99 with 1993-94 = 100 and 1999 to 2004-05 with 1999-2000 = 100.

The data on rate and volume of unemployment is presented in 32 tables.

Table 5.2.1 presents unemployment rates among males and females separately for rural and urban India. The data are given for the years, 1977-78, 1983, 1987-88, 1993-94, 1999-2000, 2004-05 and 2005-06 in terms of three alternative definitions: usual status, current daily and current weekly status. This table permits comparisons over time, between sexes and rural and urban areas.

Table 5.2.2 gives estimates of the number of unemployed according to the "usual status" among rural males, rural females, urban males and urban females for the years 1977-78, 1983, 1987-88, 1993-94, 1999-2000, 2004-05 and 2005-06.

Table 5.2.3 presents unemployment rates (usual status) among males and females by age group separately for rural and urban areas. The data are given for the years 1977-78, 1983, 1987-88, 1993-94, 1999-2000, 2004-05 and 2005-06.

Table 5.2.4 gives unemployment rates in different states and union territories in 2004-05 according to usual status. This table is useful in bringing out the inter-state differences in the incidence of unemployment.

Table 5.2.5 gives unemployment rates among three categories of educated persons: (i) below matriculate, (ii) matriculates and (iii) graduates. One set of rates is population based, and the other labour force based.

Tables 5.2.6 to 5.2.12 give the number of unemployed among degree holding and diploma holding engineers in 18 states for the years 2001 to 2005.

Data presented in table 5.2.6 relate to all branches of engineering, while that in the succeeding six tables relate to individual branches of engineering, namely civil (Table 5.2.7), chemical (Table 5.2.8), electrical (Table 5.2.9), electronics (Table 5.2.10), mechanical (Table 5.2.11) and metallurgy (Table 5.2.12).

Table 5.2.13 provides data on the number of employment exchanges, number newly registered, number of vacancies notified, number placed and the number on the live register. The data are given for the years from 1985 to 2006.

Table 5.2.14 depicts the data on special categories. These categories are women, scheduled caste, scheduled tribe, other backward classes and disabled persons etc. Table gives the detailed account of Registration, placement, total live register and percentage of live register of category to total live register of five years i.e., 2001, 2002, 2003, 2004 and 2005.

Table 5.2.15 gives the number of applicants on Live Register of Employment Exchanges by educational level. The educational levels are (i) matriculate, (ii) under graduate, (iii) graduate and (iv) post graduate. The graduate and post graduate are further given by broad faculties as (i) arts, (ii) science, (iii) commerce, (iv) engineering, (v) medicine, (vi) agriculture, (vii) education and (viii) others. The data relate to the years 1981, 1986, 1991, 1996 and 2001 to 2004.

Tables 5.2.16 to 5.2.32 give the percentage of fresh engineers absorbed in gainful activities within two years of completion of their degree/diploma course. The figures are provided for the years 1994 to 2001 of West Bengal & Tamil Nadu in the Tables 5.2.16 & 5.2.26; year 1998 to 2002 of Karnataka, Assam, Rajasthan & Orissa in Tables 5.2.17, 5.223, 5.2.27 & 5.2.28; for years 1983 to 1994 of Bihar in Table 5.2.18; year 1985 to 1999 of Uttar Pradesh in Tables 5.2.19; year 1999 to 2002 of Madhya Pradesh, Kerala & Punjab in tables 5.2.20, 5.2.24 & 5.2.31; year 1994 to 2000 of Maharashtra, Gujarat & Jammu and Kashmir in Tables 5.2.21, 5.2.29 and 5.2.30; year 1998 to 2001 of Andhra Pradesh in table 5.2.22; and year starting from 1994 to 2002 of Chandigarh in table 5.2.25.

Tables 5.3.1 to 5.3.7 provide data on stocks of different categories of educated/ trained manpower in the country for selected years. Based on this data an inference may be drawn for future. Apart from this, a training plan could be prepared for the educational policy makers and the planners.

Table 5.3.1 relates to graduates in medicine, dentistry, agricultural science and veterinary science.

Tables 5.3.2 and 5.3.3 pertain to post-graduates and graduates in arts, science and commerce.

Table 5.3.4 relates to engineers. This provides an incite into the availability of manpower in technical field.

Table 5.3.5 and 5.3.6 provide information for 20 select disciplines of engineering degree and 15 select disciplines of diploma holders respectively.

Table 5.3.7 relates to three categories of nursing personnel (i) general nurses, (ii) auxiliary nurse midwives, and (iii) health visitors.

The table 5.4.1 provides data on industrial selections for all India the selected years viz., 1961, 1971,1981 to 2002. It gives the number of registered trade unions, membership of unions submitting returns and average membership per union submitting returns.

Table 5.4.2 provides data for selected year i.e. 1981 to 2005 on the number of disputes, number of workers involved, number of mandays lost and average number of workers involved per dispute.

Table 5.4.3 gives number of disputes classified by cause for various years i.e. 1971 to 2002. The data would be useful for the manpower planners and particularly the policy makers to plan that if the number of disputes increases due to various causes, what type of requirements would arise.

(i) Wages, Salaries and Wage Differentials

Table 5.1.1: Average Annual Earnings per Employee in Manufacturing Industry—All India

(Rupee)

Code No.	*Industry@*	*1980-81*	*1985-86*	*1990-91*	*1995-96*	*1996-97*	*1998-99*	*1999-00*	*2000-01*
20-21	Food Products	2,972	7,657	14,151	25,073	29,313	55,466	61,281	67,361
22.	Beverages, Tobacco and Tobacco Products	2,751	6,163	8,461	14,439	16,469	75,146	83,932	101,156
23.	Cotton Textiles	7,709	12,665	20,202	31,766	33,392	146,756	162,888	245,821
24.	Wool, Silk and Synthetic Fibre	8,451	13,488	22,733	36,433	38,890	97,667	109,448	110,318
25.	Jute, Hemp and Mesta Textile	7,886	13,381	22,535	36,901	39,602	58,187	66,318	68,452
26.	Textile Products (including wearing Apparel other than Footwear)	5,800	8,918	14,892	24,218	27,136	48,566	57,718	63,067
27.	Wood and Wood Products	3,991	6,910	10,887	18,398	21,908	99,326	99,750	122,414
28.	Paper and Paper Products, Printing and Publishing	8,487	14,624	25,465	46,528	52,212	67,419	73,850	79,040
29.	Leather and Leather Products	7,141	10,715	15,824	25,415	27,791	72,660	119,870	119,595
30.	Rubber, Plastic, Petroleum and Coal Products	10,296	17,797	35,138	59,004	62,164	102,949	106,421	141,803
31.	Chemical and Chemical Products	11,636	20,439	27,073	50,513	53,130	94,338	109,499	132,274
32.	Non-Metallic Mineral Products	6,127	9,874	15,960	29,823	34,350	91,322	102,535	117,669
33.	Basic Metal and Alloys	11,161	19,138	31,379	60,641	63,562	75,229	118,976	105,819
34.	Metal Products and Parts except Machinery and Transport Equipments	8,156	14,002	21,626	40,833	41,770	104,621	124,080	135,729
35.	Machinery Tools and Parts	10,325	19,118	31,459	56,533	64,020	63,976	100,044	98,083
36.	Electrical Machinery and Appliances	11,752	20,646	33,889	*	*	59,199	62,683	70,535
37.	Transport Equipments and Parts	11,199	20,602	34,124	63,048	66,668	153,905	30,000	45,429
38.	Other Manufacturing Industries	9,459	15,279	23,238	41,400	46,078	—	—	—
40.	Electricity	9,802	19,285	37,840	65,072	80,775	56586	57,570	57,971

Notes : * Figures are included in industry Machinery Tools and Parts.
@ on the basis of NIC 1998.

Source: Central Statistical Organisation, *Annual Survey of Industries—Factory Sector.*

Table 5.1.2: Average Wage/Salary Received by Regular Wage/Salaried Employee Per Day, 2005-06
(Rupee)

Rural India

Industry Division	*Educational Level*									
	Not Literate		*Literate up to Middle*		*Secondary & Higher Secandary*		*Graduate and above*		*All*	
	Male	*Female*	*Male*	*Female*	*Male*	*Female*	*Male*	*Female*	*Male*	*Female*
Agriculture (o)	57.10	43.39	60.59	71.44	127.39	272.56	285.19	71.12	81.83	56.11
	(53.39)	(45.65)	(66.27)	(54.41)	(149.40)	(134.61)	(200.33)	(105.32)	(71.16(	(54.51)
Mining & Quarrying (1)	96.63	78.72	113.10	47.45	261.41	0.00	253.03	32.14	177.54	69.80
	(174.13)	(84.88)	(217.64)	(212.29)	(323.41)	(83.29)	(341.46)	(–)	(246.43)	(82.75)
Manu-factaring (2)	68.07	47.98	93.98	53.27	82.41	60.81	158.35	70.01	94.08	53.24
	(58.36)	(26.53)	(74.41)	(36.26)	(103.40)	(47.26)	(160.67)	(89.21)	(90.60)	(38.24)
Manu-factureing (3)	78.61	44.17	80.36	34.27	100.37	129.81	172.98	99.55	110.06	42.44
	(75.63)	(38.40)	(84.51)	(58.54)	(109.43)	(62.12)	(534.81)	(219.58)	(146.72)	(57.95)
Electricity, Gas and Water (4)	229.60	60.95	192.84	213.24	187.31	318.85	551.31	0.00	287.42	214.39
	(142.41)	(168.63)	(202.95)	(178.57)	(260.51)	(290.91)	(306.55)	(111.91)	(246.32)	(253.95)
Cons-truction (5)	81.94	59.56	99.14	181.58	96.70	418.57	156.24	0.00	99.69	231.78
	(85.59)	(82.64)	(100.19)	(44.21)	(111.08)	(101.70)	(223.09)	(136.09)	(106.79)	(90.80)
Trade (6)	58.30	45.15	61.55	37.97	73.25	44.43	94.51	83.71	67.44	47.38
	(65.35)	(34.72)	(66.67)	(40.70)	(86.57)	(67.51)	(108.34)	(136.45)	(75.34)	(51.15)
Transport & Storage (7)	128.14	111.43	102.50	75.54	138.69	108.19	284.95	243.93	122.24	142.38
	(98.28)	(87.75)	(112.79)	(102.54)	(138.45)	(105.32)	(235.17)	(256.22)	(126.96)	(135.75)
Services (8)	316.21	38.22	143.00	170.26	180.44	73.63	369.74	189.12	244.24	147.33
	(51.82)	(100.00)	(126.43)	(97.35)	(193.12)	(89.95)	(278.29)	(157.28)	(200.71)	(143.72)
Services (9)	74.65	35.50	146.03	67.58	204.32	108.36	244.12	169.68	203.78	107.90
	(101.07)	(34.70)	(133.20)	(50.55)	(197.20)	(105.74)	(256.93)	(174.18)	(203.66)	(113.66)
Private hhs. with Employed Person	40.72	40.85	92.46	43.67	98.39	42.07	46.03	0.00	83.19	41.98
	(50.74)	(29.18)	(66.68)	(34.10)	(88.14)	(54.90)	(137.67)	(–)	(67.80)	(31.27)
Others (10)	–	–	–	–	–	–	–	–	–	–
	(–)	(–)	(–)	(–)	(–)	(–)	(250.00)	(–)	(250.00)	(–)
All	84.05	41.40	95.65	61.17	148.87	102.18	252.99	170.58	138.74	87.71
	(72.47)	(35.74)	(98.59)	(47.75)	(158.04)	(100.19)	(270.02)	(172.70)	(144.93)	(85.53)

Notes: (*i*) Figures relate to the worker of age-group (15-59).

(*ii*) Figures in Parenthesis indicate for year 2004-05.

Source: National Sample Survey Organisation :

Report No. 515 & 522 *Employment and Unemployment Situation in India, 1999-2000 and 2004-05 and 2005-06.*

Table 5.1.3: Average Wage/Salary Received by Regular Wage Salaried Employee Per Day, 2005-06
(Rupee)

Urban India

Industry Division	Educational Level									
	Not Literate		*Literate up to Middle*		*Secondary & Higher Secondary*		*Graduate and above*		*All*	
	Male	*Female*	*Male*	*Female*	*Male*	*Female*	*Male*	*Female*	*Male*	*Female*
Agriculture [0]	60.18	51.95	129.48	44.98	126.39	168.48	308.81	100.00	159.67	58.05
	(68.83)	(55.60)	(70.66)	(73.45)	(182.06)	(74.20)	(237.37)	(225.56)	(104.80)	(79.59)
Mining & [1] Quarrying	308.44	178.67	285.87	109.42	355.62	505.02	519.85	610.67	358.72	342.36
	(266.71)	(154.15)	(248.61)	(75.78)	(348.64)	(714.29)	(806.61)	(351.30)	(359.41)	(186.30)
Manu-facturing [2]	89.56	43.72	94.53	54.98	142.85	82.23	255.68	227.12	125.01	79.37
	(79.41)	(34.23)	(88.45)	(53.25)	(122.10)	(70.71)	(218.85)	(235.10)	(113.22)	(65.58)
Manu-facturing [3]	106.88	69.74	110.88	62.79	179.15	94.06	346.02	226.16	190.46	92.71
	(106.70)	(54.81)	(108.62)	(45.81)	(176.79)	(113.24)	(362.06)	(219.39)	(189.41)	(102.16)
Electricity, Gas and Water [4]	225.98	146.87	232.56	166.64	259.91	341.03	451.74	441.94	298.35	403.72
	(159.10)	(127.06)	(188.21)	(103.33)	(325.56)	(240.48)	(523.53)	(422.72)	(340.51)	(233.34)
Construction [5]	125.30	89.31	107.59	74.82	114.19	278.46	459.74	302.13	193.38	143.84
	(81.03)	(69.08)	(115.36)	(122.35)	(106.45)	(147.59)	(376.45)	(253.59)	(171.47)	(191.75)
Trade [6]	73.27	37.70	84.16	63.60	102.78	56.27	192.56	174.37	105.94	77.62
	(62.44)	(48.81)	(76.41)	(53.63)	(112.21)	(95.07)	(208.97)	(204.85)	(103.47)	(104.53)
Transport & Storage [7]	121.85	95.46	133.96	90.14	205.66	94.29	398.69	325.02	218.07	186.22
	(104.74)	(90.72)	(138.84)	(144.69)	(211.92)	(228.99)	(361.17)	(414.48)	(207.57)	(278.41)
Services [8]	105.29	82.59	148.68	185.70	201.88	241.31	407.08	297.10	328.10	280.99
	(64.01)	(45.77)	(122.25)	(108.36)	(174.19)	(131.04)	(501.69)	(372.60)	(360.15)	(304.07)
Services [9]	138.51	82.59	164.13	86.22	229.47	161.34	347.14	268.60	267.66	203.42
	(126.80)	(78.53)	(150.01)	(116.16)	(239.72)	(186.33)	(345.63)	(247.12)	(265.72)	(205.35)
Private hhs with Employed Person	68.57	38.38	99.03	61.20	100.13	36.02	127.30	41.01	92.30	46.36
	(78.77)	(38.20)	(89.82)	(42.77)	(62.95)	(51.67)	(164.08)	(67.61)	(86.94)	(41.26)
Others [10]	–	–	–	–	–	–	276.71	–	276.71	–
	(–)	(–)	(–)	(–)	(134.00)	(66.71)	(–)	(–)	(134.00)	(66.71)
All	106.10	53.10	117.82	69.32	183.40	142.77	350.39	273.80	205.81	158.23
	(98.79)	(48.70)	(111.44)	(64.79)	(182.58)	(150.41)	(366.76)	(269.17)	(203.28)	(153.19)

Notes: (i) Figures in [ ] Brackets are industrial codes of National Industrial Classification.

(ii) Figures in Parenthesis indicate for year 2004-05.

Source: National Sample Survey Organisation :
Report No. 515 & 522, *Employment and Unemployment Situation in India 2004-05 and 2005-06.*

Table 5.1.4: Average Wage Received by Casual Labourers per Day by Type of Operation *(Rupee)*

Rural India

Category	*Status Broad Industry*	*Type of Operation*	*1999-2000*		*2004-2005*	
			Male	*Female*	*Male*	*Female*
Casual Labourers in Public Works	(41)		48.14	38.06	65.22	49.20
Casual Labourers in Other Types of Works	(51) 01-05 (a)	Manual Work in Cultivation	39.09	27.91	46.81	32.51
		Ploughing	41.81	32.73	51.69	35.04
		Sowing	38.78	28.37	45.05	32.63
		Transplanting	39.15	29.22	49.79	35.91
		Weeding	34.68	25.74	41.59	29.92
		Harvesting	39.21	29.24	46.73	33.62
		Other cultivation activities	39.27	27.65	46.98	32.90
	(b)	Manual work in other agricultural activities	44.84	30.65	54.73	39.62
		Forestry	46.45	33.34	53.23	34.67
		Plantation	61.59	41.30	74.60	53.10
		Animal Husbandry	28.11	21.88	35.43	28.79
		Fisheries	57.74	55.73	93.61	42.68
		Other agricultural activities	42.64	27.96	47.36	34.12
	10-99 (c)	Non-Manual work in Cultivation and other than Cultivation	42.80	29.30	63.33	43.38
	(d)	Manual work in non-agricultural and activities other than Cultivation	58.71	36.19	69.51	43.76
	01-99	All	44.84	29.01	54.53	34.56

Source: National Sample Survey Organisation :

(*i*) Report No. 455, *Employment and Unemployment Situation in India*, 1999-2000, Key Results.

(*ii*) Report No. 515, *Employment and Unemployment Situation in India*, 2004-2005.

Table 5.1.5: Average Wage Received by Casual Labourers Per Day by Industry
(Rupee)

Urban India

Industry Division	*1999-2000* Male	*1999-2000* Female	*2004-2005* Male	*2004-2005* Female	*2005-2006* Male	*2005-2006* Female
(0) Agriculature, Hunting, Forestry and Fishing	49.14	32.15	56.71	34.29	67.31	37.11
(1) Mining and Quarrying	76.65	54.67	76.35	36.84	78.56	60.84
(2) Manufacturing	62.88	35.64	63.53	37.67	72.21	41.53
(3) Manufacturing	69.13	50.69	75.37	45.43	85.06	46.05
(4) Electricity, Gas and Water	74.24	—	85.89	45.98	89.39	31.67
(5) Construction	69.00	50.20	84.78	57.07	86.70	58.38
(6) Wholesale and Retail Trade & Restaurants and Hotels	53.65	45.63	60.39	40.90	73.24	50.41
(7) Transport, Storage and Communication	63.64	49.63	81.32	38.85	84.60	32.78
(8) Financial, Insurance, Real Estate and Business Services	64.85	32.83	89.63	32.34	92.63	63.94
(9) Community, Social and Personal Services	55.19	28.95	67.91	46.68	72.58	44.55
(1-9) Total Non-Agricultural	64.27	40.18	76.06	47.39	82.16	47.55
All India	62.26	37.71	74.22	43.41	80.52	44.37

Source: National Sample Survey Organisation :
(i) Report No. 455, *Employment and Unemployment in India, 1999-2000,* Key Results.
(ii) Report No. 515, *Employment and Unemployment in India,* 2004-2005.
(iii) Report No. 522, Employment and Unemployment in India, 2005-2006.

Table 5.1.6: Ratio of Emoluments of Degree Engineers to Diploma Engineers in Select Disciplines and States, 1997

Discipline	*Andhra Pradesh*	*Assam*	*Chandi-garh*	*Gujarat*	*Himachal Pradesh*	*Jammu and Kashmir*	*Karna-taka*	*Kerala*	*Punjab*
1. Civil	2.96	1.89	1.80	1.83	1.36	2.44	1.64	3.29	1.85
2. Mechanical	2.63	1.97	2.04	2.85	-	1.94	2.29	3.93	2.40
3. Electrical	2.29	2.42	2.14	1.87	1.41	1.61	2.47	3.88	3.25
4. Chemical	2.05	5.17	-	2.13	-	-	1.75	5.77	2.32
5. Electronics	3.68	-	1.75	3.85	-	-	2.93	4.54	2.96

Source: NTMIS, AICTE, Govt. of India.

Table 5.1.7: Average Labour Cost per Manday Worked by State/Union Territory

(*All Industries*)

State/ Union Territory	*Average labour cost per manday (Rs.)*			
	Census Sector		*Sample Sector*	
	1999-2000	*2000-01*	*1999-2000*	*2000-01*
States				
1. Andhra Pradesh	117.30	130.51	104.68	94.25
2. Assam	172.56	145.15	71.61	73.40
3. Bihar	330.24	256.67	86.78	68.60
4. Chhattisgarh	—	322.15	—	88.60
5. Delhi	229.17	211.66	389.10	167.23
6. Goa	365.94	334.06	195.67	171.18
7. Gujarat	249.41	226.80	144.67	122.63
8. Haryana	282.21	256.19	145.02	142.00
9. Himachal Pradesh	122.30	151.99	139.17	124.73
10. Jammu & Kashmir	158.68	158.32	131.77	113.56
11. Jharkhand	—	406.99	—	96.07
12. Karnataka	238.34	220.93	137.14	139.33
13. Kerala	208.01	220.60	137.56	142.32
14. Madhya Pradesh	261.15	231.35	130.01	145.92
15. Maharashtra	336.02	325.53	194.04	176.27
16. Manipur @	52.50	57.75	—	—
17. Meghalaya @	89.15	101.23	—	—
18. Nagaland @	70.76	70.71	—	—
19. Orissa	227.31	264.29	87.57	75.41
20. Punjab	186.77	180.11	116.64	115.21
21. Rajasthan	195.42	194.42	120.52	120.34
22. Tamil Nadu	213.39	199.64	105.95	109.37
23. Tripura @	86.25	87.13	—	—
24. Uttar Pradesh	246.41	212.40	116.31	122.10
25. Uttaranchal	—	423.11	—	126.28
26. West Bengal	259.57	258.02	132.86	126.86
Union Territories				
1. Andaman and Nicobar Islands @	119.97	116.70	—	—
2. Chandigarh	313.86	307.69	183.65	182.21
3. Dadra and Nagar Haveli	126.94	154.34	131.13	122.31
4. Daman and Diu	113.05	126.97	104.98	106.28
5 Pondicherry	183.94	183.30	135.36	113.03
All India	235.25	230.93	137.38	126.21

Notes: The census sector covers industries employing 50 or more workers with power and 100 or more workers without power. The sample sector covers industries employing 10-49 workers with power and 20-99 workers without power.

@ Covered on census basis.

P — Provisional.

Source: Labour Bureau, *Indian Labour Year Book, 2004.*

Table 5.1.8: Average Monthly Emoluments Received by the Fresh Engineers (Civil)

State	*Emoluments Received by Degree Holders (Rs.)*					*Emoluments Received by Diploma Holders (Rs.)*				
	1988-90	*1998-2000*	*2001-2003*	*2002-2004*	*2003-2005*	*1988-90*	*1998-2000*	*2001-2003*	*2002-2004*	*2003 2005*
1. Andhra Pradesh	2,696	7,600	9,220	NA	7,752	–	3,876	3,110	NA	4,156
2. Assam	2,408	6,649	6,633	9,575	NA	1,706	3,352	3,722	4,130	NA
3. Chandigarh	2,736	16,111	NA	15,529	17,542	–	2,500	NA	6,000	7,833
4. Chattisgarh	–	–	–	–	13,725	–	–	–	–	5,525
5. Delhi	–	–	22,510	16,264	17,243	–	–	4,608	5,872	7,803
6. Gujarat	1,446	4,874	NA	NA	NA	1,041	2,306	NA	NA	NA
7. Haryana	–	9,340	14,970	15,128	20,014	–	3,339	4,463	7,964	6,336
8. Himachal Pradesh	–	7,133	4,620	12,300	10,240	2,350	3,388	3,845	5,850	4,906
9. Jammu & Kashmir	2,259	4,920	NA	8,188	10,541	1,607	2,751	NA	5,066	6,182
10. Karnataka	2,105	6,076	6,147	6,742	9,400	–	3,300	3,741	4.069	4,678
11. Kerala	1,824	6,644	7,437	7,101	7,383	1,378	2,747	2,261	2,572	3,120
12. Madhya Pradesh	–	15,620	14,654	16,346	14,769	–	2,541	4,340	4,480	4,528
13. Orissa	2,067	7,715	12,226	11,211	19,343	1,584	3,011	2,874	3,799	6,575
14. Punjab	2,558	7,200	7,536	9,504	9,953	1,590	2,991	4,062	4,359	5,528
15. Rajasthan	1,950	9,256	10,144	9,870	NA	1,430	4,036	4,591	4,100	NA
16. Tamil Nadu	1,644	5,320	6,414	NA	10,973	984	2,686	3,519	NA	3,660
17. Uttar Pradesh	2,855	10,095	NA	NA	NA	1,431	3,095	NA	NA	NA
18. West Bengal	2,100	9,701	9,621	12,535	12,337	–	3,777	3,859	4,467	5,230

Notes: (–) Implies Discipline does not exist/Data not available.

NA – Not Available.

Source: NTMIS, AICTE, Govt. of India.

Table 5.1.9: Average Monthly Emoluments Received by the Fresh Engineers (Mechanical)

State	*Emoluments Received by Degree Holders (Rs.)*					*Emoluments Received by Diploma Holders (Rs.)*				
	1988-90	*1998-2000*	*2001-2003*	*2002-2004*	*2003-2005*	*1988-90*	*1998-2000*	*2001-2003*	*2002-2004*	*2003-2005*
1. Andhra Pradesh	2,586	11,984	8,306	NA	8,174	1,056	5,668	3,160	NA	4,171
2. Assam	2,636	8,772	10,411	15,604	NA	1,543	3,050	3,500	3,630	NA
3. Chandigarh	3,643	11,857	NA	17,101	19,566	—	4,379	NA	7,500	6,298
4. Chhattisgarh	—	—	—	—	15,689	—	—	—	—	5,905
5. Delhi	—	—	17,251	16,331	20,731	—	—	4,695	6,166	7,393
6. Gujarat	1,692	6,319	NA	NA	NA	1,087	2,806	NA	NA	NA
7. Haryana	—	7,499	13,412	11,001	11,122	—	3,800	5,180	3,580	6,548
8. Himachal Pradesh	—	7,900	12,874	11,616	11,000	2,100	5,640	4,316	5,250	4,033
9. Jammu & Kashmir	2,910	3,500	NA	8,606	12,149	2,500	3,858	NA	3,378	4,969
10. Karnataka	2,293	7,880	7,740	9,552	11,732	1,257	3,128	3,377	3,995	4,669
11. Kerala	2,440	10,190	11,305	10,931	10,892	1,337	2,983	2,879	3,161	3,320
12. Madhya Pradesh	—	13,760	15,298	17,513	20,475	—	3,613	6,047	5,070	5,713
13. Orissa	2,750	11,756	9,117	12,312	22,589	1,638	3,133	3,090	4,103	5,315
14. Punjab	2,830	9,330	10,115	9,371	10,315	1,446	3,265	4,218	4,764	4,928
15. Rajasthan	1,990	11,370	10,866	11,996	NA	1,540	3,458	3,416	3,847	NA
16. Tamil Nadu	2,080	8,363	7,526	NA	10,058	967	2,736	3,770	NA	3,814
17. Uttar Pradesh	2,869	11,725	NA	NA	NA	1,462	3,130	NA	NA	NA
18. West Bengal	2,813	16,860	13,898	12,725	12,872	1,148	3,999	4,313	4,923	5,000

Notes: (—) Implies Discipline does not exist/Data not available.
NA – Not Available.
Source: NTMIS, AICTE, Govt. of India.

Table 5.1.10: Average Monthly Emoluments Received by the Fresh Engineers (Electrical)

State	Emoluments Received by Degree Holders (Rs.)					Emoluments Received by Diploma Holders (Rs.)				
	1988-90	1998-2000	2001-2003	2002-2004	2003-2005	1988-90	1998-2000	2001-2003	2002-2004	2003-2005
1. Andhra Pradesh	2,646	11,386	9,177	NA	10,209	1,337	4,936	4,010	NA	4,394
2. Assam	2,867	12,890	10,067	10,020	NA	1,779	2,617	NA	3,333	NA
3. Chandigarh	2,904	17,492	NA	26,020	19,917	–	3,778	NA	4,813	5,951
4. Chattisgarh	–	–	–	–	17,000	–	–	–	–	8,662
5. Delhi	–	–	20,253	21,399	22,577	–	–	4,470	6,148	8,374
6. Gujarat	2,247	6,255	NA	NA	NA	1,112	2,534	3,833	NA	NA
7. Haryana	–	9,734	11,997	12,580	11,500	–	2,996	3,867	4,380	5,154
8. Himachal Pradesh	–	9,058	12,078	10,000	15,102	1,320	2,912	3,475	3,325	4,306
9. Jammu & Kashmir	2,909	–	NA	15,800	12,810	2,394	2,859	NA	3,793	7,048
10. Karnataka	2,341	8,032	8,494	10,411	13,059	1,009	3,260	3,438	4,115	4,426
11. Kerala	2,579	8,950	9,524	9,712	13,573	1,510	2,790	2,456	3,021	3,328
12. Madhya Pradesh	–	15,833	11,089	16,511	18,504	–	3,233	6,228	3,834	4,576
13. Orissa	2,878	10,240	10,389	9,625	25,996	1,739	3,779	2,931	3,065	4,796
14. Punjab	2,462	9,074	9,660	9,169	8,557	1,822	3,890	2,970	4,615	4,340
15. Rajasthan	1,960	10,989	11607	10,405	NA	1,670	3,596	NA	3,190	NA
16. Tamil Nadu	2,612	8,311	7,200	NA	9,543	882	2,591	3,000	NA	3,659
17. Uttar Pradesh	3,037	15,890	NA	NA	NA	1,518	2,860	NA	NA	NA
18. West Bengal	2,635	11,353	13,695	14,685	14,741	935	4,689	4,133	4,615	4,037

Notes: (–) Implies Discipline does not exist/Data not available.

NA – Not Available.

Source: NTMIS, AICTE, Govt. of India.

Table 5.1.11: Average Monthly Emoluments Received by the Fresh Engineers (Chemical)

State	Emoluments Received by Degree Holders (Rs.)					Emoluments Received by Diploma Holders (Rs.)				
	1988-90	1998-2000	2001-2003	2002-2004	2003-2005	1988-90	1998-2000	2001-2003	2002-2004	2003-2005
1. Andhra Pradesh	3,136	7,979	7,025	NA	8,056	1,831	4,281	3,425	NA	4,220
2. Assam	2,477	13,731	10,750	9,167	NA	2,203	4,900	6,100	6,667	NA
3. Chandigarh	2,560	13,134	NA	25,663	17,895	—	—	—	—	—
4. Chhattisgarh	—	—	—	—	18,507	—	—	—	—	—
5. Delhi	—	—	26,776	9,000	16,000	—	—	4,100	6,000	8,290
6. Gujarat	2,569	6,263	NA	NA	NA	1,250	3,733	NA	NA	NA
7. Haryana	—	6,300	12,000	9,000	20,431	—	3,685	3,881	4,326	5,167
8. Jammu and Kashmir	2,408	—	NA	NA	5,500	—	—	NA	NA	—
9. Karnataka	2,560	8,880	8,572	9,649	12,993	1,288	3,075	4,908	4,055	3,831
10. Kerala	2,738	8,550	11,996	7,488	9,696	1,972	2,691	2,078	3,807	4,554
11. Madhya Pradesh	—	11,254	10,471	18,892	18,395	—	6,375	NA	NA	NA
12. Orissa	2,863	16,462	8,500	12,239	27,063	2,122	2,730	2,250	3,406	3,710
13. Punjab	—	7,613	11,959	7,374	11,623	—	2,805	5,146	3,615	4,857
14. Rajasthan	1,940	9,256	14,776	13,273	NA	—	4,667	4,765	4,833	NA
15. Tamil Nadu	2,251	7,162	6,607	NA	8,071	1,496	3,117	3,526	NA	4,996
16. Uttar Pradesh	2,803	13,455	NA	NA	NA	1,859	2,760	NA	NA	NA
17. West Bengal	2,723	13,007	14,804	14,910	14,749	—	—	4,700	6,256	6,256

Notes: (—) Implies Discipline does not exist in the state/Data not available.

NA – Not Available.

Source: NTMIS, AICTE, Govt. of India.

Table 5.1.12: Average Monthly Emoluments Received by the Fresh Engineers (Electronics)

State	*Emoluments Received by Degree Holders during (Rs.)*					*Emoluments Received by Diploma Holders during (Rs.)*				
	1988-90	*1998-2000*	*2001-2003*	*2002-2004*	*2003-2005*	*1988-90*	*1998-2000*	*2001-2003*	*2002-2004*	*2003-2005*
1. Andhra Pradesh	2,711	14,231	12,006	NA	11,591	1116		3,260	NA	4,525
2. Assam	3,174	13,883	17,922	18,443	NA	1985	4,145	3,344	3,908	NA
3. Chandigarh	3,765	17,895	NA	21,413	16,790	1275	2,575	NA	4,553	6,886
4. Chhattisgarh	—	—	—	—	—	—	—	—	—	5,566
5. Delhi	—	—	19,237	22,945	20,826	—	—	4,567	6,340	6,148
6. Gujarat	2,105	7,743	NA	NA	NA	—	2,597	NA	NA	NA
7. Haryana	—	7,117	13,786	13,018	16,099	—	3,785	5,566	3,938	5,427
8. Himachal Pradesh	—	11,278	13,660	15,711	19,663	—	2,903	4,915	6,340	3,548
9. Jammu & Kashmir	—	—	NA	13,167	12,469	—	—	NA	3,577	6,065
10. Karnataka	2,561	11,020	10,670	13,837	15,590	1178	3,091	3,645	3,778	4,258
11. Kerala	2,283	12,625	10,868	12,809	15,637	1462	2,701	2,393	2,671	3,133
12. Madhya Pradesh	—	1,8523	17,584	24,039	24,657	—	3,346	7,186	3,486	3,708
13. Punjab	2,700	10,627	12,432	11,775	13,539	2190	3,191	4,204	5,067	4,777
14. Orissa	2,727	17,858	10,702	10,266	22,411	—	3,283	2,871	4,615	4,404
15. Rajasthan	2,190	14,298	13,271	11,950	NA	—	3,892	4,000	3,317	NA
16. Tamil Nadu	2,630	11,235	11,470	NA	12,559	900	2,836	5,153	NA	3,319
17. Uttar Pradesh	2,905	16,275	NA	NA	NA	1614	3,290	NA	3,537	NA
18. West Bengal	2,794	1,4839	16,476	16,015	17,368	1050	4,623	5,354	5,538	6,204

Notes: (—) Implies Discipline does not exist in the state/Data not available.

NA – Not Available.

Source: NTMIS, AICTE, Govt. of India.

Table 5.1.13: Consumer Price Index

Years	*Agricultural Labourers*	*Industrial Workers*	*Urban non-manual Employees*
	Old Series (At 1980-81 Prices)		
1980-81	100.0	100.0	100.0
1985-86	138.2	154.6	153.9
1986-87	144.8	168.1	166.1
1987-88	159.2	183.5	181.0
1988-89	179.2	200.0	196.2
1989-90	188.9	212.7	209.2
1990-91	203.3	237.2	232.3
1991-92	242.5	269.3	264.0
1992-93	272.4	295.0	291.4
	Old Series (At 1993-94 Prices)		
1993-94	100.0	100.0	100.0
1994-95	111.9	110.1	109.7
1995-96	124.0	121.3	119.9
1996-97	131.4	132.6	131.0
1997-98	135.6	141.7	139.8
1998-99	150.8	160.3	156.0
	New Series (At 1999-2000 Prices)		
1999-00	100.0	100.0	100.0
2000-01	99.7	103.8	105.6
2001-02	100.8	108.3	111.0
2002-03	103.9	112.6	115.2
2003-04	108.2	116.8	119.5
2004-05	111.1	121.5	123.8
2005-06	115.4	126.7	129.7
2006-07	124.4	135.3	138.3

Source: Central Statistical Organisation, *National Accounts Statistics—2008.*

Figure 5.1.A

CONSUMER PRICE INDEX (AT 1999-2000 PRICES)

For details see Table 5.1.13

(ii) Unemployment

Table 5.2.1: Unemployment Rates

Years	*Status*	*Rural*		*Urban*	
		Male	*Female*	*Male*	*Female*
1977-78	(i) Usual Status	2.2	5.5	6.5	17.8
	(ii) Current Weekly	3.6	4.1	7.1	10.9
	(iii) Current Daily	7.1	9.2	9.4	14.5
1983	(i) Usual Status	2.1	1.4	5.9	6.9
	(ii) Current Weekly	3.7	4.3	6.7	7.5
	(iii) Current Daily	7.5	9.0	9.2	11.0
1987-88	(i) Usual Status	2.8	3.5	6.1	8.5
	(ii) Current Weekly	4.2	4.4	6.6	9.2
	(iii) Current Daily	4.6	6.7	8.8	12.0
1993-94	(i) Usual Status	2.0	1.3	5.4	8.3
	(ii) Current Weekly	3.1	2.9	5.2	7.9
	(iii) Current Daily	5.6	5.6	6.7	10.4
1999-2000	(i) Usual Status	2.1	1.5	4.8	7.1
	(ii) Current Weekly	3.9	3.7	5.6	7.3
	(iii) Current Daily	7.2	7.0	7.3	9.4
2004-2005	(i) Usual Status	2.1	3.1	4.4	9.1
	(ii) Current Weekly	3.8	4.2	5.2	9.0
	(iii) Current Daily	8.0	8.7	7.5	11.6
2005-06	(i) Usual Status	2.5	2.2	4.8	7.9
	(ii) Current Weekly	4.3	3.3	5.8	7.7
	(iii) Current Daily	8.3	7.5	7.9	10.1

Notes: The figures represent size of unemployment as percent of labour force :

(i) Usual status approach with a reference period of 365 days preceding the date of survey.

(ii) Current weekly status approach with a reference period of 7 days preceding the date of survey.

(iii) Current daily status approach with each day of the 7 days preceeding the date of survey as the reference period.

(iv) Rates for 2001-02 are based on thin sample.

Sources : National Sample Survey Organisation :

Sarvekshana, Vol. V, July 77-June 78, 32nd Round
Vol. XI, Jan.-Dec.-1983, 38th Round
Special No., July 87-June 88, 43rd Round
Vol. XX. July 93 - June 94, 50th Round

Report Nos. 458, 490, 515 and 522 , *Employment and Unemployment Situation in India,* 1999-2000, 2004-05 and 2005-06.

Figure 5.2.B

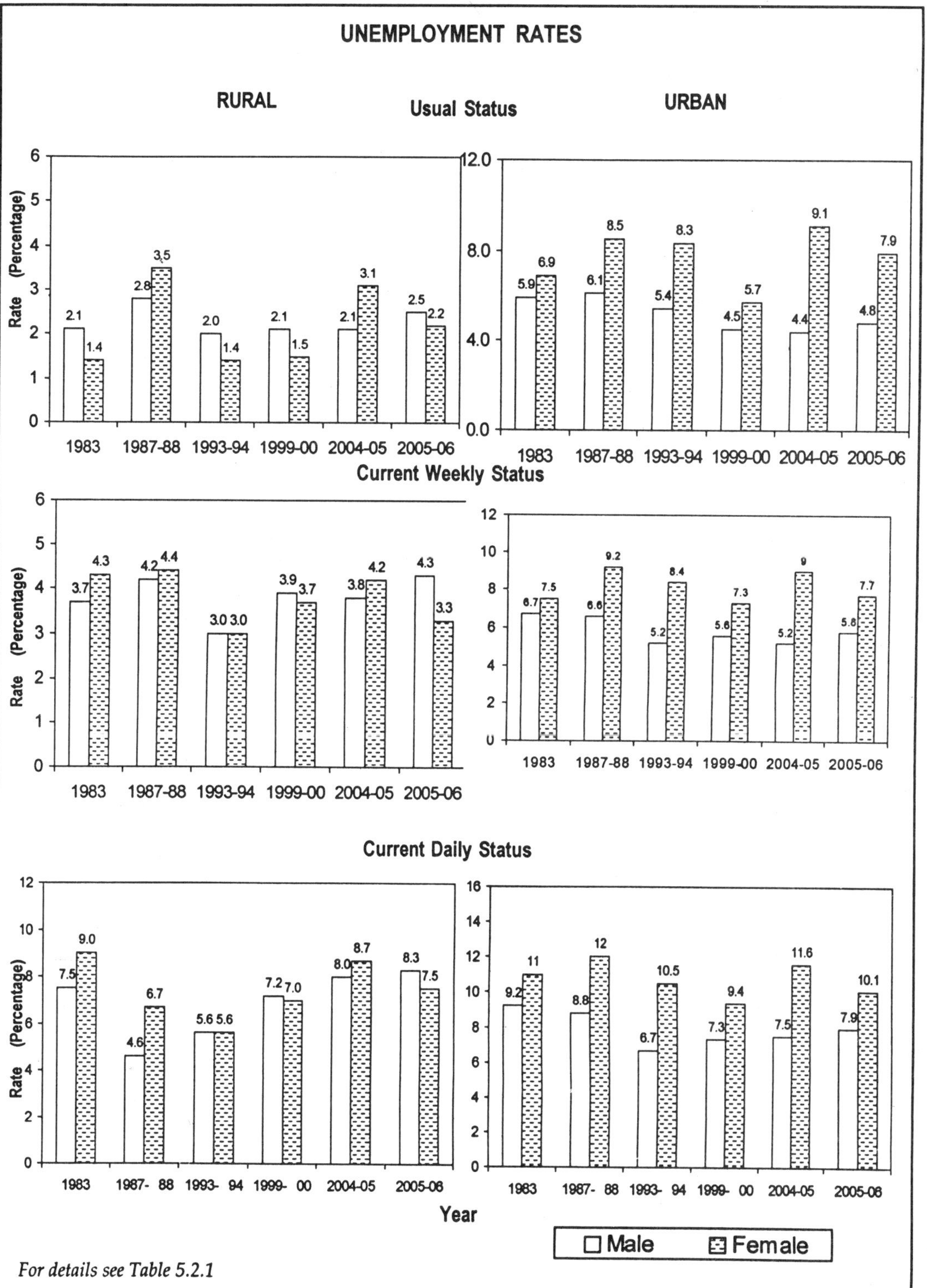

For details see Table 5.2.1

Table 5.2.2: Estimates of Unemployment

(Million)

Years	*Rural*			*Urban*		
	Male	*Female*	*Person*	*Male*	*Female*	*Person*
1977-78	3.1	3.5	6.6	2.6	1.7	4.3
1983	3.2	0.9	4.1	2.9	0.7	3.6
1987-88	4.5	3.1	7.6	3.5	1.3	4.8
1993-94	3.7	1.0	4.7	3.6	1.2	4.8
1999-2000	3.2	1.0	4.2	2.9	0.9	3.8
2004-2005	4.0	2.0	5.9	1.4	0.4	1.8
2005-2006	4.2	1.4	5.6	3.1	1.1	4.2

Note: Figures relate to usual status of individuals.

Source: National Sample Survey Organisation :

(*i*) *Sarvekshana Special Number, 43rd Round.*

(*ii*) *Report Nos. 409, 458, 515 & 522 Employment and Unemployment Situation in India, 1993-94, 1999-2000, 2004-05 & 2005-06.*

Table 5.2.3: Age-Specific Unemployment Rates

Years	*Age Group*									
	15-29		*30-44*		*45-59*		*60 and above*		*Total**	
	Male	*Female*	*Male*	*Female*	*Male*	*Female*	*Male*	*Female*	*Male*	*Female*
					RURAL					
1977-78	4.9	8.5	0.6	4.1	0.4	3.0	0.3	2.0	2.2	5.5
1983	4.7	2.8	0.5	0.5	0.2	0.4	0.2	0.6	2.1	1.4
1987-88	6.2	5.4	0.9	2.4	0.5	1.9	0.5	1.8	2.8	3.5
1993-94	4.9	3.1	0.4	0.6	0.1	0.2	0.0	0.0	2.0	1.4
1999-2000	4.3	2.7	0.4	0.2	0.3	0.0	0.2	0.0	2.1	1.5
2004-2005	3.0	1.8	0.4	0.5	0.0	0.3	0.0	0.0	1.0	0.7
2005-2006	4.6	3.0	0.4	0.4	0.2	0.1	0.3	0.4	1.9	1.3
					URBAN					
1977-78	14.0	31.4	1.3	10.4	1.0	4.8	1.5	2.2	6.5	17.8
1983	12.2	15.5	1.4	2.1	0.7	0.7	0.6	9.1	5.9	6.9
1987-88	13.6	18.8	1.2	3.5	0.7	1.1	1.1	1.1	6.1	8.5
1993-94	10.8	19.5	1.1	2.8	0.4	0.4	0.2	0.0	5.4	8.3
1999-2000	10.8	13.9	1.3	2.2	0.4	0.5	0.0	0.0	4.8	7.1
2004-2005	6.0	3.2	1.0	1.2	0.7	0.0	0.0	0.0	2.4	1.3
2005-2006	10.5	13.6	1.3	2.5	0.6	0.1	0.2	0.0	4.4	6.5

Notes: The figures represent size of unemployment as percent of labour force.
The figures of different Rounds relate to the usual status.
* Total includes figures for ages 5-14 also.

Source: National Sample Survey Organisation :
Report Nos. 409, 458, 515 & 522 *Employment and Unemployment Situation in India, 1993-94, 1999-2000, 2004-05 and 2005-06.*

Table 5.2.4: Unemployment Rates by State/Union Territory, 2005-06

State/Union Territory	*Rural*		*Urban*	
	Male	*Female*	*Male*	*Female*
States				
1. Andhra Pradesh	0.6 (1.0)	0.3 (0.4)	2.7 (3.6)	0.6 (3.8)
2. Arunachal Pradesh	NA (1.1)	NA (0.6)	NA (1.1)	NA (2.8)
3. Assam	1.4 (2.4)	0.7 (3.1)	4.0 (6.9)	1.9 (9.1)
4. Bihar	0.7 (1.8)	0.1 (0.3)	4.1 (6.7)	0.5 (4.1)
5. Chhatisgarh	0.1 (0.8)	0.1 (0.3)	2.9 (3.8)	1.0 (2.4)
6. Delhi	0.8 (2.1)	0.0 (0.0)	1.2 (4.6)	0.3 (6.4)
7. Goa	3.7 (9.1)	4.8 (15.7)	5.7 (7.6)	3.7 (11.8)
8. Gujarat	0.8 (0.8)	0.1 (0.2)	2.0 (2.3)	0.0 (2.9)
9. Haryana	2.2 (2.8)	0.0 (1.0)	2.1 (3.2)	0.6 (7.5)
10. Himachal Pradesh	0.8 (1.6)	0.5 (2.0)	1.5 (1.7)	1.6 (10.1)
11. Jammu & Kashmir	1.7 (1.7)	0.0 (1.3)	3.7 (3.7)	1.0 (10.9)
12. Jharkhand	1.3 (2.0)	0.1 (0.1)	4.9 (7.5)	1.9 (2.3)
13. Karnataka	1.2 (0.7)	0.2 (0.8)	2.8 (1.9)	0.9 (5.7)
14. Kerala	3.0 (5.1)	4.7 (20.1)	1.6 (6.2)	6.7 (33.4)
15. Madhya Pradesh	0.6 (0.7)	0.0 (0.1)	2.1 (3.1)	0.3 (1.6)
16. Maharashtra	1.0 (1.5)	0.2 (0.3)	2.9 (3.5)	1.2 (4.1)
17. Manipur	NA (1.4)	NA (0.7)	NA (5.2)	NA (6.3)
18. Meghalaya	NA (0.1)	NA (0.5)	NA (3.5)	NA (3.5)
19. Mizoram	NA (0.5)	NA (0.1)	NA (1.6)	NA (2.6)
20. Nagaland	NA (2.2)	NA (1.4)	NA (4.6)	NA (7.2)
21. Orissa	2.8 (3.1)	1.2 (8.3)	3.8 (9.0)	1.7 (26.6)
22. Punjab	2.3 (3.3)	0.8 (4.9)	2.3 (2.9)	1.3 (14.0)
23. Rajasthan	0.6 (1.2)	0.0 (0.1)	1.9 (2.8)	0.2 (2.9)
24. Sikkim	NA (2.8)	NA (1.5)	NA (3.6)	NA (4.3)
25. Tamil Nadu	1.1 (1.2)	0.5 (1.1)	2.3 (2.9)	1.0 (4.8)
26. Tripura	NA (9.6)	NA (32.0)	NA (16.6)	NA (56.8)
27. Uttaranchal	0.1 (2.0)	0.0 (0.4)	0.9 (4.2)	0.5 (10.2)
28. Uttar Pradesh	0.6 (0.7)	0.0 (0.3)	1.8 (3.5)	0.2 (2.5)
29. West Bengal	2.2 (2.2)	0.1 (3.3)	3.6 (5.6)	0.6 (8.4)
30. North-Eastern States	2.1 (NA)	0.9 (NA)	3.0 (NA)	3.5 (NA)
Union Territories				
Group of UTs	2.5 (NA)	0.5 (NA)	1.7 (NA)	2.2 (NA)
1. Andaman and Nicoba Islands	NA (3.7)	NA (12.3)	NA (6.5)	NA (17.2)
2. Chandigarh	NA (2.5)	NA (4.8)	NA (3.1)	NA (7.5)
3. Dadra and Nagar Haveli	NA (3.1)	NA (3.6)	NA (1.3)	NA (9.1)
4. Daman and Diu	NA (0.4)	NA (0.0)	NA (2.8)	NA (3.3)
5. Lakshadweep	NA (0.9)	NA (57.1)	NA (11.1)	NA (51.5)
6. Pondicherry	NA (9.4)	NA (3.2)	NA (4.1)	NA (19.5)
All India	1.1 (1.6)	0.4 (1.8)	2.5 (3.8)	1.0 (6.9)

Notes: Figures relate to usual status of individuals.The figures represent size of unemployment as per cent of labour force.
NA : Data is not available.
Figures in parenthesis indicate for the year 2004-05.

Source: National Sample Survey Organisation :
Report Nos. 515 & 522, *Employment & Unemployment Situation in India 2004-2005 & 2005-2006.*

Table 5.2.5: Unemployment Rates for Educated Persons

Year / Educational Level	Population Based: Male Rural	Population Based: Male Urban	Population Based: Female Rural	Population Based: Female Urban	Labour Force Based: Male Rural	Labour Force Based: Male Urban	Labour Force Based: Female Rural	Labour Force Based: Female Urban
1977-78								
Below Matric	N.A	N.A	N.A	N.A	N.A	N.A	N.A	N.A
Matric	9.80	7.29	15.43	9.43	13.02	10.08	45.84	42.37
Graduate	17.56	8.19	24.89	15.68	19.72	9.31	44.81	35.92
1983								
Below Matric	1.18	3.83	0.35	0.67	1.34	4.55	0.93	3.54
Matric	7.76	6.51	7.96	4.00	10.45	9.08	33.50	29.01
Graduate	11.35	6.39	15.60	7.44	12.78	7.31	41.48	21.08
1987-88								
Below Matric	1.62	4.00	1.10	0.89	1.85	4.82	2.81	4.84
Matric	7.80	6.20	8.80	3.70	10.51	8.80	33.46	22.80
Graduate	13.50	6.40	14.90	7.90	14.98	7.40	37.30	21.01
1993-94								
Below Matric	0.80	2.53	0.20	0.60	0.16	3.04	0.57	3.21
Matric	5.51	4.89	4.51	3.03	7.65	7.15	22.52	20.90
Graduate	12.10	5.50	15.50	7.30	13.25	6.38	34.60	20.56
1999-2000								
Below Matric	0.65	1.81	0.16	0.34	1.12	3.48	0.58	2.67
Matric	4.35	4.43	3.18	2.05	5.85	6.53	16.39	16.31
Graduate	9.61	5.63	14.12	4.92	10.69	6.61	31.26	16.26
2004-05								
Below Matric	0.76	2.11	0.37	0.62	0.87	2.52	0.72	2.48
Matric	2.80	2.87	3.79	2.07	3.72	4.26	11.59	14.14
Graduate	5.64	4.94	13.08	5.97	6.22	5.85	27.95	17.04
Diploma/ Certificate Course	6.78	6.76	15.82	8.85	7.40	7.87	24.78	15.38
2005-06								
Below Matric	0.69	1.82	0.19	0.14	1.31	3.84	0.59	1.04
Matric	3.11	3.16	2.46	1.51	4.28	4.80	9.03	12.03
Graduate	5.74	4.82	7.16	4.85	6.36	5.62	17.13	14.37
Diploma/ Certificate Course	6.40	5.90	11.09	6.50	7.15	7.34	20.47	15.71

Notes: Figures relate to usual status of individuals.The figures represent size of unemployment of a given educational level as percent of population/labour force of that educational level.

Matric Includes Higher secondary also.

Sources: National Sample Survey Organisation :

Sarvekshana Vol. V, July 77-June 78, 32nd Round.
Vol. XI, Jan.-Dec 1983, 38th Round.
Special No., July 87-June 88, 43rd Round.
Vol. XX. July 93 -June 94, 50th Round.

Report Nos. 458, 515 & 522, *Employment and Unemployment Situation in India*, 1999-2000, 2004-05 & 2005-06

Figure 5.2.C

UNEMPLOYMENT RATES FOR EDUCATED PERSONS (LABOUR FORCE BASED)

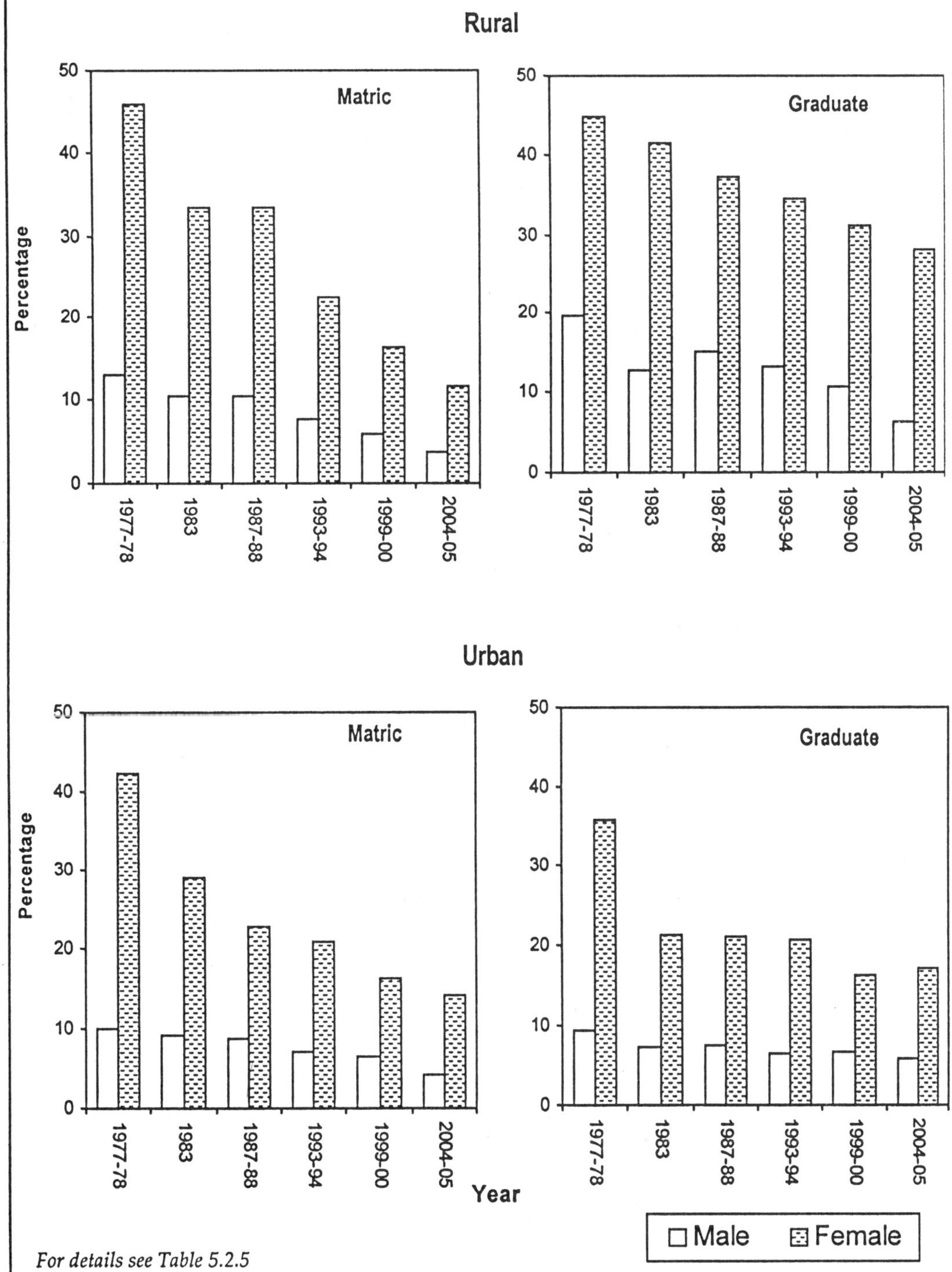

For details see Table 5.2.5

Table 5.2.6: Number of Total Unemployed Engineers by Select States

State	Degree Level					Diploma Level				
	2001	2004	2005	2006	2007	2001	2004	2005	2006	2007
1. Andhra Pradesh	5,713	11,865	NA	NA	48,372	8,398	9,581	NA	NA	16,687
2. Assam	583	474	884	579	NA	1,484	704	1,181	1,114	NA
3. Chandigarh	223	239	35	188	196	377	428	78	257	334
4. Chhattisgarh	—	—	—	—	1,421	—	—	—	—	707
5. Delhi	619	440	371	436	1,027	1,783	1,763	1,489	1,190	1,126
6. Gujarat	2,740	7,642	NA	NA	NA	5,178	8,829	NA	NA	NA
7. Haryana	—	1,206	1,029	2,585	2,855	—	1,242	858	2,288	1,843
8. Himachal Pradesh	118	333	527	68	NA	297	338	320	233	NA
9. Jammu & Kashmir	540	768	378	851	1,094	916	1,098	803	1,180	1303
10. Karnataka	5,919	12,771	12,146	14,342	17,123	10,776	11,251	13,001	10,673	12,553
11. Kerala	1,171	2,115	1,129	1,568	2,799	6,143	11,276	8,147	8,449	8,034
12. Madhya Pradesh	3,224	2,362	4,780	NA	6,688	4,783	3,443	3,752	NA	4,406
13. Maharashtra	—	27,639	NA	NA	NA	—	29,298	NA	NA	NA
14. Orissa	832	3,267	7,677	6,530	5,382	4,322	6,037	7,197	10,394	11,008
15. Punjab	726	2,038	3,008	1,922	2,324	1,196	4,521	3,751	2,840	2,329
16. Rajasthan	1,126	1,453	2,291	3,674	NA	1,744	2,347	2,250	1,769	NA
17. Tamil Nadu	18,181	49,752	51,831	NA	60,320	30,903	69,348	46,191	NA	42,022
18. Uttar Pradesh	662	—	NA	NA	NA	7,495	—	NA	NA	NA
19. West Bengal	1,012	1,616	1,854	2676	3,459	2,141	2,838	3,910	4,122	4168

Notes: The figures exclude the outturn of the year under consideration.
(—) Implies Course does not exist in the State/Data not available.
NA-Not Available

Source: NTMIS, AICTE, Govt. of India.

Table 5.2.7: Number of Unemployed Engineers by Select States (Civil)

State	Degree Level					Diploma Level				
	2001	2004	2005	2006	2007	2001	2004	2005	2006	2007
1. Andhra Pradesh	728	1,013	NA	NA	1,789	890	1,776	NA	574	NA
2. Assam	180	116	237	126	NA	615	163	289	270	NA
3. Chandigarh	40	66	0	30	17	27	29	1	32	6
4. Chhattisgarh	–	–	–	–	67	–	–	–	–	79
5. Delhi	118	101	26	75	120	205	59	31	50	16
6. Gujarat	363	884	NA	NA	NA	752	816	NA	NA	NA
7. Haryana	–	55	24	36	20	–	165	127	67	63
8. Himachal Pradesh	50	49	53	15	NA	55	78	70	8	NA
9. Jammu & Kashmir	131	205	37	142	173	146	157	114	187	255
10. Karnataka	802	1,105	1,326	671	1,118	1,190	749	873	NA	408
11. Kerala	277	440	198	242	331	1,016	1,442	936	996	923
12. Madhya Pradesh	470	115	88	NA	87	249	188	259	NA	258
13. Maharashtra	–	1,730	NA	NA	NA	–	3,067	NA	NA	1944
14. Orissa	94	138	289	168	191	477	947	1,241	1,755	1,629
15. Punjab	111	105	163	64	21	85	180	161	84	84
16. Rajasthan	249	260	203	339	NA	182	187	119	96	NA
17. Tamil Nadu	772	1,706	1,807	NA	1,756	4,597	3,859	3,952	NA	3,815
18. Uttar Pradesh	125	—	NA	NA	NA	1720	—	NA	NA	NA
19. West Bengal	112	124	159	116	105	382	846	982	802	1,155

Notes: The figures exclude the outturn of the year under consideration.
(–) Implies Course does not exist in the state/Data not available.
NA-Not Available.

Source: NTMIS, AICTE, Govt. of India.

Table 5.2.8: Number of Unemployed Engineers by Select States (Chemical)

	State	Degree Level					Diploma Level				
		2001	2004	2005	2006	2007	2001	2004	2005	2006	2007
1.	Andhra Pradesh	181	619	NA	NA	1,427	32	92	NA	NA	191
2.	Assam	20	12	20	22	NA	46	25	76	80	–
3.	Chandigarh	34	34	4	41	17	–	–	–	–	–
4.	Chhattisgarh	–	–	–	–	54	–	–	–	–	–
5.	Delhi	30	12	21	21	55	–	19	NA	24	5
6.	Gujarat	263	915	NA	NA	NA	167	494	NA	NA	NA
7.	Haryana	–	37	25	42	17	–	33	28	32	36
8.	Jammu & Kashmir	–	13	NA	–	9	–	–	NA	–	–
9.	Karnataka	54	292	270	195	181	47	41	51	44	31
10.	Kerala	42	66	47	56	126	57	162	214	152	162
11.	Madhya Pradesh	102	64	149	NA	59	8	18	-	NA	5
12.	Maharashtra	–	778	NA	NA	NA	–	598	NA	NA	NA
13.	Orissa	9	69	225	189	134	183	119	211	214	200
14.	Punjab	80	188	266	126	64	–	111	72	51	42
15.	Rajasthan	62	100	54	67	NA	–	36	16	20	NA
16.	Tamil Nadu	451	2,246	1,374	NA	1,320	251	2,675	845	NA	685
17.	Uttar Pradesh	32	–	NA	NA	NA	32	–	NA	NA	NA
18.	West Bengal	92	212	112	113	87	–	16	38	32	20

Notes: The figures exclude the outturn of the year under consideration.
(—) Implies Discipline does not exist in the state/Data not available.
NA-Not Available.

Source: NTMIS, AICTE, Govt. of India.

Table 5.2.9: Number of Unemployed Engineers by Select States (Electrical)

State	Degree Level					Diploma Level				
	2001	2004	2005	2006	2007	2001	2004	2005	2006	2007
1. Andhra Pradesh	992	2,063	NA	NA	10,157	1,394	1,099	NA	NA	2,767
2. Assam	69	121	159	183	NA	288	123	189	209	NA
3. Chandigarh	26	31	0	17	8	60	42	3	32	18
4. Chhattisgarh	—	—	—	—	136	—	—	—	—	234
5. Delhi	102	92	54	62	88	62	153	133	24	97
6. Gujarat	384	1,490	NA	NA	NA	1,045	2,757	NA	NA	NA
7. Haryana	—	196	102	232	74	—	236	233	81	87
8. Himachal Pradesh	36	118	162	19	NA	162	47	36	39	NA
9. Jammu & Kashmir	99	140	104	173	213	196	260	193	271	219
10. Karnataka	1,030	1,169	1,239	1,445	1,473	1,071	873	1,209	786	824
11. Kerala	229	381	288	163	469	924	1,271	1,087	1,103	853
12. Madhya Pradesh	711	288	481	NA	257	1703	940	1,108	NA	1198
13. Maharashtra	—	1,056	NA	NA	NA	—	1,504	NA	NA	NA
14. Orissa	282	768	1,348	870	558	1,267	1,733	1,869	2,267	2,165
15. Punjab	74	262	368	253	330	380	704	474	430	477
16. Rajasthan	134	246	530	684	NA	305	629	689	310	NA
17. Tamil Nadu	3,628	7,791	455	NA	10,444	6,078	13,524	1,667	NA	8,796
18. Uttar Pradesh	147	—	NA	NA	NA	1,318	—	NA	NA	NA
19. West Bengal	135	216	331	318	445	579	714	985	974	847

Notes: The figures exclude the outturn of the year under consideration.
(—) Implies Discipline does not exist in the state/Data not available.
NA-Not Available.

Source: NTMIS, AICTE, Govt. of India.

Table 5.2.10: Number of Unemployed Engineers by Select States (Electronics)

State	Degree Level					Diploma Level				
	2001	2004	2005	2006	2007	2001	2004	2005	2006	2007
1. Andhra Pradesh	1,236	1,652	NA	NA	4,257	2,537	2,600	NA	NA	4092
2. Assam	9	10	34	22	NA	80	74	151	147	NA
3. Chandigarh	8	11	0	6	16	66	129	8	30	28
4. Chhattisgarh	–	–	–	–	–	–	–	–	–	16
5. Delhi	50	41	122	59	265	232	199	281	301	316
6. Gujarat	310	254	NA	NA	84	192	512	NA	NA	NA
7. Haryana	–	279	343	735	734	–	194	97	572	293
8. Himachal Pradesh	18	59	147	21	887	42	48	51	85	NA
9. Jammu & Kashmir	147	184	173	312	NA	238	286	238	321	294
10. Karnataka	1,365	2,646	3,223	3,415	645	2,504	2,894	2,751	2,581	3,004
11. Kerala	175	224	162	307	13,523	1,497	2,508	1,236	1,345	1,637
12. Madhya Pradesh	737	120	306	NA	NA	411	118	99	NA	173
13. Maharashtra	–	2,718	NA	NA	11,042	–	787	NA	NA	NA
14. Orissa	163	675	1,599	1,514	1,720	642	619	715	1,230	1,507
15. Punjab	142	361	820	488	276	228	1138	1,071	590	566
16. Rajasthan	57	126	392	889	NA	359	437	396	276	NA
17. Tamil Nadu	3,998	9,135	11,808	NA	–	5,189	8,517	7,605	NA	7,924
18. Uttar Pradesh	200	–	NA	NA	NA	2530	--	NA	NA	NA
19. West Bengal	83	196	391	489	649	133	155	229	294	405

Notes: The figures exclude the outturn of the year under consideration.
(—) Implies Discipline does not exist in the state/Data not available.
NA-Not Available.

Source: NTMIS, AICTE, Govt. of India.

Table 5.2.11: Number of Unemployed Engineers by Select States (Mechanical)

State	Degree Level					Diploma Level				
	2001	2004	2005	2006	2007	2001	2004	2005	2006	2007
1. Andhra Pradesh	1,090	3,383	NA	NA	6,441	1,811	1,840	NA	NA	2,977
2. Assam	221	173	293	176	NA	190	146	276	224	NA
3. Chandigarh	15	21	7	8	13	49	67	3	24	33
4. Chhattisgarh	–	–	–	–	266	–	–	–	–	110
5. Delhi	161	77	47	73	154	109	231	154	102	122
6. Gujarat	557	1,627	NA	NA	NA	1,740	2,606	NA	NA	NA
7. Haryana	–	246	166	472	389	–	138	134	194	197
8. Himachal Pradesh	–	37	68	6	NA	24	24	22	31	NA
9. Jammu & Kashmir	163	193	36	149	196	107	142	109	143	120
10. Karnataka	1,399	3,252	1,196	2,556	2,896	2,255	2,797	2,792	2,211	2,417
11. Kerala	304	432	186	390	492	1,143	1,732	1,205	1,369	1,057
12. Madhya Pradesh	602	445	1,015	NA	1,054	1,327	885	877	NA	1,109
13. Maharashtra	–	4,711	NA	NA	NA	–	4,802	NA	NA	NA
14. Orissa	109	698	1,750	1,207	752	1,056	1,154	1,750	2,097	2,018
15. Punjab	127	317	681	279	297	142	434	347	211	290
16. Rajasthan	262	237	299	414	NA	271	297	300	257	NA
17. Tamil Nadu	4,407	8,676	8,567	NA	5,373	6,829	17,307	9,834	NA	5,412
18. Uttar Pradesh	111	–	NA	NA	NA	1,852	–	NA	NA	NA
19. West Bengal	224	541	243	202	375	819	843	1,109	1,366	1,205

Notes: The figures exclude the outturn of the year under consideration.
(–) Implies Discipline does not exist in the state/Data not available.
NA-Not Available.

Source: NTMIS, AICTE, Govt. of India.

Table 5.2.12: Number of Unemployed Engineers by Select States (Metallurgy)

State	Degree Level					Diploma Level				
	2001	2004	2005	2006	2007	2001	2004	2005	2006	2007
1. Andhra Pradesh	20	62	NA	—	59	32	92	NA	—	78
2. Chandigarh	10	14	0	7	0	—	—	—	—	—
3. Chhattisgarh	—	—	—	—	—	—	—	—	—	33
4. Gujarat	27	61	NA	—	—	7	44	NA	—	—
5. Karnataka	5	8	22	19	13	11	29	—	9	16
6. Madhya Pradesh	56	—	—	—	—	118	—	—	—	—
7. Maharashtra	—	NA	—	—	—	—	NA	56	—	—
8. Orissa	10	33	52	58	32	132	377	308	234	121
9. Rajasthan	22	32	15	55	—	—	—	—	—	—
10. Tamil Nadu	44	568	155	—	160	47	—	65	—	42
11. West Bengal	47	39	8	50	46	7	19	10	10	9

Notes: The figures exclude the outturn of the year under consideration.
(—) Implies Discipline does not exist in the state/Data not available.
NA-Not Available.

Source: NTMIS, AICTE, Govt. of India.

Table 5.2.13: Employment Exchange Characteristics

Years	Number of Employment Exchanges $	Number (Lakh)			
		Registration	Vacancies Notified	Placement	Live Register at the end of period
1985	800	58.21	6.75	3.88	262.70
1986	821	55.35	6.23	3.51	301.31
1987	835	60.12	6.01	3.34	302.47
1988	840	59.63	5.43	3.28	300.50
1989	849	65.70	6.00	2.89	327.76
1990	851	65.41	4.91	2.64	346.19
1991	854	62.36	4.59	2.53	363.00
1992	860	53.01	4.20	2.39	367.58
1993	887	55.32	3.85	2.31	362.75
1994	891	59.27	3.96	2.05	366.91
1995	895	58.58	3.86	2.15	367.42
1996	914	58.72	4.24	2.33	374.30
1997	934	63.22	3.93	2.75	391.40
1998	945	58.52	3.59	2.33	400.90
1999	955	59.66	3.29	2.21	403.71
2000	958	60.42	2.85	1.78	413.44
2001	938	55.53	3.04	1.69	419.96
2002	939	50.64	2.20	1.43	411.71
2003	945	54.63	2.56	1.55	413.89
2004	947	53.73	2.75	1.38	404.58
2005	947	54.37	3.49	1.73	393.48
2006	947	72.89	3.58	1.77	414.66

Note: $ At the end of the year.

Source: Directorate General of Employment and Training : *Employment Exchange Statistics, 2007.*

Table 5.2.14: Employment Exchange Assistance to Special* Categoies

(in Lakhs)

Year and Categories	*Registration*	*Placement*	*Total Live Register*
1	2	3	4
2001			
All	55.33	0.18	419.96 (100.00)
Women	15.41	0.31	108.85 (25.92)
Scheduled Caste	–	–	–
Scheduled Tribe	–	–	–
Other Backward Classes	–	–	–
Disabled Persons	0.60	0.04	5.10 (1.21)
2002			
All	50.64	0.14	411.71 (100.00)
Women	13.43	0.26	106.50 (25.87)
Scheduled Caste	–	–	–
Scheduled Tribe	–	–	–
Other Backward Classes	–	–	–
Disabled Persons	0.59	0.03	5.33 (1.23)
2003			
All	54.63	0.16	413.89 (100.00)
Women	14.49	0.27	107.52 (25.98)
Scheduled Caste	7.05	0.19	66.28 (16.01)
Scheduled Tribe	3.47	0.08	23.10 (5.58)
Other Backward Classes	9.23	0.17	82.32 (19.89)
Disabled Persons	0.66	0.05	6.62 (1.60)
2004			
All	53.73	0.14	404.58 (100.00)
Women	15.52	0.25	107.12 (26.48)
Scheduled Caste	7.19	0.16	64.70 (15.99)
Scheduled Tribe	2.78	0.08	22.18 (5.48)
Other Backward Classes	9.52	0.14	82.05 (20.28)
Disabled Persons	0.52	0.03	5.66 (1.40)
2005			
All	54.37	0.17	393.48 (100.00)
Women	16.07	0.32	106.06 (26.95)
Scheduled Caste	6.90	0.17	63.53 (16.14)
Scheduled Tribe	2.73	0.10	22.29 (5.66)
Other Backward Classes	9.43	0.14	79.11 (20.10)
Disabled Persons	0.57	0.03	5.79 (1.47)
2006			
All	25.37	0.31	414.66 (100.00)
Women	–	–	–
Scheduled Caste	–	–	–
Scheduled Tribe	–	–	–
Other Backward Classes	–	–	–
Disabled Persons	–	–	–

Notes: (–) Data is not available.
Figures in parenthesis indicate the percentage of total Live Register.

Source: Ministry of Labour and Employment : *Annual Report, 2006-2007*.

Figure 5.2.D

EMPLOYMENT EXCHANGE CHARACTERISTICS

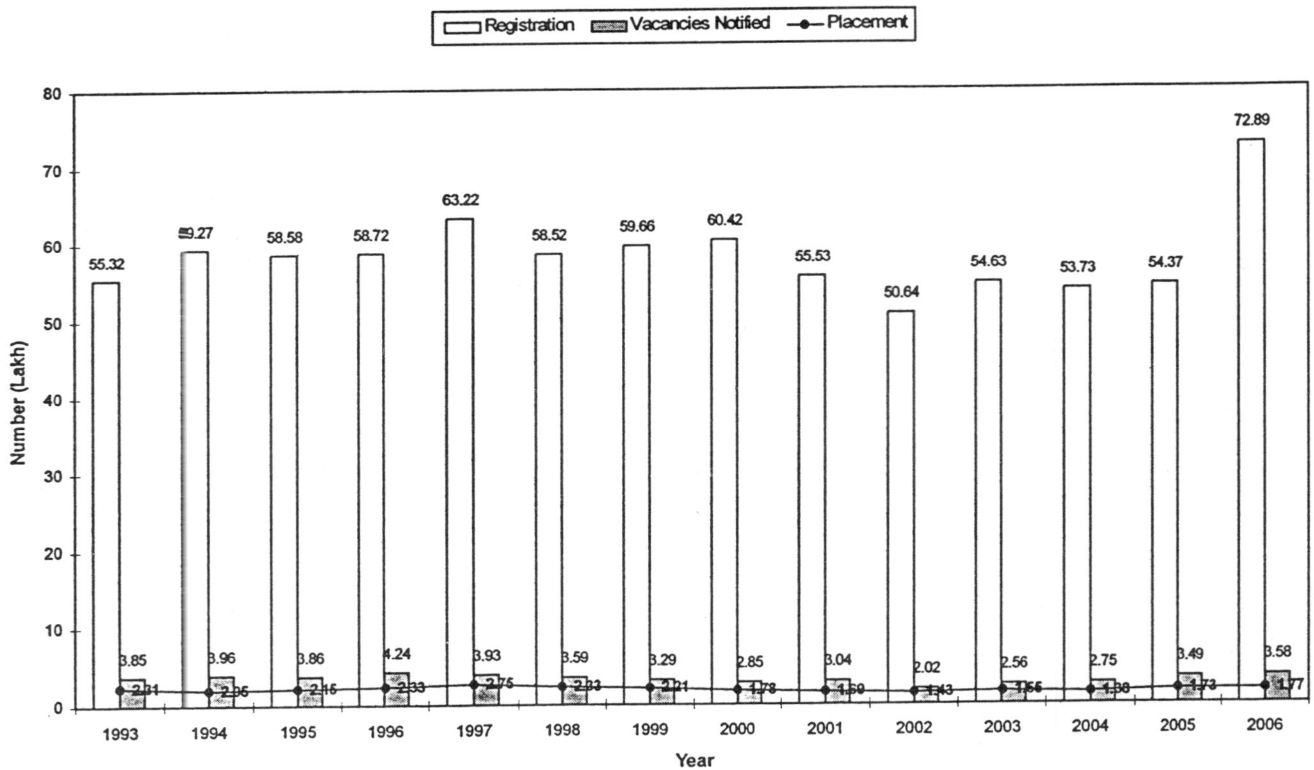

For details see Table 5.2.13

Table 5.2.15: Educational Level of Applicants on Live Register

(*Thousands*)

Educational Level	*1981*	*1986*	*1991*	*1996*	*2001*	*2002*	*2003(P)*	*2004 (P)*
1. Matriculates	5878.1	8682.0	13110.9	14529.7	17337.4	16841.7	17019.8	16,442.6
2. Undergraduates (Including Higher Sec./Intermediate)	2325.5	3806.0	5516.4	6243.2	7681.7	7715.5	7882.4	7,568.1
3. Graduates	1542.9	2306.6	3387.5	3977.3	5273.7	5110.7	5304.6	5,252.5
(i) Arts	751.8	1066.7	1398.3	1614.4	2133.4	2067.4	2145.8	2124.7
(ii) Science	337.2	467.6	659.9	696.9	987.7	957.2	993.5	983.7
(iii) Commerce	251.6	429.1	611.3	640.7	772.1	748.2	776.6	769.0
(iv) Engineering	19.9	38.3	124.3	165.9	216.8	210.1	218.1	216.0
(v) Medicine	15.6	23.8	30.8	28.6	47.6	46.2	48.0	47.5
(vi) Agriculture	13.0	24.9	31.7	27.8	36.1	35.0	36.3	42.8
(vii) Education	127.1	225.6	442.4	632.8	797.6	772.9	802.2	815.5
(viii) Others	26.7	30.4	88.8	170.2	282.4	273.7	284.1	253.2
4. Postgraduates	141.9	293.1	419.7	515.1	**	**	**	**
(i) Arts	81.8	162.9	213.5	261.5	**	**	**	**
(ii) Science	28.0	57.4	90.9	103.6	**	**	**	**
(iii) Commerce	17.8	36.1	57.3	65.7	**	**	**	**
(iv) Engineering	1.6	0.7	4.1	5.5	**	**	**	**
(v) Medicine	0.8	1.9	2.9	3.3	**	**	**	**
(vi) Agriculture	0.9	1.5	2.7	4.7	**	**	**	**
(vii) Education	7.3	22.8	31.5	47.2	**	**	**	**
(viii) Others*	3.7	9.9	16.8	23.7	**	**	**	**
Total	9888.4	15087.7	22434.5	25265.3	29153.6	29667.9	30206.8	29,263.2

Notes: P : Provisional.
* Others includes veterinary, Law and others.
** Included in the Graduates.

Source: Directorate General of Employment and Training: *Employment Exchange Statistics*, 2007.

Figure 5.2.E

APPLICANTS ON LIVE REGISTER BY BROAD EDUCATIONAL LEVEL

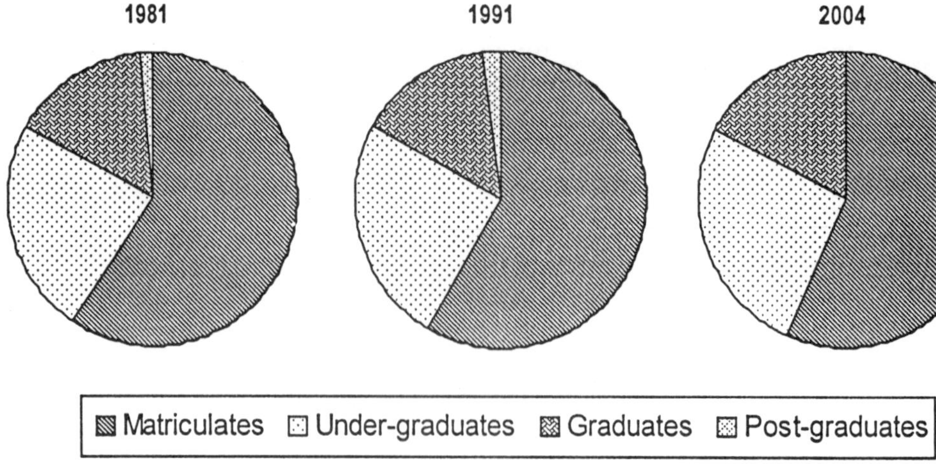

For details see Table 5.2.15

Figure 5.2.F

GRADUATES AND ABOVE APPLICANTS ON LIVE REGISTER BY FACULTY

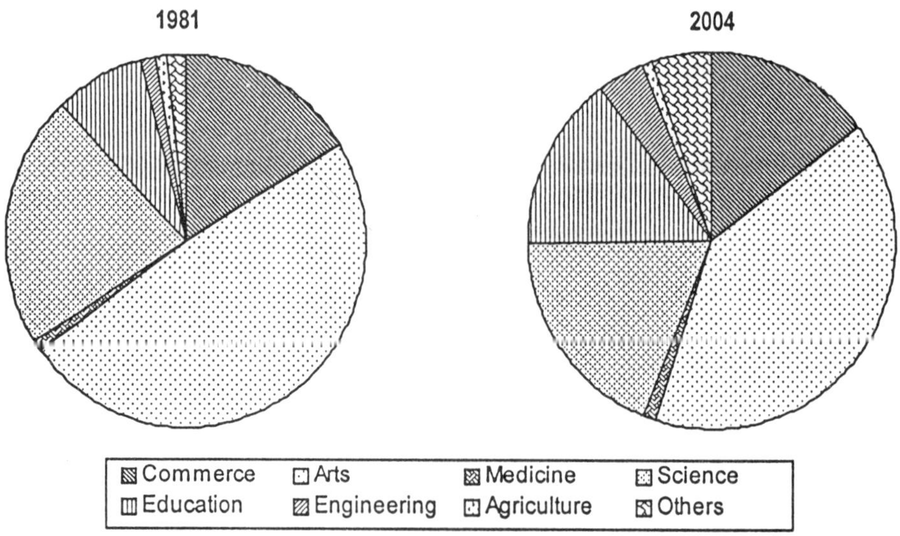

For details see Table 5.2.15

Table 5.2.16: Percentage of Fresh Engineers Absorbed* in Gainful Activities (West Bengal)

Degree

Course	1998	1999	2000	2001	2002	2003
Civil	75	78	80	87	85	90
Mechanical	81	86	71	82	81	82
Electrical	84	85	76	79	85	84
Chemical	87	92	63	85	85	86
Metallurgy	74	77	75	94	78	78
Mining	75	81	100	100	94	95
Electronics	82	100	95	79	85	91
Architecture	71	78	81	100	100	100
Instrumentation and Electronics	76	79	92	90	83	84
Computer Science/Tech.	81	100	84	84	90	93
Agriculture	86	100	100	100	100	100
Leather Tech.	63	71	100	91	91	88
Industrial	100	100	100	100	100	100
Production	82	86	91	93	100	94
Textile	65	79	88	92	88	88
Food Tech.	–	82	70	100	94	92
Energy	–	100	100	100	–	100
Aerospace	–	100	75	100	100	100
Ceramic	–	76	100	100	96	96
Manufacturing	–	100	100	100	94	92
Marine Tech.	–	100	100	100	98	100
Printing	–	100	100	100	89	90
Plastic & Rubber (Polymer Science)	–	90	91	91	92	92
Geology (Polymer Science)	–	–	71	92	100	100
Jute & Fibre Tech.	–	–	77	100	–	86
Power Plant	–	–	100	92	94	94
Applied Physics	–	–	–	–	92	83
Electronics & Instrumentation	–	–	–	–	91	92
Optics & Optics Electronics	–	–	–	–	100	100
Radio Physics & Electronics	–	–	–	–	93	96
Information Tech.	–	–	–	–	91	92
Instrumentation	–	–	–	–	100	100

Diploma

Course	1994	1999	2000	2001	2002	2003
Civil	64	70	66	63	65	62
Mechanical	72	56	68	59	60	59
Electrical	63	64	60	57	58	59
Mining	67	57	67	71	72	96
Architecture	48	84	90	89	89	91
Electronics	76	57	72	71	77	70
Printing Tech.	83	100	85	82	84	84
Instrumentation	78	64	76	78	82	72
Metallurgy	54	82	50	74	72	67
Automobile	90	76	81	71	97	77
Computer Sc.	55	75	55	63	58	65
Chemical	–	90	66	59	73	69
Production	–	–	–	73	100	85
Computer Appl.	–	–	–	–	64	60
Information Tech.	–	–	–	–	–	77
Medical Elec.	–	–	–	–	80	55
Mod. Off. Practice	–	–	–	–	67	100

Notes: * Within two years of completion of the course.

(–) Implies Discipline does not exist in the state/Data not available.

Source: NTMIS, AICTE, Govt. of India.

Table 5.2.17: Percentage of Fresh Engineers Absorbed* in Gainful Activities (Karnataka)

Course	Degree				
	1999	2000	2001	2002	2003
Civil	100	69	67	81	79
Mechanical	73	61	62	83	80
Electrical	71	62	61	78	78
Chemical	68	56	66	80	89
Metallurgy	95	80	71	69	86
Electronics & Telecommn.	78	62	60	83	81
Textile	73	59	63	80	80
Architecture Indl.	71	73	80	63	89
Production	63	58	65	75	76
Instrument Tech.	68	62	87	87	75
Automobile	73	52	52	81	87
Computer Science	82	75	68	88	88
Information Science	80	80	100	91	91
Mining	24	47	67	61	86
Agriculture Tech.	–	79	46	44	81
Bio-Medical	–	66	60	78	90
Ceramic & Cement	–	100	100	100	100
Environment Engg.	–	70	54	50	65
Polymer Tech.	–	42	86	57	100
Printing Tech.	–	65	–	72	100
Telecommunication	–	52	58	86	81
Transportation	–	57	67	100	100

Course	Diploma				
	1999	2000	2001	2002	2003
Civil	66	62	60	72	89
Mechanical	76	61	60	72	71
Electrical	69	63	61	71	65
Chemical	63	81	60	81	76
Metallurgy	84	79	61	86	89
Electronics & Telecommn.	59	57	66	62	59
Textile	100	64	93	75	43
Instrument Tech.	79	60	55	66	76
Automobile	80	57	62	75	66
Cement & Ceramics	–	14	100	100	50
Cinematography	–	84	–	–	–
Architecture	100	89	42	68	71
Heat Power Tech.	100	67	36	84	14
Machine Tool Tech.	86	50	67	91	70
Mining	74	50	69	100	36
Polymer Tech.	100	25	78	59	100
Printing Tech.	100	50	43	93	83
Welding & Sheet Metal	–	67	38	100	100
Business Mgmt.	–	68	19	100	100
Commercial Practice	–	57	57	54	51
Custom Design & Dress Making	–	49	41	43	–
Library Science	–	60	43	33	26
Civil Draftmanship	–	50	50	34	34
Computer Science	–	59	54	58	56
Sugar and Paper	–	–	94		
Others (Leather Tech./Cinemetography/Sound & TV)	–	–	53	85	100
Apparel Design & Fabric Tech.	–	–	–	–	51
Information Science	–	–	–	–	26

Notes: * Within two years of completion of the course. (–) Implies Discipline does not exist in the state/Data not available.

Source: NTMIS, AICTE, Govt. of India.

Table 5.2.18: Percentage of Fresh Engineers Absorbed* in Gainful Activities (Bihar)

Course	Degree				Course	Diploma			
	1983	1984	1993	1994		1983	1984	1993	1994
Civil	63	18	50	67	Civil	34	35	NA	41
Mechanical	80	65	95	82	Mechanical	44	32	23	51
Electrical	74	70	89	77	Electrical	42	30	31	50
Chemical	66	62	47	67	Metallurgy	65	60	61	65
Metallurgy	69	59	82	78	Mining	52	49	40	51
Mining	81	73	100	88	Electronics & Telecommn.	61	53	63	64
Electronics & Telecomm.	73	75	100	84	Textile Tech.	90	78	100	95
Production Engg	69	70	94	67	Ceramics	100	100	100	100
Petroleum	100	100	NA	100					

Note: * Within Two Years of Completion of the Course.

NA – Data not available

Source: NTMIS, AICTE, Govt. of India.

Table 5.2.19: Percentage of Fresh Engineers Absorbed* in Gainful Activities (Uttar Pradesh)

	Degree						*Diploma*					
Course	*1985*	*1988*	*1994*	*1998*	*1999*	*Course*	*1984*	*1985*	*1988*	*1994*	*1998*	*1999*
Civil	77	72	82	63	71	Civil	65	57	46	67	41	54
Mechanical	90	93	93	80	84	Mechanical	52	66	59	62	60	41
Electrical	86	100	98	85	87	Electrical	46	65	43	59	43	48
Chemical	89	100	94	100	100	Chemical	93	100	100	91	100	65
Metallurgy	99	88	98	–	–	Electronics	78	56	72	75	44	41
Mining	100	100	100	–	–	Architecture	76	75	54	84	–	–
Electronics	88	100	98	88	80	Leather Tech.	100	100	58	82	–	–
Aeronautical	100	100	100	–	–	Ceramics	100	100	85	92	–	–
Architecture	100	100	100	–	–	Computer	–	–	–	–	100	89
Industrial Engg.	100	100	96	–	–	Dairy Engg.	94	90	78	77	–	–
Textile	82	86	100	88	100	Foot Wear						
Plastic Tech.	94	100	100	–	–	Tech.	75	100	57	79	–	–
Bio-Chemical	100	100	97	–	–	Automobile	57	57	65	67	–	–
Food Tech.	94	100	96	–	–	Material Mgmt.	55	73	80	75	–	–
Paint Tech.	100	100	100	–	–	Refrigerator &						
Oil Tech.	95	88	100	–	–	Air Condn.	71	100	72	75	–	–
Leather Tech.	90	100	100	–	–	Tool Tech.	71	–	–	–	–	–
Computer Sc.	100	100	100	100	100	Public Health	48	–	–	99	–	–
Agriculture	68	84	78	67	–	Production	76	–	–	69	–	–
Ceramics	100	100	100	–	–	Construction						
Man-Made						Tech.	–	–	–	–	–	–
Fibre Tech.	100	100	100	–	–	Printing Tech.	77	100	100	89	–	100
Production	–	–	–	100	–	Sales Mgt.	46	100	89	75	–	–
Paper Tech.	100	–	–	–	–	Instrument						
Textile Tech.	100	100	100	–	–	and Control	86	100	93	90	–	–

Notes: * Within two years of completion of the course.
(–) Implies Discipline does not exist in the state/Data not avavilable.
Source: NTMIS, AICTE, Govt. of India.

Table 5.2.20: Percentage of Fresh Engineers Absorbed* in Gainful Activities (Madhya Pradesh)

Degree

Course	1999	2000	2001	2002	2003
Civil	22	44	90	61	100
Mechanical	53	80	44	49	94
Electrical	64	76	46	36	94
Chemical	74	62	29	23	78
Mining	53	—	—	-	—
Electronics	71	74	20	38	100
Electronics and Telecommn.	48	77	42	17	86
Architecture	28	33	37	16	92
Computer	78	71	66	48	93
Industial Production	36	69	100	29	100
Electrical and Instrurmentation	34	78	61	20	100
Agriculture Engg.	73	89	84	-	—
Appropiate Tech.	34	—	—	-	—
B.Pharma	40	44	—	-	—
Food Tech.	53	—	—	-	—
Textile	33	48	43	43	80
Production Engg.	—	—	21	-	—
Automobile	—	—	—	—	100
Fire Tech.	—	—	—	—	87
Information Tech.	—	—	—	—	96

Diploma

Course	1999	2000	2001	2002	2003
Civil	27	42	31	26	52
Mechanical	48	43	44	18	50
Electrical	45	31	24	18	41
Mining	6	65	32	32	—
Electronics and Telecommn.	30	39	13	17	88
Architecture	30	61	89	65	67
Printing Tech.	47	33	—	-	47
Textile Tech.	66	24	74	-	—
Automobile	92	92	—	36	54
Costume Design and Dress Making	17	33	6	18	3
Optometry and Refraction	67	65	92	19	—
Medical Lab. Tech.	37	50	38	17	9
Chemical	20	28	—	-	—
Computer	69	36	13	43	81
Production Engg.	25	55	38	51	—
Applied Videography	39	32	—	-	—
Cement Tech.	37	25	78	78	80
Electronics	53	42	18	14	47
Food Tech.	41	—	16	75	60
Garment Tech.	57	36	—	-	—
Interior Decor.	43	50	35	27	60
Manufacturing	74	25	—	-	—
Petrochemical	100	17	—	-	71
Pharmacy	28	—	—	-	—
Plastic Tech.	29	27	33	22	60
Refrigiration & A.C.	82	66	—	-	—
Elect. & Inst.	57	—	—	-	—
Industrial Elex.	30	88	—	-	—
Modern Office Mgt.	22	40	16	30	43
Beauty Culture	—	15	33	100	100
C.T.M.	—	44	—	-	100
Mechatronics	—	73	—	-	-
P.D.C.A.		43	-	-	100
Mining & Mine Survey	—	—	26	34	49
Textile Design	—	—	50	55	60

Notes: * Within two years of completion of course.

(—) Implies Discipline does not exist in the state/Data not available.

Source: NTMIS, AICTE, Govt. of India.

Table 5.2.21: Percentage of Fresh Engineers Absorbed* in Gainful Activities (Maharashtra)

Course	Degree 1994	1996	1999	2001
Civil	96	91	46	68
Mechanical	93	95	58	79
Electrical	87	97	55	80
Chemical	96	96	70	83
Metallurgy	93	93	100	63
Electronics & Telecom.	96	97	100	60
Production	87	87	51	68
Aeronautical	100	100	100	50
Instrumentation	100	89	100	57
Textile Mfg.	96	100	100	60
Architecture	96	100	76	78
Textile Chemistry	—	100	80	87
Food Tech.	87	100	75	69
Oil Tech.	100	78	100	68
Plastic Tech.	100	77	100	59
Petrochemical Tech.	90	100	100	75
Pharmaceutical Engg.	95	100	87	—
Cellulose Tech.	100	100	100	55
Intermediate Dye Tech.	100	100	100	—
Automobile	—	—	—	72
Computer Science	—	—	—	83
Construction	—	—	—	58
Paint Tech.	—	—	—	76
Printing Tech.	—	—	—	59
Power Electronics	—	—	—	63
Agricultural	—	—	—	43
Bio-Medical	—	—	—	100
Sugar Engg.	—	—	—	52

Course	Diploma 1994	1996	1999	2000
Civil	93	90	49	78
Mechanical	100	87	63	75
Electrical	95	100	62	74
Chemical	92	61	69	70
Metallurgy	95	71	84	66
Mining	93	79	60	50
Electronics	94	71	70	63
Textile Mfg.	97	90	70	68
Food Tech.	100	86	100	62
Plastic Tech.	97	67	62	64
Petrochemical Tech.	—	—	—	88
Production	96	100	83	81
Sound and T.V.	—	—	—	50
Man-Made Fibre	100	83	67	36
Textile Tech	100	96	51	70
Leather Tech.	100	86	82	52
Digital Electronics	—	100	68	71
Dress Making and Fashion Tech.	—	100	100	47
Knitting Tech.	92	90	75	43
Letter Press	—	100	60	57
Offset Printing	—	—	—	52
Computer Tech.	—	—	—	61
Medical Electronics	—	—	—	79
Interior Design	—	—	—	71
Plant Engg.	—	—	—	54
Automobile	—	—	—	59
Electrical Power System	—	—	—	97
Electronics & Radio	—	—	—	50
Information Tech.	—	—	—	83
Fibre Mfg.	—	—	—	46

Notes: * Within two year of completion of course.
(—) Implies Discipline does not exist in the state/Data not available.

Source: NTMIS, AICTE, Govt. of India.

Table 5.2.22 Percentage of Fresh Engineers Absorbed* in Gainful Activities (Andhra Pradesh)

Degree

Course	1998	1999	2000	2001	2003
Civil	67	57	54	56	48
Mechanical	59	53	46	36	46
Electrical	60	67	48	59	49
Chemical	59	50	43	31	37
Metallurgy	50	68	66	50	62
Mining	82	50	35	57	72
Electronics and Telecommn.	75	55	67	57	45
Automobile	61	–	–	–	–
Electronics & Control Eng.	53	–	–	–	53
Architecture	80	46	66	100	34
Marine Engg.	75	100	–	–	–
Computer Science	89	64	65	54	56
Production Engg.	44	59	38	28	35
Bio Medical	100	66	–	20	58
Instrumentation	–	–	58	50	58
Printing	–	–	77	–	84
Food Processing	–	–	77	46	–
Electronics & Instrumentation	–	–	–	32	49
Information Technology	–	–	–	66	58
Textile Technology	–	–	–	100	74
Electronics & Communication Engg.	–	–	–	–	48

Diploma

Course	1998	1999	2000	2001	2003
Civil	51	56	49	48	44
Mechanical	44	49	43	50	54
Electrical	53	47	29	42	46
Chemical	64	63	38	43	52
Metallurgy	67	–	67	14	56
Mining	90	45	37	29	51
Computer Engg.	41	44	35	34	67
Architectural Asstt. ship	49	40	78	43	50
Printing Tech.	79	27	–	–	51
Textile Tech.	64	–	55	100	72
Ceramics	69	–	–	19	56
Leather Tech.	100	–	–	–	–
Electronics & Communication	–	33	32	13	37
Automobile	–	36	49	45	48
Hotel Mgt.	–	50	–	–	–
Electronics & Instrument	–	41	–	–	–
Bio-Medical Engg.	–	–	–	80	44
Computer & Commercial Practice	–	–	–	35	36
Electrical Instrumentaion Engg.	–	–	34	34	
Garment Tech.	–	–	–	32	57
Footware Tech.	–	–	–	–	66
Sugar Tech.	–	–	–	–	44
TV & Sound Engg.	–	–	–	–	62

Notes: * Within two years of completion

(–) Implies discipline does not exist in the state/Data not available.

Source: NTMIS, AICTE, Govt. of India.

Table 5.2.23: Percentage of Fresh Engineers Absorbed* in Gainful Activities (Assam)

Degree

Course	1998	1999	2000	2002
Civil	57	54	65	59
Mechanical	56	100	63	66
Electrical	65	59	51	56
Chemical	100	100	95	84
Electronics and Telecommn.	100	100	94	88
Computer Science	100	100	93	95
Instrumentation	42	100	50	48

Diploma

Course	1998	1999	2000	2002
Civil	21	55	26	39
Mechanical	19	46	24	34
Electrical	14	46	15	15
Chemical	18	–	38	22
Textile	0	100	14	50
Electronics and Telecommn.		48	40	36
Handloom Technology	78	67	46	100
Architectural Asstt.	100	–	38	60
Automobile	100	–	–	22
Computer Engg.	–	57	29	48
Textile Chem.	–	15	44	–

Notes: * Within two years of completion of course.

(–) Implies Discipline does not exist in the state/Data not available.

Source: NTMIS, AICTE, Govt. of India.

Table 5.2.24: Percentage of Fresh Engineers Absorbed* in Gainful Activities (Kerala)

Course	*Degree* 2000	2001	2002	2003**
Civil	61	82	72	78
Mechanical	77	100	83	86
Electrical	77	84	100	84
Electronics and commn.	93	100	100	100
Naval Arch.	92	100	100	100
Chemical	69	100	100	55
Computer Sc.	91	100	100	100
Industrial Engg.	89	100	100	100
Production-cum-Plant Engg.	61	100	89	100
Architectural Engg.	78	100	100	100
Instrumentation and Control	76	100	100	100
Bio-Medical	92	100	100	85
Agriculture	–	100	–	70
Applied Electronics & Instrumentation	–	100	71	100
Fire Art	–	75	100	–
Information Technology	–	100	100	100
Polymer Engineering	–	100	77	55
Polymer Scinece & Rubber Technology	–	79	70	100
Safety & Fire Engg.	–	100	100	100
Electronics & Instrumentation	–	–	–	100

Course	*Diploma* 2000	2001	2002	2003
Civil	40	48	48	50
Mechanical	36	38	41	52
Electrical	45	37	33	47
Electronics	59	45	45	38
Textile	38	58	42	38
Printing	46	33	46	48
Automobile	53	51	67	60
Chemical	30	12	26	21
Polymer Tech.	31	82	74	60
Instrumentation Tech.	30	12	22	45
Applied Electronics	42	55	50	50
Architecture Engg.	100	100	70	77
Computer	63	51	50	50
Wood Tech.	79	100	80	88
Tool & Die	72	100	62	100
Medical Electronics	64	82	70	92
Telecommunication	–	50	48	57
Bio-medical	–	54	54	43
Commercial Practice	–	24	26	14
Computer Appl. & Business Mgmt.	–	20	26	47
Computer Hardware Maint.	–	58	52	64
Electronics & Avionics	–	45	–	70
Electronics & Communication	–	38	36	40
Electronics & Instrumentation	–	31	39	45
Electronics & Production	–	54	47	45
Quantity Survey & Construction Management	–	100	–	–
Information Tech.	–	–	–	52

Notes: * Within two years of completion of the course.

** With in one year of completion of the course.

(–) Implies Discipline does not exist in the state/Data not available.

Source: NTMIS, AICTE, Govt. of India.

Table 5.2.25: Percentage of Fresh Engineers Absorbed* in Gainful Activities (Chandigarh)

	Degree						*Diploma*				
Course	*1998*	*1999*	*2000*	*2002*	*2003*	*Course*	1998	1999	2000	2002	2003
Architecture	81	97	84	100	100	Architecture	66	44	53	50	67
Aeronautical	75	67	100	100	78	Civil	100	75	25	54	92
Civil	75	65	52	68	100	Electrical	49	24	32	44	70
Chemical	76	98	78	87	86	Electronics	31	14	26	65	64
Electrical	84	69	80	83	100	Mechanical	67	93	44	67	65
Electronics	96	100	93	94	100	Interior Decoration	26	51	58	100	37
Mechanical	100	100	84	92	84	Library Sc.	–	21	–	–	25
Metallurgy	42	92	74	100	100	Instrumentation	–	–	–	–	100
Production	100	96	79	85	80	Med. Lab. Tech.	–	–	–	–	48
Computer Sc.	–	100	100	87	100	Modern Office Practice	–	–	–	–	29
Fine Arts	–	–	–	–	33						
Food Tech.	–	–	–	–	100						

Notes: * Within two years of completion of the course.

(–) Implies Discipline does not exist in the state/Data not avaliable.

Source: NTMIS, AICTE, Govt. of India.

Table 5.2.26: Percentage of Fresh Engineers Absorbed* in Gainful Activities (Tamil Nadu)

Degree

Course	1994	1998	1999	2001	2003
Aerospace	—	—	—	50	180
Applied Electronics & Instrumentation	—	—	—	62	60
Applied Geology	—	—	—	22	47
Applied Math	—	—	—	17	81
Applied Science	—	—	—	6	44
Automobile	84	48	67	54	59
Agriculture	90	—	68	24	62
Architecture	100	70	43	30	75
Aeronautical	71	100	56	38	87
Civil	83	50	62	38	69
Chemical	81	63	47	23	60
Ceramic Tech.	100	—	—	—	—
Computer Sc.	92	64	63	35	61
Electrical	80	100	60	43	33
Electronics and Comm.	90	51	50	33	60
Electrical & Electronics	—	55	44	27	56
Electronics & Instrumentation	—	100	82	40	67
Electronics	95	100	—	31	68
Instrumentation	95	47	50	44	56
Industrial Engg.	—	70	60	5	58
Industrial Management	85	—	50	40	38
Leather Tech.	100	40	41	11	75
Mechanical	83	51	51	29	73
Metallurgical	98	43	58	11	72
Mining	—	70	70	33	76
Naval Architecture	96	100	40	—	100
Production Engg.	90	64	51	60	—
Transport Engg.	—	—	85	35	56
Ocean Engg.	—	—	59	42	78
Rubber Tech.	—	—	74	47	100
Petroleum Engg.	—	—	53	—	57
Polymer	—	—	—	50	79
Textile Tech.	—	—	—	47	67
Urban Engg.	—	—	—	33	61
Geo Information	—	—	—	44	75
Geo Engg.	—	—	—	52	83
Industrial Bio Tech.	—	—	—	30	81
Information Tech.	—	—	—	40	65
Instrumentation & Control Engg.	—	—	—	31	53
Instrument Tech.	—	—	—	50	50
Printing Tech.	—	—	—	41	54
Plastic & Rubber Tech.	—	—	—	—	56
Production Tech.	—	—	—	—	51
Structual Engg.	—	—	—	—	59
Applied Chemistry	—	—	—	—	76
Applied Physics	—	—	—	—	56
Avionics Engg.	—	—	—	—	100
Bio-Technology	—	—	—	—	53
Marine Engg.	—	—	—	—	58
Mechatronics Engg.	—	—	—	—	100

Diploma

Course	1994	1998	1999	2001	2003
Agri. & Farm Equipment	—	—	—	27	46
Ceramic	—	—	—	16	82
Foundary Tech.	—	—	—	15	40
Garments	—	—	—	16	59
Industrical Electronics	—	—	—	41	59
Industrical Safety	—	—	—	13	68
Automobile	82	37	46	13	53
Agriculture Engg.	50	48	26	9	60
Architecture Asstt.	92	32	33	—	48
Aeronautical	100	—	—	—	—
Civil Engg.	81	47	59	47	61
Chemical	79	42	38	10	66
Commercial Practice	81	31	20	7	45
Costume Design and Dress Making	100	37	14	12	52
Electrical Engg.	73	—	60	28	51
Electronics and Comm.	—	30	40	—	47
Electronics	82	—	33	36	43
Instrument Tech.	100	100	—	87	40
Leather Tech.	96	47	51	32	45
Mechanical Engg.	76	46	41	10	70
Machine Tool Repairs	—	89	42	26	80
Printing Tech.	88	43	69	24	56
Polymer Tech.	92	47	19	—	45
Production Tech.	100	43	100	20	66
Paint Tech.	100	—	34	—	50
Refrigeration & AC	100	67	67	8	65
Textile Tech.	85	69	69	26	69
Tool Design	—	67	39	10	—
Textile Processing	—	91	67	21	68
Textile Design	—	42	19	42	76
Computer Tech.	—	44	36	9	50
Mining Geology	—	—	58	20	—
Textile Mfg.	—	—	47	53	63
Petrochemicals Tech.	—	—	40	7	33
Information Tech.	—	—	—	33	58
Intermediates & Dyes.	—	—	—	60	—
Design & Drafting	—	—	—	33	65
Knitting Tech.	—	—	—	10	50
Man-made Fibre	—	—	—	17	58
Mechatronics	—	—	—	50	60
Tool & Die	—	—	—	10	63
Civil & Rural Engg.	—	—	—	—	26
Cosmetology	—	—	—	—	66
Electrical & Electronics	—	—	—	—	51
Footwear Tech.	—	—	—	—	56
Instrumentation & Control Engg.	—	—	—	—	63
Instrumentation Engg.	—	—	—	—	59
Marine Engg.	—	—	—	—	65
Metallurgy	—	—	—	—	63
Paper Technology	—	—	—	—	70
Electronics Instrumentation	—	—	—	—	63
Petroleum Engg.	—	—	—	—	64
Plastic & Rubber Tech.	—	—	—	—	52
Production Engg.	—	—	—	—	31
Sugar Tech.	—	—	—	—	57

Notes: * Within two years of completion of the course.
(—) Implies discipline does not exist in the state/Data not available.

Source: NTMIS, AICTE, Govt. of India.

Table 5.2.27: Percentage of Fresh Engineers Absorbed* in Gainful Activities (Rajasthan)

Degree

Course	1998	1999	2000	2002
Civil	46	35	51	48
Chemical	87	83	62	84
Agriculture	17	27	75	53
Computer Tech.	72	92	100	88
Electrical	70	45	72	60
Electronics	69	69	89	72
Electrical & Electronics	—	—	92	88
Architecture	43	43	23	64
Mechanical	69	67	73	70
Metallurgical	69	79	61	46
Mining	57	31	31	37
Instrumentation	78	62	91	70
Information System	—	—	100	72
Textile Chem.	—	—	100	100
Textile Tech.	—	—	58	83
Production & Industrial Engg.	—	—	64	55
Engineer Teem	—	—	—	100

Diploma

Course	1998	1999	2000	2002
Automobile	—	100	50	73
Civil	35	45	44	55
Costume Design	38	40	26	20
Electrical	24	25	32	52
Electronics	35	33	42	60
Mechanical	48	47	49	58
Mining	—	67	—	—
Production	—	97	100	100
Refrigeration & AC	—	—	33	100
Textile	—	44	36	40
Computer	43	58	72	36
Chemical	21	33	47	60
Architecture	—	—	86	100
Instrumentation	—	—	47	67
Printing Tech.	—	—	46	100
Agriculture	—	—	29	29

Notes: * Within two years of completion of the course.
(—) Implies discipline does not exist in the state/Data not available.
Source: NTMIS, AICTE, Govt. of India.

Table 5.2.28: Percentage of Fresh Engineers Absorbed* in Gainful Activities (Chhattisgarh)

Degree

Course	2003
Civil	82
Chemical	87
Computer	96
Ele. & Tele. Communication	83
Electrical	82
Information Technology	93
Mechanical	79
Mining	73

Diploma

Course	2003
Architecture	100
CDDM	33
Civil	67
Computer	50
Ele. & Tele. Communication	24
Electrical	44
Electronics	67
Interior Decoration	63
Instrumentation Control	33
Information Tech.	38
Mechanical	66
Mettalurgy	77
Mining & Mine Survey	38
Modern Office Mgt.	54

Notes: * Within two years of completion of the course.
(—) Implies discipline does not exist in the state/Data not available.
Source: NTMIS, AICTE, Govt. of India.

Table 5.2.29: Percentage of Fresh Engineers Absorbed* in Gainful Activities (Orissa)

Course	Degree 1998	1999	2000	2001	2002	2003
Civil	66	73	71	40	77	80
Chemical	67	77	84	47	55	70
Electrical Engg.	62	72	72	40	63	67
Electronics & Comm.	62	73	79	36	58	52
Mechanical	65	72	71	41	56	66
Metallurgy	65	65	89	66	72	81
Mining	67	50	42	30	85	72
Computer Science	72	87	78	33	69	67
Electronics	—	49	—	24	—	—
Textile	61	100	81	50	42	79
Applied Electric	—	78	89	71	—	—
Agriculture	—	56	56	17	53	17
Architecture Engg.	—	65	64	70	71	69
Ceramic Engg.	—	100	100	65	80	90
Manufacturing Sc.	—	—	67	84	78	68
Applied Electronics & Instrument Engg.	—	—	89	71	—	—
Instrumentation	—	—	88	—	—	—
Electrical & Electro. Engg.	—	—	—	—	—	70
Electro. & Instru. Engg.	—	—	—	—	—	77
Information Tech.	—	—	—	—	—	76

Course	Diploma 1998	1999	2000	2001	2002	2003
Automobile	19	30	17	27	31	18
Architecture	20	—	33	73	25	33
Civil	18	14	17	15	17	20
Chemical	15	16	48	15	15	—
Electronics & Teleco.	13	7	11	10	13	15
Electrical Engg.	14	8	8	8	14	19
Mechanical	17	14	14	10	18	26
Metallurgy	26	12	8	15	32	37
Mining	13	14	7	23	23	38
Textile Technology	70	19	67	33	25	25
Computer Science	14	26	8	19	31	18
Chemical	27	—	48	—	15	9
Food Processing & Preservation	—	25	28	21	29	8
Hotel Mgt. & Catering Tech.	—	15	100	—	—	—
Garment Designing & Dress Making	—	17	58	67	83	28
Rural Tech	—	—	33	11	36	—
Cinemetography	—	—	—	75	53	20
Film & Video Editing	—	—	—	50	100	31
Sound & TV Engg.	—	—	—	25	54	21
Computer Prog. & Application	—	—	—	23	33	40
Applied Electronics & Instrument Engg.	—	—	—	7	47	30
Modern Office Management	—	—	—	11	13	13
Beauty Culture	—	—	—	—	—	33
Ceranic Engg.	—	—	—	—	—	42
Drilling Engg.	—	—	—	—	—	25
Information Tech.	—	—	—	—	—	7
Lib. & Information Sc.	—	—	—	—	—	17
Plastics Mould Tech.	—	—	—	—	—	83
Tool & Die Making	—	—	—	—	—	75

Notes: * Within two years of completion of the course.
(—) Implies discipline does not exist in the state/Data not available.

Source: NTMIS, AICTE, Govt. of India.

Table 5.2.30: Percentage of Fresh Engineers Absorbed* in Gainful Activities (Gujarat)

	Degree					*Diploma*			
Course	*1994*	*1998*	*1999*	*2000*	*Course*	*1994*	*1998*	*1999*	*2000*
Civil	81	65	61	59	Automobile	75	60	53	35
Chemical	91	67	62	57	Architectural	74	64	57	62
Electrical	88	64	52	49	Civil	69	56	60	59
Electronics	88	71	70	73	Ceramic	72	—	62	58
Mechanical	91	74	59	58	Chemical	—	45	37	27
Metallurgy	96	—	78	21	Commercial Practice	74	—	—	19
					Dairy	97	—	—	—
Production	88	65	52	24	Electrical	76	38	27	28
Textile	92	72	NA	—	Mechanical	79	55	43	40
Dairy	88	97	92	86	Metallurgical	96	54	—	38
Instrumentation					Man-Made				
and Control	82	70	62	65	Fibre Tech.	85	—	48	48
Architecture	97	64	74	53	Printing Tech.	91	40	57	66
Rubber Technology	—	100	58	60	Electrical & Radio	—	—	—	—
Plastic Technology	—	60	78	70	Textile Chemistry	—	44	65	80
Industrial Engg.	—	90	27	38	Textile Manuf.	91	70	46	53
Computer Engg.	—	85	68	80	Computer Engg.	—	56	55	35
Agriculture Engg.	—	—	70	63	Electronics &				
Construction	—	—	75	66	Comm.	—	44	55	36
Environmental Engg.	—	—	65	31	Instrumentation				
Power Electronics	—	—	81	50	& Control Engg.	—	44	47	54
Textile Tech.	—	—	80	59	Petrochemical	—	54	46	49
Textile Engg.	—	—	79	95	Plastic Engg.	—	—	36	39
Interior Design	—	—	79	67	Power Electro.	—	—	41	25
Water Resources Mang.	—	—	65	72	Textile Tech.	—	—	45	36
Textile Processing	—	—	100	57	Textile Processing	—	—	54	48
Pharmacy	—	—	55	—	Water Resource				
Information Tech.	—	—	—	47	Mgt.	—	—	67	—
Electronics & Comm.	—	—	—	69	Pharmacy	—	—	37	—

Notes: * Within two years of completion of the course.
(—) Implies discipline does not exist in the state/Data not available.
Source: NTMIS, AICTE, Govt. of India.

Table 5.2.31: Percentage of Fresh Engineers Absorbed* in Gainful Activities (Jammu & Kashmir)

Degree

Course	1994	1997	1999	2000	2002	2003
Civil	50	14	71	22	76	61
Chemical	100	—	—	29	—	90
Electrical	67	23	33	50	25	47
Electronics & Communication	34	—	69	8	27	48
Mechanical	80	—	45	43	86	39
Metallurgical	100	—	—	—	—	—
Computer Tech.	—	—	—	95	91	44
Information Tech.	—	—	—	—	—	52

Diploma

Course	1994	1997	1999	2000	2002	2003
Automobile	100	—	—	60	—	8
Civil	37	24	35	12	50	33
Electrical	68	48	24	27	34	38
Mechanical	58	12	34	50	33	52
Architecture	24	24	56	50	56	20
Electronics and comm.	50	52	31	5	16	23
Computer	—	—	24	59	77	32
Textile	—	—	—	18	—	—
Agri.	—	—	—	—	12	8
Modern Office Practice	—	—	—	—	—	56
Commercial Practice		—	—	—	25	—

Notes: * Within two years of completion of the course.
(—) Implies discipline does not exist in the state/Data not available.
Source: NTMIS, AICTE, Govt. of India.

Table 5.2.32: Percentage of Fresh Engineers Absorbed* in Gainful Activities (Punjab)

Degree

Course	2000	2001	2002	2003
Agriculture	76	88	79	88
Civil	60	45	77	95
Electrical	51	41	65	75
Instrumentation	[illegible]	92	84	86
Mechanical	66	57	86	86
Electronics	67	58	77	82
Textile Tech.	58	64	86	84
Production Engg.	58	56	68	100
Industrial Engg.	43	78	72	100
Chemical	56	45	70	86
Computer Science	75	81	87	94
Architecture	—	53	100	100
Food Technology	—	76	100	79
Leather Technology	—	30	100	100
Textile Chem.	—	—	—	100
Information Tech.	—	—	—	67

Diploma

Course	2000	2001	2002	2003
Civil	43	32	66	67
Electrical	20	30	28	53
Footwear Tech.	—	55	33	100
Knitting Tech.	100	76	79	82
Leather Tech.	70	58	100	80
Mechanical	56	49	69	80
Architecture	45	21	37	59
Textile Tech.	79	70	52	80
Electronics	38	18	34	55
Chemical	49	42	61	67
Computer Sci.	39	43	36	67
Garment Tech.	40	28	54	71
Library Sci.	19	21	—	—
Medical Lab Tech.	41	50	—	41
Production	35	42	33	75
Textile Chemistry	84	59	79	67
M.O.P.	24	19	27	49
Tool & Die Tech.	63	36	100	88
Plastic Tech.	60	68	75	81
Instrumentation	—	39	38	53
Civil Aerodrome	—	—	—	100
Fashion Design	—	—	—	57
Textile Design	—	—	—	74

Notes: * Within two years of completion of the course.
(—) Implies discipline does not exist in the state/Data not available.
Source: NTMIS, AICTE, Govt. of India.

(iii) Supply

Table 5.3.1: Estimated Stock of Graduates in Select Professional Courses

Years	*Medicine (Allopathy)*	*Dentistry*	*Agriculture Science*	*Veterinary Science*
1971	123,500	3,950	58,950	14,840
1981	219,510	8,000	105,750	24,430
1985	253,410	9,790	130,490	28,150
1991*	296,400	13,930	168,360	34,360
1992*	304,000	14,770	174,950	35,470
1993*	312,000	15,670	181,630	36,610
1994*	320,750	16,630	188,420	37,790
1995*	330,000	17,600	195,200	39,000
1996*	339,800	18,600	202,300	40,200
1997*	349,800	19,700	209,400	41,400
1998*	359,700	20,700	216,500	42,700
1999*	369,900	21,800	223,800	44,000
2000*	380,500	22,900	231,200	45,300
2001*	391,900	24,000	238,600	46,700

Notes: Stock is taken at the beginning of the year.
* Projected.

Source: IAMR, *Estimates of Stock of Different Categories of Educated Manpower up to 2001 A.D.*

Table 5.3.2: Estimated Stock of Postgraduates in General Education

Years	*Arts*	*Science*	*Commerce*
1971	438,820	134,910	48,270
1981	1,113,570	292,360	148,300
1985	1,499,340	360,610	230,210
1991*	2,185,340	482,050	403,640
1992*	2,327,140	507,480	441,110
1993*	2,475,630	534,370	481,050
1994*	2,631,200	562,790	523,780
1995*	2,797,600	593,400	570,500
1996*	2,973,000	626,100	620,600
1997*	3,151,700	660,300	673,600
1998*	3,341,300	695,500	728,500
1999*	3,526,300	730,600	783,800
2000*	3,718,400	767,100	841,700
2001*	3,917,278	805,041	902,504

Notes: Stock is taken at the beginning of the year.
* Projected.

Source: IAMR, *Estimates of Stock of Different Categories of Educated Manpower up to 2001 A.D.*

Figure 5.3.G

STOCK OF GRADUATES AND ABOVE IN SELECT PROFESSIONAL COURSES

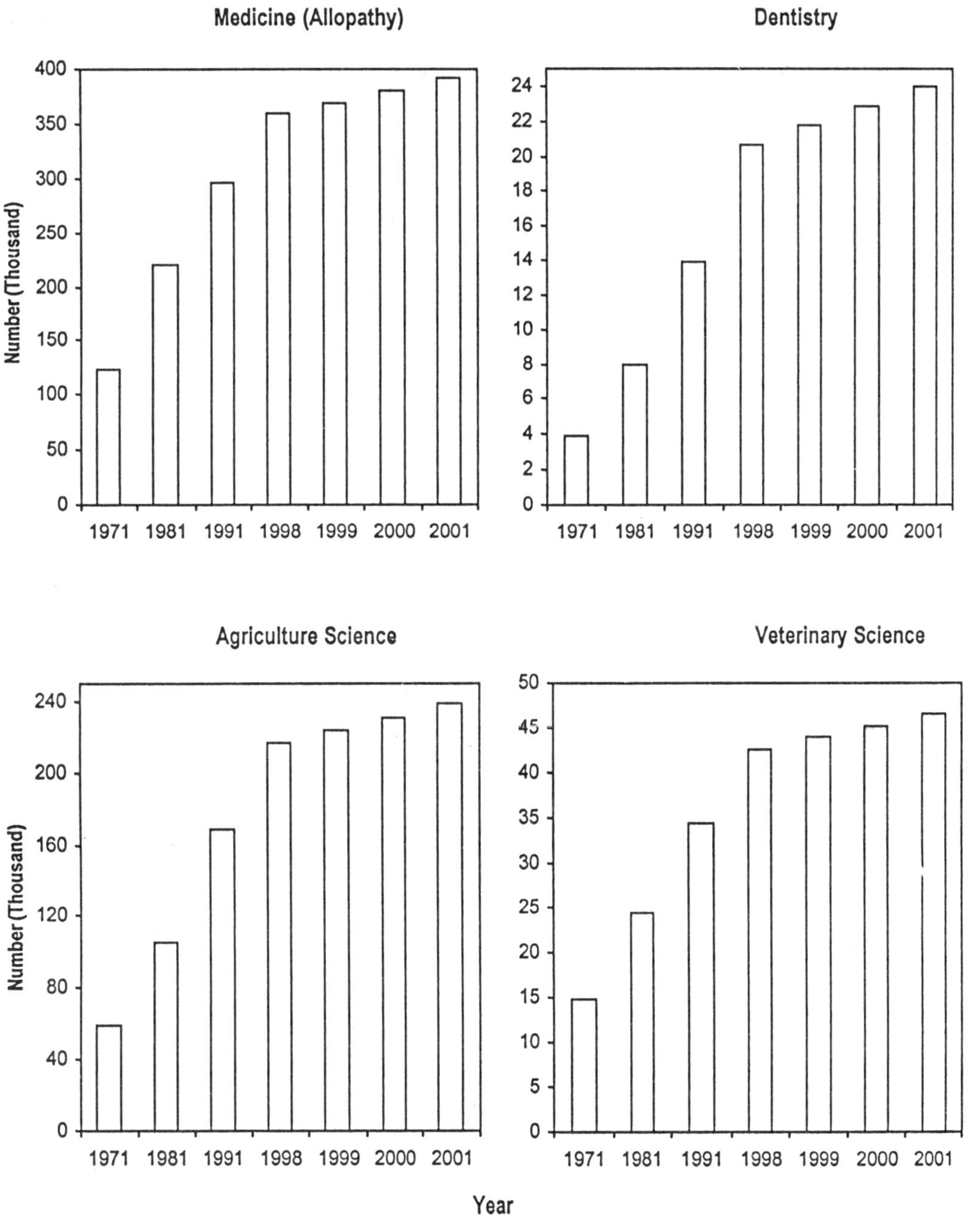

For details see Table 5.3.1

Table 5.3.3: Estimated Stock of Graduates in General Education

Years	*Arts*	*Science*	*Commerce*
1971	1,339,400	625,590	318,560
1981	3,242,560	1,434,580	1,054,160
1985	4,039,840	1,767,880	1,514,700
1991	5,501,850	2,430,330	2,468,030
1992	5,796,420	2,568,290	2,672,620
1993	6,101,340	2,712,020	2,888,820
1994	6,410,110	2,859,670	3,110,820
1995	6,705,100	3,004,600	3,328,000
1996	7,008,600	3,154,900	3,552,800
1997	7,322,700	3,311,100	3,786,300
1998	7,663,100	3,479,300	4,037,800
1999	8,023,000	3,655,400	4,301,300
2000	8,392,800	3,837,700	4,573,600
2001	8,768,995	4,024,899	4,853,079

Notes: Stock is taken at the beginning of the year.
Source: IAMR, *Estimates of Stock of Different Categories of Educated Manpower up to 2001 A.D.*

Table 5.3.4: Estimated Stock of Engineers*

(Hundred)

Year	*Degree Holders*	*Diploma Holders*	*Total*
1971	1745	2304	4049
1981	3049	4258	7307
1986	3908	6014	9922
1990	4922	7978	12900
1991	5196	8593	13789
1992	5558	9111	14669
1993	5977	9701	15678
1994	6449	10260	16709
1995	6981	10978	17959
1996	7533	11731	19264
1997	8065	12422	20487
1998	8591	13123	21714
1999	9137	13795	22932
2000	9695	14560	24255
2001	10244	15317	25561
2002	10783	16067	26850
2003	11832	17205	29037

Notes: Stock is taken at the beginning of the year.
* Refers to the stock in the working age group.
Source: NTMIS, AICTE, Govt. of India.

Figure 5.3.H

STOCK OF GRADUATES AND POST-GRADUATES IN GENERAL EDUCATION

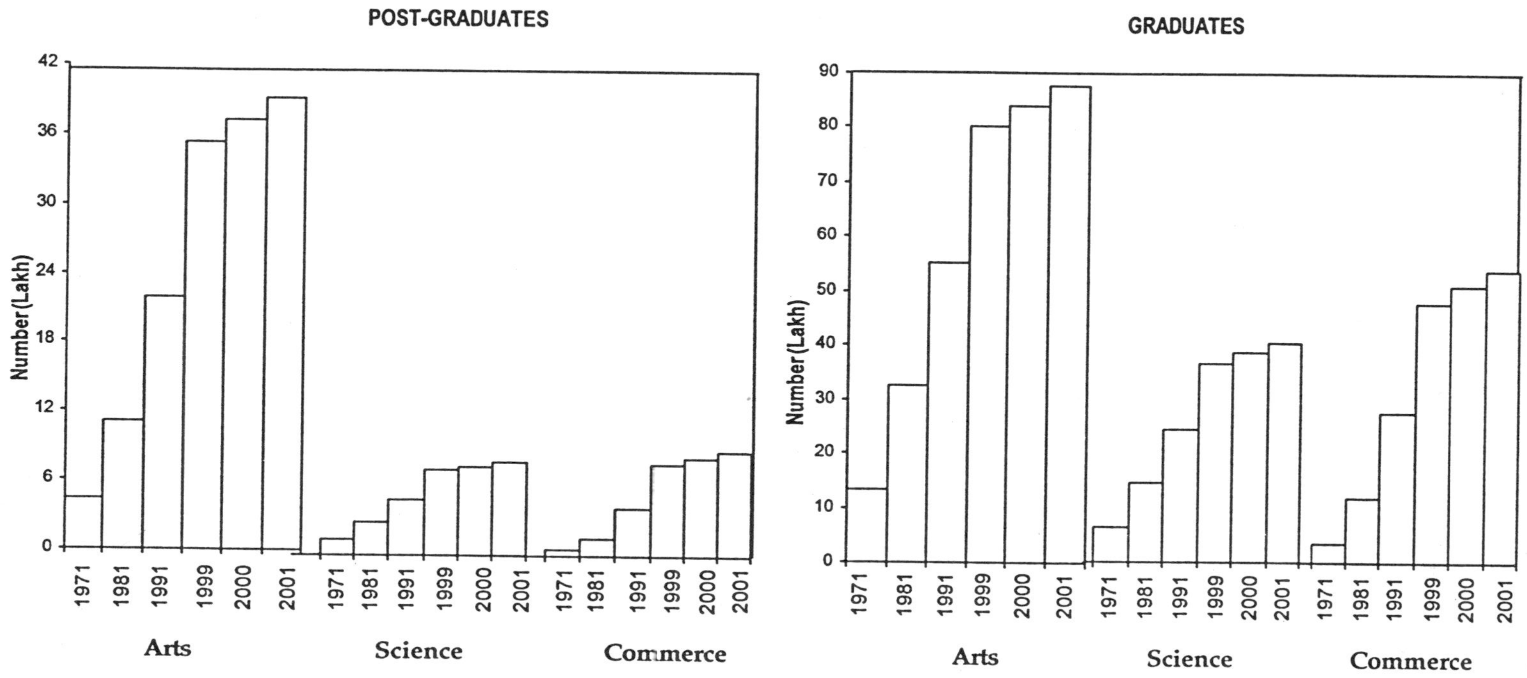

For details see Tables 5.3.2 and 5.3.3

Table 5.3.5: Estimated Stock of Engineers* by Select Disciplines (Degree)

Discipline	1991	1992	1993	1994	1995	1996	1997	1998	1999	2000	2001	2002	2003
1. Civil	126,980	133,590	140,480	146,790	153,690	160,470	166,750	172,830	178,860	184,860	190,760	196,560	200,544
2. Mechanical	138,030	145,370	153,540	162,870	172,860	184,810	194,810	204,620	214,430	224,210	233,820	243,280	256,518
3. Electrical	90,180	94,310	98,700	102,920	108,050	113,890	119,720	125,640	131,970	138,250	144,430	150,500	156,000
4. Chemical	28,300	29,480	30,580	31,960	33,520	35,490	37,590	39,670	41,760	43,830	45,850	47,850	50,951
5. Electronics & Telecomm.	45,970	53,100	61,650	72,120	82,410	93,740	104,850	115,580	132,020	148,320	164,340	180,090	190,284
6. Metallurgy	13,440	13,710	14,040	14,380	14,790	15,301	15,990	16,690	17,370	18,050	18,710	19,370	19,875
7. Mining	4,730	4,910	5,290	5,760	6,170	6,590	6,990	7,380	7,800	8,210	8,610	9,010	9,357
8. Automobile	1,350	1,500	1,770	2,060	2,360	2,720	2,960	3,250	3,490	3,720	3,950	4,180	4,390
9. Aeronautical	1,570	1,620	1,690	1,760	1,830	1,900	1,980	2,070	2,150	2,220	2,300	2,370	2,459
10. Agriculture	3,170	3,230	3,420	3,650	3,880	4,120	4,300	4,490	4,680	4,860	5,040	5,220	5,550
11. Production	5,270	6,290	7,630	9,240	11,030	12,970	14,840	16,680	18,600	20,500	22,360	24,190	26,152
12. Sugar	1,240	1,290	1,310	1,340	1,430	1,540	1,610	1,640	1,670	1,700	1,730	1,750	1,773
13. Oil	610	640	680	730	770	810	880	940	1,000	1,060	1,120	1,180	1,213
14. Textile	8,220	8,450	8,740	9,180	9,680	10,280	10,770	11,300	11,900	12,490	13,080	13,650	14,226
15. Architecture	10,160	10,740	11,540	12,320	13,330	14,450	15,740	16,910	18,150	19,390	20,600	21,800	23,073
16. Food	890	920	950	1,020	1,090	1,150	1,230	1,300	1,390	1,480	1,570	1,650	1,766
17. Instrumentation	3,080	3,780	4,550	5,920	7,540	9,470	11,360	13,340	15,190	17,040	18,850	20,640	22,259
18. Ceramic	620	830	870	980	980	1,040	1,100	1,140	1,200	1,260	1,320	1,370	1,656
19. Leather	650	680	710	730	760	810	850	8,80	930	970	1,020	1,060	1,161
20. Others	35,160	41,270	49,330	59,020	71,800	8,4420	96,810	109,370	122,350	136,210	149,830	163,230	193,979
Total	519,640	555,790	597,680	644,930	698,090	753,260	806,520	859,100	913,740	969,540	1024,380	1078,290	1183,186

Notes: Stock is taken at the beginning of the year.

* Refer to the stock in the working age-group.

Source: NTMIS, AICTE, Govt. of India.

Table 5.3.6: Estimated Stock of Engineers* by Select Disciplines (Diploma)

Discipline	1991	1992	1993	1994	1995	1996	1997	1998	1999	2000	2001	2002	2003
1. Civil	268850	280630	291510	300470	309220	318750	328490	338690	348150	358460	368660	378,760	386,238
2. Mechanical	230860	244190	257980	271230	286650	303100	319600	336620	352750	370270	387620	404,790	421,514
3. Electrical	166270	174590	182700	190230	199310	208830	218200	228680	238690	248770	258770	268,630	275,668
4. Chemical	6020	6690	7410	8320	9360	10800	12360	13880	15410	16930	18430	19,920	21,675
5. Electronics & Telecomm.	39290	46730	55770	65610	81090	95450	109710	124790	144900	165120	185140	204,960	216,261
6. Metallurgy	3760	3890	4100	4320	4610	4920	5170	5490	5800	6120	6440	6,750	7,178
7. Mining	7850	8380	8910	9480	10180	10790	11220	11660	12090	12530	12960	13,390	13,705
8. Automobile	14410	15910	17590	19170	20950	22640	24260	25890	27570	29300	31010	32,710	34,816
9. Agriculture	1460	1550	1650	1750	1850	1940	2050	2180	2300	2420	2540	2,660	2,782
10. Hotel Mgmt.	3580	3640	3870	4130	4550	5110	5580	6070	6540	7010	7470	7,930	8,323
11. Leather Tech.	2400	2490	2550	2630	2860	3020	3230	3430	3620	3810	4000	4,180	4,378
12. Production	3300	3690	4260	4690	5100	5660	6220	6804	7380	7380	7960	9,090	9,453
13. Textile Tech.	18700	19440	20530	21500	22820	24150	25280	26410	27650	28880	30100	31,310	32,104
14. Printing Tech.	8310	8640	9010	9410	9830	10300	10660	11000	11340	11670	12010	12,340	12,790
15. Others	84200	90670	101,730	112290	128590	146580	161100	175230	189300	205660	221870	237,900	273,606
Total	859260	911080	970,070	1025,980	1097,780	1173,120	1242,170	1312,310	1379,490	1455,990	1531,720	1606,690	1720,491

Notes: Stock is taken at the beginning of the Year.
* Refer to the stock in the working age -group.

Source: NTMIS, AICTE, Govt. of India.

Table 5.3.7: Stock of Registered Nursing Personnel

Year	*General Nurses*	*Auxiliary Nurse Midwives*	*Health Visitors*
1993	449,351	203,451	22,144
1994	512,495	229,304	24,411
1995	562,966	278,172	26,046
1996	565,696	283,195	26,578
1997	607,376	301,691	24,824
1998	671,341	335,485	32,249
1999	737,280	380,593	32,249
2000	776,355	419,077	35,890
2001	805,827	428,568	35,904
2005*	908,962	521,593	50,715

Notes: At the beginning of the year.
*As on 31st December, 2005
Registered with Nursing Council of India.

Sources: (*i*) Central Statistical Organisation, *Statistical Abstract* – 2003.
(*ii*) Directorate General of Health Services : Central Bureau of Health Intelligence, National Health Profile, 2006.

Figure 5.3.I

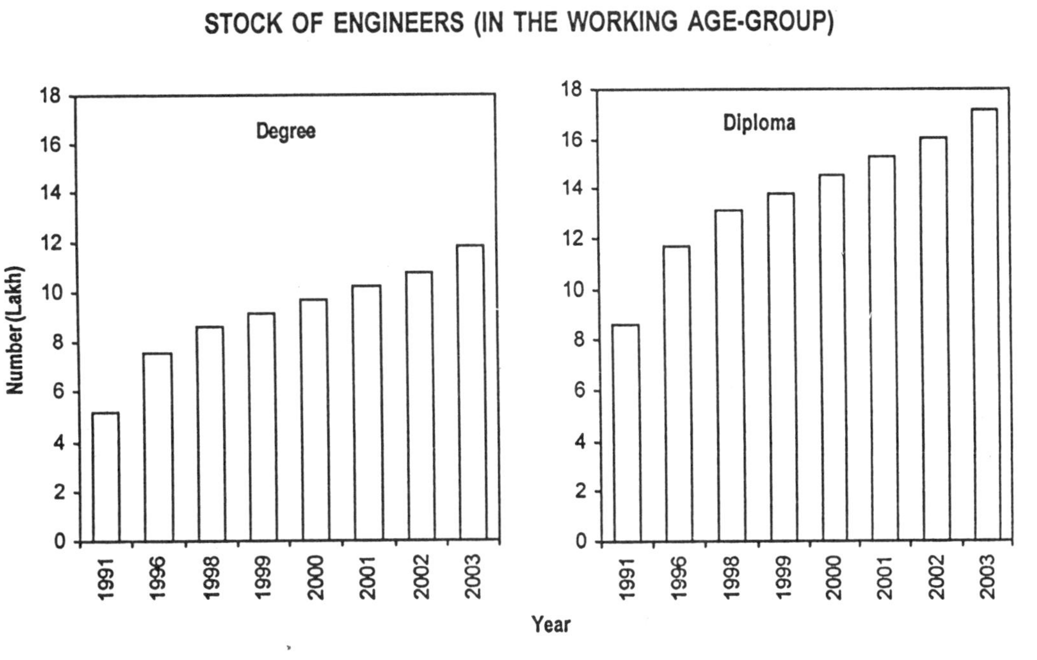

For details see Table 5.3.5 and 5.3.6

Figure 5.3.J

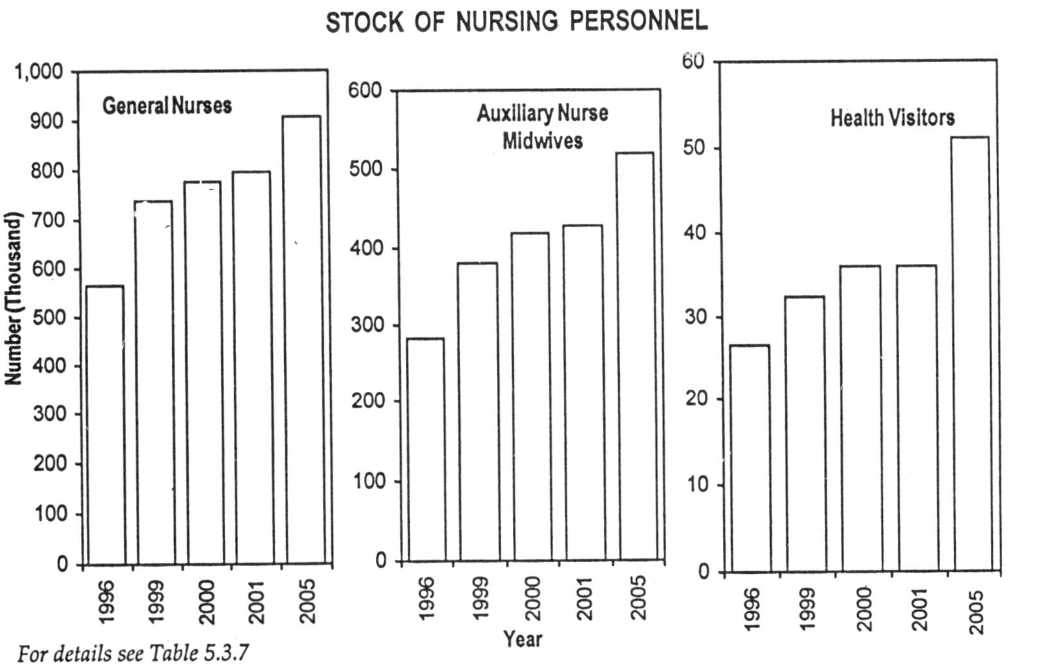

For details see Table 5.3.7

(iv) Industrial Relations

Table 5.4.1: Number of Registered Trade Unions and Their Membership

Year	*Number of Registered Trade Unions(E)*	*Number of Union submitting Returns*	*Membership of Union submitting Returns (000s)*			*Average Membership per Union submitting Returns*
			Men	*Women*	*Total**	
1961	11,312	6,813	3,618	395	4,013	589
1971	22,484	9,029	5,083	387	5,410	606
1981	37,539	6,682	5,012	385	5,397	808
1986	48,030	11,365	7,368	819	8,187	720
1987	49,329	11,063	7,211	748	7,959	719
1988	50,048	8,730	6,334	739	7,073	810
1989	52,210	9,758	8,207	1,088	9,295	953
1990	52,016	8,828	6,181	838	7,019	795
1991	53,535	8,418	5,507	594	6,101	725
1992	55,680	9,165	5,148	663	5,746	627
1993	55,784	6,806	2,636	498	3,134	460
1994	56,872	6,277	3,239	855	4,094	652
1995	57,952	8,162	5,675	863	6,538	801
1996	58,988	7,242	4,250	1,351	5,601	773
1997	60,660	8,872	6,504	905	7,409	835
1998	61,992	7,403	6,104	1,145	7,250	979
1999	64,817	8,152	5,190	1,218	6,407	786
2000	66,056	7,253	4,507	910	5,420	747
2001	66,624	6,531	NA	NA	5,874	899
2002	68,544	7,812	NA	NA	6,974	893
2003	74,649	7,258	NA	NA	6,278	865
2004	74,403	5,242	NA	NA	3,396	648

Notes: Figures relate to the entire Indian Union except Jammu and Kashmir up to 1984.
E = Estimated. NA : Data is not available
* Total may not tally to sex-wise break up because information in respect of certain Unions is not available by sex.

Sources: (*i*) Labour Bureau, *Indian Labour Year Book*, 2005.
(*ii*) Labour Bureau, Pocket Book of Labour Statistics, 2007.

Table 5.4.2: Industrial Disputes and Workers Involved

Year	Number of Disputes	Number of Workers Involved (000s)	Number of Mandays Lost (000s)	Average Size Workers Involved per Dispute
1981	2,589	1,588	36,584	613
1986	1,892	1,645	32,748	869
1991	1,810	1,342	26,428	741
1992	1,714	1,252	31,259	731
1993	1,393	954	20,301	685
1994	1,201	846	20,983	705
1995	1,066	990	16,290	929
1996	1,166	939	20,285	805
1997	1,305	981	16,971	752
1998	1,097	1,289	22,062	1175
1999	927	1,311	26,787	1414
2000	771	1,418	28,763	1,840
2001	674	688	23,767	1,020
2002	579	1,079	26,586	1,864
2003	552	1,816	30,256	3,290
2004	477	2,072	23,866	4,344
2005	456	2,914	29,665	6,390
2006^{P1}	430	1,810	20,324	4,209

Note: P_1 — Provisional.
Sources: (i)Labour Bureau, *Indian Labour Year Book.*
(ii)Ministry of Labour, *Annual Report, relevent years.*

Table 5.4.3: Disputes* Classified by Cause

Year	Causes								
	Wages and All-owances	Bonus	Perso-nnel	Retren-chment	Leave and hrs. of work	Indisci-pline and Violence	Others	Not known	Total
1971	935	384	467	149	39	97	643	29	2,752
1981	728	207	456	94	43	244	681	136	2,589
1986	460	173	343	73	23	271	445	104	1,892
1988	473	117	229	59	18	268	535	46	1,745
1989	425	108	300	39	21	275	558	60	1,786
1990	442	72	236	54	23	285	659	54	1,825
1991	435	70	270	39	18	335	300	38	1,505
1992	387	134	265	29	28	373	242	33	1,491
1993	362	94	254	21	23	272	326	41	1,393
1994	354	92	194	19	17	202	302	21	1,201
1995	320	79	195	10	21	159	253	29	1,066
1996	284	96	213	10	21	212	283	47	1,166
1997	305	112	261	7	31	259	293	37	1,305
1998	233	123	175	8	14	232	263	49	1097
1999	203	84	124	10	9	203	243	51	927
2000	158	66	84	12	7	197	208	39	771
2001^{P}	166	44	74	9	1	156	167	57	674
2002	118	37	78	12	3	171	136	24	579

Notes: * Includes both public and private sector Industrial disputes. P – Provisional.
Source: Labour Bureau, *Indian Labour Year Book,* 2004.

Figure 5.4.K

GROWTH OF TRADE UNIONS AND THEIR MEMBERSHIP

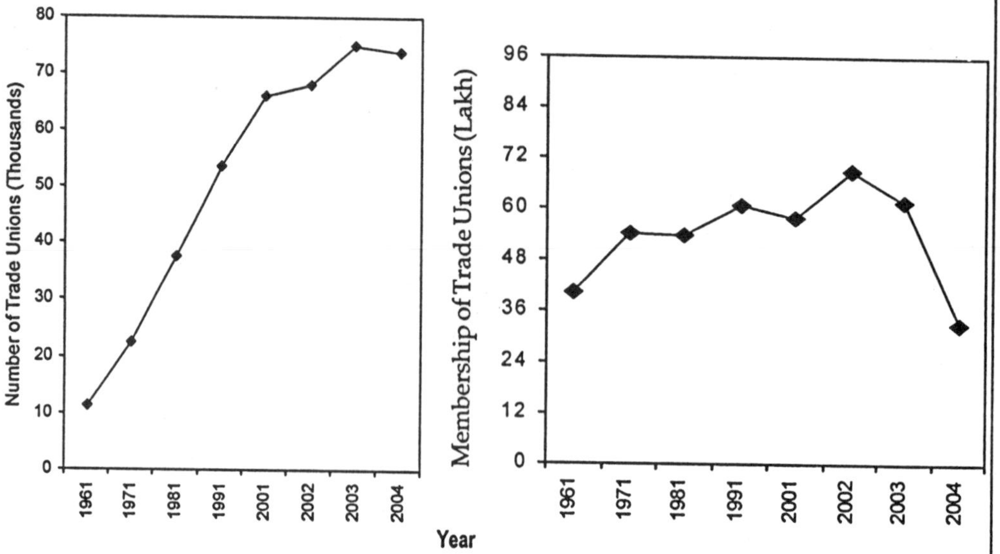

For details see Table 5.4.1

Figure 5.4.L

NUMBER OF INDUSTRIAL DISPUTES AND WORKERS INVOLVED

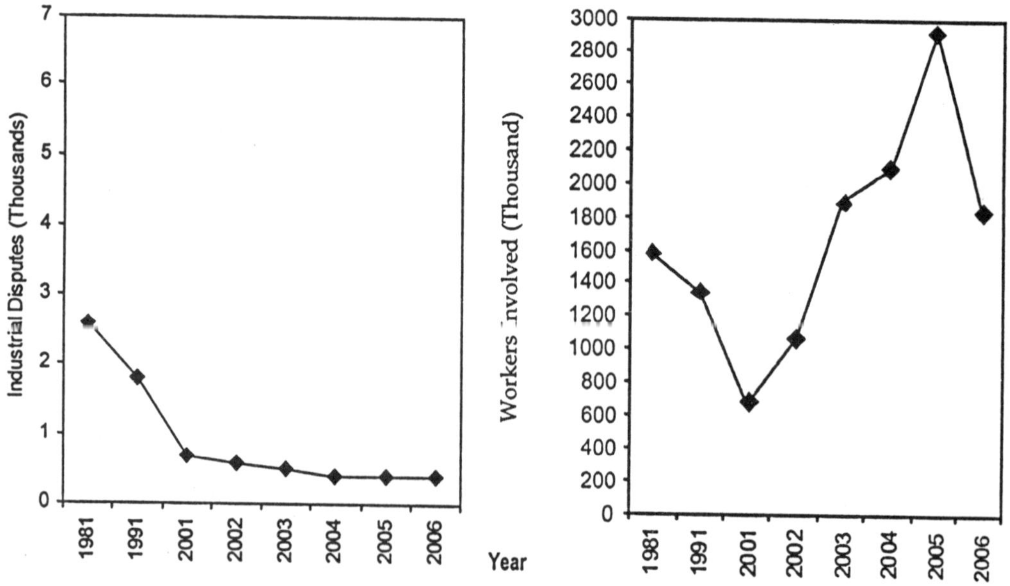

For details see Table 5.4.2

SECTION 6

Gender Issues

Dr. Rashmi Agrawal
Vijay K. Saxena

Section VI
Gender Issues

Gender equality and women's empowerment have been in focus of all human developmental interventions, national and international, for some decades. The United Nations Millennium Development Goals place a premium on the basic human rights to food, education, health care and decent living and stress upon achieving universal primary education, promoting gender equality and empowering women within a specific time frame. However, in spite of a number of positive interventions made by various countries including India aimed at bringing about gender parity, discrimination against women still persists in several walks of life. Women are being discriminated against from the very start of life (female foeticide was not uncommon in the past) through development as a child (sons get a preferential treatment in the families) and participation in economic, social and political affairs (female participation being abysmally low), and gender equality remains a distant dream. Higher female infant child mortality rates, marriages at an early age, unequal access to literacy and education and to economic activities and incomes and to ownership of the assets are some of the indicators that show the extent of discrimination against women.

This section 'Gender Issues (table 6.1 to 6.26) provides information on socio-economic status of women as well as on some of the demographic variables. These statistics on various items have been obtained from a number of sources such as population census of Registrar General of India and reports of the National Sample Survey Organisation, Department of Rural Employment and Poverty Alleviation, Ministry of Law and Justice, Ministry of Rural Development, Election Commission of India, etc. Some of the tables provide time series data that help in a quick analysis of changes taking place in gender related matters.

Table 6.1 indicates the infant mortality rates (IMR) by sex over a period of two decades. The table shows that while the IMR is coming down for both males and females, the rate for females is generally higher than for males. A positive trend however is that IMR has been coming down over the years, both for boys and girls – from about 96 per 1000 live births in 1986 to 59 in 2006 in case of the latter. Age-specific mortality rates presented in Table 6.2 indicate that mortality rates for females are higher than those for males at all ages up to 24 and fall rapidly after that age. This information can be related to the information available in Table 6.3 providing the mean age at marriage. The mean age at marriage, which was about 15 years in 1951, has risen to 20 years in 2005. Higher mortality rates for females till the age of 24 could be explained to some extent in terms of low mean age at marriage for women and the subsequent child-bearing period. The most worrisome part is the sex-differential in the rate of mortality rates in the age group of under 5. Although during the last two decades the under five-mortality rate in case of women has come down by more than half, this is still high when compared to their male counterparts.

Mortality rate is one of the major indicators of the state of health of population. Higher mortality rates in case of women are clear indications of their non-accessibility of health care facilities due to prevailing social attitudes. A girl child is often neglected, looked upon as a liability and denied access to adequate nutrition and health facilities. In-depth research studies are needed to ascertain the factors that are responsible for higher mortality rates of women in certain age groups as compared to men. The availability of health facilities for women should also be benchmarked for modifications in policies.

Early marriage is another phenomenon that prevents development of women and their empowerment. The situation is changing for the better as stated earlier but the change is very slow (Table 6.3 and Tables 6.5 to 6.8). The fact that The average age of marriage of females has increased from about 15 years to 20 years during the last half a century, even in 2001 almost a quarter of women in the age group 15-19 have been recorded as married instead of being in educational institutions (Tables 6.5 and 6.6), speaks for itself. Tables 6.7 and 6.8 provide information regarding age-specific marital status of women according to rural and urban population. The situation is worse in rural areas. About 29 per cent of the women get married in rural areas during the age of 15 to 19 years. This data shows the need to create greater awareness about this aspect specially in rural areas.

Data on female-headed households and average size of such households can be seen in Table 6.4. The information is available on rural-urban residence basis. The percentage of female-headed households in rural areas is slightly higher than in urban areas. The percentage of such households is almost stable at around 9 to 10 till 2000. The data for the year 2005 shows slight increase from 9 to about 11 per cent. The average size of female-headed households is almost constant.

Education is one of the important indicators of human development. The Millennium Development Goals aim at achieving universal primary education and promoting gender equality, specially in the field of education. It is said that if a woman is educated the entire family is educated. Education of women not only makes the family literate but it is also one of the essential components for empowering women. Education enables them to understand and realise their rights in all spheres including economic, social and political, and improves their employability. A number of initiatives have been taken in the country to provide education to all without any gender bias. Special facilities are being provided for education of girl child under various state-sponsored schemes. 'Sarva Shiksha Abhiyan', 'Mid-day Meal Scheme', 'Free Books to Children', Adult Education programmes are some of the initiatives that have been taken by the government to promote the education. In spite of these efforts, India continues to be at very low levels of female literacy and education in absolute terms as well as in relation to men. Table 6.9 provides educational levels of the population area-wise and gender-wise. About three-fourths of the women in rural areas and more than 36 per cent in urban areas are still illiterate. A wide gap between male and female literacy as well as rural-urban female literacy can be observed. The gender gaps have no doubt narrowed down but still persist at all stages of education. The data for 2001 show that only 11.0 per cent of the females were able to continue their education up to and beyond matriculation and higher secondary and only 2.4 per cent attained graduation and above qualifications, compared to men in whose case the corresponding percentages were about 19.6 per cent and 4.8 per cent respectively. The data on technical education reveals a very pathetic indication. Education and training are extremely essential if India has to compete with other countries in economic, social and political development. Efforts in this direction are needed in a mission mode.

Women's participation in economic activities is another indicator of their mainstreaming and empowerment. The extent of their participation in economic activities and gender differences in diverse fields of activity can be observed from tables 6.10, 6.11 and 6.12. Table 6.10 shows the distribution of female main workers (as defined in census) by their educational level according to rural and urban residence as per the 2001 census. It can be observed from this table that over 67 per cent of female main workers in rural areas were illiterate. Looking at the tables 6.10 and 6.12 together, it is observed that generally these illiterate women are working in agriculture and allied activities, and mining and quarrying operations. In urban areas also 36.4 per cent of female main workers were illiterates. The percentage of illiterate male workers is much lower than that of illiterate female workers in both rural and urban areas. It may also be seen that an almost negligible proportion of female main workers in rural areas are technically trained. In urban areas their percentage is only 4.10. It can be concluded that the fruits of education are yet to be enjoyed by women especially in rural areas.

Tables 6.11& 6.12 show the female main workers by industry. Comparable data for 1991 and 2001 indicate some changes in the industrial affiliation of women workers. There has been an increase of female main workers in the areas of manufacturing, wholesale and retail trade including restaurants and hotels. A very sharp increase of female main workers can be observed in the community, social and personal services. Their numbers in these services have increased from 4.91 million in 1991 to 22.40 million in 2001. Some of the identified industries where the number of females is more than that of males are bidi manufacturing, manufacturing of matches, spinning and weaving, domestic services and welfare services (Table 6.16). These data indicate that most of the employment available for women is in the relatively less paid and insecure informal sector to be, and that is the reason that they are more vulnerable to exploitation. Another conclusion that can be drawn from the data is that women have not been able to any appreciable degree, to come out of their stereotypical traditional roles in which they are supposed to do the household work and kindred activities. Even when they come out for work outside home, they are drawn to the same traditional activities, which points to the continued segmentation of labour market based on gender.

Women are yet to break the glass-ceiling in many areas of the world of work.

Table 6.14 presents information on the employment services available to women job seekers, which shows that the number of them registered with employment exchanges has been constantly increasing over the last 15 years. Table 6.13 provides the status of craftsmen training available through women ITIs in various states and women wings in these ITIs. The table which provides information about government run ITIs as well as privately run ITIs shows that some of the small States and Union Territories do not have any woman ITI or women's wing in the ITIs. There are several states which have only government run ITIs and their number is very small to cater to the needs of the educated youth including women. Women ITIs which are privately run are only in a very few states. This inadequacy of the institutional network obviously is a major factor contributing to the present status of technically trained women in the country as discussed earlier. It can be concluded that the country needs more training infrastructure (formal and informal) to cater to the needs of youth in general and of women in particular.

The relationship between fertility rates and education of women has great demographic implications. Fertility rates by level of education of women have been depicted in Table 6.15. The data show that fertility rate decreases with higher levels of education. The decline is visible even after primary education. This emphasises the point made earlier that education is extremely essential for women in order to achieve the goal of socio-economic and political development of the country.

Table 6.17 indicates the percentage distribution of migrants by sex and reason. The overwhelming reason for female migration is marriage, with about three quarters of women migrating for this reason. Unlike in the case of men, employment-related migration is very limited among women. The reason for migration in case of women has not changed during the last two decades. It is noteworthy that more and more women are migrating because of marriage. Employment related migration has declined, in case of women from 1.9 per cent in 1981 to 1.7 per cent in 2001 and in case of male, from 31.8 per cent to 28.1 per cent in the same period. Results show that women still have the secondary status in the society and they are considered the homemakers or care givers so far as their economic independence is concerned.

Poverty alleviation is one of the crucial goals of Indian planning. A number of schemes for generating wage and self-employment in rural and urban areas have been introduced to reduce poverty in the country. Tables 6.18 and 6.19 show the percentage shares of women among beneficiaries of these programmes. The percentage share of women beneficiaries under self-employment like Swaranjayanti Gramin Swarozgar Yojana (SGSY) has increased over the years. In 2007-08, 61 per cent of women were beneficiaries of such programmes. This is an encouraging development, but it should also be kept in mind that these gains to a large extent, have been due to earmarking of benefits for women under these programmes and the large share of women self help groups in the benefits. State-wise women beneficiaries in National Rural Employment Guarantee Scheme can be seen in Table 6.19. Data reveals that women's share has increased from 39.1 per cent in February, 2007 to 43.2 per cent in January, 2008. State-wise analysis shows that maximum women beneficiaries (82.0 per cent) of NREGA are in Tamil Nadu followed by Rajasthan (69.0 per cent) and Arunachal Pradesh is a laggard state with no women beneficiary.

Governance is one of the crucial issues of development in modern era. Although Constitution of India guarantees equal opportunities for all, there is a gap between the planning and implementation. There are two aspects to governance and gender issues - the role of public services in general in promoting a gender-egalitarian society and an equitable share for women in the governance. In spite of the widespread efforts in development of women, the discrimination against them still exists, correction of which requires a change in the mindset and attitudes of the society. Gender bias in decision making activities can be witnessed from the data shown in tables 6.20 to 6.26. Out of a total of 610 judges in the high courts (2008) only 34 (5.6 per cent) are women judges (Table 6.20). Regional variations can also been seen from this table. A number of states like Chhatisgarh, Jammu & Kashmir, Jharkhand, Sikkim and Uttaranchal have no women judges. The situation is no better in major States. The major educationally forward State of Kerala has only two woman judge out of a total of 25 judges. The situation in the context of representatives of women in primary services like administrative services and police services is also not very encouraging. Only 10 per cent of the IAS officers and 3 per cent of IPS officers were women in 2000 (table 6.21). The representation of women in the Lok Sabha has trippled during the last 50 years, but they still constitute only 10.7 per cent of all the members. The proposed one-third reservation in parliamentary seats has to be viewed against this dismal picture. The situation has not changed in case of women members in the Upper House of Parliament. Their representations have remained between 7 to 9 per cent in the last 29 years.

An attempt has been made to give powers to rural women through 73rd & 74th amendments of the Constitution. 50 per cent reservation has been provided to women in panchayats. Tables 6.24 to 6.26 provide a picture of women representatives in Village, Intermediate and District Panchayats at State level. The scenario appears to be encouraging in as much as about 30 per cent of those representing panchayats are women as per constitutional amendment. State-wise variations may be observed. Should it be concluded that reservations for women in every field are mandatory for their mainstreaming? A related question would be whether such reservation has actually resulted in it al transfer of power to women.

The principle of equal treatment for men and women in the society has received considerable attention at national and international levels and efforts have been made to narrow down gender gap. But the data presented in the above tables show that there is a long way to go to achieve the goal. While the achievements made in the country in this direction must not be underestimated, we have to be concerned about the pace at which the changes are taking place. Apart from accelerating the approach towards gender equality, it should also be ensured that the fruits of programmes undertaken to achieve this goal should reach the target groups.

The major issues that emerge from the above discussion and need immediate and continuous attention are gender bias in respect of major development indicators such as mortality rates and accessibility to health facilities; educational and technical levels; mean age at marriage; economic participation etc. A very few women are taking up decision making roles which calls for change in social orientation of the society as a whole which profess for varying orientation for males and females. Mainstreaming and empowerment of women are possible only when their participation in various socio-economic areas is facilitated followed by their accessibility of facilities. Besides, it would require general awareness among women about their rights. A change in the mindset of the society is a prerequisite for meeting the goal of women empowerment.

Table 6.1: Infant Mortality Rate by Sex

Years	Female	Male	Total
1986	97	96	96
1990	81	78	80
1991**	80	81	80
1992**	80	79	79
1993**	75	73	74
1994**	75	73	74
1995**	76	73	74
1996**	73	71	72
1997**	73	70	71
1998**	73	70	72
1999*	71	70	70
2000*	69	67	68
2001*	68	64	66
2002*	65	62	63
2003*	64	57	60
2004	58	58	58
2005	61	56	58
2006	59	56	57

Notes: ** Excludes Jammu & Kashmir and Nagland. * Excludes Nagaland (Rural).
Source: Registrar General and Census Commissioner of India : *Sample Registration System, Statistical Report* and *SRS Bulletin.*

Table 6.2: Age-Specific Mortality Rate by Sex

Age Group	1981		1991		1996*		1999		2000	
	Female	Male	Female	Male	Female	Male	Female	Male	Female	Male
0-4	43.3	39.2	27.5	25.6	25.6	22.2	21.1	19.8	20.6	18.6
5-9	4.4	3.7	2.9	2.6	2.7	2.0	2.1	1.6	2.0	1.5
10-14	1.7	1.8	1.6	1.4	1.4	1.2	1.3	1.2	1.3	1.2
15-19	3.0	1.9	2.5	1.8	1.9	1.4	2.1	1.7	2.2	1.6
20-24	3.8	2.4	3.1	2.5	2.7	2.0	2.8	2.3	2.7	2.2
25-29	4.0	2.5	3.3	2.9	2.5	2.5	2.8	2.9	2.7	2.9
30-34	4.2	3.7	2.9	3.3	2.8	2.9	2.7	3.5	2.8	3.3
35-39	4.3	4.6	3.6	4.2	2.8	3.9	2.8	4.8	3.0	4.4
40-44	5.2	6.5	3.9	5.1	3.9	5.7	4.0	5.9	3.3	5.5
45-49	7.5	9.5	5.7	9.1	5.3	7.9	5.3	8.5	8.1	5.3
50-54	10.9	15.3	9.1	13.4	9.0	12.7	8.3	12.1	7.4	12.2
55-59	17.0	23.8	13.8	21.2	13.6	17.9	13.0	19.4	13.4	19 1
60-64	29.6	36.3	24.0	33.0	23.8	29.7	19.1	27.0	19.7	26.6
65-69	41.3	51.7	37.5	45.9	32.4	41.5	33.0	40.8	32.3	44.2
70+	92.8	98.6	86.8	96.5	80.4	92.6	NA	NA	NA	NA
All Ages	12.7	12.4	9.7	10.0	8.9	9.1	8.2	8.9	8.9	8.1

Note: * Excludes Jammu and Kashmir.
Source: Registrar General and Census Commissioner of India : *Sample Registration System, Statistical Report.*

Figure 6.A

AGE-SPECIFIC MORTALITY RATE BY SEX

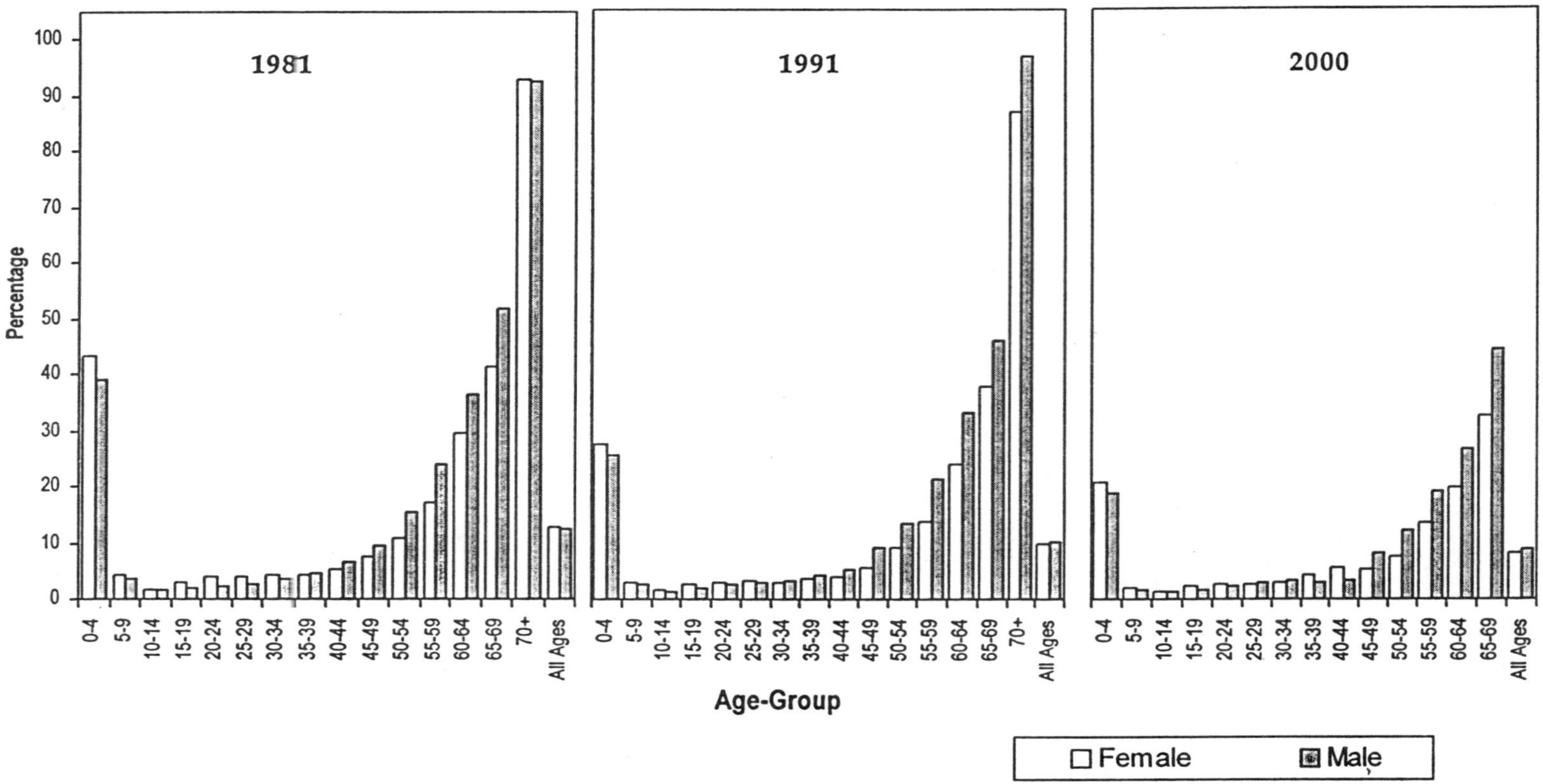

For details see Table 6.2

Table 6.3: Mean Age at Marriage by Sex

Years	*Female*	*Male*
1951	15.4	19.9
1961	16.1	22.3
1971	17.1	22.7
1981	17.9	23.3
1991	19.3	24.0
1996	19.4	–
2001	19.9	–
2002	20.0	–
2003	20.1	–
2004	20.4	–
2005	20.2	–

Note: Figures for 1951, 1961, 1971, 1981 and 1991 are singulate mean age of marriage based on population census data; 1995-2003 figures are the mean age at effective marriage based on Sample Registration System.

Source: Registrar General of India, Population of India : ESCAP Country Monograph No. 10 and Female age at Marriage, *Census of India*, occasional paper No. 7 of 1988 and *SRS Statistical Reports*.

Table 6.4: Female Headed Households and their Average Size

Years	*Rural/ Urban*	*Households (Million)*	*Female Headed Households (Million)*	*Percent Female Headed Household*	*Average Size of Female Headed Households*
1984	Rural	100.53	9.70	9.65	3.5
	Urban	33.99	2.95	8.68	3.7
1988	Rural	108.36	11.22	10.36	3.3
	Urban	34.28	3.40	9.92	3.5
1994	Rural	119.53	11.64	9.74	3.2
	Urban	43.45	4.59	10.56	3.2
2000	Rural	137.42	14.33	10.43	3.5
	Urban	51.52	4.85	9.41	3.5
2005	Rural	150.17	16.95	11.29	3.4
	Urban	56.98	6.34	11.12	3.5
2006	Rural	154.29	NA	NA	4.8
	Urban	54.44	NA	NA	4.3

Note: Data for 1984, 1988, 1994, 2000 and 2005 are based on 39th (January-June, 1984), 43rd (July 1987-June 1988), 50th (July 1993-June 1994), 55th Round (July 1999-June 2000) and 61st Round (July 2004-June 2005) resectively.

Source: National Sample Survey Organisation :
(i) Report No. 351, 1989; *Sarvekshana*, Special number; 43rd Round; (ii) Report Nos. 409, 458, 515 and 522.

Table 6.5: Age-Specific Marital Status of Total Persons (of Age 10 years & above), 2004-05

(Thousand)

Age	Marital Status																	
	Never Married			Married			Widowed			Divorced/Separator			Non-Responsed			Total		
Group	Female	Male	Person	Female	Male	Person	Female	Male	Person	Female	Male	Person	Female	Male	Person			
10-14	52457	60148	11263	38	3215	575	0.	0	0	0	0	0	0	0	0	52843	60363	113206
	(99.3)	(99.6)	(99.5)	(0.7)	(0.4)	(0.5)	(0.0)	(0.0)	(0.0)	(0.0)	(0.0)	(0.0)	(0.0)	(0.0)	(0.0)	(100.0)	(100.0)	(100.0)
15-19	35109	49679	84778	8635	1570	10211	32	0	0	55	37	95	0	0	0	43799	51286	95085
	(80.1)	(96.9)	(89.1)	(19.7)	(3.0)	(10.7)	(0.1)	(0.0)	(0.0)	(0.1)	(0.1)	(0.2)	(0.0)	(0.0)	(0.0)	(100.0)	(100.0)	(100.0)
10-19	**87565**	**109827**	**19740**	**9021**	**1784**	**10786**	**36**	**0**	**0**	**59**	**42**	**104**	**0**	**0**	**0**	**96642**	**111649**	**208291**
	(90.7)	**(98.4)**	**(94.8)**	**(9.3)**	**(1.6)**	**(5.1)**	**(0.0)**	**(0.0)**	**(0.0)**	**(0.0)**	**(0.0)**	**(0.1)**	**(0.0)**	**(0.0)**	**(0.0)**	**(100.0)**	**(100.0)**	**(100.0)**
20-24	10948	29098	40050	31665	13696	45342	204	72	233	246	72	319	0	0	0	43095	42910	86005
	(25.4)	(67.8)	(46.6)	(73.5)	(31.8)	(57.7)	(0.5)	(0.2)	(0.3)	(0.6)	(0.2)	(0.4)	(0.0)	(0.0)	(0.0)	(100.0)	(100.0)	(100.0)
25-29	2156	10615	12780	35285	26802	62072	453	170	630	337	167	532	0	27	0	38231	37818	76048
	(5.6)	(28.1)	(16.8)	(92.3)	(70.9)	(81.6)	(1.2)	(0.5)	(0.8)	(0.9)	(0.5)	(0.7)	(0.0)	(0.0)	(0.0)	(100.0)	(100.0)	(100.0)
30-34	757	2913	3658	35945	31178	67088	929	250	1185	390	162	560	0	0	0	38012	34479	72491
	(2.0)	(8.4)	(5.0)	(94.6)	(90.4)	(92.6)	(2.4)	(0.7)	(1.6)	(1.0)	(0.5)	(0.8)	(0.0)	(0.0)	(0.0)	(100.0)	(100.0)	(100.0)
20-34	**13861**	**42627**	**56488**	**102895**	**71676**	**174502**	**1619**	**510**	**2111**	**979**	**409**	**1430**	**0**	**27**	**0**	**119337**	**115207**	**234544**
	(11.6)	**(37.0)**	**(24.1)**	**(86.2)**	**(62.2)**	**(74.4)**	**(1.4)**	**(0.4)**	**(0.9)**	**(0.8)**	**(0.4)**	**(0.6)**	**(0.0)**	**(0.0)**	**(0.0)**	**(100.0)**	**(100.0)**	**(100.0)**
35-39	423	1098	1556	32550	33284	65847	1817	396	2200	386	165	542	0	0	0	35176	34969	70145
	(1.2)	(3.2)	(2.2)	(92.5)	(95.2)	(93.9)	(5.2)	(1.1)	(3.1)	(1.1)	(0.5)	(0.8)	(0.0)	(0.0)	(0.0)	(100.0)	(100.0)	(100.0)
40-44	204	543	732	24978	28236	53200	2130	586	2708	294	135	448	0	0	0	27587	29500	57087
	(0.7)	(1.8)	(1.3)	(90.5)	(95.4)	(93.2)	(7.7)	(2.0)	(4.7)	(1.1)	(0.5)	(0.8)	(0.0)	(0.0)	(0.0)	(100.0)	(100.0)	(100.0)
35-44	**627**	**1641**	**2288**	**57528**	**61520**	**119047**	**4011**	**1003**	**4983**	**675**	**299**	**985**	**0**	**0**	**0**	**62764**	**64469**	**127233**
	(1.0)	**(2.5)**	**(1.8)**	**(91.6)**	**(95.4)**	**(93.6)**	**(6.4)**	**(1.6)**	**(3.9)**	**(1.0)**	**(0.5)**	**(0.7)**	**(0.0)**	**(0.0)**	**(0.0)**	**(100.0)**	**(100.0)**	**(100.0)**
45-49	150	325	467	20041	25005	45035	3124	838	3991	249	98	348	0	0	0	23545	26266	49812
	(0.6)	(1.2)	(0.9)	(85.1)	(95.2)	(90.4)	(13.3)	(3.2)	(8.0)	(1.0)	(0.4)	(0.7)	(0.0)	(0.0)	(0.0)	(100.0)	(100.0)	(100.0)
50-54	132	249	363	14058	18311	32358	3724	1036	4754	141	54	188	0	0	0	18052	19650	37701
	(0.7)	(1.3)	(1.0)	(77.9)	(93.1)	(85.9)	(20.6)	(5.3)	(12.6)	(0.8)	(0.3)	(0.5)	(0.0)	(0.0)	(0.0)	(100.0)	(100.0)	(100.0)
55-59	100	187	286	10547	13807	24357	4055	1044	5110	89	44	134	0	0	0	14805	15082	29887
	(0.7)	(1.2)	(1.0)	(71.3)	(91.5)	(81.5)	(27.4)	(7.0)	(17.1)	(0.6)	(0.3)	(0.4)	(0.0)	(0.0)	(0.0)	(100.0)	(100.0)	(100.0)
45-49	**383**	**761**	**1116**	**44646**	**57123**	**101750**	**11314**	**3067**	**14476**	**466**	**195**	**655**	**0**	**0**	**0**	**56402**	**60998**	**117400**
	(0.6)	**(1.1)**	**(0.9)**	**(79.0)**	**(93.6)**	**(86.6)**	**(20.0)**	**(5.0)**	**(12.3)**	**(0.8)**	**(0.3)**	**(0.5)**	**(0.0)**	**(0.0)**	**(0.0)**	**(100.0)**	**(100.0)**	**(100.0)**
60+	382	430	803	14484	27506	41950	20518	6405	26920	124	103	192	0	0	0	35465	34418	69884
	(1.0)	(1.2)	(1.2)	(40.8)	(79.9)	(60.0)	(59.9)	(18.6)	(38.5)	(0.3)	(0.3)	(0.3)	(0.0)	(0.0)	(0.0)	(100.0)	(100.0)	(100.0)
All Ages	**102847**	**155218**	**25823**	**228460**	**219637**	**448075**	**36983**	**10725**	**47457**	**2321**	**1055**	**3030**	**0**	**0**	**0**	**370611**	**386741**	**757352**
	(27.0)	**(40.1)**	**(34.1)**	**(61.6)**	**(56.0)**	**(59.8)**	**(10.0)**	**(2.8)**	**(6.3)**	**(0.6)**	**(0.3)**	**(0.4)**	**(0.0)**	**(0.0)**	**(0.0)**	**(100.0)**	**(100.0)**	**(100.0)**

Notes: (1) Total may not tally due to rounding off.
(2) Figures in Parenthesis indicate the percentage.

Source: National Sample Survey Organisation : Report No. 515, Employment and Unemployment Situation in India, 2004-05.

Table 6.6: Age-Specific Marital Status of Population, 2001 (Total)

(Thousand)

Age Group	Never Married			Married			Widowed			Divorced/Separator			Total		
	Female	Male	Person	Female	Male	Person	Female	Male	Person	Female	Male	Person	Female	Male	Person
<10 Years	114910	123854	238764	0	0	0	0	0	0	0	0	0	114910	123854	238764
	(100.0)	(100.0)	(100.0)	(0.0)	(0.0)	(0.0)	(0.0)	(0.0)	(0.0)	(0.0)	(0.0)	(0.0)	(100.0)	(100.0)	(100.0)
10-14	57702	64978	122680	1407	602	2009	79	29	108	25	24	49	59214	65633	124847
	(97.4)	(99.0)	(98.3)	(2.5)	(0.9)	(1.6)	(0.1)	(0.1)	(0.1)	(0.0)	(0.0)	(0.0)	(100.0)	(100.0)	(100.0)
15-19	34774	51073	85847	11316	2805	14121	95	32	127	91	30	121	46276	53940	100216
	(75.1)	(94.6)	(85.7)	(24.5)	(5.2)	(14.1)	(0.2)	(0.1)	(0.1)	(0.2)	(0.1)	(0.1)	(100.0)	(100.0)	(100.0)
20-24	9979	30206	40185	32899	15914	48813	294	112	406	272	88	360	43443	46321	89764
	(23.0)	(65.2)	(44.8)	(75.7)	(34.4)	(54.4)	(0.7)	(0.2)	(0.5)	(0.6)	(0.2)	(0.3)	(100.0)	(100.0)	(100.0)
25-29	2366	11531	13897	38548	29666	68244	573	228	801	348	133	481	41865	41557	83422
	(5.7)	(27.7)	(16.7)	(92.2)	(71.4)	(81.8)	(1.4)	(0.5)	(1.0)	(0.7)	(0.4)	(0.5)	(100.0)	(100.0)	(100.0)
30-34	808	3253	4061	34781	33631	68412	958	337	1295	366	141	507	39912	37362	74274
	(2.2)	(8.7)	(5.5)	(94.2)	(90.0)	(92.1)	(2.6)	(0.9)	(1.7)	(1.0)	(0.4)	(0.7)	(100.0)	(100.0)	(100.0)
35-39	467	1202	1659	32183	34255	66438	1538	447	1985	358	135	493	34535	36039	70574
	(1.4)	(3.3)	(2.4)	(93.2)	(95.1)	(94.0)	(4.4)	(1.2)	(2.8)	(1.0)	(0.4)	(0.7)	(100.0)	(100.0)	(100.0)
40-44	304	635	939	23287	28579	51866	1994	554	2548	274	111	385	25859	29879	55738
	(1.2)	(2.1)	(1.7)	(90.1)	(95.7)	(93.0)	(7.7)	(1.8)	(4.6)	(1.0)	(0.4)	(0.7)	(100.0)	(100.0)	(100.0)
45-49	202	403	605	19591	23739	43330	2549	640	3189	199	86	285	22541	24868	47409
	(0.9)	(1.6)	(1.3)	(87.0)	(95.5)	(91.4)	(11.3)	(2.6)	(6.7)	(0.8)	(0.3)	(0.6)	(100.0)	(100.0)	(100.0)
50-54	152	312	464	13070	18608	31678	3377	863	4240	136	69	205	16736	19852	36588
	(0.9)	(1.6)	(1.3)	(78.1)	(93.7)	(86.6)	(20.2)	(4.3)	(11.6)	(0.8)	(0.4)	(0.5)	(100.0)	(100.0)	(100.0)
55-59	98	199	297	10803	12534	23337	3089	806	3895	80	44	124	14070	13583	27653
	(0.7)	(1.5)	(1.1)	(76.8)	(93.3)	(84.3)	(22.0)	(5.9)	(14.1)	(0.5)	(0.3)	(0.4)	(100.0)	(100.0)	(100.0)
60-64	151	255	406	8126	11950	20076	5573	1336	6909	80	46	126	13931	13586	27517
	(1.1)	(1.9)	(1.5)	(58.3)	(88.0)	(73.0)	(40.0)	(9.8)	(25.1)	(0.6)	(0.3)	(0.4)	(100.0)	(100.0)	(100.0)
65-69	123	196	319	5514	8065	13579	4648	1180	5828	50	30	80	10335	9472	19807
	(1.2)	(2.1)	(1.6)	(53.4)	(85.1)	(68.6)	(45.0)	(12.5)	(29.4)	(0.4)	(0.3)	(0.4)	(100.0)	(100.0)	(100.0)
70-74	108	190	298	2496	5995	8491	4545	1318	5863	32	24	56	7181	7528	14709
	(1.5)	(2.5)	(2.0)	(34.8)	(79.0)	(57.7)	(63.3)	(17.8)	(39.9)	(0.4)	(0.3)	(0.4)	(100.0)	(100.0)	(100.0)
75-79	57	108	165	1225	2454	3679	1193	691	2684	13	11	24	3288	3263	6551
	(1.7)	(3.3)	(2.5)	(37.3)	(75.2)	(56.2)	(60.6)	(21.2)	(41.0)	(0.4)	(0.3)	(0.3)	(100.0)	(100.0)	(100.0)
80+	145	212	357	1033	2559	3592	2925	1134	4059	16	14	30	4120	3919	8039
	(3.5)	(5.4)	(4.4)	(25.1)	(65.3)	(44.7)	(71.0)	(28.9)	(50.5)	(0.4)	(0.3)	(0.4)	(100.0)	(100.0)	(100.0)
All Ages	223048	289620	512668	236773	231820	468593	34290	9729	44019	2343	988	3331	496453	532157	1028610
	(44.9)	(54.4)	(49.8)	(47.7)	(43.6)	(45.6)	(6.9)	(1.8)	(4.3)	(0.5)	(0.2)	(0.3)	(100.0)	(100.0)	(100.0)
Age not Stated	712	1011	1723	462	464	926	61	23	84	3	3	6	1238	1500	2738
	(57.5)	(67.4)	(62.9)	(37.3)	(30.9)	(33.8)	(4.9)	(1.5)	(3.1)	(0.3)	(0.2)	(0.2)	(100.0)	(100.0)	(100.0)
Less than 18	196436	219715	416151	4870	1521	6391	128	45	123	56	37	93	201490	221319	422809
	(97.5)	(99.3)	(98.5)	(2.4)	(0.7)	(1.5)	(0.1)	(0.0)	(0.0)	(0.0)	(0.0)	(0.0)	(100.0)	(100.0)	(100.0)
Less than 21	211597	250986	462583	22122	6872	28994	256	90	346	195	75	270	234171	258023	492194
	(90.4)	(97.2)	(94.0)	(9.4)	(2.7)	(5.9)	(0.1)	(0.0)	(0.1)	(0.1)	(0.0)	(0.0)	(100.0)	(100.0)	(100.0)

Note: Figures in Parenthesis indicate the percentage.
Source: Registrar General and Census Commissioner of India, *Census of India–2001.*

Table 6.7: Age-Specific Marital Status of Population, 2001 (Rural)

(Thousand)

Age Group	Never Married			Married			Widowed			Divorced/Separator			Total		
	Female	Male	Person	Female	Male	Person	Female	Male	Person	Female	Male	Person	Female	Male	Person
<10 Years	88613	94952	183565	0	0	0	0	0	0	0	0	0	88613	94952	183565
	(100.0)	(100.0)	(100.0)	(0.0)	(0.0)	(0.0)	(0.0)	(0.0)	(0.0)	(0.0)	(0.0)	(0.0)	(100.0)	(100.0)	(100.0)
10-14	42550	48076	90626	1154	487	1641	58	22	80	18	17	35	43780	48602	92382
	(97.3)	(98.9)	(98.1)	(2.6)	(10.0)	(1.8)	(0.1)	(0.1)	(0.1)	(0.0)	(0.0)	(0.0)	(100.0)	(100.0)	(100.0)
15-19	22934	35336	58270	9233	2364	11597	72	26	98	74	22	26	32313	37749	70062
	(71.0)	(93.6)	(83.2)	(28.6)	(6.3)	(16.6)	(0.2)	(0.1)	(0.1)	(0.2)	(0.0)	(0.1)	(100.0)	(100.0)	(100.0)
20-24	5136	18477	23613	24702	12486	37188	221	93	314	212	71	283	30271	31128	61399
	(17.0)	(59.4)	(38.5)	(81.6)	(40.1)	(60.6)	(0.7)	(0.3)	(0.5)	(0.7)	(0.2)	(0.4)	(100.0)	(100.0)	(100.0)
25-29	1144	6493	7637	27479	21595	49074	423	186	609	261	104	365	29308	28377	57685
	(3.9)	(22.9)	(13.2)	(93.8)	(76.1)	(85.1)	(1.4)	(0.7)	(1.1)	(0.9)	(0.4)	(0.6)	(100.0)	(100.0)	(100.0)
30-34	421	1834	2255	24753	23482	48235	697	268	965	269	105	374	26140	25689	51829
	(1.6)	(7.1)	(4.4)	(94.7)	(91.4)	(93.1)	(2.7)	(1.1)	(1.8)	(1.0)	(0.4)	(0.7)	(100.0)	(100.0)	(100.0)
35-39	246	703	949	22481	23726	46207	1090	354	1444	260	99	359	24077	24881	48958
	(1.0)	(2.8)	(2.0)	(93.4)	(95.4)	(94.4)	(4.5)	(1.4)	(2.9)	(1.1)	(0.4)	(0.7)	(100.0)	(100.0)	(100.0)
40-44	162	387	549	16383	19517	35900	1401	436	1837	199	80	279	18145	20420	38565
	(0.9)	(1.9)	(1.4)	(90.3)	(95.6)	(93.1)	(7.7)	(2.1)	(4.8)	(1.1)	(0.4)	(0.7)	(100.0)	(100.0)	(100.0)
45-49	103	252	355	13903	16208	30111	1781	501	2282	144	63	207	15931	17024	32955
	(0.6)	(1.5)	(1.1)	(87.3)	(95.2)	(91.4)	(11.2)	(2.9)	(6.9)	(0.9)	(0.4)	(0.6)	(100.0)	(100.0)	(100.0)
50-54	78	206	284	9385	12879	22265	2403	676	3079	99	51	150	11965	13813	25778
	(0.6)	(1.5)	(1.1)	(78.4)	(93.2)	(86.4)	(20.1)	(4.9)	(11.9)	(0.8)	(0.4)	(0.6)	(100.0)	(100.0)	(100.0)
55-59	51	134	185	8095	8789	16874	2193	626	2819	58	34	92	10398	9573	19971
	(0.5)	(1.4)	(0.9)	(77.9)	(91.7)	(84.5)	(21.1)	(6.5)	(14.1)	(0.5)	(0.4)	(0.5)	(100.0)	(100.0)	(100.0)
60-64	92	185	277	6191	8858	15049	4163	1063	5231	60	36	96	10505	10147	20652
	(0.9)	(1.8)	(1.3)	(58.9)	(87.3)	(72.9)	(39.6)	(10.5)	(25.3)	(0.6)	(0.4)	(0.5)	(100.0)	(100.0)	(100.0)
65-69	76	142	218	4209	5979	10188	3424	925	4349	37	24	61	7746	7071	14817
	(1.0)	(2.0)	(1.4)	(53.4)	(84.5)	(68.8)	(44.2)	(13.1)	(29.4)	(0.5)	(0.3)	(0.4)	(100.0)	(100.0)	(100.0)
70-74	66	134	200	18954	4555	6449	3399	1039	4438	24	19	43	5382	5747	11129
	(1.2)	(2.3)	(1.8)	(35.2)	(79.3)	(57.9)	(63.2)	(18.1)	(39.9)	(0.4)	(0.3)	(0.4)	(100.0)	(100.0)	(100.0)
75-79	33	71	104	944	1811	3755	1433	521	1954	9	8	17	2418	2412	4830
	(1.3)	(3.0)	(2.2)	(39.0)	(75.1)	(57.0)	(59.3)	(21.6)	(40.5)	(0.4)	(0.3)	(0.3)	(100.0)	(100.0)	(100.0)
80+	98	148	246	778	1948	2726	2146	876	3022	11	11	22	3033	2983	6016
	(3.2)	(5.0)	(4.1)	(25.7)	(65.3)	(45.3)	(70.8)	(29.4)	(50.2)	(0.3)	(0.3)	(0.4)	(100.0)	(100.0)	(100.0)
All Ages	162300	208231	370531	171904	164951	336895	24946	7634	32580	1738	7460	2484	360888	381602	742490
	(45.0)	(53.5)	(49.9)	(47.6)	(42.5)	(45.4)	(6.9)	(2.0)	(4.4)	(0.5)	(2.0)	(0.3)	(100.0)	(100.0)	(100.0)
Age not Stated	499	700	1199	319	316	635	41	17	58	2	2	4	862	1035	1897
	(58.0)	(67.6)	(63.2)	(37.0)	(30.6)	(33.5)	(4.8)	(1.6)	(3.1)	(0.2)	(0.2)	(0.2)	(100.0)	(100.0)	(100.0)
Less than 18	147378	164779	312157	4030	1254	5284	94	35	129	43	26	69	151544	166095	317639
	(93.3)	(99.2)	(98.3)	(2.7)	(0.8)	(1.8)	(0.0)	(0.0)	(0.0)	(0.0)	(0.0)	(0.0)	(100.0)	(100.0)	(100.0)
Less than 21	156468	185698	342166	17716	5712	23428	1193	73	266	156	57	213	174534	191540	366074
	(89.6)	(97.0)	(93.5)	(10.2)	(3.6)	(6.4)	(0.1)	(0.0)	(0.1)	(0.1)	(0.0)	(0.0)	(100.0)	(100.0)	(100.0)

Note: Figures in Parenthesis indicate the percentage..
Source: Registrar General and Census Commissioner of India, *Census of India–2001.*

Table 6.8: Age-Specific Marital Status of Population, 2001. (Urban)

(Thousand)

Age Group	Never Married			Married			Widowed			Divorced/Separator			Total		
	Female	Male	Person	Female	Male	Person	Female	Male	Person	Female	Male	Person	Female	Male	Person
<10 Years	26297	28902	551899	0	0	0	0	0	0	0	0	0	26297	28902	551899
	(100.0)	(100.0)	(100.0)	(0.0)	(0.0)	(0.0)	(0.0)	(0.0)	(0.0)	(0.0)	(0.0)	(0.0)	(100.0)	(100.0)	(100.0)
10-14	15152	16902	32054	254	115	369	21	7	28	7	7	14	15434	17030	32464
	(98.2	(99.2)	(99.7)	(1.6)	(0.7)	(1.1)	(0.1)	(0.0)	(0.1)	(0.1)	(0.1)	(0.1)	(100.0)	(100.0)	(100.0)
15-19	11840	15737	27577	2083	441	2524	23	6	29	17	7	24	13962	16192	30154
	(84.8)	(97.2)	(91.5)	(14.9)	(2.8)	(8.4)	(0.2)	(0.0)	(0.1)	(0.1)	(0.0)	(0.0)	(100.0)	(100.0)	(100.0)
20-24	4843	11729	16572	8196	3428	11624	73	19	92	59	18	77	13172	15193	28365
	(36.7)	(77.2)	(58.4)	(62.2)	(22.6)	(41.0)	(0.6)	(0.1)	(0.3)	(0.5)	(0.1)	(0.3)	(100.0)	(100.0)	(100.0)
25-29	1222	5038	6260	11099	8071	79170	150	42	192	87	29	116	12557	13180	25737
	(9.7)	(38.2)	(24.3)	(88.4)	(61.3)	(74.5)	(1.2)	(0.3)	(0.7)	(0.7)	(0.2)	(0.5)	(100.0)	(100.0)	(100.0)
30-34	387	1419	1806	10028	10149	20177	261	69	330	97	36	133	10772	11673	22445
	(3.6)	(12.2)	(8.0)	(93.1)	(86.9)	(79.9)	(2.4)	(0.6)	(1.5)	(0.9)	(0.3)	(0.6)	(100.0)	(100.0)	(100.0)
35-39	211	499	710	9702	10528	20230	448	93	541	97	36	133	10458	11157	21615
	(2.0)	(4.5)	(3.3)	(92.8)	(94.4)	(93.3)	(4.3)	(0.8)	(2.5)	(0.9)	(0.3)	(0.6)	(100.0)	(100.0)	(100.0)
40-44	142	248	390	6905	9061	15966	593	118	711	75	31	106	7715	9458	170173
	(1.8)	(2.6)	(2.3)	(89.5)	(95.8)	(93.0)	(7.7)	(1.3)	(4.1)	(1.0)	(0.3)	(0.6)	(100.0)	(100.0)	(100.0)
45-49	99	151	250	5688	7531	13219	768	139	907	55	22	77	6610	7844	14454
	(1.5)	(1.9)	(1.7)	(86.1)	(96.0)	(91.5)	(11.6)	(1.8)	(6.3)	(0.8)	(0.3)	(0.5)	(100.0)	(100.0)	(100.0)
50-54	75	106	181	3684	5730	9414	974	187	1161	38	17	55	4771	6039	10810
	(1.6)	(1.7)	(1.7)	(77.2)	(94.9)	(87.1)	(20.4)	(3.1)	(10.7)	(0.8)	(0.3)	(0.5)	(100.0)	(100.0)	(100.0)
55-59	48	64	122	2707	3756	6463	895	180	1075	22	10	32	3672	4010	7682
	(1.3)	(1.6)	(1.5)	(73.7)	(93.7)	(84.1)	(24.4)	(4.4)	(14.0)	(0.6)	(0.3)	(0.4)	(100.0)	(100.0)	(100.0)
60-64	59	70	129	1936	3092	5028	1410	268	1678	21	9	30	3425	3440	6865
	(1.7)	(2.0)	(1.9)	(56.5)	(89.5)	(73.2)	(41.2)	(7.8)	(24.4)	(0.6)	(0.3)	(0.4)	(100.0)	(100.0)	(100.0)
65-69	47	54	101	1305	2086	3391	1224	255	1479	13	6	19	2589	2401	4990
	(1.8)	(2.2)	(2.0)	(50.4)	(86.9)	(68.2)	(47.3)	(10.6)	(29.6)	(0.5)	(0.3)	(0.4)	(100.0)	(100.0)	(100.0)
70-74	42	57	99	602	1440	2042	1146	278	1424	9	5	14	1798	1781	3579
	(2.4)	(3.1)	(2.8)	(33.5)	(80.9)	(57.1)	(63.7)	(15.7)	(39.8)	(0.4)	(0.3)	(0.3)	(100.0)	(100.0)	(100.0)
75-79	25	36	61	281	643	924	560	170	730	4	2	6	870	851	1721
	(2.8)	(4.3)	(3.5)	(32.3)	(75.5)	(53.7)	(64.4)	(19.9)	(42.4)	(0.4)	(0.3)	(0.4)	(100.0)	(100.0)	(100.0)
80+	46	65	111	256	610	866	779	258	1037	5	3	8	1086	936	2022
	(4.3)	(6.9)	(5.5)	(23.5)	(65.2)	(42.8)	(71.8)	(27.5)	(51.3)	(0.4)	(0.4)	(0.4)	(100.0)	(100.0)	(100.0)
All Ages	60748	81388	142136	64868	66830	131698	9344	2094	110438	605	242	847	135566	150554	286120
	(44.8)	(54.0)	(49.7)	(47.9)	(44.4)	(46.0)	(6.9)	(1.4)	(4.0)	(0.4)	(0.2)	(0.3)	(100.0)	(100.0)	(100.0)
Age not Stated	213	310	523	143	148	291	20	6	26	1	1	2	377	465	842
	(56.6)	(66.7)	(62.1)	(37.9)	(31.8)	(34.6)	(5.2)	(1.3)	(3.1)	(0.3)	(0.2)	(0.2)	(100.0)	(100.0)	(100.0)
Less than 18	49058	54936	103994	840	267	1107	34	10	44	13	11	24	49945	55224	105169
	(98.2)	(99.5)	(98.9)	(1.7)	(0.5)	(1.1)	(0.1)	(0.0)	(0.0)	(0.0)	(0.0)	(0.0)	(100.0)	(100.0)	(100.0)
Less than 21	55129	65288	120417	4406	1160	5566	63	17	80	39	18	57	59636	66484	126120
	(92.4)	(98.2)	(95.5)	(7.4)	(1.8)	(4.4)	(0.1)	(0.0)	(0.1)	(0.1)	(0.0)	(0.0)	(100.0)	(100.0)	(100.0)

Note: Figures in Parenthesis indicate the percentage..
Source: Registrar General and Census Commissioner of India, *Census of India–2001.*

Table 6.9: Comparative Educational Level of Female Population, 2001

(Percent)

Educational Level	*Rural*			*Urban*			*Total*		
	Female	*Male*	*Person*	*Female*	*Male*	*Person*	*Female*	*Male*	*Person*
Illiterate	61.67	41.42	51.26	36.68	24.96	30.51	54.85	36.76	45.49
	(75.15)	(52.93)	(63.69)	(46.15)	(31.24)	(38.28)	(67.83)	(47.25)	(57.15)
Literate without	14.86	18.63	16.79	13.87	14.27	14.08	14.58	17.40	16.04
educational level*	(8.25)	(12.81)	(10.60)	(10.99)	(11.74)	(11.38)	(8.94)	(12.53)	(10.80)
Primary	11.68	15.79	13.79	15.54	15.47	15.50	12.73	15.70	14.26
	(8.64)	(14.14)	(11.48)	(14.36)	(15.04)	(14.72)	(10.08)	(14.38)	(12.32)
Middle	5.73	9.98	7.92	10.02	11.86	10.99	6.91	10.51	8.77
	(4.89)	(10.17)	(7.61)	(11.46)	(14.08)	(12.84)	(6.55)	(11.19)	(8.96)
Matric Secondary/	5.22	11.34	8.37	16.52	21.61	19.20	8.31	14.24	11.38
Higher Secondary	(2.61)	(8.04)	(5.41)	(11.99)	(18.40)	(15.38)	(4.98)	(10.75)	(7.97)
Non-Technical Diploma or	0.01	0.02	0.02	0.05	0.11	0.08	0.03	0.05	0.04
Certificate not equal to Degree	(0.04)	(0.09)	(0.07)	(0.13)	(0.13)	(0.13)	(0.06)	(0.10)	(0.08)
Technical Diploma or Certificate	0.09	0.33	0.21	0.32	1.08	0.72	0.15	0.54	0.36
not equal to Degree	(0.06)	(0.22)	(0.14)	(0.25)	(0.89)	(0.59)	(0.11)	(0.40)	(0.26)
Graduate and above	0.74	2.49	1.64	7.00	10.64	8.92	2.44	4.80	3.66
	(0.36)	(1.60)	(1.00)	(4.67)	(8.48)	(6.68)	(1.45)	3.40	2.46
Total	100.00	100.00	100.00	100.00	100.00	100.00	100.00	100.00	100.00
Total Population (Million)	360.89	381.60	742.49	135.57	150.55	286.12	496.45	532.16	1028.61
	(301.53)	(321.27)	(622.80)	(101.83)	(113.94)	(215.77)	(403.36)	(435.21)	(838.57)

Note: * Includes figures for educational levels not classifiable.
Figures in Parenthesis indicate the Percentage of 1991 (Excludes Jammu and Kashmir).

Source: Registrar General and Census Commissioner of India, *Census of India 1991 and 2001.*

Table 6.10: Distribution of Female Main Workers by Educational Level, 2001

Educational Level	*Rural*			*Urban*			*Total*		
	Female	*Male*	*Person*	*Female*	*Male*	*Person*	*Female*	*Male*	*Person*
Illiterate	67.02	34.46	42.99	36.42	15.11	18.36	61.66	28.74	36.40
	(82.33)	(50.09)	(52.20)	(46.96)	(22.84)	(25.98)	(77.78)	(43.27)	(51.02)
Literate but below Matric/Secondary	26.86	45.53	40.63	27.98	38.31	36.74	27.06	43.39	39.59
Higher Secondary	(14.93)	(37.28)	(31.64)	(21.52)	(38.25)	(36.07)	(15.77)	(37.52)	(32.64)
Matric/Secondary/ Higher Secondary/	4.66	15.62	12.75	14.56	28.06	26.00	6.39	19.30	16.30
Inter/Pre-university (Below Graduate)	(2.02)	(10.19)	(8.13)	(14.01)	(24.17)	(22.85)	(3.56)	(13.68)	(11.40)
Technical Diploma or	0.27	0.45	0.41	1.53	1.55	1.55	0.49	0.78	0.71
Certificate not equal to Degree	(0.18)	(0.28)	(0.26)	(1.62)	(1.33)	(1.37)	(0.37)	(0.54)	(0.51)
Graduate and above	0.92	3.45	2.79	15.41	14.42	14.57	3.46	6.69	5.94
Other than Technical Degree	(0.54)	(2.18)	(1.77)	(15.89)	(13.41)	(13.73)	(2.52)	(4.99)	(4.43)
Technical Degree or	0.27	0.49	0.43	4.10	2.55	2.78	0.94	1.10	1.06
Diploma equal to Degree or Post-graduate Degree	(NA)	(NA)	(NA)	(NA)	(NA)	(NA)	(NA)	(NA)	(NA)
Total	100.00	100.00	100.00	100.00	100.00	100.00	100.00	100.00	100.00
Total Main Workers (Million)	60.08	169.10	229.18	12.77	71.05	83.82	72.85	240.15	313.00
	(56.00)	(166.29)	(222.29)	(8.27)	(55.37)	(63.64)	(64.27)	(221.66)	(285.93)

Note: Main workers are those who work for 183 days or more in a year.
Figures in Parenthesis indicate the percentage of 1991 (Excludes Jammu and Kashmir)
NA–Data not available.

Source: Registrar General and Census Commissioner of India, *Census of India 1991 and 2001.*

Figure 6.B

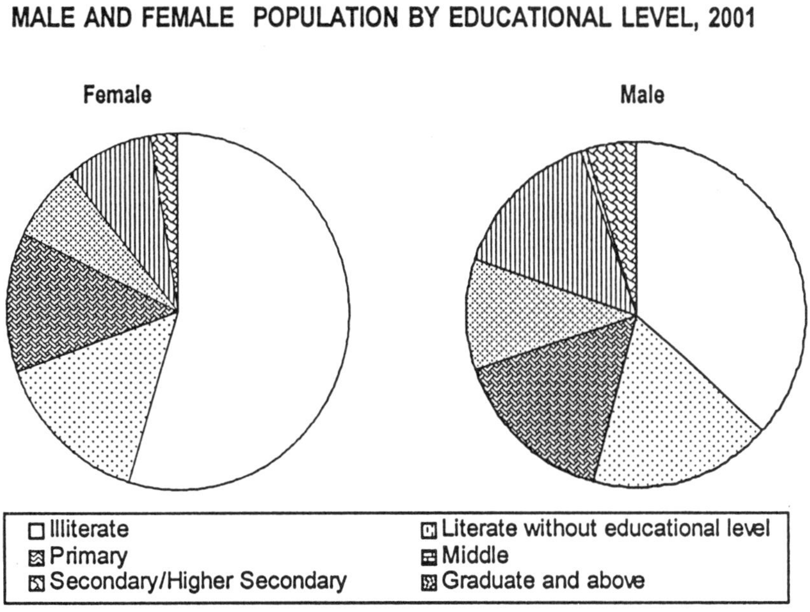

For details see Table 6.9

Figure 6.C

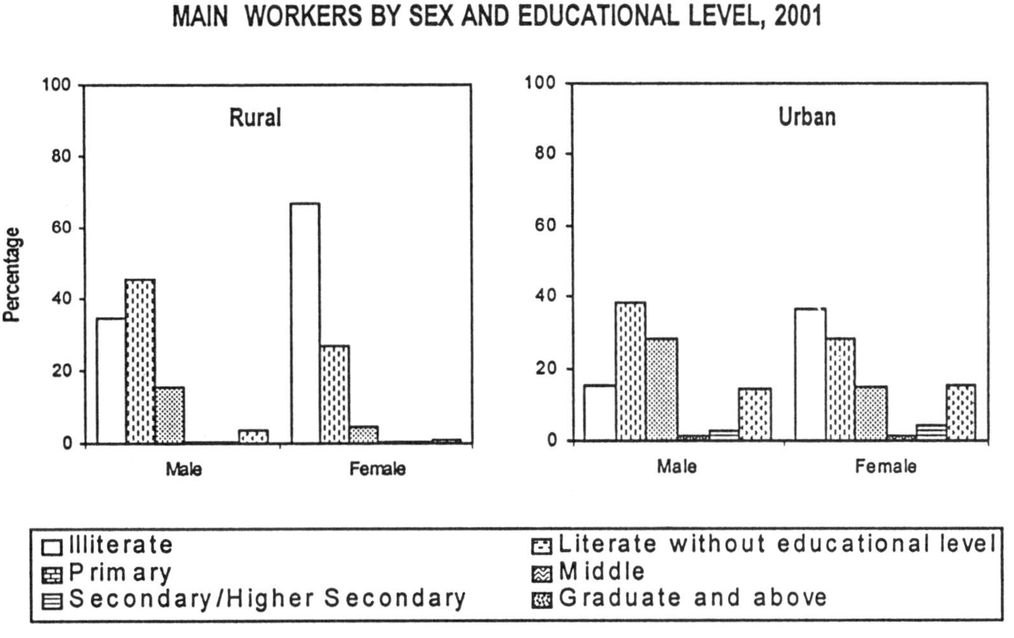

For details see Table 6.10

Table 6.11: Female Main Workers by Industry, 1991

(Million)

Industrial Classification (NIC)	Total			Urban		
	Female	Male	Person	Female	Male	Person
0. Agriculture, Hunting, Forestry & Fishing	52.04	139.66	191.70	1.87	6.82	8.69
1. Mining and Quarrying	0.22	1.61	1.83	0.06	0.71	0.77
2&3. Manufacturing	4.84	24.55	29.38	1.84	14.32	16.16
4. Electricity, Gas and Water	0.05	1.20	1.25	0.03	0.68	0.71
5. Construction	0.42	5.23	5.65	0.28	3.07	3.35
6. Wholesale and Retail Trade and Restaurants and Hotels	1.15	16.46	17.61	0.62	10.71	11.33
7. Transport, Storage and Communication Services	0.24	8.13	8.37	0.18	5.24	5.42
8. Financial, Insurance, Real Estate and Business Services	0.25	2.64	2.89	0.21	2.03	2.24
9. Community, Social and Personal Services	4.91	21.12	26.03	3.10	11.15	14.25
10. Activities not Adequately Defined	0.16	1.06	1.23	0.08	0.64	0.72
Total Workers	64.27	221.66	285.93	8.27	55.37	63.64

Note: Main workers are those who work for 183 days or more in a year. Totals may not tally due to rounding off.

Source: Registrar General and Census Commissioner of India, *Census of India 1991.*

Table 6.12: Female Main Workers by Industry, 2001

(Million)

Industrial Classification (NIC)	Total			Urban		
	Female	Male	Person	Female	Male	Person
0. Agriculture, Hunting, Forestry & Fishing	51.37	126.04	177.41	1.77	5.07	6.84
1. Mining and Quarrying	0.31	1.92	2.23	0.07	0.78	0.85
2&3. Manufacturing	8.10	30.54	38.65	3.07	16.68	19.75
4. Electricity, Gas and Water	0.08	1.41	1.49	0.06	0.80	0.86
5. Construction	1.08	10.86	11.94	0.61	5.67	6.29
6. Wholesale and Retail Trade and Restaurants and Hotels	2.18	26.91	29.10	1.16	17.07	18.22
7. Transport, Storage and Communication Services	0.38	11.82	12.20	0.27	7.04	7.32
8. Financial, Insurance, Real Estate and Business Services	1.52	8.02	9.54	0.98	5.56	6.54
9. Community, Social and Personal Services	22.40	7.68	30.08	4.75	12.24	16.99
10. Activities not Adequately Defined	NA	NA	NA	NA	NA	NA
Total Workers	72.71	239.92	312.63	12.74	70.91	83.65

Note: Main workers are those who work for 183 days or more in a year. Totals may not tally due to rounding off.

Source: Registrar General and Census Commissioner of India, *Census of India 2001.*

State/Union Territoty	Goverment		Private		Total	Total
	WITIs	Women Wing	WITIs	Women Wingh		Seats
1	2	3	4	5	6	7
States						
Andhra Pradesh	23	10	4	17	54	3,980
Arunachal Pradesh	1	–	–	–	1	80
Assam	5	5	1	–	11	864
Bihar	7	–	–	–	7	432
Chhattisgarh	8	5	–	–	13	488
Delhi	3	7	29	2	41	2,760
Goa	–	–	–	–	–	0
Gujarat	6	24	3	–	33	2,160
Haryana	31	–	8	–	39	2,460
Himachal Pradesh	16	–	–	–	16	1,140
Jammu & Kashmir	10	44	–	–	54	1,246
Jharkhand	6	—	—	–	6	544
Karnataka	17	–	11	–	28	2,260
Kerala	8	–	1	–	9	1,334
Madhya pradesh	14	–	–	–	14	846
Maharashtra	15	476	8	89	588	13,702
Manipur	1	7	–	–	8	192
Meghalaya	1	–	–	–	1	52
Mizoram	–	–	–	–	–	0
Nagaland	1	0	–	–	1	112
Orissa	10	–	5	–	15	928
Punjab	38	32	–	–	70	4,564
Rajasthan	8	5	4	–	17	928
Sikkim	–	–	–	–	–	0
Tamil Nadu	12	3	12	–	27	2,568
Tripura	1	–	–	–	1	116
Uttaranchal	4	5	–	–	9	560
Uttar Pradesh	11	48	8	–	67	3,852
West Bengal	4	12	1	–	17	640
Union Territories						
Andaman & Nicobar Islands	–	–	–	–	–	0
Chandigarh	1	–	–	–	1	280
Dadra & Nagar Haveli	–	1	–	–	1	16
Daman & Diu	–	–	–	–	–	0
Lakshdweep	–	0	–	–	0	0
Pondicherry	2	1	–	–	3	232
Total	264	285	95	108	1,152	49,336

Notes: * As on October, 2007.

– Nil.

Source: Ministry of Labour and Employment, *Annual Report*, 2007-08.

Table 6.14: Performance of Employment Exchanges in respect of Women Job-Seekers

(Thousand)

Year	*Registration*	*Placement*	*Live Register of Women*	*Total Live Register*	*% of Live Register of Women to Total*
1992	1,160.9	44.2	7,652.9	36,758.4	20.8
1993	1,226.2	42.4	7,865.3	36,275.5	21.7
1994	1,316.5	42.1	8,044.5	36,691.5	21.9
1995	1,376.0	43.6	8,020.3	36,742.3	21.8
1996	1,446.9	50.1	8,379.5	37,429.6	22.4
1997	1,609.1	61.5	9,032.7	39,139.9	23.1
1998	1,518.0	42.0	9,526.1	40,089.9	23.8
1999	1,616.7	53.0	9,932.7	40,371.4	24.6
2000	1,646.3	35.7	10,457.3	41,343.6	25.3
2001	1,540.8	31.5	10,884.8	41,995.9	25.9
2002	1,343.1	25.9	10,649.5	41,171.2	25.9
2003	1,448.8	26.7	10,752.3	41,388.7	26.1
2004	1,551.5	24.5	10,711.6	40,457.6	26.5
2005	1,606.9	32.4	10,605.6	39,347.8	27.0
2006	2,537.4	31.3	11,781.0	41,466.0	28.4

Source: Ministry of Labour and Employment, Annual Report, 2007-08.

Table 6.15 : Fertility Indicators by Level of Education of Women, 2000

(Percent)

Indicators	*Age group*	*Educational Level*								
		Illiterate	*Literate*							
			Total literate	*Without any formal education*	*Below primary*	*Primary*	*Middle*	*Class X*	*Class XII*	*Graduate and above*
				Total						
Age specific fertility rates	15-19	96.1	35.0	94.5	67.6	34.4	23.4	18.7	14.3	22.5
	20-24	289.4	191.5	284.5	298.1	194.6	187.5	143.5	87.4	94.5
	25-29	229.8	159.8	195.5	212.2	149.7	144.9	143.9	124.5	126.8
	30-34	134.9	70.9	109.7	90.1	60.5	55.7	61.3	62.4	63.2
	35-39	78.4	25.9	52.5	32.9	17.9	20.7	17.7	22.1	24.8
	40.44	32.6	7.8	17.1	9.7	6.1	7.2	3.7	3.0	4.5
	45-49	11.4	2.3	6.4	2.7	1.3	2.4	1.0	0.5	0.0
General fertility rate		128.1	87.9	117.1	124.3	80.4	74.8	72.3	63.9	71.4
Total fertility rate		4.4	2.5	3.8	3.6	2.3	2.2	1.9	1.6	1.7
				Rural						
Age specific fertility rate	15-19	98.5	39.3	94.3	71.5	35.0	25.1	21.2	18.3	16.7
	20-24	288.2	202.0	268.2	300.0	191.6	183.5	142.5	96.7	87.6
	25-29	230.6	161.9	184.1	211.4	145.3	146.7	132.0	125.1	123.9
	30-34	134.6	72.4	107.8	89.1	59.6	58.2	55.4	56.0	67.0
	35-39	81.6	30.2	54.5	35.7	21.0	23.0	21.0	25.3	33.7
	40-44	33.7	9.5	18.6	11.0	7.2	6.0	3.5	6.0	11.2
	45-49	12.3	2.7	6.4	3.0	2.0	1.0	1.8	0.6	0.0
General fertility rate		130.1	93.4	115.2	128.3	81.2	77.4	74.4	71.4	77.9
Total fertility rate		4.4	2.6	3.7	3.6	2.3	2.2	1.9	1.6	1.7
				Urban						
Age specific fertility rate	15-19	75.4	24.4	96.9	49.1	32.4	19.5	15.2	11.2	30.5
	20-24	299.6	170.6	383.9	291.3	203.3	196.6	145.0	79.4	97.6
	25-29	223.9	156.1	257.8	214.4	159.7	141.4	158.8	123.6	127.9
	30-34	137.8	68.2	119.7	93.3	62.3	51.5	67.7	67.5	62.0
	35-39	58.3	19.7	44.6	26.0	12.1	17.5	14.9	20.2	22.8
	40-44	25.0	5.5	10.7	6.4	4.1	8.8	3.8	1.8	3.2
	45-49	6.3	1.8	6.3	2.2	0.3	4.0	0.5	0.4	0.0
General fertility rate		113.8	77.6	126.3	111.7	78.2	69.8	69.8	58.3	69.3
Total fertility rate		4.1	2.2	4.6	3.4	2.4	2.2	2.0	1.5	1.7

Source: Sample Registeration System, *Statistical Report, 2000.*

Table 6.16 : Industries which Employed more Females than Males, 1991

Description	*NIC Group*	*Number of workers* *Female*	*Male*	*Percent Female*
1. Processing, Canning and Preserving of Fish, crustacea and similar foods	203	14,215	13,938	51
2. Processing of edible nuts	215	61,761	31,092	67
3. Manufacture of bidi	226	1,454,224	648,316	69
4. Cotton Spinning other than in mills (charkha)	231	150,159	109,718	58
5. Preparatory operations (including carding and combing) on coir fibres	252	17,975	9,471	65
6. Spinning, weaving and finishing of coir textiles	255	53,936	30,974	64
7. Manufacturing of matches	307	91,638	40,816	69
8. Welfare services rendered by organisations operating on a no profit basis for the promotion of welfare of the community such as relief societies, creches, homes for the aged and physically handicapped, etc.	941	170,177	99,921	63
9. Domestic Services	960	562,396	410,527	58

Source: Registrar General and Census Commissioner of India, *Census of India 1991.*

Table 6.17 : Percentage Distribution of Migrants by Reason

Reasons	*1981*		*1991*		*2001*	
	Female	*Male*	*Female*	*Male*	*Female*	*Male*
Employment	1.9	31.8	1.8	27.0	1.7	28.1
Education	1.0	5.1	0.8	4.8	0.4	2.5
Family Moved	14.3	30.3	11.0	26.6	14.2	29.3
Marriage	73.4	3.3	76.1	4.0	69.6	2.3
Others*	9.4	29.5	10.3	37.6	14.1	37.7
Total	100.0	100.0	100.0	100.0	100.0	100.0
Total (Million)	145.2	62.5	167.8	64.3	221.2	93.4

Note: * Include business, natural calamities like drought, floods, etc.
Source: Registrar General and Census Commissiner of India, Census of India 1981, 1991 and 2001.

Table 6.18: Share of Women in Employment Generated Under Poverty Alleviation Programmes

Rural India

Years	*Total number of families assisted under self employment Programmes SGSY (Million Families)*	*Percent share of Women*	*Total no. of mandays generated under wage employment programmes SGRY (Million Mandays)*	*Percent share of Women*	*Women Benefitted under DWCRA (in lakh)*
1985-86	3.2	11.52	564.0	9.67	1.01
1988-89	4.0	24.53	691.5	20.75	0.98
1989.90	3.6	27.00	864.4	22.04	0.90
1990-91	3.1	32.29	873.8	24.64	1.10
1993-94	2.8	35.47	1075.3	22.82	2.69
1994-95	2.5	35.42	1225.7	22.25	5.92
1995-96	2.3	34.16	1239.4	29.67	6.97
1996-97	1.7	31.39	730.1	30.52	5.82
1997-98	1.9	36.63	855.0	28.72	4.60
1998-99	1.6	37.56	649.7	27.69	5.77
1999-00	0.9	44.62	546.9	28.14	@
2000-2001	1.0	40.73	486.7	27.56	@
2001-2002	0.9	41.16	523.0	27.61	@
2002-2003	0.8	46.31	748.3	26.11	@
2003-2004	0.9	52.41	856.0	26.59	@
2004-2005*	0.6	53.60	540.0	24.85	@
2005-2006	1.1	57.56	821.8	25.53	@
2006-2007	1.7	73.71	424.1	23.76	@
2007-2008**	0.8	61.17	117.4	28.32	@

Notes : * as on 31-1-2005 @ Merged in SGSY w.e.f. 1..4.1999

** as on 31-12-2007

IRDP : Integrated Rural Development Programme

TRYSEM : Training of Rural Youth for Self Employment

NREP : National Rural Employment Programme (during 1985-89)

RLEGP : Rural Landless Employment Guarantee Programme (during 1985-89)

JRY : Jawahar Rozgar Yojana (since 1989-90)

EAS : Employment Assurance Scheme (since 1993-94)

SGSY : Swarnjayanti Gram Swarozgar Yojana launched since Ist April 1999 in place of earlier self employment programmes such as IRDP+TRYSEM

SGRY : Sampoorna Grameen Rozgar Yojana launched since 25th Sept. 2001 in place of earlier wage employment programmes such as NREP+RLEFP+JRY+EAS.

Sources : (1) Department of Rural Employment and Poverty Alleviation : 'Report of the working group on Rural Poverty Alleviation Programmes for the Tenth Five Year Plan 2002-2007.

(2) Ministry of Rural Development, *Annual Report* of the relevant various years.

Table 6.19: Share of Women in National Rural Emploment Guarantee Scheme

(Lakhs)

State	*No. of House-holds who have demanded employment*	*No. of Households Provided employment*	*Mandays*					
			Total	*S.C.*	*S.T.*	*Other*	*Woman*	*% of Women*
States								
Andhra Pradesh	38.18	38.18	1245.42	335.72	158.56	751.14	715.98	57.5
	(17.88)	(17.88)	(503.32)	(154.78)	(63.2)	(285.34)	(264.45)	(52.5)
Arunachal Pradesh	0.00	0.00	0.00	0.00	0.00	0.00	0.00	0.00
	(0.17)	(0.17)	(4.53)	(0.00)	(4.53)	(0.00)	(1.36)	(30.0)
Assam	8.89	8.56	281.20	22.94	121.05	137.21	96.71	34.4
	(5.00)	(4.47)	(295.87)	(27.85)	(130.41)	(137.61)	(64.76)	(21.9)
Bihar	24.02	24.02	498.07	210.39	13.76	273.93	126.05	25.3
	(8.94)	(8.87)	(297.24)	(138.86)	(4.61)	(153.76)	(50.54)	(17.0)
Chhattisgarh	17.60	17.60	835.47	128.04	345.84	361.28	341.50	40.9
	(11.23)	(10.45)	(467.90)	(47.92)	(233.19)	(186.79)	(172.31)	(36.8)
Gujarat	1.98	1.98	63.67	3.10	41.00	19.57	31.07	48.8
	(1.47)	(1.47)	(67.89)	(5.02)	(39.63)	(23.23)	(35.33)	(52.0)
Haryana	0.51	0.51	26.35	15.15	0.00	11.20	9.69	36.8
	(0.39)	(0.39)	(17.35)	(10.45)	(0.00)	(6.90)	(4.91)	(28.3)
Himachal Pradesh	2.14	2.02	109.37	23.60	28.54	57.22	29.98	27.4
	(0.57)	(0.53)	(17.34)	(5.17)	(4.14)	(8.03)	(1.76)	(10.1)
Jammu & Kashmir	0.93	0.92	27.94	2.07	5.57	20.30	0.20	0.72
	(0.39)	(0.16)	(9.65)	(0.63)	(1.59)	(7.42)	(0.01)	(0.10)
Jharkhand	12.48	12.42	554.48	114.00	236.63	203.85	125.51	22.64
	(8.69)	(8.46)	(308.14)	(74.17)	(124.32)	(109.65)	(106.83)	(34.7)
Karnataka	3.36	3.35	137.37	42.26	28.84	66.27	71.08	51.7
	(5.09)	(4.79)	(163.41)	(54.28)	(34.23)	(74.90)	(84.28)	(51.6)
Kerala	1.26	1.21	34.65	5.15	6.54	22.96	23.10	66.7
	(0.67)	(0.60)	(7.41)	(1.03)	(0.79)	(5.58)	(3.92)	(52.9)
Madhya Pradesh	38.64	38.64	2048.04	363.94	1009.94	674.16	875.75	42.8
	(26.19)	(25.82)	(1590.73)	(266.66)	(769.92)	(554.15)	(688.04)	(43.2)
Maharashtra	2.36	2.36	119.31	22.05	40.12	57.14	47.07	39.4
	(1.91)	(1.91)	(0.00)	(0.00)	(0.00)	(0.00)	(0.00)	(0.00)
Manipur	0.86	0.64	15.34	0.02	15.22	0.11	3.80	24.8
	(0.18)	(0.18)	(8.26)	(0.00)	(8.26)	(0)	(3.31)	(40.1)
Meghalaya	0.76	0.76	35.70	0.19	30.77	4.74	12.03	33.7
	(0.13)	(0.13)	(2.01)	(0.00)	(2.01)	(0.00)	(0.50)	(24.9)

State	No. of Households who have demanded employment	No. of Households Provided employment	Mandays					
			Total	S.C.	S.T.	Other	Woman	Year of Women
States								
Mizoram	0.84 (0.19)	0.84 (0.07)	26.31 (2.37)	0.00 (0.00)	26.31 (2.37)	0.00 (0.00)	10.07 (0.78)	38.3 (32.9)
Nagaland	0.34 (0.28)	0.21 (0.28)	4.48 (11.82)	0.00 (0.00)	4.48 (11.82)	0.00 (0.00)	1.74 (3.54)	38.8 (29.9)
Orissa	8.44 (12.77)	8.31 (12.64)	293.68 (506.64)	71.01 (122.51)	134.38 (248.03)	88.29 (136.10)	109.88 (166.58)	37.4 (32.9)
Punjab	0.36 (0.31)	0.36 (0.31)	12.16 (11.08)	9.18 (8.15)	0.00 (0.00)	2.99 (2.93)	1.67 (3.82)	13.7 (34.5)
Rajasthan	19.84 (10.94)	19.84 (10.94)	1135.27 (806.21)	223.04 (121.84)	546.89 (522.39)	365.35 (161.98)	788.02 (516.87)	69.4 (64.1)
Sikkim	0.08 (0.04)	0.07 (0.04)	2.12 (1.55)	0.16 (0.01)	1.18 (1.48)	0.78 (0.06)	0.25 (0.30)	11.8 (19.3)
Tamil Nadu	9.06 (5.08)	9.06 (5.08)	546.23 (129.13)	311.82 (66.41)	11.31 (2.40)	223.10 (60.32)	447.21 (62.26)	81.9 (48.2)
Tripura	4.21 (0.67)	4.18 (0.67)	129.96 (45.58)	21.31 (7.76)	51.46 (27.81)	57.19 (10.01)	52.51 (34.34)	40.4 (75.3)
Uttaranchal	1.49 (1.07)	1.49 (1.07)	50.38 (26.46)	14.74 (6.55)	1.14 (0.39)	34.50 (19.52)	22.34 (7.47)	44.3 (28.2)
Uttar Pradesh	38.03 (24.20)	37.89 (23.26)	891.84 (617.64)	477.84 (351.21)	19.58 (20.37)	394.42 (246.06)	126.14 (98.67)	14.1 (16.0)
West Bengal	38.59 (25.73)	37.52 (24.25)	479.02 (280.98)	172.18 (86.86)	61.20 (38.10)	245.63 (156.02)	82.54 (45.04)	17.2 (16.0)
All India	275.56 (170.20)	272.96 (164.91)	9603.53 (6200.51)	2589.91 (1585.14)	2940.30 (2296.01)	4073.31 (2346.36)	4151.88 (2426.48)	43.2 (39.1)

Notes: * As on Mid January, 2008

The Figure is Parenthesis indicate as on February 2007.

Source: Ministry of Rural Development, Annual Report, 2007-08.

Table 6.20: Women Judges in Supreme Court/High Courts, 2008*

Sl. No.	Name of Court	Number of Judges: Total	Men	Women	Percentage of Women to total
	Supreme Court	23	23	0	0.0
	High Court				
1.	Allahabad	78	75	03	3.8
2.	Andhra Pradesh	16	14	02	12.5
3.	Bombay	63	57	06	9.5
4.	Calcutta	40	38	02	5.0
5.	Chhatishgarh	06	06	0	0.0
6.	Delhi	38	34	04	10.5
7.	Gauhati	20	19	01	5.0
8.	Gujarat	29	26	03	10.3
9.	Himachal Pradesh	10	10	00	0.0
10.	Jammu & Kashmir	11	11	00	0.0
11.	Jharkhand	10	10	00	0.0
12.	Karnataka	31	30	01	3.2
13.	Kerala	25	23	02	8.0
14.	Madhya Pradesh	41	38	03	7.3
15.	Madras	45	42	03	6.7
16.	Orissa	19	18	01	5.3
17.	Patna	26	24	02	7.7
18.	Punjab & Haryana	34	33	01	2.9
19.	Rajasthan	34	34	00	0.0
20.	Sikkim	02	02	00	0.0
21.	Uttaranchal	09	09	00	0.0
	Total	610	576	34	5.6

Note : * Figures as on 14th August, 2008.

Source : Department of Justice, Ministry of Law and Justice, New Delhi.

Table 6.21 : Representatives of Women in Premier Services

Service	1987 Total	1987 Women	1987 Percentage	1997 Total	1997 Women	1997 Percentage	2000 Total	2000 Women	2000 Percentage
IAS	4,204	339	8.06	4,991	512	10.26	5,159	535	10.37
IPS	2,418	21	0.87	3,045	67	2.20	3,301	110	3.33
Total	6,622	360	5.44	8,036	579	7.21	8,460	645	7.62

Source: Department of Personnel and Training, Govt. of India.

Table 6.22: Representation of Women in Lok Sabha

Lok Sabha	*Years*	*Total Number of Seats*	*Number of Women Member*	*Percent to Total*
1st	1952	499	22	4.4
2nd	1957	500	27	5.4
3rd	1962	503	34	6.8
4th	1967	523	31	5.9
5th	1971	521	22	4.2
6th	1977	544	19	3.5
7th	1980	544	28	5.1
8th	1984	544	44	8.1
9th	1989	517	27	5.2
10th	1991	544	39	7.2
11th	1996	544	40*	7.4
12th	1998	543	43	7.9
13th	1999	543	49	9.0
14th	2004	543	45	8.3
15th	2009	542	58	10.7

Notes: * One MP nominated by the President.
Source: Election Commission of India.

Table 6.23: Representation of Women in Rajya Shbha

Years	*Total*	*Women Member*	*Percent to Total*
1990	245	24	9.8
1992	245	17	6.9
1994	245	20	8.2
1996	245	18	7.3
1997	245	22	7.3
1998	245	19	7.8
1999	245	19	7.8
2000	245	22	9.0
2001	245	22	9.0
2004	245	28	11.4
2005	245	25	10.2
2009	236	21	8.9

Source: Election Commission of India.

Table 6.24: State-wise Representatives of Women in Village Panchayat

S.No.	State/ Union Territories	No. of Village Panchayats	Village Panchayats Representatives		
			Total Member	Women Member	Percentage of Women to Total
1	2	3	4	5	6
	States				
1.	Andhra Pradesh	21,913	2,77,027	68,736	24.8
2.	Arunachal Pradesh	1,747	NA	NA	NA
3.	Assam	2,489	23,471	7851	33.5
4.	Bihar	8,471	1,56,582	40,553	25.9
5.	Chhattisgarh	9,139	1,66,124	41,913	25.3
6.	Goa	190	1,439	457	31.8
7.	Gujarat	13,819	1,24,198	40,985	33.0
8.	Haryana	6,034	73,002	18,356	25.2
9.	Himachal Pradesh	3,037	25,371	6,822	26.8
10.	Jammu & Kashmir	2,683	—	—	—
11.	Jharkhand	3,746	NA	NA	NA
12.	Karnataka	5,659	89,343	35,922	40.2
13.	Kerala	991	13,259	4,801	36.2
14.	Madhya Pradesh	22,029	3,14,847	1,06,491	33.9
15.	Maharashtra	28,553	2,55,194	77,548	30.4
16.	Manipur	166	1,722	611	35.5
17.	Orissa	6,234	1,18,961	31,414	26.4
18.	Punjab	12,445	75,968	27,108	35.7
19.	Rajasthan	9,189	1,53,732	39,450	25.7
20.	Sikkim	159	1,195	322	26.9
21.	Tamil Nadu	12,618	97,458	26,181	26.9
22.	Tripura	537	5,685	1,895	33.3
23.	Uttaranchal	7,227	2,61,915	18,041	6.8
24.	Uttar Pradesh	52,028	6,08,383	2,30,865	37.9
25.	West Bengal	3,360	51,200	11,497	22.5
	Sub-Total (A)	2,34,463	28,96,076	8,37,819	28.9
	Union Territories				
1.	Andaman and NicobarIslands	67	759	261	34.4
2.	Chandigarh	17	217	55	25.4
3.	Dadra and Nagar Havel	11	169	45	26.6
4.	Daman and Diu	10	63	17	27.0
5.	Lakshadweep	10	79	30	38.0
6.	Pondicherry	98	NA	NA	NA
	Sub-Total (B)	213	1,287	408	31.7
	Total (A+B)	2,34,676	28,97,363	8,38,227	28.9

Notes: As on April 2004 NA: Information is not available
— Nil
Arunachal Pradesh— Panchayat Elections held on 2.04.2003 expect on Tirap District.
Jammu & Kashmir— Has not adopted the Consitution (Seventy-Third) Amendment Act 1992.
Jharkhand— Elections to the local bodies are yet to be conducted.
Meghalaya, Mizoram, & Nagaland— Have traditional Councils.
Delhi— Panchayati Raj System is yet to be revised.

Source: Ministry of Rural Development, Govetment of India

Table 6.25: State-wise Representatives of Women in Intermediate Panchayat

S.No.	State/ Union Territories	No. of Intermediate Panchayats	Intermediate Panchayats Representatives		
			Total Member	Women Member	Percentage of Women to Total
1	2	3	4	5	6
	States				
1.	Andhra Pradesh	1,095	19,536	4,919	25.2
2.	Arunachal Pradesh	150	NA	NA	NA
3.	Assam	203	2,148	746	34.5
4.	Bihar	531	15,676	4,065	26.0
5.	Chhattisgarh	146	3,545	906	25.5
6.	Goa	—	—	—	—
7.	Gujarat	225	4,161	1,393	33.5
8.	Haryana	114	3,272	842	25.8
9.	Himachal Pradesh	75	2,220	562	25.3
10.	Jammu & Kashmir	—	—	—	—
11.	Jharkhand	211	NA	NA	NA
12.	Karnataka	175	3,537	1,375	38.9
13.	Kerala	152	1,638	629	38.4
14.	Madhya Pradesh	313	6,456	2,159	33.4
15.	Maharashtra	349	4,284	1,407	32.9
16.	Manipur	—	—	—	—
17.	Orissa	314	8,415	2,188	26.0
18.	Punjab	140	2,480	813	32.8
19.	Rajasthan	237	7,165	1,908	26.6
20.	Sikkim	—	—	—	—
21.	Tamil Nadu	385	6,570	1,770	27.0
22.	Tripura	23	299	106	35.5
23.	Uttaranchal	95	3,225	1,133	35.1
24.	Uttar Pradesh	813	51,870	18,580	35.8
25.	West Bengal	333	8,579	1,923	22.4
	Sub-Total (A)	6,079	1,55,076	47,424	30.6
	Union Territories				
1.	Andaman and NicobarIslands	7	67	25	37.3
2.	Chandigarh	1	21	6	28.6
3.	Dadra and Nagar Havel	—	—	—	—
4.	Daman and Diu	—	—	—	—
5.	Lakshadweep	—	—	—	—
6.	Pondicherry	10	NA	NA	NA
	Sub-Total (B)	18	88	31	35.2
	Total (A+B)	6,097	1,55,164	47,455	30.6

Notes: As on April 2004 NA: Information is not available — Nil

Arunachal Pradesh— Panchayat Elections held on 2.04.2003 expect on Tirap District.

Jammu & Kashmir— Has not adopted the Consitution (Seventy-Third) Amendment Act 1992.

Jharkhand— Elections to the local bodies are yet to be conducted.

Meghalaya, Mizoram, & Nagaland— Have traditional Councils.

Delhi— Panchayati Raj System is yet to be revised.

Manipur, Sikkim, Dadar and Nagar Haveli, Daman and Diu, Lakshadweep—Intermediate Panchayat does not exist..

Source: Ministry of Rural Development, Govetment of India

Table 6.26: State-wise Representatives of Women in District Panchayat

S.No.	State/ Union Territories	No. of District Panchayats	District Panchayats Representatives: Total Member	Women Member	Percentage of Women to Total
1	2	3	4	5	6
	States				
1.	Andhra Pradesh	22	1,459	364	24.9
2.	Arunachal Pradesh	15	NA	NA	NA
3.	Assam	20	390	117	30.0
4.	Bihar	38	1,572	410	26.1
5.	Chhattisgarh	16	389	95	24.4
6.	Goa	2	50	17	34.0
7.	Gujarat	25	819	275	33.6
8.	Haryana	19	423	109	25.8
9.	Himachal Pradesh	12	338	87	25.8
10.	Jammu & Kashmir	—	—	—	—
11.	Jharkhand	22	NA	NA	NA
12.	Karnataka	27	930	339	36.4
13.	Kerala	14	307	105	34.2
14.	Madhya Pradesh	45	734	248	33.8
15.	Maharashtra	33	2,081	658	31.6
16.	Manipur	4	61	22	36.1
17.	Orissa	30	1,150	296	25.8
18.	Punjab	17	279	89	31.9
19.	Rajasthan	32	1,372	364	26.5
20.	Sikkim	4	121	29	23.9
21.	Tamil Nadu	29	656	173	26.4
22.	Tripura	4	82	28	34.2
23.	Uttaranchal	13	345	119	34.5
24.	Uttar Pradesh	71	2,126	788	37.1
25.	West Bengal	18	723	156	21.6
	Sub-Total (A)	532	16,407	4,888	29.8
	Union Territories				
1.	Andaman and Nicobar Islands	1	30	10	33.3
2.	Chandigarh	1	13	3	23.1
3.	Dadra and Nagar Havel	1	16	4	25.0
4.	Daman and Diu	1	25	10	40.0
5.	Lakshadweep	1	22	8	36.4
6.	Pondicherry	1	—	35	33.0
	Sub-Total (B)	5	106	35	33.0
	Total (A+B)	537	16,513	4,923	29.8

Notes: As on April 2004 NA: Information is not available
— Nil
Arunachal Pradesh— Panchayat Elections held on 2.04.2003 expect on Tirap District.
Jammu & Kashmir— Has not adopted the Consitution (Seventy-Third) Amendment Act 1992.
Jharkhand— Elections to the local bodies are yet to be conducted.
Meghalaya, Mizoram, & Nagaland— Have traditional Councils.
Delhi— Panchayati Raj System is yet to be revised.

Source: Ministry of Rural Development, Govetment of India

SECTION 7

International Comparisons

Dr. Shachi Joshi
Vijay K. Saxena

Section VII

International Comparisons

This section captures the information relating to socio-economic, educational, health and demographic indicators from various countries of the world. The countries have been grouped as SAARC Countries , Other Asian and Pacific Countries, African Countries,North America Countries,South America Countries and European Countries.These indicators have been compared and contrasted in different tables for the purpose of a better understanding.

Table 7.1 provides broad dimensions of population, area, density and urbanization ratios. The figures show that Asia has some of the most densely populated and least urbanized countries in the world (China being at the top with a population of 1312 million and India on the second with 1110.0 million). Bangladesh is the worst and Australia and Canada are the least densely populated countries of the world with respective figures of 1198 and 3 per sq. km. in terms of sex ratio, there is not much variation amongst the countries. All the SAARC countries have less number of females per 1000 males, which is in line with the gender discrimination prevalent in these countries whereas European countries have higher sex ratios.

Highest percentage of urban population is in United Kingdom (89.7) SAARC Countries present the lowest percentage of urban population. Table 7.2 depicts the vital statistics of population in various countries. Crude birth rate is high among all the African Countries with Uganda having highest birth rate (47.0) and fertility rate (6.7).

Among SAARC Countries Nepal has the highest birth rate (29.0) and Sri Lanka the lowest (19.0). Europe has the lowest fertility rate followed by North America. Death rate and infant mortality rate is also higher in African Countries.

Maternal mortality ratio (MMR) is also high among African Countries. Many SAARC countries show poor health system also reiterates the fact that government interventions and health sector reforms have still to make a mark in these developing countries.

Table 7.3 provides information on dependency rates and adult literacy rates. Dependency rate is highest in Uganda (108.3) followed by Zambia (99.7). Republic of Korea shows the lowest dependency rate (39.6). No significant change in dependency rate is seen 2001 to 2015.

Adult literacy rates shows that many Asian and Pacific Countries have been able to achieve high literacy rates among its adult population.

Table 7.4 deals with the labour force including participation rate, gender composition and its distribution over broad sectors like agriculture, industry and services. Interestingly, most countries of the world have a similar pattern in terms of gender composition except for Bhutan, where participation of women in labour force is more than the males (57.1%). Pakistan has the lowest percentage of women (27.3%) in labour force. As far as total labour force is concerned, China tops with 780.5 million followed by India 438.0 million persons in labour force.

In the agriculture sector, Argentina and United Kingdom have the lowest proportion of male in labour force (2 per cent) and Ghana and Uganda have the highest proportion (60 per cent) while the rate of female participation is lowest in USA and UK (1 per cent) and highest in India and Uganda (77 per cent).

In the Industry sector, labour force participation in males is highest in Germany (41 per cent) and lowest in Uganda (11 per cent) while the female percentage is lowest in Australia and United Kingdom (9 per cent) and highest in Sri Lanka (35 per cent).

In the services sector, proportion of male labour force is highest (67 per cent) in Nigeria and lowest (27 per cent) in Ghana while in the case of female participation the highest is (90 per cent) in United Kingdom and lowest (10 per cent) in India.

The participation of females in economic activity (Age 15 and above) by sectors is given in Table 7.5. Uganda has the highest percentage (79.7) and Pakistan has the lowest (32.7 per cent) of females participating in economic activities. Among the SAARC countries Bangladesh has the highest (52.7) percentage of females participating in economic activities. As regards female employment in broad economic sectors is concerned, Zambia has the highest (78 per cent) participation of females in Agriculture. Malaysia has the highest percentage of females in economic activities relating to industrial sector. In service sector, United Kingdom (90 per cent) and USA (90 per cent) have the highest and Bangladesh has the lowest participation of females in economic activities.

The importance, the different national governments place on the need for social sector investments in terms of both financial and human capital resources, is evident from table 7.6 and 7.7. Table 7.6 shows that Indonesia has the lowest (0.9 per cent) and Maldives has the highest expenditure (7.1 per cent) on education as percentage of GDP in the world. On health, Germany and France spend the highest percentage of GDP with 8.9 Per cent, while Pakistan ranks lowest with spending of 0.4 per cent of GDP. Percentage of population residing below poverty line is highest in African countries, Nigeria scoring the highest with 70.8 per cent.

Table 7.7 provides details of available doctors, nurses, scientists, technicians and teachers in relation to population. In terms of population per doctor, the South Africa records 226 as the lowest, while Nepal records 25000 as highest. In terms of population per nurse, Philippines records 22 as the lowest and Bangladesh and Nepal as the highest with 20,000. For Technicians in R&D, Pakistan records 41 per million as the lowest and France, 2873 as the highest. In terms of scientists and engineers in Research & Development, Nigeria records as lowest with 15 per million and Japan with 5287 per million as the highest. The pupil-teacher ratio at primary level in Germany and USA with 14 as the lowest while for Bangladesh, it is 51 as the highest. At the secondary level, Argentina records 8 as the lowest while Philippines records 36 as the highest.

Table 7.8 shows sex-segregated life expectancies of different countries. Life expectancy in respect of males at birth is lowest in Zambia with 40.3 and highest in Japan with 78.7 while for female it is lowest in Zambia (40.6) and highest in Japan (85.7). Table 7.9 provides comparative data on human development indices. The tables depicts that in terms of rank, two countries, namely Sri Lanka and Maldives have better position amongst the SAARC countries. Most of the African countries lag for behind in comparison to the developed European and North and South American countries and also to other Asia and Pacific countries.

Table 7.10 provides participation of women in political activities. Germany has the highest participation of women in government at Ministerial Level (46.2 per cent) followed by South Africa (41.4 per cent). In Bhutan and Russian Federation, no women holds any ministerial position. As regards the participation of women in Parliament, it is observed that New Zealand has the highest participation (32.2 per cent) of women holding seats in lower or Single House while in Upper House or Senator (35.5 per cent) seats are occupied by Women in Canada.

Table 7.1: Population Characterstics in Select Countries

Country	Population Estimates as on mid year (Million)		Surface Area sq km. (000's)	Sex Ratio	Density of Population per sq. km.		Uraban Population as percent to total population[b]	
	2006	2015*	2005		1998	2006	2004	2015*
SAARC								
1. Bangladesh	156.0	180.1	144	94	867	1198	25.1	29.9
2. Bhutan	0.6	0.7	47	93	13	14	11.1	14.8
3. India	1110.0	1302.5	3287	93	289	373	28.7	32.0
4. Maldives	0.3	0.4	0.3	—	900	1,001	29.6	34.8
5. Nepal	28.0	32.8	147	95	155	193	15.8	20.9
6. Pakistan	159.0	190.7	796	92	186	206	34.9	39.6
7. Sri Lanka	20.0	20.0	66	99	285	308	15.1	15.7
Other Asian and Pacific								
8. China	1,312.0	1388.6[a]	9635[a]	94	131	141	40.4	49.2
9. Indonesia	223.0	251.6	1905	101	107	123	48.1	58.5
10. Malaysia	26.0	30.0	330	98	65	79	67.3	75.4
11. Philippines	86.0	101.1	300	99	251	289	62.7	69.6
12. Rep.of Korea	48.0	49.1	99	100	469	490	80.8	83.1
13. Thailand	63.0	66.8	513	99	119	124	32.3	36.2
14. Australia	21.0	22.4	7741	100	2	3	88.2	89.9
15. Japan	128.0	126.6	378	103	334	350	65.8	68.2
16. New Zealand	4.1	4.5	268	102	14	16	86.2	87.4
Africa								
17. Ghana	23.0	27.3	239	101	80	101	47.8	55.1
18. Kenya	37.0	46.2	580	100	50	64	20.7	24.1
19. Nigeria	145.0	175.7	924	102	115	159	48.2	55.9
20. South Africa	47.0	50.3	1219	101	32	39	59.3	64.1
21. Uganda	30.0	40.0	241	102	87	152	12.6	14.5
22. Zambia	12.0	13.8	753	103	12	16	35.0	37.0
North America								
23. Canada	33.0	35.2	9985	102	3	4	80.1	81.4
24. USA	299.0	329.0	9632	105	29	33	80.8	83.7
South America								
25. Argentina	39.0	42.7	2780	102	13	14	90.1	91.6
26. Brazil	189.0	210.0	8515	101	19	22	84.2	88.2
Europe								
27. France	61.0	63.7	552	105	107	111	76.7	79.0
28. Germany	82.0	81.8	357	108	230	236	75.2	76.3
29. Russian Federation	143.0	136.5	17098	106	9	9	73.0	72.6
30. United Kingdom	61.0	62.8	244	108	240	250	89.7	90.6

Notes: * Data refer to medium varriant projections.

(a) Population estimates include Taiwan, province of China.

(b) Because data are based on National definition of what constitutes a city or metropolitan area, cross-country comparisons should be made with caution.

Sources: (*i*) UN, *Population and Vital Statistics Report*, Statistical Papers Series A, Vol. LV, No. 1.

(*ii*) UNDP : *Human Development Report-2007/2008.*

(*iii*) World Bank : *World Development Indicators*, 2008.

Table 7.2: Vital Statistics of Population in Select Countries

Country	Crude Birth Rate (Per 1000 population)		Crude Death Rate (Per 1000 population)		Infant-Mortality Rate (Per 1000 live births)		Total Fertility Rate	Annual Population Growth Rate (%)	Maternal Mortality Ratio (Per 100000 live births)
	2006	2000-05*	2006	2000-05*	2006	2000-05*	2006	1990-2006	1990-2006[a]
SAARC									
1. Bangladesh	25.0	29.9	8.0	8.7	52	67.0	2.9	2.0	322
2. Bhutan	41.4[3]	34.8	14.4[3]	8.6	67[4]	53.6	2.9	1.9[f]	260[e]
3. India	24.0	25.0	8.0	8.1	57	40.0	2.5	1.7	301
4. Maldives	41.7[3]	17.7[1]	8.0[3]	3.9[1]	35[4]	17.4[1]	2.8	2.6[f]	140[e]
5. Nepal	29.0	34.0	8.0	9.9	46	70.9	3.1	2.3	281
6. Pakistan	26.0	36.3	7.0	9.7	78	86.5	3.9	2.4	533
7. Sri Lanka	19.0	17.3[P]	6.0	6.0[d]	11	17.3	1.9	1.0	43
Other Asian and Pacific									
8. China	12.0	14.3	7.0	7.0	20	36.5	2.0	0.9	48
9. Indonesia	20.0	20.0	7.0	7.1	26	39.5	2.2	1.4	307
10. Malaysia	21.0	24.5	4.0	4.4[2]	10	7.9[2]	2.7	2.3	28
11. Philippines	26.0	26.0	5.0	5.2	24	29.0	3.3	2.1	172
12. Rep.of Korea	9.0	12.8	5.0	5.9	5	7.1	1.1	0.8	20
13. Thailand	15.0	19.6	8.0	6.1	7	25.4	1.8	1.0	24
14. Australia	13.0	12.7[1]	7.0	6.6	5	5.3[1]	1.8	1.2	–
15. Japan	9.0	9.4[2]	9.0	7.6[2]	3	3.2[2]	1.3	0.2	8
16. New Zealand	14.0	14.8[2]	7.0	7.0[2]	5	6.1[2]	2.1	1.2	15
Africa									
17. Ghana	30.0	32.6	9.0	10.4	76	62.1	3.9	2.4	210[e]
18. Kenya	39.0	34.1	12.0	13.7	79	58.7	5.0	2.8	414
19. Nigeria	40.0	39.5	17.0	13.3	99	78.5	5.4	2.7	–
20. South Africa	23.0	24.6	21.0	17.1	56	59.2	2.7	1.9	150
21. Uganda	47.0	50.6	14.0	17.2	78	93.9	6.7	3.2	505
22. Zambia	40.0	41.5	19.0	18.8	102	79.6	5.3	2.3	729
North America									
23. Canada	11.0	10.6[1]	7.0	7.3[1]	5	5.3[1]	1.5	1.0	–
24. USA	14.0	14.7[2]	8.0	8.7[2]	6	6.9[2]	2.1	1.1	8
South America									
25. Argentina	18.0	18.2[1]	8.0	7.6[1]	14	16.3[1]	2.3	1.1	39
26. Brazil	19.0	19.2	6.0	7.0[2]	19	38.3	2.3	1.5	76
Europe									
27. France	13.0	13.1[1]	9.0	8.9[1]	4	4.4[1]	2.0	0.5	10
28. Germany	8.0	9.0[1]	10.0	10.0[1]	4	4.4[1]	1.3	0.2	8
29. Russian Federation	10.0	9.1[1]	15.0	15.6[1]	14	14.6[1]	1.3	(–) 0.2	23
30. United Kingdom	12.0	11.2[1]	10.0	10.1[1]	5	5.5[1]	1.9	0.3	7

Notes: * Estimated.

1. Data is provisional and correspond to the year 2001.
2. Data is provisional and correspond to the year 2002.
3. Data is provisional corrspond to the year 1995.
4. Data refer to year 2004.

a. Data repoted by national authoritias. Data refer to the most recent year available during the period specified.
c. Data refer for the years 2000-05.
d. Population estimates include Taiwan, Province of China.
e. Data refer to year 1990-2004.
f. Data refer to years 1975-2004.

Sources: (*i*) UNDP : *Human Development Report—2007/2008.*
(*ii*) *Population and Vital Statistics Report*, Series A, Vol. LV, No. 1.
(*iii*) World Bank : *World Development Indicators*, 2008.

Figure 7.A

CRUDE BIRTH AND DEATH RATES IN SELECT COUNTRIES-2000-05

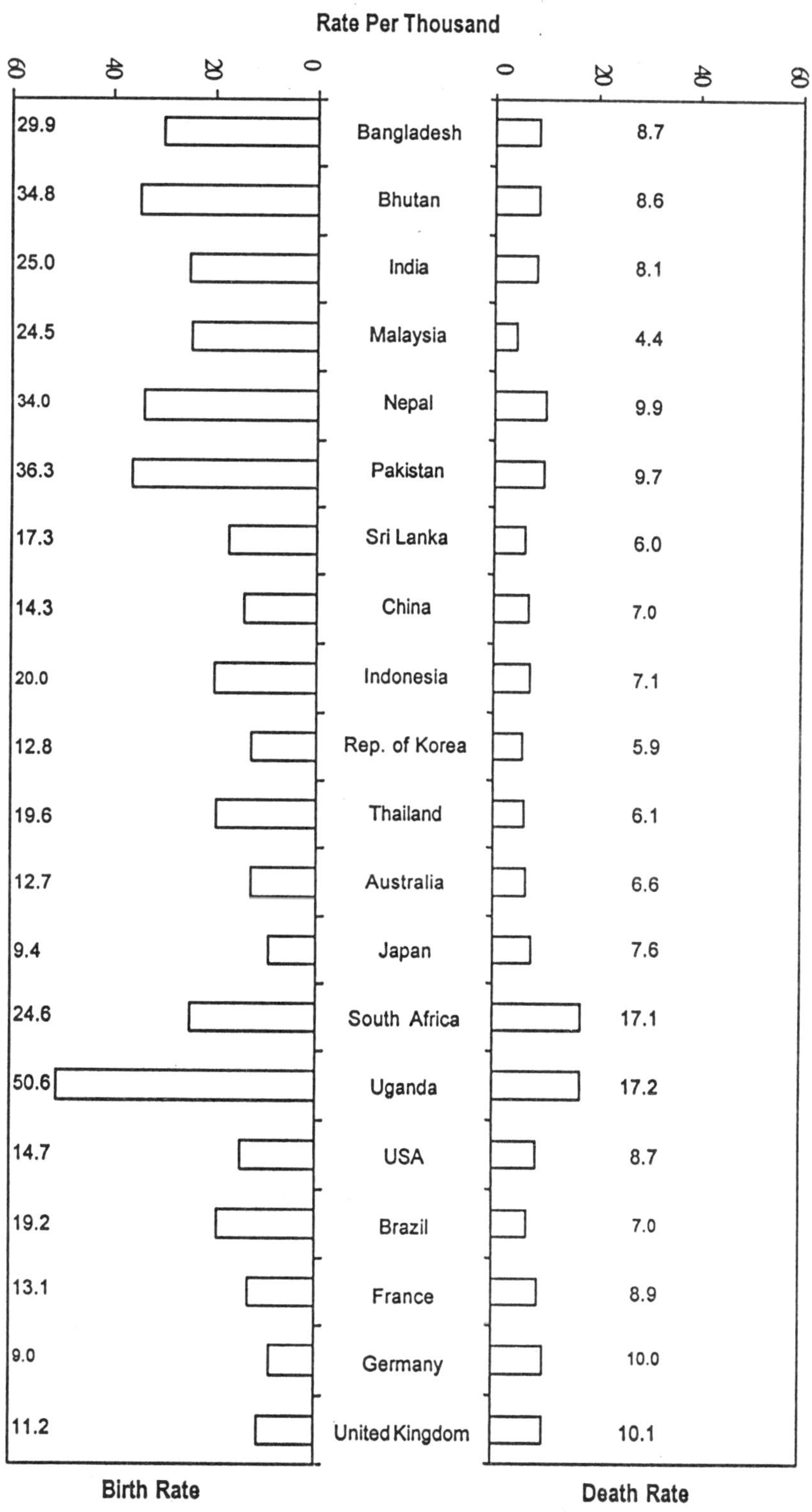

For details see Table 7.2

Table 7.3: Dependency Rates and Adult Literacy Rates in Select Countries

Country	*Population Aged 0-14 years (Percentage)*		*Population Aged 65+ years (Percentage)*		*Dependency rate*		*Adult Literacy rate*
	2005	*2015[a]*	*2005*	*2015[a]*	*2001*	*2015*	*2004*
SAARC							
1. Bangladesh	35.2	31.1	3.5	4.3	67.4	72.4	41.1[e]
2. Bhutan	33.0	24.9	4.6	5.4	87.3	87.3	47.0[C]
3. India	33.0	28.7	5.0	5.8	69.2	69.2	61.0
4. Maldives	34.0	29.0	3.8	3.9	90.7	86.7	96.3
5. Nepal	39.0	34.1	3.7	4.2	82.9	80.3	48.6
6. Pakistan	37.2	32.1	3.9	4.3	83.4	81.9	49.9
7. Sri Lanka	24.2	21.4	6.5	9.3	51.0	48.7	90.7
Other Asian and Pacific							
8. China	21.6	18.5	7.7	9.6	47.5	46.4	90.9
9. Indonesia	28.4	24.9	5.5	6.6	56.4	54.6	90.4
10. Malaysia	31.4	27.3	4.4	5.8	63.5	61.7	88.7
11. Philippines	36.2	32.5	3.8	4.7	69.2	67.6	92.6
12. Rep. of Korea	18.6	13.7	9.4	13.3	39.6	39.3	98.0[bc]
13. Thailand	21.7	19.7	7.8	10.2	46.5	45.0	92.6
14. Australia	19.5	17.9	13.1	16.1	49.6	48.7	99.0
15. Japan	13.9	12.5	19.7	26.2	45.4	46.8	99.0
16. New Zealand	21.5	19.4	12.2	14.7	52.8	52.2	99.0
Africa							
17. Ghana	39.0	35.1	3.6	4.3	88.7	86.2	57.9
18. Kenya	42.6	42.5	2.7	2.6	89.7	85.2	73.6
19. Nigeria	44.3	41.3	2.9	3.0	87.7	85.6	66.8[e]
20. South Africa	32.1	30.2	4.2	5.5	63.9	62.8	82.4[d]
21. Uganda	49.4	48.0	2.5	2.3	108.3	108.8	66.8
22. Zambia	45.7	43.4	2.9	3.0	99.7	97.7	68.0[d]
North America							
23. Canada	17.6	15.6	13.1	16.1	47.0	46.4	99.0
24. USA	20.8	19.8	12.3	14.1	52.4	51.5	99.0
South America							
25. Argentina	26.4	23.9	10.2	11.1	60.6	59.8	97.2
26. Brazil	27.8	25.4	6.1	7.7	53.7	51.4	88.6
Europe							
27. France	18.4	17.8	16.3	18.5	53.0	53.0	99.0
28. Germany	14.4	12.9	18.8	20.9	46.6	46.8	99.0
29. Russian Federation	15.1	15.9	13.8	13.1	46.6	44.2	99.4[h]
30. United Kingdom	18.0	17.2	16.1	18.1	54.0	53.5	99.0

Notes: (*a*) Data refer to medium-variant projections.
(*b*) *For purpose of calculating the HDI, a value of 99.0% was applied.*
(*c*) *UNICEF, 2004.*
(*d*) *Data refer to the most recent year available between 1995 and 1999.*
(*e*) *In the absence of recent data, estimates from UNSECO Instittite for Statistics 2003, based on outdated Census or survey information were used and should be interpreted with caution.*

Sources: (*i*) UNDP : *Human Development Report, 2007/2008* (for 2005 and 2015).
(*ii*) The World Bank : *World Development Indicators 2003* (for depandency Ratio of 2001).

Table 7.4: Labour Force Participation Rates by Broad Sector in Select Countries

Country	*Labour force (in million) 2006*	*Women's Share in labour force 2006*	*Percentage of Work force 2003-2006*[a]					
			Agriculture		*Industry*		*Services*	
		(Percent)	*Male*	*Female*	*Male*	*Female*	*Male*	*Female*
SAARC								
1. Bangladesh	71.0	36.7	50	59	12	18	38	23
2. Bhutan	NA	57.1	NA	NA	NA	NA	NA	NA
3. India	438.0	28.1	53*	77*	19*	13*	28*	10*
4. Maldives	NA	NA	NA	NA	NA	NA	NA	NA
5. Nepal	10.8	40.5	75**	91**	4**	1**	20**	8**
6. Pakistan	59.6	27.3	38	67	21	15	41	18
7. SriLanka	8.4	32.3	32[b@]	40[b@]	40[b@]	35[b@]	29[b@]	25[b@]
OtherAsianPacific								
8. China	780.5	44.1	NA	NA	NA	NA	NA	NA
9. Indonesia	109.2	37.9	43	41	20	15	37	44
10. Malaysia	11.6	36.0	16	11	35	27	49	62
11. Philippines	38.4	40.2	45	25	17	12	39	64
12. Rep.of Korea	24.5	40.8	7	9	34	17	59	74
13. Thailand	36.5	46.7	44	41	22	19	34	41
14. Australia	10.5	44.8	5	3	31	9	65	88
15. Japan	66.2	40.8	4	5	35	18	59	77
16. NewZealand	2.2	46.1	9	5	32	11	59	84
Africa								
17. Ghana	10.3	47.8	60[@]	50[@]	14[@]	15[@]	27[@]	36[@]
18. Kenya	16.7	44.2	20*	16*	23*	10*	57*	75*
19. Nigeria	52.7	35.3	4*	2*	30*	11*	67*	87*
20. SouthAfrica	20.0	37.9	13	7	33	14	54	79
21. Uganda	12.6	48.4	60[c]	77[c]	11[c]	5[c]	29[c]	18[c]
22. Zambia	5.0	42.6	NA	NA	NA	NA	NA	NA
NorthAmerica								
23. Canada	17.9	46.1	4[c]	2[c]	32[c]	11[c]	64[c]	88[c]
24. USA	157.0	45.9	2	1	30	10	68	90
SouthAmerica								
25. Argentina	18.8	43.1	2[c]	1[c]	33[c]	11[c]	66[c]	88[c]
26. Brazil	93.1	42.9	25[c]	16[c]	27[c]	13[c]	48[c]	71[c]
Europe								
27. France	27.3	45.5	5	2	35	12	60	85
28. Germany	41.0	45.1	3	2	41	16	56	82
29. Russian Federation	73.5	48.8	12	8	38	21	50	71
30. United Kingdom	30.8	45.4	2	1	33	9	65	90

Notes: a. Data are for the most recent year available, *b. – Less than 0.5.,* c. Limited coverage.
NA: Not available
* Data refer in the years 1998-2001
** Data refer in the years 1990-92.
@ Data refer in the years 2000-05.

Source: The World Bank : *World Development Indicators—2008.*

Figure 7.B

WORK FORCE PARTICIPATION RATES BY BROAD SECTOR IN SELECT COUNTRIES-2003-05

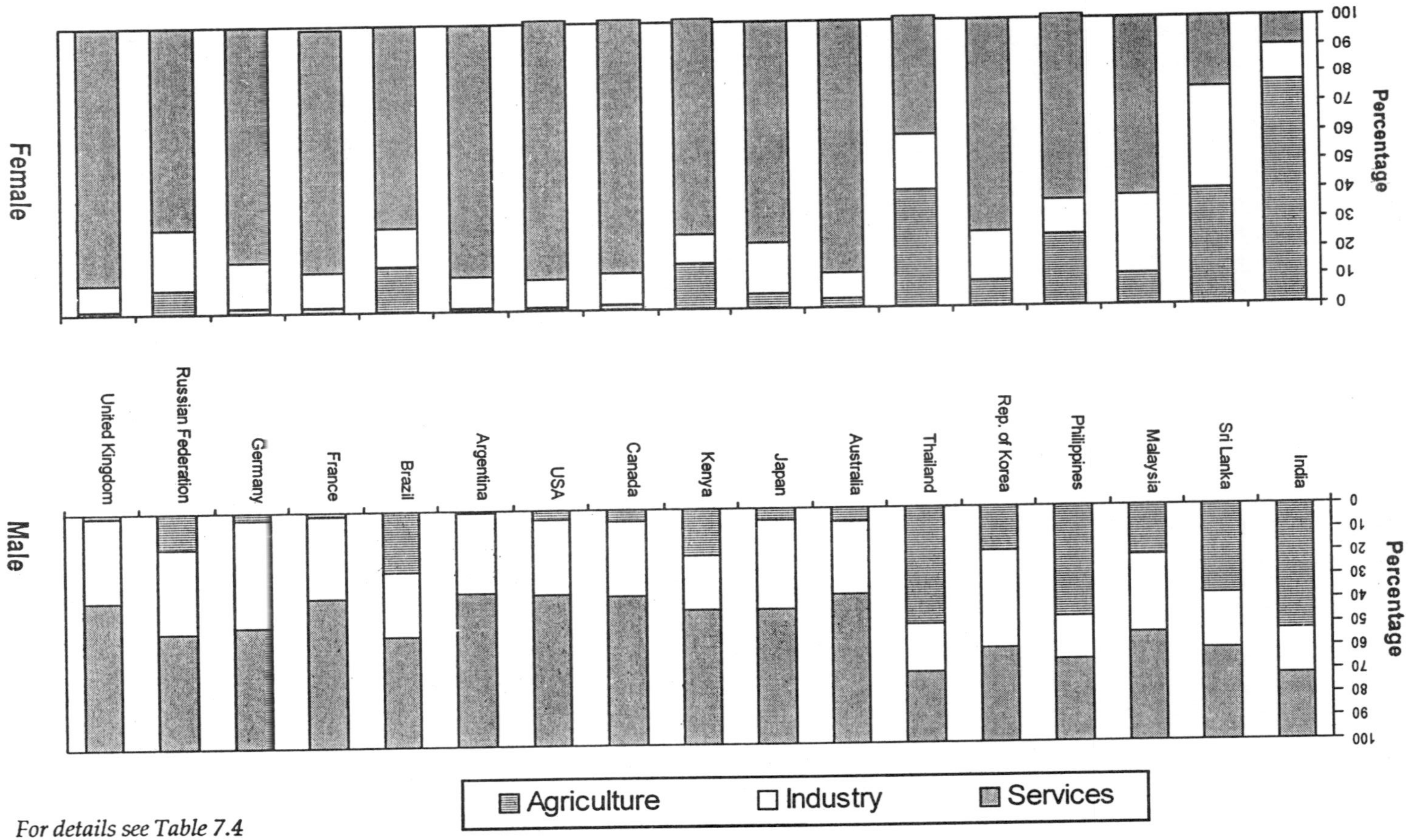

For details see Table 7.4

Table 7.5: Percentage of Female Economic Activity Rates and Employment by Board Sector Economic Activity in Select Countries

Country	Economic Activity (Age 15 and Older Rate 2005)	Female Employment by Board Sector Economic Activity (Percentate)[a]		
		Agriculture (1995-2005)	Industry (1995-2005)	Services (1995-2005)
SAARC				
1. Bangladesh	52.7	58	18	23
2. Bhutan	46.7	NA	NA	NA
3. India	34.0	NA	NA	NA
4. Maldives	48.5	5	24	39
5. Nepal	49.9	NA	NA	NA
6. Pakistan	32.7	65	16	20
7. Sri Lanka	34.9	40	35	25
Other Asian and Pacific				
8. China	68.8	NA	NA	NA
9. Indonesia	51.0	45	15	40
10. Malaysia	46.5	11	27	62
11. Philippines	54.7	25	12	64
12. Rep.of Korea	50.2	9	17	74
13. Thailand	65.6	41	19	41
14. Australia	56.4	3	9	88
15. Japan	48.3	5	18	77
16. New Zealand	60.4	5	11	84
Africa				
17. Ghana	70.3	50	15	36
18. Kenya	69.1	16	10	75
19. Nigeria	45.4	2	11	87
20. South Africa	45.9	7	14	79
21. Uganda	79.7	77	5	17
22. Zambia	66.0	78	2	20
North America				
23. Canada	60.5	2	11	88
24. USA	59.6	1	10	90
South America				
25. Argentina	53.3	1	11	88
26. Brazil	56.7	16	13	71
Europe				
27. France	48.2	3	12	84
28. Germany	50.8	2	16	82
29. Russian Fedn.	54.3	8	21	71
30. United Kingdom	55.2	1	9	90

Notes : N.A.–Data not available.

a. The percentate shares of employment by economic activity may not sum to 100 because of rounding or the omission of activities not classified.

Source : UNDP : *Human Development Report*, 2007/2008

Table 7.6: Expenditure on Education and Health as Percentage to GDP in Select Countries

Country	GDP* per capita (PPPUS$) 2005	GDP* Annual Growth Rate 1990-2005	Public Expenditure on Education (as % of GDP) 2006	Public Expenditure on Health (as % of GDP) 2005	Percentage of Population below poverty line ($ 1 a day) 1990-2005[e]
SAARC					
1. Bangladesh	2053	2.9	2.5	0.8	41.3
2. Bhutan	—	5.6	5.6[d]	3.0[g]	—
3. India	3452[c]	4.2	3.8	1.0	34.3
4. Maldives	—	—	7.1	6.3[g]	—
5. Nepal	1550	2.0	3.4[h]	1.6	24.1
6. Pakistan	2370	1.3	2.6	0.4	17.0
7. Sri Lanka	4595	3.7	—	1.9	5.6
Other Asian and Pacific					
8. China	6757[b]	8.8	1.9[h]	1.8	9.9
9. Indonesia	3843	2.1	0.9[h]	1.0	7.5
10. Malaysia	10882	3.3	6.2	1.9	2.0
11. Philippines	5137	1.6	2.7	1.2	14.8
12. Rep.of Korea	22029	4.5	4.6	3.1	2.0
13. Thailand	8677	2.7	4.2	2.2	2.0
14. Australia	31794	2.5	4.6	5.9	—
15. Japan	31267	0.8	3.7	6.7	—
16. New Zealand	24996	2.1	6.5	6.9	—
Africa					
17. Ghana	2480[c]	2.0	5.4	2.1	44.8
18. Kenya	1240	(–)0.1	6.9	2.1	22.8
19. Nigeria	1128	0.8	—	1.2	70.8
20. South Africa	11110[c]	0.6	5.4	3.6	10.7
21. Uganda	1454[c]	3.2	5.2	2.0	—
22. Zambia	1023	(–)0.3	2.0	2.7	63.8
North America					
23. Canada	33375	2.2	5.2[h]	6.8	—
24. USA	41890[a]	2.1	5.6	7.2	—
South America					
25. Argentina	14280	1.1	3.8	4.5	6.6
26. Brazil	8402	1.1	4.0	3.5	7.5
Europe					
27. France	30386	1.6	5.8	8.9	—
28. Germany	29461	1.4	4.6	8.2	—
29. Russian Fedn.	10845	(–)0.1	3.5	3.2	—
30. United Kingdom	33230	2.5	5.4	7.1	—

Notes: GDP-Gross Domestic Product. * Value expressed at constent prices.

a. In theory, for the United States the value of GDP in Purchasing Power Parity (PPP) US dollars should be the same as that in US dollars, but practical issues arising in the calculation of the PPP US dollar GDP prevent this.

b. Estimate based on a bilateral comparision between China and the United States (Ruoen and Kai 1995).

c. Estimates are based on regression.

d. Data rafer to 2003.

e. Data refer the most recent year available during the period specified.

f. Data refer to a UNESCO Institute for Statistics estimate when national estimate is not available.

g. Data refer to 2004.

h. Data refer to 2002-05.

Sources: (*i*)UNDP : *Human Development Report-2007/2008.*

(*ii*)The World Bank : *World Development Indications,* 2005 (For Annual growth).

(*iii*)The World Bank : World Development Indications, 2008.

Figure 7.C

PUBLIC EXPENDITURE ON HEALTH (AS PERCENT OF GDP) IN SELECT COUNTRIES—2005

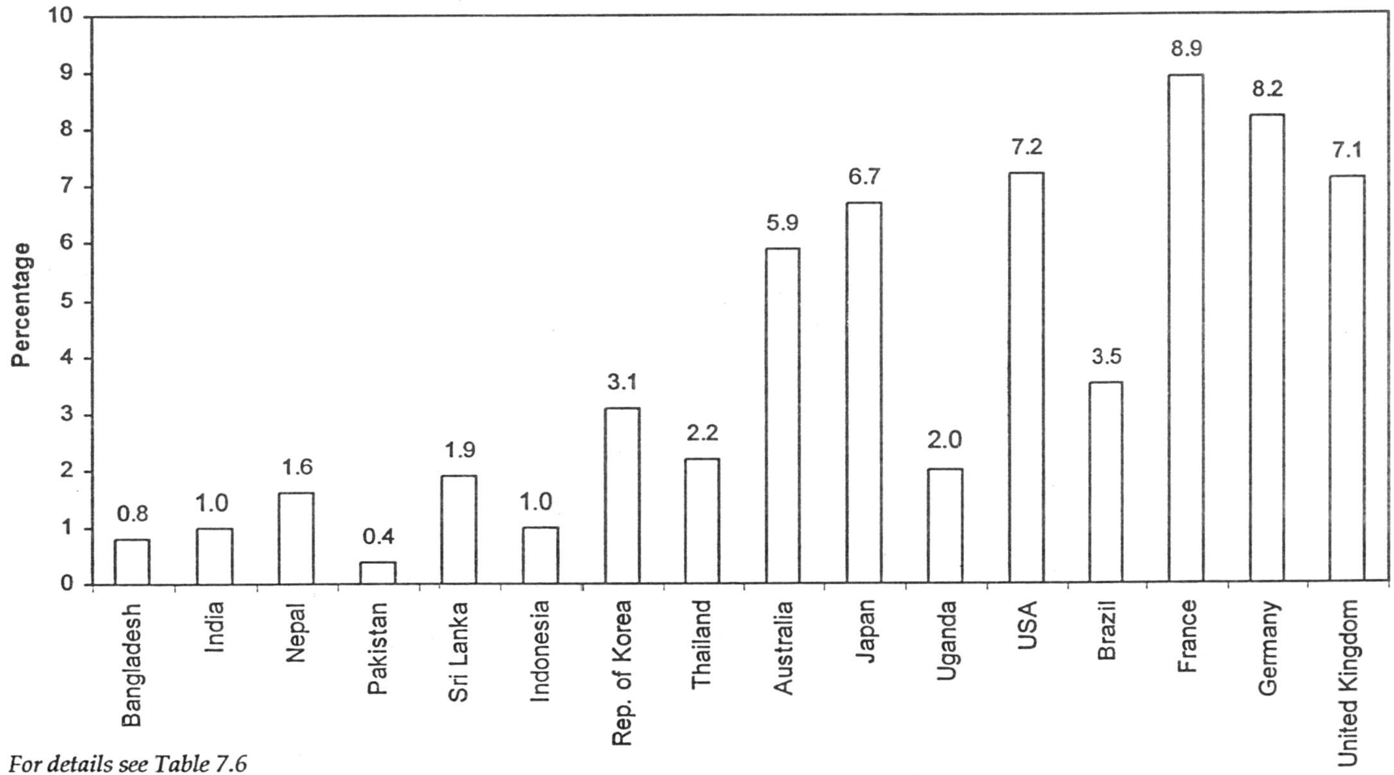

For details see Table 7.6

Table 7.7: Human Capital Formation Indicators in Select Countries

Country	*Population Per Doctor* 1990-02	*Population Per Nurse* 1993	*Technicians in R&D (Per million people)* 2000-05	*Scientists & Engineers in R&D (Per million people)* 1990-2005	*Pupil-teacher ratio* Primary 2002	Secondary 1995
SAARC						
1. Bangladesh	5000	20000	33*	51	51	28
2. Bhutan	6250	16667	—	—	30*	13
3. India	2083	—	102***	119	40	25
4. Nepal	25000	20000	137	59	40	34
5. Pakistan	1471	3126	41	75	39	19
6. Sri Lanka	2439	893	72	128	22	22
Other Asian an Pacific						
7. China	599	1136	200*	708	18	16
8. Indonesia	6250	1493	—	207	20	14
9. Malaysia	1471	625	64	299	17	19
10. Philippines	806	22	22*	48	35	36
11. Rep.of Korea	578	431	567*	3187	28	24
12. Thailand	4167	1010	208*	287	18	20
13. Australia	385	—	797*	3759	16**	12
14. Japan	508	—	528*	5287	19	—
15. New Zealand	442	—	833*	3945	16	14
Africa						
16. Ghana	16667	—	—	—	32	19
17. Kenya	1143	4348	—	—	40	16
18. Nigeria	5263	704	76*	15	37	NA
19. South Africa	226	511	110	307	36	28
20. Uganda	20000	3571	15***	24	49	17
21. Zambia	14286	—	16***	51	51	—
North America						
22. Canada	538	—	1,467	3597	17[e]	19
23. USA	362	—	—	4605	14	15
South America						
24. Argentina	340	1852	338	720	17	8
25. Brazil	633	2439	395	344	16	11
Europe						
26. France	330	—	2873*	3213	19	—
27. Germany	282	—	1,056	3261	14	14
28. Russian Federation	236		550	3319	17	12
29. United Kingdom	610	—	1017*	2706	17	13

Notes: * Data relate to 1987-97.
** Data relate to 1995.
*** Data relate to 1996-2002.
e. Data relate to 2002.

Sources: 1. UNDP : *Human Development Report, 2007/2008.*
2. *World Education Report–1998.*
3. The World Bank : *World Development Indicaters, 2008* (for Technicians in R & D.)

Table 7.8: Life Expectancy at Birth in Select Countries

(Years)

Country	2001		2003		2004		2005	
	Male	*Female*	*Male*	*Female*	*Male*	*Felame*	*Male*	*Felame*
SAARC								
1. Bangladesh	60.1	60.9	62.1	63.7	62.5	64.2	62.3	64.0
2. Bhutan	61.3	63.8	61.7	64.2	62.2	64.6	63.1	66.5
3. India	62.8	64.0	61.8	65.0	62.1	65.3	62.3	65.3
4. Maldives	67.4	66.3	67.1	66.1	67.4	66.6	66.6	67.6
5. Nepal	59.4	58.9	61.2	62.0	61.6	62.4	62.1	62.9
6. Pakistan	60.6	60.3	62.8	63.2	63.2	63.6	64.3	64.8
7. Sri Lanka	69.6	75.5	71.5	76.8	71.7	77.0	67.9	75.6
Other Asian and Pacific								
8. China	68.6	72.9	69.9	73.5	70.2	73.7	71.0[a]	74.3[a]
9. Indonesia	64.3	68.2	64.9	68.8	65.3	69.2	67.8	71.6
10. Malaysia	70.4	75.3	70.9	75.6	71.1	75.8	71.4	76.1
11. Philippines	67.6	71.6	68.3	72.5	68.6	72.8	68.9	73.3
12. Rep. of Korea	71.4	79.0	73.3	80.6	73.7	80.9	74.3	81.5
13. Thailand	64.9	73.2	66.3	73.8	66.7	74.0	65.0	74.5
14. Australia	76.3	81.9	77.7	82.8	77.9	83.0	78.5	83.3
15. Japan	77.7	84.7	78.4	85.4	78.6	85.6	78.7	85.7
16. New Zealand	75.6	80.6	76.8	81.3	77.0	81.5	77.7	81.8
Africa								
17. Ghana	56.2	59.3	56.3	57.3	56.5	57.4	58.7	59.5
18. Kenya	44.9	47.9	48.1	46.3	48.5	46.5	51.1	53.1
19. Nigeria	51.3	52.3	43.1	43.6	43.2	43.5	46.0	47.1
20. South Africa	47.7	54.4	46.8	50.2	45.7	48.2	49.5	52.0
21. Uganda	43.9	45.4	46.9	47.6	47.9	48.6	49.1	50.2
22. Zambia	33.3	33.4	37.9	36.9	38.2	37.1	40.3	40.6
North America								
23. Canada	76.5	81.8	77.4	82.4	77.6	82.6	77.9	82.6
24. USA	74.0	79.7	74.6	80.0	74.8	80.2	75.2	80.4
South America								
25. Argentina	70.3	77.4	70.7	78.2	70.9	78.4	71.1	78.6
26. Brazil	63.7	72.3	66.6	74.6	67.0	74.8	68.1	75.5
Europe								
27. France	74.9	82.6	75.9	83.0	76.0	83.1	76.6	83.7
28. Germany	74.9	81.0	75.7	81.5	75.9	81.7	76.2	81.8
29. Russian Federation	60.6	72.9	59.0	72.1	58.9	72.0	58.7	72.1
30. United Kingdom	75.4	80.4	76.0	80.6	76.2	80.8	76.7	81.2

Note: a. *The data for China do not include Hong Kong and Macao, SARs of China*

Source: UNDP: *Human Development Report, 2007/2008.*

Figure 7.D

MALE AND FEMALE LIFE EXPECTANCY AT BIRTH IN SELECT COUNTRIES-2005

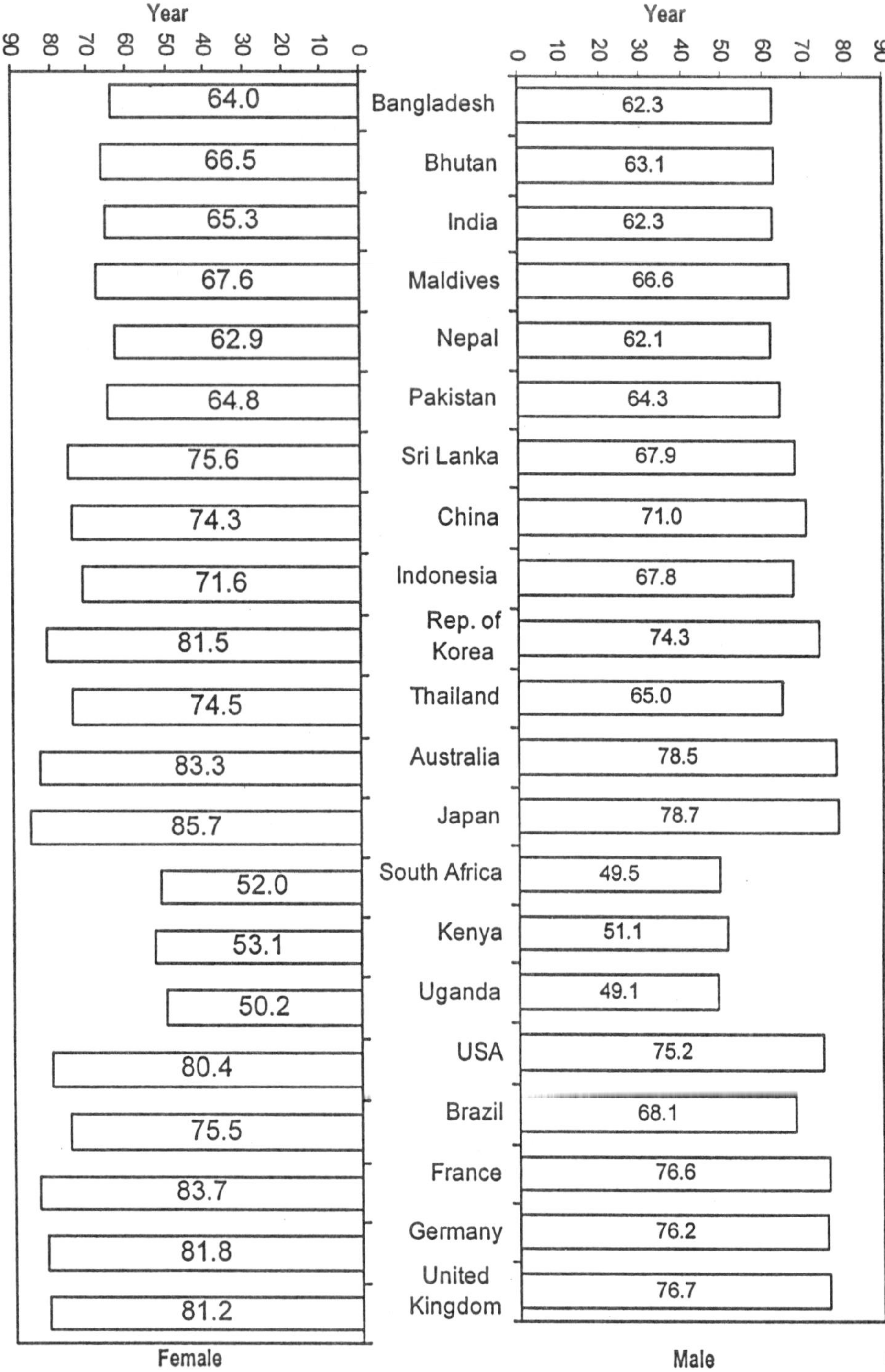

For details see Table 7.8

Table 7.9: Human Development Indices in Select Countries

Country	Human Development Index (HDI) 2005	Gender Relaed Development Index (GDI)	Gender Empower-ment Measure (GEM)	Human Poverty Index (HPI-1) (Percent)
SAARC				
1. Bangladesh	0.547	0.539	0.379	40.5
2. Bhutan	0.579	—	—	38.9
3. India	0.619	0.600	—	31.3
4. Maldives	0.741	0.744	0.437	17.0
5. Nepal	0.534	0.520	0.351	38.1
6. Pakistan	0.551	0.525	0.377	36.2
7. Sri Lanka	0.743	0.735	0.369	17.8
Other Asian and Pacific				
8. China	0.777	0.776	0.534	11.7
9. Indonesia	0.728	0.721	—	18.2
10. Malaysia	0.811	0.802	0.504	8.3
11. Philippines	0.771	0.768	0.590	15.3
12. Rep. of Korea	0.921	0.910	0.510	—
13. Thailand	0.781	0.779	0.472	10.0
14. Australia	0.962	0.960	0.847	12.1*
15. Japan	0.953	0.942	0.557	11.7*
16. New Zealand	0.943	0.935	0.811	—
Africa				
17. Ghana	0.553	0.549	—	32.3
18. Kenya	0.521	0.521	—	30.8
19. Nigeria	0.470	0.456	—	37.3
20. South Africa	0.674	0.667	—	23.5
21. Uganda	0.505	0.501	—	34.7
22. Zambia	0.434	0.425	—	41.8
North America				
23. Canada	0.961	0.956	0.820	10.9*
24. USA	0.951	0.937	0.762	15.4*
South America				
25. Argentina	0.869	0.865	0.728	4.1
26. Brazil	0.800	0.798	0.490	9.7
Europe				
27. France	0.952	0.950	0.718	11.2*
28. Germany	0.935	0.931	0.831	10.3*
29. Russian Federation	0.802	0.801	0.489	—
30. United Kingdom	0.946	0.944	0.783	14.8*

Notes: (-) Data not availble. a. Data refer to Human Development Report, 2005.
* Data refer to HPI-2.

Source: UNDP: *Human Development Report, 2007/2008.*

Table 7.10 : Percentage of Women's Political Participation

Country	Government at Ministerial (% to total)[a] 2005	Seats in Parliament held (% of total)	
		Lower or Single House 2007	Uppr house or Senate 2007
SAARC			
1. Bangladesh	8.3	15.1[d]	—
2. Bhutan	0.0	2.7	—
3. India	3.4	8.3	10.7
4. Maldives	11.8	12.0	—
5. Nepal	7.4	17.3[f]	—
6. Pakistan	5.6	21.3	17.0
7. Sri Lanka	10.3	4.9	—
Other Asian and Pacific			
8. China	6.3	20.3	—
9. Indonesia	10.8	11.3	—
10. Malaysia	9.1	9.1	25.7
11. Philippines	25.0	22.5	18.2
12. Rep. of Korea	5.6	2.0	13.4
13. Thailand	7.7	8.7	—
14. Australia	20.0	24.7	35.5
15. Japan	12.5	9.4	14.5
16. New Zealand	23.1	32.2	—
Africa			
17. Ghana	11.8	10.9	—
18. Kenya	10.3	7.3	—
19. Nigeria	10.0	6.4	7.3
20. South Africa	41.4	32.8[c]	33.3[c]
21. Uganda	23.4	29.8	—
22. Zambia	25.0	14.6	—
North America			
23. Canada	23.1	20.8	35.0
24. USA	14.3	16.3	16.0
South America			
25. Argentina	5.9	20.4	13.0
26. Brazil	11.4	8.8	12.3
Europe			
27. France	17.6	12.2	16.9
28. Germany	46.2	31.6	21.7
29. Russian Federation	0.0	9.8	3.4
30. United Kingdom	28.6	19.7	18.9

Notes: a. Data are as of 1st January, 2005. The total included Deputy Prime Ministers and Ministers. Prime Ministers who hold ministerial portfoilos and Vice Presidents and heads of ministerial level departments or agencies who exercise a ministerial function in the government structure are slso included.

b. Data are as of 31st May, 2006 unless otherwise specified. The percentage was calculated using as a refernce the number of total seats filled in Parliament at the time.

c. The figures on the distribution of seats do not include the 36 special rotating delegates appointed on an adhoc basis. The share given are therefore calculated on the basis of the 54 permanent seats.

d. In 2004 the number of seats in Parliament was raised from 300 to 345, with the additional 45 reserved seats for women. These reserved seats were filled in September and October, 2005, being allocated to political parties in proportion to their share of the National vote received in the 2001 election.

– Not applicable.

Source: UNDP: *Human Development Report, 2007/2008.*

Glossary

Activity Status: The engagement of the economically active population of a country categorised as employed, unemployed or out of labour force, on the basis of activities pursued by them during a specific reference period counted in days or weeks.

Admission: The number of students enrolled at the commencement of a course or programme of education or instruction.

Age-specific Fertility Rate: The annual number of live births per thousand women of a specific age-group.

Age-specific Labour Force Participation Rate: The percentage of population of different age-groups in the labour force at a given period of time as a proportion of the total population in the corresponding age-groups.

Age-specific Mortality Rate: The annual number of deaths in a specific age-group per thousand population in the same age-group.

Agricultural Enterprise: An agricultural enterprise is defined as a unit engaged in livestock production, agricultural services, hunting, trapping and game propagation, forestry, logging and fishing. Enterprises engaged in activities pertaining to agricultural production and plantations have not been covered under the census.

Apprenticeship: A system under which an employer undertakes by contract to engage a person, in order to train him for a trade or occupation for a period the duration of which has been fixed in advance under a contract.

Birth Rate: The annual number of births per thousand of mid-year population.

Brain drain: The international out-migration of highly skilled and professionally qualified manpower, particularly from developing to developed countries.

Casual Labour: A person casually engaged in farm or non-farm enterprises of others (both household and non-household), in return for wages on a daily basis. If engaged for a pre-determined period, such casual labour is termed as temporary labour provided the work engagement is less than 180 days in any period of 365 days.

Capital Formation: The creation of capital, that is, the process by which money capital is saved or accumulated and converted into capital goods.

Census: The total count of a country's population on a given day of the year or over a period of weeks. The term is also used to denote 100% coverage in a survey.

Current Outlay: Corresponds broadly to expenditure on revenue account in the plan schemes. It is expenditure other than that classified as investment.

Community Health Centre: A referral institution for four primary health centres for every 80,000 to 120,000 population.

Death Rate: Annual number of deaths per thousand of population.

Density of Population: The number of persons inhabiting in an area per square kilometre at a given point of time.

Dependency Ratio: The ratio of dependents (those under 15 and those over 64) to the working-age population, aged 15-64.

Disabled: A person significantly challenged in the exercise of abilities to perform an activity in the manner or within the range considered normal for a human being. It excludes illness/injury of recent origin (morbidity) resulting in temporary loss of ability to see, hear, speak or more.

Disabled (Incidence rate): The number of persons per 1,00,000 persons whose onset of disability (by birth or otherwise) has been rated during a specified period of 365 days preceeding the date of survey is termed incidence of disability in a population.

Disabled (Prevalence rate): The number of disabled persons per 1,00,000 persons.

Drop-out Rate: The Drop-out rate is the percentage of children to total enrolment dropping out of the school education system in a particular year.

Educational Expenditure: Expenditure incurred by educational institutions throughout the country or expenditure incurred on educational purposes by government. It includes private educational expenditure in the form of fees paid by or on behalf of students or regular contributions made by the management or private educational institutions, ad-hoc contributions, donations and subscriptions for particular educational projects.

Educational Institution: An institution in which a course of study followed is that which is prescribed or recognised by a University or Duty Constituted Board of education. Such institutions are open to inspection and their students are ordinarily eligible for admission to public examinations and tests conducted for certification by a government or university or Board or any authorised agency.

Educational Stage: The stage of educational progression beginning (as in India) from pre-primary, primary (I to V) and continuing through middle school (VI to VIII), high/higher secondary (IX to XII) to higher education (graduate and above).

Educated Unemployed: All educated persons, who are out of work and seeking employment during a reference period.

Emoluments: The total sum of pay plus allowances and money value of perquisites and benefits. .

Enrolment: Students on rolls in educational institutions for undergoing systematic instruction in a course of study.

Enterprise: An enterprise is an undertaking engaged in production and/or distribution of goods and/or services not for the sole purpose of own consumption. Workers of an enterprise may comprise members of the household or hired workers or both. The activities of an enterprise may be carried out at one or more than one distinct location. An enterprise may be owned or operated by a single household or several households jointly (on a partnership basis) or in an incorporated form or by a constitutional body or a government.

Establishment: An establishment is the part or whole of an enterprise engaged in economic activities with the assistance of at least one hired worker on a fairly regular basis.

Extended SNA Activity: These are activities including household maintenance care for children, sick and elderly included in the System of National Accounts.

Fertility Rate (age-specific): The number of live births in a particular age-group per thousand mid-year female population of the same age-group.

Fertility Rate (general): The number of live births in a year per thousand mid-year female population in the reproductive age-group (15-49) years.

Fertility Rate (total): The cumulative value of age-specific fertility rates at the end of the child bearing ages which gives a measure of Total Fertility Rate (TFR). This indicates the average number of children expected to be born per woman during her entire reproductive span assuming that the age specific fertility rates, to which she is exposed, would continue to be the same without mortality.

Financial Outlay: The sum of 'Current Outlay' and 'Investment'.

Gainful Activity: An activity from which a person earns money, or money equivalent, or in which he assists in the production of marketable goods and services.

General Fertility Rate: The annual number of live births per thousand women in the reproductive age-group (15-49).

Gross Attendance Ratio: Same as Gross enrolment ratio.

Gross Domestic Product (GDP): The total output of goods and services for final use produced in an economy, by both residents and non-residents, regardless of the allocation to domestic and foreign claims.

Gross Enrolment Ratio: The gross enrolment ratio is the number of students enrolled in a level of education—whether or not they belong in the relevant age-group for that level—as a percentage of the population in the relevant age group for that level. For example, the enrolment in classes, I-V, irrespective of relevant age as a percentage of estimated population in the age group 6-11. Hence, the total percentage may be more than 100 percent in some cases.

Gross National Product (GNP): This comprises GDP plus net factor incomes from abroad, which are incomes that residents receive from abroad for factor services (labour land capital), less similar payments (outflows) to non-residents who contribute to the domestic economy.

Health Expenditure: Expenditure on health comprises the expenditure both current and capital, by all government offices, departments, establishments and other bodies that are agencies or instruments of the central authority of a country in hospitals, clinics and maternity and dental centers with a major medical component on national health and medical insurance schemes and on family planning, preventive care and treatments.

Household: A household comprises a group of persons who commonly live together and take their meals from a common kitchen, unless exigencies of work prevent any of them from doing so.

Household Size: The total number of resident members of a household constitutes its size.

Incremental Capital Output Ratio (ICOR) is measured as the ratio of investment rate to growth rate for a particular period.

Infant Mortality Rate (IMR): The annual number of deaths under one year of age per thousand live births.

Industry: Industry is any systematic activity for the production of goods and services that involves work and marketable value arising from a nexus of collaboration involving more than one person. The notion clusters economic value-adding activities of a similar nature into what are termed sectors such as manufacturing, trade, construction, commerce etc.

In-migration: The crossing of a defined geographical boundary in a given time by persons in the process of changing their residence and entering a given area from other areas of the same country.

Investment: Expenditure on the creation of physical assets (e.g., building, plant and equipment) including expenditure on personnel required for putting up these assets. This expression corresponds broadly to expenditure on capital account.

Labour Force: The group of persons within a given minimum and maximum age, who, during a specified time period, are engaged or are willing to be engaged in some economic activity.

Labour Force Participation Rate (LFPR): The size of the labour force as a percentage of total population at a given period of time.

Labour Productivity: The term expresses the degree to which labour is utilised effectively. Labour productivity is the value of production (products or material services) per worker employed in production. It is calculated with reference to some unit of time (hour, day, month, or year) or cost per unit of output. Generally, output per man-hour is used as a measure of productivity as an approximation to output per unit of total input, because the latter is not available or cannot be calculated within a reasonable margin of error.

LFPR for Educated Persons: This represents size of labour force of a given educational level as percent of population of that educational level.

Literate: A person who can both read and write with understanding in any language.

Literacy Rate: The percentage of people aged seven and above who can both read and write with understanding in any language.

Life Expectation at Birth: The average number of years expected to be lived at the time of birth, if current mortality trends were to continue.

Live Register: The record of personal details of persons in the labour force who are registered in search of job. This could include either the unemployed or the employed who are in search of better prospects. It is called live because registration is valid for one year. It has to be renewed every year to keep it alive. The live register indicates in broad terms the stock of job seekers but not their flow.

Labour Cost: It is the sum total of all the expenditure incurred by the employers torwards labour such as wages/salaries, bonuses, provident fund, pension, gratuity, educational, recreational, etc.

Manpower: In a broad sense, manpower is identical with human resources. In a restricted sense, it refers to that component of human resources that is distinguished by characteristics of skill resulting from education and training. In the latter sense it includes categories such as engineering, technical, scientific and medical personnel at all levels of skill.

Main Worker: One engaged in any economically productive activity for 183 days or six months or more during a year.

Marginal worker: One who worked for less than six months or 183 days in the year.

Maternal Mortality Rate (MMR): The annual number of deaths of women from pregnancy-related causes per 1,00,000 live births.

Migration: The geographical movement of individuals or groups of individuals.

Morbidity Rate: The number (per 1000 person) of persons reporting ailment during 15 days preceding the date of survey.

Moving Average: This is a simple means of smoothening out fluctuations in a data series by calculating a number of averages covering overlapping periods of the series.

National Income: The total sum of incomes accruing within a year to all factors of production supplied by the normal residents of a country, before deduction of direct taxes, and equals sum of compensation to employees, income from incorporated enterprises, rent, interest and dividend accruing to households, savings of corporations, direct taxes on corporations and general government income from property and entrepreneurship. It is identically equal to the net national product at factor cost. (UN Yearbook of National Accounts Statistics).

Net Attendance Ratio: Same as Net Enrolment Ratio.

Net Enrolment Ratio: The number of students enrolled in a level of education who belong to the relevant age group, as a percentage of the population in that age group.

Net Domestic Product (NDP): Equals gross domestic product minus depreciation, which is an allowance for capital consumption.

Non-agricultural Enterprise: Enterprise engaged in activities other than agriculture and allied activities.

Non-Recurring Educational Expenditure: Covers expenditure on buildings (other than maintenance), equipments, libraries, etc., of educational institution.

Non-SNA activity: Activities related to learning, social and cultural, mass media, personal care and self maintenance are categorized as activities not counted in the system of national accounts activities.

Occupation: Occupation classifies or brings together individuals doing similar work, regardless of the industry in which this work is performed and status of employment of individual.

Operational Holding: All land which is used wholly or partly for agricultural production and is operated as one technical unit by one person alone or with others without regard to title, legal form, size or location.

Organized Sector: The sector of the economy which is covered under one piece of legislation or as other for purposes of counting the level of employment, production, etc. In India, the term 'organized sector' is used to cover all establishments in the public sector and non-agricultural establishments employing 10 or more workers in the private sector. Other of establishments and farm-activities form the unorganized sector.

Out-of-labour Force: By definition, total population minus persons in the labour force represents persons 'not in the labour force'. The 'out-of-labour force' group includes students, persons engaged in home duties (like housewife or other family members), persons unable to work because of permanent disability, chronic illness or old age, inmates of penal institutions, hospitals, homes for the aged, infirm or destitute, retired persons and persons who choose not to work.

Out-migration: Crossing of a defined geographical boundary in a given time by persons leaving one area to reside in another area.

Outturn: The number of persons who, on completion of a course of study, are declared by some competent examining body as having qualified in the respective examination.

Own-account Enterprise: An enterprise owned and operated with the help of household labour only.

Paramedical Manpower: The supporting persons qualified in medical education/training, who help the physicians and doctors in the overall discharge of medical service to the community. These persons generally have formal education with professional training (diploma or certificate course in hygiene, nursing and medical care). Paramedical manpower includes nurse-aides, nursing assistants, medical assistants and physician's assistants.

Per-capita Income: Gross national product divided by a country's population.

Prevalence Rate: The ratio between the number of spells of ailment suffered at any time during the reference period and the population exposed to the risk. It measures the frequency of illnesses prevailing during the reference period.

Poverty Line: A minimum subsistence level expressed either as basic money income or the cost of minimum requirements of a 'basket' of essential goods and services.

Primary Sector: Agriculture, forestry, fishing, hunting, mining and quarrying industries.

Principal Status: The status of activity on which a person spent relatively longer time prior to the date of survey is considered the principal usual status of the person.

Private Consumption: The market value of all goods and services, including durable products (such as cars, washing machines and home computers), purchased or received as income in kind by households and non-profit institutions. It excludes purchases of dwellings but includes imputed rent for owner occupied dwellings.

Private Sector: Enterprises managed by a single person or a group of private persons incorporated or otherwise with little or no participation of the Government in terms of management or shares.

Private Expenditure on Education: It is the sum total of all the expenditure incurred by student on education (towards fees, books and stationery, uniform, transport, private coaching, study tour, etc.).

Public Sector: The activity wholly or partly controlled by government or regulated by an Act of Parliament. This sector includes establishments under Central and State Governments, Quasi-Government establishments and local bodies.

Pupil-teacher Ratio: The average number of students per teacher for a particular type of school.

Primary Health Centre (PHC): For every 30000 population in plains area and 20,000 population in hilly and tribal areas.

Recurring Educational Expenditure: Expenditure incurred every year for running educational institutions. Broadly speaking, it includes expenditure on salaries of staff, contingencies, recurring expenditure on equipments, maintenance of furniture, scholarships, stipends and other financial concessions, hostel charges (except mess bills) games and sports, direction, inspection, etc.

Regular Salaried/Wage Employee: A person working in other's farm or non farm activities, both household and non-household, and getting in return salary or wages on a regular basis (and not on the basis of daily or periodic renewal of work contract)for more than 180 days in any period of 365 days.

Registered Factories: All factories employing 10 or more workers where power is used and 20 or more workers where power is not used.

Small Scale Industry(SSI): The SSIs are industrial undertakings in which the investment in fixed assets in plant and machinery, whether held on ownership terms or on lease or by hire-purchase, does not exceed Rupees 1,00,00,000.

Secondary Sector: Industry covering manufacturing, electricity, gas and water supply and construction are included in secondary sector.

Self Employed: A person who works for profit or fees in his own industry, business, or profession. He is not employed either for pay or profit by someone else. He may employ person/persons to work in his enterprise, e.g., a doctor, who may employ an assistant.

Sex Ratio: Number of females per thousand males in a given year.

Stock of Educated Persons: Total number of persons within each of the educational categories at any given time, either employed in the production process or looking for work or not currently involved in the labour force.

Sub-centre: A locus every 5000 population in the plains and 3000 population in hilly and tribal areas.

Subsidiary Status: A 'non-worker' (on the basis of principal usual activity status) who pursued some gainful activity in a subsidiary capacity is considered to be usually working in subsidiary capacity.

System of National Accounts (SNA): The 1993 System of National Accounts contains a coherent, consistent and integrated set of macro-economics accounts and balance sheets based on a set of internationally agreed concepts and definitions, classifications and accounting rules. The economic accounts provide a comprehensive and detailed record of the complex economic activities taking place within economy of transaction between the different institutional sectors and/or their sub-sectors.

SNA Activity: The SNA activities consist of primary production activities like crop farming, animal husbandry, fishing, forestry, processing and storage, mining and quarrying; secondary activities like construction, manufacturing and activities like trade, business and services.

Tertiary Sector: Industry trade and commerce, transport, storage and communications and other services represent the tertiary sector.

Total Fertility Rate (TFR): Average number of children that would be born to a woman if she experiences the current fertility pattern throughout her reproductive span (15-49 years).

TUS – (Time Use Survey) Time use survey aim to identify, classify and quantify the main types of activities that people engage, on an average, during a defined period of time.

Urban Area: An urban area is defined as follows:

(a) All statutory towns, i.e., all places with a municipal corporation, municipal board, cantonment board or notified town area.

(b) All other places which satisfy the following criteria :

- (i) A minimum population of 5000;
- (ii) 75 percent of male working population engaged in non-agricultural and allied activities; and
- (iii) A density of population of at least 400 persons per sq. km. (or 1000 per sq. mile).

Unemployed: Persons looking for work who have not worked during a specified reference period.

Unemployment Rate: The number of unemployed persons expressed as a percentage of the total labour force.

Value Added: The value created at each stage of production measured as the difference between the (untaxed) transferred price of goods or services and the cost of producing them.

Vocational Education: Vocational Education refers to skills and knowledge for employment in a particular occupation (or a group of related occupations) in any field of economic activity.

Working Children: Those who are in age group 5-14 and engaged in some gainful activity.

Work Force: The aggregate of persons within a given minimum and maximum age, who during the reference period are gainfully employed.

Workforce Participation Rate (WPR): The size of workforce as percent of total population at a point of time.

Youth: The United Nations, after studying practices in various countries has suggested 15-24 years for defining youth. However, in India, Department of Youth Affairs and Sports, the nodal department for different activities relating to youths has defined youth as the population in the age-group 15-35 years. In most of the statistical operations in the country age-wise data are generally presented in 5 years age-groups, such as 0-4, 5-9, 10-14, 15-19, 20-24, 25-29, 30-34. Due to this constraint, data on youth presented in tables pertain to 15-34 years age-group.

Index to Indicators

INDEX TO INDICATORS

Abbreviations

ABBREVIATIONS

AICTE	All India Council for Technical Education
ANM	Auxiliary Nurse Midwife
APL	Above Poverty Line
ASI	Annual Survey of Industry
ASMR	Age Specific Mortality Rate
ATI	Advance Training Institute
B.E.	Budget Estimated
BPL	Below Poverty Line
CBHI	Central Bureau of Health Intelligence
CC	Conventional Contraceptives
CGHS	Central Government Health Services
CHC	Community Health Centre
CPI	Consumer Price Index
CSO	Central Statistical Organization
CTI	Central Training Institute
D Sc	Diploma in Science
DCI	Dental Council of India
DE	Directory Establishment
DGE&T	Directorate General Employment &Training
DGHS	Director General Health Services
DHTP	Degree Holders and Technological Personnel
DOPT	Department of Personnel and Training
DST	Department of Science and Technology
EAP	Entrepreneurship Awareness Programme
EAS	Employment Assurance Scheme
EDP	Entrepreneurship Development Programme
EMI	Employment Market Information
ESCAP	Economic and Social Commission for Asia and the Pacific
ESI	Employment State Insurance
ESIS	Employee State Insurance Scheme
GAR	Gross Attendance Ratio
GDP	Gross Domestic Product
GDI	Gender Development Index
GER	Gross Enrolment Ratio
GNP	Gross National Product
GOI	Government of India
HDI	Human Development Index
HDR	Human Development Report
HRD	Human Resource Development
IAMR	Institute of Applied Manpower Research
IAS	Indian Administrative Service
ICOR	Incremental Capital Output Ratio
IIT	Indian Institute of Technology
IMR	Infant Mortality Rate
INC	Indian Nursing Council
IRDP	Integrated Rural Development Program
ITI	Industrial Training Institute
IUD	Intra Uterine Devices
JRY	Jawahar Rozgar Yojana
KVIC	Khadi and Village Industries Commission
LFPR	Labour Force Participation Ratio
LHV	Lady Health Visitors
LMIS	Labour Market Information System
LS	Lok Shaba
M Phil	Master of Philosophy
MBBS	Bachelor of Medicine Bachelor of Science
MCA	Master of Computer Application
MCI	Medical Council of India
MHFW	Ministry of Health and Family Welfare
MHRD	Ministry of Human Resource Development

MLM	Ministry of Labour and Employment
MMR	Maternal Mortality Rate
MPW	Multi Purpose Worker
NAR	Net Attendance Ratio
NAS	National Accounts Statistics
NPC	National Productivity Council
NCAER	National Council for Applied Economic Research
NDE	Non Directory Establishment
NDP	Net Domestic Product
NIC	National Industrial Classification
NPNL	Please see page.131 of 2005
NREP	National Rural Employment Programme
NSDP	Net State Domestic Product
NSS	National Sample Survey
NSSO	National Sample Survey Organisation
NTMIS	National Technical Manpower Information System
NVTI	National Vocational Training Institute
OAE	Own Account Enterprises
OBC	Other Backward Castes
P&T	Post and Telegram
PAP	Proportion of Ailing Persons
PCNSDP	Per Capita Net State Domestic Product
PG	Post Graduate
PHC	Primary Health Centre
PhD	Doctor of Philosophy
R&D	Research and Development
RE	Revised Estimate
RGCCI	Registrar General and Census Commissioner of India
RHD	Rural Health Division
RLEGP	Rural Landless Employment Guarantee Programme
RS	Rajya Sabha
RVTI	Regional Vocational Training Institute
SAARC	South Asian Association for Regional Cooperation
SC	Schedule Caste
SDES	State Directorate of Economic Survey
SGRY	Sampoorna Grameen Rozagar Yojana
SGSY	Swarnjayanthi Gram Swarozgar Yojana
SIDO	Small Industries Development Organization
SRS	Sample Registration System
SSI	Small Scale Industries
ST	Schedule Tribal
TFYP	Tenth Five Year Plan
TRYSEM	Training of Rural Youth for Self Employment
TUS	Time Use Survey
UG	Under Graduate
UGC	University Grants Commission
UK	United Kingdom
UN	United Nations
UNDP	United Nations Development Programme
USA	United States of America
UT	Union Territory
WB	World Bank
WDI	World Development Indicators
WFPR	Work Force Participant Rate
WITI	Woman Industrial Training Institutes